I & II THESSALONIANS
I & II TIMOTHY
TITUS, PHILEMON

THE PREACHER'S OUTLINE & SERMON BIBLE®

I & II THESSALONIANS
I & II TIMOTHY
TITUS, PHILEMON

THE PREACHER'S OUTLINE & SERMON BIBLE®

NEW TESTAMENT

NEW INTERNATIONAL VERSION

Leadership Ministries Worldwide
Chattanooga, TN

**THE PREACHER'S OUTLINE & SERMON BIBLE® - THESSALONIANS-PHILEMON
NEW INTERNATIONAL VERSION**

Copyright © 1988 by ALPHA-OMEGA MINISTRIES, INC.

All Rights Reserved

The Holy Bible, New International Version
Copyright © 1973, 1978, 1984 by International Bible Society
Used by permission of Zondervan Bible Publishers

All other Bible study aids, references, indexes, reference materials
Copyright © 1991 by Alpha-Omega Ministries, Inc.

**All rights reserved. No part of this publication may be reproduced, stored
in a retrieval system, or transmitted in any form or by any means—electronic,
mechanical, photo-copy, recording, or otherwise—without the prior
permission of the copyright owners.**

Previous Editions of **The Preacher's Outline & Sermon Bible®**,
New International Version NT   Copyright © 1998
King James Version NT   Copyright © 1991, 1996, 2000
by Alpha-Omega Ministries, Inc.

Please address all requests for information or permission to:
Leadership Ministries Worldwide
PO Box 21310
Chattanooga, TN 37424-0310
Ph.# (423) 855-2181   FAX (423) 855-8616   E-Mail info@outlinebible.org
http://www.outlinebible.org

Library of Congress Catalog Card Number: 98-67967
International Standard Book Number: 978-1-57407-085-9

**LEADERSHIP MINISTRIES WORLDWIDE
CHATTANOOGA, TN**

Printed in the United States of America

2   3   4   5   6   16   17   18   19   20

LEADERSHIP MINISTRIES WORLDWIDE

DEDICATED

To all the men and women of the world
who preach and teach the Gospel of
our Lord Jesus Christ and
to the Mercy and Grace of God

&

- Demonstrated to us in Christ Jesus our Lord.

  In him we have redemption through his blood, the forgiveness of sins, in accordance with the riches of God's grace. (Ep.1:7)

- Out of the mercy and grace of God, His Word has flowed. Let every person know that God will have mercy upon him, forgiving and using him to fulfill His glorious plan of salvation.

  For God so loved the world that he gave his one and only Son, that whoever believes in him shall not perish but have eternal life. For God did not send his Son into the world to condemn the world, but to save the world through him. (Jn.3:16-17)

  This is good, and pleases God our Savior, who wants all men to be saved and to come to a knowledge of the truth. (1 Ti.2:3-4)

The Preacher's Outline & Sermon Bible®

is written for God's servants to use in their study, teaching, and preaching of God's Holy Word...

- to share the Word of God with the world.
- to help believers, both ministers and laypersons, in their understanding, preaching, and teaching of God's Word.
- to do everything we possibly can to lead men, women, boys, and girls to give their hearts and lives to Jesus Christ and to secure the eternal life that He offers.
- to do all we can to minister to the needy of the world.
- to give Jesus Christ His proper place, the place the Word gives Him. Therefore, no work of Leadership Ministries Worldwide—no Outline Bible Resources—will ever be personalized.

ACKNOWLEDGMENTS AND BIBLIOGRAPHY

Every child of God is precious to the Lord and deeply loved. And every child as a servant of the Lord touches the lives of those who come in contact with him or his ministry. The writing ministries of the following servants have touched this work, and we are grateful that God brought their writings our way. We hereby acknowledge their ministry to us, being fully aware that there are many others down through the years whose writings have touched our lives and who deserve mention, but whose names have faded from our memory. May our wonderful Lord continue to bless the ministries of these dear servants—and the ministries of us all—as we diligently labor to reach the world for Christ and to meet the desperate needs of those who suffer so much.

THE GREEK SOURCES

Expositor's Greek Testament, Edited by W. Robertson Nicoll. Grand Rapids, MI: Eerdmans Publishing Co., 1970.

Robertson, A.T. *Word Pictures in the New Testament*. Nashville, TN: Broadman Press, 1930.

Thayer, Joseph Henry. *Greek-English Lexicon of the New Testament*. New York: American Book Co, n.d.

Vincent, Marvin R. *Word Studies in the New Testament*. Grand Rapids, MI: Eerdmans Publishing Co., 1969.

Vine, W.E. *Expository Dictionary of New Testament Words*. Old Tappan, NJ: Fleming H. Revell Co., n.d.

Wuest, Kenneth S. *Word Studies in the Greek New Testament*. Grand Rapids, MI: Eerdmans Publishing Co., 1966.

THE REFERENCE WORKS

Cruden's Complete Concordance of the Old & New Testament. Philadelphia, PA: The John C. Winston Co., 1930.

Josephus' *Complete Works*. Grand Rapids, MI: Kregel Publications, 1981.

Lockyer, Herbert. Series of books, including his books on *All the Men, Women, Miracles, and Parables of the Bible*. Grand Rapids, MI: Zondervan Publishing House, 1958-1967.

Nave's Topical Bible. Nashville, TN: The Southwestern Co., n.d.

The Amplified New Testament. (Scripture Quotations are from the Amplified New Testament, Copyright 1954, 1958, 1987 by the Lockman Foundation. Used by permission.)

The Four Translation New Testament. (Including King James, New American Standard, Williams - New Testament in the Language of the People, Beck - New Testament in the Language of Today.) Minneapolis, MN: World Wide Publications.

The New Compact Bible Dictionary, Edited by T. Alton Bryant. Grand Rapids, MI: Zondervan Publishing House, 1967.

The New Thompson Chain Reference Bible. Indianapolis, IN: B.B. Kirkbride Bible Co., 1964,

THE COMMENTARIES

Barclay, William. *Daily Study Bible Series*. Philadelphia, PA: Westminster Press, Began in 1953.

Bruce, F.F. *The Epistle to the Ephesians*. Westwood, NJ: Fleming H. Revell Co., 1968.

_____. *Epistle to the Hebrews*. Grand Rapids, MI: Eerdmans Publishing Co., 1964.

_____. *The Epistles of John*. Old Tappan, NJ: Fleming H. Revell Co., 1970.

Criswell, W.A. *Expository Sermons on Revelation*. Grand Rapids, MI: Zondervan Publishing House, 1962-66.

ACKNOWLEDGMENTS AND BIBLIOGRAPHY
THE COMMENTARIES
(continued)

Greene, Oliver. *The Epistles of John*. Greenville, SC: The Gospel Hour, Inc., 1966.

____. *The Epistles of Paul the Apostle to the Hebrews*. Greenville, SC: The Gospel Hour, Inc., 1965.

____. *The Epistles of Paul the Apostle to Timothy & Titus*. Greenville, SC: The Gospel Hour, Inc., 1964.

____. *The Revelation Verse by Verse Study*. Greenville, SC: The Gospel Hour, Inc., 1963.

Henry, Matthew. *Commentary on the Whole Bible*. Old Tappan, NJ: Fleming H. Revell Co.

Hodge, Charles. *Exposition on Romans & on Corinthians*. Grand Rapids, MI: Eerdmans Publishing Co., 1972-1973.

Ladd, George Eldon. *A Commentary On the Revelation of John*. Grand Rapids, MI: Eerdmans Publishing Co., 1972-1973.

Leupold, H.C. *Exposition of Daniel*. Grand Rapids, MI: Baker Book House, 1969.

Morris, Leon. *The Gospel According to John*. Grand Rapids, MI: Eerdmans Publishing Co., 1971.

Newell, William R. *Hebrews, Verse by Verse*. Chicago, IL: Moody Press, 1947.

Strauss, Lehman. *Devotional Studies in Galatians & Ephesians*. Neptune, NJ: Loizeaux Brothers, 1957.

____. *Devotional Studies in Philippians*. Neptune, NJ: Loizeaux Brothers, 1959.

____. *James, Your Brother*. Neptune, NJ: Loizeaux Brothers, 1956.

____. *The Book of the Revelation*. Neptune, NJ: Loizeaux Brothers, 1964.

Tasker, RVG. *The Gospel According to St. John*. "Tyndale New Testament Commentaries." Grand Rapids, MI: Eerdmans Publishing Co., 1960.

The New Testament & Wycliffe Bible Commentary, Edited by Charles F. Pfeiffer & Everett F. Harrison. New York: The Iverson Associates, 1971. Produced for Moody Monthly. Chicago Moody Press, 1962.

The Pulpit Commentary, Edited by H.D.M. Spence & Joseph S. Exell. Grand Rapids, MI: Eerdmans Publishing Co., 1950.

Thomas, W.H. Griffith. *Hebrews, A Devotional Commentary*. Grand Rapids, MI: Eerdmans Publishing Co., 1970.

____. *Outline Studies in the Acts of the Apostles*. Grand Rapids, MI: Eerdmans Publishing Co., 1956.

____. *St. Paul's Epistle to the Romans*. Grand Rapids, MI: Eerdmans Publishing Co., 1946.

____. *Studies in Colossians & Philemon*. Grand Rapids, MI: Baker Book House, 1973.

Tyndale New Testament Commentaries. Grand Rapids, MI: Eerdmans Publishing Co., Began in 1958.

Walker, Thomas. *Acts of the Apostles*. Chicago, IL: Moody Press, 1965.

Walvoord, John. *The Thessalonian Epistles*. Grand Rapids, MI: Zondervan Publishing House, 1973.

ABBREVIATIONS

&	=	and	O.T.	=	Old Testament
Bc.	=	because	p./pp.	=	page/pages
Concl.	=	conclusion	Pt.	=	point
Cp.	=	compare	Quest.	=	question
Ct.	=	contrast	Rel.	=	religion
e.g.	=	for example	Rgt.	=	righteousness
f.	=	following	Thru	=	through
Illust.	=	illustration	v./vv.	=	verse/verses
N.T.	=	New Testament	vs.	=	versus

THE BOOKS OF THE OLD TESTAMENT

Book	Abbreviation	Chapters	Book	Abbreviation	Chapters
GENESIS	Gen. or Ge.	50	Ecclesiastes	Eccl. or Ec.	12
Exodus	Ex.	40	The Song of Solomon	S. of Sol. or Song	8
Leviticus	Lev. or Le.	27	Isaiah	Is.	66
Numbers	Num. or Nu.	36	Jeremiah	Jer. or Je.	52
Deuteronomy	Dt. or De.	34	Lamentations	Lam.	5
Joshua	Josh. or Jos.	24	Ezekiel	Ezk. or Eze.	48
Judges	Judg. or Jud.	21	Daniel	Dan. or Da.	12
Ruth	Ruth or Ru.	4	Hosea	Hos. or Ho.	14
1 Samuel	1 Sam. or 1 S.	31	Joel	Joel	3
2 Samuel	2 Sam. or 2 S.	24	Amos	Amos or Am.	9
1 Kings	1 Ki. or 1 K.	22	Obadiah	Obad. or Ob.	1
2 Kings	2 Ki. or 2 K.	25	Jonah	Jon. or Jona.	4
1 Chronicles	1 Chron. or 1 Chr.	29	Micah	Mic. or Mi.	7
2 Chronicles	2 Chron. or 2 Chr.	36	Nahum	Nah. or Na.	3
Ezra	Ezra or Ezr.	10	Habakkuk	Hab.	3
Nehemiah	Neh. or Ne.	13	Zephaniah	Zeph. or Zep.	3
Esther	Est.	10	Haggai	Hag.	2
Job	Job or Jb.	42	Zechariah	Zech. or Zec.	14
Psalms	Ps.	150	Malachi	Mal.	4
Proverbs	Pr.	31			

THE BOOKS OF THE NEW TESTAMENT

Book	Abbreviation	Chapters	Book	Abbreviation	Chapters
MATTHEW	Mt.	28	1 Timothy	1 Tim. or 1 Ti.	6
Mark	Mk.	16	2 Timothy	2 Tim. or 2 Ti.	4
Luke	Lk. or Lu.	24	Titus	Tit.	3
John	Jn.	21	Philemon	Phile. or Phm.	1
The Acts	Acts or Ac.	28	Hebrews	Heb. or He.	13
Romans	Ro.	16	James	Jas. or Js.	5
1 Corinthians	1 Cor. or 1 Co.	16	1 Peter	1 Pt. or 1 Pe.	5
2 Corinthians	2 Cor. or 2 Co.	13	2 Peter	2 Pt. or 2 Pe.	3
Galatians	Gal. or Ga.	6	1 John	1 Jn.	5
Ephesians	Eph. or Ep.	6	2 John	2 Jn.	1
Philippians	Ph.	4	3 John	3 Jn.	1
Colossians	Col.	4	Jude	Jude	1
1 Thessalonians	1 Th.	5	Revelation	Rev. or Re.	22
2 Thessalonians	2 Th.	3			

HOW TO USE
The Preacher's Outline & Sermon Bible®

Follow these easy steps to gain maximum benefit from The POSB.

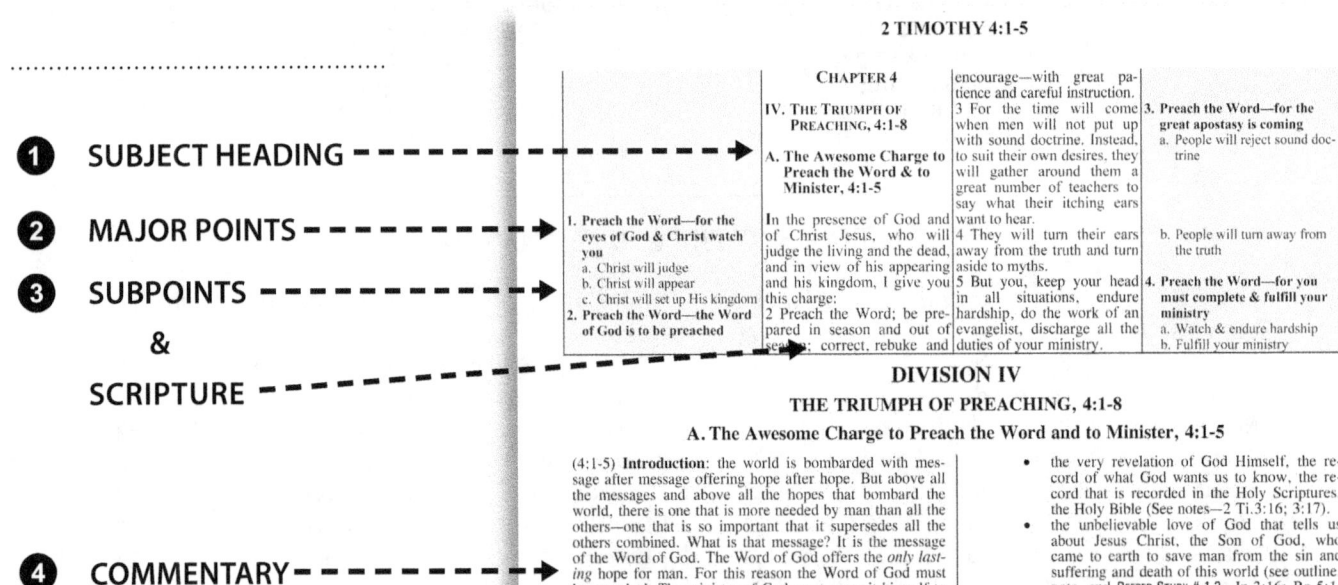

1 SUBJECT HEADING

2 MAJOR POINTS

3 SUBPOINTS & SCRIPTURE

4 COMMENTARY

1 Glance at the **Subject Heading**. Think about it for a moment.

2 Glance at the **Subject Heading** again, and then the **Major Points** (1, 2, 3, etc.). Do this several times, reviewing them together while quickly grasping the overall subject.

3 Glance at **both** the **Major Points** and **Subpoints** together while reading the **Scripture**. Do this slower than Step 2. Note how these points sit directly beside the related verse and simply restate what the Scripture is saying—in Outline form.

4 Next read the **Commentary**. Note that the *Major Point Numbers* in the Outline match those in the Commentary. When applicable, a small raised number (**DS1, DS2, etc.**) at the end of a Subject Heading or Outline Point directs you to a related **Deeper Study** in the Commentary (not shown here).

Finally, read the **Thoughts** and **Support Scripture** (not shown).

As you read and re-read, pray that the Holy Spirit will bring to your attention exactly what you should preach and teach. May God bless you richly as you study and teach His Word.

The POSB contains everything you need for sermon preparation:

1. **The Subject Heading** describes the overall theme of the passage and is located directly above the Scripture (keyed *alphabetically*).

2. **Major Points** are keyed with an outline *number* guiding you to related commentary. Note that the Commentary includes *"Thoughts"* (life application) and abundant Supporting Scriptures.

3. **Subpoints** explain and clarify the Scripture as needed.

4. **Commentary** is fully researched and developed for every point.

   - **Thoughts (in bold)** help apply the Scripture to real life.
   - **Deeper Studies** provide in-depth discussions of key words or phrases.

Woe to me if I do not preach the gospel!
(1 Co.9:16)

FIRST THESSALONIANS

1 THESSALONIANS

INTRODUCTION

AUTHOR: Paul, the Apostle.

Paul's authorship is seldom questioned. *Thessalonians* is listed in the Marcion Canon (about A.D. 140) and referred to in the Muratorian Fragment. It is quoted by Irenaeus (about A.D. 180). (Leon Morris. *The Epistles of Paul to the Thessalonians*. "Tyndale New Testament Commentaries," ed. by RVG Tasker. Grand Rapids, MI: Eerdmans, 1956, p.16.)

DATE: Probably A.D. 50-52. This date is fairly certain; Paul was in Corinth when he wrote the letter to the *Thessalonians*.

Luke says that Gallio was deputy of Achaia and that Paul was arrested in Corinth and brought before him (Acts 18:12). Just when Paul appeared before Gallio is not known. But an inscription at Delphi places Gallio's procounselship in the year of A.D. 51. Roman procounsels took office for only one year, beginning in early summer. Therefore, Gallio held office in A.D. 50-51 or A.D. 51-52. This would place Paul in Corinth in A.D. 50, and the writing of the letter between A.D. 50-52.

TO WHOM WRITTEN: "To the church of the *Thessalonians*" (1 Th.1:1). See Special Features, The Church.

PURPOSE: To encourage the church to stand fast against persecution.

Paul encourages the church by doing four things.

1. He commends their strong faith and love and hope (1 Th.1:3f).

2. He answers the malicious charges against himself (1 Th.2:1f).

3. He encourages the church to stand fast against persecution and to live holy lives (1 Th.3:1-4:12).

4. He reinforces the great hope of the Lord's return and the resurrection of those who have already passed on (1 Th.4:13f).

SPECIAL FEATURES:

1. The City of Thessalonica. The great city was the capital and the largest city of Macedonia. (See Map—Introduction to Acts.) It had been founded by Cassander, the top military officer of Alexander the Great, after Alexander had died. Under the Romans the city had been made free because of its loyalty to Rome. As a free city it was allowed its own government and local laws. At its height, the city reached a population of 200,000. The city had a natural harbor, but the primary factor contributing to the city's greatness was that it lay right on the Roman road, the Egnatian Way. In fact, the great road ran right through Thessalonica. It was the main street of the city, stretching all the way from the Adriatic Sea to the Middle East. Trade and commerce bristled with all the accompanying vice that follows such a metropolitan center.

2. The Church of Thessalonica. It was a great day when Paul walked into the city of Thessalonica bringing the news of the glorious gospel. Because of the city's strategic location and commercial importance, the gospel was bound to spread out beyond to the world rather rapidly. The great city of Thessalonica was the second great European city to be evangelized. Paul had just been evangelizing in Philippi when he entered Thessalonica. Paul preached in the synagogue for only three Sabbaths before he was forced by the Jews to leave the synagogue (Acts 17:2). Paul apparently moved into homes, preaching wherever he was allowed. He had so much success that the Jews eventually attacked and forced him to flee for his life. He took Silas and Timothy (Acts 17:10-14) and proceeded to Berea for a brief ministry. But the Jews pursued him and he was forced to leave Berea for Athens (Acts 17:13f). However, he was able to leave Silas and Timothy behind to continue the ministry. While in Athens, he sent for Timothy, but dispatched him right back to Thessalonica (1 Th.3:2f). Paul himself went on to Corinth where he was soon joined by Silas and Timothy with good news from the Thessalonian church (Acts 18:5). His heart was so warmed by this report that he sat down and wrote the Thessalonian letter.

The converts were mainly Gentiles, including a large number of devout Greeks and prestigious women. Many, especially women, were sick of the immoral society of that day. They had turned to Judaism because of its moral teachings, yet they sensed the bondage of its legalistic thrust and rejected its national prejudices. Therefore, their hearts were ripe for the message of liberty and love preached by the gospel. The church at Thessalonica...

- was founded on Paul's second missionary journey (Acts 17:1f).
- was revisited by Paul (1 Cor.16:5).
- included some Jews and a large number of Greeks and influential women (Acts 17:4; 2 Th.3:4, 7-8).
- did not support Paul. He worked at a secular job while there (1 Th.2:9); however, he did receive financial help from the church at Philippi (Ph.416).
- suffered persecution (1 Th.2:14).
- was well organized (1 Th.5:12).
- had several prominent believers known by name: Jason (Acts 176), Gaius (Acts 19:29), Aristarchus (Acts 19:29; 20:4), and Secundus (Acts 20:4).

3. *Thessalonians* is "An Early Epistle Written by the Apostle Paul." It is one of the earliest New Testament writings.

4. *Thessalonians* is "An Early Epistle that Proclaims Christ to be Lord" (1 Th.1:1, 3, 6, 10; 2:15; 3:8, 11-13; 4:1-2, 13-18; 5:1-2, 9-10, 23, 28; cp. Acts 17:7).

5. *Thessalonians* is "An Epistle that Proclaims the Doctrine of the Second Coming" (1 Th.4:13f).

6. *Thessalonians* is "An Epistle of Great Encouragement for a Person Facing Persecution" (1 Th.1:6f; 2:2f; 2:14f; 3:3f).

7. *Thessalonians* is "An Epistle Written to Warn Believers of the Danger of Sexual Impurity" (1 Th.4:1-10).

8. *Thessalonians* is "An Epistle Written to Charge Believers with the Most Practical Rules of Behavior" (1 Th. 5:12-22).

9. *Thessalonians* is "An Epistle with a Great Evangelistic and Missionary Challenge" (1 Th.1:8-12; 2:12-13; 3:12-13; 4:1-12; 5:1f).

10. *Thessalonians* is "An Epistle Written from the Heart and Soul of a Committed Minister." Wycliffe Bible Commentary has a moving description of this point. (David A. Hubbard, *First & Second Thessalonians*. "The New Testament & Wycliffe Bible Commentary," ed. by Charles

F. Pfeiffer and Everett F. Harrison. Produced for Moody Monthly by the Iversen Associates, N.Y., 1971, p.803f.)

> *"In these letters Paul lays bare not so much his subject as his soul: Here the beat of the apostle's warm heart is audible. He compares himself to a gentle nurse (1 Thess.2:7), a firm father (2:11), and a homeless orphan (in the Greek of 2:17). He shows himself ready to spend and be spent for the spreading of the Gospel. It is Paul, the man, who confronts us, gentle in his strength, loving in his exhortations, dauntless in his courage, guileless in his motives—a man (as Carl Sandburg said of Abraham Lincoln) 'of steel and velvet, hard as rock and soft as drifting fog.'"*

OUTLINE OF 1 THESSALONIANS

THE PREACHER'S OUTLINE & SERMON BIBLE® is *unique*. It differs from all other Study Bibles & Sermon Resource Materials in that every Passage and Subject is outlined right beside the Scripture. When you choose any *Subject* below and turn to the reference, you have not only the Scripture, but you discover the Scripture and Subject *already outlined for you—verse by verse*.

For a quick example, choose one of the subjects below and turn over to the Scripture, and you will find this marvelous help for faster, easier, and more accurate use.

In addition, every point of the Scripture and Subject is *fully developed in a Commentary with supporting Scripture* at the bottom of the page. Again, this arrangement makes sermon preparation much easier and faster.

Note something else: The Subjects of First Thessalonians have Biblical titles, but they have also been given *practical titles or titles of application* which sometimes have more appeal to people. This *benefit* is clearly seen for use on billboards, bulletins, church newsletters, etc.

A suggestion: For the quickest overview of First Thessalonians, first read *all the major titles* (I, II, III, etc.), then come back and read the subtitles.

OUTLINE OF 1 THESSALONIANS

I. **THE MODEL CHURCH, 1:1-3:13**

   A. The Model Church: A Strong Church or Work, 1:1-4
   B. The Model Church: A Strong Conversion, 1:5-10
   C. The Model Church: A Strong and True Minister, 2:1-12
   D. The Model Church: A Strong People, 2:13-20
   E. The Model Church: A Strong Faith, 3:1-10
   F. The Model Church: A Strong Love, 3:11-13

II. **THE MODEL WALK OR LIFE, 4:1-12**

   A. A Walk that Pleases God (Part I): A Life of Purity, 4:1-8
   B. A Walk that Pleases God (Part II): Four Practical Duties, 4:9-12

III. **THE COMING AGAIN OF JESUS CHRIST, 4:13-5:24**

   A. The Lord's Return and the Resurrection, 4:13-5:3
   B. The Lord's Return and the Believer's Behavior, 5:4-11
   C. The Lord's Return and Behavior in the Church, 5:12-28

1 THESSALONIANS

	CHAPTER 1
	
	I. THE MODEL CHURCH, 1:1-3:13
	
	A. The Model Church: A Strong Church or Work 1:1-4
		you.
		2 We always thank God for all of you, mentioning you in our prayers.
		3 We continually remember before our God and Father your work produced by faith, your labor prompted by love, and your endurance inspired by hope in our Lord Jesus Christ.
		4 For we know, brothers loved by God, that he has chosen you,
			God & in the Lord
			4 **It is a church possessing God's supreme gifts: Grace & peace, v.1**
			5 **It is a church that stirs prayer, v.2**
			6 **It is a church stirred up to work**
			  a. Stirred by faith
			  b. Stirred by love
			  c. Stirred by hope
			7 **It is a church seen to be chosen by God**

1 **It is a church that has ministers who are faithful to the church** 2 **It is a church of the people** 3 **It is a church founded in**	Paul, Silas and Timothy, To the church of the Thessalonians in God the Father and the Lord Jesus Christ: Grace and peace to		

DIVISION I

THE MODEL CHURCH, 1:1-3:13

A. The Model Church: A Strong Church or Work, 1:1-4

(1:1-4) **Introduction**: the introductory verses give us a clear picture of a strong church. The picture painted in these verses is a model for all churches. It is the picture of a church strong in carrying on a work for the Lord.
1. It is a church that has ministers who are faithful to the church (v.1).
2. It is a church of the people (v.1).
3. It is a church founded in God and in the Lord (v.1).
4. It is a church possessing God's supreme gifts: grace and peace (v.1).
5. It is a church that stirs prayer (v.2).
6. It is a church stirred up to work (v.3).
7. It is a church seen to be chosen by God (v.4).

1 (1:1) **Church**: a strong church has ministers who are faithful to the church. Note that Paul was not writing this letter alone. Silas and Timothy joined him in exhorting the church. Why is this an exhortation from three ministers? Because these particular ministers had been the three who had founded and ministered to the church throughout the early years of its ministry. Of course Paul had been the head minister, but the other two had worked just as faithfully for the Lord in their call to be associates.

The point is this: the Thessalonica church was strong because its ministers had remained faithful to the church. From every indication they had continued to stay in touch with the church and to exhort the believers through visits and letters as long as they were living and able to minister.
⇒ Paul visited the church when he returned to the area on his third missionary journey (Acts 20:1-2).
⇒ Timothy made a special visit to the church for the very purpose of helping the church through a difficult time and to establish and comfort the believers in their faith (1 Th.3:1-6).
⇒ All three ministers wrote the church at least two times, this letter of First Thessalonians and the second letter to the Thessalonians (1 Th.1:1; 2 Th.1:1).

Thought 1. How many churches lack strength because their ministers have not remained faithful in exhorting them...
• to follow on with the Lord?
• to follow and support their present ministers?

Note how Paul, probably the greatest minister who has ever lived, acknowledged Silas and Timothy as equal to him.

They preached the good news in that city and won a large number of disciples. Then they returned to Lystra, Iconium and Antioch, strengthening the disciples and encouraging them to remain true to the faith. "We must go through many hardships to enter the kingdom of God," they said. (Acts 14:21-22)

For the grace of God that brings salvation has appeared to all men. It teaches us to say "No" to ungodliness and worldly passions, and to live self-controlled, upright and godly lives in this present age, while we wait for the blessed hope—the glorious appearing of our great God and Savior, Jesus Christ, who gave himself for us to redeem us from all wickedness and to purify for himself a people that are his very own, eager to do what is good. These, then, are the things you should teach. Encourage and rebuke with all authority. Do not let anyone despise you. (Titus 2:11-15)

2 (1:1) **Church**: a strong church is a church of the people. Paul did not address the letter to "the church at Thessalonica," but to "the church *of the Thessalonians*." The church was the people, the people who had accepted Jesus Christ as their Lord and Savior. Without people who are committed to the Lord there is no church. The letter was not addressed to a particular group of leaders, but to all the people of the church. Every believer was important, and it took every one of them to make up the church. A strong church is a church of the people, a church...
• that is comprised of all the people.
• that is built upon all the people.
• that acknowledges the importance of all the people.
• that involves and uses the gifts of all the people.
• that recognizes and esteems the presence and contribution of all the people.

Thought 1. Several things will always weaken a church:
⇒ Building the church upon a few people or leaders.
⇒ Ignoring and neglecting the needs of some members.
⇒ Failing to involve and use the gifts of some members.

For by the grace given me I say to every one of you: Do not think of yourself more highly than you ought, but rather think of yourself with sober judgment, in accordance with the measure of faith God has given you. Just as each of us has one body with many members, and these members do not all have the same function, so in Christ we who are many form one body, and each member belongs to all the others. (Rom 12:3-5)

The body is a unit, though it is made up of many parts; and though all its parts are many, they form one body. So it is with Christ. For we were all baptized by one Spirit into one body—whether Jews or Greeks, slave or free—and we were all given the one Spirit to drink. Now the body is not made up of one part but of many. (1 Cor 12:12-14)

It was he who gave some to be apostles, some to be prophets, some to be evangelists, and some to be pastors and teachers, To prepare God's people for works of service, so that the body of Christ may be built up until we all reach unity in the faith and in the knowledge of the Son of God and become mature, attaining to the whole measure of the fullness of Christ. (Eph 4:11-13)

3 (1:1) **Church—Jesus Christ, Deity**: a strong church is founded "in God the Father and the Lord Jesus Christ." Jesus Christ is said to be equal with God the Father. God is acknowledged as the Father of the Lord Jesus Christ. This is the distinctive belief upon which the church is built. We believe that "God so loved the world, that He gave His *one and only Son*, that whoever believes in Him shall not perish but have eternal life" (Jn.3:16).
⇒ We believe that God the Father sent His Son, the Lord Jesus Christ, into the world to save us from perishing and to give us eternal life.
⇒ We believe that the Lord Jesus Christ is the Son of God.
⇒ We believe that the Lord Jesus Christ is *the Lord* sent from heaven, that He is God, the eternal Son embodied in human flesh and sent to earth by God the Father.
⇒ We believe that the Lord Jesus Christ is *Jesus the Carpenter* from Nazareth.
⇒ We believe that the Lord Jesus Christ is *the Christ*, the Messiah and Savior who had been promised from the very beginning of history.

As stated, it is upon this confession that the church is built. This confession is the one distinctive mark of the church.

Thought 1. A church that is not founded upon *God the Father and the Lord Jesus Christ* is not a church, not a true church, no matter what it may call itself. It is nothing more than...
• a man-created fellowship
• a man-created gathering
• a man-created assembly
• a man-created body
• a man-created meeting
• a man-created worship

"But what about you?" he asked. "Who do you say I am?" Simon Peter answered, "You are the Christ, the Son of the living God." Jesus replied, "Blessed are you, Simon son of Jonah, for this was not revealed to you by man, but by my Father in heaven. And I tell you that you are Peter, and on this rock I will build my church, and the gates of Hades will not overcome it. (Mat 16:15-18)

Jesus said to them, "Have you never read in the Scriptures: "'The stone the builders rejected has become the capstone ; the Lord has done this, and it is marvelous in our eyes'? (Mat 21:42)

He is "'the stone you builders rejected, which has become the capstone.' (Acts 4:11)

That if you confess with your mouth, "Jesus is Lord," and believe in your heart that God raised him from the dead, you will be saved. (Rom 10:9)

Built on the foundation of the apostles and prophets, with Christ Jesus himself as the chief cornerstone. (Eph 2:20)

For in Scripture it says: "See, I lay a stone in Zion, a chosen and precious cornerstone, and the one who trusts in him will never be put to shame." (1 Pet 2:6)

Who is the liar? It is the man who denies that Jesus is the Christ. Such a man is the antichrist—he denies the Father and the Son. No one who denies the Son has the Father; whoever acknowledges the Son has the Father also. (1 John 2:22-23)

If anyone acknowledges that Jesus is the Son of God, God lives in him and he in God. (1 John 4:15)

4 (1:1) **Church—Grace—Peace**: a strong church possesses God's supreme gifts—grace and peace.

1. Grace (charis) means the undeserved favor and blessings of God (see DEEPER STUDY # 1, *Grace*—Tit.2:11-15; note—Ro.4:16; note and DEEPER STUDY # 1—1 Cor.1:4 for more discussion). No church can be strong...
• without the favor of God.
• without the blessings of God.

When we see a strong church, the hand of God is immediately noticed: the hand that favors the church and blesses it. What is it that brings the hand of God's grace to a church? Note the exact wording of this verse: "To the church...*in God the Father and the Lord Jesus Christ*: Grace and peace to you." Grace comes *from* God our Father and from the Lord Jesus Christ. God pours His grace out upon the church that commits itself to the confession...

1 THESSALONIANS 1:1-4

- that God is our Father.
- that Jesus is the Lord Jesus Christ.

The church that really commits itself to this confession is the church that God favors and blesses, that experiences the outpouring of His grace. Every strong church is a church that is confessing God to be the Father of the Lord Jesus Christ and confessing the Lord Jesus Christ to be the *one and only* Son of God. When this confession is forcefully made and demonstrated by a church, it is then that the grace (favor and blessings) of God the Father and the Lord Jesus Christ pours forth.

> **Grace and peace to you from God our Father and the Lord Jesus Christ. Praise be to the God and Father of our Lord Jesus Christ, who has blessed us in the heavenly realms with every spiritual blessing in Christ. (Eph 1:2-3)**
>
> **For it is by grace you have been saved, through faith—and this not from yourselves, it is the gift of God—not by works, so that no one can boast. For we are God's workmanship, created in Christ Jesus to do good works, which God prepared in advance for us to do. (Eph 2:8-10)**
>
> **I became a servant of this gospel by the gift of God's grace given me through the working of his power. Although I am less than the least of all God's people, this grace was given me: to preach to the Gentiles the unsearchable riches of Christ, (Eph 3:7-8)**
>
> **The grace of our Lord was poured out on me abundantly, along with the faith and love that are in Christ Jesus. Here is a trustworthy saying that deserves full acceptance: Christ Jesus came into the world to save sinners—of whom I am the worst. (1 Tim 1:14-15)**

2. Peace (eirene) means to be bound, joined, and woven together. It means to be assured, confident, and secure in the love and care of God. It means to sense and know that God will...

- guide
- provide
- strengthen
- sustain
- deliver
- encourage
- empower
- bless

But again, note that peace comes only from God our Father and the Lord Jesus Christ. In order to have the peace of God and Christ, a church has to have a strong confession...

- in God as the Father of the Lord Jesus Christ.
- in Jesus as the Lord Jesus Christ.

The Father and Christ alone can bring peace to the hearts of men, and that peace can be given only to those who come to God for peace. The Father and Christ cannot give peace to a person who does not come to God for peace.

The point is this: a strong church is a body of people who know and experience the peace of God as they walk throughout the world day by day.

> **Peace I leave with you; my peace I give you. I do not give to you as the world gives. Do not let your hearts be troubled and do not be afraid. (John 14:27)**
>
> **"I have told you these things, so that in me you may have peace. In this world you will have trouble. But take heart! I have overcome the world." (John 16:33)**
>
> **Therefore, since we have been justified through faith, we have peace with God through our Lord Jesus Christ, (Rom 5:1)**
>
> **The mind of sinful man is death, but the mind controlled by the Spirit is life and peace; (Rom 8:6)**
>
> **But now in Christ Jesus you who once were far away have been brought near through the blood of Christ. For he himself is our peace, who has made the two one and has destroyed the barrier, the dividing wall of hostility, (Eph 2:13-14)**
>
> **And through him to reconcile to himself all things, whether things on earth or things in heaven, by making peace through his blood, shed on the cross. (Col 1:20)**

5 (1:2) **Church—Prayer**: a strong church stirs prayer. This is a crucial trait, for God has ordained prayer to be the medium through which He blesses and moves in behalf of people.

> **If you believe, you will receive whatever you ask for in prayer." (Mat 21:22)**
>
> **If you remain in me and my words remain in you, ask whatever you wish, and it will be given you. (John 15:7)**
>
> **What causes fights and quarrels among you? Don't they come from your desires that battle within you? You want something but don't get it. You kill and covet, but you cannot have what you want. You quarrel and fight. You do not have, because you do not ask God. When you ask, you do not receive, because you ask with wrong motives, that you may spend what you get on your pleasures. (James 4:1-3)**

Why has God chosen prayer to be the medium through which He acts for man? Because *sharing and talking* together are the way all persons communicate, fellowship, and commune together. This is true both with men and God. Prayer requires our presence, sharing, and talking; and God wants to fellowship and commune with us. Few persons heed this fact; few persons take prayer seriously. Nevertheless a strong church encourages people to pray, and it stirs people to pray for it and its ministry. Note that Paul gave thanks to God always for the Thessalonian church.

6 (1:3) **Church**: a strong church is a church that is stirred up and aroused to work. Three things stir and arouse the church to work.

1. Faith stirs the church to work. When a person believes in Jesus Christ, truly believes, he is stirred to work and serve the Lord Jesus. The same is true with a body of believers, the church. The stronger the belief of the people in Christ, the stronger they will work for the Lord. A strong faith stirs, arouses, activates, and energizes believers to work and carry out the mission of Christ.

> In addition to all this, take up the shield of faith, with which you can extinguish all the flaming arrows of the evil one. (Eph 6:16)
>
> What good is it, my brothers, if a man claims to have faith but has no deeds? Can such faith save him? Suppose a brother or sister is without clothes and daily food. If one of you says to him, "Go, I wish you well; keep warm and well fed," but does nothing about his physical needs, what good is it? In the same way, faith by itself, if it is not accompanied by action, is dead. (James 2:14-17)
>
> For everyone born of God overcomes the world. This is the victory that has overcome the world, even our faith. Who is it that overcomes the world? Only he who believes that Jesus is the Son of God. (1 John 5:4-5)

2. Love stirs the church to work. The word "work" (kopou) means to toil; to labor to the point of exhaustion; to arduously labor. When a person truly loves Christ, he is prompted and driven to arduously labor for Christ. Note: the believer who is driven by love is the believer who has really seen the love of Christ. He is always conscious that Christ has taken his sins upon Himself and borne the punishment for them. The believer knows that he is ever so short of the glory of God, and that he deserves to be punished as the transgressor of God's law. But he knows and walks around with the deep sense that Christ bore his punishment for him. It is the wonderful love of Christ that stirs the believer to love Christ ever so much. Therefore, he does all he can to please Christ and to fulfill the joy of Christ. This is what Paul meant when he said *"Christ's love compels me" to serve Him* (see note—2 Cor.5:14-16 for more discussion).

> For Christ's love compels us, because we are convinced that one died for all, and therefore all died. And he died for all, that those who live should no longer live for themselves but for him who died for them and was raised again. (2 Cor 5:14-15)
>
> And the second is like it: 'Love your neighbor as yourself.' (Mat 22:39)
>
> "A new command I give you: Love one another. As I have loved you, so you must love one another. By this all men will know that you are my disciples, if you love one another." (John 13:34-35)
>
> Love must be sincere. Hate what is evil; cling to what is good. (Rom 12:9)
>
> Let no debt remain outstanding, except the continuing debt to love one another, for he who loves his fellowman has fulfilled the law. The commandments, "Do not commit adultery," "Do not murder," "Do not steal," "Do not covet," and whatever other commandment there may be, are summed up in this one rule: "Love your neighbor as yourself." Love does no harm to its neighbor. Therefore love is the fulfillment of the law. (Rom 13:8-10)
>
> We who are strong ought to bear with the failings of the weak and not to please ourselves. (Rom 15:1)
>
> May the Lord make your love increase and overflow for each other and for everyone else, just as ours does for you. (1 Th 3:12)
>
> And let us consider how we may spur one another on toward love and good deeds. Let us not give up meeting together, as some are in the habit of doing, but let us encourage one another—and all the more as you see the Day approaching. (Heb 10:24-25)
>
> Now that you have purified yourselves by obeying the truth so that you have sincere love for your brothers, love one another deeply, from the heart. (1 Pet 1:22)

3. Hope in the Lord Jesus Christ stirs the church to endure in its work and labor. The word "endurance" (hupomones) means steadfastness, perseverance. Our hope is in the Lord Jesus Christ: we know He will...

- guide
- strengthen
- provide
- sustain
- deliver
- bless

In addition, we know that the Lord is going to transfer us into heaven at the end of this life and reward us according to our labor here on earth. Therefore, strong believers and churches are driven to endure in hope—to continue on in their arduous labor for Christ. (See DEEPER STUDY # 4, *Inheritance*—Ro.8:17 for more discussion.)

Thought 1. There are several reasons why a man works.
⇒ There is forced labor: a man is forced to work.
⇒ There is a sense of duty: a man feels obligated to work.
⇒ There is the need to meet necessities: a man has needs that have to be met.
⇒ There is the wish to gain more: a man works to build up wealth.

When a man accepts Christ, his motive for working changes. He now serves and works for Christ (Eph.6:5-9; Col.3:22-4:1). His faith in the new world Christ is creating stirs him to work for Christ. His love for Christ and for others stirs him to work in order to share the gospel with the world (1 Th.1:6-9). His hope in the return of Christ to set up His kingdom causes him to labor with endurance (1 Th.1:3). (Note: the source of this thought is unknown. If it comes from some published material, please advise us and we will give credit for it in future printings.)

> For everything that was written in the past was written to teach us, so that through endurance and the encouragement of the Scriptures we might have hope. (Rom 15:4)
>
> The faith and love that spring from the hope that is stored up for you in heaven and that you have already heard about in the word of truth, the gospel (Col 1:5)
>
> May our Lord Jesus Christ himself and God our Father, who loved us and by his grace gave us eternal encouragement and good hope, encourage your hearts and strengthen you in every good deed and word. (2 Th 2:16-17)

It teaches us to say "No" to ungodliness and worldly passions, and to live self-controlled, upright and godly lives in this present age, while we wait for the blessed hope—the glorious appearing of our great God and Savior, Jesus Christ, (Titus 2:12-13)

Praise be to the God and Father of our Lord Jesus Christ! In his great mercy he has given us new birth into a living hope through the resurrection of Jesus Christ from the dead, and into an inheritance that can never perish, spoil or fade—kept in heaven for you, (1 Pet 1:3-4)

7 (1:4) **Church**: a strong church is seen to be chosen by God. The word "chosen" (eklogen) means that the church has been selected and chosen by God. This means two things.

1. Believers are chosen by God to be His *beloved people*. God has called believers out of the world and away from the old life which the world offered, the old life of sin and death. He has called believers to be separated and set apart to Himself and the new life He offers, the new life of righteousness and eternity.

The LORD appeared to us in the past, saying: "I have loved you with an everlasting love; I have drawn you with lovingkindness. (Jer 31:3)

"For God so loved the world that he gave his one and only Son, that whoever believes in him shall not perish but have eternal life. (John 3:16)

No, the Father himself loves you because you have loved me and have believed that I came from God. (John 16:27)

But God demonstrates his own love for us in this: While we were still sinners, Christ died for us. (Rom 5:8)

But because of his great love for us, God, who is rich in mercy, made us alive with Christ even when we were dead in transgressions—it is by grace you have been saved. (Eph 2:4-5)

How great is the love the Father has lavished on us, that we should be called children of God! And that is what we are! The reason the world does not know us is that it did not know him. (1 John 3:1)

2. Believers are chosen to be *brothers loved by God*; they are called to hold one another ever so closely to their hearts and to count one another as precious and deeply loved.

"A new command I give you: Love one another. As I have loved you, so you must love one another. By this all men will know that you are my disciples, if you love one another." (John 13:34-35)

Be devoted to one another in brotherly love. Honor one another above yourselves. (Rom 12:10)

Love is patient, love is kind. It does not envy, it does not boast, it is not proud. (1 Cor 13:4)

Be kind and compassionate to one another, forgiving each other, just as in Christ God forgave you. (Eph 4:32)

If you have any encouragement from being united with Christ, if any comfort from his love, if any fellowship with the Spirit, if any tenderness and compassion, then make my joy complete by being likeminded, having the same love, being one in spirit and purpose. (Phil 2:1-2)

Therefore, as God's chosen people, holy and dearly loved, clothe yourselves with compassion, kindness, humility, gentleness and patience. (Col 3:12)

For this very reason, make every effort to add to your faith goodness; and to goodness, knowledge; and to knowledge, self-control; and to self-control, perseverance; and to perseverance, godliness; and to godliness, brotherly kindness; and to brotherly kindness, love. (2 Pet 1:5-7)

We know that we have passed from death to life, because we love our brothers. Anyone who does not love remains in death. (1 John 3:14)

Thought 1. Note two strong lessons.
1) The proof that a church is truly chosen by God is that...
   - the members act like the *loved people of God*.
   - the members treat each other as *loved brothers*.
2) A people can show that being chosen is only a false profession...
   - by acting like they are not the loved of God—living in sin and shame, dirt and pollution, worldliness and greed.
   - by treating one another as anything but brothers loved by God: being critical and divisive, prideful and arrogant, angry and hurtful, envious and prejudiced, superior and super-spiritual.

Who will bring any charge against those whom God has chosen? It is God who justifies. (Rom 8:33)

Therefore I endure everything for the sake of the elect, that they too may obtain the salvation that is in Christ Jesus, with eternal glory. (2 Tim 2:10)

Who have been chosen according to the foreknowledge of God the Father, through the sanctifying work of the Spirit, for obedience to Jesus Christ and sprinkling by his blood: Grace and peace be yours in abundance. (1 Pet 1:2)

1 THESSALONIANS 1:5-10

	B. The Model Church: A Strong Conversion, 1:5-10	Macedonia and Achaia. 8 The Lord's message rang out from you not only in Macedonia and Achaia—your faith in God has become known everywhere. Therefore we do not need to say anything about it, 9 For they themselves report what kind of reception you gave us. They tell how you turned to God from idols to serve the living and true God, 10 And to wait for his Son from heaven, whom he raised from the dead—Jesus, who rescues us from the coming wrath.	other believers a. They sounded forth the word themselves b. Their testimony was spread abroad

1 They had ministers who preached the gospel as it should be preached
  a. Ministers who did not preach just words
  b. Ministers who preached in power and in the Holy Spirit and deep conviction
  c. Ministers who lived what they preached
2 They received the Word (the gospel) despite opposition & persecution
3 They became examples to
	5 Because our gospel came to you not simply with words, but also with power, with the Holy Spirit and with deep conviction. You know how we lived among you for your sake.
	6 You became imitators of us and of the Lord; in spite of severe suffering, you welcomed the message with the joy given by the Holy Spirit.
	7 And so you became a model to all the believers in
			4 They turned to God from idols
			  a. Turned to serve the living God
			  b. Turned to wait for Christ's return
			  c. Turned to escape the wrath of God

DIVISION I

THE MODEL CHURCH, 1:1-3:13

B. The Model Church: A Strong Conversion, 1:5-10

(1:5-10) **Introduction**: Paul says that the Thessalonian church was a *pattern*. He says that they were examples not only to the heathen, but also to believers. Their example is primarily found in their strong conversion and in their thundering forth the Word of the Lord (v.8).

1. They had ministers who preached the gospel as it should be preached (v.5).
2. They received the Word (the gospel) despite opposition and persecution (v.6).
3. They became examples to other believers (v.7-8).
4. They turned to God from idols (v.9-10).

1 (1:5-6) **Ministers**: the model church had ministers who preached the gospel as it should be preached. When Paul went to Thessalonica, he went for one purpose and for one purpose only: to preach the gospel and to minister to the needs of people. Note three striking lessons.

1. Paul did not preach in word only; that is, he did not preach mere words, depending upon his own ability to influence people. He did not stand before people using nothing but his own words to reach people. His preaching was not dependent upon...

- his eloquence
- his ability
- his wisdom
- his novel ideas
- his charisma
- his appearance

When Paul stood before people and preached, he was not concerned with words and eloquence, nor with whether or not people thought he was a good preacher. He was concerned with only one thing: sharing the Word of God and the gospel of the Lord Jesus Christ. Paul knew that God honored His Word and His Word only.

> He said to them, "Go into all the world and preach the good news to all creation. (Mark 16:15)

> I am not ashamed of the gospel, because it is the power of God for the salvation of everyone who believes: first for the Jew, then for the Gentile. (Rom 1:16)

> When I came to you, brothers, I did not come with eloquence or superior wisdom as I proclaimed to you the testimony about God. For I resolved to know nothing while I was with you except Jesus Christ and him crucified. (1 Cor 2:1-2)

> My message and my preaching were not with wise and persuasive words, but with a demonstration of the Spirit's power, so that your faith might not rest on men's wisdom, but on God's power. (1 Cor 2:4-5)

> This is what we speak, not in words taught us by human wisdom but in words taught by the Spirit, expressing spiritual truths in spiritual words. (1 Cor 2:13)

> For the kingdom of God is not a matter of talk but of power. (1 Cor 4:20)

> Yet when I preach the gospel, I cannot boast, for I am compelled to preach. Woe to me if I do not preach the gospel! (1 Cor 9:16)

> Now, brothers, I want to remind you of the gospel I preached to you, which you received and on which you have taken your stand. By this gospel you are saved, if you hold firmly to the word I preached to you. Otherwise, you have believed in vain. For what I received I passed on to you as of first importance : that Christ died for our sins according to the Scriptures, that he was buried, that he was raised on the third day according to the Scriptures, (1 Cor 15:1-4)

> For we do not preach ourselves, but Jesus Christ as Lord, and ourselves as your servants for Jesus' sake. (2 Cor 4:5)

> Preach the Word; be prepared in season and out of season; correct, rebuke and encourage—with great patience and careful instruction. (2 Tim 4:2)

> For the word of God is living and active. Sharper than any double-edged sword, it penetrates even to dividing soul and spirit, joints and marrow; it judges the thoughts and attitudes of the heart. (Heb 4:12)

1 THESSALONIANS 1:5-10

2. Paul preached in power and in the Holy Spirit and with deep conviction.

   a. Preaching in "power" (dunamis) means preaching in the power and energy of God Himself. This is what is so often missed and misunderstood. The gospel is not mere words nor just sharing an idea. Words and ideas are, of course, involved; but the gospel is more, much more. The gospel is the *power of God* at work in the human heart. The gospel is the power of God operating, working, stirring, convicting, and energizing a person to believe and accept the Lord Jesus Christ.

      This is the reason it is so important for the preacher to be completely surrendered to God—living ever so closely to Him—living and moving and having his being in the Lord. The preacher must be under the control of God so that the power of God can rest upon and flow through his life. The preacher must become nothing but an instrument in the hands of God. Then and only then can the gospel—the very power of God—flow through his preaching like it should.

> **But you will receive power when the Holy Spirit comes on you; and you will be my witnesses in Jerusalem, and in all Judea and Samaria, and to the ends of the earth." (Acts 1:8)**
>
> **I am not ashamed of the gospel, because it is the power of God for the salvation of everyone who believes: first for the Jew, then for the Gentile. (Rom 1:16)**
>
> **For it is God who works in you to will and to act according to his good purpose. (Phil 2:13)**
>
> **For the word of God is living and active. Sharper than any double-edged sword, it penetrates even to dividing soul and spirit, joints and marrow; it judges the thoughts and attitudes of the heart. (Heb 4:12)**
>
> **Therefore this is what the LORD God Almighty says: "Because the people have spoken these words, I will make my words in your mouth a fire and these people the wood it consumes. (Jer 5:14)**
>
> **"Is not my word like fire," declares the LORD, "and like a hammer that breaks a rock in pieces? (Jer 23:29)**

   b. Preaching in the Holy Spirit means that the Holy Spirit was also working in the hearts of people. He was doing what God had sent Him to earth to do: convict the hearts of the hearers and convince them of the truth of the gospel:
    ⇒ that Jesus Christ did die for their sins.
    ⇒ that Jesus Christ does provide righteousness for men; that His righteousness does stand for the righteousness of men.
    ⇒ that Jesus Christ did bear the judgment and punishment of sin for men.

> **When he [the Holy Spirit] comes, he will convict the world of guilt in regard to sin and righteousness and judgment [all born by Christ]: in regard to sin, because men do not believe in me; in regard to righteousness, because I am going to the Father, where you can see me no longer; and in regard to judgment, because the prince of this world now stands condemned. (John 16:8-11)**

   c. Preaching in full assurance is a critical point. How can a minister preach and have the assurance that his preaching will bear fruit? How can he be assured that the power of God and of the Holy Spirit will rest upon his preaching? The answer is found in what is said in the following point, point three.

3. Paul lived what he preached. He lived a life that was completely surrendered to Christ. He lived and moved and had his being in Christ, walking and living ever so closely to Him. Conviction and confidence come from obedience—knowing that we are doing what we should be doing. It comes from knowing that we please God—that we are living pure and clean lives, praying and studying God's Word every day and witnessing to the saving grace of the Lord Jesus Christ. When we know that we are pleasing God, then we know that His presence and power will be upon us.
  ⇒ Obedience is the secret to assurance.
  ⇒ Obedience is the secret to the presence and power of God upon our lives and preaching.
  ⇒ Obedience is the secret to bearing fruit through preaching. This was the secret of Paul. Paul obeyed God; therefore, Paul was convinced that his preaching would be in power and in the Holy Spirit.

Thought 1. The world has yet to see what God will do with a man who obeys Him—totally and completely obeys Him—obeys Him...
- by living a pure and clean life.
- by praying and studying God's Word every day.
- by witnessing and sharing the saving grace of the Lord Jesus Christ.

> **Then he said to them all: "If anyone would come after me, he must deny himself and take up his cross daily and follow me. (Luke 9:23)**
>
> **Therefore, I urge you, brothers, in view of God's mercy, to offer your bodies as living sacrifices, holy and pleasing to God—this is your spiritual act of worship. Do not conform any longer to the pattern of this world, but be transformed by the renewing of your mind. Then you will be able to test and approve what God's will is—his good, pleasing and perfect will. (Rom 12:1-2)**
>
> **No, I beat my body and make it my slave so that after I have preached to others, I myself will not be disqualified for the prize. (1 Cor 9:27)**
>
> **Do you not know that your body is a temple of the Holy Spirit, who is in you, whom you have received from God? You are not your own; you were bought at a price. Therefore honor God with your body. (1 Cor 6:19-20)**
>
> **We demolish arguments and every pretension that sets itself up against the**

knowledge of God, and we take captive every thought to make it obedient to Christ. (2 Cor 10:5)

And to put on the new self, created to be like God in true righteousness and holiness. (Eph 4:24)

Since, then, you have been raised with Christ, set your hearts on things above, where Christ is seated at the right hand of God. Set your minds on things above, not on earthly things. For you died, and your life is now hidden with Christ in God. When Christ, who is your life, appears, then you also will appear with him in glory. (Col 3:1-4)

Let us draw near to God with a sincere heart in full assurance of faith, having our hearts sprinkled to cleanse us from a guilty conscience and having our bodies washed with pure water. (Heb 10:22)

We know that we have come to know him if we obey his commands. (1 John 2:3)

Dear children, let us not love with words or tongue but with actions and in truth. This then is how we know that we belong to the truth, and how we set our hearts at rest in his presence (1 John 3:18-19)

Thought 2. The point is this: the Thessalonians had a preacher who preached the gospel as it should be preached. They had a minister who surrendered his life totally to Christ: he *lived and preached* Christ and Christ alone. What a dynamic example for us! When we *live and preach* like we should, then our preaching will be in power and in the Holy Spirit. The presence and power of God Himself will rest upon our lives and ministries.

2 (1:6) **Decision**: they received the Word (the gospel) despite opposition and persecution. Remember: unbelieving Jews had opposed Paul and aroused some of the city troublemakers against him. The persecution became so threatening that Paul had been forced to flee the city (cp. Acts 17:4-10). However, his absence did not stop the persecution. In fact, it seems that the attack upon the church and its young believers became even more fierce. The Jews had convinced some of the Gentile citizens—some countrymen of the believers—to join them in trying to stop the gospel and destroy the church (cp. 1 Th.2:14). But note what Paul says:

⇒ The gospel still bore fruit. Some persons still received the Word and accepted Christ despite the opposition and persecution.

Do not be afraid of those who kill the body but cannot kill the soul. Rather, be afraid of the One who can destroy both soul and body in hell. (Mat 10:28)

For it has been granted to you on behalf of Christ not only to believe on him, but also to suffer for him, (Phil 1:29)

In fact, everyone who wants to live a godly life in Christ Jesus will be persecuted, (2 Tim 3:12)

⇒ The Holy Spirit rewarded the believers' commitment to Christ. He stirred joy in their hearts and lives, giving them full assurance of their eternal salvation and deliverance from death.

Though you have not seen him, you love him; and even though you do not see him now, you believe in him and are filled with an inexpressible and glorious joy, (1 Pet 1:8)

Yet to all who received him, to those who believed in his name, he gave the right to become children of God— (John 1:12)

The Spirit himself testifies with our spirit that we are God's children. Now if we are children, then we are heirs—heirs of God and co-heirs with Christ, if indeed we share in his sufferings in order that we may also share in his glory. (Rom 8:16-17)

One other fact is important: the believers became imitators (mimetai) of Paul and Christ. Is it right for people to imitate and follow preachers and other outstanding Christian leaders? A.T. Robertson gives an excellent answer to the question:

"It is a daring thing to expect people to 'imitate' the preacher, but Paul adds 'and of the Lord,' for he only expected or desired 'imitation' as he himself imitated the Lord Jesus, as he expressly says in 1 Cor.11:1. The peril of it all is that people so easily and so readily imitate the preacher when he does not imitate the Lord." (A.T. Robertson. *Word Pictures in the New Testament*, Vol.4. Nashville, TN: Broadman Press, 1931, p.11.)

Follow my example, as I follow the example of Christ. (1 Cor 11:1)

Thought 1. There are two striking lessons in this point.
1) Nothing, absolutely nothing, should keep a person from receiving the Word of the gospel—not even opposition and persecution.
2) Believers—preachers and laymen alike—must guard their lives ever so closely and make sure they are living for Christ and living ever so diligently for Him. Why? Because others are watching and following us—some child, some adult, some neighbor, some friend. There are people who look up to us and follow after us. Whether or not we like the fact, they are. Therefore, it behooves us to follow Christ as perfectly as we can.

Follow my example, as I follow the example of Christ. (1 Cor 11:1)
Be imitators of God, therefore, as dearly loved children (Eph 5:1)
So then, just as you received Christ Jesus as Lord, continue to live in him, (Col 2:6)
We do not want you to become lazy, but to imitate those who through faith and patience inherit what has been promised. (Heb 6:12)
If we claim to have fellowship with him yet walk in the darkness, we lie and do not live by the truth. (1 John 1:6)

1 THESSALONIANS 1:5-10

3 (1:7-8) **Witnessing—Testimony:** the model church became examples to other believers. This is a striking point: this young church was so committed to the Lord that their testimony spread all over the world. Note this: when Rome had conquered Greece, it had divided the country into two provinces, the northern province being Macedonia and the southern province being Achaia. Paul clearly says that the testimony of the church had spread all over Greece, both northern Greece and southern Greece. Then he adds that their faith had spread out beyond the borders of Greece. This must mean all over the world, for Thessalonica was a major commercial center where salesmen, tradesmen, and businessmen visited from all over the world. Just imagine the witnessing the church and its believers must have been doing day by day. Their excitement and enthusiasm for Christ and the opposition and persecution against them must have been the talk of the city and world.

> **Thought 1.** What a glorious testimony and dynamic example of witnessing! What a lesson for us today! How desperately we need to get to the task of living for Christ and being a testimony for Him.

> But you will receive power when the Holy Spirit comes on you; and you will be my witnesses in Jerusalem, and in all Judea and Samaria, and to the ends of the earth." (Acts 1:8)
> For we cannot help speaking about what we have seen and heard." (Acts 4:20)
> It is written: "I believed; therefore I have spoken." With that same spirit of faith we also believe and therefore speak, (2 Cor 4:13)
> So do not be ashamed to testify about our Lord, or ashamed of me his prisoner. But join with me in suffering for the gospel, by the power of God, (2 Tim 1:8)
> In everything set them an example by doing what is good. In your teaching show integrity, seriousness (Titus 2:7)
> These, then, are the things you should teach. Encourage and rebuke with all authority. Do not let anyone despise you. (Titus 2:15)
> Brothers, as an example of patience in the face of suffering, take the prophets who spoke in the name of the Lord. (James 5:10)
> But in your hearts set apart Christ as Lord. Always be prepared to give an answer to everyone who asks you to give the reason for the hope that you have. But do this with gentleness and respect, (1 Pet 3:15)
> Come and listen, all you who fear God; let me tell you what he has done for me. (Psa 66:16)
> "You are my witnesses," declares the LORD, "and my servant whom I have chosen, so that you may know and believe me and understand that I am he. Before me no god was formed, nor will there be one after me. (Isa 43:10)
> I have posted watchmen on your walls, O Jerusalem; they will never be silent day or night. You who call on the LORD, give yourselves no rest, (Isa 62:6)
> Then those who feared the LORD talked with each other, and the LORD listened and heard. A scroll of remembrance was written in his presence concerning those who feared the LORD and honored his name. (Mal 3:16)

4 (1:9-10) **Conversion—Repentance—Idolatry:** the model church turned to God from idols. Remember that Paul had been forced to flee from Thessalonica for his life. The only way he knew how the young church and its believers were holding up was from others who had been to Thessalonica to visit or conduct business. What he had heard thrilled his heart: the believers were standing fast in the gospel he had preached. There were three things in particular that struck him about their testimony.

1. The believers had turned to God from idols. John Walvoord makes an important point: they turned to God from idols, not from idols to God (*The Thessalonian Epistles*. Grand Rapids, MI: Zondervan, 1973, p.17).
   ⇒ They did not seek to clean up their own lives by themselves. They did not try to reform themselves by turning away from idols and then turning to God.
   ⇒ They turned to God first, then with God's help and strength, they repented and turned away from idols.

> Peter replied, "Repent and be baptized, every one of you, in the name of Jesus Christ for the forgiveness of your sins. And you will receive the gift of the Holy Spirit. (Acts 2:38)
> Repent, then, and turn to God, so that your sins may be wiped out, that times of refreshing may come from the Lord, (Acts 3:19)
> Repent of this wickedness and pray to the Lord. Perhaps he will forgive you for having such a thought in your heart. (Acts 8:22)
> In the past God overlooked such ignorance, but now he commands all people everywhere to repent. (Acts 17:30)
> Let the wicked forsake his way and the evil man his thoughts. Let him turn to the LORD, and he will have mercy on him, and to our God, for he will freely pardon. (Isa 55:7)
> "But if a wicked man turns away from all the sins he has committed and keeps all my decrees and does what is just and right, he will surely live; he will not die. (Ezek 18:21)

What is an idol? It is crucial to understand exactly what an idol is. Very simply, every man has an idea of what God is like and what God allows and does not allow. Some men take their ideas and make images of them by carving wood or melting and molding metal or porcelain. Other men just hold the images in their mind and picture God as being like this or like that. Either image is as much an idol as the other. An idol is merely an image of some god created by the mind of man—an image other than the God revealed by the Scripture (cp. Ro.1:21).

Note the sharp contrast made between these images of man's mind and God: God is the living and true God; the images are only the lifeless and false notions of men.

> "Therefore since we are God's offspring, we should not think that the divine being is like gold or silver or stone—an image made by man's design and skill. (Acts 17:29)

> For although they knew God, they neither glorified him as God nor gave thanks to him, but their thinking became futile and their foolish hearts were darkened. Although they claimed to be wise, they became fools and exchanged the glory of the immortal God for images made to look like mortal man and birds and animals and reptiles. (Rom 1:21-23)

> By his power God raised the Lord from the dead, and he will raise us also. Do you not know that your bodies are members of Christ himself? Shall I then take the members of Christ and unite them with a prostitute? Never! Do you not know that he who unites himself with a prostitute is one with her in body? For it is said, "The two will become one flesh." But he who unites himself with the Lord is one with him in spirit. Flee from sexual immorality. All other sins a man commits are outside his body, but he who sins sexually sins against his own body. (1 Cor 6:14-18)

> You cannot drink the cup of the Lord and the cup of demons too; you cannot have a part in both the Lord's table and the table of demons. (1 Cor 10:21)

> Dear children, keep yourselves from idols. (1 John 5:21)

> The LORD saw how great man's wickedness on the earth had become, and that every inclination of the thoughts of his heart was only evil all the time. (Gen 6:5)

> See, I am setting before you today a blessing and a curse—the blessing if you obey the commands of the LORD your God that I am giving you today; the curse if you disobey the commands of the LORD your God and turn from the way that I command you today by following other gods, which you have not known. (Deu 11:26-28)

> "I am the LORD; that is my name! I will not give my glory to another or my praise to idols. (Isa 42:8)

2. The believers had turned to God because of the promise of Christ's return. It was *God's Son* who was returning to earth, the Person who had died for them so that they might be acceptable to God and live with Him forever. They believed with all their hearts that they were to live with God forever. This was the reason they were waiting for the return of Christ. The word "wait" is in the present tense. This means that their hope for the return of Christ was alive. They expected Christ to return at any moment and eagerly looked for Him to rent the skies. Their expectation was a daily expectation.

> So you also must be ready, because the Son of Man will come at an hour when you do not expect him. (Mat 24:44)

> "Yes, it is as you say," Jesus replied. "But I say to all of you: In the future you will see the Son of Man sitting at the right hand of the Mighty One and coming on the clouds of heaven." (Mat 26:64)

> So he called ten of his servants and gave them ten minas. 'Put this money to work,' he said, 'until I come back.' (Luke 19:13)

> At that time they will see the Son of Man coming in a cloud with power and great glory. (Luke 21:27)

> "Do not be amazed at this, for a time is coming when all who are in their graves will hear his voice and come out—those who have done good will rise to live, and those who have done evil will rise to be condemned. (John 5:28-29)

> In my Father's house are many rooms; if it were not so, I would have told you. I am going there to prepare a place for you. And if I go and prepare a place for you, I will come back and take you to be with me that you also may be where I am. (John 14:2-3)

> "Men of Galilee," they said, "why do you stand here looking into the sky? This same Jesus, who has been taken from you into heaven, will come back in the same way you have seen him go into heaven." (Acts 1:11)

> Therefore you do not lack any spiritual gift as you eagerly wait for our Lord Jesus Christ to be revealed. (1 Cor 1:7)

> Therefore judge nothing before the appointed time; wait till the Lord comes. He will bring to light what is hidden in darkness and will expose the motives of men's hearts. At that time each will receive his praise from God. (1 Cor 4:5)

> For the Lord himself will come down from heaven, with a loud command, with the voice of the archangel and with the trumpet call of God, and the dead in Christ will rise first. After that, we who are still alive and are left will be caught up together with them in the clouds to meet the Lord in the air. And so we will be with the Lord forever. Therefore encourage each other with these words. (1 Th 4:16-18)

> May God himself, the God of peace, sanctify you through and through. May your whole spirit, soul and body be kept blameless at the coming of our Lord Jesus Christ. (1 Th 5:23)

> To keep this command without spot or blame until the appearing of our Lord Jesus Christ, (1 Tim 6:14)

> It teaches us to say "No" to ungodliness and worldly passions, and to live self-controlled, upright and godly lives in this present age, while we wait for the blessed hope—the glorious appearing of our great God and Savior, Jesus Christ, (Titus 2:12-13)

> So Christ was sacrificed once to take away the sins of many people; and he will appear a second time, not to bear sin, but to bring salvation to those who are waiting for him. (Heb 9:28)

1 THESSALONIANS 1:5-10

> And now, dear children, continue in him, so that when he appears we may be confident and unashamed before him at his coming. (1 John 2:28)

Note one other significant fact. How do we know that Christ is going to return to earth and take believers to live with God forever? Because God raised up Christ from the dead. By resurrecting Christ, God...
- proved that He is the God of all power.
- proved that He has the power to raise the dead.
- proved that He is going to do just as Christ taught: raise all men, some to eternal life and some to eternal death, that is, to be eternally separated from God.

> And who through the Spirit of holiness was declared with power to be the Son of God by his resurrection from the dead: Jesus Christ our Lord. (Rom 1:4)
>
> For if the dead are not raised, then Christ has not been raised either. And if Christ has not been raised, your faith is futile; you are still in your sins. Then those also who have fallen asleep in Christ are lost. (1 Cor 15:16-18)
>
> And his incomparably great power for us who believe. That power is like the working of his mighty strength, which he exerted in Christ when he raised him from the dead and seated him at his right hand in the heavenly realms, (Eph 1:19-20)
>
> Praise be to the God and Father of our Lord Jesus Christ! In his great mercy he has given us new birth into a living hope through the resurrection of Jesus Christ from the dead, (1 Pet 1:3)

3. The believers had turned to God to escape the wrath of God. Note this: a day of wrath is coming; it has to come, for man and his universe are corruptible and imperfect and are in rebellion against God. The world is already condemned; the day of wrath is already set. But this is the glorious news of the gospel: we can be delivered from the wrath to come. The word "rescues" (ruomenon) means to deliver us right out of the wrath. The picture is that of God rescuing and lifting us up out of the wrath.

> Whoever believes in him is not condemned, but whoever does not believe stands condemned already because he has not believed in the name of God's one and only Son. (John 3:18)
>
> Whoever believes in the Son has eternal life, but whoever rejects the Son will not see life, for God's wrath remains on him." (John 3:36)
>
> The wrath of God is being revealed from heaven against all the godlessness and wickedness of men who suppress the truth by their wickedness, (Rom 1:18)
>
> But among you there must not be even a hint of sexual immorality, or of any kind of impurity, or of greed, because these are improper for God's holy people. Nor should there be obscenity, foolish talk or coarse joking, which are out of place, but rather thanksgiving. For of this you can be sure: No immoral, impure or greedy person—such a man is an idolater—has any inheritance in the kingdom of Christ and of God. Let no one deceive you with empty words, for because of such things God's wrath comes on those who are disobedient. (Eph 5:3-6)
>
> Put to death, therefore, whatever belongs to your earthly nature: sexual immorality, impurity, lust, evil desires and greed, which is idolatry. Because of these, the wrath of God is coming. (Col 3:5-6)
>
> The nations were angry; and your wrath has come. The time has come for judging the dead, and for rewarding your servants the prophets and your saints and those who reverence your name, both small and great— and for destroying those who destroy the earth." (Rev 11:18)

1 THESSALONIANS 2:1-12

	CHAPTER 2 C. The Model Church: A Strong & True Minister,^{DS1} 2:1-12	you or anyone else. As apostles of Christ we could have been a burden to you, 7 But we were gentle among you, like a mother caring for her little children. 8 We loved you so much that we were delighted to share with you not only the gospel of God but our lives as well, because you had become so dear to us. 9 Surely you remember, brothers, our toil and hardship; we worked night and day in order not to be a burden to anyone while we preached the gospel of God to you. 10 You are witnesses, and so is God, of how holy, righteous and blameless we were among you who believed. 11 For you know that we dealt with each of you as a father deals with his own children, 12 Encouraging, comforting and urging you to live lives worthy of God, who calls you into his kingdom and glory.	& authority of position

1 He has a full & fruitful ministry—not an empty & fruitless ministry
2 He preaches boldly
  a. In great trials, even imprisonment
  b. In facing opposition
3 He preaches a pure gospel, lives a clean life, & does not deceive people
4 He preaches to please God, not men
 	
5 He does not preach for what he can get out of it
  a. Does not use flattery
  b. Is not greedy
6 He does not preach for glory nor for prestige
	You know, brothers, that our visit to you was not a failure.
	2 We had previously suffered and been insulted in Philippi, as you know, but with the help of our God we dared to tell you his gospel in spite of strong opposition.
	3 For the appeal we make does not spring from error or impure motives, nor are we trying to trick you.
	4 On the contrary, we speak as men approved by God to be entrusted with the gospel. We are not trying to please men but God, who tests our hearts.
	5 You know we never used flattery, nor did we put on a mask to cover up greed—God is our witness.
	6 We were not looking for praise from men, not from
			7 He preaches gently & lovingly
			  a. As a mother
			  b. As giving his own soul
			
			8 He preaches, laboring night & day
			  a. With great labor & hardship
			  b. With no charge
			
			9 He preaches with a clean life, an impeccable life
			
			10 He preaches as a father—tenderly giving direction
			
			11 He preaches with one objective—edification

DIVISION I

THE MODEL CHURCH, 1:1-3:13

C. The Model Church: A Strong and True Minister, 2:1-12

(2:1-12) **Introduction**: remember the church at Thessalonica was under heavy persecution. The Jewish religionists had risen up against Paul and the church and were set on destroying both. They enlisted all the Gentile citizens they could to join their attack. They convinced the people that the preaching of Christ would destroy their freedom and affect their jobs and businesses. The persecution became so violent that Paul was forced to flee for his life. However, his absence did not stop the persecution. The attacks against the church and its believers continued. One form which the persecution took was to destroy the reputation of Paul. Accusation after accusation was leveled against Paul, and rumor after rumor was spread about him.

Paul's purpose in writing this passage was to strengthen and build up the believers in Christ. To do so he had to answer and correct the charges against him. Paul knew how easily people are influenced by charges and rumors and how easily they become exaggerated. He wanted no question and no misunderstanding about him and the ministry of Christ. He was a minister of Christ, a true minister, and the gospel of Christ was true. This meant that their faith was valid. They were truly saved and made acceptable to God by the death of Christ, and they were going to live eternally in God's kingdom and glory (v.12). The point is this: this passage gives us the picture of a strong minister—the kind of minister and servant of Christ that every believer should be.

1. He has a full and fruitful ministry—not vain and fruitless (v.1).
2. He preaches boldly (v.2).
3. He preaches a pure gospel, lives a clean life, and does not deceive people (v.3).
4. He preaches to please God, not men (v.4).
5. He does not preach for what he can get out of it (v.5).
6. He does not preach for glory nor for the prestige and authority of position (v.6).
7. He preaches gently and lovingly (v.7-8).
8. He preaches, laboring night and day (v.9).
9. He preaches with a clean life, an impeccable life (v.10).
10. He preaches as a father—tenderly giving direction (v.11).
11. He preaches with one objective—edification (v.12).

(2:1-12) **Another Outline**: A Strong Minister.
1. Background (v.1).
  a. Opponents slandered Paul.
  b. He was not a failure.
2. His boldness (v.2).
3. His message: a pure gospel (v.3).
4. His motive (v.4-6).
  a. Not to please men but God.
  b. Not flattering words.
  c. Not for greed.
  d. Not for glory.
  e. Not even claiming due rights.

1 THESSALONIANS 2:1-12

5. His testimony (v.7-11).
   a. A gentle man (v.7-8).
   b. A laboring man (v.9).
   c. A clean man (v.10).
   d. A fatherly man (v.11a).
6. His fatherly approach (v.11).
7. His one objective: edification (v.12).

DEEPER STUDY # 1
(2:1-12) Paul, Charges Against: this passage shows the charges being leveled against Paul by those who were trying to destroy his reputation (see notes, *Introduction*—1 Th.2:1-12; 2 Cor.1:12-22).

1 (2:1) **Paul, Accusations Against—Minister, Faithfulness**: the strong and true minister has a full and fruitful ministry, not a failure (gegonen) ministry. The word failure means empty, ineffective, and fruitless. Paul reminds the believers that his ministry among them was not an empty and fruitless ministry. People had been ministered to and some had even accepted Christ and experienced a genuine conversion. They were now living for Christ—living for Him through the most difficult of times, even persecution. Therefore, the charge that his ministry was empty and fruitless was false. God had His hand upon him and God was blessing his ministry.

2 (2:2) **Minister—Preaching**: the strong minister preaches boldly even when there is opposition. Right before Paul had launched his mission into Thessalonica, he had been shamefully mistreated and imprisoned by some businessmen in Philippi, and he was forced by the city officials to leave the city. However, this did not discourage Paul. He did not give up the ministry because he had been persecuted. He moved on to another city, Thessalonica. But note what he faced in Thessalonica: persecution—the same mistreatment and attacks. Did this discourage and cause him to give up the ministry? No! He continued to boldly preach the gospel despite the opposition and conflict. The point is this: bold preaching is proof of a true and strong minister. A true and strong minister knows that God has called him and he knows why God has called him: to preach the gospel. Therefore, he boldly preaches regardless of circumstances. His bold preaching of the gospel is one of the strongest answers to his critics.

> **Thought 1.** Note what bold preaching means. It means to preach "His gospel [God's]" not to lambast one's critics. The pulpit is not the place to deal with critics; it is the place for preaching the gospel of God—the place where the unsearchable riches of Christ are to be proclaimed. This is exactly what Paul did despite the critics of the gospel who opposed him.
>
> **As you go, preach this message: 'The kingdom of heaven is near.' (Mat 10:7)**
> **He said to them, "Go into all the world and preach the good news to all creation. (Mark 16:15)**
> **"Go, stand in the temple courts," he said, "and tell the people the full message of this new life." (Acts 5:20)**
> **At once he began to preach in the synagogues that Jesus is the Son of God. (Acts 9:20)**
> **It is because of him that you are in Christ Jesus, who has become for us wisdom from God—that is, our righteousness, holiness and redemption. (1 Cor 1:30)**
> **For we do not preach ourselves, but Jesus Christ as Lord, and ourselves as your servants for Jesus' sake. (2 Cor 4:5)**
> **Preach the Word; be prepared in season and out of season; correct, rebuke and encourage—with great patience and careful instruction. (2 Tim 4:2)**

> **Thought 2.** The word "dared" (eparresiasametha) means to speak boldly and freely; to speak out and to speak publicly without fear. Too many fail to witness for Christ because they fear ridicule, embarrassment, mockery, and persecution. They are secret believers of Christ instead of bold witnesses for Christ.

3 (2:3) **Minister**: the strong and true minister preaches a pure gospel, lives a clean life, and does not deceive people. Three things are said here.

1. The strong minister preaches a pure gospel. His appeal, the gospel he preaches, is not based upon error (planes). Paul did not add to nor take away from the Word of God.

⇒ He did not tip-toe around or bypass controversial subjects because of opposition.
⇒ He did not attempt to tickle the ears of people by preaching only the subjects that they liked; he did not neglect the whole counsel of God's Word.
⇒ He did not concentrate on pleasing subjects in order to win the approval of people; he did not neglect the subjects of sin and judgment.
⇒ He did not preach in order to secure personal acceptance and support nor to gain a personal following.
⇒ He did not preach to secure his livelihood nor to strengthen his position as pastor.
⇒ He did not preach his own ideas nor the novel ideas of others. He did not follow the latest theological fashion in order to appear up-to-date and well-read.

Paul preached the pure gospel, the pure Word of God. The message of Jesus Christ was not his creation; it was the act of God, the glorious gospel of salvation which God had sent to men through His Son. Paul was not the creator of the message; God was.

⇒ Paul was only the messenger of God—a mere man whom God had employed to proclaim His message.
⇒ Paul was only the ambassador of God—a mere servant chosen to deliver the King's message to the world of men.

The point is this: Paul had no right to change the message. He had absolutely nothing to do with formulating the gospel of Christ. Therefore, he preached the gospel exactly as God had given it. He preached the pure gospel, the pure Word of God, and he did it without deviating one iota from it.

2. The strong minister lives a pure and clean life. The word "impure" (akatharsias) has to do with moral uncleanness and impurity (William Barclay. *The Letters to the Philippians, Colossians, and Thessalonians*. "The Daily Study Bible." Philadelphia, PA: The Westminster Press, 1959, p.220). Paul was being charged with immorality. A.T. Robertson quotes Lightfoot and points out that this may be

startling, to think that Paul was accused of immorality. However, such an accusation was not to be unexpected because of the immoral society of the day, a society so immoral that it had permeated some of the very religions of the day. Paul clearly says that he was not guilty. He had not used the ministry nor his position in the ministry to attract women. He had not lived an impure life. (A.T. Robertson. *Word Pictures in the New Testament*, Vol.4, p.16.)

Thought 1. Note two lessons that we must always keep in mind as the followers and servants of God.
1) Some believers—ministers and laymen alike—have rumors spread about them. Rumors, of course, damage and hurt and often destroy the testimony and ministry of people. But most tragic of all, rumors always affect the name of Christ and turn some people away from the gospel and from any chance of ever being reached for Christ. The persons who begin and spread rumors that destroy people shall face the wrath of God regardless of their profession to know God.
2) Some believers—ministers and laymen alike—fall and commit immorality. This, of course, stirs wild imaginations in those who are most hurt by the fall of the believer, wild imaginations of immoral behavior heaped upon immoral behavior. The hurt person shares his or her hurt with dear friends, and from this, rumors begin. Before long, rumor is built upon rumor. Unfortunately, this goes on until about all that is known is rumor and what has been imagined. As the followers and ministers of Christ, we must always remember this: if the fallen person is a genuine believer, a true follower of the Lord Jesus Christ, one of two things will happen...
- The fallen believer will repent and confess his sin to God, and God will forgive him. God will also begin to use him again—sometimes more effectively than ever before. Why? Because God is a God of restoration. If He were not, few if any of us would ever be serving Him. This is a fact that we desperately need to learn.
- God will take the fallen believer on home to be with Him. Some genuine believers do slip into sin and enslavement—a point beyond which they are willing to return to Christ. Now note: only God knows when a believer is unwilling to repent and when he has reached the point where he will never repent. At that point, the believer is never again to be a witness for Christ. In fact, his life and testimony are only doing damage and cutting the heart of Christ beyond imagination. Therefore, God has no choice but to take him on home to be with Him. (See outline and note, *Judgment*—1 Cor.11:27-30 for more discussion.)

For you know what instructions we gave you by the authority of the Lord Jesus. It is God's will that you should be sanctified: that you should avoid sexual immorality; that each of you should learn to control his own body in a way that is holy and honorable, not in passionate lust like the heathen, who do not know God; and that in this matter no one should wrong his brother or take advantage of him. The Lord will punish men for all such sins, as we have already told you and warned you. (1 Th 4:2-6)

Avoid every kind of evil. May God himself, the God of peace, sanctify you through and through. May your whole spirit, soul and body be kept blameless at the coming of our Lord Jesus Christ. (1 Th 5:22-23)

Dear friends, I urge you, as aliens and strangers in the world, to abstain from sinful desires, which war against your soul. (1 Pet 2:11)

3. The strong minister does not deceive people. There is no deception about him at all.
   a. Paul did not deceive people by preaching a false gospel. He was not out...
   - to secure a personal following.
   - to earn a living.
   - to serve in a respectable profession.
   - to live a comfortable life.

   Paul was sincere and genuine: he preached a true gospel. And he was out only to share that gospel so that men might come to know the only living and true God.
   b. Paul did not deceive people by the life he lived. He did not preach one thing and live another. He was not unclean, immoral, and dirty. He lived a pure and righteous life before God and the people.

If you point these things out to the brothers, you will be a good minister of Christ Jesus, brought up in the truths of the faith and of the good teaching that you have followed. (1 Tim 4:6)

He must hold firmly to the trustworthy message as it has been taught, so that he can encourage others by sound doctrine and refute those who oppose it. For there are many rebellious people, mere talkers and deceivers, especially those of the circumcision group. (Titus 1:9-10)

You must teach what is in accord with sound doctrine. (Titus 2:1)

4 (2:4) **Minister**: the strong and true minister preaches and ministers to please God, not men. Most men do not want to hear...
- about sin and judgment.
- about the utter necessity of men to depend upon the death of Christ in order to be saved.
- about the demand that a person commit all he is and has to Christ in order to meet the needs of a desperate world.

The preaching of the truth is not always popular, not with a worldly and unbelieving people. Therefore, when a minister is thrown in the midst of a people who are worldly, he can be tempted to tone down his message to please the people. The temptation can be especially strong if his livelihood is at risk.

However, note what Paul says: he sought only to please God, not men. There were two strong reasons why.

1 THESSALONIANS 2:1-12

1. First, God was the Person who had trusted him with the gospel, not men. God owned the gospel, and He was the Person who had called Paul to proclaim the gospel. Men had nothing to do with the formulation of the gospel nor with calling Paul. God would take care of him as he preached the gospel. God had called him to preach; therefore, he was God's. Consequently, he could trust God to take care of him if men reacted against the gospel and attacked him.

2. Second, God alone would try his heart and judge him. He was to stand and give an account for his ministry some day, and he was to stand before God, not before men. Men might be able to cause some difficulty for him on earth, but God would cause difficulty for him through all eternity if he abused or opposed the gospel of God.

> But no one would say anything publicly about him for fear of the Jews. (John 7:13)
>
> The one who sent me is with me; he has not left me alone, for I always do what pleases him." (John 8:29)
>
> For they loved praise from men more than praise from God. (John 12:43)
>
> Slaves, obey your earthly masters in everything; and do it, not only when their eye is on you and to win their favor, but with sincerity of heart and reverence for the Lord. (Col 3:22)
>
> On the contrary, we speak as men approved by God to be entrusted with the gospel. We are not trying to please men but God, who tests our hearts. (1 Th 2:4)
>
> Finally, brothers, we instructed you how to live in order to please God, as in fact you are living. Now we ask you and urge you in the Lord Jesus to do this more and more. (1 Th 4:1)
>
> By faith Enoch was taken from this life, so that he did not experience death; he could not be found, because God had taken him away. For before he was taken, he was commended as one who pleased God. (Heb 11:5)
>
> Fear of man will prove to be a snare, but whoever trusts in the LORD is kept safe. (Prov 29:25)
>
> "I, even I, am he who comforts you. Who are you that you fear mortal men, the sons of men, who are but grass, (Isa 51:12)

5 (2:5) **Ministers**: the strong and true minister does not preach and minister for what he can get out of it.

1. The word "flattery" (kolakeias) always means the kind of flattery that is given in order to get something out of people (William Barclay. *The Letters to the Philippians, Colossians, and Thessalonians*, p.221). Paul did not flatter people in order to secure their friendship, following, or support. He, of course, commended people; and his letters in the New Testament show that he commended them quite often. But he did it truthfully, always covering the weak areas that people needed to strengthen as well as their strong and commendable areas.

> I will show partiality to no one, nor will I flatter any man; (Job 32:21)
>
> May the LORD cut off all flattering lips and every boastful tongue (Psa 12:3)
>
> Whoever says to the guilty, "You are innocent"— peoples will curse him and nations denounce him. (Prov 24:24)
>
> A lying tongue hates those it hurts, and a flattering mouth works ruin. (Prov 26:28)
>
> He who rebukes a man will in the end gain more favor than he who has a flattering tongue. (Prov 28:23)
>
> Whoever flatters his neighbor is spreading a net for his feet. (Prov 29:5)

2. The word greed shows that Paul was accused of being in the ministry out of greed; that he had chosen the ministry to earn a livelihood and to make money. Paul emphatically denies this and says that his lifestyle proves it. He declares that the church knows the fact and that God is witness to the truth.

> Then he said to them, "Watch out! Be on your guard against all kinds of greed; a man's life does not consist in the abundance of his possessions." (Luke 12:15)
>
> Do not repay anyone evil for evil. Be careful to do what is right in the eyes of everybody. (Rom 12:17)
>
> Let no debt remain outstanding, except the continuing debt to love one another, for he who loves his fellowman has fulfilled the law. (Rom 13:8)
>
> For we are taking pains to do what is right, not only in the eyes of the Lord but also in the eyes of men. (2 Cor 8:21)
>
> Put to death, therefore, whatever belongs to your earthly nature: sexual immorality, impurity, lust, evil desires and greed, which is idolatry. (Col 3:5)
>
> "From the least to the greatest, all are greedy for gain; prophets and priests alike, all practice deceit. (Jer 6:13)
>
> My people come to you, as they usually do, and sit before you to listen to your words, but they do not put them into practice. With their mouths they express devotion, but their hearts are greedy for unjust gain. (Ezek 33:31)

6 (2:6) **Minister**: the strong and true minister does not preach or minister for glory nor for the prestige and authority of a position. Note two things.

1. Paul says that he did not seek the glory, prestige, honor, or recognition of people. He was not out to be recognized as a *great preacher or good minister*. He was not seeking to be recognized as a leader or as a man of position and authority.

> Not so with you. Instead, whoever wants to become great among you must be your servant, and whoever wants to be first must be your slave—just as the Son of Man did not come to be served, but to serve, and to give his life as a ransom for many." (Mat 20:26-28)
>
> The greatest among you will be your servant. (Mat 23:11)
>
> How can you believe if you accept praise from one another, yet make no effort to obtain the praise that comes from the only God ? (John 5:44)

Whoever serves me must follow me; and where I am, my servant also will be. My Father will honor the one who serves me. (John 12:26)

For, "All men are like grass, and all their glory is like the flowers of the field; the grass withers and the flowers fall, (1 Pet 1:24)

For he will take nothing with him when he dies, his splendor will not descend with him. (Psa 49:17)

He will call upon me, and I will answer him; I will be with him in trouble, I will deliver him and honor him. (Psa 91:15)

Therefore the grave enlarges its appetite and opens its mouth without limit; into it will descend their nobles and masses with all their brawlers and revelers. (Isa 5:14)

The more the priests increased, the more they sinned against me; they exchanged their Glory for something disgraceful. (Hosea 4:7)

2. Paul says that he had the right to assert his authority as an apostle of Christ. Being a minister of God is a great honor, and men should respect and appreciate the call. But the minister of God must not exalt his authority, for he has been called by God Himself, called to serve the sovereign Majesty of the universe. He must not be demanding and ordering people around. God has not called the minister to hold a position of honor and authority, but to minister and preach the gospel.

7 (2:7-8) **Minister**: the strong and true minister preaches and ministers gently and lovingly. What Paul says is descriptive and it shows the deep love he held for the church and its believers at Thessalonica.

1. Paul was as gentle toward them as a mother who nurses her children. The idea is that the minister must minister to his people with...

- tenderness
- care
- warmth
- intensity
- affection
- love

He must treat them as precious, as his most beloved people, holding them ever so closely to his heart.

2. Paul's affection for his people was so strong that he preached the gospel to them in the midst of adversity and great opposition. And he was willing to do even more: he was willing to pour out his soul for them; to sacrifice his very life to make sure that they came to know Christ and the eternal salvation that was in Him. Note that Paul says he was willing to sacrifice his life for one simple reason: they were dear (agapetoi) to him. The word dear means beloved, very dear. They were his beloved people.

So be on your guard! Remember that for three years I never stopped warning each of you night and day with tears. (Acts 20:31)

Therefore, my brothers, you whom I love and long for, my joy and crown, that is how you should stand firm in the Lord, dear friends! (Phil 4:1)

And the Lord's servant must not quarrel; instead, he must be kind to everyone, able to teach, not resentful. (2 Tim 2:24)

Now that you have purified yourselves by obeying the truth so that you have sincere love for your brothers, love one another deeply, from the heart. (1 Pet 1:22)

8 (2:9) **Minister**: the strong and true minister preaches and ministers, laboring night and day. John Walvoord makes a striking point: Paul did not have a five day nor a forty hour week. He did not work until four or five o'clock nor until dark and then have the rest of the day for himself (*The Thessalonian Epistles*, p.30).

Paul was the servant of Christ to meet the desperate needs of the world and to reach men with the glorious news that Christ could save them from death and give them eternal life. How could he rest and relax when people in every city and community were dying every day? He, of course, needed sleep and rest as all men do; but it is clear from Paul's letters that he slept and rested only as he needed. He was not slothful nor lazy when it came to sleeping and lounging around. Note why: he did not want to be chargeable to any man. What did he mean? Just what God says: that every minister and believer has the blood of the world upon his hands and will be held accountable for getting the message out to them—the message that they can be saved from death and receive eternal life.

But everyone who hears these words of mine and does not put them into practice is like a foolish man who built his house on sand. (Mat 7:26)

Do you not say, 'Four months more and then the harvest'? I tell you, open your eyes and look at the fields! They are ripe for harvest. Even now the reaper draws his wages, even now he harvests the crop for eternal life, so that the sower and the reaper may be glad together. (John 4:35-36)

Jesus said, "You have now seen him; in fact, he is the one speaking with you." Then the man said, "Lord, I believe," and he worshiped him. (John 9:37-38)

So then, men ought to regard us as servants of Christ and as those entrusted with the secret things of God. Now it is required that those who have been given a trust must prove faithful. (1 Cor 4:1-2)

Pray continually; give thanks in all circumstances, for this is God's will for you in Christ Jesus. (1 Th 5:17-18)

That conforms to the glorious gospel of the blessed God, which he entrusted to me. I thank Christ Jesus our Lord, who has given me strength, that he considered me faithful, appointing me to his service. (1 Tim 1:11-12)

And at his appointed season he brought his word to light through the preaching entrusted to me by the command of God our Savior, (Titus 1:3)

"That servant who knows his master's will and does not get ready or does not do what his master wants will be beaten with many blows. (Luke 12:47)

When I say to the wicked, 'O wicked man, you will surely die,' and you do not speak out to dissuade him from his ways, that wicked man will die for his sin, and I will hold you accountable for his blood. But if you do warn the wicked man to turn from his ways and he does not do so, he

1 THESSALONIANS 2:1-12

will die for his sin, but you will have saved yourself. (Ezek 33:8-9)

9 (2:10) **Minister**: the strong and true minister preaches and ministers with a clean life, an impeccable life. Paul says...
- that he lived a holy life before God: a life separated from the world and set apart totally to God.
- that he lived a just and righteous life before men: a life that loved and treated men just as God said and just as he wanted them to treat him.
- that he lived a blameless life before both God and man.

> So I strive always to keep my conscience clear before God and man. (Acts 24:16)
>
> Therefore I urge you to imitate me. (1 Cor 4:16)
>
> Follow my example, as I follow the example of Christ. (1 Cor 11:1)
>
> So that you may become blameless and pure, children of God without fault in a crooked and depraved generation, in which you shine like stars in the universe (Phil 2:15)
>
> Join with others in following my example, brothers, and take note of those who live according to the pattern we gave you. (Phil 3:17)
>
> Whatever you have learned or received or heard from me, or seen in me—put it into practice. And the God of peace will be with you. (Phil 4:9)
>
> What you heard from me, keep as the pattern of sound teaching, with faith and love in Christ Jesus. (2 Tim 1:13)

10 (2:11) **Minister**: the strong and true minister preached as a father, tenderly giving direction. The minister is not only like a mother (see note—1 Th.2:7-8), but he is also like a father. Three fatherly functions are listed.

⇒ The minister encourages just like a father: directs, guides, and teaches.

> For you can all prophesy in turn so that everyone may be instructed and encouraged. (1 Cor 14:31)
>
> Therefore encourage each other with these words. (1 Th 4:18)
>
> Therefore encourage one another and build each other up, just as in fact you are doing. (1 Th 5:11)
>
> Command and teach these things. (1 Tim 4:11)

⇒ The minister comforts just like a father: encourages, consoles, supports, sustains, holds up, lifts up, relieves and eases pain.

> If you have any encouragement from being united with Christ, if any comfort from his love, if any fellowship with the Spirit, if any tenderness and compassion, then make my joy complete by being like-minded, having the same love, being one in spirit and purpose. (Phil 2:1-2)
>
> Preach the Word; be prepared in season and out of season; correct, rebuke and encourage—with great patience and careful instruction. (2 Tim 4:2)
>
> He must hold firmly to the trustworthy message as it has been taught, so that he can encourage others by sound doctrine and refute those who oppose it. (Titus 1:9)
>
> These, then, are the things you should teach. Encourage and rebuke with all authority. Do not let anyone despise you. (Titus 2:15)

⇒ The minister urges just like a father: testifies, witnesses, protects, and warns.

> See to it that no one takes you captive through hollow and deceptive philosophy, which depends on human tradition and the basic principles of this world rather than on Christ. (Col 2:8)
>
> Tell Archippus: "See to it that you complete the work you have received in the Lord." (Col 4:17)
>
> Those who oppose him he must gently instruct, in the hope that God will grant them repentance leading them to a knowledge of the truth, (2 Tim 2:25)
>
> And we have the word of the prophets made more certain, and you will do well to pay attention to it, as to a light shining in a dark place, until the day dawns and the morning star rises in your hearts. (2 Pet 1:19)
>
> Therefore, dear friends, since you already know this, be on your guard so that you may not be carried away by the error of lawless men and fall from your secure position. (2 Pet 3:17)

11 (2:12) **Minister**: the strong and true minister preaches and ministers with one objective—to lead his people to live worthy of the Lord. God has given us the most glorious promise imaginable: the wonderful privilege of living forever in His kingdom and glory. Therefore, we must live worthy of that promise. We must live excellent lives—live day by day just as we should live—honoring and building up the name of God.

> So I say, live by the Spirit, and you will not gratify the desires of the sinful nature. (Gal 5:16)
>
> As a prisoner for the Lord, then, I urge you to live a life worthy of the calling you have received. (Eph 4:1)
>
> Be very careful, then, how you live—not as unwise but as wise, (Eph 5:15)
>
> So then, just as you received Christ Jesus as Lord, continue to live in him, (Col 2:6)
>
> But if we walk in the light, as he is in the light, we have fellowship with one another, and the blood of Jesus, his Son, purifies us from all sin. (1 John 1:7)
>
> Whoever claims to live in him must walk as Jesus did. (1 John 2:6)

1 THESSALONIANS 2:13-20

D. The Model Church: A Strong People, 2:13-20

1 They received the Word of God as the Word of GodDS1 a. Received it thru men b. Received it not as the Word of men, but as it is in truth, the Word of God c. Received it as it worked in their lives	13 And we also thank God continually because, when you received the word of God, which you heard from us, you accepted it not as the word of men, but as it actually is, the word of God, which is at work in you who believe.
2 They became followers of strong churches: Stood fast despite severe persecution	14 For you, brothers, became imitators of God's churches in Judea, which are in Christ Jesus: You suffered from your own countrymen the same things those churches suffered from the Jews,
3 They escaped the Jews' guilt a. Killed the Lord Jesus b. Killed the prophets c. Persecuted believers d. Did not please God	15 Who killed the Lord Jesus and the prophets and also drove us out. They displease God and are hostile to all men

e. Opposed all men
f. Shut people out
g. The result of their guilt
  1) They became full of their sins
  2) They brought wrath upon themselves
	16 In their effort to keep us from speaking to the Gentiles so that they may be saved. In this way they always heap up their sins to the limit. The wrath of God has come upon them at last.

4 They possessed a strong fellowship a. Paul had been forced to flee because of persecution b. Paul wished to return c. Paul was opposed by Satan**DS2**	17 But, brothers, when we were torn away from you for a short time (in person, not in thought), out of our intense longing we made every effort to see you. 18 For we wanted to come to you—certainly I, Paul, did, again and again—but Satan stopped us.
5 They were destined to bring glory & joy to their ministers a. To Paul b. At Christ's coming	19 For what is our hope, our joy, or the crown in which we will glory in the presence of our Lord Jesus when he comes? Is it not you? 20 Indeed, you are our glory and joy.

DIVISION I

THE MODEL CHURCH, 1:1-3:13

D. The Model Church: A Strong People, 2:13-20

(2:13-20) **Introduction**: a strong church is a church of strong people, a people who have trusted Jesus Christ as their Savior and Lord and who are continuing steadfast in Him. This passage covers the traits of a strong people.
1. They received the Word of God as the Word of God (v.13).
2. They became followers of strong churches: stood fast despite severe persecution (v.14).
3. They escaped the Jews' guilt (v.15-16).
4. They possessed a strong fellowship (v.17-18).
5. They were destined to bring glory and joy (v.19-20).

1 (2:13) **Word of God**: a strong people receive the Word of God as the Word of God. Note three facts.

1. The Thessalonian believers had received the Word through the preaching and teaching of men. Paul, Silas, and Timothy had carried and proclaimed the Word of God to them. They or some other believer had to take the Word to the Thessalonians, for there was no other way they could have received it. It takes people to communicate the Word of God. If believers did not speak and share the Word, then it would never be heard or received. It would stop dead in its tracks and no one would ever again be reached for Christ. There would never again be a branch added to the tree of life. The only way the Word of God can go forth is for believers to share it. The point is this: proclaiming and bearing witness to the Word of God is God's *ordained way* to reach the world for Christ. He has ordained the mission of proclaiming it *to men*, not to angels nor to any other creature. The duty to proclaim and bear testimony to the Word of God lies in the lap of believers. For this reason, we must proclaim and bear witness to God's Word every day of our lives. The very life of every soul upon earth rests in our hands. Paul knew this; that is the reason he had carried the Word of God to the Thessalonians.

2. The Thessalonian believers had received the Word not as the word of men, but as it is in truth, *the Word of God*. What a phenomenal statement! Paul unequivocally declares that the Word he proclaimed was not the word of men, but the Word of God Himself. He further adds "but as it actually is, the word of God." Do you and I believe that the Word of God is the Word of God?
⇒ The Thessalonians believed it.
⇒ Paul believed it.
⇒ But do you and I believe it? Really believe it?

Remember: what Paul preached was the Old Testament Scriptures and the mysteries of Christ which God had revealed directly to him (cp. Ro.16:25-26; 1 Cor.2:7; Eph.1:9; 3:4, 9; Col.1:27; 2:2; 4:3; 2 Tim.3:16). Most people—by far most—do not believe that the Word of God (the Bible) is the Word of God. They receive the Word of God only as the word of men.
⇒ They think that the Word of God is only of men.
⇒ Some think that the New Testament is only what the early apostles and believers could remember about Christ and conclude from His teaching.
⇒ Some think that the Old Testament is only the religious book and religious fables of the Jews, written by their great religious leaders.
⇒ Some think that the Bible is the great religious book chosen by God to use in the lives of people when it is proclaimed. Sitting on the shelf, they say that the Bible is not the Word of God, but when it is read or proclaimed, it becomes the Word of God; God uses its message to move upon the hearts of people and convict them.

However, note a critical point, a point so critical that it can be the determining factor that affects a man's eternal destiny: both the Bible and Paul claim that the Word of God is not the word of men, but the Word of God. "*It*

1 THESSALONIANS 2:13-20

actually is, the Word of God." And the Thessalonian church and its believers received it as the Word of God. (See DEEPER STUDY # 1, *Word of God*—1 Th.2:13 for more discussion.)

3. The Thessalonian believers received the Word so that it could work and operate in their lives. The verse says that it is God who *is at work in you who believe*. But what is it that we believe? The Word of God. If we do not believe the Word of God, there is nothing left to believe but the word of men. And the best that men can give us is messages and words that stir us to greater...

- self-improvement
- self-development
- self-image
- works
- goodness
- morality
- justice
- equality
- commitment

All of this is good, but it has one terrible flaw: it ends. Everything about man ends when man dies. The messages and words of men can do no more than what man can do, and man can do no more than die and continue in his terrible separation from life and God. Man cannot save himself. This is the reason man must hope and trust that God is love and has loved us enough to speak to us—speak accurately and clearly. If God cares no more than to leave us in the dark about how to become acceptable to Him, then we never want to have to face Him. Why? Because He could not be a God of love—not if He has left us in a dark, evil, and destructive world—left us groping and grasping to find our way to Him. A God of love would love and speak to us clearly and accurately, without any error, so that we could unmistakably know Him, ourselves, and the world:

⇒ who we are
⇒ why we are here
⇒ why things are the way they are
⇒ where we are going

This is the glorious gospel: God has loved us and has given us His Word, the very Word of God itself, the Holy Scriptures. Some of the Thessalonians believed in the Word of God. Therefore, God worked in their hearts and lives, converting and growing them to be more and more like His dear Son, the Lord Jesus Christ.

> **But blessed are your eyes because they see, and your ears because they hear. (Mat 13:16)**
>
> **But the one who received the seed that fell on good soil is the man who hears the word and understands it. He produces a crop, yielding a hundred, sixty or thirty times what was sown." (Mat 13:23)**
>
> **But the seed on good soil stands for those with a noble and good heart, who hear the word, retain it, and by persevering produce a crop. (Luke 8:15)**
>
> **Those who accepted his message were baptized, and about three thousand were added to their number that day. (Acts 2:41)**
>
> **Now the Bereans were of more noble character than the Thessalonians, for they received the message with great eagerness and examined the Scriptures every day to see if what Paul said was true. (Acts 17:11)**
>
> **And we also thank God continually because, when you received the word of God, which you heard from us, you accepted it not as the word of men, but as it actually is, the word of God, which is at work in you who believe. (1 Th 2:13)**

DEEPER STUDY # 1

(2:13) **Word of God**: the Bible claims to be the Word of God (see notes—2 Tim.3:16; note and DEEPER STUDY # 1,2—2 Pt.1:19-21 for more discussion).

⇒ The *unity of Scripture* indicates an origin that could come only from one mind, God's mind (see note and DEEPER STUDY # 2—2 Pt.1:19-21).
⇒ Scripture has changed millions of lives for God.
⇒ Fulfilled prophecy and archeology substantiate a divine origin. (See note and DEEPER STUDY # 1—Lk.3:23-38; DEEPER STUDY # 3—Jn.1:45; Master Subject Index for more discussion).

In fact, the unique feature of the Bible is that it has always been *exhaustively substantiated* to be the Word of God by any approach of investigation that is *serious and honest*. But note: both *seriousness and honesty* are necessary for the truth to be received. No less evidence could be expected from the mind and providence of God. For God can speak only the truth, and any pure investigation of truth can only substantiate His Word. But in saying this, it is necessary to recall that faith is an element in substantiating anything. Therefore, in accepting the Bible as the Word of God, faith is involved; it is one of the elements required.

However, the supreme authority for accepting the Bible as the Word of God is Jesus Christ. If we believe in the divine mission of Christ and His apostles, then we must believe that the Bible is the Word of God (Jn.5:39).

That Jesus Christ was a historical person is fact.
⇒ That Jesus Christ *claims* to be the Son of God is fact.
⇒ That Jesus Christ *is* the Son of God is faith.

That the Bible is an historical book is fact.
⇒ That the Bible *claims* to be the Word of God is fact.
⇒ That the Bible *is* the Word of God is faith.

> **We have not received the spirit of the world but the Spirit who is from God, that we may understand what God has freely given us. This is what we speak, not in words taught us by human wisdom but in words taught by the Spirit, expressing spiritual truths in spiritual words. (1 Cor 2:12-13)**
>
> **And we also thank God continually because, when you received the word of God, which you heard from us, you accepted it not as the word of men, but as it actually is, the word of God, which is at work in you who believe. (1 Th 2:13)**
>
> **Do your best to present yourself to God as one approved, a workman who does not need to be ashamed and who correctly handles the word of truth. (2 Tim 2:15)**
>
> **All Scripture is God-breathed and is useful for teaching, rebuking, correcting and training in righteousness, (2 Tim 3:16)**
>
> **In the past God spoke to our forefathers through the prophets at many times and in various ways, (Heb 1:1)**

> Trying to find out the time and circumstances to which the Spirit of Christ in them was pointing when he predicted the sufferings of Christ and the glories that would follow. (1 Pet 1:11)
>
> Above all, you must understand that no prophecy of Scripture came about by the prophet's own interpretation. For prophecy never had its origin in the will of man, but men spoke from God as they were carried along by the Holy Spirit. (2 Pet 1:20-21)
>
> I want you to recall the words spoken in the past by the holy prophets and the command given by our Lord and Savior through your apostles. (2 Pet 3:2)
>
> The revelation of Jesus Christ, which God gave him to show his servants what must soon take place. He made it known by sending his angel to his servant John, (Rev 1:1)
>
> Then I heard a voice from heaven say, "Write: Blessed are the dead who die in the Lord from now on." "Yes," says the Spirit, "they will rest from their labor, for their deeds will follow them." (Rev 14:13)

2 (2:14) **Church**: strong people become followers of strong churches. They stand fast in Christ despite trials, even when facing severe persecution. Note that it was their own countrymen who were persecuting them, both Jew and Gentile, but the instigators were the Jews.

> But the Jews were jealous; so they rounded up some bad characters from the marketplace, formed a mob and started a riot in the city. They rushed to Jason's house in search of Paul and Silas in order to bring them out to the crowd. (Acts 17:5)

This is exactly what was happening with the Judean churches. It was their own countrymen who were persecuting them. Therefore, Paul was able to say to the Thessalonian believers that they were following the great example of the Judean churches: they were standing firm for Christ even as the Judean churches were.

Thought 1. Note two lessons.
1) Nothing cuts and threatens us like the opposition from those who are closest to us: our family, friends, neighbors, and countrymen. When those whom we love the most oppose us, the temptation to give in is strongest. But we must never give in, for our eternal destiny is at stake. We must continue on with Christ, trusting Him to take care of us and to win many of our persecutors to Christ through the testimony of our steadfastness.

   This was what the Judean believers did, and it was what the Thessalonian believers did. It must also be what we do: stand fast for Christ no matter what opposition may confront us.
2) One of the strongest helps when facing persecution is to look to the example of others who have stood strong against opposition. This is what the Thessalonian believers did: they followed the example of the Judean churches. The faithfulness of both the Judean and Thessalonian believers stands as a strong example for us.

> I am sending you out like sheep among wolves. Therefore be as shrewd as snakes and as innocent as doves. "Be on your guard against men; they will hand you over to the local councils and flog you in their synagogues. On my account you will be brought before governors and kings as witnesses to them and to the Gentiles. (Mat 10:16-18)
>
> Remember the words I spoke to you: 'No servant is greater than his master.' If they persecuted me, they will persecute you also. If they obeyed my teaching, they will obey yours also. (John 15:20)
>
> In that day you will no longer ask me anything. I tell you the truth, my Father will give you whatever you ask in my name. (John 16:23)
>
> For it has been granted to you on behalf of Christ not only to believe on him, but also to suffer for him, (Phil 1:29)
>
> In fact, everyone who wants to live a godly life in Christ Jesus will be persecuted, (2 Tim 3:12)

3 (2:15-16) **Jews, Sins of—Persecution—Church**: a strong church escapes the guilt of the Jews. This may seem like a strange way to word this point, but what is in mind is this.

⇒ A person either stands in support of Christ or in opposition to Christ.
⇒ A church either stands in support of Christ or in opposition to Christ.

The Jewish persecutors stood in opposition to Christ, in opposition to God's very own Son. And remember: they were religionists, a body of religious people who were set on destroying the Christian church in the name of religion. But the Thessalonian church and its believers stood in support of Christ; therefore, they escaped whatever guilt hangs over a person's head for opposing God's Son. The Thessalonian believers were free of the terrible sins and guilt that the Jews had committed in the name of religion. What were the sins and guilt of the Jews? Paul lists them, and the indictment is one of the most terrible ever drawn up against man.

1. They killed the Lord Jesus. Note the title "Lord." They thought they were killing only a man, only a carpenter from Nazareth, but they were actually killing the *Lord*. By Lord is meant all that is included in the title: the Lord God, the One who came *out of heaven* itself, the very Son of God Himself. The terrible guilt is clearly seen:
   ⇒ the guilt of killing a person.
   ⇒ the guilt of killing the Lord Himself.

2. They killed their own prophets. This was a charge that has often been leveled at the Jews.

> So you testify against yourselves that you are the descendants of those who murdered the prophets. (Mat 23:31)
>
> Was there ever a prophet your fathers did not persecute? They even killed those who predicted the coming of the Righteous One. And now you have betrayed and murdered him— (Acts 7:52)

1 THESSALONIANS 2:13-20

3. They persecuted Christian believers. They not only rejected the gospel, but they wanted to destroy the message and those who followed and proclaimed it. They did not want anyone following Christ.

> **The priests and the captain of the temple guard and the Sadducees came up to Peter and John while they were speaking to the people. They were greatly disturbed because the apostles were teaching the people and proclaiming in Jesus the resurrection of the dead. They seized Peter and John, and because it was evening, they put them in jail until the next day. (Acts 4:1-3)**
>
> **Now those who had been scattered by the persecution in connection with Stephen traveled as far as Phoenicia, Cyprus and Antioch, telling the message only to Jews. (Acts 11:19)**
>
> **But the Jews were jealous; so they rounded up some bad characters from the marketplace, formed a mob and started a riot in the city. They rushed to Jason's house in search of Paul and Silas in order to bring them out to the crowd. (Acts 17:5)**

4. They did not please God. No person can please God if he stands in opposition to Christ. The only way a person can please God is to surrender his life to Christ—to give all he is and has to Christ. The Jews were not about to do this. Nothing was going to break them away from their own religious ceremonies and ideas about religion.

5. They were contrary to all men. They opposed and hated anyone who did not believe as they did. They should have loved those who differed, but instead they bitterly despised them. This is the difference between Christianity and Judaism and so many other religions. We who believe do claim that Christ and the Holy Scriptures are the truth, but we do not hate and oppose those who differ with us. We love them and do all we can to reach out and help them. We help to meet the needs of every man, even if he goes to his grave never accepting Christ. We love him; therefore, we want him to know the truth. But if he rejects Christ, we do not cast him off. We will continue to help him any way we can—in love.

6. They tried to stamp out the Word of God lest some person be saved. Just imagine trying to stop God's Word. How in the world can a man stop the Word of God? The answer is self-evident. Even a world of men could not stop God's Word. This is the foolishness of men, and it was the foolishness of the Jews.

7. Now, note the results of the sins of the Jews. First, they filled up their sin;—they heaped up their sins to the limit; their sin became full and overflowed and kept on overflowing. What a terrible indictment. The idea is that they sinned so much that they reached the point of no return. Returning to God was impossible (Leon Morris. *The Epistles of Paul to the Thessalonians.* "Tyndale New Testament Commentaries," p.57).

Second, the wrath of God is come upon the Jews to the uttermost. The idea is that the judgment of God upon the Jews was certain, for they had...

- killed His Son, the Lord Jesus.
- killed His prophets.
- persecuted His church followers.
- stood against all men.
- tried to stamp out His Word so that other people might not be saved.

Think for a moment: if Jesus Christ is truly God's Son, then the judgment of God upon the Jewish unbelievers is inevitable. In fact, His judgment upon any person or people who stands in opposition to Christ in inevitable. No man shall be able to escape His judgment.

> **Whoever believes in the Son has eternal life, but whoever rejects the Son will not see life, for God's wrath remains on him." (John 3:36)**
>
> **The wrath of God is being revealed from heaven against all the godlessness and wickedness of men who suppress the truth by their wickedness, (Rom 1:18)**
>
> **But for those who are self-seeking and who reject the truth and follow evil, there will be wrath and anger. (Rom 2:8)**
>
> **Let no one deceive you with empty words, for because of such things God's wrath comes on those who are disobedient. (Eph 5:6)**
>
> **In their effort to keep us from speaking to the Gentiles so that they may be saved. In this way they always heap up their sins to the limit. The wrath of God has come upon them at last. (1 Th 2:16)**
>
> **And give relief to you who are troubled, and to us as well. This will happen when the Lord Jesus is revealed from heaven in blazing fire with his powerful angels. He will punish those who do not know God and do not obey the gospel of our Lord Jesus. They will be punished with everlasting destruction and shut out from the presence of the Lord and from the majesty of his power (2 Th 1:7-9)**

4 (2:17-18) **Church—Fellowship**: a strong church possesses a strong fellowship. The fellowship of the Thessalonians was so strong that Paul just longed to return to them. Remember: he had been forced to flee the city because his life was being threatened by the persecution that had risen against the gospel. The ache of Paul's heart for the Thessalonians and their fellowship is seen in his emphasis:

⇒ he had been taken from them in person, but "not in thought."
⇒ he "intensely longed" (spoudazo) to return: eagerly sought to return; made a serious, concentrated effort to return.
⇒ he "abundantly" or exceedingly sought to return.
⇒ he sought to return "with every effort": with zeal, with intense longing, with strong passion.

Just imagine a fellowship of believers so strong that such effort is exerted by Paul to be present with them. What a fellowship they must have had—even in the face of persecution.

However, note: Paul's return to the Thessalonian believers had been hindered by Satan. The word "hindered" means to cut in a road; to make a road impassable (A.T. Robertson. *Word Pictures in the New Testament*, Vol.4, p.24). It means to put up a roadblock for the purpose of stopping an expedition (William Barclay. *The Letters to the Philippians, Colossians, and Thessalonians*, p.225). When a church is as strong as the Thessalonian church, Satan is bound to do all he can to weaken it and stop its growth. One of the primary ways to weaken a church is to attack the minister of the church. This was his strategy in Thessalonica. What was the roadblock that Satan threw against Paul?

⇒ Was it some illness? (2 Cor.12:7; Gal.4:13).
⇒ Was it some serious problem in Corinth where Paul was ministering—some serious problem that had been stirred up by Satan to keep Paul there and to prevent his return to Thessalonica? Remember: Corinth was full of carnal believers, prime prospects for Satan's attack (1 Th.3:1).

Just what the hindrance was is not known. But the point to note is the strength of the believers' fellowship in Thessalonica—a fellowship so strong that Paul longed to return and share in it with the believers.

> We loved you so much that we were delighted to share with you not only the gospel of God but our lives as well, because you had become so dear to us. (1 Th 2:8)
>
> Now that you have purified yourselves by obeying the truth so that you have sincere love for your brothers, love one another deeply, from the heart. (1 Pet 1:22)

DEEPER STUDY # 2
(2:18) **Satan—Paul, View of Satan**: Paul never downplayed the work and activity of Satan. He recognized the existence and activity of some terrible *force of evil*—some terrible *supernatural spirit of evil*—some terrible person in the spiritual world who is revealed in Scripture as Satan or the devil. Paul saw Satan...
- as the tempter who tempts men (1 Th.3:5).
- as the "evil one" (Greek, 2 Th.3:3).
- as the god of this age (2 Cor.4:4).
- as the ruler of the kingdom of the air (Eph.2:2).

5 (2:19-20) **Witnessing**: a strong church is destined to bring glory and joy. To whom? To the believers...
- who founded the church.
- who reached the believers for the Lord.
- who ministered and taught the church.
- who carried on the work of the church.

Paul clearly says that the Thessalonian believers were his hope and joy and crown. When? In the day when the Lord Jesus Christ will return and they will all stand in His presence.

⇒ What a hope! The return of the Lord Jesus Christ.
⇒ What a joy! Joining the Lord Jesus Christ with all the believers whom we have known, reached, and grown in Christ down here on earth.
⇒ What a crown! To offer to Christ all the dear people we have *had a part* in reaching and growing for the Lord.

Note the word "crown" (stephanos). It is the victor's crown, the crown worn by the athlete after he has won the contest. The picture is that we are in a contest, a spiritual struggle against Satan for the souls of men. Therefore, we must strain and struggle and fight for the souls of men. A crown awaits us, a crown that we will miss unless there are souls to present to Christ.

Thought 1. Have you ever won a soul to Christ? A single soul? How many?

⇒ Ten souls?
⇒ Twenty souls?
⇒ Fifty souls?
⇒ One hundred souls?

The crown in which we will glory awaits the person who will be able to present souls to the Lord in that day. Let us all ask God to touch our hearts and help us to win souls for Him. He will if we will only ask in sincerity.

> "Come, follow me," Jesus said, "and I will make you fishers of men." (Mat 4:19)
>
> And goes home. Then he calls his friends and neighbors together and says, 'Rejoice with me; I have found my lost sheep.' I tell you that in the same way there will be more rejoicing in heaven over one sinner who repents than over ninety-nine righteous persons who do not need to repent. (Luke 15:6-7)
>
> The first thing Andrew did was to find his brother Simon and tell him, "We have found the Messiah" (that is, the Christ). (John 1:41)
>
> Philip found Nathanael and told him, "We have found the one Moses wrote about in the Law, and about whom the prophets also wrote—Jesus of Nazareth, the son of Joseph." (John 1:45)
>
> Even now the reaper draws his wages, even now he harvests the crop for eternal life, so that the sower and the reaper may be glad together. (John 4:36)
>
> The church sent them on their way, and as they traveled through Phoenicia and Samaria, they told how the Gentiles had been converted. This news made all the brothers very glad. (Acts 15:3)
>
> Though I am free and belong to no man, I make myself a slave to everyone, to win as many as possible. To the Jews I became like a Jew, to win the Jews. To those under the law I became like one under the law (though I myself am not under the law), so as to win those under the law. (1 Cor 9:19-20)
>
> For what is our hope, our joy, or the crown in which we will glory in the presence of our Lord Jesus when he comes? Is it not you? Indeed, you are our glory and joy. (1 Th 2:19-20)
>
> Let us fix our eyes on Jesus, the author and perfecter of our faith, who for the joy set before him endured the cross, scorning its shame, and sat down at the right hand of the throne of God. (Heb 12:2)
>
> Remember this: Whoever turns a sinner from the error of his way will save him from death and cover over a multitude of sins. (James 5:20)
>
> Snatch others from the fire and save them; to others show mercy, mixed with fear—hating even the clothing stained by corrupted flesh. (Jude 1:23)

1 THESSALONIANS 3:1-10

	CHAPTER 3	way the tempter might have tempted you and our efforts might have been useless.	c. Must know that the labor & gospel of the minister is not empty
	E. The Model Church: A Strong Faith, 3:1-10		
1 Paul's extreme anxiety for the church	So when we could stand it no longer, we thought it best to be left by ourselves in Athens.	6 But Timothy has just now come to us from you and has brought good news about your faith and love. He has told us that you always have pleasant memories of us and that you long to see us, just as we also long to see you.	**3 A strong faith is a faith that gives forth an excellent testimony**
a. He sent a most dependable minister to them	2 We sent Timothy, who is our brother and God's fellow worker in spreading the gospel of Christ, to strengthen and encourage you in your faith,		
b. His purpose: To strengthen and encourage them		7 Therefore, brothers, in all our distress and persecution we were encouraged about you because of your faith.	**4 A strong faith is a faith that stirs the heart of its pastor & fellow believers**
2 A strong faith is not moved by trials	3 So that no one would be unsettled by these trials. You know quite well that we were destined for them.	8 For now we really live, since you are standing firm in the Lord.	a. Stirs comfort
a. Must know that one is appointed to trials	4 In fact, when we were with you, we kept telling you that we would be persecuted. And it turned out that way, as you well know.	9 How can we thank God enough for you in return for all the joy we have in the presence of our God because of you?	b. Stirs renewed life & purpose
			c. Stirs joy
b. Must know that the temptation to cave in is of Satan himself	5 For this reason, when I could stand it no longer, I sent to find out about your faith. I was afraid that in some	10 Night and day we pray most earnestly that we may see you again and supply what is lacking in your faith.	d. Stirs prayer

DIVISION I

THE MODEL CHURCH, 1:1-3:13

E. The Model Church: A Strong Faith, 3:1-10

(3:1-10) Introduction: this passage has to do with the faith of the Thessalonians. Their faith was strong and Paul wanted to make sure that it remained strong. He stressed their faith five times in these ten verses.
  ⇒ He wanted to comfort, that is, strengthen their *faith* (v.2).
  ⇒ He wanted to know if their *faith* was standing against the tempter's temptations (v.5).
  ⇒ He received word that their *faith* and love were strong (v.6).
  ⇒ He was comforted over their *faith* (v.7).
  ⇒ He wished to perfect their *faith* (v.10).

The one thing needed by Christian believers is a strong faith: a faith that honestly *knows Christ* and knows what it is to walk in Him day by day, trusting Him, His care and comfort and strength. What we need is a faith that stands fast, endures, and perseveres, and that grows stronger and stronger in Christ. The stronger we believe and the more faith we have, the more we can conquer in life and do the things that we should do. A strong faith in Christ enables us to triumph over the trials and temptations of life and to fulfill our purpose in life.

Many of the believers in Thessalonica had a strong faith; therefore, their faith stands as a model for us. What is a strong faith?

1. Paul's extreme anxiety for the church (v.1-2).
2. A strong faith is a faith that is not moved by trials (v.3-5).
3. A strong faith is a faith that gives forth an excellent testimony (v.6).
4. A strong faith is a faith that stirs the hearts of its pastor and fellow believers (v.7-10).

1 (3:1-2) **Stand Fast—Endurance—Church**: there was Paul's extreme anxiety for the church at Thessalonica. The believers were suffering fierce persecution by both the Jewish and Gentile citizens of the city. Remember: the Jews had savagely opposed Paul when he was in Thessalonica. They had aroused some of the rowdy men who hung around in the market place to riot against Paul and the church. The believers had been meeting in the home of Jason, but when the mob attacked the home, Paul was not there. However, because of the uproar, he was forced to flee for his life. He had hoped that his absence would squelch the persecution. But his plan failed; the persecution continued and apparently increased. The antagonists were determined to stamp out and destroy the gospel of Christ once and for all.

Paul had fled to Athens, but his heart was in Thessalonica, longing for the believers who were suffering the fierce attacks of persecution. Note what he says: he had reached a point when he could no longer bear the suspense over their welfare. They had received Christ, escaped the sin and death of this world and received eternal life. When Paul had left them, they were standing fast in their *faith*. Had they cracked under the savage attacks of persecution? Or were they standing fast? They had to stand fast; it was a must, for their eternal destiny depended upon their continuing to follow Christ. Paul could bear it no longer; he had to do something. He desperately wanted to return and stand by their side, but he knew he could not. His return would only add fuel to the persecution. What then could he do? He would do the next best thing: send his right hand man, Timothy (v.2). Timothy was a dependable servant of the Lord. He was…

- a dear brother to Paul.
- a minister of God.
- a fellow worker in the gospel of Christ.

If anyone could help the believers, he could. Note: Paul sent him to strengthen and encourage the believers in their faith.

⇒ The word "strengthen" (sterizo) means to support and establish.

⇒ The word "encourage" (parakaleo) means to and exhort.

2 (3:3-5) **Church—Faith—Standing Fast**: What is a strong faith? A strong faith is a faith that is not moved by trials. The word "unsettled" (sainesthai) is taken from a word that means to wag the tail like a dog; hence it came to mean to flatter; to deceive; to hoodwink; to beguile; to lead astray by some deceptive strategy. Leon Morris thinks this is the meaning here (*The Epistles of Paul to the Thessalonians*. "Tyndale New Testament Commentaries," p.63); so does the Greek Scholar A.T. Robertson (*Word Pictures in the New Testament*, Vol.4, p.25). This gives us some picture of the types of persecution going on.

⇒ There was an attack of spreading lies and rumors about the minister Paul: a persecution of deceit and guile; a deliberate strategy of deception. Apparently this was why the rumors of immorality and false preaching were launched against Paul. Those who opposed Paul and the gospel felt that if they could destroy Paul and his reputation, many would leave the church and some would even join forces with them against Paul (1 Th.2:3-6; 4:3-7).

⇒ There was the usual shameful treatment: mockery, ridicule, cursing, and verbal attacks against Christ and the life of righteousness to which the believers had committed themselves (1 Th.2:2).

⇒ There was direct confrontation and opposition: standing face to face with the believers and opposing their beliefs and threatening them if they spoke about Christ (1 Th.2:16).

⇒ There was physical abuse by mobs (Acts 17:5-6).

⇒ There was the use of civil authority and law against them if they continued to worship and speak about Christ (Acts 17:6-9).

Little else could be launched against the church and its believers except martyrdom itself. But note what Paul says: "So that no one would be unsettled by these trials." Despite the shameful treatment and savage attacks, the believer is not to be moved away from Christ. But when the attacks are so severe and savage, how can the believer keep from being unsettled? How can he stand fast? By knowing three things.

1. The believer must know that he is appointed to persecution. The believer shall suffer persecution. Note that Paul had taught the Thessalonians that they would suffer persecution if they accepted Christ. Why? Why does the world persecute the Christian believer so much?

a. Believers are persecuted because they are not of this world. They are *called out* of the world. They are in the world, but they are not of the world. They are separated from the behavior of the world. Therefore, the world reacts against them.

If you belonged to the world, it would love you as its own. As it is, you do not belong to the world, but I have chosen you out of the world. That is why the world hates you. (John 15:19)

b. They are persecuted because believers strip away the world's excuse for *sin*. They live and demonstrate a life of righteousness. Such living exposes the sins of people.

"If the world hates you, keep in mind that it hated me first. If I had not come and spoken to them, they would not be guilty of sin. Now, however, they have no excuse for their sin. (John 15:18, 22)

In fact, everyone who wants to live a godly life in Christ Jesus will be persecuted, (2 Tim 3:12)

c. They are persecuted because the world does not know God nor Christ. They want no God other than themselves and their own imaginations. They want to do just what they want—to fulfill their own desires, not what God wishes and demands.

They will treat you this way because of my name, for they do not know the One who sent me. (John 15:21)

They will do such things because they have not known the Father or me. (John 16:3)

d. They are persecuted because the world is deceived in its concept and belief of God. The world conceives God to be the One who fulfills their earthly desires and lusts (Jn.16:2-3). Man's idea of God is that of a *Supreme Grandfather*. They think God protects, provides, and gives no matter what a person's behavior is, just so the behavior is not too far out. They think God will accept and work all things out in the final analysis. However, the true believer teaches against this. God is love, but He is also just and demands righteousness. The world rebels against this concept of God.

They will put you out of the synagogue; in fact, a time is coming when anyone who kills you will think he is offering a service to God. They will do such things because they have not known the Father or me. (John 16:2-3)

Keeping these reasons in mind will help us to stand against persecution when it is launched against us. And stand we must, for we must reach the world for Christ—a world reeling under the terrible plight of so many desperate needs and sin, evil, corruption, death, and condemnation.

2. The believer must know that the temptation to cave in to persecution is of the tempter, of Satan himself. This is the very reason Satan has launched the persecution: to strike fear in the believer and silence him. Satan wants the believer to hush up about Christ and to desert Christ. If Satan can rattle the believer to turn away from Christ and the church, then he is able to use his desertion to affect many lives. Satan is able to destroy the faith of both the believer and those who look up to him, such as children, family, and friends.

Thought 1. The believer must keep in mind that Satan is behind all persecution and temptation to desert Christ. Remembering this will help the believer to stand fast, for no true believer wants to forsake God for Satan. His eternal destiny is at stake.

3. The believer must know that the labor and message of the minister is not empty. Christ died for our sins that we might not perish. Christ gives us eternal life—gives us the privilege of living forever and ever in the new heaven and earth that He is to create. But if we desert Christ, then all the labor that has gone into leading us to Christ is empty. The work of the minister and of those who have taught us will have been useless. We must not, therefore, give in to the temptation to move away from Christ. We must stand fast in afflictions, no matter how severe and savage. Standing fast in persecution is the sign of a strong faith.

> **Remember the words I spoke to you: 'No servant is greater than his master.' If they persecuted me, they will persecute you also. If they obeyed my teaching, they will obey yours also. (John 15:20)**
>
> "All this I have told you so that you will not go astray. They will put you out of the synagogue; in fact, a time is coming when anyone who kills you will think he is offering a service to God. They will do such things because they have not known the Father or me. I have told you this, so that when the time comes you will remember that I warned you. I did not tell you this at first because I was with you. (John 16:1-4)
>
> So that no one would be unsettled by these trials. You know quite well that we were destined for them. (1 Th 3:3)
>
> For it has been granted to you on behalf of Christ not only to believe on him, but also to suffer for him, (Phil 1:29)
>
> In fact, everyone who wants to live a godly life in Christ Jesus will be persecuted, (2 Tim 3:12)
>
> Do not be surprised, my brothers, if the world hates you. (1 John 3:13)
>
> Dear friends, do not be surprised at the painful trial you are suffering, as though something strange were happening to you. But rejoice that you participate in the sufferings of Christ, so that you may be overjoyed when his glory is revealed. If you are insulted because of the name of Christ, you are blessed, for the Spirit of glory and of God rests on you. (1 Pet 4:12-14)
>
> Be self-controlled and alert. Your enemy the devil prowls around like a roaring lion looking for someone to devour. Resist him, standing firm in the faith, because you know that your brothers throughout the world are undergoing the same kind of sufferings. (1 Pet 5:8-9)
>
> Therefore, dear friends, since you already know this, be on your guard so that you may not be carried away by the error of lawless men and fall from your secure position. (2 Pet 3:17)

3 (3:6) **Faith—Testimony**: What is strong faith? A strong faith is a faith that gives forth an excellent testimony. When Timothy returned from his mission to the Thessalonian church, he had a glowing report.

1. The believers were standing fast in *their faith in Christ*. They were not buckling under to persecution nor to the temptation to be silent about Christ. They were not forsaking their worship of Christ. In practical terms, they were continuing to study the Scriptures, pray, and worship together. And when possible, when it would not arouse opposition, they were sharing Christ and the promise of eternal life with all who would listen.

> **Then they asked him, "What must we do to do the works God requires?" Jesus answered, "The work of God is this: to believe in the one he has sent." (John 6:28-29)**
>
> In addition to all this, take up the shield of faith, with which you can extinguish all the flaming arrows of the evil one. (Eph 6:16)
>
> Holding on to faith and a good conscience. Some have rejected these and so have shipwrecked their faith. (1 Tim 1:19)
>
> Fight the good fight of the faith. Take hold of the eternal life to which you were called when you made your good confession in the presence of many witnesses. (1 Tim 6:12)
>
> Let us draw near to God with a sincere heart in full assurance of faith, having our hearts sprinkled to cleanse us from a guilty conscience and having our bodies washed with pure water. Let us hold unswervingly to the hope we profess, for he who promised is faithful. And let us consider how we may spur one another on toward love and good deeds. Let us not give up meeting together, as some are in the habit of doing, but let us encourage one another—and all the more as you see the Day approaching. If we deliberately keep on sinning after we have received the knowledge of the truth, no sacrifice for sins is left, (Heb 10:22-26)
>
> And without faith it is impossible to please God, because anyone who comes to him must believe that he exists and that he rewards those who earnestly seek him. (Heb 11:6)
>
> In the same way, faith by itself, if it is not accompanied by action, is dead. (James 2:17)
>
> For everyone born of God overcomes the world. This is the victory that has overcome the world, even our faith. Who is it that overcomes the world? Only he who believes that Jesus is the Son of God. (1 John 5:4-5)

2. The believers were standing fast in love—love for Christ, each other, and their fellow men. They were ministering and meeting the needs of all those who would receive their help. They were doing all they could to demonstrate love and care and good citizenship toward all.

> **And the second is like it: 'Love your neighbor as yourself.' (Mat 22:39)**
>
> "A new command I give you: Love one another. As I have loved you, so you must love one another. By this all men will know that you are my disciples, if you love one another." (John 13:34-35)
>
> My command is this: Love each other as I have loved you. (John 15:12)

> Who shall separate us from the love of Christ? Shall trouble or hardship or persecution or famine or nakedness or danger or sword? (Rom 8:35)
>
> Love must be sincere. Hate what is evil; cling to what is good. (Rom 12:9)
>
> This is how we know what love is: Jesus Christ laid down his life for us. And we ought to lay down our lives for our brothers. (1 John 3:16)

3. The believers also remembered their pastor, Paul, with the deepest of affection. Note that they longed to see him just as he longed to see them.

> They devoted themselves to the apostles' teaching and to the fellowship, to the breaking of bread and to prayer. (Acts 2:42)
>
> I thank my God every time I remember you. (Phil 1:3)
>
> Because of your partnership in the gospel from the first day until now, (Phil 1:5)
>
> But if we walk in the light, as he is in the light, we have fellowship with one another, and the blood of Jesus, his Son, purifies us from all sin. (1 John 1:7)

Thought 1. What a dynamic testimony of strong faith, the kind of faith every believer and church should covet:
⇒ a faith that stands fast in the face of severe opposition.
⇒ a faith that demonstrates the love of God—agape love.
⇒ a faith that longs for fellowship with its pastor.

4 (3:7-10) **Faith**: What is a strong faith? A strong faith is a faith that stirs the heart of its pastor and fellow believers. Note four significant points.

1. The strong faith of the Thessalonian believers comforted Paul, and Paul desperately needed comforting (v.7). The word "encouraged" (paraklethemen) means encouraged and strengthened. Why did Paul need encouragement and strengthening? It was not because of the Thessalonians, for Timothy's report had already comforted Paul's concern over them. Note: Paul says that he was in some "distress and persecution." The words are strong, very strong. "Distress" (ananke) means choking, intense pressure and stress. "Persecution" (thlipsis) means crushing trouble (A.T. Robertson. *Word Pictures in the New Testament*, Vol.4, p.26). Remember Paul was in Corinth when Timothy arrived with the glorious news of the strong faith of the Thessalonians. A fierce persecution had broken out against Paul and the church in Corinth, and he was dragged by the Jewish religionists to stand trial before the Roman court. He was released, but the persecution against him and the church continued (Acts 18:1-17). Apparently some threat and savagery happened to Paul that is not recorded, as so much that happened to him is left unrecorded. But whatever it was, it brought great affliction and distress to Paul. The point is this: the testimony of the Thessalonians strengthened and encouraged Paul in his ministry. Their faith in Christ was strong, and God used the testimony of their faith to help His dear servant in a time of need.

Thought 1. What a lesson for us! Our faith is used by God to strengthen and encourage others in their need. Therefore, we stand strong in faith and grow stronger and stronger in faith.

> In everything I did, I showed you that by this kind of hard work we must help the weak, remembering the words the Lord Jesus himself said: 'It is more blessed to give than to receive.'" (Acts 20:35)
>
> We who are strong ought to bear with the failings of the weak and not to please ourselves. (Rom 15:1)
>
> Carry each other's burdens, and in this way you will fulfill the law of Christ. (Gal 6:2)
>
> Remember those in prison as if you were their fellow prisoners, and those who are mistreated as if you yourselves were suffering. (Heb 13:3)

2. The strong faith of the Thessalonians stirred renewed life and purpose in Paul (v.8). Paul had been discouraged, not defeated, but discouraged because of the difficulties confronting him in Corinth. But when the news of the Thessalonian believers reached him, it ignited a renewed burst of life and purpose in him. He was stirred to minister and share Christ as never before.

Thought 1. Note how the Thessalonians were a testimony to Paul. They were suffering terrible persecution and remaining steadfast. Therefore, their steadfastness stirred him to bear the persecution launched against him. These dear people were a great encouragement to their pastor without their even knowing it. Their faithfulness was stirring him to be faithful—stirring him in one of those times when he needed encouragement.

We never know when our strength and faith are needed to help some dear believer. Therefore, we must always stand fast in the faith, so that God can use our strength wherever He wishes. Imagine having the privilege of helping and encouraging a dear servant like Paul in one of his stressful times. Every church and believer has the privilege of helping and encouraging their pastor—if they will only stand fast in their faith and grow more and more in Christ.

> Never be lacking in zeal, but keep your spiritual fervor, serving the Lord. (Rom 12:11)
>
> Therefore, my dear brothers, stand firm. Let nothing move you. Always give yourselves fully to the work of the Lord, because you know that your labor in the Lord is not in vain. (1 Cor 15:58)
>
> Whatever happens, conduct yourselves in a manner worthy of the gospel of Christ. Then, whether I come and see you or only hear about you in my absence, I will know that you stand firm in one spirit, contending as one man for the faith of the gospel (Phil 1:27)
>
> For this reason I remind you to fan into flame the gift of God, which is in you through the laying on of my hands. (2 Tim 1:6)

1 THESSALONIANS 3:1-10

> I think it is right to refresh your memory as long as I live in the tent of this body, (2 Pet 1:13)
>
> I am coming soon. Hold on to what you have, so that no one will take your crown. (Rev 3:11)
>
> Whatever your hand finds to do, do it with all your might, for in the grave, where you are going, there is neither working nor planning nor knowledge nor wisdom. (Eccl 9:10)

> Dear friends, do not be surprised at the painful trial you are suffering, as though something strange were happening to you. But rejoice that you participate in the sufferings of Christ, so that you may be overjoyed when his glory is revealed. (1 Pet 4:12-13)
>
> Our mouths were filled with laughter, our tongues with songs of joy. Then it was said among the nations, "The LORD has done great things for them." (Psa 126:2)

3. The strong faith of the Thessalonians stirred joy in Paul (v.9). Very simply, the news of the Thessalonian believers standing firm in their faith was bound to stir joy in their pastor's heart. He just burst forth praising and thanking God time and again.

> Sorrowful, yet always rejoicing; poor, yet making many rich; having nothing, and yet possessing everything. (2 Cor 6:10)
>
> Now I rejoice in what was suffered for you, and I fill up in my flesh what is still lacking in regard to Christ's afflictions, for the sake of his body, which is the church. (Col 1:24)
>
> These have come so that your faith—of greater worth than gold, which perishes even though refined by fire—may be proved genuine and may result in praise, glory and honor when Jesus Christ is revealed. Though you have not seen him, you love him; and even though you do not see him now, you believe in him and are filled with an inexpressible and glorious joy, for you are receiving the goal of your faith, the salvation of your souls. (1 Pet 1:7-9)

4. The strong faith of the Thessalonian believers stirred Paul to pray for their fellowship and growth in Christ. Paul longed to be with them so that he could continue to share and grow them in Christ. He wanted to build them up and perfect whatever weaknesses they might have. What a pastoral heart! The heart to always proclaim and teach Christ until we are all perfected into the image of Christ.

> So be on your guard! Remember that for three years I never stopped warning each of you night and day with tears. (Acts 20:31)
>
> Let us therefore make every effort to do what leads to peace and to mutual edification. (Rom 14:19)
>
> Each of us should please his neighbor for his good, to build him up. (Rom 15:2)
>
> It was he who gave some to be apostles, some to be prophets, some to be evangelists, and some to be pastors and teachers, to prepare God's people for works of service, so that the body of Christ may be built up (Eph 4:11-12)
>
> Night and day we pray most earnestly that we may see you again and supply what is lacking in your faith. (1 Th 3:10)

1 THESSALONIANS 3:11-13

	F. The Model Church: A Strong Love, 3:11-13	for each other and for everyone else, just as ours does for you.	b. The source of love: The Lord & His "agape" love
1 Paul's great prayer a. To God & Christ b. To visit the church	11 Now may our God and Father himself and our Lord Jesus clear the way for us to come to you.	13 May he strengthen your hearts so that you will be blameless and holy in the presence of our God and Father when our Lord Jesus comes with all his holy ones.	3 The great result of love a. To be presented blameless before God b. When: At the return of the Lord Jesus Christ
2 The great need: Love^{DS1} a. To love "everyone"	12 May the Lord make your love increase and overflow		

DIVISION I

THE MODEL CHURCH, 1:1-3:13

F. The Model Church: A Strong Love, 3:11-13

(3:11-13) **Introduction**: the greatest virtue in the world is love. This is the one possession that man must have if he is to have an abundant life. Without love man is nothing. Paul knew this; therefore, he went before God and prayed that the Thessalonian church and its believers might grow in love more and more. The model church will be a church that has a strong love.

1. Paul's great prayer (v.11).
2. The great need: love (v.12).
3. The great result of love (v.13).

1 (3:11) **Prayer—Jesus Christ, Deity**: this is Paul's great prayer for the Thessalonian church and its believers.

1. Note to whom Paul prays. This is a power-packed point. Paul prays to both God and Christ, and in so doing, he reveals who God is and who Christ is.
    a. Paul prays to *God Himself*: the Supreme and Majestic Being of the universe, the Supreme Intelligence, the Creator and Maker of all things, the Giver and Sustainer of life and of everything else, the Person who dwells everywhere in perfect and supreme power, knowledge, and being.

    Note that this is the picture of God that some men think about when they think of God. They think of a God who is in the heavens—in outer space someplace—a God who rules and reigns but is somewhat removed and not too interested in man. The point is this: Paul reveals that God is what some men think: supreme, majestic, ruling and reigning. But note the next point: God is more, much more.

    b. Paul prays to God *our Father*. God is a Father to us, intimately involved in our lives. He is not just in outer space ruling and reigning and being far removed from us. God our Father is right here with us; He is actively participating in our lives just as an earthly father participates in the lives of his children. Therefore Paul, as a child, approaches God our Father and asks Him for certain things; and when he asks, he knows that his Father will hear and answer. He knows because God is not only able to answer, but God is his Father.

    c. Paul prays to our Lord Jesus Christ. He prays...
    - *to our Lord*, the Supreme Majestic Ruler of the universe who has existed eternally in heaven and who loves us enough to become *our Lord*.
    - to our Lord Jesus, the Lord from heaven who loved us enough to come to earth in the person of Jesus, the Jewish carpenter from Nazareth. The Lord Jesus who was the promised Messiah and Savior of the world.

The point is this: Paul revealed that God Himself is our Father and that Jesus the Lord Himself is the Lord God from heaven—that both the Father and the Son have the nature of God; therefore, both have co-existed eternally. For this reason, Paul prayed both to God our Father and to our Lord Jesus.

2. Paul asked the Father and the Lord Jesus to direct and guide his way to the Thessalonians. He wanted both God and the Lord Jesus working to open the door for him to return to the dear believers at Thessalonica. Remember: Satan had created some terrible problems and obstacles to keep Paul from returning to the church (1 Th.2:18; 3:7). But he longed to return; therefore, he wanted both the Father and Son working on the matter. Hence, he addressed the request to both.

2 (3:12) **Love**: the great need for which Paul prayed is the supreme need of every believer—the need for love, to grow in love more and more.
⇒ The word "increase" (pleonasai) means to abound, to multiply over and over.
⇒ The word "overflow" (perisseusai) means to excel and overflow (Amplified New Testament).

As stated, the great need is to grow in love—to abound and multiply—to excel and overflow in love. But note the crucial point: the love being spoken about is not what the world means by love. This is seen in two significant points.

1. The love that we must grow in is the love that makes us love *everyone*, not just one another. Note the verse: May the Lord make your love increase and overflow for each other and for everyone else. The love we are to have is the love that *reaches out* and *overflows* and *multiplies* toward everyone. This means...

- the unattractive
- the orphan
- the sick
- the hateful
- the enemy
- the murderer
- the unclean
- the homeless
- the prisoner
- the diseased
- the spiteful
- the oppressor
- the poor
- the unclothed
- the widow and widower
- the sinner
- the opponent
- the dictator

How in the world can we love some of these people? How can we abound in love for them? How is it possible to love those who do evil to us and who treat us as enemies? Is it even practical to ask us to love everyone? Is it even humanly possible? No! It is not possible for us to love those who hate us and who stand as enemies against us—not humanly possible. But there is a way. However, there is only one way. This is the subject of the next point.

32

1 THESSALONIANS 3:11-13

2. The source of love is the Lord. There is no other source, not for the kind of love that can love everyone. This is the reason Paul went before the Lord and requested such a love. Paul knew that it was impossible for him or the Thessalonians to work up the kind of love that could reach out and abound toward everyone. A love that could love those who ignore, neglect, abuse, and shamefully treat us could only come from God. Note this: there are four kinds of love, the last of which is *agape love*, the very love of God Himself. It is this love that enables us to love *all men*. Agape love—the love that *loves all men*—is the kind of love that is to flood our hearts and lives—the kind of love that is to flow out toward every person no matter who they are (see DEEPER STUDY #1, Love—1 Th.3:12 for discussion).

> And the second is like it: 'Love your neighbor as yourself.' (Mat 22:39)
>
> "A new command I give you: Love one another. As I have loved you, so you must love one another. By this all men will know that you are my disciples, if you love one another." (John 13:34-35)
>
> My command is this: Love each other as I have loved you. (John 15:12)
>
> Love must be sincere. Hate what is evil; cling to what is good. (Rom 12:9)
>
> May the Lord make your love increase and overflow for each other and for everyone else, just as ours does for you. (1 Th 3:12)
>
> Keep on loving each other as brothers. (Heb 13:1)
>
> If you really keep the royal law found in Scripture, "Love your neighbor as yourself," you are doing right. (James 2:8)
>
> Now that you have purified yourselves by obeying the truth so that you have sincere love for your brothers, love one another deeply, from the heart. (1 Pet 1:22)
>
> Dear friends, let us love one another, for love comes from God. Everyone who loves has been born of God and knows God. (1 John 4:7)

DEEPER STUDY # 1
(3:12) **Love**: the kind of love which the believer is to have for all people is *agape love*, the great love of God Himself. (See note 4, Love—Jn.21:17 for more discussion.) The meaning of *agape love* is more clearly seen by contrasting it with the various kinds of love. There are essentially four kinds of love. Whereas the English language has only one word for *love* to describe all the affectionate experiences of men, the Greek language had a different word to describe each kind of love or affectionate experience.

1. There is *passionate love* or *eros love*. This is the physical love between sexes; the patriotic love of a person for his nation; the ambition of a person for power, wealth, or fame. Briefly stated, *eros love* is the base love of a man that arises from his own inner passion. Sometimes *eros love* is focused upon good and other times it is focused upon bad. It should be noted that *eros love* is never used in the New Testament.

2. There is *affectionate love* or *storge love*. This is the kind of love that exists between parent and child and between loyal citizens and a trustworthy ruler. *Storge love* is also not used in the New Testament.

3. There is an *endearing love* or *phileo love*. *Phileo love* is the love of a husband and wife for each other, of a brother for a brother, of a friend for the dearest of friends. It is the love that cherishes, that holds someone or something ever so dear to one's heart.

4. There is *selfless and sacrificial love* or *agape love*. Agape love is the love of the mind, of the reason, of the will. It is the love that goes so far...
- that it loves a person even if he does not deserve to be loved.
- that it actually loves the person who is utterly unworthy of being loved.

Note four significant points about agape love.

a. Selfless or agape love is the love of God, the very love possessed by God Himself. It is the love demonstrated in the cross of Christ.
⇒ It is the love of God for the *ungodly*.

> You see, at just the right time, when we were still powerless, Christ died for the ungodly. (Rom 5:6)

⇒ It is the love of God for *unworthy sinners*.

> But God demonstrates his own love for us in this: While we were still sinners, Christ died for us. (Rom 5:8)

⇒ It is the love of God for *undeserving enemies*.

> For if, when we were God's enemies, we were reconciled to him through the death of his Son, how much more, having been reconciled, shall we be saved through his life! (Rom 5:10)

b. Selfless or agape love is a gift of God. It can be experienced only if a person knows God *personally*—only if a person has received the love of God into his heart and life. Agape love has to be shed abroad (poured out, flooded, spread about) by the Spirit of God within the heart of a person.

> And hope does not disappoint us, because God has poured out his love into our hearts by the Holy Spirit, whom he has given us. (Rom 5:5)

c. Selfless or agape love is the greatest thing in all of life according to the Lord Jesus Christ.

> "The most important one," answered Jesus, "is this: 'Hear, O Israel, the Lord our God, the Lord is one. Love the Lord your God with all your heart and with all your soul and with all your mind and with all your strength.' The second is this: 'Love your neighbor as yourself.' There is no commandment greater than these." (Mark 12:29-31)

d. Selfless or agape love is the greatest possession and gift in human life according to the Scripture (1 Cor.13:1-13).

> And now these three remain: faith, hope and love. But the greatest of these is love. (1 Cor 13:13)

3 (3:13) **Love—Strengthen**: the great result of love is to be presented unblameable before God when Christ returns to earth. This is the most glorious result imaginable. Note several striking facts.

1. The word "strengthen" (sterixai) means to prop, support, confirm, fix, make fast, set. Note: it is the Lord Jesus Christ Himself who strengthens our hearts before God. No one else has the right or power to set us before God; no one else can make us acceptable to God. (Note: the word heart here refers to the whole person or personality of man.)

2. The word "blameless" (amemptous) means to be free from fault and blame; to be free from all charges (Vine). The word "holy" (hagiosune) means to be set apart and separated to God. It is the Lord Jesus Christ who can make our hearts blameless and holy before God. He alone can free us from the faults and charges of sin; He alone can present us blameless and holy before God. Just think about it: Who else has such power? Do you know such a person? The thinking and honest person has to answer no. And to be honest, if Christ does not have the righteousness and power to present us unblameable before God, then we are hopelessly doomed. Why? Because He is the only Person who has ever risen from the dead to never die again and to live eternally with God. If He is not our Savior, then we shall die and never arise, never live with God. Man's only hope is Christ—that He truthfully has the righteousness and power to set us unblameable and holy before God.

3. When is this glorious presentation to God going to take place? When Christ returns with all His saints, that is, with all the "holy and glorified people of God" (Vincent). When Christ returns, He will present all believers—every single one of us—to God:

⇒ all the believers who have died and gone to be with the Lord.
⇒ all the believers who are raptured when He returns.

What a coronation, the glorious day of our presentation before God—meeting Him face to face and being presented to Him unblameable and holy—to be with Him forever and ever! "When our Lord Jesus comes with all his holy ones!" It is the promise of God Himself and therefore it cannot be stopped! And no man should want to stop it. On the contrary, all men should prepare and welcome it. (See outline and notes—1 Th.4:13-5:3 for more discussion.)

> **In my Father's house are many rooms; if it were not so, I would have told you. I am going there to prepare a place for you. And if I go and prepare a place for you, I will come back and take you to be with me that you also may be where I am. (John 14:2-3)**
>
> **But our citizenship is in heaven. And we eagerly await a Savior from there, the Lord Jesus Christ, who, by the power that enables him to bring everything under his control, will transform our lowly bodies so that they will be like his glorious body. (Phil 3:20-21)**
>
> **When Christ, who is your life, appears, then you also will appear with him in glory. (Col 3:4)**
>
> **And when the Chief Shepherd appears, you will receive the crown of glory that will never fade away. (1 Pet 5:4)**
>
> **Dear friends, now we are children of God, and what we will be has not yet been made known. But we know that when he appears, we shall be like him, for we shall see him as he is. (1 John 3:2)**

1 THESSALONIANS 4:1-8

CHAPTER 4

II. THE MODEL WALK OR LIFE, 4:1-12

A. A Walk That Pleases God (Part I): A Life of Purity, 4:1-8

1 The earnest but tender exhortation

   a. Live to please God, & do so more & more

   b. Keep the commandments given you by the Lord Jesus

2 The commandment: God's will is your sanctification

Finally, brothers, we instructed you how to live in order to please God, as in fact you are living. Now we ask you and urge you in the Lord Jesus to do this more and more.
2 For you know what instructions we gave you by the authority of the Lord Jesus.
3 It is God's will that you should be sanctified: that you should avoid sexual immorality;
4 That each of you should learn to control his own body in a way that is holy and honorable,
5 Not in passionate lust like the heathen, who do not know God;
6 And that in this matter no one should wrong his brother or take advantage of him. The Lord will punish men for all such sins, as we have already told you and warned you.
7 For God did not call us to be impure, but to live a holy life.
8 Therefore, he who rejects this instruction does not reject man but God, who gives you his Holy Spirit.

   a. Avoiding sexual immorality
   b. Knowing how to control your body & spouse

   c. Resisting lustful passion

3 The reasons for purity
   a. Immorality cheats & wrongs a brother
   b. Immorality shall be revenged by God

   c. Immorality is not God's call; holiness is

   d. Immorality is a sin against God

DIVISION II

THE MODEL WALK OR LIFE, 4:1-12

A. A Walk that Pleases God (Part I): A Life of Purity, 4:1-8

(4:1-8) **Introduction**: this begins a major new discussion in *First Thessalonians*—the model walk or life of the believer. The model believer walks to please God. What does this mean? It means that he lives as God tells him to live, that he keeps God's commandments. Six commandments in particular are covered, one in this passage and five in the next passage. But note where the emphasis is: it is on this passage, the passage where moral purity is discussed. Why is more emphasis given to the commandment on morality than to the others? The answer is obvious. Immorality is the rampaging monster that destroys more lives, families, and nations than any other single evil. What God has to say is strong, and it must be heeded by all.

1. The earnest but tender exhortation (v.1-2).
2. The commandment: God's will is your sanctification (v.3-5).
3. The reasons for purity (v.6-8).

1 (4:1-2) **Believer's Walk**: the earnest but tender exhortation—walk to please God, and do so more and more. The Christian life is often described as a walk. Walking is a picture of moving forward and progressing step by step and day by day. It pictures the utter necessity of pleasing God every step of the day as we walk throughout life. God is interested in every step we take. And He is going to judge us on the basis of how we live and walk. Therefore, the primary concern of our lives must be to please God.

⇒ If we please God, we will be accepted by God.
⇒ If we do not please God, we will not be accepted by God.

This alone shows the utter necessity of pleasing God. We must please Him if we wish to be accepted by Him. A person is foolish not to want to be accepted by God, for to be rejected by God leads to the worst consequences that can be imagined: rejection by God Himself. Note how tender, yet strong this exhortation is.

1. The tenderness is seen in the words "ask and urge" and "brothers." By calling believers "brothers," Paul was expressing deep affection and care for them. The words "ask and urge" (erotomen) means to ask or request. But note: it always has a sense of urgency about it. Paul was tenderly requesting his dear brothers to continue to please God in their daily walk, but it was an urgent request. Their walking to please God was an absolute necessity, a necessity that carried with it great blessings for obedience and terrible judgment for disobedience (the displeasure of God).

2. The strength of the exhortation is seen in the following facts.

   a. The believers had been taught how they must live and please God. They had sat under the teachers and preachers of the Word; therefore, they were without excuse, for they knew exactly how to live and to please God. Once the believers had heard and been taught how they should live and please God, they were responsible to live that way. Pleasing God was not an option; it was a duty.

   b. The exhortation was based upon the Lord Jesus. It was what the *Lord Himself* had taught. There is no greater authority than the Lord. He is the supreme majestic Being of the universe; therefore, the exhortation to live and walk to please God is of the highest authority.

   c. The exhortation involves the actual commandments of the Lord Jesus. This is a repeat of verse one: keeping the commandments of the Lord Jesus is not an option. A commandment is a commandment, a law that is to be obeyed. In addition, it has been given by the Lord Himself. Therefore, it must be kept—regardless. We must walk and please God, and we must grow in our Christian walk day by day more and more.

2 (4:3-5) **Immorality—Sanctification—Sexual immorality**: the major commandment is sanctification, that is, moral purity. It can be stated no clearer: "This is *God's will*." There is no higher will than the will of God. When the will of God is known, then the will of God must be done. Sanctification—moral purity—is *the will of God*. The word *sanctified* means to be set apart and separated. We are to be set apart to God and His will, and His will is moral purity. Therefore, we are to be set apart to live pure lives before God. This means three things.

1. Sanctification means avoiding from sexual immorality. The word "immorality" (porneias) means all kinds of immoral sexual acts: adultery, pre-marital sex, homosexuality, and all forms of sexual deviation.

The believer is not to give his body to an immoral person, not to a prostitute or to an immoral neighbor. The believer's body belongs to Christ, which means that we are to honor Christ with our bodies. We are to take the sexual drive and energy of our bodies and use them as He has instructed:

⇒ either we dedicate our bodies solely to Him as eunuchs;
⇒ or we marry and build a family with the dynamic virtues of love and care, trust and loyalty.

2. Sanctification means that a person knows how to control his body and his spouse. Leon Morris points out that the word "body" (skeuos) can refer either to a person's own body or to a person's spouse (*The Epistles of Paul to the Thessalonians*. "Tyndale New Testament Commentaries," p.75). Both hold great meaning for the Christian believer. A believer is to know how to control his own body and how to control his spouse. A person can neglect, ignore, and abuse his body and a person can neglect, ignore, and abuse his or her spouse. In discussing a person's spouse it is important to note 1 Cor.7:4-5. Neglecting, ignoring, or abusing one's spouse can bring about temptation and can contribute significantly to the spouse becoming unfaithful and impure.

Note that the believer is to *know*, to possess his or her body and spouse in sanctification and honor. There is no excuse for ignorance in this matter nor for disobedience. The believer is to know…
- beyond a shadow of a doubt
- without equivocation
- without question

…that it is his duty to keep his body and spouse pure.

The point is strong: it is unthinkable that a believer would engage in immorality, that he would bring dishonor to his Lord and to his spouse, family, and himself. The believing husband and wife are to know that they must keep themselves and each other in a way that is holy and honorable. They must not set themselves apart to dishonorable and immoral neighbors nor to prostitutes.

I put this in human terms because you are weak in your natural selves. Just as you used to offer the parts of your body in slavery to impurity and to ever-increasing wickedness, so now offer them in slavery to righteousness leading to holiness. (Rom 6:19)

The husband should fulfill his marital duty to his wife, and likewise the wife to her husband. The wife's body does not belong to her alone but also to her husband. In the same way, the husband's body does not belong to him alone but also to his wife. Do not deprive each other except by mutual consent and for a time, so that you may devote yourselves to prayer. Then come together again so that Satan will not tempt you because of your lack of self-control. (1 Cor 7:3-5)

Since we have these promises, dear friends, let us purify ourselves from everything that contaminates body and spirit, perfecting holiness out of reverence for God. (2 Cor 7:1)

3. Sanctification means resisting the passion of lust. We must resist the passion of lust. Note the double emphasis, that is, the wording, "not in passionate lust." It means the *passion of lust*, the *enslaving power* of lust. When a person begins to lust, he can soon become enslaved to lust; he can be held by the grip of lust to such a degree that it is almost impossible to break the bondage. This is true with the…
- passion for sex
- passion for pornographic films and literature
- passion for manipulation
- passion for exposure
- passion for sexual conquest
- passion for looking
- passion for touching
- passion for romantic and immoral reading

The passion of lust is the way of the world. It is not the way of God. It is the life-style of those who do not know God. This does not mean that they do not know that sexual immorality is wrong. It means that they have rejected God and His commandments; they have chosen to live in the passion of their lusts. The believer is commanded to please God and to keep the commandments of the Lord Jesus. And the major commandment is our sanctification, that is, moral purity. Therefore, we are to avoid sexual immorality—from all forms of immoral sex (cp. Ro.1:18-32).

For you have spent enough time in the past doing what pagans choose to do—living in debauchery, lust, drunkenness, orgies, carousing and detestable idolatry. (1 Pet 4:3)

But each one is tempted when, by his own evil desire, he is dragged away and enticed. Then, after desire has conceived, it gives birth to sin; and sin, when it is full-grown, gives birth to death. (James 1:14-15)

In the same way the men also abandoned natural relations with women and were inflamed with lust for one another. Men committed indecent acts with other men, and received in themselves the due penalty for their perversion. (Rom 1:27)

Do you not know that the wicked will not inherit the kingdom of God? Do not be deceived: Neither the sexually immoral nor idolaters nor adulterers nor male prostitutes nor homosexual offenders (1 Cor 6:9)

Flee from sexual immorality. All other sins a man commits are outside his body, but he who sins sexually sins against his own body. (1 Cor 6:18)

I am afraid that when I come again my God will humble me before you, and I will be grieved over many who have sinned earlier and have not repented of the impurity, sexual sin and debauchery in which they have indulged. (2 Cor 12:21)

The acts of the sinful nature are obvious: sexual immorality, impurity and debauchery; and envy; drunkenness, orgies,

1 THESSALONIANS 4:1-8

and the like. I warn you, as I did before, that those who live like this will not inherit the kingdom of God. (Gal 5:19, 21)

Having lost all sensitivity, they have given themselves over to sensuality so as to indulge in every kind of impurity, with a continual lust for more. (Eph 4:19)

But among you there must not be even a hint of sexual immorality, or of any kind of impurity, or of greed, because these are improper for God's holy people. (Eph 5:3)

Put to death, therefore, whatever belongs to your earthly nature: sexual immorality, impurity, lust, evil desires and greed, which is idolatry. (Col 3:5)

It is God's will that you should be sanctified: that you should avoid sexual immorality; (1 Th 4:3)

For certain men whose condemnation was written about long ago have secretly slipped in among you. They are godless men, who change the grace of our God into a license for immorality and deny Jesus Christ our only Sovereign and Lord. In a similar way, Sodom and Gomorrah and the surrounding towns gave themselves up to sexual immorality and perversion. They serve as an example of those who suffer the punishment of eternal fire. (Jude 1:4, 7)

3 (4:6-8) **Immorality—Fornication—Adultery**: there are four reasons why we are to live pure lives, and the reasons stand as a severe warning to us.

1. Immorality defrauds and cheats a brother. Sexual immorality steals from a person. It either takes a wife from her husband or else it takes the husband from his wife. It is that simple—that tragic—that terrible. It steals one of the two major partners of a family, steals...
- their heart
- their affection
- their thoughts
- their purity
- their body
- their innocence
- their trust and trustworthiness

And the terrible tragedy is that none of these can ever be recovered—not completely, not fully. Once the heart, affection, thoughts, purity, body, innocence, and trust have been lost, they are lost and affected forever thereafter. The marriage and its bond of trust are gone forever. The pain and hurt always linger to some degree and the commitment and ability to totally surrender to the spouse always suffers to some degree. This is the reason God allows divorce after sexual immorality has been committed within marriage. (Note: God *allows* divorce; He *does not command* it. All parties involved in sexual immorality—no matter the situation—should stay together if the injured spouse can bear the pain long enough to recover and build strength.)

Note this: the same effects take place upon the *unmarried* when they commit sexual immorality. The person who seduces the unmarried steals from the person seduced and from the future spouse—steals the person's heart, affection, thoughts, purity, body, innocence, and trust.

> Love must be sincere. Hate what is evil; cling to what is good. Be devoted to one another in brotherly love. Honor one another above yourselves. (Rom 12:9-10)
>
> We who are strong ought to bear with the failings of the weak and not to please ourselves. Each of us should please his neighbor for his good, to build him up. (Rom 15:1-2)
>
> The entire law is summed up in a single command: "Love your neighbor as yourself." (Gal 5:14)
>
> "You shall not covet your neighbor's house. You shall not covet your neighbor's wife, or his manservant or maidservant, his ox or donkey, or anything that belongs to your neighbor." (Exo 20:17)

2. Immorality shall be revenged by God. This point needs to be heeded, especially in a promiscuous society like ours where immorality is not only accepted, but is encouraged. How can we dare say that immorality is accepted and encouraged in our society? Compare the emphasis and appeal of...
- dress in public and on the beach
- television and films
- books and magazines
- advertisements and promotions
- conversations and jokes
- suggestive words and actions that are acceptable today

The list could go on and on, but the point is this: God is going to judge immoral behavior no matter how much society accepts it. Society does not make the rules for man's behavior; God *makes the rules*. He has given the intimacy and preciousness of sex for marriage and only for marriage. And He has made it perfectly clear that any sex outside of marriage will not only be judged, but He will *personally avenge* the guilty party. Why? Because the guilty party...
- stole the life of a person.
- broke the person's trust and innocence for the rest of his or her life.

> The wrath of God is being revealed from heaven against all the godlessness and wickedness of men who suppress the truth by their wickedness, (Rom 1:18)
>
> He will punish those who do not know God and do not obey the gospel of our Lord Jesus. (2 Th 1:8)
>
> If we deliberately keep on sinning after we have received the knowledge of the truth, no sacrifice for sins is left, but only a fearful expectation of judgment and of raging fire that will consume the enemies of God. Anyone who rejected the law of Moses died without mercy on the testimony of two or three witnesses. How much more severely do you think a man deserves to be punished who has trampled the Son of God under foot, who has treated as an unholy thing the blood of the covenant that sanctified him, and who has insulted the Spirit of grace? For we know him who said, "It is mine to avenge; I will repay," and again, "The Lord will judge his people." It is a dreadful thing to fall into the hands of the living God. (Heb 10:26-31)

Marriage should be honored by all, and the marriage bed kept pure, for God will judge the adulterer and all the sexually immoral. (Heb 13:4)

Their vine comes from the vine of Sodom and from the fields of Gomorrah. Their grapes are filled with poison, and their clusters with bitterness. Their wine is the venom of serpents, the deadly poison of cobras. "Have I not kept this in reserve and sealed it in my vaults? It is mine to avenge; I will repay. In due time their foot will slip; their day of disaster is near and their doom rushes upon them." (Deu 32:32-35)

O LORD, the God who avenges, O God who avenges, shine forth. (Psa 94:1)

I will carry out great vengeance on them and punish them in my wrath. Then they will know that I am the LORD, when I take vengeance on them.'" (Ezek 25:17)

I will take vengeance in anger and wrath upon the nations that have not obeyed me." (Micah 5:15)

3. Immorality is not God's call; holiness is. When God calls us to salvation, He does not call us to live unclean lives, giving us the license to go from person to person. Such immorality...

- destroys genuine love for self and for others.
- destroys trust and trustworthiness of self and of others.
- destroys discipline and control of self and of others.
- destroys true care and concern for self and for others.
- destroys ego and esteem of self and of others.
- destroys confidence and assurance in self and in others.
- destroys loyalty and commitment within self and within others.
- destroys freedom and will within self and within others.
- destroys justice and fair treatment of others.
- destroys family and nation.

God would never call a person to do such terrible things. God calls us to holiness—to live lives that are set apart to Him and to purity, to our spouses and families. God calls us to build strong character and communities, strong families and nations. God calls us to holiness so that we can be strong enough to reach out to a world that reels under the awful weight of suffering and death. There is hope; there is salvation from evil and suffering and from death and judgment. But we must be sanctified and holy, totally set apart to building the strongest characters and families, communities and societies possible in order to reach the world.

Again, God does not call us to uncleanness and disintegration of character and society. God calls us to holiness.

Since we have these promises, dear friends, let us purify ourselves from everything that contaminates body and spirit, perfecting holiness out of reverence for God. (2 Cor 7:1)

And to put on the new self, created to be like God in true righteousness and holiness. (Eph 4:24)

But among you there must not be even a hint of sexual immorality, or of any kind of impurity, or of greed, because these are improper for God's holy people. (Eph 5:3)

Put to death, therefore, whatever belongs to your earthly nature: sexual immorality, impurity, lust, evil desires and greed, which is idolatry. (Col 3:5)

Make every effort to live in peace with all men and to be holy; without holiness no one will see the Lord. (Heb 12:14)

For it is written: "Be holy, because I am holy." (1 Pet 1:16)

Since everything will be destroyed in this way, what kind of people ought you to be? You ought to live holy and godly lives (2 Pet 3:11)

4. Immorality is a sin against God. Most persons reject this commandment of God as being *old fashioned* and *unacceptable* in an intellectual and enlightened society. But note what Scripture says: the person who rejects this commandment is rejecting God, not some man. The idea is that the preacher or teacher may be able to do little to us if we disregard the commandment. But God can take vengeance, and He will. Every human being who breaks the commandment shall receive the vengeance of God—unless he has repented and sought the forgiveness of God.

With eyes full of adultery, they never stop sinning; they seduce the unstable; they are experts in greed—an accursed brood! They have left the straight way and wandered off to follow the way of Balaam son of Beor, who loved the wages of wickedness. (2 Pet 2:14-15)

They went out from us, but they did not really belong to us. For if they had belonged to us, they would have remained with us; but their going showed that none of them belonged to us. (1 John 2:19)

But since you rejected me when I called and no one gave heed when I stretched out my hand, since you ignored all my advice and would not accept my rebuke, I in turn will laugh at your disaster; I will mock when calamity overtakes you— (Prov 1:24-26)

Note this also: God has given believers the Holy Spirit. The very presence of God in all His majesty dwells within our bodies. We must not, therefore, dirty our bodies with a harlot or some immoral and destructive neighbor. The majesty of God Himself must not be defiled. The Holy Spirit—He who is *holy*—is within us. We must, therefore, keep our bodies *holy*.

1 THESSALONIANS 4:9-12

	B. A Walk That Pleases God (Part II): Four Practical Duties, 4:9-12	Macedonia. Yet we urge you, brothers, to do so more and more.	
1 Grow in love more & more a. Because you are taught by God to do so b. Because you always need to grow in love more & more	9 Now about brotherly love we do not need to write to you, for you yourselves have been taught by God to love each other. 10 And in fact, you do love all the brothers throughout	11 Make it your ambition to lead a quiet life, to mind your own business and to work with your hands, just as we told you, 12 So that your daily life may win the respect of outsiders and so that you will not be dependent on anybody.	**2 Live a quiet life** **3 Mind your own business** **4 Work with your own hands** a. That we may win the respect of outsiders b. That we may lack no necessity

DIVISION II

THE MODEL WALK OR LIFE, 4:1-12

B. A Walk that Pleases God (Part II): Four Practical Duties, 4:9-12

(4:9-12) **Introduction**: every believer should be ambitious to please God. This passage gives four very practical ways that we can please God, four practical duties that must be obeyed.
1. Grow in love more and more (v.9-10).
2. Live a quiet life. (v.11).
3. Mind your own business (v.11).
4. Work with your own hands (v.11-12).

(4:9-12) **Another Outline**: A Strong Duty to Work.
1. The basis of work: Love (v.9).
   a. God Himself teaches love.
   b. The church shows great love—to brothers (v.10).
   c. The need: To grow more.
2. The rules for work (v.11).
   a. Be ambitious—to be quiet.
   b. Mind your own business.
   c. Work with your own hands.
3. The reasons for work (v.12).
   a. That we may live honorably before the world.
   b. That we may lack nothing.

1 (4:9-10) **Love, Brotherly—Church**: first, grow in love more and more. In the Greek the word "love" is not the word that is usually used for love. The word that is usually used for Christian love is *agape*, but the word used here is *philadelphia*, a very special kind of love. The word means *brotherly love*, the very special love that exists between the brothers and sisters within a loving family, brothers and sisters who truly cherish each other. It is the kind of love…
- that binds each other together as a family, as a brotherly clan.
- that binds each in an unbreakable union.
- that holds each other ever so deeply within the heart.
- that knows deep affection for each other.
- that nourishes and nurtures each other.
- that shows concern and looks after the welfare of each other.
- that joins hands with each other in a common purpose *under one father* (Leon Morris, *The Epistles of Paul to the Thessalonians*. "Tyndale New Testament Commentaries," p.80).

Note: Paul says there is no need for him to exhort the Thessalonians to love each other as brothers. Nevertheless, he does. Why? If there is no need, why does he encourage them to love each other? There are two reasons.
1. It was God who taught the Thessalonians to love each other. Therefore, as God's servant, Paul was driven to follow God; to stir the people of God to continue to love each other as brothers. This was and still is an absolute essential for the church.
   a. Christian believers need each other in order to make it through life. Living for Christ is not easy in a corrupt world that offers the bright lights of pleasure but ends up in suffering death. We all face temptation after temptation and trial after trial. We need the love of each other in order to stand against the temptation and to walk through the sufferings of life.
   b. The greatest threat to the church is that of internal strife and divisiveness. Nothing destroys the ministry of a church any quicker than criticism, grumbling, murmuring, gossiping, selfishness, cliquishness, and ambitiousness to have one's own way or to secure some position.

The point is this: God actually teaches believers to love each other *as brothers*. This means that God works within our hearts and stirs us to love each other. God arouses the thought within our minds—flashes the thought across our minds—the thought that we should love each other as brothers. Therefore, we are to grab hold of that thought and of the stirring within our hearts and love each other.

2. There is always the need to grow in love *more and more*. Note: the Thessalonian believers were noted for their love, not only within their own church, but throughout the whole district or state of Macedonia. But they were not yet perfected in love. No person is; therefore, there is always the need to grow and abound in love *more and more*. There is *never too much brotherly love* within the church or the world. We must, therefore, grow *more and more* in love.

> "A new command I give you: Love one another. As I have loved you, so you must love one another. By this all men will know that you are my disciples, if you love one another." (John 13:34-35)
>
> My command is this: Love each other as I have loved you. (John 15:12)
>
> Love must be sincere. Hate what is evil; cling to what is good. (Rom 12:9)
>
> You, my brothers, were called to be free. But do not use your freedom to indulge the sinful nature ; rather, serve one another in love. (Gal 5:13)
>
> Now that you have purified yourselves by obeying the truth so that you have sincere love for your brothers, love one another deeply, from the heart. (1 Pet 1:22)

1 THESSALONIANS 4:9-12

Above all, love each other deeply, because love covers over a multitude of sins. (1 Pet 4:8)

Whoever loves his brother lives in the light, and there is nothing in him to make him stumble. (1 John 2:10)

And he has given us this command: Whoever loves God must also love his brother. (1 John 4:21)

2 (4:11) **Quiet—Quietness**: second, live a quiet life. The word "ambition" (philotimeomai) means to be ambitious; to strive eagerly; to seek with all the energy a person has. The very meaning of the word *ambition* shows the supreme importance of quietness. We must seek to be quiet and learn to be quiet. Remember the church at Thessalonica was facing two critical problems.

1. It was facing the problem of persecution (1 Th.1:6; 2:14). Fellow workers, neighbors, and the public at large were ridiculing, mocking, and abusing the believers because of their faith and commitment to Christ. Most of the believers were standing fast against the persecution, but some misunderstood how they were to show their loyalty to Christ. When a believer is rejected or persecuted, Christ says that he is to *quietly* shake the dust of the place off his feet, turn, and walk away (Mt.10:14; Mk.6:4). Note: the whole thrust of the Lord's teaching in handling rejection and persecution is quietness, to leave the rejecters alone. But apparently, some of the Thessalonian believers were doing the very opposite: they were standing toe to toe with their neighbors and fellow workers and continuing to witness and proclaim the gospel. They were going too far and creating a noisy scene and embarrassing people.

2. The church was also facing the problem of some criticism and divisiveness against Paul. Some were accusing Paul of everything ranging from immoral conduct to deceitful and self-seeking preaching (1 Th.2:3f).

The point is this: we are to live a quiet and peaceable life before each other. We are not to be critical and divisive toward each other. We are to walk in a quiet and meek spirit out in the world. We are not to be abusive and arrogant in witnessing and in dealing with the world.

Thought 1. Note four thought provoking points.
1) A believer who is hurting needs to be heard, and the only way he can be heard is for us to be *quiet* and listen to him.
2) The world is hurting—everyone in the world has some hurt. Therefore, we must be *quiet* and listen for the hurt so that we can do what Christ said: minister to them.
3) The world needs the gospel, but the gospel cannot be effectively proclaimed in the midst of noise—not effectively and not in an appealing way. Noise pierces the ear and distracts. There must be quietness of atmosphere and mind for the gospel to have its most effective impact.
4) Believers must live a quiet instead of studying to be critical and divisive—live a quiet life at home, school, work, play, and church.

Make it your ambition to lead a quiet life, to mind your own business and to work with your hands, just as we told you, (1 Th 4:11)

Such people we command and urge in the Lord Jesus Christ to settle down and earn the bread they eat. (2 Th 3:12)

[Pray] for kings and all those in authority, that we may live peaceful and quiet lives in all godliness and holiness. (1 Tim 2:2)

Instead, it should be that of your inner self, the unfading beauty of a gentle and quiet spirit, which is of great worth in God's sight. (1 Pet 3:4)

Better a dry crust with peace and quiet than a house full of feasting, with strife. (Prov 17:1)

Better one handful with tranquillity than two handfuls with toil and chasing after the wind. (Eccl 4:6)

3 (4:11) **Believer, Duty**: third, mind your own business. Can you believe the Word of God says this? God actually tells us to mind our own business. Why? Because too many are busybodies and meddle in the affairs of others. What is it that causes a person to meddle in the business of others?

⇒ A person meddles because he is critical by nature. Through the years the person has criticized and murmured and talked about others so much that to meddle is just a way a life for him. The person has become a busybody by nature.

⇒ A person meddles because he fails to see his own shortcomings and failures. The busybody is always looking for the speck of sawdust (faults) in the lives of others when he has a plank in own life (Mt.7:3-5).

⇒ A person meddles because he fails to look after his own affairs like he should. A person should always be developing and enlarging his own life and affairs. Therefore, when he meddles in the affairs of others, he is neglecting his own business and the work God has given him to do.

⇒ A person meddles because he does not have enough to do. He has not committed himself to God—not enough to keep himself busy. He does not have enough to occupy his time and efforts.

What the busybody needs is to commit his life to Christ. The busybody needs to commit his life to undertake the mission of Christ. He needs to become so occupied with the things of Christ that he has no time to meddle in the affairs of others. The exhortation is strong: "mind your own business"—commit your time and energy to your own calling, the business God has given you to do.

Hold them in the highest regard in love because of their work. Live in peace with each other. (1 Th 5:13)

If you suffer, it should not be as a murderer or thief or any other kind of criminal, or even as a meddler. (1 Pet 4:15)

4 (4:11-12) **Work—Employment**: fourth, work with your own hands. The message of the gospel and of Christ's return to earth is a shocking message. The gospel declares...

• that a man can live forever.
• that Jesus Christ is coming back to earth to make a new heavens and earth that will be perfect.
• that all who truly believe in Christ will be the citizens of the new heavens and earth, worshipping and serving God the Father forever and ever.

As stated, the gospel is shocking to the world, but it offers great hope to the person who believes. The Thessalonian believers became excited over the return of the Lord and the promise of being with Him forever and ever in the new heavens and earth. They became so excited that they began to sacrifice all they could to meet the needs of people. But some went too far. Some quit their jobs in order to have more time to minister and, in an act of sacrificial commitment, they gave away *all they had*. The result was catastrophic. They were now having to sponge off the other believers in order to survive. Their action had been most unwise. Therefore, Paul commanded them: "work with your [own] hands"—quit sponging off others. Two reasons are given for labor.

1. We must labor in order to win the respect of outsiders, that is, win the respect of unbelievers. The word "respect" means to work in a commendable and honest way. Few in the world respect those who do not work. Of all people, Christians must set a dynamic example of work. One of the very purposes for which man has been put on earth is to work.

   a. Man is to work to subdue and gain dominion over the earth in all its unregulated and catastrophic forces.

   God blessed them and said to them, "Be fruitful and increase in number; fill the earth and subdue it. Rule over the fish of the sea and the birds of the air and over every living creature that moves on the ground." (Gen 1:28)

   b. Man is to work to provide the necessities of life for all men.

   The LORD God took the man and put him in the Garden of Eden to work it and take care of it. (Gen 2:15)

   c. Man is to work in order to have enough to give to the needy of the world.

   He who has been stealing must steal no longer, but must work, doing something useful with his own hands, that he may have something to share with those in need. (Eph 4:28)

2. We must labor in order to have enough to meet the necessities of life. As believers we are never to be dependent on anybody—not for a single thing that we need. We have two remarkable things providing for us:
   ⇒ our own mind and energy.
   ⇒ God Himself.

But seek first his kingdom and his righteousness, and all these things will be given to you as well. (Mat 6:33)

Thought 1. The exhortation is clear. God has no patience with people who do not work. All persons are placed on earth to contribute and to help meet the catastrophic and desperate needs of men. There is no place for the inactive in God's plan for the earth. The inactive, lazy, complacent—all are to hear the clear command of God: "Work with your hands."

He who has been stealing must steal no longer, but must work, doing something useful with his own hands, that he may have something to share with those in need. (Eph 4:28)

Make it your ambition to lead a quiet life, to mind your own business and to work with your hands, just as we told you, (1 Th 4:11)

Such people we command and urge in the Lord Jesus Christ to settle down and earn the bread they eat. (2 Th 3:12)

The LORD God took the man and put him in the Garden of Eden to work it and take care of it. (Gen 2:15; cp. Gen.3:19)

By the sweat of your brow you will eat your food until you return to the ground, since from it you were taken; for dust you are and to dust you will return." (Gen 3:19)

"'There are six days when you may work, but the seventh day is a Sabbath of rest, a day of sacred assembly. You are not to do any work; wherever you live, it is a Sabbath to the LORD. (Lev 23:3)

Dishonest money dwindles away, but he who gathers money little by little makes it grow. (Prov 13:11; cp. Pr.14:23)

All hard work brings a profit, but mere talk leads only to poverty. (Prov 14:23)

1 THESSALONIANS 4:13-5:3

	III. THE COMING AGAIN OF JESUS CHRIST, 4:13-5:24 **A. The Lord's Return & the Resurrection, 4:13-5:3** 13 Brothers, we do not want you to be ignorant about those who fall asleep, or to grieve like the rest of men, who have no hope. 14 We believe that Jesus died and rose again and so we believe that God will bring with Jesus those who have fallen asleep in him. 15 According to the Lord's own word, we tell you that we who are still alive, who are left till the coming of the Lord, will certainly not precede those who have fallen asleep. 16 For the Lord himself will come down from heaven,	with a loud command, with the voice of the archangel and with the trumpet call of God, and the dead in Christ will rise first. 17 After that, we who are still alive and are left will be caught up together with them in the clouds to meet the Lord in the air. And so we will be with the Lord forever. 18 Therefore encourage each other with these words. **CHAPTER 5** Now, brothers, about times and dates we do not need to write to you, 2 For you know very well that the day of the Lord will come like a thief in the night. 3 While people are saying, "Peace and safety," destruction will come on them suddenly, as labor pains on a pregnant woman, and they will not escape.	a. The Lord Himself will descend from heaven b. The dead in Christ will rise first c. The living will be caught up next d. The great reunion of the living with the dead will occur e. The experience of living face to face with the Lord will begin f. The present exhortation: encourage each other **4 The time of the Lord's return & of the Day of the Lord** a. A fact that should not have to be discussed b. A day that will come suddenly & unexpectedly c. A day of false security d. A day of terrible destruction & birth pains e. A day of no escape
1 The concern: Will believers be resurrected when Christ returns? a. Are not to be ignorant about the resurrection b. Are not to grieve excessively **2 The fact: Departed believers will return with Christ** a. Proof 1: Departed believers are with Christ b. Proof 2: The death & resurrection of Christ c. Proof 3: The Word of the Lord **3 The events of the Lord's return**			

DIVISION III

THE COMING AGAIN OF JESUS CHRIST, 4:13-5:24

A. The Lord's Return and the Resurrection, 4:13-5:3

(4:13-5:3) **Introduction**: this passage begins a new subject, a subject that intrigues people and offers the most glorious hope to man and his world. The subject is the return of Jesus Christ to earth and the resurrection of the dead. It is a subject that men must study and heed, for the return of the Lord will not only bring blessings to believers, it will launch the most terrifying judgment upon unbelievers.
1. The concern: Will believers be resurrected when Christ returns? (v.13).
2. The fact: departed believers will return with Christ (v.14-15).
3. The events of the Lord's return (v.16-18).
4. The time of the Lord's return and of the Day of the Lord (ch.5:1-3).

(4:13-5:11) **Another Outline**: The Lord's Return
1. Background: the concern (v.13).
   a. For the dead: will they arise?
   b. For the sorrowing
   c. For the hopeless
2. Fact 1: the dead will return with Jesus (v.14-15)
   a. The sure fact: "We believe…"
   b. The belief—gives assurance
   c. The Lord's Word—gives assurance
3. Fact 2: the Lord Himself will descend (v.16-17a)
   a. The dramatic appearance
   b. The order of resurrection: The dead should arise first—then the living
   c. The meeting place: in the clouds
4. Fact 3: believers will be reunited—eternally (v.17b)
   a. With the Lord
   b. Expected effect: comfort (v.18)

5. Fact 4: the Day of the Lord will come suddenly and unexpectedly upon the hopeless and the lost (5:1-3)
   a. A day of suddenness—unexpectancy
   b. A day of false security
   c. A day of destruction
   d. A day of birth pains
   e. A day of no escape
6. Fact 5: the Day of the Lord will not catch the believer unexpectedly and unprepared (v.4-5)
   a. Because of his nature
      1) He is a son of light, of the day
      2) He is not of the night, of darkness
   b. Because of the life he is to live (v.6)
      1) Not to sleep—although some do
      2) Not to be identified with the night or evil (v.7)
      3) To be sober and well protected (v.8)
   c. Because God has not appointed him to wrath, but to salvation (v.9)
   d. Because the Lord's return is to encourage and build up believers (v.11)

1 (4:13) **Resurrection, Of Believers**: the concern of the believers at Thessalonica involved dead believers. Would their loved ones who had died share in the resurrection when Christ returned to earth? Remember: the church at Thessalonica had just been founded; it was brand new. It was also being bitterly persecuted and was under savage attack. Some of the believers were dying; perhaps some were even being martyred and Christ had not yet returned. They were eagerly looking for that blessed hope and the glorious appearing of Jesus Christ. Would believers be resurrected when Christ returned? The Thessalonian

believers knew the gospel just as we know it: the gospel proclaims that Jesus Christ is returning to earth to receive believers unto Himself. When He returns to earth, we know...
- that living believers will be lifted up to meet Christ in the air.
- that all the glory, majesty, dominion, and power of God will be displayed in the heavens in the most spectacular scene imaginable.
- that the most glorious union and fellowship among *living believers* will take place around Christ.
- that believers who are lifted up will experience the most wonderful transformation and be given bodies that are perfected forever.
- that the world of unbelievers who are left here on earth will witness the most spectacular event ever seen by man.

But what about our loved ones who have already died? What will happen to them? Will they have a part in the spectacular return of Jesus Christ to earth? Will they have the privilege of sharing in the majestic display of God's power and in the glorious reunion of living believers with Christ? And how about their bodies? We know that our bodies—the bodies of believers who are living when Christ returns—will be transformed. They will never lie in the ground and decay and deteriorate. But what about the bodies of our loved ones who have already decayed and in some cases are scattered over the world due to war, disease, accident, and having been maimed? Are they going to share in the glorious resurrection and transformation when Christ returns?

All kinds of concerns about the resurrection arose in the minds of the Thessalonian believers just as they do in the minds of believers in every generation. The Thessalonians were *concerned* over their loved ones who had died. They were asking questions about the resurrection and the Lord's return out of concern. Unfortunately, this is not the case with many persons: they want to know about the end time out of curiosity, not out of concern. The very fact that Christ is returning should arouse the most urgent concern in us just as it did with the Thessalonian believers. Paul says two striking things to those who are concerned over the resurrection of dead believers when Christ returns.

1. Do not be ignorant about the resurrection. Study and grasp what God teaches and be comforted and challenged in the glorious hope He gives.

2. Do not grieve excessively over loved ones who die before Christ returns. We are bound to experience some sorrow and grief, but we are not to suffer grief like unbelievers who have no hope. They have reason to suffer the most terrible sorrow and grief, but not us. We have hope. William Barclay shows just how hopeless the world of unbelievers is by quoting several ancient writers:

> "Once a man dies there is no resurrection" (*Aeschylus*).
> "There is hope for those who are alive, but those who have died are without hope" (*Theocritus*).
> "When once our brief light sets, there is one perpetual night through which we must sleep" (*Catullus*)
> "I was not; I became; I am not; I care not" (*an ancient tombstone*).
> "Irene to Taonnophris and Philo, good comfort. I was as sorry and wept over the departed one as I wept for Didymas. And all things whatsoever were fitting, I did....But nevertheless against such things one can do nothing. Therefore, comfort one another" (*an ancient letter*). (William Barclay. *The Letters to the Philippians, Colossians, and Thessalonians*, p.235f.)

There is absolutely no hope for the unbelievers of the world. But there is glorious hope for the believer. Therefore, we are not to grieve excessively at the death of loved ones. There is no need, for they shall arise to meet the great God and our Savior, the Lord Jesus Christ. This is the glorious message of Christ's followers.

2 (4:14-15) **Resurrection of Believers**: the fact is forcefully declared—departed believers will return with Christ. There are three proofs of this great fact given.

1. Proof one: departed believers are with Christ; they are living with Him face to face.
   a. Note the words "in Him"—God will bring departed believers *with Jesus* when He returns. They are *with Him* now. This is exactly what Scripture teaches.

> **Jesus answered him, "I tell you the truth, today you will be with me in paradise." (Luke 23:43)**
> **Therefore we are always confident and know that as long as we are at home in the body we are away from the Lord. We live by faith, not by sight. We are confident, I say, and would prefer to be away from the body and at home with the Lord. (2 Cor 5:6-8)**
> **I am torn between the two: I desire to depart and be with Christ, which is better by far; (Phil 1:23)**

The point is this: departed believers are with the Lord, living face to face with Him. We do not have to wonder where they are. When they died, they went immediately to be with the Lord in paradise or heaven, and they will never be separated from the Lord. Therefore, when He returns to earth, He will bring all departed believers with Him.

   b. The words "asleep in him"—it is those who *sleep in Jesus* that God will bring with Him when He returns to earth. The word "asleep" is not teaching that death is a semi-conscious state, an existence somewhat like a deep sleep. As has already been shown, the believer immediately goes to be with Christ when he departs from this world. "Asleep" is simply a soft word used by believers to describe their departure from this world. It is a picture of resting from the trials and sufferings of this world. The person who believes in Jesus Christ while on this earth simply "sleeps [rests] with Jesus" throughout eternity. It is these persons—all the believers who sleep or rest in Jesus—whom God will bring with Him when He returns to earth. (See DEEPER STUDY # 1, *Sleep*—Jn.11:13 for more discussion.)

> **I tell you the truth, if anyone keeps my word, he will never see death." (John 8:51)**

And whoever lives and believes in me will never die. Do you believe this?" (John 11:26)

c. Jesus Christ is identified as God. It is God—God in the person of Jesus Christ—who will return to earth and bring departed believers with Him. Christ has the power of God because He is God. As God, Jesus Christ...
- had the power to come to earth as a man.
- had the power to die and arise from the dead.
- had the power to ascend back into heaven.
- has the power to transfer a departed believer into heaven with Him.
- has the power to return to earth.
- has the power to bring all departed believers back to earth with Him.

2. Proof two: the death and resurrection of Jesus Christ proves that departed believers will return to earth with God. Jesus Christ came to earth to die and bear the punishment of sin for man and to arise from the dead. Therefore, if we believe in Jesus Christ...
- we never have to die because He has already died for us.
- we shall arise from the dead even as He arose.

How? By believing that Jesus Christ did die and arise from the dead for us. If we believe in Jesus Christ, then when we depart this world, we go to be with him; and when He returns, we will return with Him.

The point is striking: the fact that Jesus Christ died and arose is the proof that departed believers are living with Him and will return with Him when He comes back to earth. Our hope—the glorious hope of the believer—is based upon the death and resurrection of Jesus Christ. There is no greater basis in all the world, for Jesus Christ really did die and arise from the dead. There is no question about it, not for the genuine believer, for God has given us the witness of His Spirit. Therefore, after we have departed from this earth, we will return with Christ when He comes back to earth.

> For my Father's will is that everyone who looks to the Son and believes in him shall have eternal life, and I will raise him up at the last day." (John 6:40)
>
> For what I received I passed on to you as of first importance : that Christ died for our sins according to the Scriptures, that he was buried, that he was raised on the third day according to the Scriptures, (1 Cor 15:3-4)
>
> Because we know that the one who raised the Lord Jesus from the dead will also raise us with Jesus and present us with you in his presence. (2 Cor 4:14)

3. Proof three: the Word of the Lord proves that departed believers will return to earth with God. Their bodies will actually be raised from the dead before we are caught up. This is a strong point. Paul emphatically states that this revelation has come from the Lord. Therefore, believers should want no greater assurance. What is the revelation? We who are alive when the Lord returns shall not be caught up first. The bodies of all departed believers will be resurrected first. Again, how do we know this? How do we know that this is a fact, a real event that will actually take place? By the Word of the Lord. The Lord Jesus Christ, God Himself, declared it.

> And we also thank God continually because, when you received the word of God, which you heard from us, you accepted it not as the word of men, but as it actually is, the word of God, which is at work in you who believe. (1 Th 2:13)
>
> All Scripture is God-breathed and is useful for teaching, rebuking, correcting and training in righteousness, (2 Tim 3:16)

3 (4:16-18) **Jesus Christ, Return—Resurrection of Believers**: the events of the Lord's return and of the resurrection are clearly spelled out in these verses.

1. First, the *Lord Himself* will come down from heaven. The very first event will be the appearance of the Lord God Himself. The supreme Majesty of the universe, the Lord Jesus Christ, will rent the skies and miraculously appear in all the spectacular glory, pomp, and power of heaven itself. When He appears, three spectacular events will occur.

a. The Lord God Himself will appear "with a loud command" (en keleusmati). The word means a military command. The commander-in-chief of the universe will shout louder than any voice has ever shouted—shout even as He did when He was upon earth: "[Believers] come out" (Jn.11:43).

b. The voice of the archangel will cry out. What will He cry? His shout will probably be the rallying cry for all the armies of the heavenly angels to join in the praise of the glorious event. Christ taught that the heavenly angels would be with Him when He returned to earth (Mt.24:31; 25:31; 2 Th.1:7).

c. The trumpet of God shall sound. The trumpet has always been for the purpose of arousing attention and warning. The whole universe—both earth and heaven, believers, unbelievers, and angels—will be aroused; and all unbelievers will be warned. The Lord God Himself is now appearing and the events of the end time are now being launched upon earth.

2. Second, the dead in Christ will rise first. Why will dead believers be the first to be caught up to meet the Lord? Because of the Lord's great love and care. The first expression of love and care will be shown to those dear saints who have passed through the shadow of death. It is the very nature of Christ to show tenderness and love to those who suffer the most; therefore, they who have suffered the awful fate of death will be the first to meet the Lord in the air. Now, note several facts.

a. Only departed believers will arise; no unbeliever will be resurrected, not at this point. Only those who are "dead in Christ"—who died believing in Jesus Christ—will be resurrected when the Lord rents the skies.

b. It will be the bodies of the departed believers that are resurrected. The believers themselves, that is, their spirits, are already with the Lord. Their bodies are being raised and transformed to live forever with God. The shout of the Lord to "*come out*" will call together all the atoms of a person's body, no matter where the various parts of a person's body may lie. The atoms of a person's body will be transformed to structure an eternal and perfect body.

c. The bodies of the departed believers will arise first—arise before we who are alive are caught up.

3. Third, we who are alive will be caught up right after the dead have risen. There will be a glorious transformation of our bodies just as there will be of those whose bodies have decayed in the earth. The change will be as Scripture declares: the infusion of a totally new nature.

> **For the perishable must clothe itself with the imperishable, and the mortal with immortality. (1 Cor 15:53)**

a. The nature of the believer's present body is corruptible and mortal; the nature of his new body will be imperishable and immortal.
⇒ The "perishable" and "mortal" nature means that men are earthly; that they age, deteriorate, die, decay, and decompose. Every person, no matter who he is, is earthly and will return to the earth unless Jesus returns while the person is living on the earth.
⇒ The "imperishable" and "immortal" nature means that believers will be made heavenly, that they will be transformed and given a *perfect nature* that will never age, deteriorate, die, decay, or decompose. They will be completely free from defilement and depravity. They will be given a body that is perfect, a body that is diametrically opposed to their present body, a body that is perfected forever to live with God in the new heavens and earth. (See DEEPER STUDY #1—Jn.21:1; 1 Cor.15:42-44.)

b. Note the word "must" in 1 Cor.15:53. It shows the absolute necessity for the change of man's body. If man is to live with God, his body must be changed. It is essential, a must, an absolute necessity if man is to live forever.

> **And they can no longer die; for they are like the angels. They are God's children, since they are children of the resurrection. (Luke 20:36)**
> **I tell you the truth, if anyone keeps my word, he will never see death." (John 8:51)**
> **And whoever lives and believes in me will never die. Do you believe this?" (John 11:26)**
> **To those who by persistence in doing good seek glory, honor and immortality, he will give eternal life. (Rom 2:7)**
> **For the perishable must clothe itself with the imperishable, and the mortal with immortality. (1 Cor 15:53)**
> **Now we know that if the earthly tent we live in is destroyed, we have a building from God, an eternal house in heaven, not built by human hands. (2 Cor 5:1)**
> **After that, we who are still alive and are left will be caught up together with them in the clouds to meet the Lord in the air. And so we will be with the Lord forever. (1 Th 4:17)**
> **But it has now been revealed through the appearing of our Savior, Christ Jesus, who has destroyed death and has brought life and immortality to light through the gospel. (2 Tim 1:10)**

4. Fourth, the great union of the living with the dead will take place. Note the emphatic declaration: we "will be caught up *together* with them in the clouds to meet the Lord in the air." We will be reunited with all our loved ones, and even more wonderful, all believers—our loved ones and those whom we have never known—shall all be united together with our wonderful Lord. We shall all be there together rejoicing in the presence of Him who has saved us and transformed us into perfect and eternal beings. What a day of reunion and rejoicing that will be!

5. The experience of living face to face with the Lord begins. We will be caught up and "so we will we be with the Lord forever." As wonderful as the reunion of believers will be, the most wonderful event will be seeing our Lord face to face for the very first time. What will our first thoughts be? Our first reaction? Everything will take place in the blinking of an eye. Suddenly...
• we will be standing in mid-air and transformed into perfect men and women.
• we will be standing in the clouds in the midst of teeming millions.
• we will be transformed in the midst of the spectacular glory and majesty, dominion and power of the Lord God Himself.

Is there any question what our first thoughts and response will be? The great reunion with family and believers will not be the occupation of our thoughts. Christ will be! The Lord God Himself in all His majestic glory and sovereignty will consume our attention and praise. We will be lifting up His name in the most perfect hymn of praise and adoration ever arranged. Jesus Christ Himself will be the total focus of our attention.

6. The present exhortation: encourage each other with these words. God does not reveal the events of the end time to satisfy curiosity. He tells us about the glorious events so that we can prepare and encourage each other. There is no need for discouragement on this earth; no need for extreme sorrow and grief; no need for hopelessness; and no need for ignorance. The Lord Himself has given us the most wonderful hope—the hope of living forever face to face with Him—of worshipping and serving Him forever in a new heavens and earth.

> **And they can no longer die; for they are like the angels. They are God's children, since they are children of the resurrection. (Luke 20:36)**
> **I tell you the truth, if anyone keeps my word, he will never see death." (John 8:51)**
> **And whoever lives and believes in me will never die. Do you believe this?" (John 11:26)**
> **Now we know that if the earthly tent we live in is destroyed, we have a building from God, an eternal house in heaven, not built by human hands. (2 Cor 5:1)**
> **But it has now been revealed through the appearing of our Savior, Christ Jesus, who has destroyed death and has brought life and immortality to light through the gospel. (2 Tim 1:10)**
> **He will wipe every tear from their eyes. There will be no more death or mourning or crying or pain, for the old order of things has passed away." (Rev 21:4)**

4 **(5:1-3) Jesus Christ, Return—Day of the Lord—Resurrection of Believers**: the time of the Lord's return and the day of the Lord. Paul wants to make it perfectly clear that he does not know when the Lord is returning to earth, nor does anyone else. Note five points.

1. When is the Lord returning? This is a fact that should not have to be discussed. Paul had already taught the believers that no one knows when the Lord is returning to earth; only God knows. Therefore, there is absolutely no need to discuss "times and the dates." This is strong, but a strong statement is needed with those who set dates. Note the meaning of "times" and "dates."

⇒ "Times" (chronon) means chronological time, the events that follow one another and roll in and away from one another. Paul had already covered the times, the order of events that were to happen in the end time.

⇒ "Dates" (kairon) means the particular time and the nature of the events that are to take place. Paul had already covered the critical events and discussed what would be happening in the events.

Thought 1. Note a crucial point: times and dates are periods of time that cover many years for men—years that can extend into decades and centuries. This is exactly what Paul is saying: "the times" of the end time extend over a long chronological time; but "the dates," the very nature and happening of critical periods, can be looked at and observed. When dealing with end time events, we must always keep this fact in mind.

Thought 2. Once a believer has studied the times and dates of the end time, that is, the great spectacular periods of coming events and the particular happenings of the events, he knows that only God could know when He is returning. There are just too many intricate details, ramifications, and weaving of events in the happenings of history for any man to know when the fullness of time is to arrive. Only God could know when the intricate details of events have been fulfilled. Only God could know when He is to return.

2. When is the Lord returning? When "the day of the Lord" is ready to come upon the earth. This is exactly what Paul is saying. And when is "the day of the Lord"? No man knows. It is coming as a thief in the night—suddenly and unexpectedly. Believers are to be looking for the Lord's return, but unbelievers will be caught completely off guard. To say that unbelievers will be surprised is an understatement. They will be shocked and stand in stark terror at the appearance of Christ and at the judgments that will begin to fall upon earth.

Note: "the day of the Lord" refers to the Lord's dealings with unbelievers. John Walvoord puts it in simple and striking words:

> "The Day of the Lord is a period of time in which God will deal with wicked men directly and dramatically in fearful judgment. Today a man may be a blasphemer of God, an atheist, can denounce God and teach bad doctrine. Seemingly God does nothing about it. But the day designated in Scripture as 'the day of the Lord' is coming when God will punish human sin, and He will deal in wrath and in judgment with a Christ-rejecting world. One thing we are sure of, that God in His own way will bring every soul into judgment" (*The Thessalonian Epistles*, p.76).

That day, the day when God will bring every soul into judgment, is what the Bible calls "the day of the Lord." When is Christ returning? When the earth has reached such a depraved condition that it is hopelessly lost forever and ripe for the judgments of "the day of the Lord."

> **See, the day of the LORD is coming — a cruel day, with wrath and fierce anger—to make the land desolate and destroy the sinners within it. The stars of heaven and their constellations will not show their light. The rising sun will be darkened and the moon will not give its light. I will punish the world for its evil, the wicked for their sins. I will put an end to the arrogance of the haughty and will humble the pride of the ruthless. (Isa 13:9-11)**

> **"The great day of the LORD is near—near and coming quickly. Listen! The cry on the day of the LORD will be bitter, the shouting of the warrior there. That day will be a day of wrath, a day of distress and anguish, a day of trouble and ruin, a day of darkness and gloom, a day of clouds and blackness, a day of trumpet and battle cry against the fortified cities and against the corner towers. (Zep 1:14-16)**

> **"Surely the day is coming; it will burn like a furnace. All the arrogant and every evildoer will be stubble, and that day that is coming will set them on fire," says the LORD Almighty. "Not a root or a branch will be left to them. (Mal 4:1)**

> **Enoch, the seventh from Adam, prophesied about these men: "See, the Lord is coming with thousands upon thousands of his holy ones to judge everyone, and to convict all the ungodly of all the ungodly acts they have done in the ungodly way, and of all the harsh words ungodly sinners have spoken against him." These men are grumblers and faultfinders; they follow their own evil desires; they boast about themselves and flatter others for their own advantage. (Jude 1:14-16)**

3. The day of the Lord will come when the world of unbelievers feel a great sense of security—when they are saying, "peace and safety." Some leaders throughout the world or some world organization will cooperate and be able to achieve some semblance of peace and security throughout the world. People will be reveling in the security and living it up even as they did in the days of Noah.

> **"Just as it was in the days of Noah, so also will it be in the days of the Son of Man. People were eating, drinking, marrying and being given in marriage up to the day Noah entered the ark. Then the flood came and destroyed them all. "It was the same in the days of Lot. People were eating and drinking, buying and selling, planting and building. But the day Lot left Sodom, fire and sulfur rained down from heaven and destroyed them all. "It will be just like**

this on the day the Son of Man is revealed. (Luke 17:26-30)

4. The day of the Lord will be a day of catastrophic destruction. When the world is crying out for peace and safety, a terrible destruction will be lying right over the horizon. Suddenly, out of nowhere, the great and terrible day of the Lord will fall upon the world and the unbelievers of the world. Note the phrase "destruction will come on them suddenly": it will be totally unexpected. It will be just like the birth pains that suddenly strike a woman who is with child. The pain, suffering, and destruction will be relentless.

> Wail, for the day of the LORD is near; it will come like destruction from the Almighty. Because of this, all hands will go limp, every man's heart will melt. Terror will seize them, pain and anguish will grip them; they will writhe like a woman in labor. They will look aghast at each other, their faces aflame. (Isa 13:6-8)
> Alas for that day! For the day of the LORD is near; it will come like destruction from the Almighty. (Joel 1:15)
> I will show wonders in the heavens and on the earth, blood and fire and billows of smoke. The sun will be turned to darkness and the moon to blood before the coming of the great and dreadful day of the LORD. (Joel 2:30-31)
> "The great day of the LORD is near—near and coming quickly. Listen! The cry on the day of the LORD will be bitter, the shouting of the warrior there. That day will be a day of wrath, a day of distress and anguish, a day of trouble and ruin, a day of darkness and gloom, a day of clouds and blackness, a day of trumpet and battle cry against the fortified cities and against the corner towers. I will bring distress on the people and they will walk like blind men, because they have sinned against the LORD. Their blood will be poured out like dust and their entrails like filth. Neither their silver nor their gold will be able to save them on the day of the Lord's wrath. In the fire of his jealousy the whole world will be consumed, for he will make a sudden end of all who live in the earth." (Zep 1:14-18)

5. The day of the Lord will be a day of no escape. "They will not escape" (ou me ekphugosin). This is a double negative in the Greek: they will not, by no means, escape. Judgment and destruction are an absolute surety; they will not, in no wise, escape. All human beings who have not truly trusted Jesus Christ will face the terrible day of the lord.

> "You snakes! You brood of vipers! How will you escape being condemned to hell? (Mat 23:33)
> So when you, a mere man, pass judgment on them and yet do the same things, do you think you will escape God's judgment? (Rom 2:3)
> While people are saying, "Peace and safety," destruction will come on them suddenly, as labor pains on a pregnant woman, and they will not escape. (1 Th 5:3)
> How shall we escape if we ignore such a great salvation? This salvation, which was first announced by the Lord, was confirmed to us by those who heard him. (Heb 2:3)
> See to it that you do not refuse him who speaks. If they did not escape when they refused him who warned them on earth, how much less will we, if we turn away from him who warns us from heaven? (Heb 12:25)
> Therefore this is what the LORD says: 'I will bring on them a disaster they cannot escape. Although they cry out to me, I will not listen to them. (Jer 11:11)
> Woe to you who long for the day of the LORD! Why do you long for the day of the LORD? That day will be darkness, not light. It will be as though a man fled from a lion only to meet a bear, as though he entered his house and rested his hand on the wall only to have a snake bite him. (Amos 5:18-19)
> Though they dig down to the depths of the grave, from there my hand will take them. Though they climb up to the heavens, from there I will bring them down. (Amos 9:2)

1 THESSALONIANS 5:4-11

	B. The Lord's Return & the Believer's Behavior, 5:4-11	drunk, get drunk at night.
		8 But since we belong to the day, let us be self-controlled, putting on faith and love as a breastplate, and the hope of salvation as a helmet.
		9 For God did not appoint us to suffer wrath but to receive salvation through our Lord Jesus Christ.
		10 He died for us so that, whether we are awake or asleep, we may live together with him.
		11 Therefore encourage one another and build each other up, just as in fact you are doing.
			the night & evil behavior
			3 He is to be sober & to protect himself
			  a. How: By putting on the armor of God—faith, love, & hope
			  b. The reasons
			    1) He is not appointed to wrath, but to salvation
			    2) Christ died for him
			
			4 He is to minister
			  a. To encourage others
			  b. To edify others

1 He is not to be surprised by the Lord's return
  a. Because he is not in darkness
  b. Because he is a child of light
  c. Because he is a child of the day
2 He is not to be spiritually asleep or unwatchful
 	
  a. Fact: Some do sleep
  b. Reason: Identifies him with
	4 But you, brothers, are not in darkness so that this day should surprise you like a thief.
	5 You are all sons of the light and sons of the day. We do not belong to the night or to the darkness.
	6 So then, let us not be like others, who are asleep, but let us be alert and self-controlled.
	7 For those who sleep, sleep at night, and those who get		

DIVISION III

THE COMING AGAIN OF JESUS CHRIST, 4:13-5:24

B. The Lord's Return and the Believer's Behavior, 5:4-11

(5:4-11) **Introduction**: the return of Jesus Christ is to be the most phenomenal event in all of human history. It will be the most amazing and spectacular event ever to be witnessed by the eyes of man. Its importance cannot be overstressed, for when Christ returns, both the blessing and the judgment of God will fall upon the earth. Genuine believers will be blessed and unbelievers will suffer the wrath of God. Because of this, how a believer behaves while he is on earth matters greatly to God. This passage deals with the all important subject of the *Lord's return and the believer's behavior*.

1. He is not to be surprised by the Lord's return (v.4-5).
2. He is not to be spiritually asleep or unwatchful (v.6-7).
3. He is to be sober and to protect himself (v.8-10).
4. He is to minister (v.11).

1 (5:4-5) **Believers, Nature—Jesus Christ, Return—Day of the Lord**: the believer is not in darkness; therefore, *that day* should not surprise him. *That day* refers back to the Day of the Lord—that great and terrible day of God's wrath, the awful judgment of God which is to fall upon the earth and unbelievers. Note the word "surprised" (katalambano). It means to come upon or take hold of by surprise. The day of the Lord is not to take the believer by surprise, not to come upon him like a thief, unexpectedly. There are three strong reasons why the believer is not to be caught off guard by the Day of the Lord.

1. The believer is not in darkness.
  a. The believer is not in the darkness of ignorance. He knows that the terrible day of God's judgment is coming. He has studied and been taught the Word of God. Both the preachers and teachers of God's Word have been faithful in warning the world: the Day of the Lord is coming upon the world. All must give an account of their rebellion against God and their selfish hoarding against the desperate of the world. No true believer is ignorant of the truth; no true believer dwells in the darkness of ignorance. If he is a true believer, he knows that God's judgment is to fall upon men; he knows that the Day of the Lord is coming. Therefore, he is to be anticipating it. He is not to be caught by surprise when it comes.
  b. The believer is not in the darkness of sin. He does not roam around in the world living in sin. His mind and thoughts are not consumed with the things of this world. He is not blinded by the glitter and power of possessions nor by the passions and pleasures of the flesh (sinful nature). The believer does not walk throughout the day with his thoughts glued to this earth, seldom if ever thinking about God. He is not in the darkness of sin, feeling that God is way off in outer space someplace and unconcerned with what happens on this earth. The believer is not separated from God and ignorant about God and His ways. His life is centered in God and his thoughts are *always* upon God. He knows God personally and intimately. Therefore, he knows that God is holy and just as well as loving. He knows that God *must* judge the unbelievers of the world.

2. The believer is a child of light (Greek, son). This simply means that the believer is a child of God, for God is light (1 Jn.1:5). The believer possesses the very nature of God, which is light. He knows God; therefore, he is not to be caught off guard nor surprised when the Lord comes and judges the world.

3. The believer is a child of the day. This is a wonderful truth. It means that the believer will escape the judgment of God. He is a child who is accepted by God; therefore, he will be accepted in that day of the Lord's return. He will not have to face the terrible day of the Lord and suffer the judgment of God's wrath. He is a child of the day, of God's glorious salvation and deliverance. Therefore, the believer should be looking for the Lord's return and the day of the Lord's wrath. He should not be walking in darkness with his mind and thoughts upon the world. He should be walking about, always praying and thinking about the things of God and the utter necessity to reach people for Christ, for the great and terrible day of the Lord is coming. It is right over the horizon, ever so near.

> **"You are the light of the world. A city on a hill cannot be hidden. (Mat 5:14)**

1 THESSALONIANS 5:4-11

Put your trust in the light while you have it, so that you may become sons of light." When he had finished speaking, Jesus left and hid himself from them. (John 12:36)

For this is what the Lord has commanded us: "'I have made you a light for the Gentiles, that you may bring salvation to the ends of the earth.'" (Acts 13:47)

For you were once darkness, but now you are light in the Lord. Live as children of light (Eph 5:8)

So that you may become blameless and pure, children of God without fault in a crooked and depraved generation, in which you shine like stars in the universe (Phil 2:15)

You are all sons of the light and sons of the day. We do not belong to the night or to the darkness. (1 Th 5:5)

"So may all your enemies perish, O LORD! But may they who love you be like the sun when it rises in its strength." Then the land had peace forty years. (Judg 5:31)

2 (5:6-7) **Believers, Duty**: the believer is not to sleep, but to be alert and self-controlled. *Sleep* refers to spiritual sleep. When a person is asleep, he is not alert nor involved in what is going on around him. When a believer is spiritually asleep, he is not alert nor involved in the things of God. His mind and behavior are not concerned with the things of God. He slumbers, dozes, and sleeps. A person who is spiritually asleep is not alert nor aware of what God is doing. Therefore, he will be caught off guard when the Lord returns.

But note: the believer is not to sleep. He is to be alert and self-controlled.

⇒ To be alert means to be alert and on guard to live for Christ. Remember: Christ may rent the skies any moment and return to earth; therefore, we must be watching every moment of every day.

⇒ To be self-controlled means to be rigid in discipline and control for Christ; to live a strict life of righteousness and godliness, ever looking for the return of the Lord.

Note two tragic facts about some believers—facts that should never happen to genuine believers.

1. Some do sleep. The word "others" refers to the unbelievers of the world (1 Th.4:13). But note: this exhortation is being given to believers. Therefore, some believers have a desperate need to heed this warning. They have fallen asleep spiritually. They are...

- no longer alert to the things of God.
- no longer alive to God, thinking and keeping their thoughts upon God.
- no longer worshipping God, praying and fellowshipping with God and His people.
- no longer anticipating the return of Christ.
- no longer active for God, serving and working for God.

Tragically, they are asleep. They are not alert nor living self-controlled lives. Discipline and control in righteousness and godliness are the furthest things from their minds.

2. Some are identified with the night and with evil behavior. This is exactly what Scripture is saying. The person who sleeps, sleeps in the night, and the person who gets drunk gets drunk in the night. Nighttime is usually the time when people sleep and become involved in sin. Therefore, if a believer carouses around with those who are of the night, he is identifying himself with the sinners of the world.

⇒ If a believer carouses around with the sleepers of the world—those who are asleep to the things of God—then he is identified with the sleeping unbelievers of the world.

⇒ If a believer carouses around with the drunken of the world—those who are indulgent, lustful, worldly, and fleshly—then he is identified with the drunken unbelievers of the world.

There is no other way to tell about a person. If he carouses around in the darkness of the night, then he shows himself to be of the night. If he walks around in the day, then he shows himself to be of the day.

"Therefore keep watch, because you do not know the day or the hour. (Mat 25:13)

It will be good for those servants whose master finds them watching when he comes. I tell you the truth, he will dress himself to serve, will have them recline at the table and will come and wait on them. (Luke 12:37)

"Be careful, or your hearts will be weighed down with dissipation, drunkenness and the anxieties of life, and that day will close on you unexpectedly like a trap. (Luke 21:34)

You are all sons of the light and sons of the day. We do not belong to the night or to the darkness. So then, let us not be like others, who are asleep, but let us be alert and self-controlled. (1 Th 5:5-6)

Be self-controlled and alert. Your enemy the devil prowls around like a roaring lion looking for someone to devour. (1 Pet 5:8)

I am coming soon. Hold on to what you have, so that no one will take your crown. (Rev 3:11)

"Behold, I come like a thief! Blessed is he who stays awake and keeps his clothes with him, so that he may not go naked and be shamefully exposed." (Rev 16:15)

3 (5:8-10) **Believers, Duty**: the believer is to be sober and to protect himself. The believer is to be self-controlled; that is, he must be mentally awake, alert, and watchful, and he must protect himself. He must make sure that he stays spiritually controlled and well protected.

1. How can the believer stay in control and protect himself? By putting on the armor of God. What is the armor of God?

a. There is the breastplate of faith and love. The breastplate protected the heart of the soldier. The heart of the believer must be protected. His heart must be committed and focused upon Jesus Christ and His cause for world conquest. It is the breastplate of faith and love that will protect our heart and keep it focused upon Christ and His cause.

⇒ Faith protects our heart: when we really believe that Jesus Christ saves us from sin and death and delivers us from the judgment of

God—when we really believe in Jesus Christ—then we focus our lives upon Jesus Christ. We stay sober: we live righteously and godly in this present world and look for the glorious appearing of the great God and Savior, Jesus Christ. Our faith in Christ keeps us sober.

> Then they asked him, "What must we do to do the works God requires?" Jesus answered, "The work of God is this: to believe in the one he has sent." (John 6:28-29)
> In addition to all this, take up the shield of faith, with which you can extinguish all the flaming arrows of the evil one. (Eph 6:16)
> And without faith it is impossible to please God, because anyone who comes to him must believe that he exists and that he rewards those who earnestly seek him. (Heb 11:6)
> And this is his command: to believe in the name of his Son, Jesus Christ, and to love one another as he commanded us. (1 John 3:23)

⇒ Love protects our hearts: when we really see the love of Christ for us—that He actually bore our sins and punishment on the cross—then we break before Him and bow in humble adoration and love. Love floods us, for He did so much for us. We never have to die; we never have to bear the punishment of sin—all because He loved us. Therefore, our hearts reach out to Him broken and pouring love back to Him. We stay sober: we live righteously and godly and look for His return because we love Him. Our love keeps us sober.

> "For God so loved the world that he gave his one and only Son, that whoever believes in him shall not perish but have eternal life. (John 3:16)
> But God demonstrates his own love for us in this: While we were still sinners, Christ died for us. (Rom 5:8)
> For Christ's love compels us, because we are convinced that one died for all, and therefore all died. And he died for all, that those who live should no longer live for themselves but for him who died for them and was raised again. (2 Cor 5:14-15)
> But because of his great love for us, God, who is rich in mercy, made us alive with Christ even when we were dead in transgressions—it is by grace you have been saved. (Eph 2:4-5)
> How great is the love the Father has lavished on us, that we should be called children of God! And that is what we are! The reason the world does not know us is that it did not know him. (1 John 3:1)

b. There is the helmet of the Christian soldier, the hope of salvation. There is only one way we can be prepared for the return of Christ and escape the judgment of God: we must keep our minds and lives focused upon Christ. How can we do this? By protecting our minds with the helmet of God's armor, the hope of salvation. We are to focus our minds upon the hope of salvation. We are to eat, drink, and sleep salvation—the great hope God has given. If we focus our lives upon salvation—if we live and move and have our being in the great hope God has given of living forever with Him—then we will stay sober. We will live a righteous life for Christ, and we will be eagerly waiting for the return of Christ. Our hope of salvation keeps us sober.

> For in this hope we were saved. But hope that is seen is no hope at all. Who hopes for what he already has? (Rom 8:24)
> For everything that was written in the past was written to teach us, so that through endurance and the encouragement of the Scriptures we might have hope. (Rom 15:4)
> It teaches us to say "No" to ungodliness and worldly passions, and to live self-controlled, upright and godly lives in this present age, while we wait for the blessed hope—the glorious appearing of our great God and Savior, Jesus Christ, (Titus 2:12-13)
> Praise be to the God and Father of our Lord Jesus Christ! In his great mercy he has given us new birth into a living hope through the resurrection of Jesus Christ from the dead, and into an inheritance that can never perish, spoil or fade—kept in heaven for you, (1 Pet 1:3-4)
> Dear friends, now we are children of God, and what we will be has not yet been made known. But we know that when he appears, we shall be like him, for we shall see him as he is. Everyone who has this hope in him purifies himself, just as he is pure. (1 John 3:2-3)

2. Why is the believer to stay in control and protect himself? There are two significant reasons.
   a. God has not appointed us to wrath, but to salvation. The only way to escape the wrath of God is to stay sober and focused upon Jesus Christ. When God saved us, he appointed us to receive salvation from sin, death, and judgment to come. He did not appoint us to death and wrath. Therefore, there is no excuse for a believer to fall asleep and return to the world of darkness. A person who does not have self-control will suffer the wrath of God.

> For God did not send his Son into the world to condemn the world, but to save the world through him. Whoever believes in him is not condemned, but whoever does not believe stands condemned already because he has not believed in the name of God's one and only Son. This is the verdict: Light has come into the world, but men loved darkness instead of light because their deeds were evil. (John 3:17-19)
> Whoever believes in the Son has eternal life, but whoever rejects the Son will not

see life, for God's wrath remains on him." (John 3:36)

But among you there must not be even a hint of sexual immorality, or of any kind of impurity, or of greed, because these are improper for God's holy people. Nor should there be obscenity, foolish talk or coarse joking, which are out of place, but rather thanksgiving. For of this you can be sure: No immoral, impure or greedy person—such a man is an idolater—has any inheritance in the kingdom of Christ and of God. Let no one deceive you with empty words, for because of such things God's wrath comes on those who are disobedient. (Eph 5:3-6)

Put to death, therefore, whatever belongs to your earthly nature: sexual immorality, impurity, lust, evil desires and greed, which is idolatry. Because of these, the wrath of God is coming. (Col 3:5-6)

b. Christ died for us. Note the words "awake or sleep:" they mean alive or departed. When Christ returns, whether we are still alive on the earth or departed, we shall live together with Him forever and ever. This is why He died, the very reason He went to the cross: that we might have the glorious privilege of living together with Him throughout all eternity.

You see, at just the right time, when we were still powerless, Christ died for the ungodly. (Rom 5:6)
Who gave himself for our sins to rescue us from the present evil age, according to the will of our God and Father, (Gal 1:4)
Who gave himself for us to redeem us from all wickedness and to purify for himself a people that are his very own, eager to do what is good. (Titus 2:14)

He himself bore our sins in his body on the tree, so that we might die to sins and live for righteousness; by his wounds you have been healed. (1 Pet 2:24)
For Christ died for sins once for all, the righteous for the unrighteous, to bring you to God. He was put to death in the body but made alive by the Spirit, (1 Pet 3:18)

4 (5:11) **Believers, Duty**: the believer is to minister by comforting and edifying others. God has delivered us from the wrath to come and given us the glorious hope of living face to face with Him forever. Therefore, we are not to sleep, but we are to be sober, awake, alert, and watchful for that glorious day.

⇒ We are to "encourage" (parakaleite) each other: exhort, admonish and comfort each other.

Comfort, comfort my people, says your God. (Isa 40:1)
Therefore encourage each other with these words. (1 Th 4:18)
Therefore encourage one another and build each other up, just as in fact you are doing. (1 Th 5:11)

⇒ We are to "*build each other up*" (oikodomeite) each other: strengthen and edify each other.

Let us therefore make every effort to do what leads to peace and to mutual edification. (Rom 14:19)
Each of us should please his neighbor for his good, to build him up. (Rom 15:2)
Do not let any unwholesome talk come out of your mouths, but only what is helpful for building others up according to their needs, that it may benefit those who listen. (Eph 4:29)

1 THESSALONIANS 5:12-28

	C. The Lord's Return & Behavior in the Church, 5:12-28	stances, for this is God's will for you in Christ Jesus. 19 Do not put out the Spirit's fire;	d. Do not suppress the Spirit^{DS1}
1 Behavior toward the leaders of the church a. Respect them	12 Now we ask you, brothers, to respect those who work hard among you, who are over you in the Lord and who admonish you.	20 Do not treat prophecies with contempt. 21 Test everything. Hold on to the good. 22 Avoid every kind of evil.	e. Do not treat prophecies with contempt f. Test all things: Hold on to what is good g. Avoid every kind of evil
b. Esteem them very highly in love c. Be at peace with each other	13 Hold them in the highest regard in love because of their work. Live in peace with each other.	23 May God himself, the God of peace, sanctify you through and through. May your whole spirit, soul and body be kept blameless at the coming of our Lord Jesus Christ.	**4 The results of proper behavior** a. God's Presence b. Sanctification c. Preservation of spirit, soul, & body d. Assurance of God's faithfulness
2 Behavior toward the church family a. Warn the idle b. Comfort the fainthearted c. Support the weak d. Be patient toward all e. See that no one repays evil for evil to any man	14 And we urge you, brothers, warn those who are idle, encourage the timid, help the weak, be patient with everyone. 15 Make sure that nobody pays back wrong for wrong, but always try to be kind to each other and to everyone else.	24 The one who calls you is faithful and he will do it. 25 Brothers, pray for us. 26 Greet all the brothers with a holy kiss. 27 I charge you before the Lord to have this letter read to all the brothers.	**5 The final exhortations for behavior, v.25** a. Pray for the ministers b. Greet all Christians c. Read this epistle to all Christians—study the Word of God d. The grace of our Lord rest upon you
3 Behavior toward God—personal behavior a. Rejoice always b. Pray always c. Give thanks in all things	16 Be joyful always; 17 Pray continually; 18 Give thanks in all circum-	28 The grace of our Lord Jesus Christ be with you.	

DIVISION III

THE COMING AGAIN OF JESUS CHRIST, 4:13-5:24

C. The Lord's Return and Behavior in the Church, 5:12-28

(5:12-28) **Introduction**: the behavior of man needs to be changed. There is one thing that will change it as much as anything else: seeing and grasping the Lord's return to earth. If a person really believes that Jesus Christ is returning to earth, it will radically change his life.
1. Behavior toward the leaders of the church (v.12-13).
2. Behavior toward the church family (v.14-15).
3. Behavior toward God—personal behavior (v.15-22).
4. The results of proper behavior (v.23-24).
5. The final exhortations for behavior (v.25-28).

1 (5:12-13) **Leaders—Church—Believers**: first, the believers' behavior toward church leaders. Note the word "work" (kopiontas). It means to labor to the point of exhaustion, then to keep on working; to continue working even if one has become weary; to arduously labor; to toil to the point of weariness; to work beyond what one is capable of doing. The point is forceful, and it should convict the heart of God's servant:
⇒ The minister of God is to arduously labor for his Lord.
⇒ The minister of God is to toil and toil for the church.
⇒ The minister is to labor to the point of exhaustion in ministering to people.

This is the work of the ministry; this is the demand made upon the minister's time and energy. His whole mind, body, and soul belong to the Lord and are to be poured out into the lives of God's dear people, into both the believers and the unbelievers of the world.

Now, note the three exhortations of these two verses.
1. Believers are to respect the leaders of their church. The word "respect" (eidenai) means to acknowledge, appreciate, and know the value of. Few people labor as much as a committed church leader.
   a. Take, for example, the committed minister. Compare his work with any other professional. How much time would some other professional take away from his regular duties...
- if he had to speak for thirty or more minutes at a conference this week?
- if he had to speak two or three times at the conference *to the same people*?
- if he had to speak every week—two or three times—*to the same people*; that is, he could never use the same speech?
- if he had to attend several committee meetings at the conference every week?
- if he had to visit everyone at the conference when they went into the hospital?
- if he had to visit all the family members and the close relatives of the conference members when they went into the hospital?
- if he had to counsel all the conference members and their family members when they had a serious problem?
- if he had to conduct all the funerals of the conference members and their families?
- if he had to conduct all the weddings of the daughters of the conference members?
- if he was expected to visit in the homes of most, if not all, of the conference members?
- if he was expected to visit all the newcomers and prospective members within the community of the conference?

The list could go on and on. But while the professional is doing all this, he still has to manage

1 THESSALONIANS 5:12-28

the administration of his business (the church itself).
b. Take, for example, the committed teacher of the Lord. The committed teacher works all day at some job either in the home or out at some secular job. Then when he or she gets home, think of the time spent...
- in studying and preparing the lesson.
- in praying.
- in telephoning class members.
- in visiting class members: at home and in the hospital.
- in counseling and ministering to class members.
- in fellowshipping and growing class members one on one and in groups (at meals, study groups, and at social functions).

For the committed teacher, the hours are endless, and just think, the committed teacher does this every week.

The same could be said about any church leader who is genuinely committed to the Lord and takes his or her calling seriously. The leader's service to the church and ministry is above and beyond their work week at secular jobs and their duties to civic affairs. True, they live for Christ wherever they are—at work and at civic functions. But their commitment goes beyond that: the church leader has been called by God...
- to teach, edify, and build up the church and its believers.
- to equip himself to be a dynamic witness for the Lord and to reach out to save the lost.
- to organize and minister to the desperate needs of the poor and hurting.

The point is this: believers are to respect their leaders—acknowledge, appreciate, and honor them. They deserve it.

> **I urge you, brothers, by our Lord Jesus Christ and by the love of the Spirit, to join me in my struggle by praying to God for me. (Rom 15:30)**
>
> **To submit to such as these and to everyone who joins in the work, and labors at it. (1 Cor 16:16)**
>
> **Even though my illness was a trial to you, you did not treat me with contempt or scorn. Instead, you welcomed me as if I were an angel of God, as if I were Christ Jesus himself. (Gal 4:14)**
>
> **Now we ask you, brothers, to respect those who work hard among you, who are over you in the Lord and who admonish you. (1 Th 5:12)**
>
> **The elders who direct the affairs of the church well are worthy of double honor, especially those whose work is preaching and teaching. (1 Tim 5:17)**
>
> **Remember your leaders, who spoke the word of God to you. Consider the outcome of their way of life and imitate their faith. (Heb 13:7)**

2. Believers are to highly esteem their leaders. Several significant things are said here.
   a. Leaders are to be held in high regard.
   b. Leaders are to be held in high regard *in love*: with affection, held ever so dear to a believer's heart.
   c. Leaders are to be held in high regard because of their work, that is, because of the work they do. They are ministers of the Lord and they serve Christ and the church and its believers. Believers owe much to them because of their sacrificial service. Therefore, believers are to hold them in high regard.

> **Welcome him in the Lord with great joy, and honor men like him, (Phil 2:29)**
>
> **Now we ask you, brothers, to respect those who work hard among you, who are over you in the Lord and who admonish you. Hold them in the highest regard in love because of their work. Live in peace with each other. (1 Th 5:12-13)**
>
> **And whenever Moses went out to the tent, all the people rose and stood at the entrances to their tents, watching Moses until he entered the tent. (Exo 33:8)**

3. Believers and leaders are to be at peace among themselves. Note: this exhortation is given to the leader as well as to the believer or follower. Believers are not to criticize, murmur, grumble, envy, or oppose their leaders. Differ, yes, but not oppose—unless, of course, he is acting contrary to Scripture or to the love of God's Spirit.

Leaders are not to act as lords over God's people, nor are they to lead for the sake of seeking position, boosting ego, securing recognition, receiving honor, or making a livelihood. A leader who leads for these reasons cannot feed the people of God. He does not have the presence and blessing of God which are necessary to feed the flock of God. Therefore, such leaders cause a restlessness and dissatisfaction among God's people.

The exhortation is for believers to be at peace among themselves. Both leader and people are to be totally committed to Christ, doing exactly what God has called them to do. When both are so serving, then they are at peace with each other.

> **For God is not a God of disorder but of peace. As in all the congregations of the saints, (1 Cor 14:33)**
>
> **Finally, brothers, good-by. Aim for perfection, listen to my appeal, be of one mind, live in peace. And the God of love and peace will be with you. (2 Cor 13:11)**
>
> **As a prisoner for the Lord, then, I urge you to live a life worthy of the calling you have received. Be completely humble and gentle; be patient, bearing with one another in love. Make every effort to keep the unity of the Spirit through the bond of peace. (Eph 4:1-3)**
>
> **I plead with Euodia and I plead with Syntyche to agree with each other in the Lord. (Phil 4:2)**
>
> **Live in peace with each other. (1 Th 5:13)**
>
> **Flee the evil desires of youth, and pursue righteousness, faith, love and peace, along with those who call on the Lord out of a pure heart. (2 Tim 2:22)**

2 (5:14-15) **Believers—Church**: second, the believers' behavior toward the church family. A list of exhortations is given to all believers in these two verses—exhortations that tell us how to behave toward the whole church family.

1 THESSALONIANS 5:12-28

1. Warn the "idle" (ataktous): "those who are out of line—the loafers, the disorderly, and the unruly" (the Amplified New Testament). The word idle is a military term that referred to the soldier who broke rank and did not stand in his place. Too many believers are not where they belong. (They belong in the ranks of the Lord and of the church: fellowshipping with the Lord and fellow believers; serving the Lord and ministering to believers; helping to reach the lost and ministering to the poor and needy.) But they are out in the world doing their own thing, fulfilling their own desires and lusts.

The idle must be warned and admonished. They are treading on thin ice. They are damaging their own souls and hurting others through their idle testimony. The Lord will not tolerate such idle behavior. The implication is that He will judge all idle behavior.

> I myself am convinced, my brothers, that you yourselves are full of goodness, complete in knowledge and competent to instruct one another. (Rom 15:14)
>
> I am not writing this to shame you, but to warn you, as my dear children. (1 Cor 4:14)
>
> Let the word of Christ dwell in you richly as you teach and admonish one another with all wisdom, and as you sing psalms, hymns and spiritual songs with gratitude in your hearts to God. (Col 3:16)
>
> And we urge you, brothers, warn those who are idle, encourage the timid, help the weak, be patient with everyone. (1 Th 5:14)
>
> If anyone does not obey our instruction in this letter, take special note of him. Do not associate with him, in order that he may feel ashamed. Yet do not regard him as an enemy, but warn him as a brother. (2 Th 3:14-15)
>
> Warn a divisive person once, and then warn him a second time. After that, have nothing to do with him. (Titus 3:10)

2. Comfort the faint-hearted, the "timid" (oligopsuchous): the reserved, dispirited; those who lack courage and are cowardly; those who are easily discouraged and disappointed; those who fear difficult situations. The picture is that of a person who hesitates to serve or witness; a person who fails to live for Christ because of being faint-hearted. We must not rebuke or despise them, but instead comfort, encourage, and assure them.

> But Jesus immediately said to them: "Take courage! It is I. Don't be afraid." (Mat 14:27)
>
> But Jesus came and touched them. "Get up," he said. "Don't be afraid." (Mat 17:7)
>
> Be on your guard; stand firm in the faith; be men of courage; be strong. (1 Cor 16:13)
>
> Now instead, you ought to forgive and comfort him, so that he will not be overwhelmed by excessive sorrow. (2 Cor 2:7)
>
> Finally, be strong in the Lord and in his mighty power. (Eph 6:10)
>
> Therefore encourage each other with these words. (1 Th 4:18)
>
> Therefore encourage one another and build each other up, just as in fact you are doing. (1 Th 5:11)
>
> And we urge you, brothers, warn those who are idle, encourage the timid, help the weak, be patient with everyone. (1 Th 5:14)
>
> You then, my son, be strong in the grace that is in Christ Jesus. (2 Tim 2:1)

3. Support the weak: the spiritually weak; those who yield so easily to temptation; those who are so easily burdened, discouraged, defeated, and led astray. These need to be helped (anthechesthe). The word means to cling and hold to. The weak need us clinging to them and holding them up. They need our help.

> In everything I did, I showed you that by this kind of hard work we must help the weak, remembering the words the Lord Jesus himself said: 'It is more blessed to give than to receive.'" (Acts 20:35)
>
> Accept him whose faith is weak, without passing judgment on disputable matters. (Rom 14:1)
>
> We who are strong ought to bear with the failings of the weak and not to please ourselves. (Rom 15:1)
>
> To the weak I became weak, to win the weak. I have become all things to all men so that by all possible means I might save some. (1 Cor 9:22)
>
> And we urge you, brothers, warn those who are idle, encourage the timid, help the weak, be patient with everyone. (1 Th 5:14)

4. Be patient (makrothumeo) toward all persons. Leon Morris points out that being patient is the opposite of being short-tempered. It is being consistently patient, being very patient with people (*The Epistles of Paul to the Thessalonians.* "Tyndale New Testament Commentaries," p.101). We must bear and forbear; we must suffer a long, long time with persons, no matter the situation.

> By standing firm you will gain life. (Luke 21:19)
>
> Be joyful in hope, patient in affliction, faithful in prayer. (Rom 12:12)
>
> You need to persevere so that when you have done the will of God, you will receive what he has promised. (Heb 10:36)
>
> Perseverance must finish its work so that you may be mature and complete, not lacking anything. (James 1:4)
>
> Be patient, then, brothers, until the Lord's coming. See how the farmer waits for the land to yield its valuable crop and how patient he is for the autumn and spring rains. (James 5:7)

5. Look after every believer: see that no believer repays evil for evil, wrong for wrong to any person. Note: it is understood that throughout life some people will do evil against everyone of us. This verse clearly states that we are responsible for each other and responsible for how we respond to evil. We are to be looking after each other: see to it that none of us retaliates or mistreats those who mistreat us.

⇒ If we mistreat an unbeliever, we lose all chance of reaching him for Christ.

⇒ If we mistreat another believer, we lose all chance of reaching him and growing him in Christ.

When we mistreat a person, our testimony with that person is ruined. We lose our opportunity to minister to that person. Note the exhortation: "always try to be kind to each other and to everyone else." *Always trying to be kind* is the only way we can ever reach and grow others, believers and unbelievers.

> But I tell you, Do not resist an evil person. If someone strikes you on the right cheek, turn to him the other also. (Mat 5:39)
>
> Do not repay anyone evil for evil. Be careful to do what is right in the eyes of everybody. (Rom 12:17)
>
> Do not repay evil with evil or insult with insult, but with blessing, because to this you were called so that you may inherit a blessing. (1 Pet 3:9)
>
> "'Do not seek revenge or bear a grudge against one of your people, but love your neighbor as yourself. I am the LORD. (Lev 19:18)
>
> Do not say, "I'll pay you back for this wrong!" Wait for the LORD, and he will deliver you. (Prov 20:22)
>
> Do not say, "I'll do to him as he has done to me; I'll pay that man back for what he did." (Prov 24:29)

3 (5:15-22) **Believers, Duty**: third, the believers' behavior toward God. Seven strong exhortations are to govern our behavior toward God.

1. Rejoice always; Be joyful always: God has saved us, and He looks after and cares for us. If we love God, God promises that He will take all the circumstances that attack us and work them out for good (Ro.8:28). And on top of this, He has given us eternal life, the glorious privilege of living face to face with Him and serving Him forever and ever. The believer who knows and keeps his mind upon these glorious facts can do nothing but rejoice.

> However, do not rejoice that the spirits submit to you, but rejoice that your names are written in heaven." (Luke 10:20)
>
> Rejoice in the Lord always. I will say it again: Rejoice! (Phil 4:4)
>
> Be joyful always; (1 Th 5:16)
>
> There, in the presence of the LORD your God, you and your families shall eat and shall rejoice in everything you have put your hand to, because the LORD your God has blessed you. (Deu 12:7)
>
> But let all who take refuge in you be glad; let them ever sing for joy. Spread your protection over them, that those who love your name may rejoice in you. (Psa 5:11)
>
> Rejoice in the LORD and be glad, you righteous; sing, all you who are upright in heart! (Psa 32:11)
>
> Rejoice greatly, O Daughter of Zion! Shout, Daughter of Jerusalem! See, your king comes to you, righteous and having salvation, gentle and riding on a donkey, on a colt, the foal of a donkey. (Zec 9:9)

2. Pray always—continually, without ceasing. Prayer is God's ordained way for man to receive things from Him. God moves, acts, and responds to prayer. Prayer is a law that He has established throughout the universe. Why? Because prayer stirs fellowship and communion with God and brings about a greater knowledge and understanding of God. It causes a person to learn more and more about God and stirs more and more trust as well as worship and praise of God. Prayer stirs and causes every good thing imaginable between God and man. This is the reason God destined prayer as the primary way man is to communicate with Him. This is the reason for this exhortation. Therefore, pray continually; continue and persevere in prayer: in your daily worship and quiet times and as you walk throughout the day.

> "Ask and it will be given to you; seek and you will find; knock and the door will be opened to you. (Mat 7:7)
>
> "Watch and pray so that you will not fall into temptation. The spirit is willing, but the body is weak." (Mat 26:41)
>
> Then Jesus told his disciples a parable to show them that they should always pray and not give up. (Luke 18:1)
>
> Until now you have not asked for anything in my name. Ask and you will receive, and your joy will be complete. (John 16:24)
>
> And pray in the Spirit on all occasions with all kinds of prayers and requests. With this in mind, be alert and always keep on praying for all the saints. (Eph 6:18)
>
> Pray continually; (1 Th 5:17)

3. Give thanks in all things. How can we thank God for terrible trials such as accidents and death and sin? We don't; this is not what Scripture means. What God means is to thank Him for His presence and power as we walk through such trials. In Christ Jesus there is victory and triumph over all, no matter how terrible. Therefore, in everything (not for everything)—as we walk through all—thank God for the victory He has given us through Christ.

Note the statement, "this is God's will for you in Christ Jesus concerning you." What is the will of God? All three exhortations that have just been given:

⇒ that we rejoice always.
⇒ that we pray continually.
⇒ that we give thanks in all circumstances.

> Always giving thanks to God the Father for everything, in the name of our Lord Jesus Christ. (Eph 5:20)
>
> Do not be anxious about anything, but in everything, by prayer and petition, with thanksgiving, present your requests to God. (Phil 4:6)
>
> And whatever you do, whether in word or deed, do it all in the name of the Lord Jesus, giving thanks to God the Father through him. (Col 3:17)
>
> Give thanks in all circumstances, for this is God's will for you in Christ Jesus. (1 Th 5:18)

1 THESSALONIANS 5:12-28

> For everything God created is good, and nothing is to be rejected if it is received with thanksgiving, (1 Tim 4:4)
>
> Sacrifice thank offerings to God, fulfill your vows to the Most High, (Psa 50:14)
>
> A psalm. A song. For the Sabbath day. It is good to praise the LORD and make music to your name, O Most High, (Psa 92:1)
>
> Give thanks to the LORD, call on his name; make known among the nations what he has done. (1 Chr 16:8)

4. Do not suppress the Spirit—do not put out the Spirit's fire (see DEEPER STUDY # 1—1 Th.5:19 for discussion).

5. Do not treat prophecies with contempt. Prophecy is the gift of proclaiming the gospel and of predicting the future under the influence of the Holy Spirit. Both proclamation and prediction are included in the gift. Note the exhortation: a person is not to minimize or to show contempt for the gift despite the abuse of the gift by some. (See notes, pt.6—1 Cor.12:8-10, especially see DEEPER STUDY # 1—1 Cor.14:3 for more discussion.)

> But everyone who prophesies speaks to men for their strengthening, encouragement and comfort. (1 Cor 14:3)
>
> Do not treat prophecies with contempt. (1 Th 5:20)

6. Test all things; hold on to what is good. The word "test" (dokimazete) means to test and to prove. Both the gifts and behavior of believers are to be tested. If a person claims to prophesy—whether proclaiming the gospel or predicting some event to strengthen believers for some coming trial—all should be tested. We are not to blindly accept what people say, even if it is the preacher or servant of God. Neither are we to blindly accept people themselves. Every person—what he says and does—is to be tested and proven. How? By measuring what he says and does by the Scripture. But note: the Scriptures must be studied in order to measure what people say and do. The only way to know truth from error is to the know the Scripture.

> And find out what pleases the Lord. (Eph 5:10)
>
> Test everything. Hold on to the good. (1 Th 5:21)
>
> Dear friends, do not believe every spirit, but test the spirits to see whether they are from God, because many false prophets have gone out into the world. (1 John 4:1)
>
> "I have made you a tester of metals and my people the ore, that you may observe and test their ways. (Jer 6:27)

Now, note the exhortation: when a person or a truth is proven, hold on. Hold on to what is good. Do not let a good person go: learn from him. Do not let a good doctrine or exhortation go: hang on to it, live and practice it, and teach it to others.

> Test everything. Hold on to the good. (1 Th 5:21)
>
> But Christ is faithful as a son over God's house. And we are his house, if we hold on to our courage and the hope of which we boast. (Heb 3:6)
>
> Therefore, since we have a great high priest who has gone through the heavens, Jesus the Son of God, let us hold firmly to the faith we profess. (Heb 4:14)
>
> Let us hold unswervingly to the hope we profess, for he who promised is faithful. (Heb 10:23)
>
> Remember, therefore, what you have received and heard; obey it, and repent. But if you do not wake up, I will come like a thief, and you will not know at what time I will come to you. Yet you have a few people in Sardis who have not soiled their clothes. They will walk with me, dressed in white, for they are worthy. (Rev 3:3-4)

7. Avoid every kind of evil: note closely what this exhortation says. It does not just say to avoid evil, but to avoid *every kind* of evil.
⇒ If something even appears or borders on evil, get away from it.
⇒ If there is any chance whatsoever that it could be wrong, leave it alone.
⇒ If there is even a suggestion that it could be wrong, flee it.

A believer must have nothing, absolutely nothing, to do with evil—not even the appearance of it.

> Love must be sincere. Hate what is evil; cling to what is good. (Rom 12:9)
>
> Avoid every kind of evil. (1 Th 5:22)
>
> He must turn from evil and do good; he must seek peace and pursue it. (1 Pet 3:11)
>
> And he said to man, 'The fear of the Lord—that is wisdom, and to shun evil is understanding.'" (Job 28:28)
>
> Turn from evil and do good; seek peace and pursue it. (Psa 34:14)
>
> Let those who love the LORD hate evil, for he guards the lives of his faithful ones and delivers them from the hand of the wicked. (Psa 97:10)
>
> Do not swerve to the right or the left; keep your foot from evil. (Prov 4:27)
>
> A wise man fears the LORD and shuns evil, but a fool is hotheaded and reckless. (Prov 14:16)

DEEPER STUDY # 1

(5:19) **Holy Spirit—Sin**: this is one of the four major sins against the Holy Spirit.

1. Quenching or putting out the Spirit's fire (1 Th.5:19). To put out means to stifle, to snuff out, to stop. The Holy Spirit is always working in the life of the believer to lead him to do God's will. The believer *puts out* the Spirit's work by (a) ignoring Him, (b) neglecting Him, (c) disobeying Him, or by simply (d) procrastinating. Note the context above. The command "not put out the Spirit's fire" is surrounded by a series of positive commands.

2. Grieving the Spirit (Eph.4:30). To grieve means to pain, to vex, to sadden. The Holy Spirit is pure, holy, and righteous. The believer grieves the Spirit when he...
- allows impure things to penetrate his life.
- behaves immorally.

1 THESSALONIANS 5:12-28

- acts unjustly.
- allows or participates in anything contrary to the nature of the Spirit.

Note the context. The command "Do not grieve the Holy Spirit of God" is surrounded by a series of negative commands.

3. Blasphemy against the Spirit (see note—Mt.12:31; 12:33).

4. Lying to the Holy Spirit (see note—Acts 5:3-4).

4 (5:23-24) **Believers, Duty**: the results of proper behavior. If a believer will behave properly—if a person will follow the exhortations given in this passage—he will experience four things.

1. The believer experiences the presence of the God of peace: peace means to be bound, joined, and weaved together. Only God can bind, join, and weave a person together. Only God can bring peace to a person's soul—the kind of peace that brings absolute assurance, confidence, and security to a person's heart. And note: God possesses so much peace and is so ready to give peace that He is called the God of peace. (See note, *Peace*—1 Th.1:1 for more discussion.)

> The God of peace be with you all. Amen. (Rom 15:33)
>
> The God of peace will soon crush Satan under your feet. The grace of our Lord Jesus be with you. (Rom 16:20)
>
> Finally, brothers, good-by. Aim for perfection, listen to my appeal, be of one mind, live in peace. And the God of love and peace will be with you. (2 Cor 13:11)
>
> Whatever you have learned or received or heard from me, or seen in me—put it into practice. And the God of peace will be with you. (Phil 4:9)
>
> May God himself, the God of peace, sanctify you through and through. May your whole spirit, soul and body be kept blameless at the coming of our Lord Jesus Christ. (1 Th 5:23)
>
> May the God of peace, who through the blood of the eternal covenant brought back from the dead our Lord Jesus, that great Shepherd of the sheep, (Heb 13:20)

2. The believer experiences sanctification: the word sanctification means to be set apart and separated to God. The believer who follows the exhortations of this passage is greatly blessed by God: God takes the person and sets him apart unto Himself. The person is very special to God; therefore God gives him a special relationship with Himself. And note the words "through and through": the believer is entirely set apart to God, under God's special care, protection, and provision.

> Sanctify them by the truth; your word is truth. (John 17:17)
>
> It is because of him that you are in Christ Jesus, who has become for us wisdom from God—that is, our righteousness, holiness and redemption. (1 Cor 1:30)
>
> If a man cleanses himself from the latter, he will be an instrument for noble purposes, made holy, useful to the Master and prepared to do any good work. (2 Tim 2:21)
>
> And so Jesus also suffered outside the city gate to make the people holy through his own blood. (Heb 13:12)
>
> Who have been chosen according to the foreknowledge of God the Father, through the sanctifying work of the Spirit, for obedience to Jesus Christ and sprinkling by his blood: Grace and peace be yours in abundance. (1 Pet 1:2)

3. The believer has his spirit, soul, and body preserved blameless in the day of judgment. This is the idea of the Greek text. The word "at" (en) is better translated *in*. That is, in that day when the Lord returns, the believer will be preserved blameless. He will be acceptable to God and receive a full reward. Note the three parts of man spelled out: spirit, soul, and body. The idea is that the whole man will be preserved—his body and soul as well as his spirit. Believers are not to be some ghost-like figure or some formless spirit. They are to have their bodies and souls resurrected and preserved forever. The whole person—the whole spirit, soul, and body—will live eternally with God. But note: only if the believer follows the exhortations of the Scripture.

> So that you may become blameless and pure, children of God without fault in a crooked and depraved generation, in which you shine like stars in the universe (Phil 2:15)
>
> But now he has reconciled you by Christ's physical body through death to present you holy in his sight, without blemish and free from accusation—(Col 1:22)
>
> May he strengthen your hearts so that you will be blameless and holy in the presence of our God and Father when our Lord Jesus comes with all his holy ones. (1 Th 3:13)
>
> May God himself, the God of peace, sanctify you through and through. May your whole spirit, soul and body be kept blameless at the coming of our Lord Jesus Christ. (1 Th 5:23)
>
> So then, dear friends, since you are looking forward to this, make every effort to be found spotless, blameless and at peace with him. (2 Pet 3:14)

4. The believer experiences the assurance of God, the very faithfulness of God. God called the believer; therefore, God completes His work in the believer. The work of salvation is God's work from beginning to end. If a person is not living for God, it is evidence that he is not really a true believer. But if a person is living for God by following the exhortation of Scripture, it is clear evidence that he is a true believer. He has truly been called of God. How do we know this? Because God is faithful. If God possesses a person, God continues to work in the person until the person is fully saved in the glorious day of redemption.

> The one who calls you is faithful and he will do it. (1 Th 5:24)
>
> But the Lord is faithful, and he will strengthen and protect you from the evil one. (2 Th 3:3)

> If we are faithless, he will remain faithful, for he cannot disown himself. (2 Tim 2:13)
>
> For this reason he had to be made like his brothers in every way, in order that he might become a merciful and faithful high priest in service to God, and that he might make atonement for the sins of the people. (Heb 2:17)
>
> Let us hold unswervingly to the hope we profess, for he who promised is faithful. (Heb 10:23)
>
> And from Jesus Christ, who is the faithful witness, the firstborn from the dead, and the ruler of the kings of the earth. To him who loves us and has freed us from our sins by his blood, (Rev 1:5)
>
> I saw heaven standing open and there before me was a white horse, whose rider is called Faithful and True. With justice he judges and makes war. (Rev 19:11)

5 (5:25-28) **Believers, Duty**: the final exhortation for behavior. This is the close of the *First Epistle to the Thessalonians*. The final words exhort us all when we apply them to ourselves.

1. Pray for ministers. Note that Paul does not say, "please" or "if you will." He emphatically charges: "Brothers, pray for us." All believers must pray for their ministers. And note: Paul says "us" not *me*—all of God's chosen ministers are to be prayed for by believers. We must not omit a single minister; and the idea is that we must pray often, not just every day, but often every day. What an impact would be made upon the world if we obeyed this one charge.

> I urge you, brothers, by our Lord Jesus Christ and by the love of the Spirit, to join me in my struggle by praying to God for me. (Rom 15:30)
>
> And pray in the Spirit on all occasions with all kinds of prayers and requests. With this in mind, be alert and always keep on praying for all the saints. Pray also for me, that whenever I open my mouth, words may be given me so that I will fearlessly make known the mystery of the gospel, (Eph 6:18-19)
>
> Brothers, pray for us. (1 Th 5:25)
>
> Finally, brothers, pray for us that the message of the Lord may spread rapidly and be honored, just as it was with you. (2 Th 3:1)
>
> Pray for us. We are sure that we have a clear conscience and desire to live honorably in every way. (Heb 13:18)

2. Greet all Christian brothers, and greet them intimately with care. Just how the holy kiss took place is not really known today. But it was a common practice in the early church. It is generally thought that only men kissed men and that they kissed on the cheek, but again, the facts are not really known (Leon Morris. *The Epistles of Paul to the Thessalonians*. "Tyndale New Testament Commentaries," p.109). The point is that affection and care are to be expressed between believers.

> Greet one another with a kiss of love. Peace to all of you who are in Christ. (1 Pet 5:14; cp. Ro.16:16; 1 Cor.16:20; 2 Cor.13:12)

3. Read this epistle to all believers. Why was it necessary for Paul to give this exhortation? Would the epistle not be read to the whole church when it gathered on Sunday? Were some believers bed-ridden and homebound? Was the church having to meet in several small groups in secret because of persecution? The answer is not known, but the lesson to us is clear. We must see to it that every believer studies this epistle as well as the rest of the Word of God. Every part of the Word is important and must be studied by all. No believer is to be left out whether bed-ridden or unable to attend services for any other reason.

Thought 1. What a challenge to churches! To provide ministries that will carry the Word of God out to those who are unable to worship and study at the regular service.

> Now the Bereans were of more noble character than the Thessalonians, for they received the message with great eagerness and examined the Scriptures every day to see if what Paul said was true. (Acts 17:11)
>
> "Now I commit you to God and to the word of his grace, which can build you up and give you an inheritance among all those who are sanctified. (Acts 20:32)
>
> Let the word of Christ dwell in you richly as you teach and admonish one another with all wisdom, and as you sing psalms, hymns and spiritual songs with gratitude in your hearts to God. (Col 3:16)
>
> But women will be saved through childbearing—if they continue in faith, love and holiness with propriety. (1 Tim 2:15)
>
> Beyond all question, the mystery of godliness is great: He appeared in a body, was vindicated by the Spirit, was seen by angels, was preached among the nations, was believed on in the world, was taken up in glory. (1 Tim 3:16)
>
> Like newborn babies, crave pure spiritual milk, so that by it you may grow up in your salvation, now that you have tasted that the Lord is good. (1 Pet 2:2-3)

4. The grace of our Lord Jesus Christ rest upon you (see note, *Grace*—1 Th.1:1 for discussion).

THE
OUTLINE & SUBJECT INDEX

REMEMBER: When you look up a subject and turn to the Scripture reference, you have not only the Scripture, you have *an outline and a discussion* (commentary) of the Scripture and subject.

This is one of the *GREAT VALUES* of **The Preacher's Outline & Sermon Bible®**. Once you have all the volumes, you will have not only what all other Bible indexes give you, that is, a list of all the subjects and their Scripture references, *BUT* you will also have...

- An outline of *every* Scripture and subject in the Bible.
- A discussion (commentary) on every Scripture and subject.
- Every subject supported by other Scriptures or cross references.

DISCOVER THE GREAT VALUE for yourself. Quickly glance below to the very first subject of the Index of First Thessalonians. It is:

ADULTERY
Discussed. 4:1-8

Turn to the reference. Glance at the Scripture and outline of the Scripture, then read the commentary. You will immediately see the GREAT VALUE of the INDEX of **The Preacher's Outline & Sermon Bible®**.

OUTLINE AND SUBJECT INDEX

ADULTERY
Discussed. 4:1-8
Results.
Cheats a brother. To be avenged by God. 4:6-8
Four r. 4:1-8

AFFLICTION
Meaning. 3:7-10

APPOINT - APPOINTED
The believer is **a**. to.
Afflictions. 3:3-5
Salvation. 5:9

ASSURANCE
Of the believer. Source. God will preserve the believer. 5:23-24

ATHENS
Paul visited, stayed in all alone. 3:1

BELIEVER
Duty.
Four practical duties. 4:9-12
How the **b**. is to behave in light of Christ's return. 5:4-11
How to live in light of the Lord's return. Many exhortations. 5:12-18
To be pure. 4:1-8
To be sober, alert, and watchful for the Lord's return. 5:4-11
To comfort & edify. 5:11
To live a morally pure life. 4:1-8
To mind one's own business. 4:11
To ministers.
To highly esteem. 5:12-13
To pray for **m**. 5:25
To study to be quiet. 4:11
To walk pleasing to God. 4:1-8
To watch & not be sleepy. 5:2-11
Toward God. Several exhortations. 5:16-22
Toward leaders. 5:12-13
Toward the church. Several exhortations. 2:14-15
Life - Walk. (See Related Subjects)
A model life. 4:1-12

A walk that pleases God. 4:1-8
Discussed. 4:9-12
In light of Jesus' return. 5:4-11
Marks - Characteristics.
A strong and true minister. 2:1-12
A strong conversion. 1:5-10
A strong encouragement. 3:7-10
A strong faith. 3:1-10
A strong love. 3:11-13
A strong people. 2:13-20
Name - Title.
Child of Light. 5:4-5
Child of the day. 5:4-5
Nature. Light. 5:4-11
Security of. (See **ASSURANCE; SECURITY**)
Some final words to. 5:25-28

BUILD EACH OTHER UP
Meaning. 5:11

CALL - CALLED (See **MINISTER - MINISTERS**)
Purpose of. To be excellent, virtuous. 4:3-8

CHRISTIAN - CHRISTIANS (See **BELIEVER; PROFESSION ONLY; WARNED - WARNINGS**)

CHURCH
Basis - Foundation.
A strong conversion. 1:5-10
"In" God the Father & "in" the Lord Jesus Christ. 1:1
Duty.
Discussed. 1:1-3:13; 5:12-28
To be a strong **c**. 1:1-4
To follow examples. 2:14-16
Marks - Characteristics.
A model **c**. 1:1-3:13
A strong & true minister. 2:1-12
A strong **c**. 1:1-4
A strong conversion. 1:5-10
A strong encouragement. 3:7-10
A strong faith. 3:1-6
A strong love. 3:11-13
A strong people. 2:13-20
Need - Needs. To be a strong **c**. 1:1-4

COMFORT
Meaning. 3:1-2; 5:11
Of whom.
The bereaved. 4:13-5:3
The timid, the weak. 5:14-15

CONVERSION
A strong **c**. 1:5-10
Marks of. 1:5-10

CRITICISM - CRITICIZING
Duty. To mind one's own business. 4:11

CROWN - CROWNS
Described. As a **c**. in which we will glory. 2:19-20

DARKNESS
Nature of. Not the nature of believers. 5:4-11

DATES
Meaning. 5:1-3

DAY OF THE LORD
Discussed. 4:13-5:3; 5:1-3; 5:4-5

DEATH - DEAD, THE
Described. Sleep. 4:14-15
Of believers.
Are present with the Lord. 4:14-15
What happens to dead believers. 4:13-5:3

DISTRESS
Meaning. 3:7-10

EDIFY - EDIFICATION
Meaning. 5:11

ENCOURAGEMENT
A strong **e**. 3:7-10

END TIME
Christ's return & the world's end.
Day of the Lord. 5:1-3; 5:4-5
How to behave while waiting. 5:4-11; 5:12-28
Resurrection, The. 4:13-5:3
Discussed. 4:13-5:3
The day of the Lord. 5:1-3; 5:4-5

INDEX

ESTABLISH
  Meaning. 3:1-2

EVIL
  Duty. To abstain even from the appearance of **e**. 5:22

FAITH
  Duty. To be strong in faith. 3:1-10
  What **f**. does. Stirs arduous labor. 1:3

FAITHFULNESS
  Of God. Will preserve the believer. 5:23-24

FORNICATION (See **SEXUAL IMMORALITY**)

GOD
  Misconceptions about. Far off in outer space, removed from & disinterested in man. 3:11
  Name - Title. God of peace. 5:23
  Nature.
    As a Father. Not far off in outer space, but near. 3:11
    Faithful. Will preserve the believer. 5:23-24

GOSPEL
  Duty.
    Not to preach in word only. 1:5
    Not to preach to please people. 2:5
    To preach a pure **g**. 2:3-6
    To preach the **g**. as it should be preached. 1:5

GRACE
  Meaning. 1:1

HOLY - HOLINESS
  Duty. To live a life of purity. 4:1-8

HOLY SPIRIT
  Believer's duty. Not to quench. 5:19
  Quenching. 5:19
  Sins against. Discussed. 5:19
  Work. To restrain evil. 2:6-8

HOPE
  Acts - Word of. Stirs endurance in labor. 1:3

IDLE - IDLENESS
  Discussed. Work & employment. 4:11-12
  Duty. To work & not be idle. 4:11-12

IDOLS - IDOLATRY
  Duty. To turn to God from **i**. 1:9-10

IMMORALITY
  Results.
    Cheats a brother. To be avenged by God. 4:6-8
    Results. Four **r**. 4:6-8

JESUS CHRIST
  Death. Substitutionary. Died for us. 5:8-10
  Deity. Equal with God. Prayed to. 3:11
  Described as. The Day of the Lord. 5:1-3
  Duty.
    How the believer is to behave in light of the **r**. 5:4-11
    To be watchful for the **r**. 5:4-11
    To wait for. 1:9-10
  Events.
    Shall catch up believers. 4:16-18
    Shall resurrect the dead. 4:16-18
    Will involve the return of all dead believers. 4:13-18
  Return of.
    Discussed. 4:13-5:3; 5:4-11; 5:12-28
    Duty. To wait expectantly—every day. 1:9-10
    Effect upon human behavior. 5:12-28
    Events of. 4:13-5:3

JEWS
  Sins of. 2:15-16

LABOR
  Duty.
    To work with your own hands. 4:11-12
    Why God demands that we **l**. 4:11-12

LIFE
  Duty. To walk pleasing God. 4:1-8
  Kinds of. The model **l**. 4:1-12

LIGHT
  L. is the nature of believers. 5:4-11

LORD, DAY OF
  Discussed. 5:1-3

LOVE
  Acts - work of. Stirs diligent labor. 1:3
  Discussed. 3:11-13
  Duty. To grow in love more & more. 4:9-10
  Importance of. Stirs diligent labor. 1:3
  Kinds of.
    A strong **l**. 3:11-13
    Brotherly love. 4:9-10
    Four kinds. 3:12
  Results. Presented unblameable before God. 3:13

MARRIAGE
  Duty.
    To know that one must possess his or her spouse. 4:3-5
    To know that one must take care of the needs of his or her spouse. 4:3-5

MINISTERS
  Described.
    As being like a father. 2:7-8
    As being like a mother. 2:7-8
  Discussed. A strong & true **m**. 2:1-12
  Duty.
    Not to be covetous for position, livelihood. 2:5; 2:6
    To concentrate on preaching the gospel, not eloquence. 1:5
    To labor night and day. 2:9
    To live a clean, moral life. 2:3
    To preach the gospel as it should be preached. 1:5

MORALS - MORALITY
  Discussed.
    Sexual purity. 4:1-8
    To live a **m**. life. 4:1-8

PAUL
  Accusations against.
    Discussed. 2:1-12
    Immorality. 2:3; cp. 2 Cor.1:12
  Sufferings - Trials of.
    In Corinth. Some terrible **t**. 3:7-10
    Shamefully treated. 2:2

PEACE
  Meaning. 1:1

PERSECUTION
  Of the church at Thessalonica. 2:1-12
  Types. Discussed. 3:3-5
  Why believers are **p**. 3:3-5

PERSEVERANCE
  Duty. Not to be moved by persecution. 3:3-5

POWER
  Duty. To preach the gospel in power. 1:5-10
  Source. For preaching. Discussed. 1:5

PRAYER
  Duty. To pray without ceasing. 5:17

PREACH - PREACHING
  Discussed. A strong & true minister **p**. the gospel. 1:5-10; 2:1-12
  Duty.
    To **p**. boldly. 2:2
    To **p**. in power & in the Holy Spirit. 1:5
    To **p**. the gospel. To **p**. as it should be preached. 1:5
    To please God, not man. Not to use flattering words, coveting position, livelihood. 2:5-6

PROPHECY
  Duty. Not to show contempt for the gift of **p**. 5:20

PROVE
  Duty. To **p**. all things. 5:21

QUIET - QUIETNESS
  Duty. To study to be **q**. 4:11

REJOICE - REJOICING
  Duty. To **r**. always. 5:16

REPENT - REPENTANCE
  Duty. To turn to God from idols. 1:9-10

RESURRECTION
  Discussed. 4:13-5:3
  Events. Order. Discussed. 4:13-5:3

REWARDS
  Crowns.
    Of rejoicing. 2:19-20
    Of soul-winner. 2:19-20
  Described - Identified as. Crowns. 2:19-20

SALVATION
  Assurance of. (See **ASSURANCE**)

SANCTIFICATION
  Duty. To live a moral & pure life. 4:1-8

SATAN
  Names - Titles.
    Satan. 2:18
    The tempter. 3:5
  Work - Strategy.

INDEX

To hinder the gospel & believers. 2:18
To stop & weaken the growth of churches. 2:18

SECURITY
Of God. God will preserve the believer. 5:23-24

SEXUAL IMMORALITY
Duty. To abstain from **f**. 4:1-8
Meaning. 4:3-5

SIN
Duty. To abstain even from the appearance of **s**. 5:22

SOUL-WINNING (See **WITNESSING**)
SOUL-WINNING, CROWN OF
Meaning. 2:19-20

STUDY
Duty. To **s**. to be quiet. 4:11

TEMPTATION
To abstain from even the appearance of evil. 5:22

TEST - TESTING
Duty. To test & prove all things. 5:21

THANKSGIVING
Duty. To give thanks in everything. 5:18

TIMES AND DATES, THE
Meaning. 5:1-3

WITNESS - WITNESSING
Duty. To win souls. Reason. 2:19-20
Results. A crown of rejoicing in the day of Christ. 2:19-20

WORD OF GOD
Described as. The words of God. 2:13
Discussed. 1:2-13
   Must be carried forth by men. 1:2-13
   Not the word of men, but of God. 2:13
Duty.
   To pray for the **W**. to have free course & be glorified. 3:1-2
   To receive as God's word. 2:13
Inspiration. Of God, not of men. 2:13
Nature of.
   God's word. 2:13
   Not the word of men, but God. 2:13

WORK (See **EMPLOYEE**)
Duty.
   To **w**. with your own hands. 4:11-12
   Why God demands that we **w**. Reasons. 4:11-12
Why **w**. Three reasons. 4:11-12

WRATH
Deliverance from. By Jesus. 1:9-10; 5:8-10

SECOND THESSALONIANS

2 THESSALONIANS

INTRODUCTION

AUTHOR: Paul, the Apostle.

DATE: Uncertain. Probably A.D. 50-52, soon after *First Thessalonians*.

TO WHOM WRITTEN: "To the church of the Thessalonians in God our Father and the Lord Jesus Christ" (2 Th. 1:1).

PURPOSE: Paul had two purposes for writing *Second Thessalonians*.
 1. To assure believers that God uses persecution.
    ⇒ He uses persecution to refine believers. Persecution refines believers by teaching them endurance, by teaching them to stand fast in a corruptible and dying world.
    ⇒ He uses persecution to seal believers (2 Th.1:4-6). Persecution proves that a believer is genuine and is going to inherit future glory.
    ⇒ He uses persecution to seal unbelievers (2 Th.1:4-6). Persecution seals the doom of persecutors.
 2. To correct some false ideas about the Lord's return.

SPECIAL FEATURES:
 1. The City of Thessalonica. The great city was the capital and the largest city of Macedonia. (See Map—Introduction to Acts.) It had been founded by Cassander, the top military officer of Alexander the Great, after Alexander had died. Under the Romans the city had been made free because of its loyalty to Rome. As a free city it was allowed its own government and local laws. At its height, the city reached a population of 200,000. The city had a natural harbor, but the primary factor contributing to the city's greatness was that it lay right on the Roman road, the Egnatian Way. In fact, the great road ran right through Thessalonica. It was the main street of the city, stretching all the way from the Adriatic Sea to the Middle East. Trade and commerce bristled with all the accompanying vice that follows such a metropolitan center.
 2. The Church of Thessalonica. It was a great day when Paul walked into the city of Thessalonica bringing the news of the glorious gospel. Because of the city's strategic location and commercial importance, the gospel was bound to spread out beyond to the world rather rapidly. The great city of Thessalonica was the second great European city to be evangelized. Paul had just been evangelizing in Philippi when he entered Thessalonica. Paul preached in the synagogue for only three Sabbaths before he was forced by the Jews to leave the synagogue (Ac.17:2). Paul apparently moved into homes, preaching wherever he was allowed. He had so much success that the Jews eventually attacked and forced him to flee for his life. He took Silas and Timothy and proceeded to Berea for a brief ministry (Acts 17:10-14). But the Jews pursued him and he was forced to leave Berea for Athens (Ac.17:13f). However, he was able to leave Silas and Timothy behind to continue the ministry. While in Athens, he sent for Timothy, but dispatched him right back to Thessalonica (1 Th.3:2f). Paul himself went on to Corinth where he was soon joined by Silas and Timothy with good news from the Thessalonian church (Ac.18:5). His heart was so warmed by this report that he sat down and wrote the First Letter to the *Thessalonians*. Right after receiving the letter, the believers apparently responded to Paul, asking him some questions about the Lord's return. These questions are what stirred the Second Letter to the *Thessalonians*.

The converts were mainly Gentiles, including a large number of devout Greeks and prestigious women. Many, especially women, were sick of the immoral society of that day. They had turned to Judaism because of its moral teachings, yet they sensed the bondage of its legalistic thrust and rejected its national prejudices. Therefore, their hearts were ripe for the message of liberty and love preached by the gospel. The church at Thessalonica...
- was founded on Paul's second missionary journey (Acts 17:1f).
- was revisited by Paul (1 Cor.16:5).
- included some Jews and a large number of Greeks and influential women (Acts 17:4; 2 Th.3:4, 7-8).
- did not support Paul. He worked at a secular job while there (1 Th.2:9); however, he did receive financial help from the church at Philippi (Ph.416).
- suffered persecution (1 Th.2:14).
- was well organized (1 Th.5:12).
- had several prominent believers known by name: Jason (Ac.17:6), Gaius (Ac.19:29), Aristarchus (Ac.19:29; 20:4), and Secundus (Ac.20:4).

3. *Thessalonians* is "An Early Epistle Written by the Apostle Paul." It is one of the earliest New Testament writings.

4. *Thessalonians* is "An Early Epistle that Proclaims Christ to be Lord" (1 Th.1:1, 3, 6, 10; 2:15; 3:8, 11-13; 4:1-2, 13-18; 5:1-2, 9-10, 23, 28; 2 Th.1:1-2, 8-9, 12; 2:1, 8, 13-14, 16; 3:1, 3-5, 12, 16, 18; cp. Ac.17:7).

5. *Thessalonians* is "An Epistle that Proclaims the Doctrine of the Second Coming" (1 Th.4:13f).

6. *Thessalonians* is "An Epistle of Great Encouragement for a Person Facing Persecution" (1 Th.1:6f; 2:2f; 2:14f; 3:3f).

7. *Thessalonians* is "An Epistle Written to Warn Believers of the Danger of Sexual Impurity" (1 Th.4:1-10).

8. *Thessalonians* is "An Epistle Written to Charge Believers with the Most Practical Rules of Behavior" (1 Th. 5:12-22).

9. *Thessalonians* is "An Epistle with a Great Evangelistic and Missionary Challenge" (1 Th.1:8-12; 2:12-13; 3:12-13; 4:1-12; 5:1f).

10. *Thessalonians* is "An Epistle that Gives a Glimpse into the End Times" (2 Th.1:6–2:17).

11. *Thessalonians* is "An Epistle that Proclaims the Righteous Judgment of God" (2 Th.1:6-12).

12. *Thessalonians* is "An Epistle that Describes the Day of the LORD" (2 Th.2:1-3).

13. *Thessalonians* is "An Epistle that Describes the Antichrist and His Followers" (2 Th.2:4-12).

14. *Thessalonians* is "An Epistle Written from the Heart and Soul of a Committed Minister." Wycliffe Bible Commentary has a moving description of this point. (David A. Hubbard, *First & Second Thessalonians*. "The New Testament & Wycliffe Bible Commentary," ed. by Charles F. Pfeiffer and Everett F. Harrison. Produced for Moody Monthly by the Iversen Associates, N.Y., 1971, p.803f.)

> *"In these letters Paul lays bare not so much his subject as his soul: Here the beat of the apostle's warm heart is audible. He compares himself to a gentle nurse (1 Thess.2:7), a firm father (2:11), and a homeless orphan (in the Greek of 2:17). He shows himself ready to spend and be spent for the spreading of the Gospel. It is Paul, the man, who confronts us, gentle in his strength, loving in his exhortations, dauntless in his courage, guileless in his motives—a man (as Carl Sandburg said of Abraham Lincoln) 'of steel and velvet, hard as rock and soft as drifting fog.'"*

OUTLINE OF 2 THESSALONIANS

THE PREACHER'S OUTLINE & SERMON BIBLE® is *unique*. It differs from all other Study Bibles & Sermon Resource Materials in that every Passage and Subject is outlined right beside the Scripture. When you choose any *Subject* below and turn to the reference, you have not only the Scripture, but you discover the Scripture and Subject *already outlined for you—verse by verse*.

For a quick example, choose one of the subjects below and turn over to the Scripture, and you will find this marvelous help for faster, easier, and more accurate use.

In addition, every point of the Scripture and Subject is *fully developed in a Commentary with supporting Scripture* at the bottom of the page. Again, this arrangement makes sermon preparation much easier and faster.

Note something else: The Subjects of Second Thessalonians have titles that are both Biblical and *practical*. The practical titles sometimes have more appeal to people. This *benefit* is clearly seen for use on billboards, bulletins, church newsletters, etc.

A suggestion: For the quickest overview of Second Thessalonians, first read *all the major titles* (I, II, III, etc.), then come back and read the subtitles.

OUTLINE OF 2 THESSALONIANS

I. **GREETING: THE PICTURE OF A MODEL CHURCH UNDER ATTACK & PERSECUTION 1:1-5**

II. **A GLIMPSE INTO THE END TIME, 1:6-2:17**
   A. The Righteous Judgment of God, 1:6-12
   B. The Day of the Lord, 2:1-3
   C. The Antichrist: The Man of Lawless, 2:4-9
   D. The Antichrist's Followers, 2:10-12
   E. The Salvation of God's Followers, 2:13-17

III. **FINAL WORDS, 3:1-18**
   A. Prayer and The Lord's Faithfulness, 3:1-5
   B. Work and Employment, 3:6-18

2 THESSALONIANS

CHAPTER 1

I. A GREETING: THE PICTURE OF A MODEL CHURCH UNDER ATTACK & PERSECUTION, 1:1-5

1 The ministers are faithful to the church
2 The believers have a firm foundation in God & in Christ
3 The believers know the grace & peace of God
4 The believers have a faith that grows more & more
5 The believers have a love that grows & overflows
6 The believers have a strong endurance & faith in all their trials
   a. Are a testimony to others
   b. Are a sign of God's coming judgment
   c. Are a proof that they are worthy of God's kingdom

Paul, Silas and Timothy, To the church of the Thessalonians in God our Father and the Lord Jesus Christ:
2 Grace and peace to you from God the Father and the Lord Jesus Christ.
3 We ought always to thank God for you, brothers, and rightly so, because your faith is growing more and more, and the love every one of you has for each other is increasing.
4 Therefore, among God's churches we boast about your perseverance and faith in all the persecutions and trials you are enduring.
5 All this is evidence that God's judgment is right, and as a result you will be counted worthy of the kingdom of God, for which you are suffering.

DIVISION I

GREETING: THE PICTURE OF A MODEL CHURCH UNDER ATTACK AND PERSECUTION 1:1-5

(1:1-5) Introduction: this passage is a clear picture of what it takes to make a church strong. A church never needs strength anymore than when it is under savage attack and persecution. The Thessalonian church was being fiercely persecuted, yet it was standing firm for Christ. The Thessalonian believers stand as a model church for all other churches: they are a picture of what a church should be when it is being attacked and persecuted.

1. The ministers are faithful to the church (v.1).
2. The believers have a firm foundation in God and Christ (v.1).
3. The believers know the grace and peace of God (v.2).
4. The believers have a faith that grows more and more (v.3).
5. The believers have a love that grows and overflows (v.3).
6. The believers have a strong endurance and faith in all their trials (v.4-5).

1 (1:1) **Ministers—Church**: the ministers are faithful to the church—no matter the circumstances. Ministers are always to be faithful to their churches, but there are times when ministers need to give *special attention* to their flock, *special times* when the flock of God needs to be strongly encouraged and exhorted to hold firm to Christ. The Thessalonian church was facing one of these times.

1. The church was being savagely attacked and persecuted by both the world and the religionists (see notes— 1 Th.2:1-12). They were being…
   - ridiculed
   - mocked
   - cursed
   - ostracized
   - threatened
   - rejected

There is a chance that some had even been physically attacked, beaten, and martyred (see note—1 Th.4:13). Whatever the case, the point is this: the believers desperately needed the help of their ministers; they needed their encouragement and comfort.

2. The church was confused about the return of the Lord and the great day of the Lord, and about the awful day of His wrath. Apparently some had begun to feel that the tribulation—the terrible time of trouble that is to come upon the earth—had already begun. Some felt this because of the savage persecution they were suffering. There were other matters concerning the second coming that were misunderstood as well. In fact, there was great confusion in the church about the Lord's return. These will be covered in a later passage. For now, the point to see is how confused the believers were over the return of the Lord Jesus. They needed the help of their ministers; they needed to be taught the truth about the coming again of Jesus Christ.

Thought 1. When special needs arise among believers, the minister of God must give special attention to the flock of God. It is a *very special duty* of the minister to comfort and encourage his people when they…
- suffer persecution
- need to be taught
- suffer disease or accident
- face death
- need correction
- need reproof
- need counsel

The list could go on and on, but the point is clearly seen. The minister must give special attention and help to his people when they face special needs. A church can be a model (strong) church only if its ministers are faithful—especially faithful when its people are facing trying times.

> **In everything I did, I showed you that by this kind of hard work we must help the weak, remembering the words the Lord Jesus himself said: 'It is more blessed to give than to receive.'" (Acts 20:35)**
>
> **We who are strong ought to bear with the failings of the weak and not to please ourselves. (Rom 15:1)**
>
> **Carry each other's burdens, and in this way you will fulfill the law of Christ. (Gal 6:2)**
>
> **Remember those in prison as if you were their fellow prisoners, and those who are mistreated as if you yourselves were suffering. (Heb 13:3)**

Religion that God our Father accepts as pure and faultless is this: to look after orphans and widows in their distress and to keep oneself from being polluted by the world. (James 1:27)

2 (1:1) **Church**: the believers have a firm foundation in God and Christ (see note, *Jesus Christ, Deity*—1 Th.1:1 for discussion).

3 (1:2) **Grace—Peace—Church**: the believers know the grace and peace of God (see note, *Grace*—1 Th.1:1 for discussion).

4 (1:3) **Father—Church**: the believers have a faith that grows more and more. The words growing more and more (huperauxanei) mean to grow beyond measure; to grow far beyond what would be expected. What a glorious testimony! Faith that just grows and grows more and more. Imagine a church full of believers whose faith in Christ Jesus grows explosively—beyond measure—beyond what we could ever imagine. And remember: the church was growing in faith while they were in the midst of savage persecution. This is the reason Paul says: "We ought always to thank God for you." The word "ought" (opheilomen) means compulsion and obligation. The church's growing faith compelled Paul to thank God for the church—for their faith. Imagine how a minister's heart would joy and rejoice over his people growing like the Thessalonian believers did.

What does it mean to have a growing faith? Faith in Christ simply means that a person believes in the Lord Jesus Christ; he trusts Christ to take care of his life…
- of his past life (sins and transgressions).
- of his present life (to provide the necessities, protection, deliverance, and guidance needed in life).
- of his future life (deliverance from death and judgment and the gift of eternal life).

A growing faith in Jesus Christ simply means that a person learns to trust and depend upon Christ more and more:
⇒ to provide for his daily necessities (Mt.6:33).
⇒ to deliver him through the trials and temptations of life (2 Th.2:4f).
⇒ to comfort him through the losses of life (2 Tim.4:18; 1 Pt.5:7; Ps.23:4).
⇒ to teach him the truth (2 Th.2:15; 3:3).
⇒ to guide and help him to hold fast to the teachings of Christ (2 Th.2:15; 3:4).
⇒ to strengthen him to walk a life that is separated from the world and totally dedicated to God (2 Th.3:3, 6-7).

Thought 1. A person who grows in faith is a person who learns to depend upon Christ more and more in every *area of life*—all the areas covered in the list above. What a glorious testimony to have a faith that grows more and more!

Thought 2. Too many believers have their minds upon growing and increasing in the comfort and possessions of this world. They think little, if any, about growing in faith. They are satisfied with just enough faith to salve their conscience. Growth in faith and Christ are of little concern to them.

Then Jesus said to the centurion, "Go! It will be done just as you believed it would." And his servant was healed at that very hour. (Mat 8:13)

"'If you can'?" said Jesus. "Everything is possible for him who believes." (Mark 9:23)

"Have faith in God," Jesus answered. "I tell you the truth, if anyone says to this mountain, 'Go, throw yourself into the sea,' and does not doubt in his heart but believes that what he says will happen, it will be done for him. Therefore I tell you, whatever you ask for in prayer, believe that you have received it, and it will be yours. (Mark 11:22-24)

The apostles said to the Lord, "Increase our faith!" (Luke 17:5)

In addition to all this, take up the shield of faith, with which you can extinguish all the flaming arrows of the evil one. (Eph 6:16)

Now we who have believed enter that rest, just as God has said, "So I declared on oath in my anger, 'They shall never enter my rest.'" And yet his work has been finished since the creation of the world. (Heb 4:3)

And without faith it is impossible to please God, because anyone who comes to him must believe that he exists and that he rewards those who earnestly seek him. (Heb 11:6)

If any of you lacks wisdom, he should ask God, who gives generously to all without finding fault, and it will be given to him. But when he asks, he must believe and not doubt, because he who doubts is like a wave of the sea, blown and tossed by the wind. (James 1:5-6)

And receive from him anything we ask, because we obey his commands and do what pleases him. (1 John 3:22)
for everyone born of God overcomes the world. This is the victory that has overcome the world, even our faith. Who is it that overcomes the world? Only he who believes that Jesus is the Son of God. (1 John 5:4-5)

Early in the morning they left for the Desert of Tekoa. As they set out, Jehoshaphat stood and said, "Listen to me, Judah and people of Jerusalem! Have faith in the LORD your God and you will be upheld; have faith in his prophets and you will be successful." (2 Chr 20:20)

How great is your goodness, which you have stored up for those who fear you, which you bestow in the sight of men on those who take refuge in you. (Psa 31:19)

The LORD redeems his servants; no one will be condemned who takes refuge in him. (Psa 34:22)

2 THESSALONIANS 1:1-5

> Trust in the LORD and do good; dwell in the land and enjoy safe pasture. (Psa 37:3)
>
> Commit your way to the LORD; trust in him and he will do this: (Psa 37:5)
>
> Trust in the LORD with all your heart and lean not on your own understanding; (Prov 3:5)
>
> You will keep in perfect peace him whose mind is steadfast, because he trusts in you. Trust in the LORD forever, for the LORD, the LORD, is the Rock eternal. (Isa 26:3-4)

5 (1:3) **Love—Church**: the believers have a love that grows and overflows toward one another. Note: the love being spoken about is the love of believer for believer, not for the world. In the letter of 1 Thessalonians, Paul had exhorted the church to grow more and more in love for one another. They had needed the message because there was some tension in the church surrounding the Lord's return. Paul's exhortation had worked: the church had straightened out the differences and the differing parties were now walking hand in hand with one another, overflowing and growing in love for one another. This is the reason Paul thanks God for their overflowing love.

What does it mean to overflow with love for one another? An overflowing love is the kind of love...

- that binds individuals together as a family—as the family of God.
- that binds individuals in an unbreakable union.
- that holds individuals with the deepest affection.
- that nourishes and nurtures one another.
- that shows concern and looks after the welfare of one another.
- that always cherishes one another and comforts, supports, and encourages one another regardless of differences or circumstances.

This was the kind of love that the model church at Thessalonica had. This is what an *increasing love* is. This is the kind of love every single believer is to have for all other believers.

> "A new command I give you: Love one another. As I have loved you, so you must love one another. By this all men will know that you are my disciples, if you love one another." (John 13:34-35)
>
> My command is this: Love each other as I have loved you. (John 15:12)
>
> Love must be sincere. Hate what is evil; cling to what is good. (Rom 12:9)
>
> You, my brothers, were called to be free. But do not use your freedom to indulge the sinful nature ; rather, serve one another in love. (Gal 5:13)
>
> Now that you have purified yourselves by obeying the truth so that you have sincere love for your brothers, love one another deeply, from the heart. (1 Pet 1:22)
>
> Above all, love each other deeply, because love covers over a multitude of sins. (1 Pet 4:8)
>
> Whoever loves his brother lives in the light, and there is nothing in him to make him stumble. (1 John 2:10)
>
> And he has given us this command: Whoever loves God must also love his brother. (1 John 4:21)

6 (1:4-5) **Endurance—Church**: the believers have a strong patience and faith in facing persecution and trials.

⇒ The word "perseverance" (hupomones) means to be steadfast, to endure, and to persevere. The Thessalonian believers endured and held firm to their faith in Christ through all the persecutions and trials thrown against them.

⇒ The word "trials" (thlipsesin) is a more general word than *persecutions* and refers to any kind of trial or trouble (Leon Morris. *The Epistles of Paul to the Thessalonians*. "Tyndale New Testament Commentaries," p.115). The Thessalonian believers were persevering and holding firm to their faith through all the trials of life: temptations, peer pressure, disease, accident, loss of job, death—whatever the trial was, they remained faithful to Christ. They did not buckle under and give in to the crowd nor to discouragement and despair. They held on to their faith in Christ. Note three points.

1. Their endurance and faith was a strong testimony to others. Paul says that they were so strong that he actually boasted of them to others.

> **Thought 1.** What a dynamic testimony: to stand up for Christ to such an extent that Paul would boast of them! What an example for us: to stand fast in our faith to such an extent that ministers boast of our testimony.

2. Their endurance and faith were a sign of God's coming judgment upon unbelievers. The believers received a supernatural strength—God's strength—when they were persecuted. Their strength was so forceful that it was clear that it was being given by God. The believers...

- were not becoming hysterical.
- were not retaliating.
- were not accepting the persecution like passive sheep.

Contrariwise, they demonstrated a serene peace and responded in an active love, exhorting and encouraging their persecutors to trust the Lord—all while they were in the midst of being mistreated. Their response could not be attributed to mental discipline nor to the commitment to some human cause. Why?

⇒ Because there were too many of them, and they were all standing firm and demonstrating some supernatural strength.

⇒ Because there was both the spirit of glory and of God resting upon them—the spirit of glory and of God that is promised to the believer who suffers persecution.

> If you are insulted because of the name of Christ, you are blessed, for the Spirit of glory and of God rests on you. (1 Pet 4:14)

The point is this: the presence of God and His glory in the believer is a clear sign that God exists and is going to vindicate his dear believer. He is going to judge and take vengeance upon the persecutors of His dear people. Persecution is a clear sign of God's coming judgment.

Now we know that God's judgment against those who do such things is based on truth. (Rom 2:2)

If this is so, then the Lord knows how to rescue godly men from trials and to hold the unrighteous for the day of judgment, while continuing their punishment. (2 Pet 2:9)

By the same word the present heavens and earth are reserved for fire, being kept for the day of judgment and destruction of ungodly men. (2 Pet 3:7)

Enoch, the seventh from Adam, prophesied about these men: "See, the Lord is coming with thousands upon thousands of his holy ones to judge everyone, and to convict all the ungodly of all the ungodly acts they have done in the ungodly way, and of all the harsh words ungodly sinners have spoken against him." (Jude 1:14-15)

3. Their endurance and faith proved that the believers were counted worthy of God's kingdom. Note the phrase "counted worthy" (kataxioo). It does not mean to make worthy; it means to count, reckon, and declare worthy (see note, *Justification*—Ro.5:1). A believer is not saved because he remains faithful through the sufferings of this life; he is saved because he believes in Jesus Christ as his Savior and Lord. However, when he suffers in this world and endures through the suffering, he is counted worthy of God's kingdom. He does not disappoint God. He proves his grit—that he is truly a man or a woman of God. He is worthy to enter heaven, for he has proven his faith.

By standing firm you will gain life. (Luke 21:19)

Remember the words I spoke to you: 'No servant is greater than his master.' If they persecuted me, they will persecute you also. If they obeyed my teaching, they will obey yours also. They will treat you this way because of my name, for they do not know the One who sent me. (John 15:-20-21)

In all my prayers for all of you, I always pray with joy (Phil 1:4)

In fact, everyone who wants to live a godly life in Christ Jesus will be persecuted, (2 Tim 3:12)

For we who are alive are always being given over to death for Jesus' sake, so that his life may be revealed in our mortal body. (2 Cor 4:11)

You need to persevere so that when you have done the will of God, you will receive what he has promised. (Heb 10:36)

2 THESSALONIANS 1:6-12

		II. A GLIMPSE INTO THE END TIME, 1:6-2:17
		
		A. The Righteous Judgment of God, 1:6-12
		
		6 God is just: He will pay back trouble to those who trouble you
		7 And give relief to you who are troubled, and to us as well. This will happen when the Lord Jesus is revealed from heaven in blazing fire with his powerful angels.
		8 He will punish those who do not know God and do not obey the gospel of our Lord Jesus.
		9 They will be punished with everlasting destruction and shut out from the presence of
			the Lord and from the majesty of his power
			10 On the day he comes to be glorified in his holy people and to be marveled at among all those who have believed. This includes you, because you believed our testimony to you.
			11 With this in mind, we constantly pray for you, that our God may count you worthy of his calling, and that by his power he may fulfill every good purpose of yours and every act prompted by your faith.
			12 We pray this so that the name of our Lord Jesus may be glorified in you, and you in him, according to the grace of our God and the Lord Jesus Christ.
				5 The time of judgment
				  a. When He comes to be glorified in His holy people
				  b. When He comes to be marveled at
				
				6 The escape from judgment
				  a. God must count a person worthy to escape
				  b. God must complete the work of faith in a person
				
				  c. The name of Christ must be glorified in a person

1	The purpose of judgment: To rectify injustice		

2	The executor of judgment: Jesus Christ Himself
	  a. A spectacular appearance from heaven
	  b. With angels
	  c. In flaming fire		

3	The people to be judged
	  a. All who do not know God
	  b. All who disobey the gospel		

4	The penalty of judgment
	  a. Punishment & destruction
	  b. Separation from the Lord		

DIVISION II

A GLIMPSE INTO THE END TIME, 1:6-2:17

A. The Righteous Judgment of God, 1:6-12

(1:6-12) **Introduction**: this begins the important discussion of the end time, of the end of the world. The first discussion covers the subject that most people dread and try to bypass or deny: *the righteous judgment of God*.
1. The purpose of judgment: to rectify injustice (v.6).
2. The executor of judgment: Jesus Christ Himself (v.7-8).
3. The people to be judged (v.8).
4. The penalty of judgment (v.9).
5. The time of judgment (v.10).
6. The escape from judgment (v.11-12).

(1:6-12) **Another Outline**: The Basic Questions About Judgment.
1. Why is there to be a judgment (v.6)?
2. Who will judge (v.7)?
3. Who will be judged (v.8)?
4. What will the judgment be (v.9)?
5. When will the judgment take place (v.10)?
6. How can a person escape the judgment (v.11)?

1 (1:6) **Judgment—Justice—Injustices**: the purpose of judgment is to rectify injustices. Remember: the believers at Thessalonica were suffering fierce persecution and all kinds of trouble at the hands of their neighbors and the local city government. Most of the citizens of Thessalonica wanted nothing to do with Christ, so they sought to stamp out His name, threatening and persecuting all who confessed Him. Just how serious the situation had become can be seen by looking at the account in Acts and the number of times the persecution is referred to in the two letters to the Thessalonians. Note these verses.

> But the Jews were jealous; so they rounded up some bad characters from the marketplace, formed a mob and started a riot in the city. They rushed to Jason's house in search of Paul and Silas in order to bring them out to the crowd. But when they did not find them, they dragged Jason and some other brothers before the city officials, shouting: "These men who have caused trouble all over the world have now come here, and Jason has welcomed them into his house. They are all defying Caesar's decrees, saying that there is another king, one called Jesus." When they heard this, the crowd and the city officials were thrown into turmoil. (Acts 17:5-8)

> When the Jews in Thessalonica learned that Paul was preaching the word of God at Berea, they went there too, agitating the crowds and stirring them up. (Acts 17:13)

> You became imitators of us and of the Lord; in spite of severe suffering, you welcomed the message with the joy given by the Holy Spirit. (1 Th 1:6)

> We had previously suffered and been insulted in Philippi, as you know, but with the help of our God we dared to tell you his gospel in spite of strong opposition. (1 Th 2:2)

> For you, brothers, became imitators of God's churches in Judea, which are in Christ Jesus: You suffered from your own countrymen the same things those churches suffered from the Jews, (1 Th 2:14)

> So that no one would be unsettled by these trials. You know quite well that we were destined for them. In fact, when we were with you, we kept telling you that we would be persecuted. And it turned out that way, as you well know. (1 Th 3:3-4)

> Therefore, among God's churches we boast about your perseverance and faith in

all the persecutions and trials you are enduring. (2 Th 1:4)

The suffering of the believers was terrifying; therefore, they needed encouragement. This Paul had done in the former passage (2 Th.1:3-5) and would do at the end of the present passage (2 Th.1:10-12). But something else was needed as well: the persecutors and unbelievers of the world needed to be warned. God is going to rectify all the injustices of the world. God's judgment is going to fall upon every person who has mistreated others. All unjust behavior of men will bear the terrible judgment of God, all the...

- killing
- mocking
- cursing
- gossiping
- criticizing
- defrauding
- ridiculing
- fighting
- arguing
- misusing
- rejecting
- ignoring
- cheating
- abusing
- stealing
- deceiving
- lying
- hoarding

The list could go on and on, but the point is this: we live in the midst of an evil and an unjust people. Therefore, much of the world's behavior—much of man's behavior—is evil and unjust. God *must judge* the world, for judgment is the righteous and just thing. To judge the injustices of men is the very thing that *must be done*. All the injustices of the world must be corrected. Not to judge would be the wrong and unjust thing. This is the reason God is going to judge the world. He is just and righteous Himself; therefore, His very nature demands that all the injustices and wrongs that men have inflicted upon others be judged and punished. Note how the verse is translated by others:

> "For after all it is only just for God to repay with affliction those who afflict you" (NASB, 2 Th.1:6).
>
> "Indeed, it is right for God to repay with crushing sorrows those who cause you these crushing sorrows" (Williams, 2 Th. 1:6).
>
> "It really is just for God to pay back with suffering those who make you suffer" (Beck, 2 Th.1:6).
>
> "[It is a fair decision] since it is a righteous thing with God to repay with distress and affliction those who distress and afflict you" (Amplified New Testament, 2 Th.1:6).

Do not take revenge, my friends, but leave room for God's wrath, for it is written: "It is mine to avenge; I will repay," says the Lord. (Rom 12:19)

God is just: He will pay back trouble to those who trouble you and give relief to you who are troubled, and to us as well. (2 Th 1:6)

This will happen when the Lord Jesus is revealed from heaven in blazing fire with his powerful angels. He will punish those who do not know God and do not obey the gospel of our Lord Jesus. (2 Th 1:7-8)

For if the message spoken by angels was binding, and every violation and disobedience received its just punishment, (Heb 2:2)

For we know him who said, "It is mine to avenge; I will repay," and again, "The Lord will judge his people." (Heb 10:30)

It is mine to avenge; I will repay. In due time their foot will slip; their day of disaster is near and their doom rushes upon them." (Deu 32:35)

O LORD, the God who avenges, O God who avenges, shine forth. Rise up, O Judge of the earth; pay back to the proud what they deserve. How long will the wicked, O LORD, how long will the wicked be jubilant? They pour out arrogant words; all the evildoers are full of boasting. They crush your people, O LORD; they oppress your inheritance. They slay the widow and the alien; they murder the fatherless. They say, "The LORD does not see; the God of Jacob pays no heed." Take heed, you senseless ones among the people; you fools, when will you become wise? He will repay them for their sins and destroy them for their wickedness; the LORD our God will destroy them. (Psa 94:1-8, 23)

According to what they have done, so will he repay wrath to his enemies and retribution to his foes; he will repay the islands their due. (Isa 59:18)

I will not look on you with pity or spare you; I will surely repay you for your conduct and the detestable practices among you. Then you will know that I am the LORD. (Ezek 7:4)

So I will not look on them with pity or spare them, but I will bring down on their own heads what they have done." (Ezek 9:10)

But as for those whose hearts are devoted to their vile images and detestable idols, I will bring down on their own heads what they have done, declares the Sovereign LORD." (Ezek 11:21)

2 (1:7-8) **Judgment—Jesus Christ, Return**: the executor of judgment will be Jesus Christ Himself. Note that Jesus Christ is coming to give relief to the believer as well as to judge the world. The believer will be released from the injustices, sufferings, and death of this world. As the Pulpit Commentary says:

> *"[Heaven] is rest to the weary, freedom to the enslaved, release from sorrow, suffering, and pain, relaxation from toil, ease from noise and turmoil, the quiet heaven of peace after being tossed about in the tempestuous ocean [of this world]"* (P.J. Gloag. *Second Thessalonians*. "The Pulpit Commentary," Vol.21, ed. by H.D.M. Spence and Joseph S.Exell. Grand Rapids, MI: Eerdmans, 1950, p.2).

There remains, then, a Sabbath-rest for the people of God; (Heb 4:9)

There the wicked cease from turmoil, and there the weary are at rest. (Job 3:17)

Note that the Person who will execute judgment is Jesus Christ Himself. He is personally going to *return to earth* to judge the world.

2 THESSALONIANS 1:6-12

1. His return in judgment shall be a spectacular appearance from heaven. The word "revealed" (apokalupsei) means to be unveiled and uncovered. The day is coming when Jesus Christ shall rent the heavens and return to earth in judgment. As Matthew Henry says, "He will come in all the pomp and power of the upper world" (*Matthew Henry's Commentary*. Old Tappan, NJ: Fleming H. Revell, Vol.6, p.794). He will be revealed as the Supreme Majesty and Judge of the world.

> Moreover, the Father judges no one, but has entrusted all judgment to the Son, (John 5:22)
> He commanded us to preach to the people and to testify that he is the one whom God appointed as judge of the living and the dead. (Acts 10:42)
> For he has set a day when he will judge the world with justice by the man he has appointed. He has given proof of this to all men by raising him from the dead." (Acts 17:31)
> This will take place on the day when God will judge men's secrets through Jesus Christ, as my gospel declares. (Rom 2:16)
> In the presence of God and of Christ Jesus, who will judge the living and the dead, and in view of his appearing and his kingdom, I give you this charge: (2 Tim 4:1)

2. His return in judgment will be with the angels of His power. The angels will return with Him for several purposes:

⇒ to add to the majestic glory and triumph of His person and presence.

> For the Son of Man is going to come in his Father's glory with his angels, and then he will reward each person according to what he has done. (Mat 16:27)
> "When the Son of Man comes in his glory, and all the angels with him, he will sit on his throne in heavenly glory. (Mat 25:31)
> And give relief to you who are troubled, and to us as well. This will happen when the Lord Jesus is revealed from heaven in blazing fire with his powerful angels. (2 Th 1:7)

⇒ to carry out His orders and to execute His justice and mercy.

> And the enemy who sows them is the devil. The harvest is the end of the age, and the harvesters are angels. (Mat 13:39)
> This is how it will be at the end of the age. The angels will come and separate the wicked from the righteous and throw them into the fiery furnace, where there will be weeping and gnashing of teeth. (Mat 13:49-50)
> And he will send his angels with a loud trumpet call, and they will gather his elect from the four winds, from one end of the heavens to the other. (Mat 24:31)

3. His return in judgment will be in blazing fire. This is a reference to the brilliance and glory and holiness of His appearance and to the fact that He is coming in judgment. His return in judgment will be in all the majesty and glory of God Himself—so brilliant that it will be as the blazing fire of God's pure holiness.

> "At that time the sign of the Son of Man will appear in the sky, and all the nations of the earth will mourn. They will see the Son of Man coming on the clouds of the sky, with power and great glory. (Mat 24:30)
> "When the Son of Man comes in his glory, and all the angels with him, he will sit on his throne in heavenly glory. All the nations will be gathered before him, and he will separate the people one from another as a shepherd separates the sheep from the goats. (Mat 25:31-32)
> If anyone is ashamed of me and my words in this adulterous and sinful generation, the Son of Man will be ashamed of him when he comes in his Father's glory with the holy angels." (Mark 8:38)
> And give relief to you who are troubled, and to us as well. This will happen when the Lord Jesus is revealed from heaven in blazing fire with his powerful angels. He will punish those who do not know God and do not obey the gospel of our Lord Jesus. (2 Th 1:7-8)
> Enoch, the seventh from Adam, prophesied about these men: "See, the Lord is coming with thousands upon thousands of his holy ones to judge everyone, and to convict all the ungodly of all the ungodly acts they have done in the ungodly way, and of all the harsh words ungodly sinners have spoken against him." (Jude 1:14-15)
> Look, he is coming with the clouds, and every eye will see him, even those who pierced him; and all the peoples of the earth will mourn because of him. So shall it be! Amen. (Rev 1:7)
> Fire goes before him and consumes his foes on every side. (Psa 97:3)

3 (1:8) **Judgment—Jesus Christ, Return**: the people to be judged are separated into two classes.

1. All who do not know God, the only living and true God, will be judged. Who are these persons? They are those who sin against natural revelation, who look at creation and fail to see God or to live by the laws that are clearly seen in nature and creation.

   a. Men can know God within themselves: in their own thoughts, reasonings, and consciences.

   > Since what may be known about God is plain to them, because God has made it plain to them. (Rom 1:19)
   > Since they [the heathen] show that the requirements of the law are written on their hearts, their consciences also bearing witness, and their thoughts now accusing, now even defending them. (Rom 2:15)

   b. Men can know God outside of themselves: in creation and nature, the earth and outer space. (See notes—Ro.1:19; 1:20; 1:21; 2:11-15 for more discussion.)

75

> Yet he has not left himself without testimony: He has shown kindness by giving you rain from heaven and crops in their seasons; he provides you with plenty of food and fills your hearts with joy." (Acts 14:17)
>
> For since the creation of the world God's invisible qualities—his eternal power and divine nature—have been clearly seen, being understood from what has been made, so that men are without excuse. (Rom 1:20)
>
> For the director of music. A psalm of David. The heavens declare the glory of God; the skies proclaim the work of his hands. (Psa 19:1)
>
> The heavens proclaim his righteousness, and all the peoples see his glory. (Psa 97:6)

The point is this: men can know that God gives them life and that He cares and provides for them, and that God runs everything in an orderly and lawful way, giving purpose and meaning to life. Men can look at nature and see that God is great and good; therefore, God deserves to be glorified and given thanks. But instead of seeing God and coming to know God, men have rejected Him. Instead of worshipping God...

- some worship the creation, that is, science and man—a humanistic worship.
- some worship the god of their imagination, a thought or image of what God is (a god that allows them to live as they desire).

They are the persons who are to be judged. They are the persons who do not know the living and true God, not personally—not in a personal day to day relationship.

2. All who do not obey the gospel of our Lord Jesus Christ will be judged. Who are these?
⇒ Every person who has ever heard the gospel of Jesus Christ and rejected it.
⇒ Every person who has professed the gospel of Jesus Christ but does not obey the commandments of the gospel.
⇒ Every person who has been baptized but does not obey the commandment of the gospel.
⇒ Every person who has joined the church and holds a membership in the church but does not obey the commandments of the gospel.

> But among you there must not be even a hint of sexual immorality, or of any kind of impurity, or of greed, because these are improper for God's holy people. Nor should there be obscenity, foolish talk or coarse joking, which are out of place, but rather thanksgiving. For of this you can be sure: No immoral, impure or greedy person—such a man is an idolater—has any inheritance in the kingdom of Christ and of God. Let no one deceive you with empty words, for because of such things God's wrath comes on those who are disobedient. Therefore do not be partners with them. (Eph 5:3-7)
>
> He will punish those who do not know God and do not obey the gospel of our Lord Jesus. (2 Th 1:8)
>
> For if the message spoken by angels was binding, and every violation and disobedience received its just punishment, how shall we escape if we ignore such a great salvation? This salvation, which was first announced by the Lord, was confirmed to us by those who heard him. (Heb 2:2-3)
>
> How much more severely do you think a man deserves to be punished who has trampled the Son of God under foot, who has treated as an unholy thing the blood of the covenant that sanctified him, and who has insulted the Spirit of grace? For we know him who said, "It is mine to avenge; I will repay," and again, "The Lord will judge his people." (Heb 10:29-30)

4 (1:9) **Judgment—Jesus Christ, Return**: the penalty of judgment will be terrible, but it will be deserved. Why? Because those who are to be judged had the opportunity to know God, but they chose to deny and curse Him and to walk as they desired throughout life. Note three significant facts about the penalty and punishment of judgment.

1. The word "they" (hoitines) is used in a qualitative sense; that is, it means *"persons who are such as"* deserve this punishment; "persons who are of *such a kind as to"* deserve this punishment. The Greek word clearly shows that these persons deserve the punishment of the coming judgment. (This is pointed out by A.T. Robertson, *Word Pictures in the New Testament*, Vol.4, p.44; and Leon Morris, *The Epistles of Paul to the Thessalonians*. "Tyndale New Testament Commentaries," p.119.)

2. The phrase "will be punished" (diken tisousin) means to pay the penalty. Matthew Henry says that "they did sin's work, and must receive sin's wages" (*Matthew Henry's Commentary*, Vol.6, p.795). Sinners may get away with their sin and rejection of God while on earth, but they will be punished in the final analysis.

Note another fact about the punishment. Note the Greek word for punishment (diken). It comes from the same root as righteous (dikaios). This means that the punishment will be righteous, just—exactly what the person deserves, no more, no less. A person will be measured an exact amount of punishment that he has worked while on earth. God's punishment will not be vindictive; it will be perfectly just, a punishment of retribution—a punishment that pays a person exactly what he deserves.

> And if your eye causes you to sin, gouge it out and throw it away. It is better for you to enter life with one eye than to have two eyes and be thrown into the fire of hell. (Mat 18:9)
>
> "Then he will say to those on his left, 'Depart from me, you who are cursed, into the eternal fire prepared for the devil and his angels. For I was hungry and you gave me nothing to eat, I was thirsty and you gave me nothing to drink, I was a stranger and you did not invite me in, I needed clothes and you did not clothe me, I was sick and in prison and you did not look after me.' "They also will answer, 'Lord, when did we see you hungry or thirsty or a stranger or needing clothes or sick or in prison, and did not help you?' "He will reply, 'I tell you the truth, whatever you did not do for one of the least of these, you did not do for me.' "Then they will go away to

2 THESSALONIANS 1:6-12

eternal punishment, but the righteous to eternal life." (Mat 25:41-46)

But whoever blasphemes against the Holy Spirit will never be forgiven; he is guilty of an eternal sin." (Mark 3:29)

[The Lord] His winnowing fork is in his hand to clear his threshing floor and to gather the wheat into his barn, but he will burn up the chaff with unquenchable fire." (Luke 3:17)

But for those who are self-seeking and who reject the truth and follow evil, there will be wrath and anger. There will be trouble and distress for every human being who does evil: first for the Jew, then for the Gentile; (Rom 2:8-9)

They will be punished with everlasting destruction and shut out from the presence of the Lord and from the majesty of his power (2 Th 1:9)

How much more severely do you think a man deserves to be punished who has trampled the Son of God under foot, who has treated as an unholy thing the blood of the covenant that sanctified him, and who has insulted the Spirit of grace? For we know him who said, "It is mine to avenge; I will repay," and again, "The Lord will judge his people." (Heb 10:29-30)

If this is so, then the Lord knows how to rescue godly men from trials and to hold the unrighteous for the day of judgment, while continuing their punishment. (2 Pet 2:9)

On the wicked he will rain fiery coals and burning sulfur; a scorching wind will be their lot. (Psa 11:6)

I will punish the world for its evil, the wicked for their sins. I will put an end to the arrogance of the haughty and will humble the pride of the ruthless. (Isa 13:11)

See, the LORD is coming out of his dwelling to punish the people of the earth for their sins. The earth will disclose the blood shed upon her; she will conceal her slain no longer. (Isa 26:21)

According to what they have done, so will he repay wrath to his enemies and retribution to his foes; he will repay the islands their due. (Isa 59:18)

I will punish you as your deeds deserve, declares the LORD. I will kindle a fire in your forests that will consume everything around you.'" (Jer 21:14)

At that time I will search Jerusalem [the world] with lamps and punish those who are complacent, who are like wine left on its dregs, who think, 'The LORD will do nothing, either good or bad.' (Zep 1:12)

"Surely the day is coming; it will burn like a furnace. All the arrogant and every evildoer will be stubble, and that day that is coming will set them on fire," says the LORD Almighty. "Not a root or a branch will be left to them. (Mal 4:1)

3. The words "everlasting destruction" (olethron aionion) do not mean annihilation or ceasing to exist. They mean exactly what they say in this verse: to be shut out, separated from the presence and face of the Lord and from the majesty of His power—an eternity of woe (A.T. Robertson. *Word Pictures in the New Testament*, Vol.4, p.44). They mean complete ruin and loss; to be cut off, excluded, removed, separated, extinguished, deprived, abhorred, and banished from all the good things of life.

⇒ *Complete ruin and loss*: from all that life should be.
⇒ *Cut off*: from the presence of God and from the majesty of His power and of heaven.
⇒ *Excluded*: from all joy, pleasure and satisfaction. It is utter emptiness.
⇒ *Removed*: from all companionship and associations and from all possessions. It is being left all alone and left with nothing. It is utter loneliness.
⇒ *Separated*: from the presence of all goodness and righteousness—from God and from all those who sought after righteousness. And there is no prospect of the separation ever ending, not even for an hour.
⇒ *Extinguished*: from love and affection. It is a hell of passion let loose.
⇒ *Deprived*: from the Holy Spirit restraining the force of evil. It is a hell of lawlessness.
⇒ *Abhorred*: from the bodies of glory. It is a decayed carcass (Is.66:23-24).
⇒ *Banished*: from all hope. It is being eternally lost forever, and there is no prospect of the banishment ever ending—not even for one hour.

Leon Morris quotes the Biblical scholar James Denny as saying:

> "If there is any truth in Scripture at all, this is true—that those who stubbornly refuse to submit to the gospel, and to love and obey Jesus Christ, incur at the Last Advent an infinite and irreparable loss. They pass into a night on which no morning [ever] dawns" (*The Epistles of Paul to the Thessalonians.* "Tyndale New Testament Commentaries," p.120).

Let both grow together until the harvest. At that time I will tell the harvesters: First collect the weeds and tie them in bundles to be burned; then gather the wheat and bring it into my barn.'" (Mat 13:30)

This is how it will be at the end of the age. The angels will come and separate the wicked from the righteous (Mat 13:49)

"But while they were on their way to buy the oil, the bridegroom arrived. The virgins who were ready went in with him to the wedding banquet. And the door was shut. "Later the others also came. 'Sir! Sir!' they said. 'Open the door for us!' "But he replied, 'I tell you the truth, I don't know you.' (Mat 25:10-12)

All the nations will be gathered before him, and he will separate the people one from another as a shepherd separates the sheep from the goats. (Mat 25:32)

"But he will reply, 'I don't know you or where you come from. Away from me, all you evildoers!' (Luke 13:27)

2 THESSALONIANS 1:6-12

And besides all this, between us and you a great chasm has been fixed, so that those who want to go from here to you cannot, nor can anyone cross over from there to us.' (Luke 16:26)

For, as I have often told you before and now say again even with tears, many live as enemies of the cross of Christ. Their destiny is destruction, their god is their stomach, and their glory is in their shame. Their mind is on earthly things. (Phil 3:18-19)

While people are saying, "Peace and safety," destruction will come on them suddenly, as labor pains on a pregnant woman, and they will not escape. (1 Th 5:3)

They will be punished with everlasting destruction and shut out from the presence of the Lord and from the majesty of his power (2 Th 1:9)

People who want to get rich fall into temptation and a trap and into many foolish and harmful desires that plunge men into ruin and destruction. (1 Tim 6:9)

But there were also false prophets among the people, just as there will be false teachers among you. They will secretly introduce destructive heresies, even denying the sovereign Lord who bought them—bringing swift destruction on themselves. (2 Pet 2:1)

He writes the same way in all his letters, speaking in them of these matters. His letters contain some things that are hard to understand, which ignorant and unstable people distort, as they do the other Scriptures, to their own destruction. (2 Pet 3:16)

5 (1:10) **Judgment—Jesus Christ, Return:** the time of the judgment is set. Unbelievers are going to be judged…
- when Jesus Christ comes to be glorified in His holy people and to be marveled at among all those who have believed.

Note the word "in" (en). When Jesus Christ returns, His glory is going to be seen *in His holy people*. All the world will see the wonder and glory of…
- the height of His love
- the depth of His mercy
- the length of His grace
- the breadth of His power

The Lord Jesus Christ has loved and saved us, and the height, depth, length, and breadth of His salvation is beyond imagination. His salvation far exceeds anything that we could ever know or describe. When the glory of what Jesus Christ has done for us is manifested, it will explode into such a spectacular demonstration of glory—into a spectacle that will exceed the explosion of all the brilliant lights of the heavenly bodies. The greatness of the glory and love of Jesus Christ will be seen in that day—seen in His dear saints and in all them who believe.

Note one other significant point: He will not only be glorified in that day, He will be admired. Philips' translation says, "It will be a breath-taking wonder." Leon Morris says, "the glory of that day will far surpass anything of which we can have any idea…and when we do behold it we shall be lost in amazement" (*The Epistles of Paul to the Thessalonians*. "Tyndale New Testament Commentaries," p.120).

6 (1:11-12) **Judgment:** the escape from judgment. Three things are necessary to escape judgment. Note that these two verses are a prayer of Paul for the believers.

1. A person must be counted worthy by God. How can a person be counted worthy? No person has any worthiness of his own; no person is perfect. Therefore, no person has enough goodness to stand before God, for God is perfect. If a person is to be acceptable to God, he has to approach God through faith in His Son, the Lord Jesus Christ. God accepts a person as worthy only if he comes in the name of Jesus Christ—believing in and trusting Jesus Christ to save him. The person who comes to God through Jesus Christ honors Christ, and any person who honors Christ is counted worthy by God. Note: we are not worthy; we possess no righteousness of our own. But God *counts and credits* us with righteousness because we come to Him in the perfect righteousness of His Son. We honor God's Son and God honors anyone who honors His Son.

2. God must complete the work of faith in us. We age, deteriorate, die, and decay. We cannot complete anything, not permanently. We can complete something for only a few short years at most, and even then we cannot complete anything perfectly. Nothing that we do is ever perfected. Therefore, if we are to be *saved from judgment and given eternal life*, God has to take our initial belief in Christ…
- and complete the good pleasure of His goodness in us.
- and complete the work of faith in us—complete it with omnipotent power.

3. The name of Christ must be glorified in us and we in Him. This simply means that…
- we must let Him live and move and have His being in us—every day.
- we must live and move and have our being in Him—every day.
- we must let Him be glorified in us.

This is the only way to escape judgment. A person can know that he will escape the judgment of God…
- if he has trusted Jesus Christ as his Savior and Lord.
- if he knows that God is completing the work of faith in him.
- if he is honoring the name of the Lord and letting the Lord glorify Himself in his life.

As a prisoner for the Lord, then, I urge you to live a life worthy of the calling you have received. (Eph 4:1)

And this is his command: to believe in the name of his Son, Jesus Christ, and to love one another as he commanded us. Those who obey his commands live in him, and he in them. And this is how we know that he lives in us: We know it by the Spirit he gave us. And this is his command: to believe in the name of his Son, Jesus Christ, and to love one another as he commanded us. Those who obey his commands live in him, and he in them. And this is how we know that he lives in us: We know it by the Spirit he gave us. (1 John 3:23-24)

Here I am! I stand at the door and knock. If anyone hears my voice and opens the door, I will come in and eat with him, and he with me. (Rev 3:20)

2 THESSALONIANS 2:1-3

	CHAPTER 2	prophecy, report or letter supposed to have come from us, saying that the day of the Lord has already come.
		3 Don't let anyone deceive you in any way, for that day will not come until the rebellion occurs and the man of lawlessness is revealed, the man doomed to destruction.
			b. Let nothing shake or alarm you about that day
			
			2 Let no man deceive you—watch for two events first
			   a. A great rebellion
			   b. A revelation of the antichrist

1 Guard against being shaken or alarmed by the Day of the Lord a. Look to the coming of the Lord, not to the judgment of that Day	**B. The Day of the Lord, 2:1-3** Concerning the coming of our Lord Jesus Christ and our being gathered to him, we ask you, brothers, 2 Not to become easily unsettled or alarmed by some		

DIVISION II

A GLIMPSE INTO THE END TIME, 1:6-2:17

B. The Day of the Lord, 2:1-3

(2:1-3) **Introduction**: when the Bible refers to the day of the Lord, it does not mean a single day in history. It is using the word *day* in a forceful or emphatic sense just like men do when they speak of the great day of space exploration or the great day of some world leader or the great day of creation. The day of the Lord covers a long span of time and some very significant events. In the Bible it covers the whole span of history beginning with the two events of this passage and reaching forward to the end of time. It will be a terrible time of trouble, a time that is known as that great and terrible day of judgment, the day when the wrath of God will fall upon all the meanness, viciousness, ugliness, and filthiness of men. However, note the point of this passage: no believer has to fear the day of the Lord. The day of the Lord launches God's judgment against unbelievers; it is not the judgment of believers.
  1. Guard against being shaken or alarmed by the day of the Lord (v.1-2).
  2. Let no man deceive you—watch for two events first (v.3).

1 (2:1-2) **Day of the Lord—God, Judgment of—World, Judgment of**: guard against being shaken or alarmed by the day of the Lord. The believers at Thessalonica thought the day of the Lord had begun—that great and terrible day when God's judgment is to fall upon the earth. Verse two explains why. Remember: the believers were suffering fierce persecution (see note—2 Th.1:6 for discussion). They were suffering as much as human beings could bear; apparently some were even being martyred. Verse two says that some person was even claiming...
- "that a prophecy (a message by the Spirit) had revealed to him that the day of the Lord had begun."
- that he had a special report, a special revelation from God that the day of the Lord had begun.
- that he had either received or heard about a letter from Paul that said the day of the Lord was at hand.

Combine these three claims with the suffering of savage persecution and it is easily understood why some of the believers would be *unsettled and alarmed*. In fact, the word "unsettled" means to be shaken, tossed about, agitated, shocked; and the word "alarmed" means a continued state of tension and nervousness. Paul says two quick things that we must keep in mind as we look toward the day of the Lord.

  1. Look to the coming of the Lord and toward our gathering together unto Him, not to the judgment that is coming. Note that this is an appeal from Paul, an urgent appeal: he begs his brothers in the Lord. And he begs them "by the coming of our Lord Jesus Christ and our being gathered to Him." The point is striking: the believer is to focus upon the Lord's return and not upon the judgment of the Lord's day. The day of the Lord is to be the judgment of unbelievers, not of believers. The believer is not appointed to receive the wrath of God; he is appointed to salvation. Therefore, he is not to fear the day of the Lord. He is to be looking to the glorious appearing of the great God and our Savior, Jesus Christ.

> For God did not appoint us to suffer wrath but to receive salvation through our Lord Jesus Christ. (1 Th 5:9)
> It teaches us to say "No" to ungodliness and worldly passions, and to live self-controlled, upright and godly lives in this present age, while we wait for the blessed hope—the glorious appearing of our great God and Savior, Jesus Christ, (Titus 2:12-13)

  2. Let nothing shake or alarm you about the day of the Lord: not a prophecy, nor some so-called spiritual message, nor a writing from some so-called spiritual man. Note: the best manuscripts and the great majority of commentaries translate and understand this to be the *day of the Lord*."

2 (2:3) **Day of the Lord—Apostasy, The Great—Antichrist, The**: let no man deceive you—watch for two significant events; for that day—the great and terrible day of the Lord—will not come until these two events happen. Note the emphasis upon guarding against deception: let no man deceive you *in any way*—no matter what any person says or claims or uses against you, do not let him deceive you about the day of the Lord. That terrible day—the day when God's judgment will begin to fall upon the world and its unbelievers—cannot come until these two events happen. But note: the idea is that these events *will launch* the day of the Lord, that is, the terrible judgment of God upon all those who have cursed, denied, ignored, neglected, and defamed the name of Him who is the holy Sovereign of the universe (see note, pt.2—1 Th.5:1-3 for more discussion).

  1. The first event that will launch the day of the Lord will be a great rebellion of believers against God. The word "rebellion" is much too weak for what the Greek says. The Greek is forceful: "rebellion" means apostasy, revolt, falling away. The picture is that of multitudes—millions from all over the world—rebelling and revolting against God. As the eminent scholar Leon Morris says: "In the last times there will be an outstanding manifestation of the powers of evil arrayed against God" (*The Epistles of Paul to the Thessalonians*. "Tyndale New Testament Commentaries," p.126). The point is this: before the day of the Lord—before the terrible judgment of God can come

upon the earth, there will be a great apostasy, a tragic turning away from God by millions. Note a most significant point: apostasy is one of the causes for the day of the Lord. The revolt and rebellion against God will be so massive that it will necessitate the return of Christ in judgment. Man and his world will be so evil and sinful and so immoral and unjust—so much in rebellion against God—that Christ has to return and judge the world. Most of the people in the world will have gone so far that they will be beyond ever repenting.

> **At that time many will turn away from the faith and will betray and hate each other, and many false prophets will appear and deceive many people. Because of the increase of wickedness, the love of most will grow cold, but he who stands firm to the end will be saved. (Mat 24:10-13)**
>
> **The Spirit clearly says that in later times some will abandon the faith and follow deceiving spirits and things taught by demons. Such teachings come through hypocritical liars, whose consciences have been seared as with a hot iron. (1 Tim 4:1-2)**
>
> **But mark this: There will be terrible times in the last days. People will be lovers of themselves, lovers of money, boastful, proud, abusive, disobedient to their parents, ungrateful, unholy, without love, unforgiving, slanderous, without self-control, brutal, not lovers of the good, treacherous, rash, conceited, lovers of pleasure rather than lovers of God—having a form of godliness but denying its power. Have nothing to do with them. (2 Tim 3:1-5)**
>
> **For the time will come when men will not put up with sound doctrine. Instead, to suit their own desires, they will gather around them a great number of teachers to say what their itching ears want to hear. They will turn their ears away from the truth and turn aside to myths. (2 Tim 4:3-4)**

2. The second event that will launch the day of the Lord will be the revelation of that man of lawlessness—the man doomed to destruction, that is, the antichrist himself. Note the following facts:

   a. The antichrist will be *revealed*. This fact indicates that he existed before his appearance (Leon Morris. *The Epistles of Paul to the Thessalonians*. "Tyndale New Testament Commentaries," p.126). A.T. Robertson says. "the implication is that *the man of sin* [lawlessness] is hidden somewhere who will be suddenly manifested" (*Word Pictures in the New Testament*, Vol.4, p.50).

   b. The antichrist is "the man of *lawlessness*;" the man doomed to destruction; the man who will be the very embodiment of lawlessness or total rebellion against God. He will do all he can to lead a total revolt against God—do all he can to lead every man, woman, and child to turn away from God.

   c. The antichrist is "the man of lawlessness." This means that he will be so evil that he will be just like the man of doom and destruction, of the devil himself. It also means that he is doomed to perdition; he is doomed to destruction.

   d. The antichrist is not just another evil world leader who is a mass deceiver or murderer of millions. This is not what Scripture means in this passage. Scripture speaks of other antichrists, others who will appear in the world and mislead people and do much evil upon the earth (1 Jn. 2:18; 2 Jn.7). But this Scripture is not dealing with antichrists (plural), but with the most infamous antichrist of all—the one antichrist...

   • who will launch the day of the Lord, and who must appear before the day of the Lord can come.

   • who is so terrible that his very name is "this man of lawlessness" and "the man doomed to destruction".

Note: the antichrist is not Satan, but he is said to be a man who will be sent by the very "work of Satan" (cp. 2 Th.2:9).

Thought 1. Some idea of just how evil the antichrist will be can be gleaned by thinking of some of the evil men in history. Just think: their evil was nothing compared to the evil of the antichrist. Think of the evil of such mass murderers as Hitler, Stalin, and other dictators down through history who have slaughtered millions.

> **"So when you see standing in the holy place 'the abomination that causes desolation,' [the antichrist] spoken of through the prophet Daniel—let the reader understand— (Mat 24:15)**
>
> **"When you see 'the abomination that causes desolation' [the antichrist] standing where it does not belong—let the reader understand—then let those who are in Judea flee to the mountains. (Mark 13:14)**
>
> **Don't let anyone deceive you in any way, for that day will not come until the rebellion occurs and the man of lawlessness is revealed, the man doomed to destruction. He will oppose and will exalt himself over everything that is called God or is worshiped, so that he sets himself up in God's temple, proclaiming himself to be God. (2 Th 2:3-4)**
>
> **And then the lawless one will be revealed, whom the Lord Jesus will overthrow with the breath of his mouth and destroy by the splendor of his coming. The coming of the lawless one will be in accordance with the work of Satan displayed in all kinds of counterfeit miracles, signs and wonders, (2 Th 2:8-9)**
>
> **Men worshiped the dragon because he had given authority to the beast, and they also worshiped the beast and asked, "Who is like the beast? Who can make war against him?" The beast was given a mouth to utter proud words and blasphemies and to exercise his authority for forty-two months. He opened his mouth to blaspheme God, and to slander his name and his dwelling place and those who live in heaven. He was given power to make war against the saints and to conquer them. And he was given authority over every tribe, people, language and nation. All inhabitants of the earth will worship the beast—all whose names have not been written in the book of life belonging to the Lamb that was slain from the creation of the world. He who has an ear, let him hear. (Rev 13:4-9)**

2 THESSALONIANS 2:4-9

		C. The Antichrist: The Man of Sin, 2:4-9	7 For the secret power of lawlessness is already at work; but the one who now holds it back will continue to do so till he is taken out of the way.	b. The mystery of lawlessness: Is already at work, but restrained
1	**His character** (v.3-4) a. Rebellious, apostate b. Man of lawlessness c. Doomed to destruction, hell d. Adversary, opposer to God e. Claims to be God	4 He will oppose and will exalt himself over everything that is called God or is worshiped, so that he sets himself up in God's temple, proclaiming himself to be God.	8 And then the lawless one will be revealed, whom the Lord Jesus will overthrow with the breath of his mouth and destroy by the splendor of his coming.	c. The appearance: When the restraint is removed 4 **His end** a. Slain by the Lord's breath or Word b. Destroyed by the Lord's glory
2	**His danger: Is so great it must be taught to the church**	5 Don't you remember that when I was with you I used to tell you these things? 6 And now you know what is holding him back, so that he may be revealed at the proper time.	9 The coming of the lawless one will be in accordance with the work of Satan displayed in all kinds of counterfeit miracles, signs and wonders,	5 **His work: To carry on Satan's activity in all kinds of counterfeit miracles, signs & wonders**
3	**His revelation to the world: An historical appearance** a. The time: Is set			

DIVISION II

A GLIMPSE INTO THE END TIME, 1:6-2:17

C. The Antichrist: The Man of Sin, 2:4-9

(2:4-9) Introduction: there are many antichrists who have risen throughout history to carry on Satan's work with great severity (1 Jn.2:18). However, Paul is not speaking of these men who stand against Christ and His followers. By the terms "that man of lawlessness" and "the man doomed to destruction." Paul means the most infamous antichrist who is to appear in the end time. The antichrist is to be revealed when the end time is near. He is to be Satan's instrument in the most severe way. How? By being filled with Satan's spirit (2 Th.2:9).

Paul did not identify the antichrist and 1 Jn.2:18 speaks of many antichrists. These two facts are a warning to us, a warning to guard against hastily identifying some world leader as the antichrist.

The antichrist is most assuredly a person. The descriptions of this passage, as well as others, have to be terribly misconstrued to make them fit any force or system other than a person. Our Lord's words in Mk.3:14, where He uses the masculine participle, identify him as a person. (See DEEPER STUDY # 1—Mk.13:14; DEEPER STUDY # 1—Rev. 11:7; notes—13:1-10; 13:11-18; 17:7-14. Cp. Dan.9:20-27, esp. 27.)

1. His character (v.4).
2. His danger: is so great it must be taught to the church (v.5).
3. His revelation to the world: an historical appearance (v.6-8).
4. His end (v.8).
5. His work: to carry on Satan's activity in all kinds of counterfeit miracles, signs and wonders (v.9).

1 (2:4) **Antichrist**: the character of the antichrist. There are five traits of the antichrist revealed in this verse and in the former verse (v.3-4).

1. The antichrist is the "man of lawlessness" (v.3). He will be the very embodiment of sin and lawlessness; the man who idealizes sin; the man who is the ideal sinner. He will be the man who fulfills the dreams of Satan upon earth. He will lead the perfect rebellion and revolt against God—a rebellion and revolt that will embrace practically every man, woman, and child.

2. The antichrist is "doomed to destruction, hell" (v.3). The Greek word for "destruction" (apoleias) means doom. Judas is said to be the son of destruction, of hell. But the meaning here is that the antichrist is the very embodiment of destruction of hell itself...

- he is the man of the most violent doom and destruction; the man of the most violent evil imaginable.
- the man who is more deserving of doom and perdition than anyone else who has ever lived.
- the man of doom and destruction of the devil himself, the father of doom and destruction.

3. The antichrist is the opponent of all that is called God (v.4).

> *"Who opposeth is a participle, and might well be rendered 'the opposer' or 'the adversary', a term sometimes applied to Satan (e.g. 1 Tim.5:14); indeed the Hebrew satan means 'adversary'. The word emphasizes the kinship of the 'man of lawlessness' with his master [the devil]"* (Leon Morris. *The Epistles of Paul to the Thessalonians*. "Tyndale New Testament Commentaries," p.127).

The antichrist will be the opponent of Christ: this is the very meaning of his name. He will oppose Christ and everything Christ stands for: love, mercy, morality, and justice. Instead of these, he will lead the world to live a life of immorality, injustice, selfishness, and indulgence—especially in the treatment of those who profess the name of Christ.

4. The antichrist is the "exalter of himself" (Leon Morris. *The Epistles of Paul to the Thessalonians*. "Tyndale New Testament Commentaries," p.127f). He lifts himself up above *all* others, above the measure of all others. The idea is against all others, in a hostile or antagonistic way. All peoples will either subject themselves to him or else suffer severe consequences. (Note: the picture is probably referring to imprisonment or death.) The point to see is that he is totally...

- self-centered
- power hungry
- fame crazed
- authoritarian
- dictatorial
- without values
- immoral
- unjust

2 THESSALONIANS 2:4-9

5. The antichrist claims to be God. Note exactly what is said here:.
   ⇒ He exalts himself over everything that is called God or is worshipped.

He does not just attack authority, but he attacks all religions—"everything that is called God or is worshipped." How does he do this? He sits in the temple of God and shows himself or claims that he is God. The idea is that he sets himself up as the object of worship. He actually sets himself up within the temple of God to be worshipped. A.T. Robertson, the great Biblical scholar, in his *Word Pictures in the New Testament* (Vol.4, p.50), refers to J.B. Lightfoot as pointing out some of the parallels between Christ and the antichrist:
   ⇒ both Christ and the antichrist are revealed.
   ⇒ both Christ and the antichrist are surrounded by many mysteries.
   ⇒ both Christ and the antichrist *claim to be God*.

Thought 1. This is probably referring to the worship of a state religion which will focus upon the leader of the world, the antichrist. We have a perfect example in the worship of the emperor of the old Roman empire. Images of the emperor were placed in temples all around the world and the citizens were expected to worship the state. Remember what Rome had done. It had brought peace to a war torn world. Because of this many people were willing to worship the *ideal* of the state. Think how some people worship science and technology today. And just imagine what would happen if a person arose upon the world scene who could either mobilize or force the nations of the world...
- to live at peace with each other.
- to solve the hunger problem by coordinating the growth and distribution of food for everyone in the world.
- to solve the problems of the world such as homelessness, unemployment, poverty, lack of medical care, crime, and on and on.

Imagine how the vast majority of people would worship the person and state that could bring about this kind of utopian state for the peoples of the world. Natural man would gladly follow such a leader—his science and technology, his will and desire.

Think about this as well: What would be the best way for such a leader to control the masses of the world? The masses who had always been religious? Would it not be to create a new religion, a religion focused upon the ruler and the state over which he ruled? Would not men willingly worship the ruler—his government, science, and technology—that had brought such a utopian existence upon earth for mankind?

This is exactly what happened in ancient Rome in the worship of the emperor and state. People were allowed to continue the worship of their own gods just so they acknowledged the supremacy of the emperor and the Roman state. They were to worship the state that had brought and maintained peace within the civilized world of that day. By encouraging (by law) the people to worship the emperor (the symbol of the state), the people were focused upon the government—upon the fact that the state had blessed the world with peace. (This worship of the state helped to maintain the peace throughout the Roman empire.)

2 (2:5) **Antichrist**: the importance of the antichrist is so great that it must be taught to the church. Paul had taught the Thessalonian believers all about the end time and the antichrist. The importance of the Lord's return, the day of the Lord, the great apostasy, and the rise of antichrist cannot be overstressed. Scripture declares emphatically that these events are going to happen.
   ⇒ The Lord is returning to gather His people together in the most spectacular and joyful occasion of human history.
   ⇒ The great and terrible day of the Lord is going to fall upon the earth. Unbelievers—all those who have cursed, rebelled, denied, ignored, neglected, and rejected Christ—are going to bear the justice of God.
   ⇒ The great apostasy is going to be witnessed by the earth: millions are going to turn away from Christ.
   ⇒ The antichrist is going to arise upon the world scene and bring a material utopia to the earth and some form of state worship—all in utter rebellion and denial of God Himself.

The point is this: the end times are coming upon the world. Therefore, people must be taught so that some can be saved and escape the things coming upon the earth. (See outline and notes—Mt.24:1-51 for more of a picture as to what makes the tribulation of the last days worse than what men usually suffer upon earth. A quick glance at the outlines and notes of *Revelation*, Chapters 6-18, will also show the difference.)

3 (2:6-8) **Antichrist**: the revelation of the antichrist to the world. There is to be an historical appearance of the antichrist in the world. Note the words "revealed at the proper time." The time is set: he is going to actually appear upon the world scene.

1. Right now, there is some *power of restraint* that holds back the antichrist and keeps him from appearing. However, the day is coming when *the restraining power* is to be "taken out of the way"; then the antichrist will be revealed to the world. Note that the restraining power is not identified. What or who is it? Even the best Bible scholars differ. But note three significant points.
   a. The words used are "taken out of the way," *not taken away*. There is a vast difference: the power of restraint upon the antichrist can step aside and allow the antichrist to appear and still be at work in the world. If the power of restraint was completely removed and taken away, then there would be no power of good whatsoever in the world. Therefore, the words "taken out of the way" have to be noticed. Whatever the power of restraint is, it is still present in the world working for good. It only steps aside enough to allow the antichrist to appear and to carry on his work of evil.
   b. The masculine pronoun "one" (v.7) and the neuter pronoun "what" (v.6) are both used for the restraining power. Therefore, the restraining power can be referred to as both a person and as the very embodiment of the power of good that works throughout the world. Note that the power is so strong that it controls the events of human history. That is, the restraining power can determine the exact day to step aside and let the antichrist appear.

2 THESSALONIANS 2:4-9

c. Logic has to be considered in determining who the restraining power is. When the identity is not given and there are so many varied opinions, we have to use the best logic we can. In light of this, note the following:

⇒ What is the power that restrains evil upon the earth? The power of law? Laws change from society to society and from generation to generation. What is evil to one society is good to another. Many societies consider lying, stealing, cheating, and even murder to be good if it is for the purpose of forwarding the state or government or leadership of a nation. (Compare Rome, Communism, and many dictatorships.)

⇒ What then is the true power that restrains evil upon the earth? Is it not the power of God Himself? God's power and work against sin is the whole point of this passage. Therefore, it is difficult to see how the restraining power could be anything other than the *Spirit of God* upon the earth.

Note this as well: the Holy Spirit is referred to in both the masculine and neuter genders in Scripture (cp. Jn.14:16-17; 16:13). And He is pictured as the restraining force of evil in the Old Testament (Gen.6:3).

2. The "secret power of lawlessness" is now at work in the world. This is a terrifying verse, for it says that the power that restrains evil is going to be removed—evil is going to be cut loose upon the world. God is going to remove much of the restraint that He now puts upon evil. Note the word "secret": it means something that has been hidden but is now revealed. There is, of course, so much that we do not know about lawlessness:

⇒ Why do we do things that we know are bad for us?

⇒ Why do we lie, steal, cheat, kill, curse and go to war?

⇒ Why are we so selfish that we allow barriers and feelings to build up toward husband, wife, child, parent, neighbor, friend, employer, and employee—barriers and feelings that end up destroying our lives and relationships and hurting all those around us?

⇒ Why do we indulge, hoard, bank, build, and then indulge, hoard, bank, and build more and more, neglecting the reality of a world that reels under the weight of desperate needs?

The questions could go on and on. We know better, yet we continue to do evil. Why? What is there about us that causes us to sin and then to continue on sinning when it is so bad and does so much harm? And why is it that we cannot control sin and lawlessness within ourselves, much less within our world? We cannot answer the question, not in and of ourselves. That is the secret power of lawlessness. Sin is a mystery, an unknown factor of human life. However, there is Someone who does understand sin, and there is Someone who has revealed what it is and why we are enslaved by it. The Person is God. The secret power of lawlessness has been revealed to men by God through Christ and His Holy Word. It is a matter of man listening to Christ and to the Word of God. But that is a discussion for another time.

The point is this: in the last days when it is time for the antichrist to arise, God is going to remove much of His restraint upon lawlessness. Lawlessness will be allowed to run rampant over the earth, and the rampage will be part of the judgment falling upon the earth. Men will be allowed to do their own thing and live as they desire to live. The day is coming when men will get their wish and be left to themselves without God interfering.

3. The antichrist will be revealed. He will "appear unveiled in all his naked deformity—no longer working secretly, but openly, and in an undisguised form; no longer the mystery, but the revelation of lawlessness" (*Pulpit Commentary*, Vol.21, p.25). The spirit of sin and lawlessness will find its fulfillment in the antichrist and his government. He will vent the rage of men against God that has built up for centuries upon the world. He will arise upon the earth, and the terrible rage of lawlessness will be cut loose upon mankind. Men will suffer the results of their own sin. They will sin and sin and live lawless lives and burn in their lusts for more and more. But they will never be satisfied with what they have, nor with the good and the normal and the natural. They will have more than enough, but they will lust in their passions for more and more and they will bear the terrible inner punishment of more and more...

- dissatisfaction
- emptiness
- loneliness
- unfulfillment
- insecurity
- purposelessness
- disturbance
- conflict
- sorrow
- restlessness

On the surface, these things may not look all that bad, but think about them for a moment: imagine the depth and intensity of each inner punishment when God is not present to help us through them. The horror and fear, despair and insecurity that will be consuming the souls of men cannot be described, for men have never had to live without the presence of God upon the earth to help them.

> **At that time many will turn away from the faith and will betray and hate each other, and many false prophets will appear and deceive many people. Because of the increase of wickedness, the love of most will grow cold, (Mat 24:10-12)**
>
> **But God turned away and gave them over to the worship of the heavenly bodies. This agrees with what is written in the book of the prophets: "'Did you bring me sacrifices and offerings forty years in the desert, O house of Israel? (Acts 7:42)**
>
> **For although they knew God, they neither glorified him as God nor gave thanks to him, but their thinking became futile and their foolish hearts were darkened. Although they claimed to be wise, they became fools (Rom 1:21-22)**
>
> **For although they knew God, they neither glorified him as God nor gave thanks to him, but their thinking became futile and their foolish hearts were darkened. Although they claimed to be wise, they became fools. Therefore God gave them over in the sinful desires of their hearts to sexual impurity for the degrading of their bodies with one another. They exchanged the truth of God for a lie, and worshiped and served created things rather than the Creator—who is forever praised. Amen. Because of this, God gave them over to shameful lusts. Even their women exchanged natural relations for unnatural ones. In the same way the men also abandoned natural**

relations with women and were inflamed with lust for one another. Men committed indecent acts with other men, and received in themselves the due penalty for their perversion. Furthermore, since they did not think it worthwhile to retain the knowledge of God, he gave them over to a depraved mind, to do what ought not to be done. They have become filled with every kind of wickedness, evil, greed and depravity. They are full of envy, murder, strife, deceit and malice. They are gossips, slanderers, God-haters, insolent, arrogant and boastful; they invent ways of doing evil; they disobey their parents; they are senseless, faithless, heartless, ruthless. (Rom 1:24-31)

But because of your stubbornness and your unrepentant heart, you are storing up wrath against yourself for the day of God's wrath, when his righteous judgment will be revealed. (Rom 2:5)

Do not be deceived: God cannot be mocked. A man reaps what he sows. (Gal 6:7)

The Spirit clearly says that in later times some will abandon the faith and follow deceiving spirits and things taught by demons. Such teachings come through hypocritical liars, whose consciences have been seared as with a hot iron. (1 Tim 4:1-2)

But mark this: There will be terrible times in the last days. People will be lovers of themselves, lovers of money, boastful, proud, abusive, disobedient to their parents, ungrateful, unholy, without love, unforgiving, slanderous, without self-control, brutal, not lovers of the good, treacherous, rash, conceited, lovers of pleasure rather than lovers of God—having a form of godliness but denying its power. Have nothing to do with them. (2 Tim 3:1-5)

For the time will come when men will not put up with sound doctrine. Instead, to suit their own desires, they will gather around them a great number of teachers to say what their itching ears want to hear. They will turn their ears away from the truth and turn aside to myths. (2 Tim 4:3-4)

So I gave them over to their stubborn hearts to follow their own devices. (Psa 81:12)

4 (2:8) **Antichrist**: the end of the antichrist. The Lord will make quick work of the antichrist: this is the point of this verse. The antichrist poses no threat to the Lord Himself. The power of the antichrist is as a drop of water in the Ocean—as non-existent—in comparison to the power of the Lord. Note that the antichrist will be destroyed when Christ returns to earth.

1. The Lord Jesus will slay the antichrist with the breath of His mouth. What is *the breath of Jesus' mouth*? It is the spirit of truth, holiness, and unlimited power. When Jesus speaks, what He says is of God and unstoppable. When He rents the sky to slay the antichrist, there will be no battle, for all the forces of heaven and earth combined would be as non-existent against the Lord God of the universe. Christ will speak the Word, and the antichrist will be slain. It will be like the blowing of a little breath and the dust particle is removed never to return.

Leon Morris says that the emphasis is "the ease with which the Lord will destroy the lawless one, terrible though he will be (*The Epistles of Paul to the Thessalonians.* "Tyndale New Testament Commentaries," p.132).

The Pulpit Commentary says, "The words are to be taken literally as a description of the power and irresistible might of Christ at His coming—that the mere breath of His mouth is sufficient to consume the wicked" (Vol.21, p.25f).

> But with righteousness he will judge the needy, with justice he will give decisions for the poor of the earth. He will strike the earth with the rod of his mouth; with the breath of his lips he will slay the wicked. (Isa 11:4)

2. The Lord of glory will destroy the antichrist with the splendor of His coming. The word "splendor" (epiphaneia) is a very special word. It is a word chosen by the New Testament to refer only to the coming (parousia) of the Lord. It is used only five times in all the New Testament, and in every instance it refers to the Lord's coming into the world. It refers once to His first coming (2 Tim.1:10) and four times to His second coming (1 Tim.6:14; 2 Tim.4:1, 8; Tit.2:13). The whole idea is brightness, radiance, glory, and light. Someone has pointed out that when Jesus Christ returns to earth, there will be such a spectacular display of glory and splendor that the explosion of every star in the universe could not match the sight of the Lord (source unknown). When Christ first appears, there will apparently be the energizing of a laser beam of glory zeroed in on the antichrist, and he shall be immediately destroyed by the radiance of the Lord's glory and light—quicker than we could blink an eye. Simply by showing Himself, the Lord will destroy the antichrist. Note: the word "destroy" does not mean to annihilate, but to make inoperative; to make powerless; to end; to put a stop to his evil work.

5 (2:9) **Antichrist**: the work of antichrist—to carry on the activity of Satan upon the earth. Note that the coming of the antichrist will be after the working of Satan. This means...

- that he will be the very embodiment of Satan himself.
- that he will carry on all the lying power, signs, and wonders of Satan.
- that he will carry out the very activity and work of Satan on earth.

The point to see is that Satan will have complete control over the life of the antichrist. He will be totally surrendered to Satan, and Satan will be energizing him. He will be turning as many as he possibly can away from God. Teeming millions will be listening, watching, and following the antichrist and his government upon the earth. He will demonstrate the power, signs, and wonders...

- to bring peace to earth.
- to adequately grow and distribute the food so that all may have adequate provision.
- to solve the problems of adequate health coverage, full employment, homelessness, energy crunches, and the other problems of this world.

What is wrong with this? Nothing. These are wonderful things and they all need to be solved. But the antichrist will not stop with this. He will claim supernatural power for himself, his state, and its science. Because he has done so much for men, he will insist that religions and gods take a back seat to him and his government. He will institute the seat of imperial worship. He will do all he can to turn men away from God and lead them to worship him and his state (see note—2 Th.2:4).

The problem with these claims is the problem with all the claims of men: they go no further than the grave. Men die. No matter how much peace, food, clothing, shelter, and material possessions we are able to enjoy, it all ends. All the pleasures of this earth end, for we die. We are here only a few years—barring accident and disease—and then we are gone. Therefore, the power, signs, and wonders of the antichrist can benefit a person only for the briefest of times. But not God—not the living and true God. He is interested in saving men eternally—forever and ever. This is the mammoth difference between the lies of Satan and the truth of Jesus Christ.

Note: there seems to be little if any difference between "counterfeit miracles, signs and wonders." They seem to be only for emphatic stress: stressing the fact that Satan is going to be working all he can and in every way he can through the antichrist. There is no question, if a person could solve the problems such as peace, hunger, and unemployment, it would be miraculous. But again, note: if the person began to claim that he was God and to persecute others, then his works would prove to be counterfeit miracles and signs and wonders. Why? Because they are ever so temporary. His works still leave us in the grave. They do not and cannot impart eternal life to us.

And he said to him, "I will give you all their authority and splendor, for it has been given to me, and I can give it to anyone I want to. (Luke 4:6)

And even if our gospel is veiled, it is veiled to those who are perishing. The god of this age has blinded the minds of unbelievers, so that they cannot see the light of the gospel of the glory of Christ, who is the image of God. (2 Cor 4:3-4)

For our struggle is not against flesh and blood, but against the rulers, against the authorities, against the powers of this dark world and against the spiritual forces of evil in the heavenly realms. (Eph 6:12)

The coming of the lawless one will be in accordance with the work of Satan displayed in all kinds of counterfeit miracles, signs and wonders, (2 Th 2:9)

Be self-controlled and alert. Your enemy the devil prowls around like a roaring lion looking for someone to devour. (1 Pet 5:8)

2 THESSALONIANS 2:10-12

	D. The Antichrist's Followers, 2:10-12	11 For this reason God sends them a powerful delusion so that they will believe the lie	3 They are the deceived
1 They are the perishing	10 And in every sort of evil that deceives those who are perishing. They perish because they refused to love the truth and so be saved.	12 And so that all will be condemned who have not believed the truth but have delighted in wickedness.	4 They are the condemned a. Because they do not believe the truth b. Because they take pleasure in wickedness
2 They are the persons who do not love the truth			

DIVISION II

A GLIMPSE INTO THE END TIME, 1:6-2:17

D. The Antichrist's Followers, 2:10-12

(2:10-12) **Introduction**: this passage stands as a strong warning to all unbelievers. It reveals just who the followers of the antichrist will be. It shows who runs the risk of becoming a follower of the antichrist.
1. They are the perishing (v.10).
2. They are the persons who do not believe the truth (v.10).
3. They are the deceived (v.11).
4. They are the condemned (v.12).

1 (2:10) **Antichrist**: the followers of the antichrist are those who are perishing (apollumenois). Note the continuous action: those "who are perishing"; that is, the persons who are in the process of perishing. Even while a follower of the antichrist lives on the earth, he is perishing. He is on the road to being lost. He has turned away from God and is traveling in the opposite direction along the road that leads to perdition. The word "perishing" means to be lost, to be in the process of being destroyed or ruined, corrupted and put to death. The thing to note is this: when a person is on the road to perdition, he has *turned away* from God and is pointed in the *opposite direction*. He is *traveling away* from God. He has deliberately separated himself from God and has severed all ties with God.

Therefore, he cannot see God nor the things of God. His face and eyes are not turned toward the gospel, but toward the world that perishes. The gospel is hid to him because he is perishing, because he is traveling the road of the lost, the road of those who are perishing. He is simply facing in the wrong direction, looking away from the gospel.

> I tell you, no! But unless you repent, you too will all perish. (Luke 13:3)
>
> All who sin apart from the law will also perish apart from the law, and all who sin under the law will be judged by the law. (Rom 2:12)
>
> For the message of the cross is foolishness to those who are perishing, but to us who are being saved it is the power of God. (1 Cor 1:18)
>
> And in every sort of evil that deceives those who are perishing. They perish because they refused to love the truth and so be saved. (2 Th 2:10)
>
> But these men blaspheme in matters they do not understand. They are like brute beasts, creatures of instinct, born only to be caught and destroyed, and like beasts they too will perish. (2 Pet 2:12)
>
> If you ever forget the LORD your God and follow other gods and worship and bow down to them, I testify against you today that you will surely be destroyed. (Deu 8:19)
>
> For the LORD watches over the way of the righteous, but the way of the wicked will perish. (Psa 1:6)

Note why the followers of the antichrist will be perishing: they will be deceived by the antichrist. He will deceive them to live unrighteous lives—lives that are not right before God. And note: he will use all kinds and forms of deceit to secure the loyalty of people:
⇒ He will lead people away from the truth.
⇒ He will mistreat people by lying to them.
⇒ He will lead people to believe false ideas and untruths.
⇒ He will exalt man, government, and science.
⇒ He will cheat people out of the inheritance they could receive.
⇒ He will misguide people and keep them from knowing peace, true inner peace, true assurance, security, love, joy, and confidence—all the qualities that build the very best of lives.

2 (2:10) **Antichrist**: the followers of the antichrist are the persons who do not love the truth. The word "refused" (edechanto) means not to welcome. Note what it is that they do not welcome: the truth, the love of the truth. By truth is meant the truth of the gospel. They do not welcome the truth of the gospel; they do not love the gospel. What a terrible indictment against the followers of the antichrist. They reject the love of God. God has provided...
• the way for them to be saved.
• the way for them to escape death.
• the way for them to live eternally.
• the way for them to live victoriously over the trials and sufferings of this life.

But despite all this, they do not love the truth of the gospel. And the result is terrible: they are not saved. The followers of the antichrist will be those who have not welcomed the love of the truth—those who have rejected the love of the gospel.

> This is the verdict: Light has come into the world, but men loved darkness instead of light because their deeds were evil. (John 3:19)
>
> Whoever believes in the Son has eternal life, but whoever rejects the Son will not see life, for God's wrath remains on him." (John 3:36)
>
> I told you that you would die in your sins; if you do not believe that I am the one I claim to be, you will indeed die in your sins." (John 8:24)

2 THESSALONIANS 2:10-12

> And so that all will be condemned who have not believed the truth but have delighted in wickedness. (2 Th 2:12)
>
> See to it, brothers, that none of you has a sinful, unbelieving heart that turns away from the living God. (Heb 3:12)
>
> Though you already know all this, I want to remind you that the Lord delivered his people out of Egypt, but later destroyed those who did not believe. (Jude 1:5)

3 (2:11) **Antichrist**: the followers of the antichrist are the deceived. There are always two factors involved in deception:

⇒ the deceit of the deceiver.
⇒ the willingness of the person to reject the truth and to believe a lie.

Note verse ten above and both factors are clearly seen. Now note what this verse says: "For this reason God sends them a powerful delusion so that they will believe the lie." Does this mean that God misleads unbelievers? That God deceives people? No! Scripture shouts a thousand "nos!" A person is not deceived...

- apart from his own will.
- against his will.

A person is deceived only because he chooses to disbelieve God and His Word. What Scripture teaches is that God has set certain laws in the universe...

- laws both within man and within nature.
- laws which go into motion and take effect when man acts.

If a person does something, certain things will happen. If a person does something else, then something else will happen. Scripture teaches that unbelief is governed by these laws. For example...

- there is the law of sowing and reaping. If a person sows unbelief and deception, he shall reap unbelief and deception.

> Do not be deceived: God cannot be mocked. A man reaps what he sows. The one who sows to please his sinful nature, from that nature will reap destruction; the one who sows to please the Spirit, from the Spirit will reap eternal life. (Gal 6:7-8)

- there is the law of measure. If a person measures unbelief and deception, unbelief and deception shall be measured back to him.

> For in the same way you judge others, you will be judged, and with the measure you use, it will be measured to you. (Mat 7:2)
>
> Give, and it will be given to you. A good measure, pressed down, shaken together and running over, will be poured into your lap. For with the measure you use, it will be measured to you." (Luke 6:38)

The point is this: it is *because people reject the truth* of the gospel that they will suffer a powerful delusion and believe the lie of the antichrist. Note the words "powerful delusion" (energeian planes). The words mean a working of error. In the end time, people will work error after error, sin after sin, evil after evil. They will become stronger and stronger in their sin, harder and harder. They will become steeped in their rejection of the gospel more and more.

Leon Morris says, "It is the law of life that those who take this step [disbelieve the gospel] go further and further astray into error....Men who reject the truth are bound to end by accepting evil as true. Thereby God uses Satan as the means of punishing them" (The Epistles of Paul to the *Thessalonians*. "Tyndale New Testament Commentaries," p.134).

In the simplest of words, A.T. Robertson says, "[God] gives the wicked over to the evil which they have deliberately chosen (Ro.1:24, 26, 28)" (*Word Pictures in the New Testament*, Vol.4, p.53).

> But if your eyes are bad, your whole body will be full of darkness. If then the light within you is darkness, how great is that darkness! (Mat 6:23)
>
> But the Pharisees went out and plotted how they might kill Jesus. (Mat 12:14)
>
> But their minds were made dull, for to this day the same veil remains when the old covenant is read. It has not been removed, because only in Christ is it taken away. (2 Cor 3:14; cp. 2 Cor 4:4)
>
> They are darkened in their understanding and separated from the life of God because of the ignorance that is in them due to the hardening of their hearts. (Eph 4:18)
>
> But whoever hates his brother is in the darkness and walks around in the darkness; he does not know where he is going, because the darkness has blinded him. (1 John 2:11)
>
> Friend deceives friend, and no one speaks the truth. They have taught their tongues to lie; they weary themselves with sinning. (Jer 9:5)
>
> The heart is deceitful above all things and beyond cure. Who can understand it? (Jer 17:9)
>
> Her rich men are violent; her people are liars and their tongues speak deceitfully. (Micah 6:12)

Thought 1. What a warning to men! The followers of the antichrist will be those who are deceived about the gospel—the persons who do not believe nor love the truth of the gospel. And the great tragedy is that a person cannot reject Jesus Christ and expect things to stay as they are. God loves His Son too much to overlook His being rejected. Jesus Christ has done too much for man for God to bypass a person's unbelief and rejection. When a person has the chance to see the gospel and open his heart, but chooses not to look and closes his heart, that person suffers the consequences. He suffers more and more unbelief and deception; he becomes stronger and stronger in his rejection, believing more and more in the lie. The unbeliever is the prime target of the antichrist: it is the unbelievers who will become his followers.

4 (2:12) **Antichrist**: the followers of the antichrist are the condemned—those who take pleasure in unrighteousness. The word "condemned" (krithosin) means judged, punished. There are two reasons why the followers of the antichrist will be judged.

1. They will not believe the truth of the gospel, the truth of the Lord Jesus Christ. God loves His Son Jesus Christ—loves Him with a perfect love. Therefore, a man cannot expect God to overlook him when he...

- curses Christ
- opposes Christ
- despises Christ
- rejects Christ
- downgrades Christ
- scoffs at Christ
- dishonors Christ
- disobeys Christ
- neglects Christ
- ignores Christ
- demeans Christ
- debases Christ

Jesus Christ is the Sovereign Son of God who has sacrificially died for men. Therefore, if a person rejects the sacrificial death of Christ, he cannot expect God to overlook the dishonor done to His Son. The person can only expect the judgment of God. Remember: antichrist means *anti*, that is, against Christ. Any person who follows any of the antichrists now or the infamous antichrist in the future will be judged, condemned and punished by God. God could do nothing else.

2. They will have pleasure in wickedness. They will be people who live wicked lives and take pleasure in their wickedness. They will be people who love their sins.

   a. They will lust with their eyes and love to feed their imaginations with what they look at.
- ⇒ They will be people who look and lust after pornographic literature.
- ⇒ They will be people who look and lust after those who dress to expose their bodies and attract attention.
- ⇒ They will be people who look and lust after enticing food.
- ⇒ They will be people who look and lust after the possessions of the world.

   b. They will lust with their flesh (sinful nature) and love to feed their flesh with what they lust after.
- ⇒ They will be people who lust and feed their flesh with all forms of immorality.
- ⇒ They will be people who lust and feed their flesh with all kinds of food.
- ⇒ They will be people who lust and feed their flesh with all kinds of possessions, indulging every desire and knowing little about sacrifice in order to meet the needs of the lost in the world.

   c. They will seek the pride of life, seek position, recognition, honor, power, fame, and wealth. They will focus more and more upon self and the power of man and science to give them the utopia of happiness and success.

Note the awful tragedy of all this: man is the total focus—his pleasure, desires, ambitions, image, ego, esteem. God is forgotten altogether. Man loves himself and himself alone. He looks and focuses upon himself and himself alone. God is rejected, denied, forgotten, ignored, and neglected. God is relegated to nothing more than a figment of the imagination of some superstitious people. Therefore the judgment, condemnation, and punishment of God shall fall upon those who love their unrighteousness (sin).

> **The wrath of God is being revealed from heaven against all the godlessness and wickedness of men who suppress the truth by their wickedness,** (Rom 1:18)
>
> **Because of this, God gave them over to shameful lusts. Even their women exchanged natural relations for unnatural ones. In the same way the men also abandoned natural relations with women and were inflamed with lust for one another. Men committed indecent acts with other men, and received in themselves the due penalty for their perversion. Furthermore, since they did not think it worthwhile to retain the knowledge of God, he gave them over to a depraved mind, to do what ought not to be done. They have become filled with every kind of wickedness, evil, greed and depravity. They are full of envy, murder, strife, deceit and malice. They are gossips, slanderers, God-haters, insolent, arrogant and boastful; they invent ways of doing evil; they disobey their parents; they are senseless, faithless, heartless, ruthless. Although they know God's righteous decree that those who do such things deserve death, they not only continue to do these very things but also approve of those who practice them.** (Rom 1:26-32, cp. Ro.2:8)
>
> **But among you there must not be even a hint of sexual immorality, or of any kind of impurity, or of greed, because these are improper for God's holy people. Nor should there be obscenity, foolish talk or coarse joking, which are out of place, but rather thanksgiving. For of this you can be sure: No immoral, impure or greedy person—such a man is an idolater—has any inheritance in the kingdom of Christ and of God. Let no one deceive you with empty words, for because of such things God's wrath comes on those who are disobedient.** (Eph 5:3-6)
>
> **For this reason God sends them a powerful delusion so that they will believe the lie and so that all will be condemned who have not believed the truth but have delighted in wickedness.** (2 Th 2:11-12)
>
> **How much less man, who is vile and corrupt, who drinks up evil like water!** (Job 15:16)
>
> **You love evil rather than good, falsehood rather than speaking the truth. Selah You love every harmful word, O you deceitful tongue! Surely God will bring you down to everlasting ruin: He will snatch you up and tear you from your tent; he will uproot you from the land of the living. Selah** (Psa 52:3-5)
>
> **Who delight in doing wrong and rejoice in the perverseness of evil, but the wicked will be cut off from the land, and the unfaithful will be torn from it.** (Prov 2:14, 22)
>
> **This is what the LORD says about this people: "They greatly love to wander; they do not restrain their feet. So the LORD does not accept them; he will now remember their wickedness and punish them for their sins."** (Jer 14:10)

2 THESSALONIANS 2:13-17

	E. The Salvation of God's Followers, 2:13-17	our Lord Jesus Christ. 15 So then, brothers, stand	4 The duty of salvation: To stand firm & to cling to the Word
1 Believers are saved, not condemned like the followers of antichrist	13 But we ought always to thank God for you, brothers loved by the Lord, because	firm and hold to the teachings we passed on to you, whether by word of mouth or by letter.	

2 The origin of salvation: God has chosen believers
  a. From the beginning
  b. Thru sanct. of the spirit
  c. Thru belief in the gospel
	from the beginning God chose you to be saved through the sanctifying work of the Spirit and through belief in the truth.	16 May our Lord Jesus Christ himself and God our Father, who loved us and by his grace gave us eternal encouragement and good hope,	5 The resources for salvation
			  a. God's love
			  b. Eternal encouragement
			  c. A good hope
			  d. Comfort
			  e. Strength

3 The purpose of salvation: To gain the glory of Christ	14 He called you to this through our gospel, that you might share in the glory of	17 Encourage your hearts and strengthen you in every good deed and word.	

DIVISION II

A GLIMPSE INTO THE END TIME, 1:6-2:17

E. The Salvation of God's Followers, 2:13-17

(2:13-17) **Introduction**: this passage is a contrast between the followers of the antichrist and the followers of Christ. It is a passage that should speak with force to the heart of the believer.
1. Believers are saved, not condemned (v.12) like the followers of antichrist (v.13).
2. The origin of salvation: God has chosen believers (v.13).
3. The purpose of salvation (v.14).
4. The duty of salvation: To stand firm and to cling to the Word (v.15).
5. The resources for salvation (v.16-17).

1 (2:13) **Believers—Salvation**: believers are not condemned like the followers of antichrist; they are saved. Note the word "but." It is a sharp contrast between the followers of the antichrist and the followers of the Lord. The followers of the antichrist are to be condemned, that is, judged, and punished. But the followers of the Lord are *the brothers loved* by *the Lord*. Why? Because they follow Him. They believe Him, all that He claimed: that He is truly the Son of God who has come to earth...
- to die for men.
- to save men from death and judgment.
- to give men eternal life.
- to bring assurance, love, joy, and peace to men as they walk throughout life.

Therefore, believers love the Lord with all their hearts, and they follow Him ever so diligently, doing all they can to please Him. The Lord is bound to count a person who so loves and follows Him as one of His *loved followers*. The Lord is bound to *save* any person who truly believes Him.

The point is this: believers are not to be condemned like the followers of antichrist, but saved. The great truth of salvation is the discussion of this passage.

2 (2:13) **Salvation—Chosen—God, Election**: the origin of salvation is God. "From the beginning God chose you to be saved." This is a most wonderful truth. God has *chosen* believers before the world was ever created, chosen them to salvation. God wants us to be with Him. God does not want us to be judged and condemned and separated from Him. God wants us to live with Him forever and ever.

Note: the Greek word for "chose" (heilato) is strong. It is an unusual word to use here. Leon Morris points out that this is the only time it is used in the New Testament (*The Epistles of Paul to the Thessalonians*. "Tyndale New Testament Commentaries," p.136). The word's uniqueness is this: it is one of the words that is used when God chose Israel (in the Greek Old Testament):

> **And the LORD has declared this day that you are his people, his treasured possession as he promised, and that you are to keep all his commands. (Deu 26:18)**
>
> **For you are a people holy to the LORD your God. The LORD your God has chosen you out of all the peoples on the face of the earth to be his people, his treasured possession. The LORD did not set his affection on you and choose you because you were more numerous than other peoples, for you were the fewest of all peoples. (Deu 7:6-7)**
>
> **Yet the LORD set his affection on your forefathers and loved them, and he chose you, their descendants, above all the nations, as it is today. (Deu 10:15)**

The point is this: God has chosen believers in the very same sense in which He chose Israel. Believers are as chosen by God as Israel was. God loves us from the depths of His heart, and He wants us to be secure in the fact that He has *chosen us*. Our salvation is secure because it is based upon His having chosen us.

1. God has chosen believers to be saved "*from the beginning*," that is, before the foundation of the world. This is a most glorious truth: God saw us *as saved* before we were ever born. He chose us to be saved before He ever created the world. Just think of the security in this. If God saw us as *saved* before the earth was made—if God saw us *saved* before we were ever born, then there is no way we can be lost and removed from His love and care. This is what Jesus meant when He said:

> **I give them eternal life, and they shall never perish; no one can snatch them out of my hand. My Father, who has given them to me, is greater than all; no one can**

89

snatch them out of my Father's hand. (John 10:28-29)

What security! Having been chosen by God to salvation—chosen from the beginning, from eternity past—before the earth was ever established. There is no judgment or condemnation for the believer; the believer will not be judged and condemned with the followers of the antichrist nor with any other unbelievers.

For he chose us in him before the creation of the world to be holy and blameless in his sight. In love (Eph 1:4)

Note a most crucial point: in the Bible the truth of God's choice (election and predestination) is not so much a statement of theology or philosophy—it is more a message that speaks to the spiritual experience of the believer. If the pure logic of philosophy and theology is applied, then God's choice says that God chooses some for heaven and others for a terrible hell. But this is simply not what God means in the passages dealing with *His choice*, and this fact needs to be given close attention by all ministers. What God wants believers to do is to take heart, for He has assured their salvation and given them the greatest security imaginable. This is what He means by His having *chosen* us to be saved. (See notes—Jn.6:44-46; Ro.8:29 for more discussion.) The next two points show how salvation takes place, both God's part and man's part.

2. God has chosen believers "*through the sanctifying work of the Spirit.*" The word "sanctifying" means to set apart or be separated unto God. We must always remember this fact (too many forget it and thereby become inconsistent in their theology and teaching of the Word). A man is a dead spirit; therefore, he can do nothing spiritually just as a dead body can do nothing physically. The natural man prefers self and sin; therefore, if a man with a dead spirit is to come to Christ, he has to be acted upon and drawn by God. Both God's Spirit and man have a part in salvation. The part of God's Spirit is to move upon the heart of a man and stir him to set apart his life unto God. How does the Spirit of God do this?

   a. The Holy Spirit quickens or makes alive the gospel to a man's mind so that he *sees it as never before*. He sees, understands, grasps as never before that "the Father...has sent" Christ to feed and nourish man (to save and to give him life).

In reply Jesus declared, "I tell you the truth, no one can see the kingdom of God unless he is born again." (John 3:3)

For just as the Father raises the dead [spiritually dead] and gives them life, even so the Son gives life to whom he is pleased to give it. (John 5:21)

The Spirit gives life; the flesh counts for nothing. The words I have spoken to you are spirit and they are life. (John 6:63)

And if the Spirit of him who raised Jesus from the dead is living in you, he who raised Christ from the dead will also give life to your mortal bodies through his Spirit, who lives in you. (Rom 8:11)

As for you, you were dead in your transgressions and sins, (Eph 2:1)

But because of his great love for us, God, who is rich in mercy, made us alive with Christ even when we were dead in transgressions—it is by grace you have been saved. (Eph 2:4-5)

You were taught, with regard to your former way of life, to put off your old self, which is being corrupted by its deceitful desires; to be made new in the attitude of your minds; (Eph 4:22-23)

And have put on the new self, which is being renewed in knowledge in the image of its Creator. (Col 3:10)

So I prophesied as he commanded me, and breath entered them; they came to life and stood up on their feet—a vast army. (Ezek 37:10)

   b. The Holy Spirit convicts a man of sin, of righteousness and of judgment, that is, of his need to be fed and nourished (saved and given life).

When he [the Holy Spirit] comes, he will convict the world of guilt in regard to sin and righteousness and judgment: (John 16:8)

   c. The Holy Spirit attracts men to the cross of Christ through its glorious provisions.

"No one can come to me unless the Father who sent me draws him, and I will raise him up at the last day. (John 6:44)

But I, when I am lifted up from the earth, will draw all men to myself." He said this to show the kind of death he was going to die. (John 12:32-33)

For the message of the cross is foolishness to those who are perishing, but to us who are being saved it is the power of God. (1 Cor 1:18)

May I never boast except in the cross of our Lord Jesus Christ, through which the world has been crucified to me, and I to the world. (Gal 6:14)

And in this one body to reconcile both of them to God through the cross, by which he put to death their hostility. (Eph 2:16)

And through him to reconcile to himself all things, whether things on earth or things in heaven, by making peace through his blood, shed on the cross. (Col 1:20)

   d. The Holy Spirit stirs a man to respond by coming to Christ.

"Come to me, all you who are weary and burdened, and I will give you rest. (Mat 11:28)

On the last and greatest day of the Feast, Jesus stood and said in a loud voice, "If anyone is thirsty, let him come to me and drink. (John 7:37)

The Spirit and the bride say, "Come!" And let him who hears say, "Come!" Whoever is thirsty, let him come; and whoever wishes, let him take the free gift of the water of life. (Rev 22:17)

Whether you turn to the right or to the left, your ears will hear a voice behind you,

saying, "This is the way; walk in it." (Isa 30:21)

"Come, all you who are thirsty, come to the waters; and you who have no money, come, buy and eat! Come, buy wine and milk without money and without cost. Why spend money on what is not bread, and your labor on what does not satisfy? Listen, listen to me, and eat what is good, and your soul will delight in the richest of fare. Give ear and come to me; hear me, that your soul may live. I will make an everlasting covenant with you, my faithful love promised to David. (Isa 55:1-3)

3. God has chosen believers through "belief in the truth," that is, through believing the gospel of the Lord Jesus Christ.
⇒ The Lord Jesus Christ has died for believers: taken their sins upon Himself and suffered the penalty, judgment, condemnation, and punishment of their sins. He has sacrificed and substituted His life for them.
⇒ The Lord Jesus Christ has risen from the dead for believers: conquered death and ascended into heaven for them.

The believers of the world believe the gospel with all their hearts: believe they will never have to die because Jesus Christ died for them—believe they shall ascend into heaven to live eternally with the Father and His Son, the Lord Jesus Christ. They believe and have entrusted their lives to this glorious truth.

The point is this: when a person really believes the truth of the gospel, God saves him. This is man's part in salvation. No person has ever been saved who did not believe the truth of the gospel. And no person who has rejected the gospel is lost because God has not chosen him. The person is lost because he rejected Christ. God will choose any person who will accept Christ. This is His Word; it is the promise of His Word. God will not force us to believe nor will He keep us from believing. The choice is every person's choice. No person is forced to receive or to reject Christ. Every person is responsible for his own decision.

"For God so loved the world that he gave his one and only Son, that whoever believes in him shall not perish but have eternal life. For God did not send his Son into the world to condemn the world, but to save the world through him. Whoever believes in him is not condemned, but whoever does not believe stands condemned already because he has not believed in the name of God's one and only Son. (John 3:16-18)

"I tell you the truth, whoever hears my word and believes him who sent me has eternal life and will not be condemned; he has crossed over from death to life. (John 5:24)

Then they asked him, "What must we do to do the works God requires?" Jesus answered, "The work of God is this: to believe in the one he has sent." (John 6:28-29)

Jesus said to her, "I am the resurrection and the life. He who believes in me will live, even though he dies; (John 11:25)

I have come into the world as a light, so that no one who believes in me should stay in darkness. (John 12:46)

But these are written that you may believe that Jesus is the Christ, the Son of God, and that by believing you may have life in his name. (John 20:31)

That if you confess with your mouth, "Jesus is Lord," and believe in your heart that God raised him from the dead, you will be saved. For it is with your heart that you believe and are justified, and it is with your mouth that you confess and are saved. (Rom 10:9-10)

And this is his command: to believe in the name of his Son, Jesus Christ, and to love one another as he commanded us. (1 John 3:23)

3 (2:14) **Salvation—Glory**: the purpose of salvation is to gain the glory of Christ. Remember: the Thessalonian believers were suffering severe persecution. Think what this verse meant to them. They were bound for glory—to obtain and share in the glory of the Lord Jesus Christ Himself. The word "glory" (doxes) means to possess perfect light and to be full of perfect light; to dwell in the perfect light, brilliance, splendor, brightness, luster, and magnificence of God. (See DEEPER STUDY # 1, *Glory*—Jn.17:22 for more discussion.)
⇒ The believer will be glorified with Christ as an *heir of God*.

The Spirit himself testifies with our spirit that we are God's children. Now if we are children, then we are heirs—heirs of God and co-heirs with Christ, if indeed we share in his sufferings in order that we may also share in his glory. (Rom 8:16-17)

⇒ The believer will be glorified by being given a body just like the body of Christ.

Who, by the power that enables him to bring everything under his control, will transform our lowly bodies so that they will be like his glorious body. (Phil 3:21)

⇒ The believer will be glorified with Christ by appearing in the glory of heaven.

When Christ, who is your life, appears, then you also will appear with him in glory. (Col 3:4)

⇒ The believer will be glorified with Christ by receiving a nature of glory, a glorious nature just like the nature of Christ.

I consider that our present sufferings are not worth comparing with the glory that will be revealed in us. (Rom 8:18)

⇒ The believer will be glorified with Christ by receiving an eternal glory.

> For our light and momentary troubles are achieving for us an eternal glory that far outweighs them all. (2 Cor 4:17)

⇒ The believer will be glorified with Christ by receiving a salvation that involves eternal glory.

> Therefore I endure everything for the sake of the elect, that they too may obtain the salvation that is in Christ Jesus, with eternal glory. (2 Tim 2:10)

⇒ The believer will be glorified with Christ by sharing in the glory to be revealed.

> To the elders among you, I appeal as a fellow elder, a witness of Christ's sufferings and one who also will share in the glory to be revealed: (1 Pet 5:1)

⇒ The believer will be glorified with Christ by receiving the light of the glory of God, and they will reign with Him for ever and ever.

> There will be no more night. They will not need the light of a lamp or the light of the sun, for the Lord God will give them light. And they will reign for ever and ever. (Rev 22:5)

4 (2:15) **Salvation**: the duty of salvation is to stand firm and to cling to the Word of God. Note the word "teachings" (paradoseis). It means all the Word of God whether it is taught or written. Leon Morris quotes J.B. Lightfoot: "The prominent idea of *paradosis* [tradition] or teachings...is that of an authority external to the teacher himself." Leon Morris himself says:

> *"This is another way of putting the truth...that the gospel is not of human origin, and the preacher is not at liberty to substitute his own thoughts for that which he has received"* (The Epistles of Paul to the Thessalonians. "Tyndale New Testament Commentaries," p.138).

We are to stand firm and cling to the Word of God. We are not to buckle under to the world and its enticements. We are not to cave in, as the followers of the antichrist will do. We are to stand firm and cling to the Word of God no matter the inducement and the opposition.

> "As the Father has loved me, so have I loved you. Now remain in my love. (John 15:9)

> Therefore, my dear brothers, stand firm. Let nothing move you. Always give yourselves fully to the work of the Lord, because you know that your labor in the Lord is not in vain. (1 Cor 15:58)

> Whatever happens, conduct yourselves in a manner worthy of the gospel of Christ. Then, whether I come and see you or only hear about you in my absence, I will know that you stand firm in one spirit, contending as one man for the faith of the gospel (Phil 1:27)

> Be self-controlled and alert. Your enemy the devil prowls around like a roaring lion looking for someone to devour. Resist him, standing firm in the faith, because you know that your brothers throughout the world are undergoing the same kind of sufferings. (1 Pet 5:8-9)

> Therefore, dear friends, since you already know this, be on your guard so that you may not be carried away by the error of lawless men and fall from your secure position. (2 Pet 3:17)

> But you are to hold fast to the LORD your God, as you have until now. (Josh 23:8)

5 (2:16-17) **Salvation**: the resources of salvation are fivefold.

1. The person who is saved receives the love of God and of Christ (see note and DEEPER STUDY # 1, Love—1 Th.3:12 for discussion).

2. The person who is saved receives eternal encouragement (paraklesin aionian). The phrase means eternal encouragement, comfort, and strength. It is a consolation and strength that cannot be shaken by anything—no matter what it is—either now or in eternity.

3. The person who is saved receives good hope. What greater hope could the believer have than to live in glory with the Lord God forever and ever (see note, *Glory*—2 Th.2:14 for discussion)? Note: our hope is given us through the grace of God and through His grace alone.

> In my Father's house are many rooms; if it were not so, I would have told you. I am going there to prepare a place for you. And if I go and prepare a place for you, I will come back and take you to be with me that you also may be where I am. (John 14:2-3)

> For the Lord himself will come down from heaven, with a loud command, with the voice of the archangel and with the trumpet call of God, and the dead in Christ will rise first. After that, we who are still alive and are left will be caught up together with them in the clouds to meet the Lord in the air. And so we will be with the Lord forever. Therefore encourage each other with these words. (1 Th 4:16-18)

4. The person who is saved receives comfort or "encouragement" (parakalesai). The word means exhortation, encouragement, admonition, comfort. Note that God and Christ are the Ones who can comfort, exhort, and encourage the believer to live like they should. When the believer comes to Christ for strength, Christ will comfort and encourage him.

5. The person who is saved is strengthened in every good word and work. The word "strengthen" (sterixai) means to establish, secure, make stable, set fast, and make firm. The one thing men long for is to be secure, strong, and firmly established in life. God is able to fulfill this longing. God is able to establish and strengthen man and to give him a strong life.

2 THESSALONIANS 3:1-5

	CHAPTER 3 **III. FINAL WORDS, 3:1-18** **A. Prayer & The Lord's Faithfulness, 3:1-5**	delivered from wicked and evil men, for not everyone has faith. 3 But the Lord is faithful, and he will strengthen and protect you from the evil one.	delivered from evil men c. Pray—because not everyone has faith **2 The Lord's faithfulness to the believer** a. God strengthens & keeps him from evil
1 The request for prayer a. Pray that the Word will spread rapidly b. Pray that believers be	Finally, brothers, pray for us that the message of the Lord may spread rapidly and be honored, just as it was with you. 2 And pray that we may be	4 We have confidence in the Lord that you are doing and will continue to do the things we command. 5 May the Lord direct your hearts into God's love and Christ's perseverance.	b. God motivates him to keep the commandments c. God stirs him into God's love d. God stirs him to persevere just as Christ persevered

DIVISION III

FINAL WORDS, 3:1-18

A. Prayer and The Lord's Faithfulness, 3:1-5

(3:1-5) **Introduction**: the main section of the letter of Second Thessalonians has been completed. This passage begins the final words ever written to the church by Paul so far as we know. In the final words, two subjects jump to the forefront immediately: prayer and the Lord's faithfulness.

1. The request for prayer (v.1-2).
2. The Lord's faithfulness to the believer (v.3-5).

1 (3:1-2) **Prayer**: there was the request for prayer. The believers at Thessalonica were suffering severe persecution and all kinds of trouble. This was one of the reasons Paul was writing to the church: to comfort and encourage them to continue on for Christ. But remember: Paul was in Corinth and he too was suffering all kinds of trouble, including persecution. He needed the presence and power of the Lord as much as anyone. As John Walvoord says:

> "Paul, too, was having his difficulties. The task committed to Paul was a very lonely one: to go from place to place, frequently coming into a strange city where not one person would welcome him. He was not entertained in the best hotel, nor was there any honorarium for him in recognition of his services. He had to find his own way, arrange for his public meetings, and somehow try to bear a testimony for Christ. Apart from fellowship with the Lord, it was a very difficult and solitary task and one in which there were many discouragements" (*The Thessalonian Epistles*, p.146).

The specific trouble at Corinth was persecution. The Jewish religionists attacked Paul and dragged him before the civil authorities. However, the case was dismissed because it was a religious matter. Paul was allowed to continue his preaching mission, but apparently the Jewish religionists continued their opposition, stirring up whatever trouble they could (cp. Acts 18:1-18 for the full story).

The point is this: Paul needed prayer; he needed believers everywhere praying for him. But note what it was he requested. He did not ask prayer...

- for comfort
- for personal needs
- for God to take him away from Corinth and to open up a new ministry elsewhere

Paul's focus was not selfish, not upon himself—not at all. His whole focus was upon the spread and success of the gospel. He wanted prayer for two things.

1. There was the need for the Word to have *spread rapidly and be honored*. The Word of God is often hindered, hampered, and stymied. Too often, it has no power or influence among a people. Why?

⇒ opposition
⇒ unprepared hearts
⇒ sleepy eyed listeners
⇒ daydreaming minds
⇒ unprepared and carnal preachers and teachers

The list could go on and on, but the great need of the hour is for the Word of God to spread rapidly and be honored in the pulpits and pews, classrooms and homes, streets and places of this nation and world.

"Spread rapidly" means to run. It is a picture of an Olympian athlete running in a race, the picture of the Word of God spreading all over because it is...

- focused
- active
- strong
- urgent
- unflinching
- vigorous
- powerful

If the Word of God had spread rapidly, it would be honored; that is, souls would be saved and lives changed. People would be freed...

- from sin and its enslavement
- from guilty consciences
- from immoral and evil behavior
- from unjust treatment
- from ignorance
- from worldliness

People would no longer experience emptiness, loneliness, purposelessness, or lostness. They would be set free to know the Lord and to commit their lives to reaching and meeting the needs of a world full of desperate people. Note: this is exactly what had happened to the Thessalonian believers. The Word of God had spread rapidly among the Thessalonians; therefore, many had been converted to the Lord (cp. 1 Th.1:5; 2:1, 13).

> **When the Gentiles heard this, they were glad and honored the word of the Lord; and all who were appointed for eternal life believed. (Acts 13:48)**
>
> **Because our gospel came to you not simply with words, but also with power,**

with the Holy Spirit and with deep conviction. You know how we lived among you for your sake. (1 Th 1:5)

And we also thank God continually because, when you received the word of God, which you heard from us, you accepted it not as the word of men, but as it actually is, the word of God, which is at work in you who believe. (1 Th 2:13)

The law of the LORD is perfect, reviving the soul. The statutes of the LORD are trustworthy, making wise the simple. The precepts of the LORD are right, giving joy to the heart. The commands of the LORD are radiant, giving light to the eyes. The fear of the LORD is pure, enduring forever. The ordinances of the LORD are sure and altogether righteous. They are more precious than gold, than much pure gold; they are sweeter than honey, than honey from the comb. By them is your servant warned; in keeping them there is great reward. (Psa 19:7-11)

He sends his command to the earth; his word runs swiftly. (Psa 147:15)

Thought 1. Believers should always be praying for the ministers and teachers of the gospel—that the Word of God might have spread rapidly as it is preached and taught. And they should pray every day for every preacher and teacher they know. Think for a moment: What would happen if the believers of a single church prayed often every day for their minister and teachers? One thing is known: God could not sit still, for He would know that those believers were as sincere and genuine as they could be. He would know that they desperately wanted to reach their community for Christ.

2. There was the need for believers to be delivered from unreasonable and wicked men. Again, remember the situation of Paul, how he was being attacked in Corinth. He knew what it was like to be opposed by wicked people who would not listen to reason.

Ministers, teachers, and believers alike are sometimes opposed and attacked by unreasonable and wicked people. Think how unreasonable the attacks are. Why would people want to oppose and attack a person who preaches and teaches...

- love
- joy
- peace
- morality
- discipline
- brotherhood
- salvation
- eternal life

Why would people want to attack a person who preaches and teaches that God loves the world—that He has provided the way for man to escape death and to live forever and that the *fountain of youth* has been revealed? A reasonable and honest person would never oppose or attack a person who was preaching and teaching this message. But note: not all people are reasonable and good. As Scripture says, all persons do not have faith (v.2). In fact, the world is full of unreasonable and evil persons, persons who want to live like they want without any interference from God. They deny and ignore God—deny and ignore the evidence within the world and within their hearts and thoughts that God exists and that His love and judgments are real. Therefore, they oppose anything that reminds them of eternity, of a coming day of judgment. They want nothing to do with a message that puts restrictions upon their behavior, especially a message that demands so much love—a love that demands that we give all we are and have to meet the needs of the dying and poor masses of the world.

Believers, ministers and laymen alike, need to be delivered from such unreasonable and evil persons. When people lack reason and morality, goodness and honesty, conscience and decency, they are dangerous. They can hinder both the messenger and the message of the gospel. Therefore, believers need to be constantly praying for God to deliver His people from unreasonable and evil persons.

I urge you, brothers, by our Lord Jesus Christ and by the love of the Spirit, to join me in my struggle by praying to God for me. Pray that I may be rescued from the unbelievers in Judea and that my service in Jerusalem may be acceptable to the saints there, (Rom 15:30-31)

And pray in the Spirit on all occasions with all kinds of prayers and requests. With this in mind, be alert and always keep on praying for all the saints. Pray also for me, that whenever I open my mouth, words may be given me so that I will fearlessly make known the mystery of the gospel, for which I am an ambassador in chains. Pray that I may declare it fearlessly, as I should. (Eph 6:18-20)

Brothers, pray for us. (1 Th 5:25)

If this is so, then the Lord knows how to rescue godly men from trials and to hold the unrighteous for the day of judgment, while continuing their punishment. (2 Pet 2:9)

2 (3:3-5) **Jesus Christ, Faithfulness of:** there is the faithfulness of the Lord to the believer. The Lord Jesus Christ is faithful. Believers may fail us: when we stand in the greatest need, when people oppose and persecute us, when the most terrible trials confront us—believers may fail...

- to pray
- to encourage
- to support
- to speak kindly
- to help

But not the Lord. The Lord God is faithful. He will do four things for the believer.

1. The Lord will strengthen the believer and keep him from evil.

⇒ The word "strengthen" (sterixei) means to establish, secure, make stable or firm, and set fast.

⇒ The word "protect" (phulaxei) means to guard, keep.

⇒ The word "evil" can refer both to evil behavior and to the evil one, that is, Satan.

The point is this: the Lord is faithful, even if we fail to help one another. God will strengthen and guard us against Satan and his evil followers. In fact, the Lord will strengthen and guard us against all evil no matter what it is. Even if the evil seems to be conquering us, it will not—not in the final analysis.

⇒ God will deliver us by working all things out for good.

And we know that in all things God works for the good of those who love him,

who have been called according to his purpose. (Rom 8:28)

⇒ God will deliver us by overcoming our failures and completing His work of salvation in us.

Being confident of this, that he who began a good work in you will carry it on to completion until the day of Christ Jesus. (Phil 1:6)

That is why I am suffering as I am. Yet I am not ashamed, because I know whom I have believed, and am convinced that he is able to guard what I have entrusted to him for that day. (2 Tim 1:12)

To him who is able to keep you from falling and to present you before his glorious presence without fault and with great joy—to the only God our Savior be glory, majesty, power and authority, through Jesus Christ our Lord, before all ages, now and forevermore! Amen. (Jude 1:24-25)

⇒ God will deliver us by delivering us from death.

The Lord will rescue me from every evil attack and will bring me safely to his heavenly kingdom. To him be glory for ever and ever. Amen. (2 Tim 4:18)

2. The Lord will motivate the believer to keep His commandments. The Lord actually works within and energizes the believer to will and do God's pleasure, that is, to keep His commandments. When we *sense a stirring*, some energy being aroused within our hearts to do good, that is the Spirit of God working within us. The Lord will never leave the believer, not completely; so long as the believer is on earth, the Lord will continue to work within him, to stir and energize him to keep God's commandments. This is the reason Paul had confidence in the Thessalonian believers, that they would keep the commandments of the Word that had been taught them.

Thought 1. This is a critical fact: a person can tell if he is a true believer or not by the working of the Lord within his heart. If a person keeps the commandments of God, then it is evidence that the Lord is working within his heart; however, if a person is not keeping the commandments of God, then it is evidence that the Lord does not live within his heart and is not working within him.

We know that we have come to know him if we obey his commands. (1 John 2:3)

Dear children, let us not love with words or tongue but with actions and in truth. This then is how we know that we belong to the truth, and how we set our hearts at rest in his presence (1 John 3:18-19)

We know that we live in him and he in us, because he has given us of his Spirit. (1 John 4:13)

Anyone who believes in the Son of God has this testimony in his heart. Anyone who does not believe God has made him out to be a liar, because he has not believed the testimony God has given about his Son. (1 John 5:10)

3. The Lord directs the believer's heart into the love of God. This means both God's love for us and our love for God. The word "direct" (kateuthunai) means to make straight or to be straight. It means to remove obstacles out of the way or to open up. The Lord Jesus Christ takes the genuine believer and opens up his heart; He straightens, directs, and focuses the believer's heart upon the love of God. The result is that the believer learns to love God more and more. His attention and focus becomes more and more set upon God's love. Therefore, when trials, trouble, temptation, and evil attack the believer, he is able to stand in the love of God and overcome the attack.

"For God so loved the world that he gave his one and only Son, that whoever believes in him shall not perish but have eternal life. (John 3:16)

Keep yourselves in God's love as you wait for the mercy of our Lord Jesus Christ to bring you to eternal life. (Jude 1:21)

Love the LORD your God with all your heart and with all your soul and with all your strength. (Deu 6:5)

And now, O Israel, what does the LORD your God ask of you but to fear the LORD your God, to walk in all his ways, to love him, to serve the LORD your God with all your heart and with all your soul, (Deu 10:12)

Love the LORD, all his saints! The LORD preserves the faithful, but the proud he pays back in full. (Psa 31:23)

4. The Lord also directs the believer to endure just as Christ persevered. To endure in what? In patiently waiting for Christ's return. The Lord Jesus Christ stirs the genuine believer to keep his eyes upon His return. Therefore, when evil strikes, the believer endures and perseveres—stands in strength and patience—keeping his eyes and heart focused upon the glorious hope of Christ, the hope of conquering death and of living forever and ever in perfection with God, the hope of ruling and reigning throughout the whole universe for Christ.

The faith and love that spring from the hope that is stored up for you in heaven and that you have already heard about in the word of truth, the gospel (Col 1:5)

May God himself, the God of peace, sanctify you through and through. May your whole spirit, soul and body be kept blameless at the coming of our Lord Jesus Christ. (1 Th 5:23)

To keep this command without spot or blame until the appearing of our Lord Jesus Christ, (1 Tim 6:14)

It teaches us to say "No" to ungodliness and worldly passions, and to live self-controlled, upright and godly lives in this present age, while we wait for the blessed hope—the glorious appearing of our great God and Savior, Jesus Christ, (Titus 2:12-13)

Praise be to the God and Father of our Lord Jesus Christ! In his great mercy he has given us new birth into a living hope through the resurrection of Jesus Christ from the dead, (1 Pet 1:3)

And now, dear children, continue in him, so that when he appears we may be confident and unashamed before him at his coming. (1 John 2:28)

2 THESSALONIANS 3:6-18

	B. Work & Employment, 3:6-18	11 We hear that some among you are idle. They are not busy; they are busybodies.	d. Because idlers tend to be busybodies
1 Keep away from every brother who lives in idleness—who does not work	6 In the name of the Lord Jesus Christ, we command you, brothers, to keep away from every brother who is idle and does not live according to the teaching you received from us.	12 Such people we command and urge in the Lord Jesus Christ to settle down and earn the bread they eat.	2 Work—every one of you a. Earn your own living—settle down b. Do not get tired of doing good
a. Because he disobeys the instructions of God		13 And as for you, brothers, never tire of doing what is right.	
b. Because you have the example of committed workers	7 For you yourselves know how you ought to follow our example. We were not idle when we were with you,	14 If anyone does not obey our instruction in this letter, take special note of him. Do not associate with him, in order that he may feel ashamed.	3 Discipline the idler: Disassociate from him a. That he may feel ashamed
1) Paul worked night & day	8 Nor did we eat anyone's food without paying for it. On the contrary, we worked night and day, laboring and toiling so that we would not be a burden to any of you.	15 Yet do not regard him as an enemy, but warn him as a brother.	b. Warn him as a brother
2) Paul had the ministerial right to be supported, but he did not exercise it	9 We did this, not because we do not have the right to such help, but in order to make ourselves a model for you to follow.	16 Now may the Lord of peace himself give you peace at all times and in every way. The Lord be with all of you. 17 I, Paul, write this greeting in my own hand, which is the distinguishing mark in all my letters. This is how I write.	4 The conclusion: The believer receives three possessions in Christ a. A great peace b. A special & personal fellowship
c. Because you must work or lose your right to eat	10 For even when we were with you, we gave you this rule: "If a man will not work, he shall not eat."	18 The grace of our Lord Jesus Christ be with you all.	c. The grace & strength of Jesus Christ

DIVISION III

FINAL WORDS, 3:1-18

B. Work and Employment, 3:6-18

(3:6-18) Introduction: this passage concludes the letter of Second Thessalonians. It deals with a very significant subject for our day and time: work and employment. The workplace is full of disorderly workers, workers who slack off and do as little as possible; workers who are eyewatchers, who work only when they see the boss coming. In addition to these, there are many in our society who could be working, but they choose not to work because of laziness and slothfulness; and they have found a way to sponge off the government, social services, churches, and neighbors. The result is that a tragic dullness and a spirit of *give me* has pervaded the workplace and nation. As stated, this is the subject of this passage, a much needed subject.

1. Keep away from every brother who is idle—who does not work (v.6-11).
2. Work—every one of you (v.12-13).
3. Discipline the idler, disassociate from him (v.14-15).
4. The conclusion: the believer receives three possessions in Christ (v.16-18).

1 (3:6-11) **Employee—Employment—Labor—Work**: keep away from every brother who lives in idleness, that is, who does not work. Note: this is a very strong command. It has the force of a military command: it is given "in the name of the Lord Jesus Christ," the supreme commander. There is to be no discussion about the matter. What is being said is to be obeyed.

"Keep away from every brother who is idle" (v.6). Who are the idle? Those who do not work. A strange thing had happened in the Thessalonian church. Some of the believers had become excited over the return of the Lord and the promise of being with Him forever in the new heavens and earth. They became so excited that they began to sacrifice all they could to meet the needs of people. But some went too far. They ignored the Lord's words that only God knew when He would be returning, and they began to project dates and declare that His return was about to take place. Therefore, some quit their jobs in order to have more time to minister, and in an act of sacrificial commitment they gave away *all they had*. The result was catastrophic. They were now having to sponge off the other believers in order to survive. Their action had been most unwise—unwise because believers are to *live life* as it should be lived so long as they are upon earth. Believers are to set the example as to how life is to be lived, and work is certainly one of the duties of men. Therefore, of all people believers are to set an example in work. They are to be the very best workmen possible. Quitting work and not working is idle behavior; it is totally unacceptable for a true believer. It is so unacceptable that believers are commanded to keep away from non-workers.

⇒ What does the Lord mean by "keep away" (stellesthai)? The word means to stay away from the idle worker; to have no fellowship with him. His behavior is not to be indulged or condoned. We are not to put our stamp of approval upon him, nor are we to run the risk of becoming identified with him.

⇒ Who are the idle? They are the slothful, the lazy. They are the persons who refuse to work or who shirk their work or are slack in their work.

There are four reasons why we are to withdraw from the idle worker.

1. The idle worker disobeys the instructions of God (v.6). Note the word "teaching" (paradosin). It means all

the Word of God, whether taught or written (2 Th.2:15). Paul says that he had taught the believers the commandments of God that deal with work; therefore, they are without excuse. They know better than to sit around idle. If they continue to be idle, slothful, and lazy, the other believers are to keep away from them. They are deliberately disobeying the instructions of God.

> "Who then is the faithful and wise servant, whom the master has put in charge of the servants in his household to give them their food at the proper time? It will be good for that servant whose master finds him doing so when he returns. (Mat 24:45-46)
>
> Never be lacking in zeal, but keep your spiritual fervor, serving the Lord. (Rom 12:11)
>
> He who has been stealing must steal no longer, but must work, doing something useful with his own hands, that he may have something to share with those in need. (Eph 4:28)
>
> Slaves, [employees] obey your earthly masters with respect and fear, and with sincerity of heart, just as you would obey Christ. (Eph 6:5)
>
> Slaves, [employees] obey your earthly masters in everything; and do it, not only when their eye is on you and to win their favor, but with sincerity of heart and reverence for the Lord. (Col 3:22)
>
> Make it your ambition to lead a quiet life, to mind your own business and to work with your hands, just as we told you, (1 Th 4:11)
>
> Such people we command and urge in the Lord Jesus Christ to settle down and earn the bread they eat. (2 Th 3:12)
>
> Teach slaves to be subject to their masters in everything, to try to please them, not to talk back to them, (Titus 2:9)
>
> We do not want you to become lazy, but to imitate those who through faith and patience inherit what has been promised. (Heb 6:12)
>
> Slaves, [employees] submit yourselves to your masters with all respect, not only to those who are good and considerate, but also to those who are harsh. (1 Pet 2:18)
>
> The LORD God took the man and put him in the Garden of Eden to work it and take care of it. (Gen 2:15)
>
> By the sweat of your brow you will eat your food until you return to the ground, since from it you were taken; for dust you are and to dust you will return." (Gen 3:19)
>
> Whatever your hand finds to do, do it with all your might, for in the grave, where you are going, there is neither working nor planning nor knowledge nor wisdom. (Eccl 9:10)

2. The idle worker has the example of committed workers. The believers of Thessalonica had the example of Paul; we have the example of committed workers in our day. Paul worked *day and night* so that he would not owe any man anything (v.7-8). As a minister of the gospel, he had the right to be supported by believers so that he could be free to minister more. But he refused to exercise that right. Why? So that he could set a dynamic example of a diligent worker for the believers (v.9). Note: Paul says "follow our example" in being a diligent worker:

⇒ You "yourselves know how you ought to follow our example" (v.7).
⇒ We have set an example "for you to follow" (v.9).

Thought 1. There is absolutely no excuse for a Christian to be idle, slothful, or lazy at his work. Paul set a dynamic example for us, and there are examples of other dynamic Christian workers who surround us. And if by chance there are no examples around us, then we should be following the example of Christ (the carpenter) and Paul (the tentmaker). We should be setting an example for other believers in diligent work.

> After this, Paul left Athens and went to Corinth. There he met a Jew named Aquila, a native of Pontus, who had recently come from Italy with his wife Priscilla, because Claudius had ordered all the Jews to leave Rome. Paul went to see them, and because he was a tentmaker as they were, he stayed and worked with them. (Acts 18:1-3)
>
> You yourselves know that these hands of mine have supplied my own needs and the needs of my companions. In everything I did, I showed you that by this kind of hard work we must help the weak, remembering the words the Lord Jesus himself said: 'It is more blessed to give than to receive.'" (Acts 20:34-35)
>
> And when I was with you and needed something, I was not a burden to anyone, for the brothers who came from Macedonia supplied what I needed. I have kept myself from being a burden to you in any way, and will continue to do so. (2 Cor 11:9)
>
> Surely you remember, brothers, our toil and hardship; we worked night and day in order not to be a burden to anyone while we preached the gospel of God to you. (1 Th 2:9)
>
> Nor did we eat anyone's food without paying for it. On the contrary, we worked night and day, laboring and toiling so that we would not be a burden to any of you. (2 Th 3:8)

3. The idle worker must work or lose his right to eat (v.10). This fact is stated as clearly as it can be: "If a man will not work, he shall not eat." Note that this is a command, a command that Paul had preached when he was with the church. Note this fact as well: the commandment deals with those who choose to be idle and refuse to work. It is not dealing with those who are honestly unable to work due to disability or being unable to find employment. If a person is able to work, he is to work. If he refuses, he is not to be fed; he is not to be allowed to sponge off the church, community, or society. There is no excuse for a person not working if he is able to work—not in the sight of God. Too many in the world—millions—are desperate

and destitute, dying within and without from loneliness, emptiness, starvation, disease, and sin. Almost every church or social service can put us to work in reaching a world of desperate and dying people who need our help and attention. In God's words: "We gave you this rule: If a man will not work, he shall not eat."

> We want each of you to show this same diligence to the very end, in order to make your hope sure. We do not want you to become lazy, but to imitate those who through faith and patience inherit what has been promised. (Heb 6:11-12)
>
> Never be lacking in zeal, but keep your spiritual fervor, serving the Lord. (Rom 12:11; cp. Mt.25:24-27)
>
> Let no debt remain outstanding, except the continuing debt to love one another, for he who loves his fellowman has fulfilled the law. (Rom 13:8)
>
> Come back to your senses as you ought, and stop sinning; for there are some who are ignorant of God—I say this to your shame. (1 Cor 15:34)
>
> For it is light that makes everything visible. This is why it is said: "Wake up, O sleeper, rise from the dead, and Christ will shine on you." (Eph 5:14)
>
> Allow no sleep to your eyes, no slumber to your eyelids. (Prov 6:4)
>
> Go to the ant, you sluggard; consider its ways and be wise! It has no commander, no overseer or ruler, yet it stores its provisions in summer and gathers its food at harvest. How long will you lie there, you sluggard? When will you get up from your sleep? A little sleep, a little slumber, a little folding of the hands to rest—and poverty will come on you like a bandit and scarcity like an armed man. (Prov 6:6-11)
>
> He who gathers crops in summer is a wise son, but he who sleeps during harvest is a disgraceful son. (Prov 10:5)
>
> He who works his land will have abundant food, but he who chases fantasies lacks judgment. (Prov 12:11)
>
> One who is slack in his work is brother to one who destroys. (Prov 18:9)
>
> Laziness brings on deep sleep, and the shiftless man goes hungry. (Prov 19:15)
>
> The sluggard's craving will be the death of him, because his hands refuse to work. All day long he craves for more, but the righteous give without sparing. (Prov 21:25-26)
>
> For drunkards and gluttons become poor, and drowsiness clothes them in rags. (Prov 23:21)

4. The idle worker tends to be a busybody. The mind of man is an active thing. What we tend to overlook is this: the mind is *always active*; it is never still. It is either thinking positive thoughts or negative and evil thoughts. The point is this: an idle person has an idle mind. His mind is not set upon positive thoughts, but negative and evil thoughts. An idle mind is the devil's playground. This is the reason why so many idle persons—regardless of their age—get into trouble. The trouble can range all the way from becoming a busybody to murder.

The present passage is dealing with Christians and the trouble caused by being a busybody. Too many believers are busybodies, that is, poking themselves into other people's affairs, tattling, gossiping, and spreading all kinds of talk and rumors. They just go about speaking all kinds of things that they should not. Why? Because they do not stay busy for the Lord by helping and ministering to the needs of those within the community who are hurting, lonely, desperate, dying, and lost.

> We hear that some among you are idle. They are not busy; they are busybodies. (2 Th 3:11)
>
> Besides, they get into the habit of being idle and going about from house to house. And not only do they become idlers, but also gossips and busybodies, saying things they ought not to. (1 Tim 5:13)
>
> If you suffer, it should not be as a murderer or thief or any other kind of criminal, or even as a meddler. (1 Pet 4:15)
>
> "'Do not go about spreading slander among your people. "'Do not do anything that endangers your neighbor's life. I am the LORD. (Lev 19:16)

2 (3:12-13) **Employee**: work—every one of you. Again, this is a forceful command, a command that comes from the Lord Jesus Christ. But note: it is also an exhortation, a stirring challenge that comes from the Lord. The Lord is not cold or hard about the matter. If a believer has been mistaken about how he should work—if he has been slothful and slack in his work—the Lord will forgive. But the believer must confess his wrong and repent. He must repent by beginning to work and earn his own living. And note how we are to go about earning our living: "*to settle down.*" This is in contrast to being a busybody. We are to work with a quiet spirit and mind our own business; we are not to poke ourselves in other people's business. We are to settle down and be efficient workers, not inefficient busybodies who are always walking about gabbing about other people and their affairs.

Note one other point: do not be weary in well-doing—never tire of doing what is right. Do not let the idlers discourage you, but stick to your job: be diligent and persevere. Do not slack off no matter what others do. Be a dynamic example for the Lord.

> "Who then is the faithful and wise servant, whom the master has put in charge of the servants in his household to give them their food at the proper time? It will be good for that servant whose master finds him doing so when he returns. (Mat 24:45-46)
>
> Never be lacking in zeal, but keep your spiritual fervor, serving the Lord. (Rom 12:11)
>
> He who has been stealing must steal no longer, but must work, doing something useful with his own hands, that he may have something to share with those in need. (Eph 4:28)
>
> Slaves [employees], obey your earthly masters [employers] with respect and fear,

and with sincerity of heart, just as you would obey Christ. (Eph 6:5)

Make it your ambition to lead a quiet life, to mind your own business and to work with your hands, just as we told you, (1 Th 4:11)

Such people we command and urge in the Lord Jesus Christ to settle down and earn the bread they eat. (2 Th 3:12)

3 (3:14-15) **Employee—Idler**: discipline the idler, have no company with him. Keep away from him and have no fellowship with him. Note why: that he may feel ashamed. The hope is that his shame will motivate him to get up and get to work.

However, the idle person is not to be disciplined as an enemy, but as a brother. The discipline is not to be done in a spirit of some superior, but in the spirit of a fellow believer, admonishing and warning him of what the Lord has to say about the matter.

The importance of the discipline is seen in the exactness of the words of Paul. Paul says, "take special note of him"; that is, mark him out and disapprove of his behavior. Let him know that his refusal to work is not acceptable. Do not condone and indulge his idleness. Keep away and have no fellowship with him. Also warn him: warning is essential. He must be admonished. Warning and letting him experience shame are his only hope of changing. Being warned and feeling shame might stir him to repent, to get up and get to work.

And we urge you, brothers, warn those who are idle, encourage the timid, help the weak, be patient with everyone. (1 Th 5:14)

He [Adam] answered, "I heard you in the garden, and I was afraid because I was naked; so I hid." (Gen 3:10)

And prayed: "O my God, I am too ashamed and disgraced to lift up my face to you, my God, because our sins are higher than our heads and our guilt has reached to the heavens. (Ezra 9:6)

My disgrace is before me all day long, and my face is covered with shame (Psa 44:15)

4 (3:16-18) **Conclusion**: the believer has three great possessions in Christ. Note: this is a prayer of Paul for all the believers of the church.

1. The believer receives peace from "the Lord of peace Himself." Note the phrase "At all times and in every way." The believer receives peace "at all times and in all ways—under all circumstances and conditions, whatever comes" (Amplified New Testament). (See note, *Peace*—1 Th.1:1 for discussion.)

2. The believer receives fellowship, a very special and personal fellowship. The church was dear to Paul. He sensed ever so deeply a close tie, a spiritual fellowship that bound his heart to the believers. Thus, he became concerned and was aroused to write and deal with the problems that had infiltrated the church. He wrote because of the special bond of fellowship between him and the church. (See DEEPER STUDY # 3, *Fellowship*—Acts 2:42 for more discussion.)

Note: it was Paul's practice to dictate his letters to a secretary and then to sign them. This is what he means by the statement, "I, Paul, write this greeting in my own hand, which is the distinguishing mark in all my letters. This is how I write" (v.17).

3. The believer receives grace—the undeserved favor and strength of Jesus Christ (see note, *Grace*—1 Th.1:1 for discussion).

THE
OUTLINE & SUBJECT INDEX

REMEMBER: When you look up a subject and turn to the Scripture reference, you have not only the Scripture, you have *an outline and a discussion* (commentary) of the Scripture and subject.

This is one of the *GREAT VALUES* of **The Preacher's Outline & Sermon Bible®**. Once you have all the volumes, you will have not only what all other Bible indexes give you, that is, a list of all the subjects and their Scripture references, *BUT* you will also have...

- An outline of *every* Scripture and subject in the Bible.
- A discussion (commentary) on every Scripture and subject.
- Every subject supported by other Scriptures or cross references.

DISCOVER THE GREAT VALUE for yourself. Quickly glance below to the very first subject of the Index of Second Thessalonians. It is:

ANTICHRIST
Appearance. When he will **a**.
After God takes the restraints off sin. 2:6-8

Turn to the reference. Glance at the Scripture and outline of the Scripture, then read the commentary. You will immediately see the GREAT VALUE of the INDEX of **The Preacher's Outline & Sermon Bible®**.

OUTLINE AND SUBJECT INDEX

ANTICHRIST
Appearance. When he will **a**.
After God takes the restraints off sin. 2:6-8
After two events. 2:3
Described.
Man of sin (lawlessness). 2:3
Son of perdition. 2:3
That wicked (one). 2:8
Discussed. 2:4-9
End of. Slain & destroyed by Christ. 2:8
Followers of. Discussed. 2:10-12
How **a**. rises to power.
A political ruler. 2:4-9
A religious ruler. 2:4
Nature - Character.
Discussed. 2:4
Embodiment of Satan. 2:8
Work.
To carry on Satan's work. 2:9
To set up imperial or state worship. 2:4

APOSTASY
Meaning. 2:3

ASSURANCE
Comes by. God's faithfulness. 3:3-5
Of believer. Discussed. 2:13

BELIEVERS
Life - Walk. (See Related Subjects)
In light of the end times. 2:13-17

BRIGHTNESS
Meaning. 2:8

CALL - CALLED (See **MINISTER - MINISTERS**)
Purpose of. To obtain glory. 2:14

CHOSEN
Discussed. 2:13
Meaning. 2:13

CHURCH
Basis - Foundation. A model **c**. 1:1-5
Persecuted - Persecution. (See **PERSECUTION**)
Matures a **c**. 1:3-5
Problems. Ignorance of the antichrist. 2:3; 2:5

CHURCH DISCIPLINE
Of idle workers. 3:6-18

CONSOLATION (See **ENCOURAGEMENT**)

DAY OF THE LORD
Discussed. 2:1-3

DECEIVE - DECEPTION
Who deceives. Antichrist. 2:9; 2:10
Who is **d**. Discussed. 2:11

DESTRUCTION
Meaning. 1:9

DIRECT
Meaning. 3:3-5

ELECTION
Discussed. 2:13

EMPLOYEE
Discussed.
Discipline of idle workers. 3:6-18
Work & employment. 3:6-18

EMPLOYMENT
Discussed. Work & **e**. 3:6-18

ENCOURAGMENT
Meaning. 2:16-17

END TIME
Christ's return and the world's end.
Day of the Lord. 2:1-3
Glimpse into the end time. 1:6-2:17
Judgment of unbelievers. 2:12

Two events necessary before Christ's return. 2:1-3

ENDURANCE
Meaning. 1:4

ESTABLISH (See **STRENGTHEN**)
Meaning. 3:3-5

EVIL
Meaning. Means both evil & the evil one or Satan. 3:3-5
Restraint of. By God. 2:6-8

FAITH
Discussed. A growing faith. 1:3
Kinds. A growing faith. 1:3

FAITHFULNESS
Of Christ. To the believer. In three areas. 3:3-5

FALLING AWAY
In the end time. Discussed. 2:3

GLORY
Of believer. Discussed. 2:14
Of Jesus Christ. When He returns. 1:10

GOD
Faithfulness of. Discussed. 3:1-5

HELL
Described.
Everlasting destruction. 1:9
From the presence of the Lord. 1:9
Who is to be in **h**.
Those who do not know God. 1:8
Those who do not obey the gospel. 1:8

HOLY SPIRIT
Restrains sin. 2:6-8

INDEX

JESUS CHRIST
    Faithfulness of. To the believer. In three areas. 3:3-5
    Results. The righteous judgment of God. 1:6-12
    Return - Second Coming. (See **END TIMES**)
        Described. As "that day." 1:10
    When C. is to return. After two events. 2:3

JUDGMENT
    Described. As punishment and destruction. 1:9
    Discussed. Righteousness of God. 1:6-12
    How God judges.
        Allows life to perish & become corruptible. 2:10-12
        By allowing a judicial judgment. 2:11
    Kinds. Judicial **j**. of God. 1:9; 2:11; 2:12
    Man and **j**. Man is perishing; he is condemned now. 2:10-12
    Of followers of antichrist. Discussed. 2:11; 2:12
    When - Time of.
        The day of the Lord. 2:1-3
        When Christ returns. 1:6-12

JUSTICE
    Fact.
        All injustices to be corrected. 1:6
        Is essential. 1:6

KEEP (See **PROTECT**)

LABOR - LABORERS
    Duty.
        Discussed. 3:6-18
        To withdraw from disorderly **l**. 3:6-11

LAWLESSNESS, MAN OF
    Antichrist, The. 2:3

LAZY - LAZINESS
    Discussed. Work & employment. 3:6-18

LORD, DAY OF THE
    Discussed. 2:1-3

LOVE
    Kinds.
        Abounding **l**. 1:3
        Brotherly **l**. 1:3

MAN
    Depravity. Is damned & perishing. 2:12

MAN OF SIN
    Antichrist, The. 2:3-4

MORAL UNIVERSE
    The universe is **m**. 1:6

PATIENCE
    Meaning. 1:4

PAUL
    Ministry. Did not receive support for **m**. Worked. 3:6-11

PAYBACK
    Discussed. 1:6

PERDITION
    Meaning. 2:4

PERISH - PERISHING
    Meaning. 1:9
    Who the **p**. are. Discussed. 2:10

PERSECUTION
    Duty. To pray for deliverance. 3:1-2
    Example. Picture of a model church under **p**. 1:1-5
    How to overcome. Picture of a model church under **p**. 1:1-5
    Is a sign of coming judgment. 1:5
    Of Thessalonian church. Described. 1:6
    Results. Proves a person's faith—that he is worthy of heaven. 1:5

PRAYER
    Duty.
        To pray for deliverance from persecution. 3:1-2
        To pray for the Word of God to spread rapidly free course. 3:1-2

PROTECT
    Meaning. 3:3-5

PUNISHMENT
    Meaning. 1:9

RECOMPENSE (See **PAYBACK**)

RELIGION, STATE
    To be enforced by antichrist. 2:4

SALVATION
    Discussed. 2:13-17
    Duty. To stand fast & cling to the Word of God. 2:15
    Resources. Fivefold. 2:16-17

SECURITY
    Of Believers. Discussed. 2:13

SIN
    Fact. Is presently restrained. 2:6
    Restraint of. By God. 2:6-8

SIN, MAN OF
    Antichrist, The. 2:3

SLOTHFUL
    Discussed. Work & employment. 3:6-18

SON OF PERDITION
    Antichrist, The. 2:3

STABLISH (See **STRENGTHEN**)

STRENGTHEN
    Meaning. 2:16-17

TEACHING - TRAINING (See **CHRISTIAN FAITH; DOCTRINE**)
    Duty. To **t**. about the antichrist. 2:5

TRIALS - TRIBULATION
    Deliverance through. How the church progresses under **t**. 1:4-5

UNIVERSE
    Fact. Injustices shall be rectified. 1:6

WORK
    Discussed. 3:6-18
    Disorderly **w**. 3:6-11

WORLD
    Nature of. Is moral. 1:6

FIRST

TIMOTHY

1 TIMOTHY

INTRODUCTION

AUTHOR: Paul, the Apostle.

DATE: Uncertain. Probably A.D. 61-64.

The books of *First Timothy* and *Titus* seem to have been written while Paul was traveling and ministering between two Roman imprisonments. The date depends upon the answer to this question: Did Paul suffer one or two Roman imprisonments? The book of *Acts* mentions only one imprisonment and closes with Paul in prison in Rome. It says nothing about his death. As one discusses this question, one major thing needs to be kept in mind. Paul prayed fervently that God would release him from prison. And he asked others to pray fervently for his release (Ph.1:25-26; Phile.22). Did God answer his prayer as requested? No one knows for sure. However, several factors point rather decisively to his being released and later suffering a second imprisonment.

1. The Life and Movements of Paul. Paul says in Tit.1:5 that he had been to Crete on a mission tour. And in Tit.3:12 he says that he was spending the winter in Nicopolis. These events do not fit in with any of the accounts in *Acts*. The evidence seems to be that God answered his prayer and had him released from prison.

2. The Life and Movements of Paul's Companions. Note the following two examples, and there are others. In 1 Tim.1:3 Paul says that he told Timothy to stay in Ephesus. But there is no record of this event in Scripture. Paul had made only two visits to Ephesus. One was a very short visit with little if any ministry. There is no mention whatsoever about Timothy (Acts 18:19-22). The second was his three year ministry in which Timothy had a part. But when it came time for Paul to move on, he sent Timothy and Erastus to Macedonia. He did not ask Timothy to stay in Ephesus. When then did Paul tell Timothy to stay in Ephesus? There just is no record of such a visit in Scripture. Thus all indications point to a third visit by Paul and Timothy—a visit after his first imprisonment and before an unrecorded second imprisonment.

Again, in 2 Tim.4:20 Paul writes, "I left Trophimus sick in Miletus." Paul was in Miletus before his first Roman imprisonment, but he did not leave Trophimus there sick (Acts 20:17). Trophimus went on to Rome with Paul (Acts 21:29). When then was Trophimus left at Miletus sick? The only clear answer seems to be that Paul made another visit to Miletus—after his first imprisonment and right before a second unrecorded imprisonment.

3. The Time Sequence Between the Writing of the Prison Epistles and the Pastoral Epistles. The Prison Epistles (*Ephesians, Philippians, Colossians,* and *Philemon*) were written while Paul was in prison in Rome. He says so in each epistle. Note the following example: Philemon 24 says that Demas is a follower of Christ, but 2 Tim.4:10 says that he had deserted. The letter to Timothy was definitely written after the prison letter to Philemon. When? The evidence points toward a time after his first imprisonment and before a second unrecorded imprisonment. This seems to be the only clear explanation.

As stated above, *First Timothy* and *Titus* seem to have been written right after Paul had been released from his first imprisonment in Rome and was traveling about ministering. At some point in those few years he was rearrested and imprisoned in Rome for a second time. He wrote *Second Timothy* either before his release (when he began a mission tour into Spain) or before his execution. His execution was probably between A.D. 65-68.

TO WHOM WRITTEN: "To Timothy, my true son in the faith" (1 Tim.1:2). Timothy's father was a Greek and an unbeliever, but his mother was a Jew and a believer. Her name was Eunice and his grandmother's name was Lois (2 Tim.1:5). Timothy was not circumcised; hence it would seem that he was educated in Greek ways and customs (Acts 16:3). When Paul met Timothy, Timothy was already a Christian believer with a strong testimony, so strong in fact that Paul arranged for him to become his missionary partner (Acts 16:1f). Timothy's maturity and importance are seen in Acts 16 when the word "he" of verse one is changed very rapidly to "they" of verse four. Timothy became a son to Paul (1 Cor.4:17). He was esteemed so highly and loved so deeply by Paul that Paul said he was the one man whose mind was at one with his own (Ph.2:19). He was probably chosen by Paul to become Paul's successor (see note—Ph.1:1). From this point on, he was seen either ministering with Paul or else being sent out by Paul to minister to certain churches. He was with Paul in Paul's first imprisonment (Col.1:1; Phile.1). Apparently, Paul was released from prison and Timothy began to travel with him again (see First Timothy, Introduction, Date). On this journey Paul left him in Ephesus to correct some errors that had arisen, while Paul himself traveled on into Macedonia to visit the churches there. Soon thereafter Paul was arrested and imprisoned in Rome a second time. As soon as possible Timothy joined him (2 Tim.4:11, 21), but this time Timothy was imprisoned also. However Timothy was later released (Heb.13:23), while Paul was either beheaded or released and began a mission tour into Spain. (See *Second Timothy, Introduction, Date*. Also see note, *Timothy—Ph.2:19-24* for more discussion.)

PURPOSE: Paul had three purposes for writing Timothy.

1. To encourage Timothy in his Christian life and walk.
2. To warn against false teaching and doctrinal error.
3. To teach the qualifications and order of officials in the church. Believers needed to know how to behave in the church: "you will know how people ought to conduct themselves in God's household." (1 Tim.3:15).

SPECIAL FEATURES:

1. *First Timothy* is "A Pastoral Epistle." There are two other Pastoral Epistles: *Second Timothy* and *Titus*. They are called Pastoral Epistles because they deal primarily with the pastoral care, oversight, and organization of the church. They tell believers how they ought to behave in the house of God (1 Tim.3:15). Interestingly, the term *pastoral* has a long history. It was first used by Thomas Aquinas in A.D. 1274. He called *First Timothy* "an epistle of pastoral rule" and Second Timothy "an epistle of pastoral care." The term "Pastoral Epistles," however, began to be widely used only after D.N. Berdot (A.D. 1703) and Paul Anton (A.D. 1726) so described them (Donald Guthrie. *The Pastoral Epistles*. "The Tyndale New Testament Commentaries." Grand Rapids, MI: Eerdmans, 1972, p.11).

2. *First Timothy* is "A Personal Epistle." It was written to a young disciple who was loved as a son. The epistle is filled with warm and affectionate feelings and filled with instructions that were to govern Timothy's personal behavior.

3. *First Timothy* is "An Ecclesiastical Epistle." It was written to answer questions about church organization, doctrinal purity, and personal behavior. Two things were happening. First, the number and sizes of churches were growing rapidly, and second, the apostles were aging. In both cases the apostles were just unable to personally reach and instruct all the churches; therefore, they had to write if the churches were to be rooted and grounded in the Lord.

4. *First Timothy* is "An Apologetic Epistle." It is a defense of the faith. The first rumblings and early development of false teaching had just begun to appear (Gnosticism. See Colossians, Introductory Notes, Purpose.) Therefore, Paul warns the believers and defends the truth against heretical and false teaching.

OUTLINE OF 1 TIMOTHY

THE PREACHER'S OUTLINE & SERMON BIBLE® is *unique*. It differs from all other Study Bibles & Sermon Resource Materials in that every Passage and Subject is outlined right beside the Scripture. When you choose any *Subject* below and turn to the reference, you have not only the Scripture, but you discover the Scripture and Subject *already outlined for you—verse by verse*.

For a quick example, choose one of the subjects below and turn over to the Scripture, and you will find this marvelous help for faster, easier, and more accurate use.

In addition, every point of the Scripture and Subject is *fully developed in a Commentary with supporting Scripture* at the bottom of the page. Again, this arrangement makes sermon preparation much easier and faster.

Note something else: The Subjects of First Timothy have titles that are both Biblical and *practical*. The practical titles sometimes have more appeal to people. This *benefit* is clearly seen for use on billboards, bulletins, church newsletters, etc.

A suggestion: For the quickest overview of First Timothy, first read *all the major titles* (I, II, III, etc.), then come back and read the subtitles.

OUTLINE OF 1 TIMOTHY

INTRODUCTION: THE MINISTER AND HIS YOUNG DISCIPLE, 1:1-2

I. **FALSE AND TRUE TEACHERS IN THE CHURCH, 1:3-20**

   A. The Danger of False Teachers, 1:3-11
   B. The Testimony of a True Minister, 1:12-17
   C. The Young Minister (Charge 1): To be a Warrior, 1:18-20

II. **DUTIES AND ORDER IN THE CHURCH, 2:1-3:13**

   A. The First Duty of the Church—Pray, 2:1-8
   B. The Women of the Church, 2:9-15
   C. The Overseers of the Church, 3:1-7
   D. The Deacons of the Church, 3:8-13

III. **BEHAVIOR AND RELATIONSHIPS IN THE CHURCH, 3:14-6:21**

   A. The Description of the Church, 3:14-16
   B. The Warning About False Teachers and Their Apostasy, 4:1-5
   C. The Young Minister (Charge 2): To Be a Good Minister, 4:6-16
   D. The Spirit of Relationships, 5:1-2
   E. The Responsibilities to Christian Widows, 5:3-16
   F. The Elders or Officials, 5:17-20
   G. The Young Minister (Charge 3): To Be an Impartial Minister, 5:21-25
   H. The Believing Slaves or Employees, 6:1-2
   I. The False Teachers, 6:3-5
   J. The Secret of Contentment, 6:6-10
   K. The Young Minister (Charge 4): To Be a Man of God, 6:11-16
   L. The Rich Man and The Minister: The Final Charge, 6:17-21

1 TIMOTHY

	CHAPTER 1	of God our Savior and of Christ Jesus our hope,	a. By command of God b. By God our Savior c. By Christ our hope
	INTRODUCTION: THE MINISTER & HIS YOUNG DISCIPLE, 1:1-2	2 To Timothy my true son in the faith: Grace, mercy and peace from God the Father and Christ Jesus our Lord.	**2 The disciple's privilege & need**^{DS1} a. A true son in the faith b. His need: Grace, mercy,^{DS2} & peace^{DS3}
1 The minister's call & credentials: An apostle	Paul, an apostle of Christ Jesus by the command		

INTRODUCTION: THE MINISTER AND HIS YOUNG DISCIPLE, 1:1-2

(1:1-2) **Introduction**: this is a strong but warm and tender greeting. It is a greeting that has royalty in it, the kind of royalty that exists in a man who is the ambassador of a King. The ambassador is writing to his dear son. This is exactly what Paul is claiming when he says that he is an apostle: he is the ambassador of God Himself. But note the tenderness as well as the royalty of his greeting. He is not only an ambassador, a person of royalty, he is also a father. He has *fathered* his son in the faith. He has devoted his life and energy to his son over the past years, and his son has become a disciple of his wonderful Lord. Now he wishes to pass on the royalty of the Lord's command.

The one thing needed within the church is the royal ministry of making disciples, of nourishing and nurturing men and women as sons and daughters of the faith. This is the challenge of this greeting. In seeing the relationship that existed with Paul and Timothy, we should be challenged more and more to make disciples—to get to the task of growing leaders within God's church.

1. The minister's call and credentials: an apostle (v.1).
2. The disciple's privilege and need (v.2).

1 (1:1) **Minister, Call—Apostle**: the minister's call and credentials. Paul calls himself an apostle of Christ Jesus. The word "apostle" (apostolos) means a person who is sent out or sent forth. An apostle is a representative, an ambassador, an envoy, a person who is sent out into one country to represent another country. Three things are true of the apostle:

⇒ he belongs to the king or country who sends him out.
⇒ he is commissioned to be sent out.
⇒ he possesses all the authority and power of the person who sends him out.

Paul makes three forceful points.

1. He was an apostle by the command of God. The word command (epitagen) means to be under orders; to be placed under obligation. It is the instructions given by some high official that must be carried out, for example, the word of a king. The word *command* has the sense of compulsion, force, and necessity.

Paul—the minister of God—was a man sent forth by the command and order of the King of kings, God Himself. The compulsion, force, and necessity of God's command drove him to be a minister of Christ Jesus.

> **Thought 1.** The stress of Paul upon his apostleship seems to indicate that Timothy was to share the letter of First Timothy with the church as a whole. What Paul was writing to Timothy was coming from an apostle of Christ; therefore, the whole church was to heed the exhortations.

2. He was an apostle because of *God our Savior*. This is one of the great titles of God. God is the *first source* of our salvation. We are saved because God loves us.

> "For God so loved the world that he gave his one and only Son, that whoever believes in him shall not perish but have eternal life. (John 3:16)

If God did not love us, we would not be saved. We would be wiped off the face of the earth, utterly destroyed, condemned, and punished throughout all of eternity without any hope of ever being saved. But God does love us; therefore, He has provided the way for us to be saved. God is our Savior.

The point is this: since God is our Savior, man never has to die; he can be delivered from sin, death, and judgment to come. This is another reason Paul was driven to serve Christ. People all around him were...

- enslaved by sin.
- gripped by death.
- doomed to face the judgment of God.

Therefore, Paul was driven to represent Christ Jesus in this world of sin and death. He was forced by the inner compulsion of God our Savior to carry the glorious message of salvation to the whole world: the message that God is interested in the whole world. God is our Savior.

> And my spirit rejoices in God my Savior, (Luke 1:47)
> This is good, and pleases God our Savior, who wants all men to be saved and to come to a knowledge of the truth. For there is one God and one mediator between God and men, the man Christ Jesus, who gave himself as a ransom for all men—the testimony given in its proper time. (1 Tim 2:3-6)
> (And for this we labor and strive), that we have put our hope in the living God, who is the Savior of all men, and especially of those who believe. (1 Tim 4:10)
> A faith and knowledge resting on the hope of eternal life, which God, who does not lie, promised before the beginning of time, and at his appointed season he brought his word to light through the preaching entrusted to me by the command of God our Savior, (Titus 1:2-3)
> And not to steal from them, but to show that they can be fully trusted, so that in every way they will make the teaching about God our Savior attractive. (Titus 2:10)

> But when the kindness and love of God our Savior appeared, he saved us, not because of righteous things we had done, but because of his mercy. He saved us through the washing of rebirth and renewal by the Holy Spirit, whom he poured out on us generously through Jesus Christ our Savior, so that, having been justified by his grace, we might become heirs having the hope of eternal life. (Titus 3:4-7)
>
> To the only God our Savior be glory, majesty, power and authority, through Jesus Christ our Lord, before all ages, now and forevermore! Amen. (Jude 1:25)

3. He was an apostle because of Christ Jesus who is our hope. Men long and hope for all kinds of things...
- recognition, acceptance, esteem, friends.
- security and victory over the trials of life.
- deliverance from death and eternal life.

The reason man longs for these things is because he lacks them. Even if he possesses some sense of them, he still senses a great deal of lack: a great deal of emptiness, incompleteness, unfulfillment, and insecurity within his soul. Why? Because the human soul can never be at rest until it has the absolute assurance that it is *acceptable to God and is going to live forever*. The human soul was made for God and for the hope of God. Therefore, there is only one way a person can ever have this absolute assurance: Christ Jesus must live within his heart. Christ Jesus is a person's hope of glory (Col.1:27). When a person receives Christ Jesus into his heart and life, the divine nature of Christ...
- makes the person acceptable to God.
- gives the person the recognition, acceptance, and friendship of God and of all other believers (the church).
- gives the person security and gives him supernatural power to conquer the trials of life.
- delivers the person from death and gives him the inheritance of eternal life.

On top of all this, the most wonderful thing happens: Christ gives the person the *absolute assurance and hope* of all these. The person becomes complete, perfectly complete and satisfied in Christ Jesus our hope (Col.2:10).

The point is this: since Christ is our hope, Paul was driven to serve Christ. He was forced by the inner compulsion to offer the hope of Christ to a world that was gripped by the hopelessness of despair, trouble, and death.

> To them God has chosen to make known among the Gentiles the glorious riches of this mystery, which is Christ in you, the hope of glory. (Col 1:27)
>
> Praise be to the God and Father of our Lord Jesus Christ! In his great mercy he has given us new birth into a living hope through the resurrection of Jesus Christ from the dead, and into an inheritance that can never perish, spoil or fade—kept in heaven for you, (1 Pet 1:3-4)
>
> Dear friends, now we are children of God, and what we will be has not yet been made known. But we know that when he appears, we shall be like him, for we shall see him as he is. Everyone who has this hope in him purifies himself, just as he is pure. (1 John 3:2-3)
>
> Why are you downcast, O my soul? Why so disturbed within me? Put your hope in God, for I will yet praise him, my Savior and my God. (Psa 43:5)

Thought 1. William Barclay says that *Christ our hope* became one of the most precious titles for Christ in the early church. He quotes two ancient writers to illustrate his point:

> "Ignatius of Antioch, when he was on his way to execution in Rome, writes to the Church in Ephesus: 'Be of good cheer in God the Father and in Jesus Christ our common hope' (Ignatius, To the Ephesians 21:2). Polycarp writes: 'Let us therefore persevere in our hope and the earnest of our righteousness, who is Jesus Christ' (Epistle of Polycarp 8)." (*The Letters to Timothy, Titus, and Philemon.* "Daily Study Bible." Philadelphia, PA: The Westminster Press, 1956, p.22.)

2 (1:2) **Discipleship—Timothy—Minister**: the disciple's privilege and need. Timothy was greatly privileged, for he was treated as a son by a minister of God, even by Paul himself. (See Author—Introduction.) Note that Paul calls Timothy "my true son in the faith." When Paul first met Timothy, Timothy was only ten to twelve years old. But even at that young age, his love for the Lord was apparently strong and noticed by Paul. When Paul returned to Lystra on his next missionary journey, Paul was so stricken with Timothy's spiritual maturity that he invited him to become a disciple. Later, Paul was to say that Timothy was the one person whose mind was as one with his own (Ph.2:19). Paul took him under his wing and began to disciple him in the Lord—to teach him all he knew. What a wonderful privilege: to be discipled by Paul the apostle. (See DEEPER STUDY # 1, *Timothy*—1 Tim.1:2; DEEPER STUDY # 1—Acts 16:1-3; note—Ph.2:22-24.)

Note the greeting by Paul. He names three qualities that a disciple must possess.

1. There is the grace of God and of Christ (see DEEPER STUDY # 1, *Grace*—Tit.2:11-15 for discussion).

2. There is the mercy of God and of Christ (see note, *Mercy*—1 Tim.1:2 for discussion).

3. There is the peace of God and of Christ. Peace (eirene) means to be bound, joined, and weaved together. It means to be assured, confident, and secure in the love and care of God. It means to have a sense, a consciousness, a knowledge that God will...
- provide
- guide
- strengthen
- sustain
- deliver
- encourage
- save
- give life, real life, both now and forever

A person can experience true peace only as he comes to know Jesus Christ. Only Christ can bring peace to the human heart, the kind of peace that brings deliverance and assurance to the human soul.

Again, it is an absolute essential for the minister and disciple of Christ to know the peace of God and Christ. How can the minister share the gospel of peace unless he has peace with God? The answer is obvious: you cannot share that which you do not possess.

Peace I leave with you; my peace I give you. I do not give to you as the world gives. Do not let your hearts be troubled and do not be afraid. (John 14:27)

"I have told you these things, so that in me you may have peace. In this world you will have trouble. But take heart! I have overcome the world." (John 16:33)

Therefore, since we have been justified through faith, we have peace with God through our Lord Jesus Christ, (Rom 5:1)

The mind of sinful man is death, but the mind controlled by the Spirit is life and peace; (Rom 8:6)

But the fruit of the Spirit is love, joy, peace, patience, kindness, goodness, faithfulness, gentleness and self-control. Against such things there is no law. (Gal 5:22-23)

I will lie down and sleep in peace, for you alone, O LORD, make me dwell in safety. (Psa 4:8)

DEEPER STUDY # 1
(1:2) **Timothy**: Timothy was just a child when Paul visited Lystra on his first mission (about five or six years before). He was probably somewhere around ten to twelve years old. He was still a young man when Paul wrote his first letter to Timothy (1 Tim.4:12). All this means Timothy was somewhere around eighteen years old when Paul met him on his second mission to Lystra.

It is also possible that Paul led Timothy to the Lord on his first mission tour, but it is more probable that Timothy's mother and grandmother led him to the Lord.

Acts seems to read as though Paul did not know or remember Timothy from his first mission (Acts 16:1-3). In either case, his spiritual maturity at this point was strong enough for Paul to challenge him to join his mission corps. The facts of his life seem to be as follows:

Timothy's father was a Greek and an unbeliever, but his mother was a Jew and a believer. Her name was Eunice and his grandmother's name was Lois (2 Tim.1:5). Timothy was not circumcised; hence it would seem that he was educated in Greek ways and customs (Acts 16:3). When Paul met Timothy, Timothy was already a Christian believer with a strong testimony, so strong in fact that Paul arranged for him to become his missionary partner (Acts 16:1f). Timothy's maturity and importance are seen in Acts 16 when the word "he" of verse one is changed very rapidly to "they" of verse four. Timothy became a son to Paul (1 Cor.4:17). He was esteemed so highly and loved so deeply by Paul that Paul said he was the one man whose mind was at one with his own (Ph.2:19). He was probably chosen by Paul to become Paul's successor (see note—Ph.1:1). From this point on, he was seen either ministering with Paul or else being sent out by Paul to minister to certain churches. He was with Paul during Paul's first imprisonment (Col.1:1; Phile.1). Apparently, Paul was released from prison and Timothy began to travel with him again (see 1 Timothy, Introduction, Date). On this journey Paul left him in Ephesus to correct some errors that had arisen, while Paul himself traveled on into Macedonia to visit the churches there. Soon thereafter Paul was arrested and imprisoned in Rome a second time. As soon as possible Timothy joined him (2 Tim.4:11, 21), but this time Timothy was imprisoned also. However, Timothy was later released (Heb.13:23), while Paul was either beheaded or released and began a mission tour into Spain. (See note, *Timothy*—Ph.2:19 for more discussion.)

DEEPER STUDY # 2
(1:2) **Mercy**: (eleos) feelings of pity, compassion, affection, kindness. It is a desire to succor; to tenderly draw unto oneself and to care for. Two things are essential in order to have mercy: seeing a need and being able to meet that need. God sees our need and feels for us (Eph.2:1-3). Therefore, He acts; He has mercy upon us...
- God withholds His judgment.
- God provides a way for us to be saved.

Mercy arises from a heart of love: God has mercy upon us because He loves us. His mercy has been demonstrated in two great ways:
⇒ God has withheld His judgment from us—withheld it even when we deserve it.
⇒ God has provided a way for us to be saved through the Lord Jesus Christ.

When Jesus Christ died, He died for our sins. He took our sins upon Himself and bore the judgment of sin for us. Therefore, if we trust Christ as our Savior, God *does not count* sin against us. Instead, He *counts the righteousness* of Christ for us. We become acceptable to God through the righteousness of Christ. The great mercy of God is...
- that He allowed Christ, His very own Son, to die for us. He actually allowed His own Son to bear the punishment of our sins for us.
- that he loves us so much that He will forgive our sins if we will only trust Christ.

The point is this: it is absolutely necessary for both the minister and the disciple to know and possess the mercy of God and of Christ. A person who has not experienced the mercy of God does not know God. Of all people, the minister and disciple of Christ must know the mercy of God.

DEEPER STUDY # 3
(1:2) **Peace**: see note 2, pt.3—1 Tim.1:2.

1 TIMOTHY 1:3-11

	I. FALSE AND TRUE TEACHERS IN THE CHURCH 1:3-20 **A. The Danger of False Teachers, 1:3-11**	meaningless talk. 7 They want to be teachers of the law, but they do not know what they are talking about or what they so confidently affirm. 8 We know that the law is good if one uses it properly.	**4** False teachers put ambition & personal ideas above the truth **5** False teachers put self-righteousness above God's gospel
1 False teachers teach a different doctrine	3 As I urged you when I went into Macedonia, stay there in Ephesus so that you may command certain men not to teach false doctrines any longer	9 We also know that law is made not for the righteous but for lawbreakers and rebels, the ungodly and sinful, the unholy and irreligious; for	a. They do not understand the law & its purposes 1) Law is not given to righteous men, but to unrighteous men: To everyone who is
2 False teachers give heed to speculations & controversies rather than God's work	4 Nor to devote themselves to myths and endless genealogies. These promote controversies rather than God's work—which is by faith.	those who kill their fathers or mothers, for murderers, 10 For adulterers and perverts, for slave traders and liars and perjurers—and for whatever else is contrary to	guilty of any of these—to all of us 2) Law is given to restrain men

3 False teachers put empty discussion above love
  a. Above a pure heart
  b. Above a good conscience
  c. Above a sincere faith
	5 The goal of this command is love, which comes from a pure heart and a good conscience and a sincere faith.
	6 Some have wandered away from these and turned to
		the sound doctrine
		11 That conforms to the glorious gospel of the blessed God, which he entrusted to me.
			b. They do not understand the real measuring rod: The gospel

DIVISION I

FALSE AND TRUE TEACHERS IN THE CHURCH, 1:3-11

A. The Danger of False Teachers, 1:3-11

(1:3-11) **Introduction—Minister**: this is the first charge to the young minister—*to be a defender of the faith*. The young minister must guard against and correct false teachers. (See the general outline for the other charges to the young minister.)
1. False teachers teach a different doctrine (v.3).
2. False teachers give heed to speculations and controversies rather than God's work (v.4).
3. False teachers put empty discussion above love (v.5-6).
4. False teachers put ambition and personal ideas above the truth (v.7).
5. False teachers put self-righteousness above God's gospel (v.8-11).

1 (1:3) **Teachers, False—Doctrine**: false teachers teach a different doctrine. Timothy was in Ephesus and Paul was in Macedonia, a great distance apart. Ephesus was in Asia and Macedonia was in Europe, north of Greece. Note that Paul had to urge Timothy to stay at Ephesus. The church was in trouble because false teaching had seeped in, and the church needed Timothy. Apparently, Timothy felt incapable and wanted to join Paul until Paul could return to Ephesus and handle the situation himself. However, false teaching is so serious a matter that it has to be handled immediately when it raises its ugly head. Therefore, Timothy had to remain in Ephesus so that he could command the church to stop the false teaching. The word "command" (parangello) is a strong word. It is a military word that means to pass commands down through the ranks. Timothy was to *give orders and command* the false teachers to stop teaching false doctrine, and if this did not work, he was to order and command the church to handle the false teachers. This says several things about the church at Ephesus.

1. The leaders had not heeded the word of Paul when he had met with them earlier (Acts 20:17-38). He had warned them about false teachers.

> Keep watch over yourselves and all the flock of which the Holy Spirit has made you overseers. Be shepherds of the church of God, which he bought with his own blood. I know that after I leave, savage wolves will come in among you and will not spare the flock. Even from your own number men will arise and distort the truth in order to draw away disciples after them. So be on your guard! Remember that for three years I never stopped warning each of you night and day with tears. (Acts 20:28-31)

2. The leaders had not insisted upon the purity of the gospel as Paul had done and taught. They had allowed the Word of God to become corrupted.

> However, I consider my life worth nothing to me, if only I may finish the race and complete the task the Lord Jesus has given me—the task of testifying to the gospel of God's grace." Now I know that none of you among whom I have gone about preaching the kingdom will ever see me again. Therefore, I declare to you today that I am innocent of the blood of all men. For I have not hesitated to proclaim to you the whole will of God. (Acts 20:24-27)

> "Now I commit you to God and to the word of his grace, which can build you up and give you an inheritance among all those who are sanctified. (Acts 20:32)

Unlike so many, we do not peddle the word of God for profit. On the contrary, in Christ we speak before God with sincerity, like men sent from God. (2 Cor 2:17)

3. Timothy was to command the ministers, teachers, and leaders to preach no other doctrine than the doctrine of God's Word.
⇒ They were not to add to the doctrine of God's Word.
⇒ They were not to take away from the doctrine of God's Word.
⇒ They were not to formulate new doctrines for the church.

They were not to make what they thought were improvements nor to correct what they thought were defects in the Word of God. They were not to change or alter the Word of God to any degree whatsoever. In the clear words of this verse: "command certain men not to teach false doctrine any longer."

> I am astonished that you are so quickly deserting the one who called you by the grace of Christ and are turning to a different gospel—which is really no gospel at all. Evidently some people are throwing you into confusion and are trying to pervert the gospel of Christ. But even if we or an angel from heaven should preach a gospel other than the one we preached to you, let him be eternally condemned! As we have already said, so now I say again: If anybody is preaching to you a gospel other than what you accepted, let him be eternally condemned! (Gal 1:6-9)
>
> Then they understood that he was not telling them to guard against the yeast used in bread, but against the teaching of the Pharisees and Sadducees. (Mat 16:12)
>
> See to it that no one takes you captive through hollow and deceptive philosophy, which depends on human tradition and the basic principles of this world rather than on Christ. (Col 2:8)
>
> Do not be carried away by all kinds of strange teachings. It is good for our hearts to be strengthened by grace, not by ceremonial foods, which are of no value to those who eat them. (Heb 13:9)

2 (1:4) **Teachers, False**: false teachers give heed to speculations and controversies rather than God's work. No better description of false teaching could be given than what this verse gives:

> Nor to devote themselves to myths and endless genealogies. These promote controversies rather than God's work—which is by faith. (1 Tim 1:4)

1. The word "myths" (muthois) refers to *all forms* of false and fictional teaching or doctrine. It means the *false ideas* and speculations of men about God and Christ and the teachings of God's Word. The doctrines of men are only speculations, fables, narratives, stories, fictions, and falsehoods (A.T. Robertson. *Word Pictures in the New Testament*, Vol.4, p.561).

> Have nothing to do with godless myths and old wives' tales; rather, train yourself to be godly. (1 Tim 4:7)
>
> They will turn their ears away from the truth and turn aside to myths. (2 Tim 4:4)
>
> And will pay no attention to Jewish myths or to the commands of those who reject the truth. (Titus 1:14)
>
> We did not follow cleverly invented stories when we told you about the power and coming of our Lord Jesus Christ, but we were eyewitnesses of his majesty. (2 Pet 1:16)

2. The word "genealogies" refers to those who take comfort in a godly heritage. The Jews were guilty of this. They took great pride in their godly forefathers, so much so that they felt that the godliness of their forefathers rubbed off on them. The more godly forefathers they had in their roots, the more prestigious and acceptable they felt before God and men. They felt that the stronger their roots, the more man and God would accept and esteem them. Note the reference to "endless genealogies." There were apparently those who were spending enormous amounts of time in structuring and discussing the godly heritage of the past. Apparently, the practice had seeped into the church. There were those...
- who were stressing heritage over Christ.
- who were depending upon a godly heritage for salvation instead of trusting Christ.
- who were spending more time in genealogies than in edifying and building up the godliness of the church.
- who were concentrating upon questions and theories rather than upon building godly behavior among believers.

Thought 1. Some persons take great comfort in their godly heritage. They actually feel that God would never reject them...
- because of their godly wives, husbands, children, parents.
- because they have a godly pastor or friend with whom they are close.

> Produce fruit in keeping with repentance. And do not begin to say to yourselves, 'We have Abraham as our father.' For I tell you that out of these stones God can raise up children for Abraham. (Luke 3:8)
>
> Then they hurled insults at him and said, "You are this fellow's disciple! We are disciples of Moses! (John 9:28)
>
> If you are convinced that you are a guide for the blind, a light for those who are in the dark, (Rom 2:19)
>
> Who can bring what is pure from the impure? No one! (Job 14:4)
>
> 'I am pure and without sin; I am clean and free from guilt. (Job 33:9)
>
> Many a man claims to have unfailing love, but a faithful man who can find? (Prov 20:6)
>
> Who can say, "I have kept my heart pure; I am clean and without sin"? (Prov 20:9)

All a man's ways seem right to him, but the LORD weighs the heart. (Prov 21:2)

Those who are pure in their own eyes and yet are not cleansed of their filth; (Prov 30:12)

3 (1:5-6) **Teachers, False—Love—Conscience—Faith**: false teachers put empty discussion above love. The end of God's commandment to men is love (agape, God's kind of love). Therefore, ministers and teachers are to focus upon growing in love and in teaching love. The great call of believers is…

- to know the love of God and to love God.
- to love each other as brothers in the Lord.
- to love the lost of the world so much that we are driven to take the gospel to them.

But note where this kind of love comes from. Its source is not found in men; it does not just arise out of the heart of man. The love which we are to know and possess comes from three sources.

⇒ Love comes from a pure heart: a heart forgiven by God and cleansed from all impurities; a heart that is not weighed down by selfishness, worldliness, envy, covetousness, and immorality.

⇒ Love comes from a good conscience: a conscience that knows there is nothing between it and God, between it and men; a conscience that knows it has been true to God's Word and has taught no error.

⇒ Love comes from a sincere faith: a faith that is set upon God and His Word, that holds to God's Word and trusts and teaches God's Word and God's Word only.

The end of God's commandment—of all that God has ever said to man—is love. Therefore, a true believer commits his life to learn more and more about the love of God and to teach the love of God more and more. But to do this he must be totally committed…

- to having a pure heart before God.
- to having a good (clear) conscience before God.
- to following *the faith*, that is, the teachings and doctrine of God's Word.

However, this is not true with some—not true with false teachers. Note exactly what Scripture says: some have wondered and turned away to empty discussions. The term "meaningless talk" sounds just like what false teaching amounts to: meaningless talk. The term means empty arguments, discussions, and speculations—the speculative ideas of men about God, Christ, and the Word of God. Note that false teachers swerve and turn aside from the doctrines of God's Word to meaningless talk.

The Spirit clearly says that in later times some will abandon the faith and follow deceiving spirits and things taught by demons. Such teachings come through hypocritical liars, whose consciences have been seared as with a hot iron. (1 Tim 4:1-2)

For there are many rebellious people, mere talkers and deceivers, especially those of the circumcision group. (Titus 1:10)

"Would a wise man answer with empty notions or fill his belly with the hot east wind? Would he argue with useless words, with speeches that have no value? (Job 15:2-3)

At the beginning his words are folly; at the end they are wicked madness— (Eccl 10:13)

4 (1:7) **Teachers, False**: false teachers put their own ambition and personal ideas above the truth. The picture is that of a person who is ambitious..

- to be recognized as an original teacher or preacher.
- to be recognized as a creative person.
- to be recognized as the creator of a novel idea or doctrine.
- to be recognized as the author of a new concept or doctrine.
- to be recognized as the founder of a new movement.

The picture is that of a person who so desires to fit in with the latest fashion of teaching that he neglects or ignores the truth. He disregards the truth in order to fit in with his peers. The false teacher's ambition is allowed to cloud his understanding of the truth.

Barclay points out that the false teacher who is ambitious often…

- demonstrates arrogance instead of humility.
- focuses upon teaching rather than learning.
- looks down upon simple-minded people.
- regards those who do not agree with his conclusions as ignorant fools. (*The Letters to Timothy, Titus, and Philemon*, p.37.)

They worship me in vain; their teachings are but rules taught by men.'" (Mat 15:9)

Jesus replied, "You are in error because you do not know the Scriptures or the power of God. (Mat 22:29)

He was in the world, and though the world was made through him, the world did not recognize him. He came to that which was his own, but his own did not receive him. (John 1:10-11)

(They still did not understand from Scripture that Jesus had to rise from the dead.) (John 20:9)

Such teachings come through hypocritical liars, whose consciences have been seared as with a hot iron. (1 Tim 4:2)

If anyone teaches false doctrines and does not agree to the sound instruction of our Lord Jesus Christ and to godly teaching, he is conceited and understands nothing. He has an unhealthy interest in controversies and quarrels about words that result in envy, strife, malicious talk, evil suspicions and constant friction between men of corrupt mind, who have been robbed of the truth and who think that godliness is a means to financial gain. (1 Tim 6:3-5)

For the time will come when men will not put up with sound doctrine. Instead, to suit their own desires, they will gather around them a great number of teachers to say what their itching ears want to hear. (2 Tim 4:3)

They must be silenced, because they are ruining whole households by teaching things they ought not to teach—and that for the sake of dishonest gain. (Titus 1:11)

But there were also false prophets among the people, just as there will be false teachers among you. They will secretly introduce destructive heresies, even denying the sovereign Lord who bought them—bringing swift destruction on themselves. Many will follow their shameful ways and will bring the way of truth into disrepute. In their greed these teachers will exploit you with stories they have made up. Their condemnation has long been hanging over them, and their destruction has not been sleeping. (2 Pet 2:1-3)

5 (1:8-11) **Teachers, False—Law, The**: false teachers put self-righteousness above God's gospel. These verses show that the false teachers who had infiltrated the church were Jewish legalists. These said that a person became acceptable to God...

- by Christ *and the law*.
- by receiving Christ *plus keeping the law*.
- by becoming righteous in Christ *and by doing* the righteousness of the law.

They rejected the teaching that a person was saved by grace through faith *alone*. To them a person could not be saved unless he...

- became good enough to please God.
- did enough good to make himself acceptable to God.

What is wrong with this? There is nothing wrong with doing good, but there is a great deal wrong with *thinking and teaching* that a person can do *enough good* to make himself acceptable to God. God is perfect; therefore, a person would have to become perfect to be acceptable to God.

⇒ Man is already short of perfection; he is already imperfect; therefore, he can never be acceptable to God—not by any merit or work of his own.

⇒ Man already comes so short and is so sinful, he can never stop coming short and sinning. Every man comes short, sins, fails, trespasses, and transgresses—no matter who he is. He is depraved and lives a depraved life—a life short of God's glory (Ro.3:23).

This is the reason God gave man the law: not to show man that he is righteous (lawful), but to show him just how far short he really is of God's glory—how unrighteous he is and how much he needs the love and grace of God. God gave the law to show man how much he needs a Savior, the Lord Jesus Christ, the Son of God Himself. This is what man fails to see. This is what the false teachers fail to see.

1. False teachers do not understand the law and its purposes. God gave the law to man to show him how short he comes (unrighteousness) and to restrain evil. Note this:

⇒ The law was given to man—to all men.
⇒ The law was not made for the righteous, but for the unrighteous.
⇒ Therefore, all men must be unrighteous because the law was given to all men.

Scripture gives a list of the people to whom God gave the law. Note how the list covers all of society. Every person is guilty of having broken the law of God.

a. The law is given to the lawbreakers and rebels: all who fail to live as God wills and commands. If a person could fail just once (he can't, but if he could), he would still need the law to let him know that he is short of the standard and has to pay the penalty and must not violate the standard any more.

b. The law is given to the ungodly and sinful: all who act contrary to God's nature and come short of perfection.

c. The law is given to the unholy and irreligious: all who refuse to set their lives apart to God and dedicate themselves to God; all who deny and question God and spiritual things and exalt themselves and this world above God and the spiritual world.

d. The law is given to "those who strike and beat and [even] murder fathers and strike and beat and [even] murder mothers" and for other murderers (Amplified New Testament).

e. The law is given to adulterers and perverts that is, all impure and immoral persons and all homosexuals.

f. The law is given to slave traders or kidnappers.

g. The law is given to liars and to those who commit perjury.

h. The law is given to any thing else that is contrary to the sound doctrine (teaching) of God's Word.

Note how no person is left out of the list: every human being who has ever lived or ever will live needs the law, for every person is short of God's glory; that is, every man is unrighteous. Therefore, no person can ever be acceptable to God. Righteousness is not by the law—not by being good and doing good. False teachers fail to see this.

2. False teachers do not understand the real measuring rod of God: the gospel—the glorious gospel of the blessed God. The blessed God has made a way for man to become acceptable to Him. It is not the way of law and works, but the way of the gospel. When a person accepts the gospel of God, God accepts that person. What is the gospel?

> **Here is a trustworthy saying that deserves full acceptance: Christ Jesus came into the world to save sinners—of whom I am the worst. (1 Tim 1:15)**
>
> **For what I received I passed on to you as of first importance : that Christ died for our sins according to the Scriptures, that he was buried, that he was raised on the third day according to the Scriptures, (1 Cor 15:3-4)**
>
> **He himself bore our sins in his body on the tree, so that we might die to sins and live for righteousness; by his wounds you have been healed. (1 Pet 2:24)**
>
> **"For God so loved the world that he gave his one and only Son, that whoever believes in him shall not perish but have eternal life. For God did not send his Son into the world to condemn the world, but to save the world through him. Whoever believes in him is not condemned, but whoever does not believe stands condemned already because he has not believed in the name of God's one and only Son. (John 3:16-18)**

1 TIMOTHY 1:12-17

1 Christ Jesus appointed him to serve a. Christ strengthened him b. Christ considered him trustworthy c. Christ forgave his terrible sins d. Christ poured out His grace upon him	**B. The Testimony of a True Minister, 1:12-17** 12 I thank Christ Jesus our Lord, who has given me strength, that he considered me faithful, appointing me to his service. 13 Even though I was once a blasphemer and a persecutor and a violent man, I was shown mercy because I acted in ignorance and unbelief. 14 The grace of our Lord was poured out on me abundantly, along with the faith and love that are in Christ Jesus.	15 Here is a trustworthy saying that deserves full acceptance: Christ Jesus came into the world to save sinners—of whom I am the worst. 16 But for that very reason I was shown mercy so that in me, the worst of sinners, Christ Jesus might display his unlimited patience as an example for those who would believe on him and receive eternal life. 17 Now to the King eternal, immortal, invisible, the only God, be honor and glory for ever and ever. Amen.	**2 Christ saved him** a. Christ came to save sinners b. Christ has now saved the "worst" sinner c. Christ saved him as an example of His great mercy^{DS1} **3 Christ is to be praised**

DIVISION I

FALSE AND TRUE TEACHERS IN THE CHURCH, 1:3-20

B. The Testimony of a True Minister, 1:12-17

(1:12-17) **Introduction**: this passage is a contrast with the former passage (1 Tim.1:3-11), presenting a strong contrast between the true minister and false teachers. These verses cover the testimony of Paul, who was a true minister. The verses are a sharp contrast with those who are false teachers (see outline and notes—1 Tim.1:3-11). It is a passage that every minister and teacher of the church should heed.

1. Christ Jesus appointed him to serve (v.12-14).
2. Christ saved him (v.15-16).
3. Christ is to be praised (v.17).

1 (1:12-14) **Minister**: Christ Jesus appointed him to serve. Jesus Christ puts the true minister in the ministry. This is a critical fact. Paul says that he did not make himself a minister nor did other persons choose him to be a minister. He did not choose the ministry because he thought it would be a good profession nor because people thought he would make a good minister. He was in the ministry for one reason only: Christ Jesus had chosen him and put him into the ministry. Note four facts.

1. Christ Jesus *strengthened* Paul. The word "strength" (endunamoo) means to enable and give power to. The power of Paul's ministry came from Christ. Christ gave him the strength to minister. Paul's strength and power to minister did not come from his...

- trying to stir up power within himself.
- talking about the results and power in his ministry.
- trying to program strength and power into his ministry.
- trying to shout power into his preaching.

Christ Himself put Paul into the ministry; therefore Christ Himself strengthened and empowered Paul for the ministry. No person has the power to do spiritual warfare; no person can penetrate the spirits of other people. If a person is to minister to people, he must be empowered by Christ, for only Christ can penetrate the spirits of people. Therefore, the minister must possess the power of Christ.

Thought 1. This is a critical fact. It means that a person cannot make himself a minister nor can other persons choose him to be a minister—not a true minister, not a minister who pleases Christ and can be blessed by Christ. Why? Because no person can carry on a successful ministry in his own strength, not a ministry that truly reaches people for Christ and delivers them from sin, death, and the judgment to come. Only Christ can do this. This is the reason the minister must be enabled by Christ; he must minister in the strength and power of Christ.

A person who is in the ministry because he has chosen the ministry as a profession or because people thought he would make a good minister is only serving a humanistic religion. Of course, a humanistic minister—a minister who ministers only in his human strength—does some good through social and emotional development. But he does much harm in that he leads people into a false security. How? He is not able to spiritually save a person—not a single person—from sin, death, and the judgment to come. Only Christ Jesus can do this. Therefore, the only way a minister can be what he should be...

- is to be put in the ministry by Christ Jesus.
- is to be strengthened and empowered by Christ Jesus.

> **You did not choose me, but I chose you and appointed you to go and bear fruit—fruit that will last. Then the Father will give you whatever you ask in my name. (John 15:16)**
>
> **But God chose the foolish things of the world to shame the wise; God chose the weak things of the world to shame the strong. He chose the lowly things of this world and the despised things—and the things that are not—to nullify the things that are, so that no one may boast before him. (1 Cor 1:27-29)**
>
> **He [God] has made us competent as ministers of a new covenant—not of the letter but of the Spirit; for the letter kills, but the Spirit gives life. (2 Cor 3:6)**
>
> **Therefore, since through God's mercy we have this ministry, we do not lose heart. (2 Cor 4:1)**

1 TIMOTHY 1:12-17

All this is from God, who reconciled us to himself through Christ and gave us the ministry of reconciliation: that God was reconciling the world to himself in Christ, not counting men's sins against them. And he has committed to us the message of reconciliation. We are therefore Christ's ambassadors, as though God were making his appeal through us. We implore you on Christ's behalf: Be reconciled to God. God made him who had no sin to be sin for us, so that in him we might become the righteousness of God. (2 Cor 5:18-21)

I became a servant of this gospel by the gift of God's grace given me through the working of his power. (Eph 3:7)

It was he who gave some to be apostles, some to be prophets, some to be evangelists, and some to be pastors and teachers, to prepare God's people for works of service, so that the body of Christ may be built up until we all reach unity in the faith and in the knowledge of the Son of God and become mature, attaining to the whole measure of the fullness of Christ. (Eph 4:11-13)

I thank Christ Jesus our Lord, who has given me strength, that he considered me faithful, appointing me to his service. (1 Tim 1:12)

Who has saved us and called us to a holy life—not because of anything we have done but because of his own purpose and grace. This grace was given us in Christ Jesus before the beginning of time, but it has now been revealed through the appearing of our Savior, Christ Jesus, who has destroyed death and has brought life and immortality to light through the gospel. And of this gospel I was appointed a herald and an apostle and a teacher. (2 Tim 1:9-11)

2. **Christ Jesus considered him trustworthy.** This is a most wonderful thought, that Christ would consider us trustworthy. He trusts us to be faithful, and in the final analysis, He knows that we will be faithful to Him. This is one of the reasons He chooses and puts us in the ministry.

Thought 1. No matter how far down a minister falls, he should always remember that Christ Jesus considers him faithful. Christ knows that the minister of Christ will arise and begin to serve with renewed fervor. This is the reason Christ called the minister: because in the final analysis the minister will be faithful. How do we know this? Because of the forgiveness and power and faithfulness of Christ. Therefore, any minister who has fallen must arise and seek the forgiveness of Christ and begin to walk anew in the strength and power of Christ.

Thought 2. William Barclay has an excellent message for us as we deal with our dear brothers and sisters who have fallen.

"It was to Paul an amazing thing, that he, the arch-persecutor, had been chosen as the missionary and the pioneer of Christ. It was not only that Jesus Christ had forgiven him; it was that Christ had trusted him. Sometimes in human affairs we forgive a man who has committed some mistake or who has been guilty of some sin, but we make it very clear that his past makes it impossible for us to trust him again with any responsibility. But Christ had not only forgiven Paul, He had entrusted him with His work to do. The man who had been the persecutor of Christ had been made the ambassador of Christ" (*The Letters to Timothy, Titus, and Philemon*, p.48).

Now it is required that those who have been given a trust must prove faithful. (1 Cor 4:2)

If I preach voluntarily, I have a reward; if not voluntarily, I am simply discharging the trust committed to me. (1 Cor 9:17)

I have become its servant by the commission God gave me to present to you the word of God in its fullness— (Col 1:25)

On the contrary, we speak as men approved by God to be entrusted with the gospel. We are not trying to please men but God, who tests our hearts. You know we never used flattery, nor did we put on a mask to cover up greed—God is our witness. (1 Th 2:4-5)

That conforms to the glorious gospel of the blessed God, which he entrusted to me. I thank Christ Jesus our Lord, who has given me strength, that he considered me faithful, appointing me to his service. (1 Tim 1:11-12)

A faith and knowledge resting on the hope of eternal life, which God, who does not lie, promised before the beginning of time, and at his appointed season he brought his word to light through the preaching entrusted to me by the command of God our Savior, (Titus 1:2-3)

3. **Christ Jesus forgave his terrible sins.** Paul mentions three terrible sins of which he had been guilty.

⇒ Blasphemy: he had insulted, reviled, cursed, and railed the name of Christ.
⇒ Persecutor: he had been so angry at Christ that he had set out to wipe the Lord's name off the face of the earth. Therefore, he had been set against all believers—set upon destroying them all. (See note, *Church, Persecution of*—Acts 8:3 for more discussion.)
⇒ A violent man (hubristes): insolent; to treat and use others despitefully; to be brutal and violent and to enjoy it; to be in a fiery rage and to inflict it upon others. William Barclay says that the word "indicates a kind of arrogant sadism; it describes the man who is out to inflict pain and injury for the sheer joy of inflicting it....that is what Paul was once like in regard to the Christian Church. Not content with words of insult, he went to the limit of legal persecution. Not content with legal persecution, he went to the limit of sadistic brutality in his attempt to stamp out the Christian faith" (*The Letters to Timothy, Titus, and Philemon*, p.52).

However despite all this evil, God had mercy upon Paul. Paul had not known that Christ was really the true Messiah. He thought that he knew God and that his religion was the true religion. He felt that any religion that stood against his religion was to be stamped out. Therefore, when Paul attacked Christ and His followers, he did it ignorantly in unbelief. He just did not believe that Jesus Christ could possibly be the Messiah.

The point is this: God had mercy upon Paul. He took pity upon Paul despite his terrible sins (see Deeper Study # 2, Mercy—1 Tim.1:2).

> It does not, therefore, depend on man's desire or effort, but on God's mercy. (Rom 9:16)
>
> But when the kindness and love of God our Savior appeared, he saved us, not because of righteous things we had done, but because of his mercy. He saved us through the washing of rebirth and renewal by the Holy Spirit, whom he poured out on us generously through Jesus Christ our Savior, so that, having been justified by his grace, we might become heirs having the hope of eternal life. (Titus 3:4-7)
>
> Because of the Lord's great love we are not consumed, for his compassions never fail. (Lam 3:22)
>
> Who is a God like you, who pardons sin and forgives the transgression of the remnant of his inheritance? You do not stay angry forever but delight to show mercy. (Micah 7:18)

4. Christ Jesus poured out His grace upon Paul. Remember: grace means the undeserved favor and blessings of God.

⇒ Christ favored Paul even when he did not deserve it.
⇒ Christ blessed Paul even when he did not deserve it.

And note: Christ favored and blessed him *abundantly*, that is, superabundantly and beyond measure. Christ did two things for Paul.

⇒ Christ stirred *faith* in Paul: the faith to believe and trust and to serve and to keep on serving no matter the trial, problem, or fatigue.
⇒ Christ stirred *love* in Paul: the love to still reach out and do all he could for people even when they rejected, ridiculed, abused, and persecuted him. (See note—1 Tim.1:5-6 for more discussion.)

> Or do you show contempt for the riches of his kindness, tolerance and patience, not realizing that God's kindness leads you toward repentance? (Rom 2:4)
>
> And are justified freely by his grace through the redemption that came by Christ Jesus. (Rom 3:24)
>
> In him we have redemption through his blood, the forgiveness of sins, in accordance with the riches of God's grace (Eph 1:7)
>
> The grace of our Lord was poured out on me abundantly, along with the faith and love that are in Christ Jesus. (1 Tim 1:14)

> For the grace of God that brings salvation has appeared to all men. It teaches us to say "No" to ungodliness and worldly passions, and to live self-controlled, upright and godly lives in this present age, while we wait for the blessed hope—the glorious appearing of our great God and Savior, Jesus Christ, who gave himself for us to redeem us from all wickedness and to purify for himself a people that are his very own, eager to do what is good. (Titus 2:11-14)

2 (1:15-16) **Minister—Salvation**: Jesus Christ saves the true minister. Three significant points are made in these two verses.

1. Christ Jesus came into the world to save sinners. This is a trustworthy saying or statement. It is a true message that can be trusted, and the glorious message is worthy of everyone *accepting* it. Not a single person should reject or ignore the message.

"Christ Jesus came into the world to save sinners." Christ actually left the spiritual world or dimension to come into the physical world in order to save the human race. He saves us from sin, death, and the judgment to come. No matter how sinful a person is—no matter how great a sin or sins he has committed—Christ Jesus came to save him. And the person can be saved.

The point is this: every true minister has been saved by Christ or else he is not a true minister. It is just as necessary for a minister to be saved as it is for anyone else. Every person needs to be saved, and once he has been saved—no matter how terrible his sin—Christ can put him into the ministry.

> For the Son of Man came to seek and to save what was lost." (Luke 19:10)
>
> "For God so loved the world that he gave his one and only Son, that whoever believes in him shall not perish but have eternal life. For God did not send his Son into the world to condemn the world, but to save the world through him. (John 3:16-17)
>
> "As for the person who hears my words but does not keep them, I do not judge him. For I did not come to judge the world, but to save it. There is a judge for the one who rejects me and does not accept my words; that very word which I spoke will condemn him at the last day. (John 12:47-48)
>
> God exalted him to his own right hand as Prince and Savior that he might give repentance and forgiveness of sins to Israel. (Acts 5:31)
>
> Here is a trustworthy saying that deserves full acceptance: Christ Jesus came into the world to save sinners—of whom I am the worst. (1 Tim 1:15)
>
> Therefore he is able to save completely those who come to God through him, because he always lives to intercede for them. (Heb 7:25)

2. Christ Jesus has now saved the worst sinner. The worst sins in the world are the sins of...

- blasphemy: being filled with anger and malice against Christ; cursing and blaspheming His name with a bitter hostility.
- persecuting believers and trying to annihilate them off the face of the earth.
- injuring believers; being brutal and violent against believers and enjoying it.

This had been Paul, but note the wonderful truth: "Christ Jesus came into the world to save sinners." And Paul was the worst sinner; therefore, Christ Jesus had come to save him.

> **Thought 1.** Christ will save anyone who confesses that he is a sinner and that he needs to be saved—any sinner who truly confesses and repents of his sin. No matter how terrible the sin, if the person will confess and turn from his sin, Christ will save him. Why? Because Christ Jesus came to save sinners. This was His very purpose for coming into the world.

The point is this: every true minister is to know how terrible a sinner he is. He is as much a sinner as Paul was. The minister is to be as conscious of being a sinner as much as anyone else. He is to be aware that he is "the worst" of sinners or else he lacks a true sense of God's holiness and of man's depravity.

> On hearing this, Jesus said, "It is not the healthy who need a doctor, but the sick. But go and learn what this means: 'I desire mercy, not sacrifice.' For I have not come to call the righteous, but sinners." (Mat 9:12-13)
>
> When the Pharisee who had invited him saw this, he said to himself, "If this man were a prophet, he would know who is touching him and what kind of woman she is—that she is a sinner." (Luke 7:39)
>
> All the people saw this and began to mutter, "He has gone to be the guest of a 'sinner.'" (Luke 19:7)
>
> Jesus straightened up and asked her, "Woman, where are they? Has no one condemned you?" "No one, sir," she said. "Then neither do I condemn you," Jesus declared. "Go now and leave your life of sin." (John 8:10-11)
>
> But God demonstrates his own love for us in this: While we were still sinners, Christ died for us. (Rom 5:8)
>
> Peter replied, "Repent and be baptized, every one of you, in the name of Jesus Christ for the forgiveness of your sins. And you will receive the gift of the Holy Spirit. (Acts 2:38)
>
> Repent, then, and turn to God, so that your sins may be wiped out, that times of refreshing may come from the Lord, (Acts 3:19)
>
> Here is a trustworthy saying that deserves full acceptance: Christ Jesus came into the world to save sinners—of whom I am the worst. (1 Tim 1:15)
>
> He who conceals his sins does not prosper, but whoever confesses and renounces them finds mercy. (Prov 28:13)

3. Christ Jesus saved Paul as an example of His great mercy. (See DEEPER STUDY # 1—1 Tim.1:16 for more discussion.) Very simply, Paul is the prime example...

- that any sinner, no matter how terrible his sin, can be saved—if he will only receive Christ and begin to follow Him day by day.
- that any believer can be delivered from sin and from the power of sin, no matter how strong the enslavement is—if he will only receive the power of Christ and follow Him with a renewed commitment.

The point is this: the true minister is an example of the Lord's great patience. The Lord has saved the minister from sin, truly saved him; therefore, the true minister stands as a dynamic example of God's eternal mercy and eternal grace.

> That everyone who believes in him may have eternal life. "For God so loved the world that he gave his one and only Son, that whoever believes in him shall not perish but have eternal life. (John 3:15-16)
>
> "I tell you the truth, whoever hears my word and believes him who sent me has eternal life and will not be condemned; he has crossed over from death to life. (John 5:24)
>
> Jesus said to her, "I am the resurrection and the life. He who believes in me will live, even though he dies; (John 11:25)
>
> I have come into the world as a light, so that no one who believes in me should stay in darkness. (John 12:46)
>
> But these are written that you may believe that Jesus is the Christ, the Son of God, and that by believing you may have life in his name. (John 20:31)
>
> That if you confess with your mouth, "Jesus is Lord," and believe in your heart that God raised him from the dead, you will be saved. For it is with your heart that you believe and are justified, and it is with your mouth that you confess and are saved. (Rom 10:9-10)
>
> The Lord is not slow in keeping his promise, as some understand slowness. He is patient with you, not wanting anyone to perish, but everyone to come to repentance. (2 Pet 3:9)

DEEPER STUDY # 1

(1:16) **Paul, Example**: Paul was chosen to be the example for all other men. The example of what? Of unlimited patience—that God's mercy can save anyone. Paul had been the arch-persecutor of the church, storming into the homes and arresting and murdering the followers of Christ (see notes—Acts 8:1-4; 9:1-2). But God, who is patient and not willing that any should perish, reached down and had mercy upon Paul. God forgave Paul and saved him.

Paul declared a marvelous truth: if God could save him, God could save anyone. No matter how great the sinner, the patience and mercy of God are greater. Paul is proof; he is the example of God's mercy.

---

3 (1:17) **Minister—Jesus Christ—God**: Christ is to be praised. Thinking of the glorious salvation that Christ had given him led Paul to break forth into praise. This is a great doxology:

⇒ God is "the King eternal": the word eternal is literally *ages*. God is the King, the sovereign majesty of the ages, both this age and the age to come.
⇒ God is immortal: that is, incorruptible. He has no seed of corruption, no seed of aging, deterioration, or decay within His being. God cannot die. He alone has immortality (1 Tim.6:16).
⇒ God is invisible: that is, He cannot be seen by people, not with physical eyes in the physical dimension or world.
⇒ God is the only God: that is, he is the only living and true God, the only God who actually possesses intelligence and wisdom, who can truthfully interact with the world and save men.

So that with one heart and mouth you may glorify the God and Father of our Lord Jesus Christ. (Rom 15:6)

You were bought at a price. Therefore honor God with your body. (1 Cor 6:20)

Through Jesus, therefore, let us continually offer to God a sacrifice of praise—the fruit of lips that confess his name. (Heb 13:15)

But you are a chosen people, a royal priesthood, a holy nation, a people belonging to God, that you may declare the praises of him who called you out of darkness into his wonderful light. (1 Pet 2:9)

1 TIMOTHY 1:18-20

	C. The Young Minister (Charge 1): To Be a Warrior, 1:18-20	19 Holding on to faith and a good conscience. Some have rejected these and so have shipwrecked their faith.	2 The equipment & weapons of war: The faith & a good conscience^{DS1}

1 The charge: To fight the good fight
  a. Timothy's special call to the ministry
  b. His call was to stir him to fight the good fight
	18 Timothy, my son, I give you this instruction in keeping with the prophecies once made about you, so that by following them you may fight the good fight,	20 Among them are Hymenaeus and Alexander, whom I have handed over to Satan to be taught not to blaspheme.	3 The warning: Conscience can be rejected, & faith can be shipwrecked
			  a. Two specific examples
			  b. The discipline
			    1) Delivered to Satan
			    2) Corrective not punitive

DIVISION I

FALSE AND TRUE TEACHERS IN THE CHURCH, 1:3-20

C. The Young Minister (Charge 1): To Be a Warrior, 1:18-20

(1:18-20) **Introduction**: this is a great study for the young minister or for any person who is sensing the call to serve God. All believers are called to be warriors for God in this world. But the minister of God is called to do more: he is called *to take charge* and *to lead* in being a warrior.
1. The charge: the fight the good fight (v.18).
2. The equipment and weapons of war: the faith and a good conscience (v.19).
3. The warning: conscience can be rejected and faith shipwrecked (v.19-20).

1 (1:18) **Minister—Spiritual Struggle and Warfare—Fight**: the charge to the young minister is forceful—fight the good fight! Paul is giving an "instruction" (paraggelian) to Timothy. The word means a command, an urgent command, a military command. It is a command that lays upon a person the most urgent and critical obligation. Donald Guthrie says, "The ministry is not a matter to be trifled with, but an order from the commander-in-chief" (*The Pastoral Epistles*. "Tyndale New Testament Commentaries," p.67). W.E. Vine points out that the "charge" is always a command from a superior that is to be transmitted to others; that is, this charge—the charge to fight a good warfare—is to be given to the young minister and he, in turn, is to pass the charge on to others (*Expository Dictionary of New Testament Words*. Old Tappan, NJ: Fleming H. Revell, 1966).

> And the things you have heard me say in the presence of many witnesses entrust to reliable men who will also be qualified to teach others. (2 Tim 2:2)

Note two points in this verse.
1. Timothy had a special call to the ministry. Remember: Timothy had a strong testimony for Christ before the church and his community (Acts 16:2). As A.T. Robertson says, "He began his ministry rich in hopes, prayers, *predictions*" (*Word Pictures in the New Testament*, Vol.4, p.565). The Holy Spirit actually *moved* upon several believers to predict that Timothy would enter the ministry and fight the good fight .

Thought 1. Note two significant points.
1) A person must be called to the ministry by the Spirit of God. The ministry is not just *another profession* where a person serves society and makes a living. The Christian ministry is the call of God—the call that puts a person right in the midst of spiritual war that fights for the souls and minds of people.

2) When a person is called by the Spirit of God, he must not reject the call. He must do exactly what Paul says: jump right into the midst of the battle and fight a good fight!

2. Timothy's call was to stir him to fight the good fight. He was never to forget his call—never to forget the predictions of his home church, the predictions that he would fight the good fight in the ministry for Christ—all for Christ. He was to keep these expectations of his home church before his mind and use them to stir him to fight for Christ.

Note: Paul is recommitting this instruction or charge to Timothy. Apparently Timothy needed to be recharged. He was facing the critical issue of false teaching in the church at Ephesus, and he was shrinking from it. But God's call was clear: he was to fight the good fight—to struggle even to the point of death if need be.

Believers, ministers and laymen alike, must never forget: the ministry is a sacred trust, a sacred commitment. God has taken the most precious and sacred thing to Him—the very gospel of His dear Son—and placed that message into the hands of men. Therefore, the minister must not fail. He must arise and charge right to the forefront of the warfare, the spiritual fight that is being fought for the souls and minds of people.

> **Thought 1.** A spiritual fight is being fought for the minds and souls of people. The minister of God is to be right in the middle of the conflict. He is God's instrument to teach men—to teach them the way to God and righteousness. If God's ministers do not fight and struggle to lead men to God, then literally millions of souls will perish without ever knowing the way to God—without ever knowing that a person can actually live forever in the presence of God. This is the reason ministers must arise and lead the charge into the battle for the minds and souls of men. So much depends upon the minister of God—so many souls, the hope and lives of so many—that he must be faithful and fight the good fight.

2 (1:19) **Minister—Spiritual Struggle and Warfare—Fight**: the equipment and weapons of war—the faith and a good conscience. Note that the young minister is to "hold"—that is, keep—the faith and a good conscience.
1. "The faith" means the truth of Christianity and of Christ and of the Word of God. It is the faith that the minister holds in Christ, in the very teachings of Christ and of the Word of God. *The faith* of the minister is the very basis, foundation, and structure of his life. *The faith* of the

1 TIMOTHY 1:18-20

Lord Jesus Christ and of the Word of God is his life. As the minister fights the spiritual battles of this life, he is to cling to the commands, instructions, and words of his commander-in-chief. He is not to turn away from the commands and words of the Lord Jesus Christ—not even for a minute.

2. The minister is to hold "a good conscience" (see DEEPER STUDY # 1, *Conscience*—1 Tim.1:19 for discussion).

DEEPER STUDY # 1
(1:19) **Conscience**: very simply stated, conscience is the inner sense of right and wrong. Contrary to what some teach, conscience does not come from training, education, society, or environment. Scripture says that conscience is innate; that is, a man is born with a consciousness of right and wrong.

> (Indeed, when Gentiles, who do not have the law, do by nature things required by the law, they are a law for themselves, even though they do not have the law, since they show that the requirements of the law are written on their hearts, their consciences also bearing witness, and their thoughts now accusing, now even defending them.) (Rom 2:14-15)

However, the conscience *has to be developed and matured* through education and environment. It is just like a small baby: it is there, existing, but it is undeveloped and immature until it is fed and taught what to do. In fact the conscience, just like a small child, is either developed or defiled—one or the other—through environment and education. Every person is born with a conscience, but its *value and health* are determined by how well it is fed and trained with righteousness and godliness. The better it is fed and taught, the more effective and valuable it will become.

The point is this: a good and healthy conscience comes from living a righteous and godly life before God. A bad and defiled conscience comes from living an unrighteous and ungodly life in this world. If a person violates his conscience (does wrong), his conscience pricks and nags him. He feels remorse, regret, and guilt. If he corrects his behavior and asks God for forgiveness, God removes the guilt—completely and totally. If he continues to violate his conscience, three things happen.

⇒ The conscience becomes hardened. It no longer directs the person. The pricking and nagging and pull to do right is dulled. The person becomes calloused and hardened to righteousness. He no longer has the direction of conscience and the consciousness of what is right. He is left alone in the world to walk in unrighteousness and ungodliness just as he wills. (See DEEPER STUDY # 1, *Unbelief*—Jn.12:39-41 for more discussion on the Judicial Judgment of God.)

⇒ Some persons refuse to listen and react against conscience, and they strike out in hostility and rebellion, living more and more unrighteously and ungodly.

⇒ Other persons refuse to listen to conscience and sense more and more failure. This can and often does lead to withdrawal and depression and all kinds of emotional and mental problems.

Scripture says the following about the conscience.
1. The work of conscience.
   a. The conscience convicts of sin.

> At this, those who heard began to go away one at a time, the older ones first, until only Jesus was left, with the woman still standing there. (John 8:9)

   b. The conscience (at least at first) bears witness to what is right even if a person does not have the law of God.

> (Indeed, when Gentiles, who do not have the law, do by nature things required by the law, they are a law for themselves, even though they do not have the law, since they show that the requirements of the law are written on their hearts, their consciences also bearing witness, and their thoughts now accusing, now even defending them.) (Rom 2:14-15)

   c. The conscience confirms the feelings and actions of a person.

> I speak the truth in Christ—I am not lying, my conscience confirms it in the Holy Spirit— (Rom 9:1)

   d. The conscience is to stir a person to live in holiness and sincerity.

> Now this is our boast: Our conscience testifies that we have conducted ourselves in the world, and especially in our relations with you, in the holiness and sincerity that are from God. We have done so not according to worldly wisdom but according to God's grace. (2 Cor 1:12)

   e. The conscience is to stir a person to commend himself to every man's conscience...
   • by renouncing deception.
   • by not destorting the Word of God.

> Rather, we have renounced secret and shameful ways; we do not use deception, nor do we distort the word of God. On the contrary, by setting forth the truth plainly we commend ourselves to every man's conscience in the sight of God. (2 Cor 4:2)

2. The source of a good, clear, pure, and healthy conscience.
   a. A good and healthy conscience comes from obeying the laws of the state.

> Therefore, it is necessary to submit to the authorities, not only because of possible punishment but also because of conscience. (Rom 13:5)

   b. A good and healthy conscience comes from love which flows from a pure heart and a sincere faith.

> The goal of this command is love, which comes from a pure heart and a good conscience and a sincere faith. (1 Tim 1:5)

   c. A good and healthy conscience comes from holding fast to one's faith and to a good conscience.

1 TIMOTHY 1:18-20

Holding on to faith and a good conscience. Some have rejected these and so have shipwrecked their faith. (1 Tim 1:19)

d. A good and healthy conscience comes from serving God.

I thank God, whom I serve, as my forefathers did, with a clear conscience, as night and day I constantly remember you in my prayers. (2 Tim 1:3)

e. A good and healthy conscience comes from being cleansed by the blood of Christ.

How much more, then, will the blood of Christ, who through the eternal Spirit offered himself unblemished to God, cleanse our consciences from acts that lead to death, so that we may serve the living God! (Heb 9:14)
Therefore, brothers, since we have confidence to enter the Most Holy Place by the blood of Jesus, by a new and living way opened for us through the curtain, that is, his body, and since we have a great priest over the house of God, let us draw near to God with a sincere heart in full assurance of faith, having our hearts sprinkled to cleanse us from a guilty conscience and having our bodies washed with pure water. (Heb 10:19-22)

f. A good and healthy conscience comes from the will to live honorably in all things.

Pray for us. We are sure that we have a clear conscience and desire to live honorably in every way. (Heb 13:18)

g. A good and healthy conscience comes from suffering unjustly for the sake of God.

For it is commendable if a man bears up under the pain of unjust suffering because he is conscious of God. (1 Pet 2:19)

h. A good and healthy conscience comes from good behavior in Christ.

Keeping a clear conscience [behavior], so that those who speak maliciously against your good behavior in Christ may be ashamed of their slander. (1 Pet 3:16)

3. Some facts about conscience.
   a. A person is to live in all good conscience.

   Paul looked straight at the Sanhedrin and said, "My brothers, I have fulfilled my duty to God in all good conscience to this day." (Acts 23:1)

   b. A person is to keep a conscience clear before God and man.

   So I strive always to keep my conscience clear before God and man. (Acts 24:16)

   c. The conscience can be weak.

   When you sin against your brothers in this way and wound their weak conscience, you sin against Christ. (1 Cor 8:12; cp. 1 Cor.8:7, 10)

   d. A person is not to do anything that would violate the conscience of another person.

   But if anyone says to you, "This has been offered in sacrifice," then do not eat it, both for the sake of the man who told you and for conscience' sake—the other man's conscience, I mean, not yours. For why should my freedom be judged by another's conscience? (1 Cor 10:28-29)

   e. Conscience can be rejected, and faith can be shipwrecked.

   Holding on to faith and a good conscience. Some have rejected these and so have shipwrecked their faith. (1 Tim 1:19)

   f. The conscience can be seared (branded either as following God or devils).

   Such teachings come through hypocritical liars, whose consciences have been seared as with a hot iron. (1 Tim 4:2)

   g. The conscience and mind are both corrupted (made impure, unclean) through defilement and unbelief.

   To the pure, all things are pure, but to those who are corrupted and do not believe, nothing is pure. In fact, both their minds and consciences are corrupted. (Titus 1:15)

   h. Keeping the law and being religious cannot make the conscience clear.

   This [tabernacle] is an illustration for the present time, indicating that the gifts and sacrifices being offered were not able to clear the conscience of the worshiper. (Heb 9:9)
   If it could, would they not have stopped being offered? For the worshipers would have been cleansed once for all, and would no longer have felt guilty for their sins. (Heb 10:2)

   i. Seeking for a good conscience toward God saves us by the resurrection of Jesus Christ.

   And this water symbolizes baptism that now saves you also—not the removal of dirt from the body but the pledge of a good conscience toward God. It saves you by the resurrection of Jesus Christ, (1 Pet 3:21)

4. Scripture mentions at least six kinds of conscience. (This idea comes from Thomas Walker. *The Acts of the Apostles*. Chicago, IL: Moody Press, 1965. p.487).

a. There is the good (clear, pure, healthy) conscience.

> Paul looked straight at the Sanhedrin and said, "My brothers, I have fulfilled my duty to God in all good conscience to this day." (Acts 23:1)
> Holding on to faith and a good conscience. Some have rejected these and so have shipwrecked their faith. (1 Tim 1:19)

b. There is a clear conscience.

> So I strive always to keep my conscience clear before God and man. (Acts 24:16)
> They must keep hold of the deep truths of the faith with a clear conscience. (1 Tim 3:9)
> I thank God, whom I serve, as my forefathers did, with a clear conscience, as night and day I constantly remember you in my prayers. (2 Tim 1:3)

c. There is a weak conscience.

> But not everyone knows this. Some people are still so accustomed to idols that when they eat such food they think of it as having been sacrificed to an idol, and since their conscience is weak, it is defiled. For if anyone with a weak conscience sees you who have this knowledge eating in an idol's temple, won't he be emboldened to eat what has been sacrificed to idols? When you sin against your brothers in this way and wound their weak conscience, you sin against Christ. (1 Cor 8:7, 10, 12)

d. There is a seared conscience.

> Such teachings come through hypocritical liars, whose consciences have been seared as with a hot iron. (1 Tim 4:2)

e. There is a corrupt conscience.

> To the pure, all things are pure, but to those who are corrupted and do not believe, nothing is pure. In fact, both their minds and consciences are corrupted. (Titus 1:15)

f. There is a guilty conscience.

> Let us draw near to God with a sincere heart in full assurance of faith, having our hearts sprinkled to cleanse us from a guilty conscience and having our bodies washed with pure water. (Heb 10:22)

3 (1:19-20) **Faith—Minister**: The warning is frightening. Conscience can be rejected, and faith can be shipwrecked. "Rejected" (aposamenoi) means to push away with force. It is a willful and deliberate pushing away of conscience. Conscience says that something is wrong and should not be done, but conscience is ignored and subdued, turned away from and denied.

When a person *continues to push his conscience away*, something terrible happens: his faith is shipwrecked. His faith is broken to pieces and destroyed. A person must live as Scripture dictates: righteously and godly. If he does not live righteously and godly, then he weakens his faith and soon dashes it upon the storms of evil, worldliness, and false doctrine. His faith is shipwrecked—because he pushed his conscience aside refusing to listen to its call to live righteously and godly. Note two points.

1. Paul gives two specific examples of men who pushed their conscience away and shipwrecked their faith.
   ⇒ Hymenaeus was the man who taught false doctrine: that the resurrection of believers had already taken place (2 Tim.2:17).
   ⇒ Alexander was probably the metalworker who opposed Paul and did him a great deal of harm (2 Tim.4:14).
2. Paul mentions the discipline which he exercised against the two men. But remember why he disciplined them: they had continued to reject the guidance of their conscience and to turn away from the faith. Therefore, Paul had handed them over to Satan. What does this mean? There are two possible explanations.
   a. The discipline means that the men must be excommunicated from the church (vs. 2, 7, 13). The idea is that outside the church—outside in the world—is the domain of Satan, whereas in the church is the domain of God (Jn.12:31; 16:11; Acts 26:18; Eph.2:12; Col.1:13; 1 Jn.5:19). The men were to be sent back to Satan's world to which they belonged. Perhaps such discipline would humiliate them and bring them to their senses. It was a discipline not only to punish them, but to awaken them to righteousness. It was a judgment that took away their Christian privileges with the hope that the discipline would stir them to repent.
   b. The discipline means more than excommunication. It is the miraculous subjection of the person to the power of Satan, to be terrified or tormented by him that they might repent and return to Christ.

   ⇒ The idea is that Paul and the church prayed for some circumstance or difficulty to arise in their lives that would stir them to repent.

People are chastised for sin and spiritual failure. In fact, it is impossible to sin and escape chastisement. Men reap what they sow. There is a spiritual power that inflicts punishment upon sin. However, this should not be surprising in our day, for modern medicine and psychology tell us that misbehavior causes physical, emotional, and mental punishment. (See notes—1 Cor.5:3-5; 11:27-30; DEEPER STUDY #1—1 Jn.5:16 for more discussion.)

Note that the discipline is remedial; that is, the two men were disciplined in order to try to lead them back to Christ. The men were delivered to Satan so that they might learn not to blaspheme.

> That is why [continuing in sin] many among you are weak and sick, and a number of you have fallen asleep. But if we judged ourselves, we would not come under judgment. When we are judged by the Lord, we are being disciplined so that we will not be condemned with the world. (1 Cor 11:30-32)

He cuts off every branch in me that bears no fruit, while every branch that does bear fruit he prunes so that it will be even more fruitful. (John 15:2)

Then Saul, who was also called Paul, filled with the Holy Spirit, looked straight at Elymas and said, "You are a child of the devil and an enemy of everything that is right! You are full of all kinds of deceit and trickery. Will you never stop perverting the right ways of the Lord? Now the hand of the Lord is against you. You are going to be blind, and for a time you will be unable to see the light of the sun." Immediately mist and darkness came over him, and he groped about, seeking someone to lead him by the hand. (Acts 13:9-11; cp. Acts 5:1-11)

Among them are Hymenaeus and Alexander, whom I have handed over to Satan to be taught not to blaspheme. (1 Tim 1:20)

And you have forgotten that word of encouragement that addresses you as sons: "My son, do not make light of the Lord's discipline, and do not lose heart when he rebukes you, (Heb 12:5; cp. v.6-11 for a complete picture)

Those whom I love I rebuke and discipline. So be earnest, and repent. (Rev 3:19)

Blessed is the man you discipline, O LORD, the man you teach from your law; (Psa 94:12)

My son, do not despise the Lord's discipline and do not resent his rebuke, because the LORD disciplines those he loves, as a father the son he delights in. (Prov 3:11-12)

Correct me, LORD, but only with justice— not in your anger, lest you reduce me to nothing. (Jer 10:24)

1 TIMOTHY 2:1-8

CHAPTER 2

II. DUTIES & ORDER IN THE CHURCH, 2:1-3:13

A. The First Duty of the Church—Pray, 2:1-8

1 Pray for everyone
  a. By requests
  b. By special prayers
  c. By intercession
  d. By thanksgiving
2 Pray for civil authorities
  a. That we may lead quiet & peaceable lives
  b. That we may lead godly & holy lives
3 Pray for all men to be saved

I urge, then, first of all, that requests, prayers, intercession and thanksgiving be made for everyone—
2 For kings and all those in authority, that we may live peaceful and quiet lives in all godliness and holiness.
3 This is good, and pleases God our Savior,
4 Who wants all men to be saved and to come to a knowledge of the truth.
5 For there is one God and one mediator between God and men, the man Christ Jesus,
6 Who gave himself as a ransom for all men—the testimony given in its proper time.
7 And for this purpose I was appointed a herald and an apostle—I am telling the truth, I am not lying—and a teacher of the true faith to the Gentiles.
8 I want men everywhere to lift up holy hands in prayer, without anger or disputing.

  a. Bc. God is our Savior & He wills for all men to be saved
  b. Bc. there is only one God, not the many gods of men
  c. Bc. there is only one Mediator who can save us
  d. Bc. Christ is the ransom for all
  e. Bc. ministers are ordained or appointed to proclaim the salvation of God

4 Pray everywhere & pray in the right spirit

DIVISION II

DUTIES AND ORDER IN THE CHURCH, 2:1-3:13

A. The First Duty of the Church—Pray, 2:1-8

(2:1-8) Introduction: this begins a significant section in the teaching of *1 Timothy*, a section that covers the duties and order of the church. The first duty of the church is basic: it is the duty of prayer.
1. Pray for everyone (v.1).
2. Pray for civil authorities (v.2).
3. Pray for all men to be saved (v.3-7).
4. Pray everywhere and pray in the right spirit (v.8).

(2:1-8) Another Outline: The First Duty of the Church: Prayer.
1. The exhortation to pray for everyone (v.1).
2. The exhortation to pray for civil authorities (v.2).
3. The reasons why we are to pray for everyone (v.3-6).
4. The place and spirit of prayer (v.7-8).

1 (2:1) **Prayer**: pray for everyone. Not a single person is to be omitted or left out. We are to pray for all persons:
⇒ the high and the low.
⇒ the educated and the uneducated.
⇒ the important and the unimportant.
⇒ the rich and the poor.
⇒ the leader and the followers.
⇒ the old and the young.
⇒ the friend and the enemy.

Pray for everyone. Do not neglect, ignore, or bypass any person. Every person needs prayer; every person needs God: His salvation, care, direction, approval, and acceptance. Therefore, pray for everyone.

Note: this is an *exhortation* ("I urge," parakaleo) to pray, which means that it is both an encouragement and a charge. The believer is both *encouraged and charged* to pray. He is given the encouragement and charge to pray just as a soldier is encouraged and charged to fight.

"First of all" stresses just how important prayer is. "First of all"—above all else, of supreme importance—put prayer first. "First of all"—before all else—pray for everyone.

Note that four kinds of prayer are mentioned. This also stresses the importance of praying for everyone.

1. There are "requests" (deeseis). This refers to the prayers that focus upon special needs—deep and intense needs. When we see special needs in the lives of people—all people—we are to seek God for them. That is, we are to be carrying the need before God with a great sense of urgency and plead and beg for the person or persons. The idea is that of intense and deep brokenness before God in behalf of others—that God would help and save the person.

Thought 1. Just think what a different world this would be, what a different community we would have if we really took the names and needs of people before God and pleaded for them in an intense brokenness and in tears. Just think...
- how many more loved ones would be saved and helped.
- how many more within our community and state and country and world would be saved and helped.
- how fewer problems would exist within society.

Scripture emphatically declares: "You do not have, because you do not ask God" (Jas.4:2).

2. There are "prayers" (proseuchas). This refers to the special times of prayer that we set aside for devotion and worship. We are to have set times for prayer, times that we set aside to worship God and when we pray for all men.

3. There is "intercession" (enteuxeis). This refers to bold praying; to standing before God in behalf of another person. Christ is our Intercessor, the One who stands between God and us in our behalf. But we are to intercede for men, to carry their names and lives before God and to boldly pray for them, expecting God to hear and answer—all in the name of Christ. We are to intercede for all men—to stand in the gap between them and God, boldly praying and asking God to be merciful and gracious in salvation and in deliverance.

1 TIMOTHY 2:1-8

4. There is "thanksgiving" (eucharistias). This means that we thank God for hearing and answering—thank Him for what He has done and is going to do for all men.

> But I tell you: Love your enemies and pray for those who persecute you, (Mat 5:44)
>
> "Ask and it will be given to you; seek and you will find; knock and the door will be opened to you. (Mat 7:7)
>
> Then Jesus told his disciples a parable to show them that they should always pray and not give up. (Luke 18:1)
>
> Jesus said, "Father, forgive them, for they do not know what they are doing." And they divided up his clothes by casting lots. (Luke 23:34)
>
> Then he fell on his knees and cried out, "Lord, do not hold this sin against them." When he had said this, he fell asleep. (Acts 7:60)
>
> And pray in the Spirit on all occasions with all kinds of prayers and requests. With this in mind, be alert and always keep on praying for all the saints. (Eph 6:18)
>
> Do not be anxious about anything, but in everything, by prayer and petition, with thanksgiving, present your requests to God. And the peace of God, which transcends all understanding, will guard your hearts and your minds in Christ Jesus. (Phil 4:6-7)
>
> Devote yourselves to prayer, being watchful and thankful. (Col 4:2)
>
> Pray continually; (1 Th 5:17)
>
> Therefore confess your sins to each other and pray for each other so that you may be healed. The prayer of a righteous man is powerful and effective. Elijah was a man just like us. He prayed earnestly that it would not rain, and it did not rain on the land for three and a half years. Again he prayed, and the heavens gave rain, and the earth produced its crops. (James 5:16-18)

2 (2:2) **Prayer—Civil Authorities**: pray for civil authorities, for kings and for all who are in authority.
⇒ No matter how good or how bad they are, pray for them.
⇒ No matter how moral or immoral they are, pray for them.
⇒ No matter how just or unjust they are, pray for them.

The thought of praying for evil rulers is shocking to some people. Just think of the evil rulers in the world even today. But remember: Nero was on the throne in Rome when Paul charged believers to pray for the king or emperor. And Nero had already burned Rome and had blamed it on Christian believers. In fact, he was presently launching a violent persecution against the believers.

> Donald Guthrie says, *"This Christian attitude towards the State is of utmost importance. Whether the civil authorities are perverted or not they must be made subjects for prayer, for Christian citizens may in this way influence the course of national affairs, a fact often forgotten except in times of special crisis"* (*The Pastoral Epistles*. "Tyndale New Testament Commentaries," p.70).
>
> Matthew Henry says, *"Pray for Kings...though the kings at this time were heathens, enemies to Christianity, and persecutors of Christians...because it is for the public good that there should be civil government, and proper persons entrusted with the administration of it"* (*Matthew Henry's Commentary*, Vol.5, p.811).

There are two reasons why we are to pray for rulers.
1. We pray for rulers so that we can live peaceful and quiet and lives. The only way the citizens of a nation can live quiet and peaceful lives is for the ruler to be filled...
• with wisdom and knowledge.
• with morality and justice.
• with courage and boldness.
• with compassion and understanding.

Therefore, believers must pray for the rulers to be filled to the brim so that the rulers can bring about peace and security throughout the land. Then and only then can the citizens of a land live peaceful and quiet lives.
2. We must pray for rulers so that we can live godly and holy lives. Believers want freedom of worship for all citizens.
⇒ They want freedom of worship, and freedom of life and choice, the right to worship and live for God without being opposed and persecuted.
⇒ They want freedom of life and choice, the right to live *holy or purposeful lives*, the right to pursue their own lives and wills without being opposed by a ruler.

Thought 1. People desire, even crave freedom: freedom of life and choice and freedom of worship. This is the reason we must pray for rulers...
• for wise and knowledgeable rulers.
• for moral and just rulers.
• for courageous and bold rulers.
• for compassionate and understanding rulers.

> Through the blessing of the upright a city is exalted, but by the mouth of the wicked it is destroyed. (Prov 11:11)
>
> Righteousness exalts a nation, but sin is a disgrace to any people. (Prov 14:34)
>
> Remind the people to be subject to rulers and authorities, to be obedient, to be ready to do whatever is good, (Titus 3:1)
>
> Show proper respect to everyone: Love the brotherhood of believers, fear God, honor the king. (1 Pet 2:17)

3 (2:3-7) **Jesus Christ, Mediator—Prayer—Salvation—Ransom—Redemption**: pray for all men to be saved, both rulers and citizens, both high and low. There are five reasons given why we are to pray for the salvation of all men, including all rulers.

1. First, God is our Savior and He wills all men to be saved and to come to a knowledge of the truth. As pointed out earlier (1 Tim.1:1), *God our Savior* is one of the great

titles for God. God is our Savior, the source of our salvation. God is the first Person who has cared for and loved man. God loves us and He is not willing that any should perish; therefore, He has taken the initiative and provided the way for us to be saved.

Note: God wills all men to be saved, but not in the sense of a decree. God has not decreed that all men be saved. This is evident by the ungodly and unrighteous lives lived by so many. God wills all men to be saved in the sense that He loves and longs for them to be saved. If any man perishes, it is his own fault. God has done all He can. He has provided the way for man to be saved. If a man is now lost, it is his own choosing.

Note the words "a knowledge of the truth." What truth is it that God wants man to know? The truth that is covered in the points that follow: that there is only one God, and there is only one Mediator who gave Himself a ransom for all—the truth that all can be saved from sin and death and judgment to come through the death of the Lord Jesus Christ. God loves man so much that He has provided *the way* for man to be saved. *That way* is the truth, and *that truth* is the truth that God wants man to know.

> **Jesus answered, "I am the way and the truth and the life. No one comes to the Father except through me. (John 14:6)**

This is the reason we should pray for all men, both rulers and citizens, high and low, educated and uneducated, moral and immoral, just and unjust, civilized and savage, saved and lost. God wants all men to be saved regardless of who they are and no matter how evil they may be.

> **The Lord is not slow in keeping his promise, as some understand slowness. He is patient with you, not wanting anyone to perish, but everyone to come to repentance. (2 Pet 3:9)**
>
> **Say to them, 'As surely as I live, declares the Sovereign LORD, I take no pleasure in the death of the wicked, but rather that they turn from their ways and live. Turn! Turn from your evil ways! Why will you die, O house of Israel?' (Ezek 33:11)**

2. Second, there is only one God, not the many gods of men. If there were many gods, then there would be many ways to reach the heavens of the gods. But there are not many gods. Logically, there could not be many gods. When we speak of God, we mean the Infinite and Supreme Majesty of the Universe. There can be only one Supreme Being, only one Infinite Being. If there should be many gods, then they would not be infinite or supreme; therefore, they would not be God.

The point is this: since there is only one God, there can be only one way to reach Him—only one way to be saved. Why? This is the discussion of the next point.

> **So then, about eating food sacrificed to idols: We know that an idol is nothing at all in the world and that there is no God but one. (1 Cor 8:4)**
>
> **One God and Father of all, who is over all and through all and in all. (Eph 4:6)**
>
> **For there are three that testify: (1 John 5:7)**
>
> **"How great you are, O Sovereign LORD! There is no one like you, and there is no God but you, as we have heard with our own ears. (2 Sam 7:22)**
>
> **For you are great and do marvelous deeds; you alone are God. (Psa 86:10)**
>
> **"You are my witnesses," declares the LORD, "and my servant whom I have chosen, so that you may know and believe me and understand that I am he. Before me no god was formed, nor will there be one after me. I, even I, am the LORD, and apart from me there is no savior. (Isa 43:10-11)**
>
> **"This is what the LORD says— Israel's King and Redeemer, the LORD Almighty: I am the first and I am the last; apart from me there is no God. (Isa 44:6)**
>
> **For this is what the LORD says— he who created the heavens, he is God; he who fashioned and made the earth, he founded it; he did not create it to be empty, but formed it to be inhabited— he says: "I am the LORD, and there is no other. (Isa 45:18)**

3. There is only one mediator between God and men. Man must have a mediator if he is to be saved, if he is to approach God and be acceptable to God. As asked above, why? Because there is only one perfect Person: God Himself. No man can stand before God, not in his own name or righteousness. Man is imperfect, and God is perfect. Man cannot make himself acceptable to God no matter what he does. *Imperfection is unacceptable to perfection*. If perfection accepted imperfection, it would no longer be perfection. Perfection has to be just and righteous, which means that it has to reject imperfection. God cannot accept imperfect man. God has to be just and righteous and reject man in all the imperfection of his thoughts and behavior.

How, then, can man become acceptable to God? God has to make man acceptable. God Himself has to handle the sin, condemnation, and death of men. But how? There was only one way: God, the Perfect Person, had to become Man. God had to come to earth in such a way that man could understand Him and understand what He was doing. This He did by partaking of flesh and blood and coming to earth in the person of His Son, the Man Christ Jesus.

⇒ God Himself had to conquer sin. He had to live a *perfect and sinless life* as a man in order to handle sin. By living a perfect and sinless life, He became the Ideal and Perfect Man, the Ideal and Perfect Righteousness that could cover and stand for all men (Heb.2:14-15).

This is part of what is meant by Jesus Christ being our Mediator. He stands before God as the Perfect Man, and He also stands between God and men as the Perfect Man. He is the Ideal Pattern of all men, of just what a man should be. Therefore, when a man really believes in Jesus Christ...

- God takes that man's belief and counts it as the righteousness of Jesus Christ.
- God accepts the man's faith and honor in His Son as righteousness.
- God lets the righteousness of His Son, Jesus Christ, cover the man.
- God accepts the man's faith as the righteousness of Jesus Christ.

Very simply stated, the man is not righteous, but God takes the man's faith in His Son and credits his faith as righteousness. Jesus Christ stands as the Mediator between God and men; He stands as the Mediator of perfection and righteousness for man. The point is this: since there is only one Mediator, we must pray for men to come to know Him. And we must rush to proclaim Him to all men so that they can know about Him and have the opportunity to follow Him.

> **The Word became flesh and made his dwelling among us. We have seen his glory, the glory of the One and Only, who came from the Father, full of grace and truth. (John 1:14)**
>
> **Jesus answered, "I am the way and the truth and the life. No one comes to the Father except through me. (John 14:6)**
>
> **Jesus answered: "Don't you know me, Philip, even after I have been among you such a long time? Anyone who has seen me has seen the Father. How can you say, 'Show us the Father'? Don't you believe that I am in the Father, and that the Father is in me? The words I say to you are not just my own. Rather, it is the Father, living in me, who is doing his work. Believe me when I say that I am in the Father and the Father is in me; or at least believe on the evidence of the miracles themselves. (John 14:9-11)**
>
> **For there is one God and one mediator between God and men, the man Christ Jesus, (1 Tim 2:5)**
>
> **But the ministry Jesus has received is as superior to theirs as the covenant of which he is mediator is superior to the old one, and it is founded on better promises. (Heb 8:6)**
>
> **For this reason Christ is the mediator of a new covenant, that those who are called may receive the promised eternal inheritance—now that he has died as a ransom to set them free from the sins committed under the first covenant. (Heb 9:15)**
>
> **For Christ did not enter a man-made sanctuary that was only a copy of the true one; he entered heaven itself, now to appear for us in God's presence. (Heb 9:24)**
>
> **To Jesus the mediator of a new covenant, and to the sprinkled blood that speaks a better word than the blood of Abel. See to it that you do not refuse him who speaks. If they did not escape when they refused him who warned them on earth, how much less will we, if we turn away from him who warns us from heaven? (Heb 12:24-25)**
>
> **My dear children, I write this to you so that you will not sin. But if anybody does sin, we have one who speaks to the Father in our defense—Jesus Christ, the Righteous One. (1 John 2:1)**

4. The man Christ Jesus gave Himself a ransom for all. The word "ransom" (antilutron) means to *exchange* something for something else. The man Christ Jesus exchanged His life for the life of man; He gave up His life for the life of man. How? By the cross. Jesus Christ took the sin and condemnation of men upon Himself and bore their judgment for them. Christ died for man; He bore the judgment of God against sin for man.

As the Ideal and Perfect Man, Christ could do this for man. Since He was the Ideal Man, His death was the ideal death. Therefore, His death can stand for and cover the death of all men. If a man really believes and trusts that the death of Jesus Christ is for him...

- God counts the death of Christ for the man.
- God actually *counts* the man as having already died in Christ.
- God accepts the man as free from the guilt and condemnation of sin because Christ has already paid the ransom price for sin and death.

This is the glorious gospel of God: man can now live forever in the presence of God. Jesus Christ gave Himself as a ransom for sin and death. When man receives Christ Jesus into his heart and begins to follow Christ...

- God gives him life now and forever, abundant life and eternal life. When the man finishes his task upon earth, God will transfer him right into His presence—quicker than a flash of lightning. The man never has to taste death.

The words "the testimony given in its proper time" mean that God sent His Son in the fullness of time, when the time had fully come. When it was time for Christ to come to earth, He came.

Now note: we must pray for men to believe that Christ died for them—pray that they might be saved. And we must rush to proclaim the glorious news that Christ Jesus has paid the ransom price for us: we can now be set free from sin, death, and condemnation. We can now live with God eternally.

> **For the life of a creature is in the blood, and I have given it to you to make atonement for yourselves on the altar; it is the blood that makes atonement for one's life. (Lev 17:11)**
>
> **Just as the Son of Man did not come to be served, but to serve, and to give his life as a ransom for many." (Mat 20:28)**
>
> **And are justified freely by his grace through the redemption that came by Christ Jesus. (Rom 3:24)**
>
> **You were bought [redeemed] at a price. Therefore honor God with your body. (1 Cor 6:20)**
>
> **You were bought at a price; do not become slaves of men. (1 Cor 7:23)**
>
> **In him we have redemption through his blood, the forgiveness of sins, in accordance with the riches of God's grace (Eph 1:7)**
>
> **In whom we have redemption, the forgiveness of sins. (Col 1:14)**
>
> **For there is one God and one mediator between God and men, the man Christ Jesus, who gave himself as a ransom for all men—the testimony given in its proper time. (1 Tim 2:5-6)**
>
> **For this reason Christ is the mediator of a new covenant, that those who are called may receive the promised eternal inheritance—now that he has died as a ransom to set them free from the sins committed under the first covenant. (Heb 9:15)**
>
> **For you know that it was not with perishable things such as silver or gold that**

you were redeemed from the empty way of life handed down to you from your forefathers, but with the precious blood of Christ, a lamb without blemish or defect. (1 Pet 1:18-19)

And they sang a new song: "You are worthy to take the scroll and to open its seals, because you were slain, and with your blood you purchased men for God from every tribe and language and people and nation. (Rev 5:9)

5. Ministers are ordained or appointed to proclaim the salvation of God. Note: Paul said three things about himself.

a. God had appointed Paul to be a preacher, a herald (kerux): a preacher is a herald, an ambassador who was appointed by a king to go forth and proclaim the message of the king. The minister is a preacher, a herald who is sent forth by God to preach the truth about Jesus Christ...
- that He is the Mediator between God and men.
- that He has given Himself as a ransom for all.

He appointed twelve—designating them apostles—that they might be with him and that he might send them out to preach (Mark 3:14)

He said to them, "Go into all the world and preach the good news to all creation. (Mark 16:15)

"Go, stand in the temple courts," he said, "and tell the people the full message of this new life." (Acts 5:20)

Preach the Word; be prepared in season and out of season; correct, rebuke and encourage—with great patience and careful instruction. (2 Tim 4:2)

For Christ did not send me to baptize, but to preach the gospel—not with words of human wisdom, lest the cross of Christ be emptied of its power. (1 Cor 1:17)

Yet when I preach the gospel, I cannot boast, for I am compelled to preach. Woe to me if I do not preach the gospel! (1 Cor 9:16)

b. God had appointed Paul to be an apostle (apostolos): a person who had been sent as a very special witness and on a very special mission. The minister is sent forth on the special mission to bear witness that Jesus Christ is the Mediator between God and men. Jesus Christ has paid the ransom price for man.

You did not choose me, but I chose you and appointed you to go and bear fruit—fruit that will last. Then the Father will give you whatever you ask in my name. (John 15:16)

We are therefore Christ's ambassadors, as though God were making his appeal through us. We implore you on Christ's behalf: Be reconciled to God. God made him who had no sin to be sin for us, so that in him we might become the righteousness of God. (2 Cor 5:20-21)

c. God had appointed Paul as a teacher (didaskalos): a person who instructs people into the faith and truth of God's Word. It is the gift to root and ground people in doctrine, reproof, correction, and righteousness.

Note Paul's stress upon his call from God: "I am telling the truth, I am not lying." God had called him to proclaim and teach the salvation in Christ Jesus. Apparently, there were some at Ephesus who questioned Paul's call and ministry.

The point is this: God has called ministers to proclaim the faith and truth of the Mediator and the great ransom price that He paid for man's salvation. Therefore, we must pray for *all men*—that they will receive the message of the minister and be saved.

One night the Lord spoke to Paul in a vision: "Do not be afraid; keep on speaking, do not be silent. For I am with you, and no one is going to attack and harm you, because I have many people in this city." So Paul stayed for a year and a half, teaching them the word of God. (Acts 18:9-11)

For two whole years Paul stayed there in his own rented house and welcomed all who came to see him. Boldly and without hindrance he preached the kingdom of God and taught about the Lord Jesus Christ. (Acts 28:30-31)

And in the church God has appointed first of all apostles, second prophets, third teachers, then workers of miracles, also those having gifts of healing, those able to help others, those with gifts of administration, and those speaking in different kinds of tongues. (1 Cor 12:28)

It was he who gave some to be apostles, some to be prophets, some to be evangelists, and some to be pastors and teachers, (Eph 4:11)

4 (2:8) **Prayer**: pray everywhere and pray in the right spirit. A person should never stop praying. He should be praying all day long as he walks throughout the day. He should develop an unbroken communion and fellowship with the Lord, praying for all men—for both the ruler and the citizen, the high and the low, the lost and the saved—all over the world. He should pray for those of his...
- home
- city
- state
- church
- community
- country

He should pray for those in...
- North America
- Central America
- India
- South America
- Africa
- Russia

...and on and on.

The believer is to pray and to keep on praying. He is to pray everywhere—no matter where he is. But note: the believer is also told how to pray.

1. He is to pray and "lift up holy hands"; that is, he is not to come before God having touched or handled "the

forbidden things" (William Barclay. *The Letters to Timothy, Titus, and Philemon*, p.74). He is not to come with sin in his life.

> **If I had cherished sin in my heart, the Lord would not have listened; (Psa 66:18)**
>
> **But your iniquities have separated you from your God; your sins have hidden his face from you, so that he will not hear. (Isa 59:2)**
>
> **No one calls on your name or strives to lay hold of you; for you have hidden your face from us and made us waste away because of our sins. (Isa 64:7)**

2. He is to pray without anger or feelings in his heart against someone else. Very simply...
- God does not accept us unless we accept others.
- God does not forgive us unless we forgive others.

> **"Therefore, if you are offering your gift at the altar and there remember that your brother has something against you, leave your gift there in front of the altar. First go and be reconciled to your brother; then come and offer your gift. (Mat 5:23-24)**
>
> **But if you do not forgive men their sins, your Father will not forgive your sins. (Mat 6:15)**
>
> **"This is how my heavenly Father will treat each of you unless you forgive your brother from your heart." (Mat 18:35)**

3. He is to pray without doubting. There is no need to pray if we do not think God is going to hear us. If we ask Him doubting, we are not trusting His presence and power to meet our need. We are actually denying God's care and power. We are destroying the name of God among men. Therefore, we must believe God when we pray.

> **Jesus entered the temple courts, and, while he was teaching, the chief priests and the elders of the people came to him. "By what authority are you doing these things?" they asked. "And who gave you this authority?" (Mat 21:23)**
>
> **Therefore I tell you, whatever you ask for in prayer, believe that you have received it, and it will be yours. (Mark 11:24)**
>
> **And without faith it is impossible to please God, because anyone who comes to him must believe that he exists and that he rewards those who earnestly seek him. (Heb 11:6)**
>
> **But when he asks, he must believe and not doubt, because he who doubts is like a wave of the sea, blown and tossed by the wind. That man should not think he will receive anything from the Lord; (James 1:6-7)**

1 TIMOTHY 2:9-15

	B. The Women of the Church, 2:9-15	12 I do not permit a woman to teach or to have authority over a man; she must be silent.	3 In church, women are not to teach nor to have authority over a man
1 **In public, women are to dress modestly**	9 I also want women to dress modestly, with decency and propriety, not with braided hair or gold or pearls or expensive clothes,	13 For Adam was formed first, then Eve.	a. Because God created in an orderly way
a. Dress modestly & sensibly		14 And Adam was not the one deceived; it was the woman who was deceived and became a sinner.	b. Because God created man & woman with different natures
b. Do not dress to attract attention	10 But with good deeds, appropriate for women who profess to worship God.		c. Because woman was deceived
c. Dress with good deeds	11 A woman should learn in quietness and full submission.	15 But women will be saved through childbearing—if they continue in faith, love and holiness with propriety.	4 **In the home, that is, in childbearing, women are to be saved if they continue to live & walk in the Lord**
2 **In church, women are to learn in silence & submissiveness**			

DIVISION II

DUTIES AND ORDER IN THE CHURCH, 2:1-3:13

B. The Women of the Church, 2:9-15

(2:9-15) **Introduction**: this is a vibrant passage of Scripture, a passage that stirs both men and women to sit up and listen. It even arouses emotions and reactions from some, in particular within societies where women's rights have become a heated issue. The subject is women in the church: the place of women in public, in the church, and in the home or in childbearing.

1. In public, women are to dress modestly (v.9-10).
2. In church, women are to learn in quietness and submissiveness (v.11-14).
3. In church, women are not to teach nor to have authority over men (v.12-14).
4. In the home, that is, in childbearing, women are to be saved if they continue to live and walk in the Lord (v.15).

1 (2:9-10) **Women—Dress—Clothing**: in public women are to dress in modest clothing. The words "dress modestly" (kosmein) refer to the dress, ornaments, and arrangement of clothing upon the body. But to dress modestly also refers to behavior and demeanor, that is, the way a woman carries herself, walks, moves, and behaves in public. Remember: this passage is being written to genuine Christian women—women who truly believe in the Lord and wish to honor the Lord and to have a strong testimony for Him. The Christian woman wants to guard her clothing and to dress modestly; she wants to watch the way she dresses, walks, moves, and behaves in public. She wants to bring honor to the Lord and to build a strong testimony—a testimony that she loves the Lord and has committed her life...

- to help people, not to seduce them.
- to serve people, not to destroy them.
- to point people to Jesus, not to attract them to herself.
- to teach people righteous behavior, not fleshly and worldly behavior.

Scripture covers three things about the adorning or dress of a true Christian woman. All three are revealing. They demonstrate exactly where a woman stands—regardless of profession: either with Christ or with the world.

1. The Christian woman is to dress and behave modestly and to keep herself under control at all times.

⇒ She is to dress modestly, with decency; that is, in public she is to dress and act modestly, somewhat reserved and shy.

⇒ She is to dress modestly, with propriety; that is, she is to dress and act appropriately, sensibly, controlled, soberly, calmly, quietly, and seriously.

2. The Christian woman is not to dress to attract attention. This is the point of these negative commands. She is not to dress herself...

- with braided hair: elaborate hair-styles—hair-styles that are so different that they break away from acceptable customs and attract attention to herself.
- with gold, or pearls, or expensive clothing: elaborate jewelry and clothing that is extravagant, ostentatious, flamboyant, and that attracts attention to herself.

Donald Guthrie says that a woman's mind is mirrored by her dress (*The Pastoral Epistles*. "Tyndale New Testament Commentaries," p.74). How true this is! How a woman dresses shows whether she lives in prayer and devotion to God or has deep feelings and desires for the world and the gaping and lustful attention of men.

3. The Christian woman is to dress herself with good works or deeds. Note exactly what this verse says: "Women *profess to worship God*." Their worship of God means that they reverence and fear God and are devoted to Him. These are the women who are committed and concerned with good works. As stated earlier, their minds are upon helping, saving, and teaching people, not upon attracting, seducing, and destroying them through lustful and immoral thoughts and sexual behavior.

Now, note a significant fact that is often ignored and sometimes tragically unknown. True beauty is inward, not outward. Think for a moment: a woman who is focused upon Christ and good deeds is at peace with herself. She is filled with assurance and confidence, and she has strong self-image and esteem. She has purpose, meaning, and significance in life and knows that she is perfectly secure and looked after by Christ. Picture such a woman:

⇒ her smile—which arises from a joy filling her whole body.
⇒ her walk—which has a spring in each step.
⇒ her dignity, calmness, serenity, confidence, security, purposefulness.

Picture her beauty. No matter what her facial features are—no matter how modest her clothing is—she is beautiful. Just how true this is can be easily seen in the opposite picture. Picture the woman who lives in and of the world,

concerned about her looks and dress and appearance. Picture...
- her smile—which arises from an emptiness and reveals a dissatisfaction with life.
- her walk and movements—which reveal an insecurity, loneliness, and fear of not being accepted for what she is within and the need to *fit in* with her peers.
- her behavior of looseness, restlessness, and her lack of purpose, meaning, and significance.

Picture this woman's behavior. Every man—even if he has known hundreds of women—knows that this woman lacks beauty, no matter how attractive her facial and body features may be. In the eyes of so many in the world, she is good for only one thing: to be used to satisfy the world's greed for money and lust for pleasure.

As stated, beauty is not in looks; beauty is from within. If a woman is beautiful within—if she is really godly and given over to good works—God floods her with a beauty that far surpasses any beauty of the flesh or clothing.

Thought 1. Christian women must be focused upon Christ and upon helping the desperate who are in the communities and cities of the world. Christian women must be focused upon godliness—fearing and reverencing God—and upon good deeds—the good deeds that are so desperately needed by the lost and poor within our communities and cities.

> **Do not offer the parts of your body to sin, as instruments of wickedness, but rather offer yourselves to God, as those who have been brought from death to life; and offer the parts of your body to him as instruments of righteousness. (Rom 6:13)**
>
> **I also want women to dress modestly, with decency and propriety, not with braided hair or gold or pearls or expensive clothes, but with good deeds, appropriate for women who profess to worship God. (1 Tim 2:9-10)**
>
> **Your beauty should not come from outward adornment, such as braided hair and the wearing of gold jewelry and fine clothes. Instead, it should be that of your inner self, the unfading beauty of a gentle and quiet spirit, which is of great worth in God's sight. For this is the way the holy women of the past who put their hope in God used to make themselves beautiful. They were submissive to their own husbands, (1 Pet 3:3-5)**

2 (2:11-14) **Women—Church**: in church women are to learn in silence and submissiveness. Two striking points are given in these verses. Remember: this passage is being written to genuine Christian women, women who truly love and wish to honor the Lord and to have a strong testimony for Him. The woman who is a true Christian wants to guard her behavior in church as well as in public.

The Christian woman is a follower of Christ, a true believer; therefore, she is to learn all she can about Christ. She is to attend church and read, listen, and study. She is to show and demonstrate her love for the Lord by learning all she can about Him. And note the spirit in which she is to learn. She is to learn...
- in a spirit of "quietness" (hesuchiai).
- in a spirit of "submission."

Thought 1. There is no difference between men and women in learning about Christ. Therefore, this verse could apply to men as well as to women. Everyone is to learn about Christ; therefore, everyone is to approach the Lord and the church in a spirit of quietness and submissiveness. This is true of any student, whether in a public school, university, or church. A student cannot learn if he is always questioning, contradicting, refuting, arguing, and differing with the teacher. A student who sits under a teacher in a spirit of arrogance, pride, and rebellion seldom learns anything. A student can learn only if he comes in a spirit of quietness and submissiveness, a willingness to listen, read, and study under his teacher. In fact, the quieter and more submissive he is to the authority of the professor, the more he is likely to learn.

Therefore, Christian women are to learn of Christ, learn in a spirit of quietness and submissiveness. They are not to be disruptive, arguing, differing, contradicting, grumbling, griping, and complaining in church. They are to learn of Christ in church, and they are to learn in a spirit of quietness and submissiveness.

> **Do your best to present yourself to God as one approved, a workman who does not need to be ashamed and who correctly handles the word of truth. (2 Tim 2:15)**
>
> **Like newborn babies, crave pure spiritual milk, so that by it you may grow up in your salvation, now that you have tasted that the Lord is good. (1 Pet 2:2-3)**

3 (2:12-14) **Women—Church**: the Christian woman is not to teach in church nor to have authority over a man. Ears perk up and eyes focus when this statement is read, and in some cases emotions are aroused, especially in societies where the struggle for women's rights are being fought. What does Scripture mean? Scripture is brief and factual. A simple statement is made: "I do not permit a woman to teach or to have authority over a man." But note: a woman is not forbidden to teach nor forbidden to hold authority. She is only forbidden to teach and to hold authority over a man. Why? Why is she allowed to teach and manage other women and children but not men?

1. Because God created in an organized and orderly fashion; He created everything to have its own order and function. In relation to human beings, God created man first, then woman. God created man...
- to be the driving force of creation.
- to plow the way.
- to take the lead.
- to be the initiator.
- to oversee the family and its welfare.

The woman was created not as a competitor but as a counterpart. She is just as unique a creation as the man and her function is just as important as the man's, but her function upon earth is not the same as man's. In the plan of God's creation, each supports, complements, and works *along the side* of the other. Therefore, within the church the teaching and administrative leadership of the church is to be headed up by the man.

2. God created man and woman with different natures. Women were created with more of an open and receptive, trusting and intuitive, tender and bearing nature. Because

of her receptive and trusting nature, she tends to believe things and to follow along more easily than man. Therefore, she is more easily deceived than man. This is what happened with Adam and Eve when they fell into sin. Eve was deceived and followed along with the temptation, but not Adam. He knew exactly what he was doing. He sinned because he loved the woman and wanted to know the pleasure of sin with her. He knew exactly what he was doing; therefore, he was in the greater wrong.

The point is this: by nature, men are built more to take the lead in teaching and administration; whereas women are built more to receive and follow.

> **Now I want you to realize that the head of every man is Christ, and the head of the woman is man, and the head of Christ is God. (1 Cor 11:3)**
>
> **Women should remain silent in the churches. They are not allowed to speak, but must be in submission, as the Law says. If they want to inquire about something, they should ask their own husbands at home; for it is disgraceful for a woman to speak in the church. (1 Cor 14:34-35)**
>
> **Wives, submit to your husbands as to the Lord. For the husband is the head of the wife as Christ is the head of the church, his body, of which he is the Savior. Now as the church submits to Christ, so also wives should submit to their husbands in everything. Husbands, love your wives, just as Christ loved the church and gave himself up for her (Eph 5:22-25)**
>
> **A woman should learn in quietness and full submission. I do not permit a woman to teach or to have authority over a man; she must be silent. (1 Tim 2:11-12)**
>
> **Wives, in the same way be submissive to your husbands so that, if any of them do not believe the word, they may be won over without words by the behavior of their wives, (1 Pet 3:1)**
>
> **For this is the way the holy women of the past who put their hope in God used to make themselves beautiful. They were submissive to their own husbands, (1 Pet 3:5)**

Thought 1. Note an important question: Does this mean that a woman is never to teach or hold authority over a man?

The New Testament gives example after example of women who held a phenomenal position and ministry in the early days of Christianity.

⇒ Mary of Nazareth was chosen by God to bear and rear and teach God's very own Son, the Lord Jesus Christ, while He was on earth (Lk.1:26-38).
⇒ Anna, a prophetess, was chosen by God to predict the future of the baby Jesus (Lk.2:36-38).
⇒ It was four women who demonstrated raw courage by standing at the foot of Jesus' cross when all the disciples had fled for their lives (Mk.15:40).
⇒ Joanna and Susanna supported the work of Christ (Lk.8:3).
⇒ Martha and Mary opened their home to Jesus time and again (Lk.10:38-39; Jn.11:5).
⇒ Mary Magdalene, because of her great love and devotion for Christ, was chosen by God to be the first to witness the Lord's resurrection (Mt.16:9; Jn.20:11-18).
⇒ Tabitha or Dorcas helped the poor of her city by clothing them (Acts 9:36-43).
⇒ Mary, the mother of John Mark, allowed the early believers to meet in her home (Acts 12:12).
⇒ Lydia courageously stepped forth and became the very first convert to Christ in Europe (Acts 16:13).
⇒ Priscilla, along with her husband Aquila, taught the truth of Christ to the young preacher, Apollos (Acts 18:26).
⇒ Philip the evangelist had four daughters who were prophetesses (Acts 21:9).
⇒ Phoebe served the church at Cenchrea, probably as a deaconess (see note, Phoebe—Ro.16:1-2).
⇒ Mary of Rome ministered to Paul and his companions (Ro.16:6).
⇒ Tryphena and Tryphosa were two ladies who labored in the Lord (Ro.16:12).
⇒ The mother of Rufus became a mother to Paul (Ro.16:13).
⇒ Euodia and Syntyche were two women who labored in the gospel (Ph.4:2-3).
⇒ The mother and grandmother of Timothy, Lois and Eunice, taught the Scriptures to Timothy from his earliest childhood (2 Tim.1:5).
⇒ The aged women were to teach the young women (Tit.2.3).

These Scriptures clearly show that women were chosen and gifted by God to hold a significant position and ministry in the early days of Christianity. But it also has to be noted that there is no clear record of a woman serving in the capacity of the head teacher or head authority in the New Testament church (pastor, overseer, or elder). Does this mean that God never raises up a woman to teach all Christians, men and women, or to hold authority on a church wide or world wide ministry? In answer to this question, we have to go before the Lord humbly and openly seek the answer for ourselves. But we must always confess that God is God; therefore, He can do what He wills in order to meet a special need. If He needs to raise up a woman to meet some special teaching or administrative need in the church, He can do it.

Thought 2. Some commentators say that this passage is to be interpreted only in the context of its day. William Barclay's comment gives an example of this position.

> *"The Christian Church did not lay down these regulations as in any sense permanent regulations, but as things which were necessary in the situation in which the early Church found itself....All the things in this chapter are mere temporary regulations laid down to meet a given situation. If we want Paul's real and permanent view on this matter, we get it in Galatians 3:28. 'There is neither Jew nor Greek, there is neither bond nor free, there is neither male nor female: for ye*

are all one in Christ Jesus.' In Christ the differences of place and honour and prestige and function within the Church were all wiped out....We must not read this passage as a barrier to all women's work and service within the Church; we must read it in the light of its Jewish background and in the light of the situation in a Greek city. And we must look for Paul's permanent views in the passage which tells us that the differences are wiped out, and that men and women, slaves and freemen, Jews and Gentiles, are all eligible to serve Christ" (*The Letters to Timothy, Titus, and Philemon*, p.78).

But note: this position is most unlikely because of the universal reference to Adam and Eve. Scripture is drawing a universal application from the creation of Adam and Eve. It is because God created in an organized and orderly way and gave specific functions to both man and woman that man is to take the lead in blazing the path through life for his family and the church.

Thought 3. There is another possible reason why God has forbidden women to stand before men in a position of teaching and authority, a reason that has perhaps been neglected in discussion. By nature men and women are attracted to each other by looking, but man by nature is the more dominant pursuer. Therefore, by nature he is probably more attracted by looking than the woman is. If a man looks at a woman long enough, he will begin to notice any feature of attractiveness about her. *This is natural and normal*, the way God made man and woman. However, when a woman *stands before* a man for a long time and the man is forced to continue looking at her, the situation becomes ready-made for temptation to attack his mind with suggestive thoughts. This is not to say that every man who sits under the teaching of a woman and who is forced to look at her is thinking immoral thoughts. It only means that when a man is forced to look and look at a woman, the temptation is more likely to happen.

4 (2:15) **Women, Fulfillment**: in the home, that is, in childbearing, the woman will be saved if she continues in faith, love, holiness, and self-control or propriety. This is a glorious promise to the true Christian woman. But what does it mean? Women still suffer pain in childbearing and some women, even Christian women, die when giving birth to a child. The verse refers back to Eve and her sin. The judgment upon her sin was that she would suffer pain in childbearing (Gen.3:16). The promise seems to mean one of three things.

1. When the promise is kept within the context of this passage, it seems to mean that the woman does not find her salvation and fulfillment through holding positions of teaching and authority but through childbearing (v.12-14). The very nature of a woman's being, the primary function of a woman's nature and call upon earth, is to carry on the human race. Therefore, the woman's salvation—that is, her ultimate fulfillment, satisfaction and completeness in life—comes through bearing and rearing children. Her salvation and completeness in life does not come from competing with men to see who blazes the paths and builds the roads through the jungles of this earth. She can do these things, but her salvation—her ultimate fulfillment and satisfaction—does not come by doing these things. Contrariwise, the woman will be saved and totally fulfilled if she...

- will continue in faith: continue believing and trusting.
- will continue in love: loving the Lord, her husband, believers, and the lost of the world.
- will continue in holiness: living a life totally set apart to Christ and His purpose.
- will continue in self-control or propriety: disciplining and controlling her life to follow Christ in all things.

2. A second possible meaning of the verse is this: the sentence of pain in childbearing (the penalty of her sin) does not prohibit a woman's salvation. She shall be saved if she continues in faith, love, holiness, and self-control.

3. There is one other possible meaning of this passage that needs to be considered. The definite article (the) is in the Greek before the word "childbearing." That is, the verse reads: "[She] will be saved through *the* childbearing." Some commentators feel that "the childbearing" refers to *the seed* of the woman, that is, to the *greatest childbearing* that has ever taken place which is the birth of Christ Himself. Therefore, the meaning is this: despite the judgment upon the woman (suffering pain in childbearing), the woman will be saved in *the supreme childbearing*, that is, in Christ.

Whatever a person's interpretation, note the condition. The promise is based upon the woman...

- already having faith in Christ.
- already knowing the love of God.
- already living a holy life.
- already controlling her life and following Christ.

> **Then they asked him, "What must we do to do the works God requires?" Jesus answered, "The work of God is this: to believe in the one he has sent." (John 6:28-29)**
>
> **And without faith it is impossible to please God, because anyone who comes to him must believe that he exists and that he rewards those who earnestly seek him. (Heb 11:6)**
>
> **And this is his command: to believe in the name of his Son, Jesus Christ, and to love one another as he commanded us. (1 John 3:23)**

1 TIMOTHY 3:1-7

	CHAPTER 3 C. The Overseers of the Church, 3:1-7 Here is a trustworthy saying: If anyone sets his heart on being an overseer, he desires a noble task. 2 Now the overseer must be above reproach, the husband of but one wife, temperate, self-controlled, respectable, hospitable, able to teach, 3 Not given to drunkenness, not violent but gentle, not quarrelsome, not a lover of money.	4 He must manage his own family well and see that his children obey him with proper respect. 5 (If anyone does not know how to manage his own family, how can he take care of God's church?) 6 He must not be a recent convert, or he may become conceited and fall under the same judgment as the devil. 7 He must also have a good reputation with outsiders, so that he will not fall into disgrace and into the devil's trap.	3 **Family qualifications: The minister or overseer must rule his own home** 4 **Spiritual qualifications** a. Must be spiritually mature b. Reason: A danger of pride 5 **Community qualifications**
1 **The office of minister or overseer** a. Is a noble task b. Is to be desired 2 **Personal qualifications**			

DIVISION II

DUTIES AND ORDER IN THE CHURCH, 2:1-3:13

C. The Overseers of the Church, 3:1-7

(3:1-7) **Introduction**: the office of an overseer is probably the same office as elder or presbyter or minister in the New Testament. All three words refer to the same person, to the minister of the gospel and of the church (see DEEPER STUDY #1, *Elder*—Tit.1:5-9 for discussion). What are the qualifications of the minister? Who should be preaching the gospel and filling the pulpits of the Lord's church? Who should be considering the ministry—what kind of person? The importance of this passage cannot be overstressed when it comes to the building and protection of God's church and people.

1. The office of minister or overseer (v.1).
2. Personal qualifications (v.2-3).
3. Family qualifications: the minister or overseer must rule his own home (v.4-5).
4. Spiritual qualifications (v.6).
5. Community qualifications (v.7).

1 (3:1) **Minister—Overseer—Elder**: the office of minister or overseer is a good work. The word "noble" (kalou) means honorable, excellent, beneficial, productive. Note that the position of the ministry is not what is stressed, but the work of the ministry. The emphasis is not the esteem and honor of the profession. The emphasis is upon the work of the ministry. It is the work that is honorable, excellent, beneficial, and productive. The work of the ministry is a "noble task."

Note another fact: the office of minister or overseer is to be desired. The word "desire" means to seek after with a strong desire; to set one's heart upon. God stirs some hearts to seek the ministry and to dedicate their lives to the work of the ministry.

> **Thought 1.** When a person is stirred to commit his life to the ministry, he must say "yes" to the Spirit of God. To say "no" to God's call is to reject God and to miss one's calling and life. It is to miss one's very purpose for being on earth.

> You did not choose me, but I chose you and appointed you to go and bear fruit— fruit that will last. Then the Father will give you whatever you ask in my name. (John 15:16)

> But eagerly desire the greater gifts. And now I will show you the most excellent way. (1 Cor 12:31)

> Follow the way of love and eagerly desire spiritual gifts, especially the gift of prophecy [proclaim the word of God]. (1 Cor 14:1)

> So it is with you. Since you are eager to have spiritual gifts, try to excel in gifts that build up the church. (1 Cor 14:12)

> It was he who gave [called and appointed] some to be apostles, some to be prophets, some to be evangelists, and some to be pastors and teachers, to prepare God's people for works of service, so that the body of Christ may be built up (Eph 4:11-12)

2 (3:2-3) **Minister—Overseer—Elder**: the minister or overseer of God must be qualified; he must meet some personal qualifications; he must be a person of great Christian character.

1. The minister or overseer must be "above reproach" (anepilempton): blameless; not open to attack; not able to be criticized by the enemy at all (*The Pulpit Commentary*, Vol.21, p.50). He must be completely above reproach.
2. The minister or overseer must be "the husband of but one wife." From the earliest times of church history, this qualification has been interpreted differently. Some have held...

- that the overseer or minister must have a wife; he must be married to be a minister.
- that the overseer or minister must never have more than one wife; he must never marry again, even if his wife died. This position holds that second marriages are completely forbidden.
- that the overseer must not have more than one wife at a time. (Remember: polygamy was the common practice of society when the church was first born).

1 TIMOTHY 3:1-7

- that an overseer must live a life of strict morality; he "must be a loyal husband, preserving marriage in all its purity" (William Barclay, *The Letters to Timothy, Titus, and Philemon*, p.87).

Thought 1. Every minister, believer, and church must go before the Lord and seek the meaning of this qualification for him or herself. But we must be honest and open to hear the Lord and then beg of Him the courage and discipline to do what He says. This is an absolute essential for all who are believers, for nothing is any more traumatic than the loss of a spouse through death or separation and divorce. And if there is ever a time that we must reach out and minister to our brothers and sisters, it is when they lose their spouses.

The point is this: should a minister or overseer be allowed to serve as a minister if he has had more than one wife, either through death or divorce? The Pulpit Commentary has an excellent comment on this point:

"If we consider the general laxity in regard to marriage, and the facility of divorce, which prevailed among Jews and Romans at this time, it must have been a common thing for a man to have more than one woman living who had been his wife. And this [was] a distinct breach of the primeval law (Gen.ii.24), [and] would properly be a bar to any one being called to the 'office of a bishop'....It is utterly unsupported by any single passage in Scripture that a second marriage should disqualify a man for the sacred ministry. As regards the opinion of the early Church, it was not at all uniform, and amongst those who held that this passage absolutely prohibits second marriages in the case of a [overseer], it was merely a part of the asceticism of the day" (Vol.21, p.51).

A.T. Robertson very simply says, *"Of one wife [mias gunaikos]. One at a time, clearly"* (*Word Pictures in the New Testament*, Vol.4, p.572).

William Barclay says, *"In its context here we can be quite certain that this means that the Christian leader must be a loyal husband, preserving marriage in all its purity"* (*The Letters to Timothy, Titus, and Philemon*, p.87).

Thompson Chain Reference Bible, in listing its subjects, simply says *"Polygamy Forbidden."*

"Haven't you read," he replied, "that at the beginning the Creator 'made them male and female,' and said, 'For this reason a man will leave his father and mother and be united to his wife, and the two will become one flesh'? So they are no longer two, but one. Therefore what God has joined together, let man not separate." (Mat 19:4-6)

Now the overseer must be above reproach, the husband of but one wife, temperate, self-controlled, respectable, hospitable, able to teach, (1 Tim 3:2)

An elder must be blameless, the husband of but one wife, a man whose children believe and are not open to the charge of being wild and disobedient. (Titus 1:6)

He must not take many wives, or his heart will be led astray. He must not accumulate large amounts of silver and gold. (Deu 17:17)

3. The minister or overseer must be temperate (nephalion): self-controlled, watchful. He must be vigilant, watch over, and control his own life and the lives of his dear people.

"Watch and pray so that you will not fall into temptation. The spirit is willing, but the body is weak." (Mat 26:41)

So be on your guard! Remember that for three years I never stopped warning each of you night and day with tears. (Acts 20:31)

So, if you think you are standing firm, be careful that you don't fall! (1 Cor 10:12)

Be on your guard; stand firm in the faith; be men of courage; be strong. (1 Cor 16:13)

Be self-controlled and alert. Your enemy the devil prowls around like a roaring lion looking for someone to devour. (1 Pet 5:8)

4. The minister or overseer must be "self-controlled" (sophrona): be sober-minded, that is, to have a mind that is sound, sensible, controlled, disciplined, and chaste—a mind that has complete control over all sensual desires. Note: if the mind is controlled, a person's whole life—his body and behavior—is controlled. He lives a life of self-control.

So then, let us not be like others, who are asleep, but let us be alert and self-controlled. For those who sleep, sleep at night, and those who get drunk, get drunk at night. But since we belong to the day, let us be self-controlled, putting on faith and love as a breastplate, and the hope of salvation as a helmet. (1 Th 5:6-8)

Now the overseer must be above reproach, the husband of but one wife, temperate, self-controlled, respectable, hospitable, able to teach, (1 Tim 3:2)

In the same way, their wives are to be women worthy of respect, not malicious talkers but temperate and trustworthy in everything. (1 Tim 3:11)

Rather he [an overseer] must be hospitable, one who loves what is good, who is self-controlled, upright, holy and disciplined. (Titus 1:8)

Teach the older men to be temperate, worthy of respect, self-controlled, and sound in faith, in love and in endurance. to be self-controlled and pure, to be busy at home, to be kind, and to be subject to their husbands, so that no one will malign the word of God. (Titus 2:2, 5)

1 TIMOTHY 3:1-7

For the grace of God that brings salvation has appeared to all men. It teaches us to say "No" to ungodliness and worldly passions, and to live self-controlled, upright and godly lives in this present age, while we wait for the blessed hope—the glorious appearing of our great God and Savior, Jesus Christ, (Titus 2:11-13)

Therefore, prepare your minds for action; be self-controlled; set your hope fully on the grace to be given you when Jesus Christ is revealed. (1 Pet 1:13)

The end of all things is near. Therefore be clear minded and self-controlled so that you can pray. (1 Pet 4:7)

5. The minister or overseer must be "respectable" (kosmion): well-behaved, orderly, composed, solid, and honest. It is a person who has good conduct, whose character and behavior stands as the ideal and pattern for others.

It [love] is not rude, it is not self-seeking, it is not easily angered, it keeps no record of wrongs. (1 Cor 13:5)
So that you may be able to discern what is best and may be pure and blameless until the day of Christ, (Phil 1:10)
In the name of the Lord Jesus Christ, we command you, brothers, to keep away from every brother who is idle and does not live according to the teaching you received from us. For you yourselves know how you ought to follow our example. We were not idle when we were with you, (2 Th 3:6-7)
Now the overseer must be above reproach, the husband of but one wife, temperate, self-controlled, respectable, hospitable, able to teach, (1 Tim 3:2)
Likewise, teach the older women to be reverent in the way they live, not to be slanderers or addicted to much wine, but to teach what is good. (Titus 2:3)

6. The minister or overseer must be "hospitable" (philoxenon): to have an open heart and home; "showing love or being a friend to the believers, especially strangers or foreigners" (Amplified New Testament). The minister helps and entertains as much as he can. He does not open his heart, home, time, or money to the things of the world; but he uses what resources he has to help and minister to people.

Share with God's people who are in need. Practice hospitality. (Rom 12:13)
Now the overseer must be above reproach, the husband of but one wife, temperate, self-controlled, respectable, hospitable, able to teach, (1 Tim 3:2)
And is well known for her good deeds, such as bringing up children, showing hospitality, washing the feet of the saints, helping those in trouble and devoting herself to all kinds of good deeds. (1 Tim 5:10)
Rather he must be hospitable, one who loves what is good, who is self-controlled, upright, holy and disciplined. (Titus 1:8)
Do not forget to entertain strangers, for by so doing some people have entertained angels without knowing it. (Heb 13:2)
Offer hospitality to one another without grumbling. (1 Pet 4:9)

7. The minister or overseer must be "able to teach": capable, skillful, and qualified to teach. William Barclay has such an excellent comment on this point that he must be quoted:

"It has been said that the duty of the Christian leader is 'to preach to the unconverted and to teach the converted.' There are two things to be said about this. It is one of the disasters of modern times that the teaching ministry of the Church has not been exercised as it should be. There is any amount of topical preaching; there is any amount of exhortation; but there is little use in exhorting a man to be a Christian when he does not know what being a Christian means. Instruction is a primary duty of the Christian preacher and leader. But the second thing is this. The finest and the most effective teaching is not done by speaking, but by being. Our ultimate duty is not to talk to men about Christ, but to show men Christ. Even the man with no gift of words can teach by living in such a way that in him men see the reflection of the Master. A saint has been defined as someone 'in whom Christ lives again'" (*The Letters to Timothy, Titus, and Philemon*, p.95).

Matthew Henry also has an excellent comment:

"This is a preaching bishop whom Paul describes, one who is both able and willing to communicate to others the knowledge which God has given him, one who is fit to teach and ready to take all opportunities of giving instruction, who is himself well instructed in the things of the kingdom of heaven, and is communicative of what he knows to others" (*Matthew Henry's Commentary*, Vol.5, p.815).

And teaching them to obey everything I have commanded you. And surely I am with you always, to the very end of the age." (Mat 28:20)
Now the overseer must be above reproach, the husband of but one wife, temperate, self-controlled, respectable, hospitable, able to teach, (1 Tim 3:2)
Command and teach these things. (1 Tim 4:11)
Those who oppose him he must gently instruct, in the hope that God will grant them repentance leading them to a knowledge of the truth, (2 Tim 2:25)

Thought 1. Note: the minister must be rooted and grounded in the Word of God in order to teach.

8. The minister or overseer must not be given to drunkenness: not be a drunkard; not sit around drinking all the time. In order to justify their right to drink, some argue that drinking wine was a common practice in the ancient world even among true Christian believers. However, we

must always remember what William Barclay so forcefully points out about the ancient world:

⇒ First, the water supply was often inadequate and dangerous.
⇒ Second, "although the ancient world used wine as the commonest of all drinks it used it most abstemiously. When wine was drunk, it was drunk in the proportion of two parts of wine to three parts of water. A man who was drunken would be disgraced in ordinary heathen society, let alone in the Church" (*The Letters to Timothy, Titus, and Philemon*, p.91).
⇒ Oliver B. Greene pointedly says:

> "All believers should abstain from strong drink in any form, but especially should a bishop observe this admonition. Concerning wine, Paul's instruction to a bishop is very clear. He is not to participate in such practice. Greek scholars tell us that the word used here implies 'sitting over wine,' habitually drinking wine, as the people did in that day—even those who professed to be very religious. Not only for his own sake should a bishop abstain from the use of wine, but also for the sake of other believers" (*The Epistles of Paul the Apostle to Timothy and Titus.* Greenville, SC: The Gospel Hour, 1964, p.114).

> **For he [John the Baptist] will be great in the sight of the Lord. He is never to take wine or other fermented drink, and he will be filled with the Holy Spirit even from birth. (Luke 1:15)**
> **It is better not to eat meat or drink wine or to do anything else that will cause your brother to fall. (Rom 14:21)**
> **"You and your sons are not to drink wine or other fermented drink whenever you go into the Tent of Meeting, or you will die. This is a lasting ordinance for the generations to come. (Lev 10:9)**
> **He [the Nazarite] must abstain from wine and other fermented drink and must not drink vinegar made from wine or from other fermented drink. He must not drink grape juice or eat grapes or raisins. (Num 6:3)**
> **Do not gaze at wine when it is red, when it sparkles in the cup, when it goes down smoothly! (Prov 23:31)**
> **"It is not for kings, O Lemuel— not for kings to drink wine, not for rulers to crave beer, (Prov 31:4)**
> **But they replied, "We do not drink wine, because our forefather Jonadab son of Recab gave us this command: 'Neither you nor your descendants must ever drink wine. (Jer 35:6)**
> **But Daniel resolved not to defile himself with the royal food and wine, and he asked the chief official for permission not to defile himself this way. (Dan 1:8)**

9. The minister or overseer must not be "violent" (me plekten): not combative or violent, not contentious or quarrelsome, not a person who strikes out and contends with another person. The minister must not be a person who strikes other people or who becomes easily upset, irritated, or aggravated with others. He uses neither hand nor tongue against anyone. On the contrary he is kind, gentle, and patient with others.

Thought 1. Note: the tongue can be used to strike out at a person as easily as the hand or fist. Many a person has been hurt and damaged by the poisonous venom of a striking tongue.

> **Do nothing out of selfish ambition or vain conceit, but in humility consider others better than yourselves. Each of you should look not only to your own interests, but also to the interests of others. (Phil 2:3-4)**
> **Keep reminding them of these things. Warn them before God against quarreling about words; it is of no value, and only ruins those who listen. (2 Tim 2:14)**
> **And the Lord's servant must not quarrel; instead, he must be kind to everyone, able to teach, not resentful. (2 Tim 2:24)**
> **Do not accuse a man for no reason— when he has done you no harm. (Prov 3:30)**
> **Starting a quarrel is like breaching a dam; so drop the matter before a dispute breaks out. (Prov 17:14)**
> **It is to a man's honor to avoid strife, but every fool is quick to quarrel. (Prov 20:3)**

10. The minister or overseer must be "gentle" (epieike): gracious, kind, patient, forbearing, reasonable, soft, and tender. The word goes beyond treating someone with justice: it treats a person graciously and tenderly. It reaches beyond justice and touches the person with a gentle hand. (See note, *Gentleness*—Ph.4:5 for more discussion.)

> **But we were gentle among you, like a mother caring for her little children. (1 Th 2:7)**
> **Not given to drunkenness, not violent but gentle, not quarrelsome, not a lover of money. (1 Tim 3:3)**
> **And the Lord's servant must not quarrel; instead, he must be kind to everyone, able to teach, not resentful. (2 Tim 2:24)**
> **To slander no one, to be peaceable and considerate, and to show true humility toward all men. (Titus 3:2)**
> **But the wisdom that comes from heaven is first of all pure; then peace-loving, considerate, submissive, full of mercy and good fruit, impartial and sincere. (James 3:17)**

11. The minister or overseer must not be quarrelsome (amachon): not contentious or a fighter. He must be a man of peace, a mild-mannered person, always under control. Again, this refers to the tongue as well as to the hands. He must be a man who is deeply touched when there is unrest, controversy, or disturbance in the church or among believers. He must be a person who is so touched that he will work and seek for peace.

> **For God is not a God of disorder but of peace. As in all the congregations of the saints, (1 Cor 14:33)**

> Finally, brothers, good-by. Aim for perfection, listen to my appeal, be of one mind, live in peace. And the God of love and peace will be with you. (2 Cor 13:11)
>
> As a prisoner for the Lord, then, I urge you to live a life worthy of the calling you have received. Be completely humble and gentle; be patient, bearing with one another in love. Make every effort to keep the unity of the Spirit through the bond of peace. (Eph 4:1-3)
>
> Flee the evil desires of youth, and pursue righteousness, faith, love and peace, along with those who call on the Lord out of a pure heart. (2 Tim 2:22)
>
> He must turn from evil and do good; he must seek peace and pursue it. (1 Pet 3:11)
>
> Turn from evil and do good; seek peace and pursue it. (Psa 34:14)

12. The minister or overseer must not be a lover of money (aphilargyros). The minister must be a person who has given all he is and has (money) to minister to people. He must not be a person who has entered the ministry as a profession or as a livelihood. He *must be supported* and given a livelihood by the church *but he is not* to be in the ministry in order to get a livelihood. He must not be a person who is *out to get,* but a person who is *committed to giving*. He must live of the gospel—God's people must support him so that he can preach the gospel—but he must be dead to the *love of money* and material possessions. He must give all that he is and has to the cause of Christ—to meet the dire needs of the desperate and dying men, women, and children of this earth. Remember: the following warnings were written to professing Christians.

> For the love of money is a root of all kinds of evil. Some people, eager for money, have wandered from the faith and pierced themselves with many griefs. (1 Tim 6:10)
>
> Your gold and silver are corroded. Their corrosion [storing, banking] will testify against you and eat your flesh like fire. You have hoarded wealth in the last days. (James 5:3)
>
> Then he said to them, "Watch out! Be on your guard against all kinds of greed; a man's life does not consist in the abundance of his possessions." (Luke 12:15)
>
> But among you there must not be even a hint of sexual immorality, or of any kind of impurity, or of greed, because these are improper for God's holy people. (Eph 5:3)
>
> Put to death, therefore, whatever belongs to your earthly nature: sexual immorality, impurity, lust, evil desires and greed, which is idolatry. (Col 3:5)
>
> Keep your lives free from the love of money and be content with what you have, because God has said, "Never will I leave you; never will I forsake you." (Heb 13:5)
>
> "You shall not covet your neighbor's house. You shall not covet your neighbor's wife, or his manservant or maidservant, his ox or donkey, or anything that belongs to your neighbor." (Exo 20:17)
>
> "From the least to the greatest, all are greedy for gain; prophets and priests alike, all practice deceit. (Jer 6:13)
>
> My people come to you, as they usually do, and sit before you to listen to your words, but they do not put them into practice. With their mouths they express devotion, but their hearts are greedy for unjust gain. (Ezek 33:31)
>
> They covet fields and seize them, and houses, and take them. They defraud a man of his home, a fellowman of his inheritance. (Micah 2:2)
>
> "Woe to him who builds his realm by unjust gain to set his nest on high, to escape the clutches of ruin! (Hab 2:9)

3 (3:4-5) **Minister—Overseer—Elder**: the minister or overseer must meet one very significant family qualification. The minister or overseer must manage his own household and manage it well. The home is a miniature of the church; the home is the proving ground for leadership in the church. The husband is the head of the home. This does not mean that he is the dictator, tyrant, or bully of the home. It means that he is the leader of the wife and children. He leads them all...
- in the building of a loving, joyful, and peaceful home.
- in the fulfillment of their life calling and task upon earth.

It means that the man is not bossed about or dominated by his wife; that he does not allow his children to disobey, rebel, or talk back to him or their mother; that he takes the lead in controlling his home for Christ and His kingdom.

Note the word "respect" (semnotes). It means dignity. The minister must manage his home with dignity, respect, and love. As the Amplified New Testament says: "With true dignity, commanding their respect in every way and keeping them respectful."

As Scripture says, "(If anyone does not know how to manage his own family, how can he take care of God's church?)" (1 Tim.3:5).

4 (3:6) **Proven—Novice—Minister—Overseer—Elder**: the minister or overseer of God must be spiritually qualified. He must not be a recent convert (me neophuton), that is, a new convert or a new church member. He must have been a convert or church member for a long time...
- long enough to have become rooted and grounded in the Lord and His Word.
- long enough to have become spiritually mature.
- long enough to have proven his testimony for Christ.
- long enough to be well known and respected by other believers.
- long enough to be able to minister to others and to teach them to minister.

Note why a recent convert must not be given a position of leadership in the church: he may become conceited and "fall under the same judgment as the devil." Satan was expelled from heaven because of pride. It was pride that caused his fall and brought condemnation upon him. When a person is given a great responsibility before he has become rooted and grounded in the faith, he is most likely going to fall and be condemned just as Satan fell and was condemned. We must always remember what Matthew

Henry points out: "Pride...is a sin that turned angels into devils" (*Matthew Henry's Commentary*, Vol.6, p.815). We must guard against pride. We must guard against putting a person in a position of leadership that will tempt him to feel more important than he is.

> **For whoever exalts himself will be humbled, and whoever humbles himself will be exalted. (Mat 23:12)**
>
> **Do nothing out of selfish ambition or vain conceit, but in humility consider others better than yourselves. Each of you should look not only to your own interests, but also to the interests of others. (Phil 2:3-4)**
>
> **When pride comes, then comes disgrace, but with humility comes wisdom. (Prov 11:2)**
>
> **Pride goes before destruction, a haughty spirit before a fall. (Prov 16:18)**
>
> **It is not good to eat too much honey, nor is it honorable to seek one's own honor. (Prov 25:27)**
>
> **You said in your heart, "I will ascend to heaven; I will raise my throne above the stars of God; I will sit enthroned on the mount of assembly, on the utmost heights of the sacred mountain. I will ascend above the tops of the clouds; I will make myself like the Most High." (Isa 14:13-14)**
>
> **You have trusted in your wickedness and have said, 'No one sees me.' Your wisdom and knowledge mislead you when you say to yourself, 'I am, and there is none besides me.' (Isa 47:10)**
>
> **"Son of man, say to the ruler of Tyre, 'This is what the Sovereign LORD says: "'In the pride of your heart you say, "I am a god; I sit on the throne of a god in the heart of the seas." But you are a man and not a god, though you think you are as wise as a god. (Ezek 28:2)**
>
> **Though you soar like the eagle and make your nest among the stars, from there I will bring you down," declares the LORD. (Oba 1:4)**

5 (3:7) **Minister—Overseer—Elder**: the minister or overseer must meet one very important community qualification. He must have a "good reputation with outsiders;" that is, he must have a good testimony before the world. Of course, there are some in the world who will criticize and slander any person who has failed and run with the world. Many in the world do not recognize conversion nor repentance and forgiveness—the simple fact that Christ can forgive and change a person. But when a person enters the ministry, he must have experienced such a significant change that it is clearly evident that he is *now following Christ*. The change in his life must be radical: a radical turning away from the world and self to Christ. The change must be so radical that even the unbelievers can see it. Then and only then can he ever hope to reach the unbelieving world for Christ.

Note why the minister must have a good reputation before the world: to that he will not fall into disgrace. The unbelievers of the world will reproach, ridicule, and mock him; and he will fall into the snare of the devil. That is, he will hesitate to bear testimony for Christ and to fulfill his duties as a minister. He will tend to withdraw and keep silent and to remain unseen as much as possible. The power of his ministry and testimony will be drastically weakened.

> **The brothers at Lystra and Iconium spoke well of him. Paul wanted to take him along on the journey, so he circumcised him because of the Jews who lived in that area, for they all knew that his father was a Greek. (Acts 16:2-3)**
>
> **First, I thank my God through Jesus Christ for all of you, because your faith is being reported all over the world. (Rom 1:8)**
>
> **But in your hearts set apart Christ as Lord. Always be prepared to give an answer to everyone who asks you to give the reason for the hope that you have. But do this with gentleness and respect, (1 Pet 3:15)**

Thought 1. A testimony before the world is essential. The world is not to choose or even have a voice in selecting church leaders. But church leaders must be respected by their day to day acquaintances. The point is *profession* verses *possession*. Those *outside* are the first to notice wrong behavior in a Christian. The Christian believer must behave like a Christian believer before he can serve as an overseer in God's church.

1 TIMOTHY 3:8-13

	D. The Deacons of the Church,^{DS1} 3:8-13	as deacons.
		11 In the same way, their wives are to be women worthy of respect, not malicious talkers but temperate and trustworthy in everything.
		12 A deacon must be the husband of but one wife and must manage his children and his household well.
		13 Those who have served well gain an excellent standing and great assurance in their faith in Christ Jesus.
			3 Family qualifications
			  a. Must have a committed wife
			  b. Must have a controlled family & home

1 Personal qualifications	8 Deacons, likewise, are to be men worthy of respect, sincere, not indulging in much wine, and not pursuing dishonest gain.		

2 Spiritual qualifications
  a. Spiritual convictions
  b. Spiritually tested—proven
	9 They must keep hold of the deep truths of the faith with a clear conscience.
	10 They must first be tested; and then if there is nothing against them, let them serve
			4 Results: Reward reaped
			  a. Community respect
			  b. Spiritual assurance

DIVISION II

DUTIES AND ORDER IN THE CHURCH, 2:1-3:13

D. The Deacons of the Church, 3:8-13

(3:8-13) **Introduction**: this passage discusses the second officer of the church, the deacon. The office of deacon is so important that the qualifications required are just as high as those demanded of a minister or overseer. In this day and time, when worldliness, immorality, and lawlessness are running so rampant, the qualifications for deacons need to be studied, heeded, and guarded ever so diligently.

1. Personal qualifications (v.8).
2. Spiritual qualifications (v.9-10).
3. Family qualifications (v.11-12).
4. Results: reward reaped (v.13).

DEEPER STUDY # 1
(3:8-13) **Deacons**: the word deacon (diakonous) means servant, minister. The first reference to deacons is in Acts (Acts 6:1-7). Deacons were appointed to help in the ministerial and administrative duties of the church (Acts 6:2). Their function was to relieve ministers so that ministers could give their "attention [continually] to prayer and to the ministry of the Word" (Acts 6:4). In particular they were chosen to minister to the day-to-day needs of believers and to the needs of widows and widowers and the poor and sick of a church. They were to relieve ministers so the ministers could *concentrate on prayer and preaching*.

> Brothers, choose seven men from among you who are known to be full of the Spirit and wisdom. We will turn this responsibility over to them and will give our attention to prayer and the ministry of the word." (Acts 6:3-4)

However, note a significant fact: this does not mean that ministers are never to meet day-to-day needs of believers nor that deacons should never share or preach the Word. In the early church both ministers and deacons served in both areas, but each *concentrated* upon their primary call and mission.

⇒ Preachers were sometimes called deacons, that is, servants.

> What, after all, is Apollos? And what is Paul? Only servants, [diakonoi] through whom you came to believe—as the Lord has assigned to each his task. (1 Cor 3:5)

> He has made us competent as ministers [diakonous] of a new covenant—not of the letter but of the Spirit; for the letter kills, but the Spirit gives life. (2 Cor 3:6)

⇒ The first deacons preached as well as ministered to the needy of the church.

> Now Stephen, [a deacon] a man full of God's grace and power, did great wonders and miraculous signs among the people. (Acts 6:8)
> Philip [a deacon] went down to a city in Samaria and proclaimed the Christ there. (Acts 8:5)

⇒ Deacons are closely linked to overseers.

> Paul and Timothy, servants of Christ Jesus, To all the saints in Christ Jesus at Philippi, together with the overseers and deacons: (Phil 1:1)

⇒ Deacons are to be spiritually equipped for their task.

> Brothers, choose seven men from among you who are known to be full of the Spirit and wisdom. We will turn this responsibility over to them (Acts 6:3; cp. 1 Tim.3:8-13)

⇒ The office of the deacon was an early development in the church.

> In those days when the number of disciples was increasing, the Grecian Jews among them complained against the Hebraic Jews because their widows were being overlooked in the daily distribution of food. So the Twelve gathered all the disciples together and said, "It would not be right for us to neglect the ministry of the word of God in order to wait on tables. Brothers, choose seven men from among you who are known to be full of the Spirit and

1 TIMOTHY 3:8-13

> wisdom. We will turn this responsibility over to them and will give our attention to prayer and the ministry of the word." (Acts 6:1-4)

1 (3:8) **Deacons—Church, Officer of**: deacons must be qualified; they must meet some personal qualifications.

1. Deacons must be "worthy of respect" (semnous): serious, honorable, revered, highly respected, noble. It is being serious-minded, the very opposite...
   - of being flippant.
   - of dishonoring oneself.
   - of being shallow by being over-talkative.
   - of having little respect because one is not grave or serious enough.
   - of having a surface religion only.

However, note that this does not mean that the deacon is to walk around with a long face, never smiling, joking, or having fun. It simply means that he is serious-minded and committed to Christ and to the mission of the church: the mission of reaching the lost and meeting the needs of the desperate of the world.

> So then, let us not be like others, who are asleep, but let us be alert and self-controlled. For those who sleep, sleep at night, and those who get drunk, get drunk at night. But since we belong to the day, let us be self-controlled, putting on faith and love as a breastplate, and the hope of salvation as a helmet. (1 Th 5:6-8)
>
> Now the overseer must be above reproach, the husband of but one wife, temperate, self-controlled, respectable, hospitable, able to teach, (1 Tim 3:2)
>
> In the same way, their wives are to be women worthy of respect, not malicious talkers but temperate and trustworthy in everything. (1 Tim 3:11)
>
> Rather he [an overseer must be] must be hospitable, one who loves what is good, who is self-controlled, upright, holy and disciplined. (Titus 1:8)
>
> Teach the older men to be temperate, worthy of respect, self-controlled, and sound in faith, in love and in endurance. to be self-controlled and pure, to be busy at home, to be kind, and to be subject to their husbands, so that no one will malign the word of God. (Titus 2:2, 5)
>
> For the grace of God that brings salvation has appeared to all men. It teaches us to say "No" to ungodliness and worldly passions, and to live self-controlled, upright and godly lives in this present age, while we wait for the blessed hope—the glorious appearing of our great God and Savior, Jesus Christ, (Titus 2:11-13)
>
> Therefore, prepare your minds for action; be self-controlled; set your hope fully on the grace to be given you when Jesus Christ is revealed. (1 Pet 1:13)
>
> The end of all things is near. Therefore be clear minded and self-controlled so that you can pray. (1 Pet 4:7)

2. Deacons must not be insincere (dilogos): bearing tales, gossiping, saying "one thing to one person and something different to another [person]" (Donald Guthrie. *The Pastoral Epistles*. Tyndale New Testament Commentaries, p.84); saying one thing to a person's face and something else behind his back.

The quality of *being sincere* is important. As a deacon ministers through visitation (going from house to house) he is often tempted to gossip or say one thing to one person and something else to another person. He is also tempted to evade or smooth talk issues. Therefore, he must be a man of integrity, a man who speaks the straight truth—a man who is as honest as the day is long.

> Besides, they get into the habit of being idle and going about from house to house. And not only do they become idlers, but also gossips and busybodies, saying things they ought not to. (1 Tim 5:13)
>
> He chose to give us birth through the word of truth, that we might be a kind of firstfruits of all he created. (James 1:18)
>
> If you suffer, it should not be as a murderer or thief or any other kind of criminal, or even as a meddler. (1 Pet 4:15)
>
> "'Do not go about spreading slander among your people. "'Do not do anything that endangers your neighbor's life. I am the LORD. (Lev 19:16)
>
> A gossip betrays a confidence, but a trustworthy man keeps a secret. (Prov 11:13)
>
> The words of a gossip are like choice morsels; they go down to a man's inmost parts. (Prov 18:8)
>
> A gossip betrays a confidence; so avoid a man who talks too much. (Prov 20:19)
>
> Without wood a fire goes out; without gossip a quarrel dies down. (Prov 26:20)

3. The deacon must not indulge in wine (see note, *Minister*, pt.8—1 Tim.3:2-3 for discussion).

4. The deacon must not pursue dishonest gain (see note, *Minister*, pt.10—1 Tim.3:2-3 for discussion).

2 (3:9-10) **Deacon—Church, Officer of**: deacons must meet three very important spiritual qualifications.

1. Deacons must keep hold of the deep truths of the faith with a clear conscience. The deep truths of the faith are given in verse 16:

"Beyond all question, the mystery of godliness is great:
  ⇒ He [God] appeared in a body
  ⇒ Was vindicated by the Spirit
  ⇒ Was seen by angels
  ⇒ Was preached among the nations
  ⇒ Was believed on in the world
  ⇒ Was taken up in glory."

A deacon must believe in the incarnation, in the glorious gospel that God has come to earth in the Person of the Lord Jesus Christ to *preach* the love and salvation of God for man. In fact, note what this verse says: a deacon must hold deep truths of the faith. He must possess and cling to it, and he must hold it in good conscience. He must believe the *whole gospel* (mystery) and not deceive the church by being hypocritical about his belief.

There is another point about conscience as well: the deacon must have a clear conscience about living and sharing the deep truths of the faith. He must not accept the call and office of deacon and then shirk his duties. He must hold the mystery of the gospel of the faith in all good conscience, that is, in sharing it faithfully with both believers and unbelievers.

> Now this is our boast: Our conscience testifies that we have conducted ourselves in the world, and especially in our relations with you, in the holiness and sincerity that are from God. We have done so not according to worldly wisdom but according to God's grace. (2 Cor 1:12)
>
> The goal of this command is love, which comes from a pure heart and a good conscience and a sincere faith. (1 Tim 1:5)
>
> Holding on to faith and a good conscience. Some have rejected these and so have shipwrecked their faith. (1 Tim 1:19)
>
> Keeping a clear conscience, so that those who speak maliciously against your good behavior in Christ may be ashamed of their slander. (1 Pet 3:16)

2. Deacons must first be tested or proved before they are called to the office of a deacon (see note, *Proven*—1 Tim.3:6 for discussion).

3. Deacons must be blameless, have nothing against them" (see note, pt.1—1 Tim.3:2-3).

3 (3:11-12) **Deacons—Church, Officer of**: deacons must meet several family qualifications. The Greek of this verse allows the verse to refer to women in the church who served as deaconesses, and indeed, many translators and commentators translate it as referring to deaconesses. However, this position seems most unlikely, for all the other verses of this passage deal with the deacons of a church. It is much more likely and logical that Paul is talking about the wives of deacons. The greater weight of the context certainly lies with this position. This is not a good passage for a person to build his case for deaconesses in the church. As a deacon visits and ministers to the women of the church, he needs his wife with him if she is able to accompany him. A strong picture of marital and family love and commitment to Christ are needed. Therefore, the deacon's wife must be as strong in the Lord as he is.

1. The deacon must have a wife who is as committed to the Lord and to the church as he is.

   a. The wife of a deacon must be "worthy of respect": serious-minded, honorable, respected, and noble (see note, pt.1—1 Tim.3:8 for discussion).
   b. The wife of a deacon must not be a "malicious talker" (me diabolous): a talebearer, gossiper; a person who goes about talking about others, stirring up mischief and disturbance.

   > Get rid of all bitterness, rage and anger, brawling and slander, along with every form of malice. (Eph 4:31)
   >
   > We hear that some among you are idle. They are not busy; they are busybodies. (2 Th 3:11)
   >
   > Besides, they get into the habit of being idle and going about from house to house. And not only do they become idlers, but also gossips and busybodies, saying things they ought not to. (1 Tim 5:13)
   >
   > If anyone considers himself religious and yet does not keep a tight rein on his tongue, he deceives himself and his religion is worthless. (James 1:26)
   >
   > The tongue also is a fire, a world of evil among the parts of the body. It corrupts the whole person, sets the whole course of his life on fire, and is itself set on fire by hell. (James 3:6)
   >
   > Brothers, do not slander one another. Anyone who speaks against his brother or judges him speaks against the law and judges it. When you judge the law, you are not keeping it, but sitting in judgment on it. (James 4:11)
   >
   > Therefore, rid yourselves of all malice and all deceit, hypocrisy, envy, and slander of every kind. (1 Pet 2:1)
   >
   > For, "Whoever would love life and see good days must keep his tongue from evil and his lips from deceitful speech. (1 Pet 3:10)
   >
   > Whoever slanders his neighbor in secret, him will I put to silence; whoever has haughty eyes and a proud heart, him will I not endure. (Psa 101:5)
   >
   > With his mouth the godless destroys his neighbor, but through knowledge the righteous escape. (Prov 11:9)
   >
   > A perverse man stirs up dissension, and a gossip separates close friends. (Prov 16:28)
   >
   > The words of a gossip are like choice morsels; they go down to a man's inmost parts. (Prov 26:22)

   c. The wife of a deacon must be temperate (see note, pt.4—1 Tim.3:2-3 for discussion).
   d. The wife of a deacon must be trustworthy in everything: completely trustworthy as a wife and mother and as a believer. She must be faithful to the Lord...
   - in her personal devotion and loyalty to the Lord.
   - in her call as a wife and mother.
   - in her commitment to the church and its services and ministry.
   - in her ministry in serving with her husband.

   > Then he said to them all: "If anyone would come after me, he must deny himself and take up his cross daily and follow me. (Luke 9:23)
   >
   > Therefore, my dear brothers, stand firm. Let nothing move you. Always give yourselves fully to the work of the Lord, because you know that your labor in the Lord is not in vain. (1 Cor 15:58)
   >
   > Let us not become weary in doing good, for at the proper time we will reap a harvest if we do not give up. (Gal 6:9)
   >
   > Therefore, prepare your minds for action; be self-controlled; set your hope fully on the grace to be given you when Jesus Christ is revealed. (1 Pet 1:13)

> But you are to hold fast to the LORD your God, as you have until now. (Josh 23:8)

2. The deacon must be the husband of one wife (see note, pt.2—1 Tim.3:2-3 for discussion).

3. The deacon must have a managed family and home (see note—1 Tim.3:4-5 for discussion).

4 (3:13) **Deacon—Testimony**: the faithful deacon experiences two results.

1. He gains an excellent standing and testimony before both God and man.

> In the same way, faith by itself, if it is not accompanied by action, is dead. (James 2:17)

2. He gains great assurance or confidence and security in the faith. He experiences more and more assurance and freedom in the Spirit of God.

> In him [Christ] and through faith in him we may approach God with freedom and confidence. (Eph 3:12)

> Let us then approach the throne of grace with confidence, so that we may receive mercy and find grace to help us in our time of need. (Heb 4:16)

> Therefore, brothers, since we have confidence to enter the Most Holy Place by the blood of Jesus.... let us draw near to God with a sincere heart in full assurance of faith, having our hearts sprinkled to cleanse us from a guilty conscience and having our bodies washed with pure water. Let us hold unswervingly to the hope we profess, for he who promised is faithful. And let us consider how we may spur one another on toward love and good deeds. (Heb 10:19, 22-24)

> In this way, love is made complete among us so that we will have confidence on the day of judgment, because in this world we are like him. (1 John 4:17)

1 TIMOTHY 3:14-16

	III. BEHAVIOR & RELATIONSHIPS IN THE CHURCH, 3:14-6:21	conduct themselves in God's household, which is the church of the living God, the pillar and foundation of the truth.	a. The house of God b. The church of the living God c. The pillar & support of the truth
	A. The Description of the Church, 3:14-16	16 Beyond all question, the mystery of godliness is great: He appeared in a body, was vindicated by the Spirit, was seen by angels, was preached among the nations, was believed on in the world, was taken up in glory.	**3 The truth of the church** a. Is confessed by all true believers b. Is the mystery of godliness: Six facts
1 The purpose of the Pastoral Epistles—that men might know how they ought to behave in the church **2 The description of the church**	14 Although I hope to come to you soon, I am writing you these instructions so that, 15 If I am delayed, you will know how people ought to		

DIVISION III

BEHAVIOR AND RELATIONSHIPS IN THE CHURCH, 3:14-6:21

A. The Description of the Church, 3:14-16

(3:14-16) **Introduction**: this passage begins a new division of subjects in 1 Timothy—the believer's behavior and relationships in the church. This first passage is one of the greatest discussions on the church in all of Scripture. It is a passage that every church and believer needs to study and heed.
1. The purpose of the Pastoral Epistles—that men might know how they ought to behave in the church (v.14).
2. The description of the church (v.15).
3. The truth of the church (v.16).

1 (3:14-15) **Church—Pastoral Epistles—Scripture**: these two verses explain why Paul was writing to Timothy and why he was later to write to Titus and Philemon. In essence these two verses give the very purpose for all the Pastoral Epistles (First and Second Timothy, Titus, and Philemon). Paul was writing to tell believers how they should behave within the church, that is, within the household or family of God. The word "conduct" (anastrephesthai) means the walk and behavior of a person; but it especially refers to how a person relates to other people. Therefore, the great concern of the Pastoral Epistles is how believers conduct themselves, how they behave in their relationships to God, to each other, and to the unbelievers of the world.

Remember: Timothy was in Ephesus and Paul was writing from Macedonia. Paul hoped to visit Ephesus and Timothy soon, but he was not quite sure that he would be able to leave Macedonia. Therefore, he was spelling out in some detail...
- how Christian believers are to conduct themselves within the church.
- how Christian believers are to behave and witness to a world that is lost and reeling under the weight of corruption and evil.

2 (3:15) **Church**: this verse gives a great description of the church, a description that spells out three great pictures of the church.
1. The church is "God's household [oikoi]." This does not refer to the building of the church, but to the household of the church, to the people of the church. The church is a body of people who have committed themselves to form a family of people, a family centered around God and His Son, the Lord Jesus Christ.

The church is a *family of people*...

- who believe in God and in His Son, the Lord Jesus Christ.
- who have committed their lives to live for Christ.
- who have based their lives upon the promise of eternal salvation promised by the Lord Jesus Christ.
- who have committed themselves to live as a family with all other believers.

Simply stated, the church is a body of people who have committed their lives to live as the family of God. God is the Father; Jesus Christ is the only begotten Son of the Father; but we, the followers of God, are the adopted children of God. Every person who truly follows God is a true member of the church, that is, of the family of God (Jn.1:12; 2 Cor.6:17-18; Gal.4:4-6).

The point is this:
⇒ How should we behave toward our Father?
⇒ How should we behave toward our brothers and sisters?

The answer is found within the family relationship.
a. The children of a family are to love, obey, and learn from the Father.

> **For whoever does the will of my Father in heaven is my brother and sister and mother." (Mat 12:50)**
> **Jesus replied: "'Love the Lord your God with all your heart and with all your soul and with all your mind.' This is the first and greatest commandment. And the second is like it: 'Love your neighbor as yourself.' (Mat 22:37-39)**
> **If anyone chooses to do God's will, he will find out whether my teaching comes from God or whether I speak on my own. (John 7:17)**
> **Whoever has my commands and obeys them, he is the one who loves me. He who loves me will be loved by my Father, and I too will love him and show myself to him." (John 14:21)**
> **Jesus replied, "If anyone loves me, he will obey my teaching. My Father will love him, and we will come to him and make our home with him. (John 14:23)**
> **Do your best to present yourself to God as one approved, a workman who does not**

need to be ashamed and who correctly handles the word of truth. (2 Tim 2:15)

But Samuel replied: "Does the LORD delight in burnt offerings and sacrifices as much as in obeying the voice of the LORD? To obey is better than sacrifice, and to heed is better than the fat of rams. (1 Sam 15:22)

b. The children of a family are to love and help each other.

And the second is like it: 'Love your neighbor as yourself.' (Mat 22:39)

"A new command I give you: Love one another. As I have loved you, so you must love one another. By this all men will know that you are my disciples, if you love one another." (John 13:34-35)

My command is this: Love each other as I have loved you. (John 15:12)

Now that you have purified yourselves by obeying the truth so that you have sincere love for your brothers, love one another deeply, from the heart. (1 Pet 1:22)

In everything I did, I showed you that by this kind of hard work we must help the weak, remembering the words the Lord Jesus himself said: 'It is more blessed to give than to receive.'" (Acts 20:35)

We who are strong ought to bear with the failings of the weak and not to please ourselves. (Rom 15:1)

Carry each other's burdens, and in this way you will fulfill the law of Christ. (Gal 6:2)

Therefore, as we have opportunity, let us do good to all people, especially to those who belong to the family of believers. (Gal 6:10)

And let us consider how we may spur one another on toward love and good deeds. (Heb 10:24)

Remember those in prison as if you were their fellow prisoners, and those who are mistreated as if you yourselves were suffering. (Heb 13:3)

2. The church is "the church of the living God." The word "church" (ekklesia) means an assembly, a gathering, a company of people who have been called out by God. But note: God is the living God; He is not some dead god. He is not some idol or figment of man's imagination. He is the living God who is actually alive and is vitally concerned with how men behave and conduct themselves. This means a most significant thing.

God calls people to His church. He calls them to join His assembly, His gathering, His company of people. But it is up to people whether or not they come to His church. He is the living God; therefore, He actually speaks to the human heart and calls people to follow Him and to live for Him. There are times when every person feels and senses the call of God within his heart to come and join His company of people. But the decision is up to the person. God loves the person; therefore, He will not force the person to come to Him.

For they themselves report what kind of reception you gave us. They tell how you turned to God from idols to serve the living and true God, and to wait for his Son from heaven, whom he raised from the dead—Jesus, who rescues us from the coming wrath. (1 Th 1:9-10)

For we know him who said, "It is mine to avenge; I will repay," and again, "The Lord will judge his people." It is a dreadful thing to fall into the hands of the living God. (Heb 10:30-31)

3. The church is the pillar and support or foundation of the truth. The church *supports* the truth just as the pillars and foundation support a building. The church props and supports the truth, holds together and binds the truth. William Barclay points out that Paul could also be thinking of the meaning of *display* (*The Letters to Timothy, Titus, and Philemon*, p.102). Pillars, whether short and small or towering and large, always appear to have an aire of stateliness that attracts attention. Therefore, the church is the pillar, the display, the demonstration of the truth that attracts people to Jesus Christ.

The church holds the truth up before a world that misbehaves and dies, yet does not have to die. The church—the family and company of God—is God's instrument upon earth to proclaim the truth to the world. What truth? The glorious truth of the Incarnation—that God has loved the world and has demonstrated His love by sending His Son to save the world (cp. v.16). This is the glorious truth that the church supports and holds ever so highly before the world.

Thought 1. A piercing question is this: How many within the church are really supporting the truth before the world? How many are really holding up the truth by behaving and conducting themselves as they should? How many are holding up the truth by proclaiming it as they should?

"Therefore everyone who hears these words of mine and puts them into practice is like a wise man who built his house on the rock. The rain came down, the streams rose, and the winds blew and beat against that house; yet it did not fall, because it had its foundation on the rock. But everyone who hears these words of mine and does not put them into practice is like a foolish man who built his house on sand. The rain came down, the streams rose, and the winds blew and beat against that house, and it fell with a great crash." (Mat 7:24-27)

For no one can lay any foundation other than the one already laid, which is Jesus Christ. (1 Cor 3:11)

Which he exerted in Christ when he raised him from the dead and seated him at his right hand in the heavenly realms, far above all rule and authority, power and dominion, and every title that can be given, not only in the present age but also in the one to come. And God placed all things under his feet and appointed him to be head over everything for the church, (Eph 1:20-22)

In this way they will lay up treasure for themselves as a firm foundation for the coming age, so that they may take hold of the life that is truly life. (1 Tim 6:19)

Nevertheless, God's solid foundation stands firm, sealed with this inscription:

"The Lord knows those who are his," and, "Everyone who confesses the name of the Lord must turn away from wickedness." (2 Tim 2:19)

As you come to him, [Christ] the living Stone—rejected by men but chosen by God and precious to him—you also, like living stones, are being built into a spiritual house to be a holy priesthood, offering spiritual sacrifices acceptable to God through Jesus Christ. (1 Pet 2:4-5)

3 (3:16) **Church—Incarnation**: this is one of the great verses of Scripture; it is the glorious truth of the church—the truth that all true believers confess before the world. It is the truth which the church and its believers must never deny, neglect, ignore, or question. It is the only truth that offers hope and salvation for man beyond the grave. Deny and destroy this truth and all are lost and doomed to death forever. Why? Because all man-made and self-proclaimed truths end in the grave. But this truth will never die, for it is the truth of God's unbelievable love, the great "mystery of godliness." What is the mystery of godliness? This is the only reference to it in the Bible, and note the truth of it: it is "beyond all question," that is, indisputable, undeniable, beyond any question. It is the truth that all genuine believers confess. And what is being confessed really happened. God has done six wonderful things for man. This is the mystery of godliness, the mystery that has now been revealed to man.

1. "God appeared in a body." God actually became a man in the person of Jesus Christ. He actually partook of flesh and blood.

   a. Jesus Christ identified with man perfectly. By becoming Man, He experienced all the trials and sufferings of men; therefore, He is able to help and deliver men through all the trials of life.

   For surely it is not angels he helps, but Abraham's descendants. For this reason he had to be made like his brothers in every way, in order that he might become a merciful and faithful high priest in service to God, and that he might make atonement for the sins of the people. Because he himself suffered when he was tempted, he is able to help those who are being tempted. (Heb 2:16-18)

   For we do not have a high priest who is unable to sympathize with our weaknesses, but we have one who has been tempted in every way, just as we are—yet was without sin. Let us then approach the throne of grace with confidence, so that we may receive mercy and find grace to help us in our time of need. (Heb 4:15-16)

   b. Jesus Christ became man in order to take away the sins of men.

   He himself bore our sins in his body on the tree, so that we might die to sins and live for righteousness; by his wounds you have been healed. (1 Pet 2:24)

   But you know that he appeared so that he might take away our sins. And in him is no sin. (1 John 3:5)

   He who does what is sinful is of the devil, because the devil has been sinning from the beginning. The reason the Son of God appeared was to destroy the devil's work. (1 John 3:8)

   c. Jesus Christ became Man in order to destroy him who had the power of death, that is, Satan.

   Since the children have flesh and blood, he too shared in their humanity so that by his death he might destroy him who holds the power of death—that is, the devil—and free those who all their lives were held in slavery by their fear of death. (Heb 2:14-15)

Thought 1. The Incarnation is indisputable, undeniable, irrefutable. It is a fact: God did come to earth in the person of Jesus Christ.

The Word became flesh and made his dwelling among us. We have seen his glory, the glory of the One and Only, who came from the Father, full of grace and truth. (John 1:14)

That God was reconciling the world to himself in Christ, not counting men's sins against them. And he has committed to us the message of reconciliation. (2 Cor 5:19)

Therefore, when Christ came into the world, he said: "Sacrifice and offering you did not desire, but a body you prepared for me; (Heb 10:5)

That which was from the beginning, which we have heard, which we have seen with our eyes, which we have looked at and our hands have touched—this we proclaim concerning the Word of life. The life appeared; we have seen it and testify to it, and we proclaim to you the eternal life, which was with the Father and has appeared to us. (1 John 1:1-2)

2. Christ was vindicated by the Spirit. When Christ walked upon earth, He proclaimed this truth: He was the Son of God who had come to earth to save all who would believe Him. But the vast majority of people did not believe Him. They denied, ignored, neglected, rebuked, mocked, questioned, argued against, and cursed Him. Many tried to use Him in order to get what they wanted, and others plotted to murder Him. But He was *truly the Son of God*; therefore, the Spirit of God vindicated Him; the Spirit of God proved His claims. How? The Spirit of God did three things.

   a. The Spirit of God enabled Christ to live a sinless and perfect life. The one thing that man knows is this: no man can live a sinless life. If a perfect life could ever be lived, it would have to be lived by God Himself as a Man, and this is exactly the point. Christ proved that He was the Son of God by living a sinless and perfect life.

   Can any of you prove me guilty of sin? If I am telling the truth, why don't you believe me? (John 8:46)

   God made him who had no sin to be sin for us, so that in him we might become the righteousness of God. (2 Cor 5:21)

1 TIMOTHY 3:14-16

But about the Son he says, "Your throne, O God, will last for ever and ever, and righteousness will be the scepter of your kingdom. You have loved righteousness and hated wickedness; therefore God, your God, has set you above your companions by anointing you with the oil of joy." (Heb 1:8-9)

For we do not have a high priest who is unable to sympathize with our weaknesses, but we have one who has been tempted in every way, just as we are—yet was without sin. (Heb 4:15)

Such a high priest meets our need—one who is holy, blameless, pure, set apart from sinners, exalted above the heavens. (Heb 7:26)

How much more, then, will the blood of Christ, who through the eternal Spirit offered himself unblemished to God, cleanse our consciences from acts that lead to death, so that we may serve the living God! (Heb 9:14)

But with the precious blood of Christ, a lamb without blemish or defect. (1 Pet 1:19)

"He committed no sin, and no deceit was found in his mouth." (1 Pet 2:22)

But you know that he appeared so that he might take away our sins. And in him is no sin. (1 John 3:5)

b. The Spirit of God vindicated Christ by giving Him the power to do the mighty works of God. Christ worked so many miraculous works of healing and ministry that John could only say that the world itself could not contain the books if they had all been recorded (Jn.21:25). The point is this: no man could do the works that Christ did. Only God Himself could perform the kind of miracles Christ did. Therefore, the very works of Christ were the proof that He is who He claimed: the Son of God Himself.

This, the first of his miraculous signs, Jesus performed at Cana in Galilee. He thus revealed his glory, and his disciples put their faith in him. (John 2:11)

He came to Jesus at night and said, "Rabbi, we know you are a teacher who has come from God. For no one could perform the miraculous signs you are doing if God were not with him." (John 3:2)

Jesus answered, "I did tell you, but you do not believe. The miracles I do in my Father's name speak for me, (John 10:25)

Do not believe me unless I do what my Father does. But if I do it, even though you do not believe me, believe the miracles, that you may know and understand that the Father is in me, and I in the Father." (John 10:37-38)

Believe me when I say that I am in the Father and the Father is in me; or at least believe on the evidence of the miracles themselves. (John 14:11)

If I had not done among them what no one else did, they would not be guilty of sin. But now they have seen these miracles, and yet they have hated both me and my Father. (John 15:24)

c. The Spirit of God vindicated Christ by raising Him from the dead. Men killed Him; they crucified Him upon the cross. But He was truly the Son of God; therefore the Spirit of God proved His claim by raising Him up from the dead.

And who through the Spirit of holiness was declared with power to be the Son of God by his resurrection from the dead: Jesus Christ our Lord. (Rom 1:4)

[The power of God] which he exerted in Christ when he raised him from the dead and seated him at his right hand in the heavenly realms, (Eph 1:20)

Praise be to the God and Father of our Lord Jesus Christ! In his great mercy he has given us new birth into a living hope through the resurrection of Jesus Christ from the dead, and into an inheritance that can never perish, spoil or fade—kept in heaven for you, (1 Pet 1:3-4)

For Christ died for sins once for all, the righteous for the unrighteous, to bring you to God. He was put to death in the body but made alive by the Spirit, (1 Pet 3:18)

3. Christ was seen by angels. The angels are *heavenly beings* who have always seen and beheld Christ. In fact, they are the very ministers of Christ who have been created to carry out His will in the other world, the spiritual world or spiritual dimension of being. Therefore, it is only natural that the angels were involved when Christ came to earth to save man. They were involved...

- in the preparation for His birth (Lk.1:26f).
- in His birth (Lk.2:8, 13).
- in His temptation (Mk.1:13).
- in His trials (Lk.22:43).
- in His resurrection (Mt.28:2f).
- in His ascension (Acts 1:10-11).

Angels are the ministering spirits of Christ who saw all that happened to Him. They saw Christ secure our salvation. The point is this: angels are living beings who have lived with Christ in a real place throughout all of eternity. Therefore, the promise of Christ—that we too shall live with Him eternally—is true. Heaven and angels are real. There is a real world, a spiritual world and dimension of being where God and Christ actually exist.

4. Christ was preached among the nations of the world. This is a glorious part of the "mystery of godliness": that Jesus Christ came to save all people, even the heathen—those who knew absolutely nothing about God and are so immoral, depraved, and corrupted, and so hopeless and helpless in life. Christ is not the exclusive Savior of the Jews nor of any other nation including America. He is the Savior of all people and all nations, both Jew and Gentile alike.

And this gospel of the kingdom will be preached in the whole world as a testimony to all nations, and then the end will come. (Mat 24:14)

Therefore go and make disciples of all nations, baptizing them in the name of the Father and of the Son and of the Holy Spirit, and teaching them to obey everything I have commanded you. And surely I am with you always, to the very end of the age." (Mat 28:19-20)

And the gospel must first be preached to all nations. (Mark 13:10)

He said to them, "Go into all the world and preach the good news to all creation. (Mark 16:15)

And repentance and forgiveness of sins will be preached in his name to all nations, beginning at Jerusalem. (Luke 24:47)

But you will receive power when the Holy Spirit comes on you; and you will be my witnesses in Jerusalem, and in all Judea and Samaria, and to the ends of the earth." (Acts 1:8)

Then I saw another angel flying in midair, and he had the eternal gospel to proclaim to those who live on the earth—to every nation, tribe, language and people. (Rev 14:6)

5. Christ was *believed on* in the world. This was the very purpose for the *Incarnation,* the very reason why Jesus Christ had come to earth: that some might believe on Him and be saved to live with God eternally. Note this: when Christ left earth and ascended into heaven, there were only one hundred and twenty who were following Him and who began to share the gospel. But within fifty years every nation of the world had been touched for Christ. Thousands upon thousands had accepted Christ—so many in fact that Paul declared that the gospel had been carried to the ends of the world.

But now revealed and made known through the prophetic writings by the command of the eternal God, so that all nations might believe and obey him—(Rom 16:26)

[The gospel] that has come to you. All over the world this gospel is bearing fruit and growing, just as it has been doing among you since the day you heard it and understood God's grace in all its truth. (Col 1:6)

If you continue in your faith, established and firm, not moved from the hope held out in the gospel. This is the gospel that you heard and that has been proclaimed to every creature under heaven, and of which I, Paul, have become a servant. (Col 1:23)

The point is this: what is the difference between the witness of the early believers and our witness today? Why were they able to reach so many and we seemingly reach so few? The answer is the truth of this point: belief. They truly believed on Christ; they rested their past, present, and future upon Him. They cast their souls and lives upon Him. They totally committed their lives to Him. They gave Him all they were and had. This kind of belief is missing today. The belief that so many have is a belief *about Christ*: that He is the Savior of the world. However, a belief about Christ is not *believing on Christ*. It is not turning one's life over to Him; not casting one's being—all that one is and has—upon Him.

The glorious "mystery of godliness" is that a person can be saved by believing on Christ—really believing on Him.

"For God so loved the world that he gave his one and only Son, that whoever believes in him shall not perish but have eternal life. (John 3:16)

"I tell you the truth, whoever hears my word and believes him who sent me has eternal life and will not be condemned; he has crossed over from death to life. (John 5:24)

Jesus said to her, "I am the resurrection and the life. He who believes in me will live, even though he dies; (John 11:25)

But these are written that you may believe that Jesus is the Christ, the Son of God, and that by believing you may have life in his name. (John 20:31)

That if you confess with your mouth, "Jesus is Lord," and believe in your heart that God raised him from the dead, you will be saved. For it is with your heart that you believe and are justified, and it is with your mouth that you confess and are saved. (Rom 10:9-10)

6. Christ was taken up in glory. This is a reference to the ascension and exaltation of Christ. He has been exalted as the Supreme Majesty of the universe, as Lord of lords, and King of kings. He is the God of the universe who rules and reigns over the universe in glory and majesty, dominion and power. Jesus Christ has completed the great work of salvation. He has been taken back into heaven, back to the very place from which He had come. He sits at the right hand of the Father, and He shall sit upon the throne of heaven until He chooses to return to earth and bring human history to its climactic consummation,

After the Lord Jesus had spoken to them, he was taken up into heaven and he sat at the right hand of God. (Mark 16:19)

But from now on, the Son of Man will be seated at the right hand of the mighty God." (Luke 22:69)

Which he exerted in Christ when he raised him from the dead and seated him at his right hand in the heavenly realms, (Eph 1:20)

But made himself nothing, taking the very nature of a servant, being made in human likeness. And being found in appearance as a man, he humbled himself and became obedient to death— even death on a cross! Therefore God exalted him to the highest place and gave him the name that is above every name, that at the name of Jesus every knee should bow, in heaven and on earth and under the earth, (Phil 2:7-10)

In a loud voice they sang: "Worthy is the Lamb, who was slain, to receive power and wealth and wisdom and strength and honor and glory and praise!" (Rev 5:12)

This is the great mystery and godliness now revealed to men.

⇒ God appeared in a body (in the person of Jesus Christ.).

⇒ Christ was justified or vindicated in the Spirit.

⇒ Christ was seen by angels, actually seen by heavenly beings.

⇒ Christ was preached to the Gentiles—to all the nations of the world.

⇒ Christ was believed on in the world.

⇒ Christ was taken up and exalted in heaven.

1 TIMOTHY 4:1-5

	CHAPTER 4	seared as with a hot iron. 3 They forbid people to marry and order them to abstain from certain foods, which God created to be received with thanksgiving by those who believe and who know the truth. 4 For everything God created is good, and nothing is to be rejected if it is received with thanksgiving, 5 Because it is consecrated by the word of God and prayer.	**3 Their doctrine** a. The error: Forbids marriage & foods b. The truth 1) God has created all things to be received with thanksgiving 2) All food created by God is good 3) All food is consecrated by the Word of God & by prayer
	B. The Warning About False Teachers & Their Apostasy, 4:1-5		
1 They will arise in the latter days of history **2 Their apostasy** a. Will abandon the faith b. Will follow deceiving spirits c. Will be hypocritical liars d. Will have seared consciences	The Spirit clearly says that in later times some will abandon the faith and follow deceiving spirits and things taught by demons. 2 Such teachings come through hypocritical liars, whose consciences have been		

DIVISION III

BEHAVIOR AND RELATIONSHIPS IN THE CHURCH, 3:14-6:21

B. The Warning About False Teachers and Their Apostasy, 4:1-5

(4:1-5) **Introduction**: this is a passage that strikes a serious warning to believers—a passage that must be taken ever so seriously by minister and laymen alike. It is the warning about false teachers and their apostasy.
1. False teachers will arise in latter times (v.1).
2. Their apostasy (v.1-2).
3. Their doctrine (v.3-5).

1 (4:1) **Apostasy—False Teachers**: the false teachers will arise in the latter days of history. The phrase "later times" means a little later on, not far out in the future. That is, false teachers were to arise within the church almost immediately and continue on through our day and on to the end of time. The point is well made: the church and the genuine believer have to be constantly on guard against false teaching. The terrible danger of false teaching always confronts the church and believer. And note: this is a revelation of the Spirit of God Himself. It is not the idea of some preacher seeking recognition because of his novel idea. It is the warning of God's Spirit. The Spirit has spoken clearly (rhetos), that is, in specific terms, in plain words, distinctly, so that there can be no question about what is being said. False teachers will arise in the later times.

2 (4:1-2) **False teachers—Apostasy**: the apostasy of the false teachers is serious, so serious that it should make us search our hearts. False teachers commit four tragic errors.
1. False teachers "abandon the faith." Note: they are within the church, within the field of religion. This passage is not dealing with the philosophies and false teachings taught by the unbelievers out in the world. It is talking about false teachers within the church itself. The Spirit of God is warning us: some preachers and some teachers will turn away from the faith and become false teachers. They will turn away from the Lord Jesus Christ, away from the death and resurrection of the Lord Jesus.

> He [Christ] was delivered over to death for our sins and was raised to life for our justification. (Rom 4:25)
> That if you confess with your mouth, "Jesus is Lord," and believe in your heart that God raised him from the dead, you will be saved. For it is with your heart that you believe and are justified, and it is with your mouth that you confess and are saved. (Rom 10:9-10)
> For what I received I passed on to you as of first importance : that Christ died for our sins according to the Scriptures, that he was buried, that he was raised on the third day according to the Scriptures, (1 Cor 15:3-4)
> He himself bore our sins in his body on the tree, so that we might die to sins and live for righteousness; by his wounds you have been healed. (1 Pet 2:24)

Thought 1. There is only one true faith that can save a person. A person can have all kinds of faith and he can have faith in all kinds of people and things and religions. But only one faith can save a person: the faith in God's Son, the Lord Jesus Christ. This is the faith from which a person must never depart.

> "For God so loved the world that he gave his one and only Son, that whoever believes in him shall not perish but have eternal life. For God did not send his Son into the world to condemn the world, but to save the world through him. Whoever believes in him is not condemned, but whoever does not believe stands condemned already because he has not believed in the name of God's one and only Son. (John 3:16-18)
> For my Father's will is that everyone who looks to the Son and believes in him shall have eternal life, and I will raise him up at the last day." (John 6:40)
> Jesus answered, "I am the way and the truth and the life. No one comes to the Father except through me. (John 14:6)
> But these are written that you may believe that Jesus is the Christ, the Son of God, and that by believing you may have life in his name. (John 20:31)

2. False teachers follow deceiving spirits and things taught by demons. There are all kinds of evil spirits

throughout the world, spirits that are set on seducing and deceiving people. They are set on leading people to follow them and their ideas and teachings. They do all they can to turn people away from the doctrine and faith of Christ. And note: the method they use is not a frontal attack, not a clear or loud declaration against the truth. They mix some truth with error. Their method is to…

- seduce
- deceive
- delude
- lure
- entice
- attract
- persuade
- charm
- appear as light and truth

> For such men are false apostles, deceitful workmen, masquerading as apostles of Christ. And no wonder, for Satan himself masquerades as an angel of light. It is not surprising, then, if his servants masquerade as servants of righteousness. Their end will be what their actions deserve. (2 Cor 11:13-15)

> For the time will come when men will not put up with sound doctrine. Instead, to suit their own desires, they will gather around them a great number of teachers to say what their itching ears want to hear. They will turn their ears away from the truth and turn aside to myths. (2 Tim 4:3-4)

> For there are many rebellious people, mere talkers and deceivers, especially those of the circumcision group. They must be silenced, because they are ruining whole households by teaching things they ought not to teach—and that for the sake of dishonest gain. (Titus 1:10-11)

3. False teachers are hypocritical liars. Very simply, they teach something different from what the Scripture says, and they know it. They know they are not teaching what Scripture says. In fact, some false teachers take pride in their stand against what they call "a literal interpretation" of Scripture. Some even mock and poke fun at those who believe and hold to the truth of Scripture. But note what is so often overlooked:

⇒ "Teaching lies" means speaking and teaching what is contrary to Scripture. This is exactly what Scripture is declaring. In the eyes of Scripture, a lie is a teaching that is contrary to the teaching of Scripture.

⇒ "Hypocritical" means the teacher knows that he is teaching contrary to Scripture. He claims to be a minister or teacher of God, Christ, and the Word (Scripture), and yet he teaches something contrary to what Scripture says. A hypocrite is a person who claims to be one thing but he is something else.

The point is this: the false teacher is a person who is a hypocritical liar. He denies, refutes, or ignores what Scripture says and he knows it; yet he claims to be a minister or teacher of Christ and the gospel. This is the person who is an instrument or tool of some seducing and deceptive spirit, who teaches the things taught by demons.

> You hypocrites! Isaiah was right when he prophesied about you: "'These people honor me with their lips, but their hearts are far from me. They worship me in vain; their teachings are but rules taught by men.'" (Mat 15:7-9)

> Then they understood that he was not telling them to guard against the yeast used in bread, but against the teaching of the Pharisees and Sadducees. (Mat 16:12)

> In the same way, on the outside you appear to people as righteous but on the inside you are full of hypocrisy and wickedness. (Mat 23:28)

> Hypocrites! You know how to interpret the appearance of the earth and the sky. How is it that you don't know how to interpret this present time? "Why don't you judge for yourselves what is right [Christ and His claims or words]? (Luke 12:56-57)

> I urge you, brothers, to watch out for those who cause divisions and put obstacles in your way that are contrary to the teaching you have learned. Keep away from them. For such people are not serving our Lord Christ, but their own appetites. By smooth talk and flattery they deceive the minds of naive people. (Rom 16:17-18)

> See to it that no one takes you captive through hollow and deceptive philosophy, which depends on human tradition and the basic principles of this world rather than on Christ. (Col 2:8)

> The Spirit clearly says that in later times some will abandon the faith and follow deceiving spirits and things taught by demons. Such teachings come through hypocritical liars, whose consciences have been seared as with a hot iron. (1 Tim 4:1-2)

> They claim to know God, but by their actions they deny him. They are detestable, disobedient and unfit for doing anything good. (Titus 1:16)

> Do not be carried away by all kinds of strange teachings. It is good for our hearts to be strengthened by grace, not by ceremonial foods, which are of no value to those who eat them. (Heb 13:9)

Thought 1. William Barclay has an excellent statement on men becoming tools of Satan and evil spirits.

> *"It was from these evil spirits and demons that this false teaching came. But though it came from the demons, it came through men….Now here is the threatening and the terrible thing. We know that God and God's Spirit are everywhere looking for men to use. God is always searching for men who will be His instruments, His weapons, His tools in the world. But here we come face to face with the terrible fact that the forces of evil are also looking for men to use. Just as God seeks men for His purposes, the forces of evil seek men for their purposes. Here is the terrible responsibility of manhood. Man can accept the service of God, or the service of the devil. Man can become an instrument of the Supreme Good or the Supreme Evil. Men are faced with the eternal choice—to whom are we to give our lives, to God or to God's*

enemy? Are we to decide to be used by God, or are we to decide to be used by the devil?" (*The Letters to Timothy, Titus, and Philemon*, p.107).

4. False teachers have consciences that are seared, that is cauterized, hardened, and insensitive. It does not bother most false teachers to teach contrary to the truth of Scripture. They can ignore and deny the Scripture and present their own ideas and it does not bother them at all. They are totally insensitive to the preachings and convictions of God's Spirit. They have no conscience and no remorse about twisting the Scriptures and the truth about Christ. They are completely past feeling any kind of movement from God's Spirit.

> Why is my language not clear to you? Because you are unable to hear what I say. (John 8:43)
>
> For this people's heart has become calloused; they hardly hear with their ears, and they have closed their eyes. Otherwise they might see with their eyes, hear with their ears, understand with their hearts and turn, and I would heal them.' (Acts 28:27) But because of your stubbornness and your unrepentant heart, you are storing up wrath against yourself for the day of God's wrath, when his righteous judgment will be revealed. (Rom 2:5)
>
> Having lost all sensitivity, they have given themselves over to sensuality so as to indulge in every kind of impurity, with a continual lust for more. (Eph 4:19)
>
> Such teachings come through hypocritical liars, whose consciences have been seared as with a hot iron. (1 Tim 4:2)
>
> Blessed is the man who always fears the LORD, but he who hardens his heart falls into trouble. (Prov 28:14)
>
> A man who remains stiff-necked after many rebukes will suddenly be destroyed—without remedy. (Prov 29:1)

3 **(4:3-5) False teachers—Apostasy**: the doctrine of the false teachers is also serious, so serious that it too should make us search our hearts.

1. The particular doctrine confronting the church at Ephesus was Gnosticism. The Gnostics felt that what really mattered in life was the spirit of man; the spirit was the only good thing in the world. Everything else in the world—all physical and material substances including the human body—was corruptible and evil. Therefore, man's task upon earth was to deny self and avoid the things of the world and to control the body as much as possible. How? By denying the body as many things as possible. Note: in the church at Ephesus, the two things being denied and forbidden were eating of meat and marriage. Some were teaching that a person could get closer to God and please Him more by being a vegetarian and by remaining single. By being free of family duties, the person could concentrate on God more.

Note one other fact about Gnosticism that is not covered in this passage but is of extreme importance. Some Gnostics took the opposite view. Since the spirit is all that matters, the body and the world do not matter. Therefore, man can do what he likes physically. He can satisfy his passions, lusts, urges, and instincts—just so he takes good care of his spirit.

Every generation has its Gnostics, people who teach the false doctrines of extreme discipline or asceticism and those who teach the false doctrines of loose living (license and indulgence).

⇒ There are those who *concentrate* upon the body and its health. They seek to overcome the evil, that is, the corruption, disease, aging, and dying of the body as much as possible. Some exercise and exercise and others become vegetarians—all struggling against the aging, weakening, and dying of the body.

⇒ There are even those today who feel they can become closer to God and more spiritual by not marrying and by eating no meat. (But remember what Scripture has just said: it is best for the minister and leaders of the church to be married. Cp. 1 Tim.3:2-13.)

⇒ There are those who live as they please—eating, drinking, partying, indulging, and living extravagantly—all doing their own thing.

The point to see is this: each gives attention to their spirit and worship only as they wish, only as much as they feel is necessary to keep their spirit in tune with God. But note: their concentration is the body and its pleasure. In one case the pleasure is the exhilaration of discipline and control; in the other case the exhilaration is the stimulating of the flesh (sinful nature) through partying and possessions.

> Anyone who breaks one of the least of these commandments and teaches others to do the same will be called least in the kingdom of heaven, but whoever practices and teaches these commands will be called great in the kingdom of heaven. (Mat 5:19)
>
> Therefore, I urge you, brothers, in view of God's mercy, to offer your bodies as living sacrifices, holy and pleasing to God—this is your spiritual act of worship. Do not conform any longer to the pattern of this world, but be transformed by the renewing of your mind. Then you will be able to test and approve what God's will is—his good, pleasing and perfect will. (Rom 12:1-2)
>
> Since you died with Christ to the basic principles of this world, why, as though you still belonged to it, do you submit to its rules: "Do not handle! Do not taste! Do not touch!"? These are all destined to perish with use, because they are based on human commands and teachings. Such regulations indeed have an appearance of wisdom, with their self-imposed worship, their false humility and their harsh treatment of the body, but they lack any value in restraining sensual indulgence. (Col 2:20-23)
>
> For there are many rebellious people, mere talkers and deceivers, especially those of the circumcision group. They must be silenced, because they are ruining whole households by teaching things they ought not to teach—and that for the sake of dishonest gain. Even one of their own prophets has said, "Cretans are always liars, evil

brutes, lazy gluttons." This testimony is true. Therefore, rebuke them sharply, so that they will be sound in the faith and will pay no attention to Jewish myths or to the commands of those who reject the truth. To the pure, all things are pure, but to those who are corrupted and do not believe, nothing is pure. In fact, both their minds and consciences are corrupted. They claim to know God, but by their actions they deny him. They are detestable, disobedient and unfit for doing anything good. (Titus 1:10-16)

2. Note how the truth destroys this life-style and teaching.
   a. God has created all things to be received with thanksgiving. And note: all things can be received even by believers, by all who believe and know the truth.
   b. All food that has been created by God is good and is not to be refused, if the believer can give thanks for it.
   c. All food is consecrated or set apart by the Word of God and prayer. If the food is approved by God's Word or can be prayed about and approved by God's Spirit, then the believer can partake of it without any qualm of conscience. Wycliffe Bible Commentary gives an excellent comment on this point:

> "The principles governing the right use...of this life are: (a) God is the Creator and his creation is good; (b) He created food for men, and those who believe and know the truth about eternal salvation will have the right attitude toward the necessities of this life, and will neither deify the created thing nor degrade and despise it, but will accept it thankfully as the Father's wise provision" (Quoted from *First and Second Timothy, Titus.* "The New Testament and Wycliffe Bible Commentary," ed. by Charles F. Pfeiffer and Everett F. Harrison. Produced for Moody Monthly by the Iversen Associates, NY, 1971, p.854).

So do not worry, saying, 'What shall we eat?' or 'What shall we drink?' or 'What shall we wear?' For the pagans run after all these things, and your heavenly Father knows that you need them. But seek first his kingdom and his righteousness, and all these things will be given to you as well. (Mat 6:31-33)

But food does not bring us near to God; we are no worse if we do not eat, and no better if we do. (1 Cor 8:8)

Eat anything sold in the meat market without raising questions of conscience, for, "The earth is the Lord's, and everything in it." If some unbeliever invites you to a meal and you want to go, eat whatever is put before you without raising questions of conscience. (1 Cor 10:25-27)

1 TIMOTHY 4:6-16

	C. The Young Minister (Charge 2): To Be a Good Minister, 4:6-16		

1 He instructs believers about false teachers, v.1-5	6 If you point these things out to the brothers, you will be a good minister of Christ Jesus, brought up in the truths of the faith and of the good teaching that you have followed.	believe.
		11 Command and teach these things.
		12 Don't let anyone look down on you because you are young, but set an example for the believers in speech, in life, in love, in faith and in purity.
			7 He commands & teaches these things
			8 He is an example to the believers
			  a. An example despite his young age
			  b. An example to all bel's.
			  c. An example in speech

2 He nourishes himself in Christian faith & doctrine			
3 He avoids frivolous speculations	7 Have nothing to do with godless myths and old wives' tales; rather, train yourself to be godly.	13 Until I come, devote yourself to the public reading of Scripture, to preaching and to teaching.	9 He devotes himself to public worship

4 He exercises himself to godliness
  a. Physical: Exercise is good
  b. Spiritual: Godliness is better
	8 For physical training is of some value, but godliness has value for all things, holding promise for both the present life and the life to come.	14 Do not neglect your gift, which was given you through a prophetic message when the body of elders laid their hands on you.	10 He does not neglect his gift
			  a. Supernaturally given
			  b. Humanly recognized & ordained

5 He is a man of reason & of purpose	9 This is a trustworthy saying that deserves full acceptance	15 Be diligent in these matters; give yourself wholly to them, so that everyone may see your progress.	11 He meditates & is diligent in giving himself wholly to the Scripture

6 He is a man who works & strives—willingly & laboriously
  a. Because God lives
  b. Because God saves
	10 (And for this we labor and strive), that we have put our hope in the living God, who is the Savior of all men, and especially of those who	16 Watch your life and doctrine closely. Persevere in them, because if you do, you will save both yourself and your hearers.	12 He guards himself & his teaching
			  a. To persevere in the faith
			  b. The purpose: To save himself & the hearers

DIVISION III

BEHAVIOR AND RELATIONSHIPS IN THE CHURCH, 3:14-6:21

C. The Young Minister (Charge 2): To Be a Good Minister, 4:6-16

(4:6-16) **Introduction**: this is one of the greatest pictures of the minister painted by Scripture. It is an excellent description of just what makes a minister a "good minister" (v.6). Note: this is the second charge given to the young minister Timothy. The minister is given the strong charge: be a *good minister*.

1. He instructs believers about false teachers (v.1-5).
2. He nourishes himself in Christian faith and doctrine (v.6).
3. He avoids frivolous speculations (v.7).
4. He exercises himself to godliness (v.8).
5. He is a man of reason and of purpose (v.9).
6. He is a man who works and strives—willingly and laboriously (v.10).
7. He commands and teaches these things (v.11).
8. He is an example to the believers (v.12).
9. He devotes himself to public worship (v.13).
10. He does not neglect his gift (v.14).
11. He meditates and is diligent in giving himself wholly to the Scripture (v.15).
12. He guards himself and his teaching (v.16).

1 (4:6) **Minister—Teaching**: the good minister and teacher instructs believers about false teachers. "These things" refers to the previous passage which warns believers to guard against false teachers (v.1-5). A good minister does all he can to lift up Jesus Christ and to warn his flock about false teachers, about those who will try to seduce and lead them astray. The Greek word "instruct" or "point these things out" (hupotithemenos) means to place under, suggest, counsel, advise. The point is this: false teaching is such a threat to the church and believers, the good minister of Jesus Christ will use every method of communication he can to instruct and protect his flock from being seduced by false teachers.

> So I will always remind you of these things, even though you know them and are firmly established in the truth you now have. I think it is right to refresh your memory as long as I live in the tent of this body, because I know that I will soon put it aside, as our Lord Jesus Christ has made clear to me. And I will make every effort to see that after my departure you will always be able to remember these things. We did not follow cleverly invented stories when we told you about the power and coming of our Lord Jesus Christ, but we were eyewitnesses of his majesty. (2 Pet 1:12-16)

> Dear friends, this is now my second letter to you. I have written both of them as reminders to stimulate you to wholesome thinking. I want you to recall the words spoken in the past by the holy prophets and the command given by our Lord and Savior through your apostles. First of all, you must understand that in the last days scoffers will come, scoffing and following their own evil desires. (2 Pet 3:1-3)

2 (4:6) **Minister**: the good minister nourishes himself on the words of *the faith*. Note that the Greek uses the definite article "*the* faith" (tes pisteos). This means the teachings of the Word of God. True doctrines are doctrines which are based upon the Scriptures. No doctrine is true (or Christian) that is not based upon the Scriptures.

Timothy had done this; he had been nourished upon the Scripture from earliest childhood (2 Tim.3:15), and he had continued to feed upon the Word of God. Paul was now encouraging him to continue the practice, for a good minister is a minister who feeds upon the Scriptures day by day.

> "Now I commit you to God and to the word of his grace, which can build you up and give you an inheritance among all those who are sanctified. (Acts 20:32)
>
> Do your best to present yourself to God as one approved, a workman who does not need to be ashamed and who correctly handles the word of truth. (2 Tim 2:15)
>
> And how from infancy you have known the holy Scriptures, which are able to make you wise for salvation through faith in Christ Jesus. All Scripture is God-breathed and is useful for teaching, rebuking, correcting and training in righteousness, (2 Tim 3:15-16)
>
> Like newborn babies, crave pure spiritual milk, so that by it you may grow up in your salvation, now that you have tasted that the Lord is good. (1 Pet 2:2-3)
>
> He humbled you, causing you to hunger and then feeding you with manna, which neither you nor your fathers had known, to teach you that man does not live on bread alone but on every word that comes from the mouth of the LORD. (Deu 8:3)
>
> I have not departed from the commands of his lips; I have treasured the words of his mouth more than my daily bread. (Job 23:12)
>
> When your words came, I ate them; they were my joy and my heart's delight, for I bear your name, O LORD God Almighty. (Jer 15:16)

3 (4:7) **Minister—False Teaching**: the good minister avoids frivolous speculations, rejects godless myths and old wives' tales. What a description of false teaching! It is nothing more than "irreverent legends—profane and impure and godless fictions, mere grandmother's tales—and silly myths" (Amplified New Testament). The *good minister* rejects all false teachings, which are nothing more than the *frivolous speculations and false notions of men*.

> In the presence of God and of Christ Jesus, who will judge the living and the dead, and in view of his appearing and his kingdom, I give you this charge: Preach the Word; be prepared in season and out of season; correct, rebuke and encourage—with great patience and careful instruction. For the time will come when men will not put up with sound doctrine. Instead, to suit their own desires, they will gather around them a great number of teachers to say what their itching ears want to hear. They will turn their ears away from the truth and turn aside to myths. (2 Tim 4:1-4)
>
> I have fought the good fight, I have finished the race, I have kept the faith. (2 Tim 4:7)
>
> This testimony is true. Therefore, rebuke them sharply, so that they will be sound in the faith and will pay no attention to Jewish myths or to the commands of those who reject the truth. To the pure, all things are pure, but to those who are corrupted and do not believe, nothing is pure. In fact, both their minds and consciences are corrupted. They claim to know God, but by their actions they deny him. They are detestable, disobedient and unfit for doing anything good. (Titus 1:13-16)
>
> We did not follow cleverly invented stories when we told you about the power and coming of our Lord Jesus Christ, but we were eyewitnesses of his majesty. For he received honor and glory from God the Father when the voice came to him from the Majestic Glory, saying, "This is my Son, whom I love; with him I am well pleased." We ourselves heard this voice that came from heaven when we were with him on the sacred mountain. And we have the word of the prophets made more certain, and you will do well to pay attention to it, as to a light shining in a dark place, until the day dawns and the morning star rises in your hearts. Above all, you must understand that no prophecy of Scripture came about by the prophet's own interpretation. For prophecy never had its origin in the will of man, but men spoke from God as they were carried along by the Holy Spirit. (2 Pet 1:16-21)

4 (4:8) *Minister*: the good minister exercises himself to godliness. The minister is compared to an athlete in these two verses. Note two things.

1. The minister is to train (gumnasia) himself in godliness as much as an Olympic athlete exercises his body. How much energy, effort, time, and dedication does an Olympic athlete put into his training? His sport is his life—unequivocally so. So it is with the minister: godliness is to be his life. All of his energy, effort, time, and dedication are to be given over to godliness. The minister is to know *no training* but the training of godliness.

> People who want to get rich fall into temptation and a trap and into many foolish and harmful desires that plunge men into ruin and destruction. For the love of money is a root of all kinds of evil. Some people, eager for money, have wandered from the faith and pierced themselves with many griefs. But you, man of God, flee from all this, and pursue righteousness, godliness, faith, love, endurance and gentleness. (1 Tim 6:9-11)
>
> It teaches us to say "No" to ungodliness and worldly passions, and to live self-controlled, upright and godly lives in this present age, while we wait for the blessed hope—the glorious appearing of our great God and Savior, Jesus Christ, (Titus 2:12-13)
>
> Since everything will be destroyed in this way, what kind of people ought you to

1 TIMOTHY 4:6-16

be? You ought to live holy and godly lives (2 Pet 3:11)

2. Physical training is of some value, but godliness has value for all things, far more profitable. The minister should exercise his body regularly; he should keep himself physically fit. But the focus of his life is to be godliness. The reason is clear: godliness bears fruit—great fruit—both in this life and in the life to come. God promises to bless the godly person now while he walks upon this earth, and eternally when he receives the life to come.

> Have nothing to do with godless myths and old wives' tales; rather, train yourself to be godly. For physical training is of some value, but godliness has value for all things, holding promise for both the present life and the life to come. (1 Tim 4:7-8)
>
> But godliness with contentment is great gain. (1 Tim 6:6)
>
> This is a trustworthy saying. And I want you to stress these things, so that those who have trusted in God may be careful to devote themselves to doing what is good. These things are excellent and profitable for everyone. (Titus 3:8)
>
> Keep his decrees and commands, which I am giving you today, so that it may go well with you and your children after you and that you may live long in the land the LORD your God gives you for all time. (Deu 4:40)
>
> Carefully follow the terms of this covenant, so that you may prosper in everything you do. (Deu 29:9)
>
> Blessed is the man who does not walk in the counsel of the wicked or stand in the way of sinners or sit in the seat of mockers. But his delight is in the law of the LORD, and on his law he meditates day and night. He is like a tree planted by streams of water, which yields its fruit in season and whose leaf does not wither. Whatever he does prospers. (Psa 1:1-3)
>
> Tell the righteous it will be well with them, for they will enjoy the fruit of their deeds. (Isa 3:10)

5 (4:9) **Minister**: the good minister is a man of reason and of purpose. All that is being said—all of the instructions to ministers—is trustworthy, and all deserves his complete acceptance.

The *good minister* knows this:
⇒ the instructions to him are trustworthy.
⇒ the instructions to him deserve his complete acceptance.

Therefore, he commits his life to do exactly what Scripture charges him to do. The good minister is a man of reason and of purpose, a man who understands and knows and commits his life to live as God says. It is the very fact that distinguishes the minister as *good*.

> Here is a trustworthy saying that deserves full acceptance: Christ Jesus came into the world to save sinners—of whom I am the worst. (1 Tim 1:15)
>
> This is a trustworthy saying that deserves full acceptance (and for this we labor and strive), that we have put our hope in the living God, who is the Savior of all men, and especially of those who believe. (1 Tim 4:9-10)
>
> Here is a trustworthy saying: If we died with him, we will also live with him; if we endure, we will also reign with him. If we disown him, he will also disown us; if we are faithless, he will remain faithful, for he cannot disown himself. (2 Tim 2:11-13)
>
> But when the kindness and love of God our Savior appeared, he saved us, not because of righteous things we had done, but because of his mercy. He saved us through the washing of rebirth and renewal by the Holy Spirit, whom he poured out on us generously through Jesus Christ our Savior, so that, having been justified by his grace, we might become heirs having the hope of eternal life. This is a trustworthy saying. And I want you to stress these things, so that those who have trusted in God may be careful to devote themselves to doing what is good. These things are excellent and profitable for everyone. But avoid foolish controversies and genealogies and arguments and quarrels about the law, because these are unprofitable and useless. (Titus 3:4-9)

6 (4:10) **Minister**: the good minister labors *and strives*. The word "labor" (kopiao) means arduous work, strenuous work. The good minister labors and labors, works and works to the point of fatigue and exhaustion; to the point that he can go no further. He exerts every ounce of energy and effort in his body for the sake of God and Christ. And note: he is even willing to strive for Christ. He continues to minister even when men ridicule, revile, mock, curse, and persecute him. Why?

⇒ Because God is the living God. The minister's work and message are based upon the truth; what he is doing is truth. It is all for the living God.
⇒ Because Jesus Christ is the Savior of all men. All men can be saved, actually delivered from the grip of sin, death, and condemnation.

Therefore the good minister must labor, no matter how difficult the struggle. He must share the glorious news: man can now be reconciled to God and live forever.

> Not so with you. Instead, whoever wants to become great among you must be your servant, and whoever wants to be first must be slave of all. (Mark 10:43-44)
>
> "My food," said Jesus, "is to do the will of him who sent me and to finish his work. (John 4:34)
>
> As long as it is day, we must do the work of him who sent me. Night is coming, when no one can work. (John 9:4)
>
> They arranged to meet Paul on a certain day, and came in even larger numbers to the place where he was staying. From morning till evening he explained and declared to them the kingdom of God and tried to convince them about Jesus from the Law of Moses and from the Prophets. (Acts 28:23)
>
> Never be lacking in zeal, but keep your spiritual fervor, serving the Lord. (Rom 12:11)

Therefore, my dear brothers, stand firm. Let nothing move you. Always give yourselves fully to the work of the Lord, because you know that your labor in the Lord is not in vain. (1 Cor 15:58)

Let us not become weary in doing good, for at the proper time we will reap a harvest if we do not give up. Therefore, as we have opportunity, let us do good to all people, especially to those who belong to the family of believers. (Gal 6:9-10)

For this reason I remind you to fan into flame the gift of God, which is in you through the laying on of my hands. (2 Tim 1:6)

But you, keep your head in all situations, endure hardship, do the work of an evangelist, discharge all the duties of your ministry. (2 Tim 4:5)

We want each of you to show this same diligence to the very end, in order to make your hope sure. We do not want you to become lazy, but to imitate those who through faith and patience inherit what has been promised. (Heb 6:11-12)

Therefore, since we are surrounded by such a great cloud of witnesses, let us throw off everything that hinders and the sin that so easily entangles, and let us run with perseverance the race marked out for us. (Heb 12:1)

Therefore, dear friends, since you already know this, be on your guard so that you may not be carried away by the error of lawless men and fall from your secure position. (2 Pet 3:17)

Whatever your hand finds to do, do it with all your might, for in the grave, where you are going, there is neither working nor planning nor knowledge nor wisdom. (Eccl 9:10)

7 (4:11) **Minister**: the *good minister* commands and teaches these things. He preaches and teaches with authority. This is the very reason God has called the minister: to command and teach the Word of God with the very authority of God. Therefore, the *good* minister is a minister who boldly declares the Word of God and the commandments of God. He does not allow the fear of men nor the danger of hardship stop him. He has been commissioned by the Lord and he stands in the strength of the Lord. Therefore, he knows that the Lord will deliver him through all the dangers of life if he will only be faithful, if he will courageously declare the Word and the commandments of God.

Therefore go and make disciples of all nations, baptizing them in the name of the Father and of the Son and of the Holy Spirit, and teaching them to obey everything I have commanded you. And surely I am with you always, to the very end of the age." (Mat 28:19-20)

He said to them, "Go into all the world and preach the good news to all creation. (Mark 16:15)

Preach the Word; be prepared in season and out of season; correct, rebuke and encourage—with great patience and careful instruction. (2 Tim 4:2)

8 (4:12) **Minister**: the *good minister* is an example to the believers. Timothy was a young man; therefore, there was the possibility that some in the church would have difficulty in accepting his ministry. How could he overcome the opposition to his being so young? There was only one way: he had to prove that he was mature well beyond his years. He had to live a mature life, a life that would be an example to the believers.

1. He was to be an example in speech: in what he said and in the way he said it. He had to control his conversation and tongue at all times, no matter the opposition.

But I tell you that men will have to give account on the day of judgment for every careless word they have spoken. For by your words you will be acquitted, and by your words you will be condemned." (Mat 12:36-37)

Let your conversation be always full of grace, seasoned with salt, so that you may know how to answer everyone. (Col 4:6)

What you heard from me, keep as the pattern of sound teaching, with faith and love in Christ Jesus. (2 Tim 1:13)

And soundness of speech that cannot be condemned, so that those who oppose you may be ashamed because they have nothing bad to say about us. (Titus 2:8)

Their voice goes out into all the earth, their words to the ends of the world. In the heavens he has pitched a tent for the sun, (Psa 19:4)

Pleasant words are a honeycomb, sweet to the soul and healing to the bones. (Prov 16:24)

A man of knowledge uses words with restraint, and a man of understanding is even-tempered. (Prov 17:27)

Words from a wise man's mouth are gracious, but a fool is consumed by his own lips. (Eccl 10:12)

2. He was to be an example in behavior. His conduct was to be disciplined and controlled. He was to demonstrate that he was a true follower and leader of the Lord, that he was living for the Lord in all godliness and righteousness.

So that you may be able to discern what is best and may be pure and blameless until the day of Christ, (Phil 1:10)

Whatever happens, conduct yourselves [behavior] in a manner worthy of the gospel of Christ. Then, whether I come and see you or only hear about you in my absence, I will know that you stand firm in one spirit, contending as one man for the faith of the gospel (Phil 1:27)

Don't let anyone look down on you because you are young, but set an example for the believers in speech, in life, in love, in faith and in purity. (1 Tim 4:12)

Who is wise and understanding among you? Let him show it by his good life, by

1 TIMOTHY 4:6-16

deeds done in the humility that comes from wisdom. (James 3:13)

> Live such good lives among the pagans that, though they accuse you of doing wrong, they may see your good deeds and glorify God on the day he visits us. (1 Pet 2:12)

3. He was to be an example in love (see Deeper Study # 1, *Love*—1 Th.3:12 for discussion).

> Those who live according to the sinful nature have their minds set on what that nature desires; but those who live in accordance with the Spirit have their minds set on what the Spirit desires. (Rom 8:5)
>
> Because those who are led by the Spirit of God are sons of God. (Rom 8:14)

4. He was to be an example in faith, that is, in faithfulness. He was to be loyal to the Lord Jesus and the church regardless of the demands, hardships, temptations, trials, or opposition. Imagine! No matter what the circumstance, the *good* minister is faithful and loyal.

> Then he said to them all: "If anyone would come after me, he must deny himself and take up his cross daily and follow me. (Luke 9:23)
>
> "Whoever can be trusted with very little can also be trusted with much, and whoever is dishonest with very little will also be dishonest with much. (Luke 16:10)
>
> Therefore, I urge you, brothers, in view of God's mercy, to offer your bodies as living sacrifices, holy and pleasing to God—this is your spiritual act of worship. (Rom 12:1)
>
> Never be lacking in zeal, but keep your spiritual fervor, serving the Lord. (Rom 12:11)
>
> Therefore, my dear brothers, stand firm. Let nothing move you. Always give yourselves fully to the work of the Lord, because you know that your labor in the Lord is not in vain. (1 Cor 15:58)
>
> Serve wholeheartedly, as if you were serving the Lord, not men, (Eph 6:7)
>
> We want each of you to show this same diligence to the very end, in order to make your hope sure. We do not want you to become lazy, but to imitate those who through faith and patience inherit what has been promised. (Heb 6:11-12)
>
> Be shepherds of God's flock that is under your care, serving as overseers—not because you must, but because you are willing, as God wants you to be; not greedy for money, but eager to serve; not lording it over those entrusted to you, but being examples to the flock. (1 Pet 5:2-3)
>
> Therefore, my brothers, be all the more eager to make your calling and election sure. For if you do these things, you will never fall, (2 Pet 1:10)
>
> So then, dear friends, since you are looking forward to this, make every effort to be found spotless, blameless and at peace with him. (2 Pet 3:14)

5. He was to be an example in purity. He was to live a moral and clean, just and honest life. He was to be free—completely free—of coveting, lusting, worldliness, self-seeking, immorality, and all other known sins. He was to live a life of purity that far exceeded the standards of the world. His heart and life were to be pure—perfectly pure.

> Blessed are the pure in heart, for they will see God. (Mat 5:8)
>
> The goal of this command is love, which comes from a pure heart and a good conscience and a sincere faith. (1 Tim 1:5)
>
> Do not be hasty in the laying on of hands, and do not share in the sins of others. Keep yourself pure. (1 Tim 5:22)
>
> "He committed no sin, and no deceit was found in his mouth." (1 Pet 2:22)
>
> So then, dear friends, since you are looking forward to this, make every effort to be found spotless, blameless and at peace with him. (2 Pet 3:14)
>
> Then you will lift up your face without shame; you will stand firm and without fear. (Job 11:15)
>
> Who may ascend the hill of the LORD? Who may stand in his holy place? He who has clean hands and a pure heart, who does not lift up his soul to an idol or swear by what is false. (Psa 24:3-4)

9 (4:13) **Minister—Public Worship**: the good minister devotes himself to public worship. There are three things in particular to which he publicly devotes himself: the reading, exhortation, and teaching of Scripture and its doctrine. Note what the major task of the minister is as he stands in the pulpit...

- He is to read the Scripture.
- He is to preach and teach the doctrines of Scripture.

> Until I come, devote yourself to the public reading of Scripture, to preaching and to teaching. (1 Tim 4:13)
>
> Preach the Word; be prepared in season and out of season; correct, rebuke and encourage—with great patience and careful instruction. (2 Tim 4:2)
>
> He must hold firmly to the trustworthy message as it has been taught, so that he can encourage others by sound doctrine and refute those who oppose it. (Titus 1:9)
>
> These, then, are the things you should teach. Encourage and rebuke with all authority. Do not let anyone despise you. (Titus 2:15)
>
> But encourage one another daily, as long as it is called Today, so that none of you may be hardened by sin's deceitfulness. (Heb 3:13)
>
> Let us not give up meeting together, as some are in the habit of doing, but let us encourage one another—and all the more as you see the Day approaching. (Heb 10:25)

Thought 1. *The New Testament and Wycliffe Bible Commentary* gives an excellent explanation of exhortation [preaching and teaching]: "Comfort, encouragement, admonition, exhortation, the whole area of ministry which would today be described as counseling, but here the context favors the ministry of preaching, expounding the Scriptures." (p.856.)

10 (4:14) **Minister**: the good minister does not neglect his gift. This refers to the spiritual gift, the special anointing given him by the Holy Spirit to be a minister. Note that the gift had been received through both prophecy and the laying on of hands by other elders or ministers of the church.

Neglect is dangerous, for it means that a minister fails to do his duty. It means that he is unfaithful and stands before God as an unfaithful minister.

> It was he who gave some to be apostles, some to be prophets, some to be evangelists, and some to be pastors and teachers, to prepare God's people for works of service, so that the body of Christ may be built up (Eph 4:11-12)
>
> Do not neglect your gift, which was given you through a prophetic message when the body of elders laid their hands on you. (1 Tim 4:14)
>
> For this reason I remind you to fan into flame the gift of God, which is in you through the laying on of my hands. (2 Tim 1:6)

11 (4:15) **Minister**: the good minister meditates and is diligent in giving himself wholly to these instructions. The good minister meditates upon the Word of God. He lives, eats, and drinks the Scripture and its instructions. And he meditates upon the application of the Scripture to his people. He holds the Bible in one hand and the daily newspaper in the other so as to apply the Scripture to the needs of the day. William Barclay has an excellent statement:

> "The great danger of the Christian leader is intellectual sloth and the shut mind. The danger is that he forgets to study and allows his thoughts to run in well-worn grooves. The danger is that he never gets outside the orbit of a limited number of favorite ideas. The danger is that new truths, new methods, the attempt to restate the faith in contemporary terms comes merely to irritate and to annoy him. The Christian leader must be a Christian thinker or he fails in his task; and to be a Christian thinker is to be an adventurous thinker so long as life lasts" (*The Letters to Timothy, Titus, and Philemon*, p.117-118).

> We demolish arguments and every pretension that sets itself up against the knowledge of God, and we take captive every thought to make it obedient to Christ. (2 Cor 10:5)
>
> Finally, brothers, whatever is true, whatever is noble, whatever is right, whatever is pure, whatever is lovely, whatever is admirable—if anything is excellent or praiseworthy—think about such things. (Phil 4:8)
>
> Be diligent in these matters; give yourself wholly to them, so that everyone may see your progress. (1 Tim 4:15)
>
> He is a double-minded man, unstable in all he does. (James 1:8)

> In your anger do not sin; when you are on your beds, search your hearts and be silent. Selah (Psa 4:4)
>
> May the words of my mouth and the meditation of my heart be pleasing in your sight, O LORD, my Rock and my Redeemer. (Psa 19:14)
>
> You will keep in perfect peace him whose mind is steadfast, because he trusts in you. (Isa 26:3)

12 (4:16) **Minister**: the good minister guards himself and his teaching. The word "watch" (epeche) means to keep a strict eye upon or to keep on paying attention to oneself and to one's teaching.

⇒ He guards his body, keeps it both morally and physically fit. He flees the temptations that assault and seduce him, and he controls his thoughts and keeps them pure from the lusts of the world and flesh (sinful nature). He neither eats too much nor succumbs to immoral thoughts or acts. He neither gives in to greed nor seeks the possessions or wealth of the world.

⇒ He guards his spirit and keeps it spiritually fit. He worships God every day and lives in God's Word and prayer all day long, and he shares the glorious gospel of Christ, witnessing to and exhorting people as he walks throughout the day.

⇒ He guards his study and teaching, avoiding the profane doctrines, teachings, notions, philosophies, ideas, and fables of men.

Note what he does. He perseveres in the instructions of the Word of God. The word "perseveres" (epimene) means to "stay by them," "stick to them," "see them through" (A.T. Robertson. *Word Pictures in the New Testament*, Vol.4, p.582). Why? Because by persevering in them, he saves both himself and those who hear him.

> All men will hate you because of me, but he who stands firm to the end will be saved. (Mat 10:22)
>
> No, I beat my body and make it my slave so that after I have preached to others, I myself will not be disqualified for the prize. (1 Cor 9:27)
>
> Do not be hasty in the laying on of hands, and do not share in the sins of others. Keep yourself pure. (1 Tim 5:22)
>
> Religion that God our Father accepts as pure and faultless is this: to look after orphans and widows in their distress and to keep oneself from being polluted by the world. (James 1:27)
>
> Therefore, prepare your minds for action; be self-controlled; set your hope fully on the grace to be given you when Jesus Christ is revealed. (1 Pet 1:13)
>
> Be self-controlled and alert. Your enemy the devil prowls around like a roaring lion looking for someone to devour. (1 Pet 5:8)
>
> Keep yourselves in God's love as you wait for the mercy of our Lord Jesus Christ to bring you to eternal life. (Jude 1:21)
>
> I am coming soon. Hold on to what you have, so that no one will take your crown. (Rev 3:11)

1 TIMOTHY 5:1-2

CHAPTER 5

D. The Spirit & Discipline of Relationships, 5:1-2

1 Older men: To be treated as fathers
2 Younger men: To be treated as brothers
3 Older women: To be treated as mothers
4 Younger women: To be treated as sisters

Do not rebuke an older man harshly, but exhort him as if he were your father. Treat younger men as brothers, 2 Older women as mothers, and younger women as sisters, with absolute purity.

DIVISION III

BEHAVIOR AND RELATIONSHIPS IN THE CHURCH, 3:14-6:21

D. The Spirit and Discipline of Relationships, 5:1-2

(5:1-2) **Introduction—Church—Minister**: there is the duty to correct and discipline various age groups. Note that these two verses picture a family. The instructions are clear: the members of a church are to treat each other as family members. In no sense is any member to be *rebuked*. "Rebuke" (epiplesso) means to be severely censured, angrily reprimanded, violently reproached. When a family church member needs to be corrected, there is to be no severity, anger, or violence involved; no contempt or disgust. A church member is to be corrected and disciplined through exhortation (parakalei), that is, through encouragement, through appeal and pleading. This passage deals with the spirit and discipline of various relationships within the church.

1. Older men: to be treated as fathers (v.1).
2. Younger men: to be treated as brothers (v.1).
3. Older women: to be treated as mothers (v.2).
4. Younger women: to be treated as sisters (v.2).

1 (5:1) **Older Men**: older men are to be treated as fathers. Older men who are true Christian believers have more experience and wisdom in dealing with life. This is not to say they are always right; sometimes they are not. But they do have the wisdom of experience. Therefore, they are not to be ignored, neglected, bypassed, overlooked, or set aside as useless. They are to be treated as a father, with affection, respect, and honor. Their ideas, opinions, counsel, and direction are to be sought. They are to be a part of the life and ministry of the church.

One other point is important as well. Because of their experience, older men sometimes hold strong opinions and become set in their ways. They can become close-minded to new ideas, ministries, and methods. The end result is sometimes tragic: misbehavior, grumbling, complaining, criticism, opposition, and division.

The point is this: if an older man ever needs to be corrected, he is to be corrected and disciplined as a father, not as an enemy. He is to be approached and exhorted, appealed to and pleaded with just as we would our earthly father.

> Children, obey your parents in the Lord, for this is right. (Eph 6:1)
> Do not rebuke an older man harshly, but exhort him as if he were your father. Treat younger men as brothers, (1 Tim 5:1)

> "Rise in the presence of the aged [gray head], show respect for the elderly and revere your God. I am the LORD. (Lev 19:32)
> So Elihu son of Barakel the Buzite said: "I am young in years, and you are old; that is why I was fearful, not daring to tell you what I know. (Job 32:6)
> Listen, my son, to your father's instruction and do not forsake your mother's teaching. (Prov 1:8)
> My son, keep your father's commands and do not forsake your mother's teaching. (Prov 6:20)
> Gray hair is a crown of splendor; it is attained by a righteous life. (Prov 16:31)
> Listen to your father, who gave you life, and do not despise your mother when she is old. (Prov 23:22)

2 (5:1) **Younger Men**: younger men are to be treated as brothers. The young are sometimes thought to know too little and to be too inexperienced to have a part in the decisions and ministry of the church. Therefore, there is the tendency to ignore and bypass them. But this is never to be. Young men are to be treated as brothers; they are to be accepted and invited and given a part in the life and ministry of the church. The older members of a church are not to show an aire of superiority in dealing with young men. They are to show brotherly affection: consideration, respect, and care.

There is another need that also sometimes arises among younger men. They need direction: there are times when younger men need to be taught, corrected, and disciplined—no matter their age. When these times arise, there is to be no aire of superiority, severe reaction, contempt, or disgust. There is to be a brotherly spirit: affection and care, exhortation and direction, guidance and teaching.

> "A new command I give you: Love one another. As I have loved you, so you must love one another. By this all men will know that you are my disciples, if you love one another." (John 13:34-35)

My command is this: Love each other as I have loved you. (John 15:12)

In everything I did, I showed you that by this kind of hard work we must help the weak, remembering the words the Lord Jesus himself said: 'It is more blessed to give than to receive.'" (Acts 20:35)

Love must be sincere. Hate what is evil; cling to what is good. (Rom 12:9)

Love does no harm to its neighbor. Therefore love is the fulfillment of the law. (Rom 13:10)

We who are strong ought to bear with the failings of the weak and not to please ourselves. Each of us should please his neighbor for his good, to build him up. (Rom 15:1-2)

Therefore, if what I eat causes my brother to fall into sin, I will never eat meat again, so that I will not cause him to fall. (1 Cor 8:13)

The entire law is summed up in a single command: "Love your neighbor as yourself." (Gal 5:14)

Carry each other's burdens, and in this way you will fulfill the law of Christ. Therefore, as we have opportunity, let us do good to all people, especially to those who belong to the family of believers. (Gal 6:2, 10)

3 (5:2) **Older Women**: older women are to be treated as mothers. Just think what a mother gives to a family and you can see what the older women can contribute to the church:

- love
- warmth
- care
- tenderness
- energy
- affection
- compassion
- nourishment
- concern
- perseverance
- protection
- provision
- kindness
- guidance
- giving
- direction
- teaching
- instruction
- discipline
- understanding

A church is totally irresponsible if it ignores its older women who are true Christian believers. Their potential contribution to the lives and fellowship of believers is immeasurable. Therefore, the church is instructed to treat its older women as mothers. They are to be loved and protected, and their softness, tenderness, guidance, understanding, instruction, and energy are to be sought and used by the church.

Again, if an older woman needs correction and discipline, it must not be done in contempt and disrespect, but rather by the appeal and pleading of encouragement.

> Do not rebuke an older man harshly, but exhort him as if he were your father. Treat younger men as brothers, (1 Tim 5:1)
>
> But if a widow has children or grandchildren, these should learn first of all to put their religion into practice by caring for their own family and so repaying their parents and grandparents, for this is pleasing to God. (1 Tim 5:4)

> Religion that God our Father accepts as pure and faultless is this: to look after orphans and widows in their distress and to keep oneself from being polluted by the world. (James 1:27)
>
> "Honor your father and your mother, so that you may live long in the land the LORD your God is giving you. (Exo 20:12)
>
> "'Each of you must respect his mother and father, and you must observe my Sabbaths. I am the LORD your God. (Lev 19:3)
>
> Listen, my son, to your father's instruction and do not forsake your mother's teaching. (Prov 1:8)
>
> My son, keep your father's commands and do not forsake your mother's teaching. (Prov 6:20)
>
> Listen to your father, who gave you life, and do not despise your mother when she is old. (Prov 23:22)

4 (5:2) **Younger Women**: younger women are to be treated as sisters. But note the added exhortation: with absolute *purity*. Lust, immoral thoughts, sex—thinking about the physical attractiveness and the bodies of the younger women—none of this is to have a place in the church. The men and women of the church are all to keep themselves pure and to treat the young Christian women as sisters. They are to be protected and guarded, nourished and taught within the church. And their energy, tenderness, understanding, and compassion are to be sought and used by the church in its ministry.

In the matter of correction and discipline, young women are not to be treated with severity or disgust, but in love, encouragement, and exhortation.

> Blessed are the pure in heart, for they will see God. (Mat 5:8)
>
> But I tell you that anyone who looks at a woman lustfully has already committed adultery with her in his heart. (Mat 5:28)
>
> Flee from sexual immorality. All other sins a man commits are outside his body, but he who sins sexually sins against his own body. (1 Cor 6:18)
>
> Now for the matters you wrote about: It is good for a man not to marry. But since there is so much immorality, each man should have his own wife, and each woman her own husband. (1 Cor 7:1-2)
>
> And live a life of love, just as Christ loved us and gave himself up for us as a fragrant offering and sacrifice to God. But among you there must not be even a hint of sexual immorality, or of any kind of impurity, or of greed, because these are improper for God's holy people. (Eph 5:2-3)
>
> Put to death, therefore, whatever belongs to your earthly nature: sexual immorality, impurity, lust, evil desires and greed, which is idolatry. (Col 3:5)
>
> It is God's will that you should be sanctified: that you should avoid sexual immorality; (1 Th 4:3)

The goal of this command is love, which comes from a pure heart and a good conscience and a sincere faith. (1 Tim 1:5)

Then they can train the younger women to love their husbands and children, to be self-controlled and pure, to be busy at home, to be kind, and to be subject to their husbands, so that no one will malign the word of God. (Titus 2:4-5)

Now that you have purified yourselves by obeying the truth so that you have sincere love for your brothers, love one another deeply, from the heart. (1 Pet 1:22)

These are those who did not defile themselves with women, for they kept themselves pure. They follow the Lamb wherever he goes. They were purchased from among men and offered as firstfruits to God and the Lamb. (Rev 14:4)

(But note: a woman must guard how she dresses and makes herself up. Although not covered in this passage, other passages cover this subject. See note—1 Tim.2:9-10).

1 TIMOTHY 5:3-16

	E. The Responsibilities to Christian Widows, 5:3-16		
1 **Christian widows are to be honored**	3 Give proper recognition to those widows who are really in need.	good deeds, such as bringing up children, showing hospitality, washing the feet of the saints, helping those in trouble and devoting herself to all kinds of good deeds.	1) Must remain unmarried 2) Must be known for good works

2 **The children & their parents**
  a. Children are to care for their widowed parents
	4 But if a widow has children or grandchildren, these should learn first of all to put their religion into practice by caring for their own family and so repaying their parents and grandparents, for this is pleasing to God.	11 As for younger widows, do not put them on such a list. For when their sensual desires overcome their dedication to Christ, they want to marry.
		12 Thus they bring judgment on themselves, because they have broken their first pledge.
			4 **The church & the younger widows & idleness**
			  a. They should not be counted permanent widows
			    1) Can desire to be remarried
			    2) Can bring judgment upon themselves

b. Widows are to live above reproach
    1) Trusting God & praying
    2) Not living for pleasure
	5 The widow who is really in need and left all alone puts her hope in God and continues night and day to pray and to ask God for help.
	6 But the widow who lives for pleasure is dead even while she lives.
		13 Besides, they get into the habit of being idle and going about from house to house. And not only do they become idlers, but also gossips and busybodies, saying things they ought not to.	3) Can become idle, gossips, & busybodies

c. Both widows & children are to obey these instructions
  d. Children are accountable to God
	7 ive the people these instructions, too, so that no one may be open to blame.
	8 If anyone does not provide for his relatives, and especially for his immediate family, he has denied the faith and is worse than an unbeliever.
		14 So I counsel younger widows to marry, to have children, to manage their homes and to give the enemy no opportunity for slander.
		15 Some have in fact already turned away to follow Satan.
			b. They should remarry
			    1) Lest they cause immoral gossip
			
			    2) Lest they turn to Satan

3 **The church & its organization of widows**
  a. The required age to be a member: Sixty
  b. Their reputation
	9 No widow may be put on the list of widows unless she is over sixty, has been faithful to her husband,
	10 And is well known for her
		16 If any woman who is a believer has widows in her family, she should help them and not let the church be burdened with them, so that the church can help those widows who are really in need.	5 **The believer is to take care of the widows in his own family**

DIVISION III

BEHAVIOR AND RELATIONSHIPS IN THE CHURCH, 3:14-6:21

E. The Responsibilities to Christian Widows, 5:3-16

(5:3-16) **Introduction**: What is the children's responsibility to their widowed parents? What is the believer's and the church's responsibility to the Christian widows under their care? These are the all important questions of this passage.
1. Christian widows are to be honored (v.3-8).
2. The children and their parents (v.4-8).
3. The church and its organization of widows (v.9-10).
4. The church and the younger widows and idleness (v.11-15).
5. The believer is to take care of the widows in his own family (v.16).

1 (5:3) **Widows—Elderly Parents**: Christian widows are to be honored. Honor means to respect and esteem, but it also means to consider and give due care. It has the idea of looking after and caring for, of giving material help. All Christian widows are to be honored, respected, and esteemed by the church. But note the phrase "widows who are really in need." This limits the material support of the church. Not all widows need help. Some widows have family and estates that can help them. The widows who have no family and inadequate finances are those who are to be helped and supported by the church. They are the widows who are to be honored with the material support of the church.

2 (5:4-8) **Widows—Children—Aged Parents**: the children and their parents. Note four significant points.
  1. Children are to care for their parents and grandparents. This is a strong statement. In fact, the very first duty of a child is to be pious at home, that is...
   * to live for Christ in the home.
   * to be responsible in caring for his own family.

A true believer is a Christian at home before he is a Christian anyplace else. His first duty as a Christian is to love and care for his own family, and this includes his parents and grandparents. His parents and grandparents loved and took care of him when he was a child; therefore, he is to return the love and care when they are no longer able to take care of themselves.

Note the declaration: this is "pleasing to God." No other action is pleasing to God. A Christian child must love and take care of the widowed parents or else they receive the disapproval of God (cp. v.8).

2. Widowed parents who are true Christians are to live above reproach. Who are "widows who are really in need," the persons who are to be cared for by the church?
⇒ The person who is "left all alone" (memo-nomene): left completely alone; without husband, children, or close kin.
⇒ The person who puts her hope in God. The Greek says who "has set her hope on God"; who has "placed her hope [and keeps it] on God" (A.T. Robertson. *Word Pictures in the New Testament*, Vol.4, p.584). Note what God declares: "Your widows too can trust in me" (Jer.49:11).
⇒ The person who continues night and day to pray.

The widow who really trusts God and focuses her life and attention upon praying day and night—that widow is a true Christian, a person who is focused upon Christ and His mission just as the church is. Therefore, the church is to look after and take care of this dear saint of God. But note the contrast: some widows live in pleasure; that is, they give themselves over to the flesh and the world. They party, get drunk, and live immoral lives. These are not to be supported by the church. The church's energy and resources are *not to be used* to indulge and give license to worldliness and sin. Such a woman is "dead even while she lives." She is *dead* to God and to the things of God. Her mind is upon her clubs and parties, the world and the flesh (sinful nature) not upon the Lord and His church and the desperate needs of a dying world.

3. Both widowed parents and children are to obey these instructions. The reason is clearly stated: so that they can be blameless before God. We shall all be held accountable...
- for children: how they treat their widowed and aged parents.
- for widowed parents: how they live when widowed and aged, whether righteous or immoral, godly or ungodly.

We must both live obeying God and doing exactly what He says. We shall either be declared *blameless* and acceptable to God or else guilty of sin and unacceptable to God.

4. Children are accountable to God. This is a frightening declaration. It clearly shows just how important God considers our treatment of widows. If a child does not take care of his family, especially those within his own household (meaning immediate family—wife, children, parents, and grandparents), two things are true of him.
⇒ He denies the faith.
⇒ He is worse than an unbeliever.

An unbeliever is a person who rejects Christ and sometimes even opposes Christ. He denies God and everything about God. The point is this: a person who does not take care of his parents (or anyone else of his household) stands opposed to God. He even denies the very existence of God by his behavior, for he shows that he does not fear God nor God's command to respect and care for his parents. How we treat our aged parents is of critical importance to God. God holds us accountable and will judge us for how we treat our fathers and mothers when they become old.

"Honor your father and your mother, so that you may live long in the land the LORD your God is giving you. (Exo 20:12)

"'Each of you must respect his mother and father, and you must observe my Sabbaths. I am the LORD your God. (Lev 19:3)

"Cursed is the man who dishonors his father or his mother." Then all the people shall say, "Amen!" (Deu 27:16)

"The eye that mocks a father, that scorns obedience to a mother, will be pecked out by the ravens of the valley, will be eaten by the vultures. (Prov 30:17)

For God said, 'Honor your father and mother' and 'Anyone who curses his father or mother must be put to death.' (Mat 15:4)

Religion that God our Father accepts as pure and faultless is this: to look after orphans and widows in their distress and to keep oneself from being polluted by the world. (James 1:27)

3 (5:9-10) **Widows—Church**: the church and its organization of widows. Apparently, the early church did what any wise church does: organized its most spiritual widows for ministry. Widows who are committed to Christ have a great potential for ministry. Once they have recovered from the loss of their spouse, their commitment, energy, time, and talents can concentrate upon Christ and the ministry of the church. The early church recognized this fact and organized the widows for a very special ministry to the needy. But note: the ministry of organization had high spiritual standards.
⇒ The widow had to be at least sixty years old. This would mean that she had probably walked with Christ and proven her faith for some years.
⇒ The widow must have been faithful to her husband. By this, she would be a strong example of purity and trustworthiness.
⇒ The widow must have a strong testimony of good works or deeds.
⇒ The widow must have reared and nourished her children as she should have: in love and care, correction and discipline, and in Christ and His church.
⇒ The widow must have been a hospitable person, opening and using her home as a ministering center for Christ. The inns of that day were "notoriously dirty, notoriously expensive, and notoriously immoral" (William Barclay. *The Letters to Timothy, Titus, and Philemon*, p.128). Therefore, Christians who were willing to open their homes to strangers traveling about showed an open heart for ministry.
⇒ The widow must have washed the saints' feet. The people of that day wore sandals and the roads and paths were dirty. Therefore, it was the common practice to have a bowl of water at the entrance of the home for guests to wash their feet. The idea is that the spiritual woman would have a humble spirit. She would have never allowed a servant to greet other Christians into her home; she would have done that herself. She would have humbly met them and cleaned their feet herself. This would show that she was willing to do the most humble and menial task in ministering to people.
⇒ The widow must have helped those in trouble, the afflicted and distressed, the suffering. This would show that she was tender and compassionate.

⇒ The widow must have devoted herself to all kinds of good deeds.

Thought 1. Every church needs to organize its widows for ministry, especially those who love the Lord and have lived for Him and are committed to the church. They can...
- be a strong example in purity and trustworthiness.
- provide a strong testimony of good works or deeds.
- minister to the children of the church and community, both the orphans and those with parents.
- minister enormously through hospitality using their homes as an outreach center.
- serve in the most humble and menial tasks of the church.
- minister to the suffering and distressed.
- be used in all the works and ministries of the church.

> In the same way, let your light shine before men, that they may see your good deeds and praise your Father in heaven. (Mat 5:16)
> We who are strong ought to bear with the failings of the weak and not to please ourselves. (Rom 15:1)
> Carry each other's burdens, and in this way you will fulfill the law of Christ. (Gal 6:2)
> Therefore, as we have opportunity, let us do good to all people, especially to those who belong to the family of believers. (Gal 6:10)
> Serve wholeheartedly, as if you were serving the Lord, not men, (Eph 6:7)
> Command them to do good, to be rich in good deeds, and to be generous and willing to share. (1 Tim 6:18)
> In everything set them an example by doing what is good. In your teaching show integrity, seriousness (Titus 2:7)
> And let us consider how we may spur one another on toward love and good deeds. (Heb 10:24)
> And do not forget to do good and to share with others, for with such sacrifices God is pleased. (Heb 13:16)
> Live such good lives [behavior] among the pagans that, though they accuse you of doing wrong, they may see your good deeds and glorify God on the day he visits us. (1 Pet 2:12)

4 (5:11-15) **Widows—Young Women—Church**: the church and the younger widows and idleness. Two significant things are said here about young widows and the early church.

1. Young widows were not allowed to serve in the church's *order of widows*. The reason given is that they might wish to marry again. This tells us that the church's *order of widows* made a vow to serve God and His church for the remainder of their lives, never again marrying.

The picture is this: a young Christian lady whose husband had just died would be gripped with bitter sorrow. She would find her most comforting solace in God Himself and in her friends at church. She could be subject to the hasty impulse of dedicating her life to God as a widow—and requesting that she be added to the church's *order of widows*. The exhortation to refuse her request is to prevent a hasty and impulsive decision. Such a decision would bring judgment to the young widow at a later date when she might wish to break her vow to God and marry again. (See outline—1 Cor.7:8-9; 7:39-40.) If she broke her vow, she would displease God, stir criticism, and lower the meaning of making vows to God and to the ministry of the church.

Another problem might also arise. Young widows have not had time to become all that mature in the Lord. Therefore, as they went from house to house in their ministry, they might tend...
- to idle time away.
- to gossip.
- to be busybodies.
- to say "things they should not say and [talk] of things they should not mention" (Amplified New Testament).

> We hear that some among you are idle. They are not busy; they are busybodies. (2 Th 3:11)
> Besides, they get into the habit of being idle and going about from house to house. And not only do they become idlers, but also gossips and busybodies, saying things they ought not to. (1 Tim 5:13)
> If you suffer, it should not be as a murderer or thief or any other kind of criminal, or even as a meddler. (1 Pet 4:15)

2. Young widows should, therefore, marry.
    a. They should marry lest they cause immoral gossip.

> So I counsel younger widows to marry, to have children, to manage their homes and to give the enemy no opportunity for slander. (1 Tim 5:14)

Thought 1. It is not wrong for a young widow to remain single if she can live for Christ and the church. But if she cannot dedicate her life to Christ and the ministry, then she should marry.

b. They should marry lest they turn away to follow Satan (v.15). Note that this verse says that some in Ephesus had turned away and gone after the world and its immoral and unclean lifestyle.

> Those on the rock are the ones who receive the word with joy when they hear it, but they have no root. They believe for a while, but in the time of testing they fall away. (Luke 8:13)
> But my righteous one will live by faith. And if he shrinks back, I will not be pleased with him." (Heb 10:38)
> He is a double-minded man, unstable in all he does. (James 1:8)
> If they have escaped the corruption of the world by knowing our Lord and Savior Jesus Christ and are again entangled in it and overcome, they are worse off at the end than they were at the beginning. (2 Pet 2:20)

Therefore, dear friends, since you already know this, be on your guard so that you may not be carried away by the error of lawless men and fall from your secure position. (2 Pet 3:17)

Do not love the world or anything in the world. If anyone loves the world, the love of the Father is not in him. For everything in the world—the cravings of sinful man, the lust of his eyes and the boasting of what he has and does—comes not from the Father but from the world. (1 John 2:15-16)

They went out from us, but they did not really belong to us. For if they had belonged to us, they would have remained with us; but their going showed that none of them belonged to us. (1 John 2:19)

You love evil rather than good, falsehood rather than speaking the truth. Selah (Psa 52:3)

This is what the LORD says about this people: "They greatly love to wander; they do not restrain their feet. So the LORD does not accept them; he will now remember their wickedness and punish them for their sins." (Jer 14:10)

5 (5:16) **Church—Widows**: the believer is to take care of the widows in his or her family. The church is not to be charged with the care of widows if there are living relatives. The responsibility is that of the families.

> Learn to do right! Seek justice, encourage the oppressed. Defend the cause of the fatherless, plead the case of the widow. (Isa 1:17)
>
> He is the one who comes after me, the thongs of whose sandals I am not worthy to untie." (John 1:27)

1 TIMOTHY 5:17-20

	F. The Elders or Officials, 5:17-20	it is treading out the grain," and "The worker deserves his wages."	Dt.25:4; Lk.10:7; 1 Cor.9:9, 14)	
1 The honor & pay of an elder a. Is conditional: Must manage the church well b. Scripture commands that they be paid (cp.	17 The elders who direct the affairs of the church well are worthy of double honor, especially those whose work is preaching and teaching. 18 For the Scripture says, "Do not muzzle the ox while	19 Do not entertain an accusation against an elder unless it is brought by two or three witnesses. 20 Those who sin are to be rebuked publicly, so that the others may take warning.		2 The discipline of an elder a. To be several witnesses b. To be rebuked publicly (before the elders or officials)

DIVISION III

BEHAVIOR AND RELATIONSHIPS IN THE CHURCH, 3:14-6:21

F. The Elders or Officials, 5:17-20

(5:17-20) **Introduction**: this is a day in which the minister of God is being attacked not only by the world, but most unfortunately, by those within the church. The attackers are causing a loss of respect for Christ and a neglect, ignoring, abuse, and persecution of the ministry as has seldom been experienced in civilization. Because of this, ministers are being neglected when it comes to meeting their financial needs and quickly deserted when gossip and rumors swirl about their heads. Whether the rumors are true or not, few people care and are willing to support the minister of God. This passage deals with both subjects—critical subjects for our day.
1. The honor and pay of an elder (v.17-18).
2. The discipline of an elder (v.19-20).

1 (5:17-18) **Elder—Minister, Financial Support**: the church is to honor its minister—esteem, respect, acknowledge, and recognize him. He is to be held within the heart of the believer and held ever so closely, and he is to be esteemed ever so highly. In fact, note what Scripture says: he is to be counted "worthy of double honor."

But note: there is a condition attached to honoring the minister. The minister to be honored is one who "direct[s] well." The word "direct" (proistemi) is a general word meaning to oversee, supervise, and look after. The minister who is worthy of double honor is the minister who labors and labors and works and works. If he is to receive double honor then he must demonstrate a double commitment to Christ and the church.

Note also that the whole ministerial staff is covered by this charge. All the ministers of a church staff are to be counted worthy of double honor. But there is one minister who is singled out: the minister who labors in the Word and doctrine, that is, who preaches and teaches. It is he upon whom so much responsibility lies: he is the minister who takes the lead in edifying and building up the believer and the church. He is the one who has to spend hours on his face before God and in the Word in order to preach and teach—this in addition to taking the lead in all the other duties and ministries of the church. If he is a committed minister, a minister who labors and labors for Christ and works and works for the church, then he is worthy of double honor.

Now, one other significant fact. The word "honor" (time) means more than just esteem and respect. It means to pay and bestow what is due. A minister is due an honorarium; he is due compensation, some pay, some wage for his labor. And, if he performs his duty well—labors and labors and works and works—then he is due double honor. Is this to be taken literally? Is the church to pay him a double salary? A.T. Robertson states that there are "numerous examples of Roman soldiers who received double pay for unusual services" (*Word Pictures in the New Testament*, Vol.4, p.588). One thing is sure: double pay means adequate, ample, sufficient, and generous financial support.

The oxen used to grind out the corn is an example. In the East, oxen have been used to pull a millstone around and around over grain. The ox were never muzzled. He was allowed to eat as much grain as he wished, for he was considered to have earned all the grain he wished. So it is to be with the minister of God. He is worthy of his labor. As he grinds and grinds away at the harvest of souls for God and His church, the minister is to be given more than enough financial support.

> **Thought 1.** Scripture has already deplored money-grabbing (1 Tim.3:3). God equally deplores inadequate compensation. The point is: if God ordained that working oxen should be cared for, how much more has He ordained the church to adequately care for the working minister!
>
> Do not muzzle an ox while it is treading out the grain. (Deu 25:4)
> Do not take along any gold or silver or copper in your belts; take no bag for the journey, or extra tunic, or sandals or a staff; for the worker is worth his keep. (Mat 10:9-10)
> Stay in that house, eating and drinking whatever they give you, for the worker deserves his wages. Do not move around from house to house. "When you enter a town and are welcomed, eat what is set before you. (Luke 10:7-8)
> For it is written in the Law of Moses: "Do not muzzle an ox while it is treading out the grain." Is it about oxen that God is concerned? (1 Cor 9:9)
> In the same way, the Lord has commanded that those who preach the gospel should receive their living from the gospel. (1 Cor 9:14)
> The elders who direct the affairs of the church well are worthy of double honor, especially those whose work is preaching and teaching. For the Scripture says, "Do not muzzle the ox while it is treading out the grain," and "The worker deserves his wages." (1 Tim 5:17-18)

2 (5:19-20) **Minister—Elder**: the discipline of an elder. (When studying church discipline, the instructions of our

Lord should always be studied. See outline and notes—Mt.18:15-20.) Matthew Henry gives an excellent exposition of verse 19, an exposition that every minister should read:

> "Here is the scripture-method of proceeding against an elder, when accused of any crime. Observe [it]. There must be an accusation; it must not be a flying uncertain report, but an accusation, containing a certain charge, [and it] must be drawn up....
>
> "This accusation is not to be received unless supported by two or three credible witnesses; and the accusation must be received before them, that is, the accused must have the accusers face to face, because the reputation of a minister is...a tender thing...therefore, before any thing be done in the least to blemish that reputation, great care should be taken [and] the thing alleged against him be well proved" (*Matthew Henry's Commentary*, Vol.6, p.825).

A very practical and warm exposition is also given by Oliver Greene:

> "It is possible for even a godly, separated, God-appointed elder to commit sin....It is possible even for those who live very near to the heart of God to be caught off guard and commit sin that will bring shame and disgrace upon the church. But we are not to accuse an elder unless there are two or more witnesses to testify that the accusation is an accomplished fact. We should never repeat anything we hear about a minister, deacon, steward, elder, Sunday school teacher or any leader in the church. If we hear reports of evil, we should investigate in the right way, through the right people—and certainly we should not discuss the situation with unbelievers. It is very clear in verse 19 that an elder must not be accused unless there are at least two or three witnesses who can prove the truth of the accusation" (*The Epistles of Paul the Apostle to Timothy and Titus*, p.202).

The discipline is clearly stated: the elder or minister is to be rebuked. The words "rebuked publicly" most likely mean before all the elders rather than before the whole church (A.T. Robertson, *Word Pictures in the New Testament*, Vol.4, p.589). To go before the whole church would only add fuel to the flame of the immature and carnal believers within the church. It would make a public spectacle before the outside world. Such would naturally damage the church's testimony—even if an attempt was made to balance the damaged image by claiming disciplinary action. Note that the point of the discipline is the correction of the sinning minister and the prevention of other ministers from sinning: that they may fear exposure and embarrassment.

William Barclay has an excellent exposition of this verse that merits being read by all ministers:

> "Those who persist in sin are to be publicly rebuked. That public rebuke had a double value. It sobered the sinner into a consideration of his ways, and wakened him into a sense of shame; and it made others have a care that they did not involve themselves in a like humiliation. The threat of publicity is no bad thing, if it keeps a man in the right way, even from fear. A wise leader will know when there is a time to keep things quiet, and a time for public rebuke. But whatever happens, the Church must never give the world the impression that it is condoning sin" (*The Letters to Timothy, Titus, and Philemon*, p.135).

In conclusion, charges made against a minister or anyone else is one of the most serious acts that a person can do. Barclay states it as well as it can be stated:

> "This would be a happier world, and the Church would be a happier Church, if people would realize that it is nothing less than a sin to spread and to repeat stories about people of whose truth *they are not, and cannot be, sure*. Irresponsible, slanderous and malicious talk does infinite damage and causes infinite heartbreak, and such talk will not go unpunished by God...." (*The Letters to Timothy, Titus, and Philemon*, p.135f).

"If your brother sins against you, go and show him his fault, just between the two of you. If he listens to you, you have won your brother over. But if he will not listen, take one or two others along, so that 'every matter may be established by the testimony of two or three witnesses.' If he refuses to listen to them, tell it to the church; and if he refuses to listen even to the church, treat him as you would a pagan or a tax collector. (Mat 18:15-17)

Jesus said to his disciples: "Things that cause people to sin are bound to come, but woe to that person through whom they come. It would be better for him to be thrown into the sea with a millstone tied around his neck than for him to cause one of these little ones to sin. So watch yourselves. "If your brother sins, rebuke him, and if he repents, forgive him. (Luke 17:1-3)

Those who sin are to be rebuked publicly, so that the others may take warning. (1 Tim 5:20)

Preach the Word; be prepared in season and out of season; correct, rebuke and encourage—with great patience and careful instruction. (2 Tim 4:2)

This testimony is true. Therefore, rebuke them sharply, so that they will be sound in the faith (Titus 1:13)

These, then, are the things you should teach. Encourage and rebuke with all authority. Do not let anyone despise you. (Titus 2:15)

Warn a divisive person once, and then warn him a second time. After that, have nothing to do with him. (Titus 3:10)

1 TIMOTHY 5:21-25

	G. The Young Minister (Charge 3): To Be An Impartial Minister, 5:21-25	Keep yourself pure. 23 Stop drinking only water, and use a little wine because of your stomach and your frequent illnesses.	4 **Charge 3: Care for the body & its weaknesses**
1 A strong charge	21 I charge you, in the sight of God and Christ Jesus and the elect angels, to keep these instructions without partiality, and to do nothing out of favoritism.	24 The sins of some men are obvious, reaching the place of judgment ahead of them; the sins of others trail behind them.	5 **Charge 4: Leave the judgment of others to God**
2 Charge 1: Minister without partiality			
3 Charge 2: Guard ordination & guard oneself	22 Do not be hasty in the laying on of hands, and do not share in the sins of others.	25 In the same way, good deeds are obvious, and even those that are not cannot be hidden.	a. Because sin is not always clearly seen b. Because good is not always clearly seen

DIVISION III

BEHAVIOR AND RELATIONSHIPS IN THE CHURCH, 3:14-6:21

G. The Young Minister (Charge 3): To Be an Impartial Minister, 5:21-25

(5:21-25) **Introduction**: this is the third personal charge given to Timothy, a charge that desperately needs to be heeded by all believers and all ministers and teachers of God's Word.
1. A strong charge (v.21).
2. Charge 1: minister without partiality (v.21).
3. Charge 2: guard ordination and guard oneself (v.22).
4. Charge 3: care for the body and its weaknesses (v.23).
5. Charge 4: leave the judgment of others to God (v.24-25).

(5:21-25) **Another Outline**: this passage could be combined with the former passage into one outline (1 Tim.5:17-25). These verses would simply become point 3. The three points would be:
1. The honor and pay of a minister (v.17-18).
2. The discipline of a minister (v.19-20).
3. The personal behavior of a minister (v.21-25).
   a. He is not to show partiality (v.21).
   b. He is to guard ordination (v.22).
   c. He is to care for the body and its weaknesses (v.23).
   d. He is to leave the judgment of others up to God (v.24-25).

1 (5:21) **Charge**: this is a strong charge, a command that opens the eyes and awakens the mind. The charge is directed to the minister of God and it is given...
- "In the sight of God, and Christ Jesus and the elect angels," that is, the angels who obeyed God and "kept their own principality [positions of authority] [Jude 6] and who did no sin [2 Pet.2:4]" (A.T. Robertson. *Word Pictures in the New Testament*, Vol.4, p.589). The angels who are "commissioned to watch over men's affairs" (Donald Guthrie. *The Pastoral Epistles*. Tyndale New Testament Commentaries, p.107). (Cp. Heb.1:14.)

The mention of all three—God, Christ, and the elect angels—shows how important these instructions are to God. He wants the message of *1 Timothy* preached and taught. Timothy was not only to appear before God, he was also to appear before the Lord Jesus Christ and the elect angels. He was to be held accountable for the way he discharged his duty to preach and teach these things. So is every other minister. We shall be held accountable for the way we preach and teach the Scripture.

2 (5:21) **Partiality—Favoritism—Prejudice**: the first charge is to minister without prejudice or partiality. Timothy faced the temptation that every minister faces:
 ⇒ being prejudiced against some people—judging some people because they have a different color skin, or belong to a different race, or are poor, or live in a different section of town.
 ⇒ showing partiality and favoritism to other people—seeking, listening, recognizing, and spending more time with certain people while ignoring others.

Scripture is clear in its warning to us about partiality, yet we continue to be prejudiced and to show partiality. As believers of the Lord—servants, teachers, and ministers of Christ—we must heed the following instructions of God.
 ⇒ We must not make decisions because we fear the face of some men, that is, their position and power.

> Do not show partiality in judging; hear both small and great alike. Do not be afraid of any man, for judgment belongs to God. Bring me any case too hard for you, and I will hear it. (Deu 1:17)

 ⇒ We must not make decisions because some leader or powerful person desires it.

> "'Do not pervert justice; do not show partiality to the poor or favoritism to the great, but judge your neighbor fairly. (Lev 19:15)

 ⇒ We must not preach and teach the Word of God with partiality; we must not hold back, fearing the face of man. We must fearlessly preach the truth for the sake of people's salvation—all people. The wealthy and powerful must repent as much as the poor and unknown.

> I charge you, in the sight of God and Christ Jesus and the elect angels,

to keep these instructions without partiality, and to do nothing out of favoritism. (1 Tim 5:21)

"So I have caused you to be despised and humiliated before all the people, because you have not followed my ways but have shown partiality in matters of the law." (Mal 2:9)

⇒ We must not accept and favor people because of their social standing, wealth, position, or power.

My brothers, as believers in our glorious Lord Jesus Christ, don't show favoritism. Suppose a man comes into your meeting wearing a gold ring and fine clothes, and a poor man in shabby clothes also comes in. If you show special attention to the man wearing fine clothes and say, "Here's a good seat for you," but say to the poor man, "You stand there" or "Sit on the floor by my feet," have you not discriminated among yourselves and become judges with evil thoughts? (James 2:1-4)

⇒ We must not admire or give more attention to some people because they have a greater advantage in looks, society, position, or popularity.

These men are grumblers and faultfinders; they follow their own evil desires; they boast about themselves and flatter others for their own advantage. (Jude 1:16)

⇒ We must not secretly show partiality.

He would surely rebuke you if you secretly showed partiality. (Job 13:10)

⇒ God clearly says: To show partiality in judging is not good.

These also are sayings of the wise: To show partiality in judging is not good: (Prov 24:23)

3 (5:22) **Ordination—Ministers:** the second charge is to guard ordination and to guard oneself. The laying on of hands here can refer to ordaining men to the ministry of the Lord Jesus Christ or to restoring the ministers who had fallen into sin and been disciplined. "The prohibition suits either situation," but the context seems to suit the restoration of fallen ministers (A.T. Robertson. *Word Pictures in the New Testament*, Vol.4, p.589). However, the charge is certainly meant for both situations, for ordaining men to the ministry of Christ is of critical importance.

1. Note the phrase "Do not be hasty." We must not rush to ordain men. The reason is clearly understood.
⇒ Young believers have not yet grown enough in the Lord. They have not yet learned to conquer the temptations and sins of the world and of their former lives (through Christ). They can easily slip back and disgrace the name of Christ and of the ministry. Therefore, all young believers must be given time to grow in Christ before they are ever ordained.
⇒ New church members must also be given time to prove their profession and call before being ordained. A person is not always what he professes to be. Ordaining someone before we know for sure that he is going to continue on for Christ and is definitely called by Christ can lead to devastating results. A new convert, a new church member, often returns to the world and its sinful ways. If he has been ordained, he brings reproach upon Christ, the church, and the ministry.

"Undue haste in Christian appointments has...led to unworthy men bringing havoc to the cause of Christ." (Donald Guthrie. *The Pastoral Epistles.* "Tyndale New Testament Commentaries," p.107).

"Before a man gains promotion in business, or in teaching, or in the army or the navy or the air force, he must give proof that he has earned it and that he deserves it. No man should ever start at the top. A man must give proof that he deserves a position of responsibility and leadership. This is doubly important in the Church; for a man who is raised to high office, and who then fails in it or brings discredit on it, brings dishonour, not only on himself, but also on the Church. In a critical world the Church cannot be too careful in regard to the kind of men whom she chooses as her leaders" (William Barclay. *The Letters to Timothy, Titus, and Philemon*, p.136).

This proposal pleased the whole group. They chose Stephen, a man full of faith and of the Holy Spirit; also Philip, Procorus, Nicanor, Timon, Parmenas, and Nicolas from Antioch, a convert to Judaism. They presented these men to the apostles, who prayed and laid their hands on them. (Acts 6:5-6)

Until I come, devote yourself to the public reading of Scripture, to preaching and to teaching. Do not neglect your gift, which was given you through a prophetic message when the body of elders laid their hands on you. (1 Tim 4:13-14)

Do not be hasty in the laying on of hands, and do not share in the sins of others. Keep yourself pure. (1 Tim 5:22)

For this reason I remind you to fan into flame the gift of God, which is in you through the laying on of my hands. (2 Tim 1:6)

You are to bring the Levites before the LORD, and the Israelites are to lay their hands on them. (Num 8:10)

So the LORD said to Moses, "Take Joshua son of Nun, a man in whom is the spirit, and lay your hand on him. (Num 27:18)

Now Joshua son of Nun was filled with the spirit of wisdom because Moses had laid his hands on him. So the Israelites listened to him and did what the LORD had commanded Moses. (Deu 34:9)

2. The minister who has fallen into sin can take great heart from this passage (cp. v.19-22). It definitely teaches that the fallen minister can be restored to the ministry—just as effectively as he was before, perhaps even more because of the praise to Christ that results through God's mercy. It is God's eternal mercy and eternal grace that reaches out and saves the fallen minister; therefore, when the minister is reached, God's mercy and grace are seen to be ever so wonderful and glorious, beyond imagination. God is praised—gloriously praised. But note the Scripture:

> Do not be hasty in the laying on of hands.... (1 Tim 5:22)

The fallen minister is not to be re-ordained or replaced in the pulpit immediately after his repentance. Ministers are to wait until he has proven...
- that his repentance is genuine.
- that his rededication and recommitment to follow Christ sticks.
- that he is being conformed and molded into the image of Jesus Christ.
- that he is committed to serving Christ and His church and is actively involved in reaching people for Christ and in ministering to the needs of the needy.

But note a critical point: this does not mean that we do not embrace the dear brother, that we withdraw fellowship from him, that we look upon him with distrust and suspicion. Contrariwise, we reach out and embrace him, love and care for him, nourish and nurture him. In fact, we do this immediately upon hearing about his fall. We go after him immediately, for he is too precious to lose to the world.

> That God was reconciling the world to himself in Christ, not counting men's sins against them. And he has committed to us the message of reconciliation. We are therefore Christ's ambassadors, as though God were making his appeal through us. We implore you on Christ's behalf: Be reconciled to God. (2 Cor 5:19-20)
>
> Brothers, if someone is caught in a sin, you who are spiritual should restore him gently. But watch yourself, or you also may be tempted. (Gal 6:1)
>
> Remember this: Whoever turns a sinner from the error of his way will save him from death and cover over a multitude of sins. (James 5:20)
>
> Above all, love each other deeply, because love covers over a multitude of sins. (1 Pet 4:8)
>
> I was enraged by his sinful greed; I punished him, and hid my face in anger, yet he kept on in his willful ways. I have seen his ways, but I will heal him; I will guide him and restore comfort to him, (Isa 57:17-18)
>
> "Return, faithless people; I will cure you of backsliding." "Yes, we will come to you, for you are the LORD our God. (Jer 3:22)
>
> But I will restore you to health and heal your wounds,' declares the LORD, 'because you are called an outcast, Zion for whom no one cares.' (Jer 30:17)

> "I will heal their waywardness and love them freely, for my anger has turned away from them. (Hosea 14:4)

3. Note that we as ministers are held responsible for those we ordain. The minister who lays hands on an unworthy man for ordination bears equal responsibility for his sins. In God's eyes the minister himself becomes guilty of the man's sins—just as guilty as the man himself. This is the meaning of the exhortation: when ordaining men do not "share in the sins of others. Keep yourself pure."

> For in the same way you judge others, you will be judged, and with the measure you use, it will be measured to you. (Mat 7:2)
>
> "Therefore come out from them and be separate, says the Lord. Touch no unclean thing, and I will receive you." (2 Cor 6:17)
>
> Do not be hasty in the laying on of hands, and do not share in the sins of others. Keep yourself pure. (1 Tim 5:22)
>
> Now that you have purified yourselves by obeying the truth so that you have sincere love for your brothers, love one another deeply, from the heart. (1 Pet 1:22)
>
> Depart, depart, go out from there! Touch no unclean thing! Come out from it and be pure, you who carry the vessels of the LORD. (Isa 52:11)

4 (5:23) **Ministers—Wine**: the third charge is to care for the body and its weaknesses. Timothy was having stomach problems of some sort and had been drinking water exclusively. Wine was used as a mild medicine in that day and time, but apparently Timothy had refused to drink it because of the Scriptural commands that a priest or minister of God must not touch the fruit of the vine when it had fermented (Num.6:3-4; Jer.35:5-7). However, Paul assures him that he is not violating the Scripture by taking a little wine as medicine. The word "little" would be what we would refer to as a tablespoon or two.

The point is this: we must take care of our bodies. Health must not be neglected. There is no excuse...
- for overeating and being flabby.
- for lying around and not exercising and being physically alert.
- for eating junk food and not eating healthy food.
- for not having periodic checkups from a physician if physicians are available in our communities.

No matter what we may think or claim, we must always remember and never forget...
- if the body is sluggish, the mind and spirit are sluggish.
- if the body is not fed oxygen, the mind is not fed oxygen.
- if the body is not energetic, the mind and spirit are not energetic.

> Therefore, I urge you, brothers, in view of God's mercy, to offer your bodies as living sacrifices, holy and pleasing to God—this is your spiritual act of worship. Do not conform any longer to the pattern of this world, but be transformed by the renewing of your mind. Then you will be able to test and approve what God's will

is—his good, pleasing and perfect will. (Rom 12:1-2)

Do you not know that your body is a temple of the Holy Spirit, who is in you, whom you have received from God? You are not your own; you were bought at a price. Therefore honor God with your body. (1 Cor 6:19-20)

5 (5:24-25) **Ministers—Judging Others**: the fourth charge is to leave judgment up to God. A minister's task is to deal with people and their sins. In fact, he is always involved with people, dealing with their weaknesses and strengths, their sins and virtues. Because of this he is often tempted to pass judgment upon people; he is tempted to look upon some as being weak and non-commital and others as being strong and decisive. But this point is an eye-opener. Judgment is to be left up to God, for only God knows the whole truth about a person. Only God knows...

- the genes and heritage and childhood of a person that affect a person so much.
- every minute and hour and day and month and breath and thought the person has lived.
- every trial and temptation the person has experienced.
- every thought and longing and hope the person has had.

Only God knows all this and all the multitudes of ramifications of each of these. Therefore, only God can judge. But as stated, we are tempted to judge when we see a person commit open sin and another person do good works. But we must not judge, for only God sees and knows everything about a person. Note how clearly Scripture states this fact.

⇒ We do not clearly see the sins of people—not always. The sins of some people are clearly seen, and they make no attempt to hide them. These people shall suffer judgment; their sins definitely point to judgment. But some people are secret sinners; they hide their sins behind closed doors and in the dark. Their sins and judgment will be exposed later—in the terrible day of judgment.

⇒ Likewise, the good works of some people are clearly seen, but the good works of others are not seen.

The point is this: we have no way to tell what is in a person's heart and life, what he is doing and thinking every moment of every day. We cannot even know our spouses or children or parents that well—not well enough to judge them. Judgment is to be left up to God, not to men—not even to ministers. In fact, the minister himself is charged: leave the judgment up to God.

"Do not judge, or you too will be judged. For in the same way you judge others, you will be judged, and with the measure you use, it will be measured to you. (Mat 7:1-2)

Be merciful, just as your Father is merciful. "Do not judge, and you will not be judged. Do not condemn, and you will not be condemned. Forgive, and you will be forgiven. (Luke 6:36-37)

You, therefore, have no excuse, you who pass judgment on someone else, for at whatever point you judge the other, you are condemning yourself, because you who pass judgment do the same things. (Rom 2:1)

Who are you to judge someone else's servant? To his own master he stands or falls. And he will stand, for the Lord is able to make him stand. (Rom 14:4)

Therefore let us stop passing judgment on one another. Instead, make up your mind not to put any stumbling block or obstacle in your brother's way. (Rom 14:13)

Therefore judge nothing before the appointed time; wait till the Lord comes. He will bring to light what is hidden in darkness and will expose the motives of men's hearts. At that time each will receive his praise from God. (1 Cor 4:5)

Because judgment without mercy will be shown to anyone who has not been merciful. Mercy triumphs over judgment! (James 2:13)

Not many of you should presume to be teachers, [judges] my brothers, because you know that we who teach will be judged more strictly. (James 3:1)

There is only one Lawgiver and Judge, the one who is able to save and destroy. But you—who are you to judge your neighbor? (James 4:12)

Don't grumble against each other, brothers, or you will be judged. The Judge is standing at the door! (James 5:9)

1 TIMOTHY 6:1-2

	CHAPTER 6
	
	H. The Believing Slaves or Employees, 6:1-2
	
	All who are under the yoke of slavery should consider their masters worthy of full respect, so that God's name and our teaching may not be slandered.
		2 Those who have believing masters are not to show less respect for them because they are brothers. Instead, they are to serve them even better, because those who benefit from their service are believers, and dear to them. These are the things you are to teach and urge on them.	2 Duty toward the Christian master (employer)
			  a. Duty 1: Do not show disrespect—they are brothers
			  b. Duty 2: Give greater service—faithfulness bears fruit

1 Duty toward any master (employer)
  a. Duty: Respect
  b. Reason: To avoid reproach			

DIVISION III

BEHAVIOR AND RELATIONSHIPS IN THE CHURCH, 3:14-6:21

H. The Believing Slaves or Employees, 6:1-2

(6:1-2) Introduction: William Barclay points out that there were millions and millions of slaves in the Roman Empire during the days of Paul. He says that there were over sixty million (*The Letters to the Philippians, Colossians, and Thessalonians*, p.141). The gospel was bound to reach many of these, and the churches all over the Empire were bound to be filled with slaves. For this reason the New Testament has much to say to slaves (1 Cor.7:21-22; Col.3:22; 4:1; 1 Tim.6:1-2; Tit.2:9-10; 1 Pt.2:18-25 and the whole book of Philemon is written about a slave named Onesimus). However, slavery is never directly attacked by the New Testament. If it had been, there would have probably been so much bloodshed the scene would have been unimaginable! The slave owners and government would have...

- attacked the church, its preachers and believers, seeking to destroy such a doctrine.
- imprisoned and executed any who refused to be silent about such a doctrine.
- reacted and killed all of the slaves who professed Christ.

The Expositors Greek Testament has an excellent statement on how Christianity went about destroying slavery. It is found in the commentary on Eph.6:5.

> "Here, as elsewhere in the NT, slavery is accepted as an existing institution, which is neither formally condemned nor formally approved. There is nothing to prompt revolutionary action, or to encourage repudiation of the position...the institution is left to be undermined and removed by the gradual operation of the great Christian principles of...
> - *the equality of men in the sight of God*
> - *a common Christian brotherhood*
> - *the spiritual freedom of the Christian man*
> - *the Lordship of Christ to which every other lordship is subordinate*" (S.D.F. Salmond. *The Epistle to the Ephesians*. "The Expositor's Greek Testament," Vol.3, ed. by W. Robertson Nicoll. Grand Rapids, MI: Eerdmans, 1970, p.377).

The instructions to slaves and masters in the New Testament are applicable to every generation of workman. As Francis Foulkes says, "...the principles of the whole section apply to employees and employers in every age, whether in the home, in business, or in the state" (*The Epistle of Paul to the Ephesians*. "Tyndale New Testament Commentaries." Grand Rapids, MI: Eerdmans, no date listed, p.167).

1. Duty toward any master (employer) (v.1).
2. Duty toward the Christian master (employer) (v.2).

1 (6:1) Slaves—Employers—Workmen: there is the slave's or workman's duty toward an unbelieving master (employer). The word "yoke" (*zugon*) means to be under bondage, enslaved, weighed down ever so heavily. Paul does not hesitate to call slavery just what it is: a yoke that does not belong upon any man. Paul is expressing a heartfelt compassion for the slaves.

Now, note the specific instructions of this passage. The duty of the slave or workman is to count his master (employer) worthy of all honor. That is...

- to respect, comply, obey, and do what the employer says and requires.
- to do a job and to do it well.
- to be thankful and appreciative for having work to do.

This is especially true when a workman commits his life to Christ. If the workman does not give a full day's work for a full day's wage, he dishonors the name of Christ. If the workman is lazy, slothful, and beating time, or if he is disrespectful, the employer knows something: the God of the new convert is a laugh, for He is inactive and dead. God has made no difference in the life of the workman. Therefore, the superior blasphemes the name of God and the teachings of the gospel.

Thought 1. An excellent application of this point is given by Oliver Greene that merits quoting in full.

> "I personally know dear men today who have been fired by their employer because they talked too much about Jesus while they were on the job; and I have also known professing Christians who did not give their employer a good day's work for the salary received, and that is not right. It is not right for Christians to use company time to witness on the job. If one can witness without robbing his employer, that is fine; but a Christian's testimony will be hurt by his being seen talking when he should be working, even though he may be talking with an unsaved person about the grace of God and the saving power of Jesus. In Romans 14:16 Paul tells us, 'Let not then your good be evil spoken of.' Christians

must be 'wise as serpents and harmless as doves.' Any Christian who has an employer must render to that employer a good day's work and proper respect, lest reproach be brought upon the Gospel.

"Young man, young woman—if you are a Christian, do not be any less alert and on the job when the boss is absent than you are when he is looking at you. Your earthly master may not always be watching you, but the Heavenly Master sees and knows all that you do. So whether your job is that of superintendent in a huge plant or janitor in a small office, never forget that if you do not give your employer a good day's work in the right spirit, you are bringing reproach upon the name of Jesus" (*The Epistles of Paul the Apostle to Timothy and Titus*, p.212f).

2 (6:2) **Slaves—Employees**: there is the slave's or workman's duty toward a believing master (employer). It is a wonderful thing when a Christian workman can have a Christian employer, for the workman can expect to be treated justly and fairly and in a brotherly spirit. However, the workman faces a serious danger, the danger of feeling that he...

- should be given special treatment.
- should be allowed to slack off some.
- should be treated with more leniency.
- should be given more consideration.
- should not be as readily corrected or rebuked for inefficiency or mistakes.

In the case of slaves in the Roman empire, or for that matter anywhere else, the slave would have faced the temptation to *despise or be disrespectful* of his master. He could have easily felt that a master, upon becoming a believer, should grant his freedom or at least show some favor. However, the fact that a master became a Christian did not mean that a believing slave was to appeal for better and easier treatment. On the contrary, the believing slave was to become the best worker he could because the master was now a Christian believer.

Once the believing slave became the best worker possible—once he began to work diligently as though he was working for Christ—then he could expect to reap some benefits from having a Christian master. He could expect to reap benefits such as fair and decent and brotherly treatment. Believing slaves were to treat believing masters as brothers, faithful and beloved, and there was to be a greater testimony because of greater production and efficiency and fruitfulness.

The point is this: the Christian workman is to give great service to a Christian employer because faithfulness bears fruit. Both the workman and employer doing the best they can will bear more fruit of the Spirit and a greater production of work. Thereby they will together bear a greater testimony for Christ.

> **Thought 1.** In reality, being a slave or a master has nothing to do with one's commitment to life and work. The believing Christian, whether slave or master, is to do the very best he can at whatever he is doing. One's state of condition or environment or circumstance has nothing to do with faithfulness to one's work. One is to do his very best no matter who or where one is. (See note—1 Cor.7:20-23; 7:24. Cp.Eph.6:6-7; Col.3:23-25.)

> **Slaves [workmen], obey your earthly masters with respect and fear, and with sincerity of heart, just as you would obey Christ. Obey them not only to win their favor when their eye is on you, but like slaves of Christ, doing the will of God from your heart. Serve wholeheartedly, as if you were serving the Lord, not men, because you know that the Lord will reward everyone for whatever good he does, whether he is slave or free. (Eph 6:5-8)**

> **Slaves, obey your earthly masters in everything; and do it, not only when their eye is on you and to win their favor, but with sincerity of heart and reverence for the Lord. Whatever you do, work at it with all your heart, as working for the Lord, not for men, since you know that you will receive an inheritance from the Lord as a reward. It is the Lord Christ you are serving. Anyone who does wrong will be repaid for his wrong, and there is no favoritism. (Col 3:22-25)**

1 TIMOTHY 6:3-5

	I. The False Teachers, 6:3-5	unhealthy interest in controversies and quarrels about words that result in envy, strife, malicious talk, evil suspicions	2 He is conceited
			3 He has a sick interest in controversial questions
1 He teaches a different doctrine a. Does not agree to the sound teachings of Christ b. Does not agree to godly teaching	3 If anyone teaches false doctrines and does not agree to the sound instruction of our Lord Jesus Christ and to godly teaching, 4 He is conceited and understands nothing. He has an	5 And constant friction between men of corrupt mind, who have been robbed of the truth and who think that godliness is a means to financial gain.	4 He has a corrupt mind & is destitute of the truth 5 He thinks religion leads to financial gain

DIVISION III

BEHAVIOR AND RELATIONSHIPS IN THE CHURCH, 3:14-6:21

I. The False Teachers, 6:3-5

(6:3-5) **Introduction**: this is a most serious and critical passage, a passage that the church must constantly study in order to keep its message and ministry pure. It deals with those who fill the pulpit and classrooms of the church, whether the positions are filled by true teachers or false teachers. Every minister, teacher, leader, and member must heed and search his heart over this description of the false teacher.
1. He teaches a different doctrine (v.3).
2. He is conceited (v.4).
3. He has a sick interest in controversial questions (v.4).
4. He has a corrupt mind and is destitute of the truth (v.5).
5. He thinks religion leads to financial gain (v.5).

1 (6:3) **Teacher, False**: the false teacher teaches a different doctrine (heterodidaskalei). (See note—1 Tim.1:3 for more discussion.) He does not teach the words of the Lord Jesus Christ. This is a terrible indictment. Imagine being in the pulpit of a Christian church and claiming to be a teacher of the Lord Jesus Christ, yet not teaching His words. How many of us are guilty of this indictment? How many of us are guilty of teaching a different, false doctrine? Two reasons are given as to why the false teacher teaches a different doctrine.
1. The false teacher does not agree to the sound teachings of our Lord Jesus Christ. The word "agree" (proserchomai) means *approach* and has the sense of "attaching oneself to" Christ (Daniel Guthrie. *The Pastoral Epistles*. "Tyndale New Testament Commentaries," p.110f). The false teacher is just not willing to attach himself to the *Lord Jesus Christ*. He is...
- not willing to confess that Jesus is the *Lord God* from heaven, the very Son of God Himself.
- not willing to confess that Jesus is the Christ, the Messiah and Savior of the world.

2. The false teacher does not agree to godly teaching. He is...
- not willing to accept the righteousness of God revealed in Jesus Christ.
- not willing to separate himself from the world nor to set his life wholly apart unto God.

One or both of these reasons are why the false teacher does not teach the wholesome words of Christ, but rather chooses to teach a different doctrine and way of life. He has committed his life to the *profession* of the ministry...
- as a way to serve mankind.
- as a way to earn a livelihood.

But he is not committed to represent Christ and His Word. As a result, the person is called a false teacher by both the Holy Scriptures and Christ.

> I am astonished that you are so quickly deserting the one who called you by the grace of Christ and are turning to a different gospel—which is really no gospel at all. Evidently some people are throwing you into confusion and are trying to pervert the gospel of Christ. But even if we or an angel from heaven should preach a gospel other than the one we preached to you, let him be eternally condemned! As we have already said, so now I say again: If anybody is preaching to you a gospel other than what you accepted, let him be eternally condemned! (Gal 1:6-9)

> Then they understood that he was not telling them to guard against the yeast used in bread, but against the teaching of the Pharisees and Sadducees. (Mat 16:12)

> See to it that no one takes you captive through hollow and deceptive philosophy, which depends on human tradition and the basic principles of this world rather than on Christ. (Col 2:8)

> Do not be carried away by all kinds of strange teachings. (Heb 13:9)

2 (6:4) **Teacher, False—Pride**: the false teacher is conceited (tetuphotai). The word means *puffed up* and proud. But note: the word includes the idea of folly; it lacks good sense. Rejecting the evidence that Jesus is the Lord—the Lord Jesus Christ—is the height of pride and folly. Such rejection just lacks good sense (source unknown).

The false teacher takes pride...
- in his views and ideas.
- in his rejection of certain portions of the Bible.
- in his knowledge that some of the stories and events in the Bible are what he calls fables.
- in his intellectual ability to dissect the truth from the falsehood about Christ.
- in his enlightenment—that he knows better than to believe in such things as the miracles, deity, virgin birth, incarnation, resurrection, ascension and the personal return of Christ to earth.
- in his new and novel concepts and ideas about Christ.

The list could go on and on, but all ministers have detected this pride in discussions with other ministers. And, tragically, we have all been guilty of feeling pride over our own ideas before. William Barclay has an excellent comment on the pride of the false teacher:

> *"His first characteristic is conceit. His first aim is self-display. His desire is not to display Christ, but to display himself. There are still preachers and teachers who are more concerned to gain a following for themselves than for Jesus Christ. They are more concerned to press their own views upon people than they are to bring to men the word of God. When people meet together for worship they are not concerned to listen to what any man thinks; they are eager to hear what God says. The great preacher and teacher is not a purveyor of his own ideas; he is an echo of God"* (*The Letters to Timothy, Titus, and Philemon*, p.146).

3 (6:4) **Teachers, False:** the false teacher has a sick interest in controversial questions. When preparing to preach and teach, the false teacher does not rely upon the primary source, the Word of God itself. He relies upon secondary sources, that is, books *about* the Bible.

The Bible just is not the basis for his life nor for his preaching and teaching. The false teacher rejects the primary source (the Bible), and turns to secondary sources *about* the Bible. In some cases, he does not even know how to study the Bible. His interest lies...

- in trying to *discover* the truth in the Bible, not in proclaiming the truth of the Bible.
- in *questioning* what is true and not true instead of living out what the Bible says.

The result, of course, is what we so often see written in the faces and minds of the false teacher and those who sit under him: many thoughts and moments of...

- disturbance and lack of peace
- emptiness and lack of purpose
- questioning and lack of meaning
- wondering if God really does exist
- wondering if there is really any meaning to religion and worship
- wondering if there is a world or life beyond this earth

Why? Because what the human heart craves is God and His Word, the knowledge and assurance of Him and His guidance.

This is only reasonable and to be expected, for God is bound to have put within man a deep, natural hunger for Him and His Word. Therefore, what the human heart craves, even the heart of the false teacher, is not controversial questions and arguments over the "sound instruction of our Lord Jesus Christ" or of the Bible. What the heart craves is to hear from God, to hear the *authoritative proclamation of the Word of God itself*.

> **For the appeal we make does not spring from error or impure motives, nor are we trying to trick you. On the contrary, we speak as men approved by God to be entrusted with the gospel. We are not trying to please men but God, who tests our hearts. (1 Th 2:3-4)**
>
> **And we also thank God continually because, when you received the word of God, which you heard from us, you accepted it not as the word of men, but as it actually is, the word of God, which is at work in you who believe. (1 Th 2:13)**
>
> **As I urged you when I went into Macedonia, stay there in Ephesus so that you may command certain men not to teach false doctrines any longer nor to devote themselves to myths and endless genealogies. These promote controversies rather than God's work—which is by faith. The goal of this command is love, which comes from a pure heart and a good conscience and a sincere faith. Some have wandered away from these and turned to meaningless talk. They want to be teachers of the law, but they do not know what they are talking about or what they so confidently affirm. (1 Tim 1:3-7)**
>
> **He is conceited and understands nothing. He has an unhealthy interest in controversies and quarrels about words that result in envy, strife, malicious talk, evil suspicions (1 Tim 6:4)**
>
> **But women will be saved through childbearing—if they continue in faith, love and holiness with propriety. (1 Tim 2:15)**
>
> **Don't have anything to do with foolish and stupid arguments, because you know they produce quarrels. And the Lord's servant must not quarrel; instead, he must be kind to everyone, able to teach, not resentful. (2 Tim 2:23-24)**
>
> **All Scripture is God-breathed and is useful for teaching, rebuking, correcting and training in righteousness, (2 Tim 3:16)**
>
> **But avoid foolish controversies and genealogies and arguments and quarrels about the law, because these are unprofitable and useless. Warn a divisive person once, and then warn him a second time. After that, have nothing to do with him. You may be sure that such a man is warped and sinful; he is self-condemned. (Titus 3:9-11)**
>
> **And we have the word of the prophets made more certain, and you will do well to pay attention to it, as to a light shining in a dark place, until the day dawns and the morning star rises in your hearts. Above all, you must understand that no prophecy of Scripture came about by the prophet's own interpretation. For prophecy never had its origin in the will of man, but men spoke from God as they were carried along by the Holy Spirit. (2 Pet 1:19-21)**

4 (6:5) **Teacher, False:** the false teacher has a corrupt mind and is destitute of the truth. His mind is corrupt in that it is not centered upon teaching the "sound instruction of our Lord Jesus Christ," (the Word of God, the Scriptures, the Bible. v.3). His mind...

- focuses upon the doctrines and theologies of men.
- focuses upon the psychologies and philosophies of men.

- focuses upon man's own energy and self-improvement, upon building up man's ego and self-image.
- focuses upon the latest religions or theological ideas.
- focuses upon the popular religious discussions that please and tickle men's ears.

The point is this: the false teacher does not focus upon the truth, the Word of God. He is destitute and empty of the truth. He does not possess nor teach the truth. He is bankrupt when it comes to the truth. However, note this: what the false teacher teaches often helps us do better. It often helps to build our ego and self-image and to achieve more in this life. Some self-help preaching is just like some self-help programs, clinics, and seminars conducted all across the nation: they are excellent in so far as they go. But they have one serious flaw: *they do not go far enough.* They do not show...

- that God is really with us and looking after us as we walk upon earth.
- that Jesus Christ has really died for our sins and risen to give us life—life that goes on forever.
- that God has really forgiven our sins and accepted us in Christ.
- that when we die, God will immediately transfer us into His presence to live with Him forever.

This kind of absolute, deep, intense assurance is missing in the false teacher and in anyone else whose mind is not focused upon "sound instruction of our Lord Jesus Christ," that is, the Word of God (v.3).

> Furthermore, since they did not think it worthwhile to retain the knowledge of God, he gave them over to a depraved mind, to do what ought not to be done [immoral]. (Rom 1:28)
>
> The sinful mind is hostile to God. It does not submit to God's law, nor can it do so. (Rom 8:7)
>
> So I tell you this, and insist on it in the Lord, that you must no longer live as the Gentiles do, in the futility of their thinking. (Eph 4:17)
>
> Do not let anyone who delights in false humility and the worship of angels disqualify you for the prize. Such a person goes into great detail about what he has seen, and his unspiritual mind puffs him up with idle notions. (Col 2:18)
>
> To the pure, all things are pure, but to those who are corrupted and do not believe, nothing is pure. In fact, both their minds and consciences are corrupted. (Titus 1:15)

5 (6:5) **Teacher, False**: the false teacher thinks religion leads to financial gain. This means at least three things.

1. Some false teachers *are concerned* with morality and virtue and with man being the best and achieving the most that he can. They believe in God, not necessarily in Christ, but in God. Therefore, they know the answer to making man and his world better is religion. Hence, they commit their lives to God and religion, to getting men to do the works of religion and to living more righteous and moral lives. They want people to be good and to do good. They think that "godliness is a means to financial gain," that it helps and benefits man and his world.

Thought 1. Note that the false teacher is right on this point: the moral teaching of religion—living moral and upright lives—is good for man. But as pointed out above, works and self-help ministers do not go far enough. They do not focus upon God's Son, the Lord Jesus Christ. And God will never accept anyone who *does not honor* His Son, for He has only one Son who is begotten of Him. That Son, the Lord Jesus Christ, is loved by God. God loves His Son with His whole being, for His Son has the very nature of God Himself. Christ has always obeyed the Father—has always lived a perfectly godly life just as the Father willed. Therefore, anyone who honors Christ shall be honored and accepted by the Father. But the converse is also true: anyone who does not honor Christ will not be honored by the Father. The craving of man's heart for God and His Word—for the deep, intense knowledge and assurance of God—comes only through Christ. Therefore, as good as they are, religion and good works do not go far enough. They do not make a person acceptable to God. God accepts only one thing: faith in Christ, His only Son. (See notes, *Justification*—1 Tim.2:3-7; Ro.5:1 for more discussion.)

> "For God so loved the world that he gave his one and only Son, that whoever believes in him shall not perish but have eternal life. For God did not send his Son into the world to condemn the world, but to save the world through him. Whoever believes in him is not condemned, but whoever does not believe stands condemned already because he has not believed in the name of God's one and only Son. (John 3:16-18)
>
> "I tell you the truth, whoever hears my word and believes him who sent me has eternal life and will not be condemned; he has crossed over from death to life. (John 5:24)
>
> Jesus answered, "I am the way and the truth and the life. No one comes to the Father except through me. (John 14:6)
>
> Therefore, since we have been justified through faith, we have peace with God through our Lord Jesus Christ, (Rom 5:1)
>
> But God demonstrates his own love for us in this: While we were still sinners, Christ died for us. (Rom 5:8)
>
> We are therefore Christ's ambassadors, as though God were making his appeal through us. We implore you on Christ's behalf: Be reconciled to God. (2 Cor 5:20)

2. Some false teachers enter the ministry as a profession and as a means to make a living. They probably have some concern for the religious welfare of people, but the major consideration in choosing to enter the ministry was this: they thought it would be a good and commendable profession and provide a good livelihood for them and their present or future family.

3. Some false teachers have commercialized religion. The false teacher is "out for profit. He looks on his teaching and preaching, not as a vocation, but as a career. He is in the business, not to serve others, but to advance

himself" (William Barclay. *The Letters to Timothy, Titus, and Philemon*, p.148).

Thought 1. Man-centered and self-help teaching is helpful, but it does not belong in the pulpit of God's church; it belongs in the conference rooms and halls of the secular world. The church must be kept pure and free in proclaiming the gospel and the supreme love of God demonstrated in His Son, the Lord Jesus Christ. If the human race fails to keep the pure Word of God flowing from the pulpits of God's church, then the human race is doomed. Why? Because when we die, that will be it. We shall be separated from God eternally. For God will only accept us if we approach Him in Christ. Therefore, the critical hour for man will always be when he sits under the preaching of the Word of God and listens to "the sound instruction of our Lord Jesus Christ and to godly teaching." When man hears the Word of God preached, he must respond and do as God says.

> I urge you, brothers, to watch out for those who cause divisions and put obstacles in your way that are contrary to the teaching you have learned. Keep away from them. (Rom 16:17)

> In the name of the Lord Jesus Christ, we command you, brothers, to keep away from every brother who is idle and does not live according to the teaching you received from us. (2 Th 3:6)

> If anyone teaches false doctrines and does not agree to the sound instruction of our Lord Jesus Christ and to godly teaching, he is conceited and understands nothing. He has an unhealthy interest in controversies and quarrels about words that result in envy, strife, malicious talk, evil suspicions and constant friction between men of corrupt mind, who have been robbed of the truth and who think that godliness is a means to financial gain. (1 Tim 6:3-5)

> Having a form of godliness but denying its power. Have nothing to do with them. (2 Tim 3:5)

> If anyone comes to you and does not bring this teaching, do not take him into your house or welcome him. Anyone who welcomes him shares in his wicked work. (2 John 1:10-11)

1 TIMOTHY 6:6-10

	J. The Secret of Contentment, 6:6-10	9 People who want to get rich fall into temptation and a trap and into many foolish and harmful desires that plunge men into ruin and destruction.
		10 For the love of money is a root of all kinds of evil. Some people, eager for money, have wandered from the faith and pierced themselves with many griefs.
			2 The secret to contentment is not money
			  a. It tempts & enslaves
			  b. It can cause many foolish & harmful desires
			  c. It plunges men into destruction
			  d. It—the love of money—is the root of all evil
			    1) Causes wandering
			    2) Causes acute mental anguish

1 The secret to contentment is godliness
  a. At birth—we brought nothing into the world
  b. At death—we take nothing out of the world
  c. Conclusion: Be content with necessities
	6 But godliness with contentment is great gain.
	7 For we brought nothing into the world, and we can take nothing out of it.
	8 But if we have food and clothing, we will be content with that.		

DIVISION III

BEHAVIOR AND RELATIONSHIPS IN THE CHURCH, 3:14-6:21

J. The Secret of Contentment, 6:6-10

(6:6-10) **Introduction**: every person strives for contentment. Contentment is the one thing we all want. We want to be fulfilled, complete, satisfied, completely self-sufficient. But when we look around, this is not what we see. What we see is a society and a world discontented, about as unfulfilled, incomplete, dissatisfied, empty, lonely, and restless as they can be. Why? Why are so many people discontented? Why are few people truly contented? This is the importance of this passage: *the secret of contentment*.

1. The secret to contentment is godliness (v.6-8).
2. The secret to contentment is not money (v.9-10).

1 (6:6-8) **Contentment—Godliness—Wealth**: the secret to contentment is godliness. "Contentment" (autarkeias) means to be *completely sufficient*, to need absolutely nothing. It means to be fulfilled, satisfied, and complete. Imagine a person who feels *wholly complete and sufficient*, who lacks absolutely nothing. This is what Scripture means by contentment. What makes a person content? What brings such contentment to the human soul? Scripture pulls no punches; it unequivocally states that it is *godliness*. Godliness alone can make a person content. Godliness alone can take a person and make him...

- fulfilled
- satisfied
- complete
- sufficient

Godliness alone can give man the sense that he lacks absolutely nothing. Imagine being so contented—so fulfilled, so satisfied, so completed, so sufficient—that you sense no lack. You just sense no need whatsoever within your innermost being and soul. This is exactly what godliness does for the human soul. This is the reason Scripture declares that godliness with contentment is great gain. No greater gain could ever come to a person than contentment.

Note that Scripture wants us to think about the three stages of life for a moment:

⇒ there is the stage of birth. At birth we brought nothing into this world. When we entered the world, we came with only two things: our bodies and life. Beyond these we were stark naked. We had nothing else.

⇒ There is the stage of death. Note that the fact of death is an absolute certainty. At death, we carry nothing—absolutely nothing—out of this world. We leave this world just as we entered it, with nothing.

⇒ There is the stage that is between birth and death—the stage of life. Life is entirely different from birth and death. There are some things that we need during life: necessities that we must have to sustain life. We need food, clothing, and shelter. The Greek word (skepasmata) for *clothing* literally means covering: it is applicable both to clothing and shelter. In order to live and complete our lives upon earth, we *need* food, clothing, and shelter. But note: we *need* nothing else. We can live and sustain life if we have these things. Therefore, a person is to be content with these. Remember the point of these verses: the secret of contentment is godliness. Godliness with contentment is *great gain*.

The point is driven home by a series of statements taken from Matthew Henry:

"If a man [has]...enough to carry him through [this world], he needs desire no more, his godliness...will be his great gain."

"Godliness is itself great gain; it is profitable to all things."

"Wherever there is true godliness, there will be contentment."

"The highest pitch of contentment [is] godliness [which makes the] happiest people in this world."

"Christian contentment...is all the wealth in the world."

"He that is godly is sure to be happy in another world."

"Godliness with contentment, this is the way to gain."

"A Christian's gain is great: it is not like the little gain of worldlings, who are so fond of a little worldly advantage."

"All truly godly people have learned with Paul: 'I have learned in whatsoever state I am, therewith to be content'" (Ph.4:11). (*Matthew Henry's Commentary*, Vol.6, p.828.)

A striking point is made by William Barclay in his Daily Study Bible (*The Letters to Timothy, Titus, and Philemon*, p.150).

"It is not that Christianity pleads for poverty. There is no special virtue in being poor, and no happiness in having a constant struggle to make ends meet. But Christianity does plead for two things.
1. 'It pleads for the realization that it is never in the power of things to bring happiness.'
2. 'It pleads for the concentration upon the things which are permanent, the things that a man can take with him when in the end he dies.'"

I am not saying this because I am in need, for I have learned to be content whatever the circumstances. (Phil 4:11)

But godliness with contentment is great gain. But if we have food and clothing, we will be content with that. (1 Tim 6:6, 8)

Keep your lives [behavior] free from the love of money and be content with what you have, because God has said, "Never will I leave you; never will I forsake you." (Heb 13:5)

Better a little with the fear of the LORD than great wealth with turmoil. (Prov 15:16)

2 (6:9-10) **Wealth—Riches—Money, Love of**: the secret to contentment is not money. This is shocking, for the rich cling and hoard their money, and the rest of mankind is forever seeking to get more and more money. But God is clear about the matter: money and wealth do not bring contentment. There are four reasons why this is true.

1. Money tempts and enslaves. How can money tempt and enslave? The answer is clearly seen. A person with money…
- can buy anything he wants when he wants.
- can go wherever he wants when he wants.
- can do just about anything he wants when he wants.

This is power within the world—what we might call worldly power. A person who has the power to buy anything, go anywhere, and do whatever he wants has worldly power.

The point is this: a person who has such power—the money to buy anything, go anywhere, and do anything—is always tempted. He is tempted to live selfishly and to hoard what he has. He is always tempted…
- to keep on buying and buying.
- to keep on going and going.
- to keep on doing and doing.

The rich are far more tempted to indulge the flesh (sinful nature) and to live extravagantly—far more tempted to live selfishly and to control and dominate people through the power of their wealth.

The rich and they who would be rich are never free from the bombardment of temptation. Therefore, the rich person never has peace. He never possesses contentment, not inward completeness and satisfaction. He never feels completely fulfilled and sufficient. This is the first reason money does not bring contentment. Money brings a bombardment of temptation, and it ensnares men in sin.

2. Money can cause many foolish and harmful desires. Think how foolish and harmful some of these things are.
⇒ How foolish are closets full of clothing: a person can wear only one set of clothing at a time and there are only so many different kinds of clothing. How foolish is it to have closets full of clothing that we can seldom wear?
⇒ How foolish is extravagance in clothes? Labels on clothes? An expensive store and an inexpensive chain store will carry the very same clothing made by the same manufacturer. Is it wise or foolish to buy the expensive clothing because of a small label with a different name?
⇒ How foolish is extravagance in eating? Eating and eating and eating—training our bodies to crave and crave more and more food. Is it foolish or wise to damage the body?
⇒ How foolish is indulgence in smoking? Walking around like a smoke stack damaging our bodies.
⇒ How foolish and harmful is selling and giving our bodies over to intoxicating drink, drugs, immorality, and greed?
⇒ How foolish and harmful is it to…
- crave and crave?
- lust and lust?
- hoard and hoard?
- indulge and indulge?
- secure and secure?
- possess and possess?

How foolish and harmful is it to feed our desires and lusts with the things, possessions, and niceties of this world when millions upon millions are hopeless and helpless and going to bed hungry, cold, and sick—all dying from lack of food, clothing, shelter, and disease? And, most tragic of all—dying without Christ and without any hope of living eternally with God. As stated, money can cause many foolish and harmful desires.

3. Money plunges men into ruin and destruction. The word "plunge" (buthizo) is a descriptive picture of wealth being "a personal monster, which plunges its victims into an ocean of complete destruction" (Donald Guthrie. *The Pastoral Epistles*. "Tyndale New Testament Commentaries," p.113). The idea is this: the person who falls into the foolish and harmful desires of this world shall be utterly destroyed and ruined, both in body and soul. And the destruction and ruin shall be for eternity (A.T. Robertson. *Word Pictures in the New Testament*, Vol.4, p.593).

For, as I have often told you before and now say again even with tears, many live as enemies of the cross of Christ. Their destiny is destruction, their god is their stomach, and their glory is in their shame. Their mind is on earthly things. (Phil 3:18-19)

While people are saying, "Peace and safety," destruction will come on them suddenly, as labor pains on a pregnant woman, and they will not escape. (1 Th 5:3)

And give relief to you who are troubled, and to us as well. This will happen when the Lord Jesus is revealed from heaven in blazing fire with his powerful angels. He will punish those who do not know God and do not obey the gospel of our Lord Jesus. They will be punished with everlasting destruction and shut out from the presence of the Lord and from the majesty of his power (2 Th 1:7-9)

People who want to get rich fall into temptation and a trap and into many foolish and harmful desires that plunge men into ruin and destruction. (1 Tim 6:9)

But we are not of those who shrink back and are destroyed, but of those who believe and are saved. (Heb 10:39)

4. Money—that is, the love of money—is a root of all kinds of evil. Note the three reasons why:
⇒ The love of money causes people to covet, and covetousness is idolatry.
⇒ The love of money causes people to wander away from the faith. It causes people to go after the lusts of this world.
⇒ The love of money causes people to pierce themselves with many griefs. The things, possessions, and lusts of this world do not satisfy nor fulfill a person's heart and life. Money cannot bring contentment to a person. The love of money only consumes and eats a person with grief (A.T. Robertson. *Word Pictures in the New Testament*, Vol.4, p.594). It pierces the heart with a void—the void of emptiness and worry, anxiety, and insecurity. Money cannot buy love, health, and deliverance from death. Money cannot buy God; it cannot buy assurance, not the assurance and confidence of living forever.

The point is this: a person craves the necessities of life; his very nature craves them. However, once man has the necessities of life, he discovers that he still craves for more. The necessities do not satisfy his inner craving and emptiness—his void, hunger, and thirst—for something more. Therefore, man seeks to satisfy his craving by getting more and more food, clothing and everything else he desires. He eats and eats, buys and buys, and goes after more and more comfort, ease, pleasure, wealth, money, and everything else he wants. But what man overlooks is this: the craving within his heart—the void, the hunger, the thirst—is not for more material possessions. It is for *spiritual satisfaction*, the *filling up* of another part of his being. His craving is for godliness. Therefore, once he has food and clothing, he has satisfied his physical craving. Enough food and clothing for today brings contentment today—but only physical contentment. What he needs after that is spiritual food, the satisfaction of his spiritual hunger. Man's contentment comes from having both his need for physical and spiritual food met. One without the other leaves him with some emptiness, some incompletion (Col.2:8-9). True contentment comes only from godliness.

Thought 1. "The love of money is a root of all kinds of evil." William Barclay points out that the great classical thinkers recognized this truth.
⇒ The great thinker Democritus said, "Love of money is the metropolis of all evils."
⇒ Seneca refers to "the desire for that which does not belong to us, from which every evil of the mind springs."
⇒ Phocylides says that "the love of money is the mother of all evils."
⇒ Philo refers to the "love of money which is the starting-place of the greatest transgressions of the Law."
⇒ Athenaeus quotes another thinker: "The belly's pleasure is the beginning and root of all evil."

William Barclay himself makes an excellent point that is worthy of note:

"Money in itself is neither good nor bad; it is simply dangerous in that the love of it may become bad. With money a man can do much good; and with money he can do much evil. With money a man can selfishly serve his own desires; and with money he can generously answer to the cry of his neighbour's need. With money a man can buy his way to the forbidden things and facilitate the path of wrong-doing; and with money he can make it easier for someone else to live as God meant him to live. Money is not an evil, but it is a great responsibility" (*The Letters to Timothy, Titus, and Philemon*, p.152).

1 TIMOTHY 6:11-16

	K. The Young Minister (Charge 4): To Be a Man of God, 6:11-16	testifying before Pontius Pilate made the good confession, I charge you	to quicken, to give life b. Because of Christ's example
1 Flee the passion for wealth (cp. v.9-10). 2 Pursue, follow after the things of God	11 But you, man of God, flee from all this, and pursue righteousness, godliness, faith, love, endurance and gentleness.	14 To keep this command without spot or blame until the appearing of our Lord Jesus Christ, 15 Which God will bring about in his own time—God, the blessed and only Ruler, the King of kings and Lord of lords,	c. Because Christ is to come again: He is to be exalted as King of kings and Lord of lords

3 Fight the fight of faith & lay hold of eternal life
  a. Are called to eternity
  b. Have witnessed to eternity
	12 Fight the good fight of the faith. Take hold of the eternal life to which you were called when you made your good confession in the presence of many witnesses.		

4 Keep this charge—keep this commandment (v.14) a. Because of God's power	13 In the sight of God, who gives life to everything, and of Christ Jesus, who while	16 Who alone is immortal and who lives in unapproachable light, whom no one has seen or can see. To him be honor and might forever. Amen.	d. Because Christ alone possesses immortality: He dwells in the transcendent e. Because Christ alone possesses an unapproachable light of God's great glory

DIVISION III

BEHAVIOR AND RELATIONSHIPS IN THE CHURCH, 3:14-6:21

K. The Young Minister (Charge 4): To Be a Man of God, 6:11-16

(6:11-16) **Introduction**: this is a straightforward charge to the minister of God. The minister is called the "*man of God.*" This is one of the great titles of the minister of God.
⇒ Moses was called "the man of God" (Dt.33:1; Ps.90, the title).
⇒ Eli was called a man of God (1 Sam.2:27).
⇒ Samuel was called a man of God (1 Sam.9:6).

A concordance will show how often the servants of God were called "the man of God." What a dynamic challenge to the minister: to be a "*man of God.*" Four charges are given to the *man of God*.
1. Flee the passion for wealth (v.11).
2. Pursue, follow after the things of God (v.11).
3. Fight the fight of faith and lay hold of eternal life (v.12).
4. Keep this charge—keep this commandment (v.13-16).

1 (6:11) **Minister—Duty**: the man of God flees the passion for wealth. A person is to flee the love of money—run away from all that has just been covered in verses 9-10. Note a shocking fact—shocking because so many people love money and the things it can buy:
⇒ the man who loves money is not a *man of God*. The man of God is the person who flees the love of money. (See former note—1 Tim.6:9-10 for more discussion.)

The man of God does not love the world nor seek after the things of the world. He flees from the love and passion of this world.

> Do not conform any longer to the pattern of this world, but be transformed by the renewing of your mind. Then you will be able to test and approve what God's will is—his good, pleasing and perfect will. (Rom 12:2)
>
> "Therefore come out from them and be separate, says the Lord. Touch no unclean thing, and I will receive you." "I will be a Father to you, and you will be my sons and daughters, says the Lord Almighty." (2 Cor 6:17-18)
>
> Do not love the world or anything in the world. If anyone loves the world, the love of the Father is not in him. For everything in the world—the cravings of sinful man, the lust of his eyes and the boasting of what he has and does—comes not from the Father but from the world. (1 John 2:15-16)

2 (6:11) **Minister**: the man of God pursues, follows after the things of God. The word "pursue" (dioke) is strong. It means to run after; to run swiftly after; to hotly pursue; to seek eagerly and earnestly. It has the idea of aiming at and pursuing until something is gained; of never giving up until we have reached our goal. There are six things the man of God is to pursue.

1. The man of God pursues righteousness (dikiaosune). Righteousness means two things.
  a. Righteousness means *being right* with God.
  ⇒ It is having a heart that is *right with God*, that has approached God exactly as He says: through His only Son, the Lord Jesus Christ.
  ⇒ It is having a heart that has *allowed God* to recreate and remake it *in righteousness*: through the Lord Jesus Christ.
  ⇒ It is having a heart that has participated in the divine nature of God (2 Pt.1:4).

> Blessed are those who hunger and thirst for righteousness, for they will be filled. (Mat 5:6)
>
> For I tell you that unless your righteousness surpasses that of the Pharisees and the teachers of the law, you will certainly not enter the kingdom of heaven. (Mat 5:20)
>
> Therefore, if anyone is in Christ, he is a new creation; the old has gone, the new has come! (2 Cor 5:17)
>
> That God was reconciling the world to himself in Christ, not counting men's sins against them. And he has committed to us the message of reconciliation. (2 Cor 5:19)
>
> And to put on the new self, created to be like God in true righteousness and holiness. (Eph 4:24)

b. Righteousness means *doing right*, that is, living exactly as God says to live. Simply stated, a righteous person is a person who *lives right*—a person who does his duty both to God and to man. He lives doing what he should do. He lives a righteous life, walking righteously before God and man day by day. As a result, he is free from guilt and has a free conscience and a strong self-image. The man of God follows and runs after righteousness.

> Come back to your senses as you ought, and stop sinning; for there are some who are ignorant of God—I say this to your shame. (1 Cor 15:34)
> Filled with the fruit of righteousness that comes through Jesus Christ—to the glory and praise of God. (Phil 1:11)

2. The man of God pursues godliness (eusebeian). Godliness means to live in the reverence and awe of God; to be *so conscious* of God's presence that one lives just as God would live if He were walking upon earth. It means to live seeking to be like God; to seek to possess the very character, nature, and behavior of God. The man of God follows and runs after godliness. He seeks to gain a consciousness of God's presence—a consciousness so intense that he actually lives as God would live if He were on earth.

Note: godliness means to be *Christlike*. Godliness is *Christlikeness*: it is living upon earth just as Christ lived.

> And we, who with unveiled faces all reflect the Lord's glory, are being transformed into his likeness with ever-increasing glory, which comes from the Lord, who is the Spirit. (2 Cor 3:18)
> And to put on the new self, created to be like God in true righteousness and holiness. (Eph 4:24)
> Set your minds on things above, not on earthly things. (Col 3:2)
> Have nothing to do with godless myths and old wives' tales; rather, train yourself to be godly. (1 Tim 4:7)
> It teaches us to say "No" to ungodliness and worldly passions, and to live self-controlled, upright and godly lives in this present age, while we wait for the blessed hope—the glorious appearing of our great God and Savior, Jesus Christ, (Titus 2:12-13)
> Since everything will be destroyed in this way, what kind of people ought you to be? You ought to live holy and godly lives (2 Pet 3:11)

3. The man of God pursues faith (pistin). Faith means both to believe and to be faithful.
⇒ The man of God seeks faith: to learn to trust God more and more; to be a man of faith, a man of great faith and belief. He wants to believe, trust, and depend upon God—to grow more and more in believing God.
⇒ The man of God seeks to be faithful: be faithful to God more and more. He wants to be loyal, obedient, and attached to God. He wants to please God in all that he does.

> Now it is required that those who have been given a trust must prove faithful. (1 Cor 4:2)
> On the contrary, we speak as men approved by God to be entrusted with the gospel. We are not trying to please men but God, who tests our hearts. (1 Th 2:4)
> I thank Christ Jesus our Lord, who has given me strength, that he considered me faithful, appointing me to his service. (1 Tim 1:12)

4. The man of God pursues love (see DEEPER STUDY # 1, *Love*—1 Th.3:12 for discussion).

5. The man of God pursues endurance (hupomonen) (see note, *Endurance* —2 Th.1:4-5 for discussion).

6. The man of God pursues gentleness (praupathian). Gentleness means to be tender, humble, mild, considerate, but strongly so. Gentleness has the strength to control and discipline, and it does so at the right time.
a. Gentleness has *a humble state of mind*. But this does not mean the person is weak, cowardly, and bowing. The meek person simply loves people and loves peace; therefore, he walks humbly among men regardless of their status and circumstance in life. Associating with the poor and lowly of this earth does not bother the gentle person. He desires to be a friend to all and to help all as much as possible.
b. Gentleness has *a strong state of mind*. It looks at situations and wants justice and right to be done. It is not a weak mind that ignores and neglects evil and wrong-doing, abuse and suffering.
⇒ If someone is suffering, gentleness steps in and does what it can to help.
⇒ If evil is being done, gentleness does what it can to stop and correct it.
⇒ If evil is running rampant and indulging itself, gentleness actually strikes out in anger. However, note a crucial point: the anger is always at the right time and against the right thing.

c. Gentleness has *strong self-control*. The gentle person controls his spirit and mind. He controls the lusts of his flesh (sinful nature). He does not give way to ill-temper, retaliation, passion, indulgence, or license. The gentle person dies to himself, to what his flesh would like to do, and he does the right thing—exactly what God wants done.

In summary, the gentle person walks in a humble, tender, but strong state of mind. He denies himself and gives utmost consideration to others. He shows a control and righteous anger against injustice and evil. A gentle man forgets self and lives for others because of what Christ has done for him.
⇒ God is gentle.

> But the fruit of the Spirit is love, joy, peace, patience, kindness, goodness, faithfulness, gentleness and self-control. Against such things there is no law. (Gal 5:22-23)

⇒ Jesus Christ was gentle.

> Take my yoke upon you and learn from me, for I am gentle and humble in heart, and you will find rest for your souls. (Mat 11:29)

1 TIMOTHY 6:11-16

⇒ Believers are to be gentle.

> **Brothers, if someone is caught in a sin, you who are spiritual should restore him gently. But watch yourself, or you also may be tempted. (Gal 6:1)**
>
> **As a prisoner for the Lord, then, I urge you to live a life worthy of the calling you have received. Be completely humble and gentle; be patient, bearing with one another in love. Make every effort to keep the unity of the Spirit through the bond of peace. (Eph 4:1-3)**
>
> **Those who oppose him he must gently instruct, in the hope that God will grant them repentance leading them to a knowledge of the truth, (2 Tim 2:25)**
>
> **To slander no one, to be peaceable and considerate, and to show true humility toward all men. (Titus 3:2)**
>
> **Therefore, get rid of all moral filth and the evil that is so prevalent and humbly accept the word planted in you, which can save you. (James 1:21)**
>
> **Who is wise and understanding among you? Let him show it by his good life, by deeds done in the humility that comes from wisdom. (James 3:13)**
>
> **Instead, it should be that of your inner self, the unfading beauty of a gentle and quiet spirit, which is of great worth in God's sight. (1 Pet 3:4)**

3 (6:12) **Minister**: the man of God must fight the good fight of faith and lay hold of eternal life. This is a picture of an athletic contest. The word fight (agonizou) means to agonize, struggle, battle, contend, and fight for the prize. It is the idea of a *desperate effort and struggle*.

Note: the believer is in a desperate struggle for eternal life. Laying hold of the prize of eternal life is the struggle. Eternal life is the goal for which the man of God is fighting. Matthew Henry described it well:

> *"Those who will get to heaven must fight their way there. There must be a conflict with corruption and temptations and...the power of darkness. Observe. It is a good fight, it is a good cause, and it will have a good [end and purpose]...Observe...*
>
> *"Eternal life is the crown proposed to us, forever encouragement to war, and to fight...*
>
> *"This we must lay hold on [eternal life], as those that are afraid of coming short of it and losing it. Lay hold, and take heed of losing your hold....*
>
> *"We are called to the fight, and to lay hold on eternal life"* (Matthew Henry's Commentary, Vol.6, p.830).

Kenneth Wuest says, *"Paul exhorts Timothy to lay hold of eternal life, he does not imply that he does not possess it. Timothy was saved, and possessed eternal life as a gift of God. What Paul was desirous of was that Timothy experience more of what this eternal life is in his life"* (The Pastoral Epistles, "Wuest's Word Studies," Vol.2. Grand Rapids, MI: Eerdmans, 1952, p.98).

Note an extremely significant point: what the profession of a minister is. When a man commits his life to the ministry, he is professing...

- that he believes in eternal life—that eternal life is a reality.
- that he and all others who trust Christ shall live forever.

He professes the reality of eternal life before "many witnesses"—all who know him and come in contact with him.

The point is this: the man of God must live up to his profession. He must do exactly what he professes: fight the good fight of the faith and take hold of eternal life.

> **All men will hate you because of me, but he who stands firm to the end will be saved. (Mat 10:22)**
>
> **No one serving as a soldier gets involved in civilian affairs—he wants to please his commanding officer. (2 Tim 2:4)**
>
> **Do you not know that in a race all the runners run, but only one gets the prize? Run in such a way as to get the prize. Everyone who competes in the games goes into strict training. They do it to get a crown that will not last; but we do it to get a crown that will last forever. Therefore I do not run like a man running aimlessly; I do not fight like a man beating the air. No, I beat my body and make it my slave so that after I have preached to others, I myself will not be disqualified for the prize. (1 Cor 9:24-27)**
>
> **The one who sows to please his sinful nature, from that nature will reap destruction; the one who sows to please the Spirit, from the Spirit will reap eternal life. (Gal 6:8)**
>
> **Consider him who endured such opposition from sinful men, so that you will not grow weary and lose heart. In your struggle against sin, you have not yet resisted to the point of shedding your blood. (Heb 12:3-4)**
>
> **I am coming soon. Hold on to what you have, so that no one will take your crown. (Rev 3:11)**

4 (6:13-16) **Minister**: the man of God must keep this commandment. What commandment? The commandment just covered in v.11-12. Five reasons are given for keeping these commandments.

1. God has the power to quicken, to give life to everything. The phrase "gives life" (zoogonountos) means to quicken; to bring forth alive (Robertson). God is life; He possesses the very energy and power of life within Himself. Therefore, God actually has the power to inject and infuse *eternal life* into us. There is no greater reason for keeping the commandments of God. If we keep His commandments, He will quicken us to live forever; He will give us eternal life.

2. Christ has set the example of a good profession before us. When Christ stood before Pilate, He said:

> Jesus said, "My kingdom is not of this world. If it were, my servants would fight to prevent my arrest by the Jews. But now my kingdom is from another place." "You are a king, then!" said Pilate. Jesus answered, "You are right in saying I am a king. In fact, for this reason I was born, and for this I came into the world, to testify to the truth. Everyone on the side of truth listens to me." (John 18:36-37)

The man of God is to make the very same profession that Christ made: Jesus Christ is King, the Supreme majesty of the universe, the "blessed and only Ruler, the King of kings and Lord of lords" (v.15). This is the second reason for keeping the commandments of God.

3. Christ is to come again and be exalted as King of kings and Lord of lords. The point is judgment. Every one of us must confront Christ: we will be called forth and be forced to stand face to face with Him. We will have to give an account of how well we kept His commandments.

⇒ "Keep [the commandment] with an eye to His second coming, when we must all give an account of the talents we have been entrusted with...
⇒ "The Lord Jesus Christ will appear; and it will be a glorious appearing....Ministers should have an eye to this appearing of the Lord Jesus Christ in all their administrations...
⇒ "Till his appearing, they [ministers] are to keep this commandment without spot, unrebukeable" (Matthew Henry. *Matthew Henry's Commentary*, Vol.6, p.831).

Jesus Christ shall return to earth and be exalted:

> Which God will bring about in his own time—God, the blessed and only Ruler, the King of kings and Lord of lords, (1 Tim 6:15)

This is the third reason why we must keep the commandments of God.

4. Christ alone possesses immortality and dwells in the transcendent and unapproachable light of God's glory. This is one of the magnificent doxologies of the Bible. Its message is powerful.

a. Christ alone has immortality: no person shall ever live forever apart from Jesus Christ.

> I tell you the truth, if anyone keeps my word, he will never see death." (John 8:51) and whoever lives and believes in me will never die. Do you believe this?" (John 11:26)

> But it has now been revealed through the appearing of our Savior, Christ Jesus, who has destroyed death and has brought life and immortality to light through the gospel. (2 Tim 1:10)

b. Christ alone dwells in the light which no man can approach unto, the glorious light of God's presence. No person shall ever approach God or dwell in the light of God's presence apart from Jesus Christ.

> Jesus answered, "I am the way and the truth and the life. No one comes to the Father except through me. (John 14:6)
> For there is one God and one mediator between God and men, the man Christ Jesus, (1 Tim 2:5)

5. Christ alone has seen and can see the light of God's presence and glory. No person shall ever be allowed to see the light of God's presence and glory apart from Christ.

> But," he said, "you cannot see my face, for no one may see me and live." (Exo 33:20)
> No one has ever seen God, but God the One and Only, who is at the Father's side, has made him known. (John 1:18)
> And the Father who sent me has himself testified concerning me. You have never heard his voice nor seen his form, (John 5:37)
> He is the image of the invisible God, the firstborn over all creation. (Col 1:15)
> Now to the King eternal, immortal, invisible, the only God, be honor and glory for ever and ever. Amen. (1 Tim 1:17)
> Who alone is immortal and who lives in unapproachable light, whom no one has seen or can see. To him be honor and might forever. Amen. (1 Tim 6:16)

Therefore, to God and Christ alone belong honor and might forever. Amen.

> *"This whole passage is a magnificent embodiment of the attributes of the living God, supreme blessedness and almighty power, universal dominion, and unchangeable being, inscrutable majesty, radiant holiness, and glory inaccessible and unapproachable by his creatures, save through the mediation of his only begotten Son"* (*Pulpit Commentary*, Vol.21, p.123).

1 TIMOTHY 6:17-21

	L. The Rich Man & the Minister: The Final Charge, 6:17-21	19 In this way they will lay up treasure for themselves as a firm foundation for the coming age, so that they may take hold of the life that is truly life.	e. Lay up wealth for the world to come

1 **The charge to the rich man**
a. Do not be arrogant
b. Do not trust in riches
c. Hope, trust in the living God
 	
d. Do good & be rich in good works: Be generous & share sacrificially
	17 Command those who are rich in this present world not to be arrogant nor to put their hope in wealth, which is so uncertain, but to put their hope in God, who richly provides us with everything for our enjoyment.
	18 Command them to do good, to be rich in good deeds, and to be generous and willing to share.
		20 Timothy, guard what has been entrusted to your care. Turn away from godless chatter and the opposing ideas of what is falsely called knowledge,
		21 Which some have professed and in so doing have wandered from the faith. Grace be with you.
			2 **The charge to the minister**
			a. Guard the faith entrusted to your care
			b. Turn away from false teaching
			  1) From godless & empty words
			  2) From false knowledge
			  3) Some have turned away from the faith

DIVISION III

BEHAVIOR AND RELATIONSHIPS IN THE CHURCH, 3:14-6:21

L. The Rich Man and the Minister: The Final Charge, 6:17-21

(6:17-21) **Introduction**: this is the final lesson and study in the book of First Timothy. The lessons have been many and the studies very helpful and stirring. This last lesson and study is no exception. It is a strong charge both to the rich of this world and to the ministers of the gospel.
1. The charge to the rich man (v.17-19).
2. The charge to the minister (v.20-21).

1 (6:17-19) **Riches—Wealth**: the final charge to the rich man. The word "command" (*paraggelle*) is a strong word. It has the force of a military command, yet it has the tenderness of an appeal to it. It means to beg and beseech a person—strongly so—to the point that the person is commanded to act. In this command God is appealing and begging the rich person, but He is doing it so strongly that it is a command. The rich person is approached in love and tenderness and an appeal is made to him, but he is expected to do exactly what God says. Five strong charges are given to the rich.

1. The rich person is not to be highminded, proud, or arrogant. The world honors money. Practically everyone in the world wants more money, and most are actually seeking more money. Few persons would turn down money. Money—the thought of riches and wealth—is so interwoven in the fabric of this world that it is probably the most honored thing in this world. The result is that the rich person is lifted up in the minds of most people. Most people want to be like the rich person. Most people put the rich person upon a pedestal. This makes it extremely difficult for a rich person to keep a proper perspective of himself.

⇒ There is great danger that the rich person will begin to think too highly of himself. There is the danger that he will become highminded, prideful, and arrogant; that he will begin to feel above other persons and to esteem himself better than others. There is the danger that he will begin to look down upon others and downplay others. The rich person—just because of his riches—must guard against feeling more important than other people. Riches and possessions do not make a person a *good person*; they do not make a person a *quality person*. Therefore, riches and possessions do not make a person *better*, *of more quality* than anyone else.

The charge is forceful: "Command those who are rich in this present world not to be arrogant." The temptation is there—always confronting the rich—because of the world's attitude toward riches. But the charge of God is clear: "[The rich are] not to be arrogant."

> **But you are not to be like that. Instead, the greatest among you should be like the youngest, and the one who rules like the one who serves. (Lk.22:26)**
>
> **For by the grace given me I say to every one of you: Do not think of yourself more highly than you ought, but rather think of yourself with sober judgment, in accordance with the measure of faith God has given you. (Ro.12:3)**
>
> **Do nothing out of selfish ambition or vain conceit, but in humility consider others better than yourselves. Each of you should look not only to your own interests, but also to the interests of others. (Ph.2:3-4)**
>
> **Humble yourselves before the Lord, and he will lift you up. (Jas.4:10)**
>
> **He has showed you, O man, what is good. And what does the Lord require of you? To act justly and to love mercy and to walk humbly with your God. (Mic.6:8)**

2. The rich person is not to trust in the *uncertainty of riches*. Riches are about the most uncertain thing in life. The world's economy is never certain, fluctuating up and down every few years; crisis follows crisis in world affairs and the markets respond and react to each crisis. Even if a person can keep his wealth in this life, disease or accident can happen overnight, and the person's wealth does him no good whatsoever. Riches—their value and benefit—may be here today, but they are just as easily gone tomorrow.

The charge is forceful: "Command those who are rich in this present world...[that they not] put their hope in wealth."

187

> The disciples were amazed at his words. But Jesus said again, "Children, how hard it is to enter the kingdom of God! (Mk.10:24)
>
> And I'll say to myself, "You have plenty of good things laid up for many years. Take life easy; eat, drink and be merry." ' "But God said to him, 'You fool! This very night your life will be demanded from you. Then who will get what you have prepared for yourself?' (Lk.12:19-20)
>
> Command those who are rich in this present world not to be arrogant nor to put their hope in wealth, which is so uncertain, but to put their hope in God, who richly provides us with everything for our enjoyment. (1 Tim.6:17)
>
> "If I have put my trust in gold or said to pure gold, 'You are my security,' if I have rejoiced over my great wealth, the fortune my hands had gained, Then these also would be sins to be judged, for I would have been unfaithful to God on high. (Job 31:24-25, 28)
>
> "Here now is the man who did not make God his stronghold but trusted in his great wealth and grew strong by destroying others!" (Ps.52:7)

3. The rich person is to *trust in God*. The word "hope" means to fix and set one's heart and life upon God. God is—He actually exists. He is living and He is the only Person who possesses every good and perfect gift. Therefore, He alone can give us...

- the good and perfect gifts necessary for this life.
- the good and perfect gifts necessary for the next life.

In fact, every *good gift* that we receive now—including riches—has come from God. This fact is not to be missed; it bears repeating: every good gift that we now have has come from God. Therefore, if we want more and more of the good things of this life, we must put our hope in God.

> Every good and perfect gift is from above, coming down from the Father of the heavenly lights, who does not change like shifting shadows. (Jas.1:17)
>
> But seek first his kingdom and his righteousness, and all these things will be given to you as well. (Mt.6:33)
>
> I have told you this so that my joy may be in you and that your joy may be complete. (Jn.15:11)
>
> Worship the Lord your God, and his blessing will be on your food and water. I will take away sickness from among you, (Ex.23:25)
>
> You care for the land and water it; you enrich it abundantly. The streams of God are filled with water to provide the people with grain, for so you have ordained it. (Ps.65:9)
>
> Praise be to the Lord, to God our Savior, who daily bears our burdens. Selah (Ps.68:19)

4. The rich person is to do good and to be rich in good works or deeds. What deeds? The deeds of a rich man are clearly stated: he is to distribute his wealth and be generous in it. Too many rich people shut their ears when they hear this. They turn their attention elsewhere, for they do not want to think about giving large amounts of money. They reject the fact that God expects them to give—to give to the point of sacrifice just like God did when He gave His Son and just like God's people do. But think about something—think honestly and realistically.

⇒ First, literally millions of people are hurting and dying every day from hunger, disease, and lack of fresh water; from ignorance, sin, loneliness, and emptiness. When God looks down upon earth and sees someone hurting and dying, and He sees us—the rich of the earth—what do you think God expects us to do? The world is one community; God expects us to meet the needs of the earth—to sacrificially meet the needs.

⇒ Second, why do you think a person has wealth? To hoard it? To bank and store it up and just let it lie around and never be used? We know better—every one of us knows better.

God expects the rich to do good and be rich in good deeds. He expects the rich to distribute and to be generous and sacrificial in meeting the needs of the lost and poor and dying of this world.

> Sell your possessions and give to the poor. Provide purses for yourselves that will not wear out, a treasure in heaven that will not be exhausted, where no thief comes near and no moth destroys. (Lk.12:33)
>
> In everything I did, I showed you that by this kind of hard work we must help the weak, remembering the words the Lord Jesus himself said: 'It is more blessed to give than to receive.'" (Acts 20:35)
>
> Share with God's people who are in need. Practice hospitality. (Ro.12:13)
>
> Therefore, as we have opportunity, let us do good to all people, especially to those who belong to the family of believers. (Gal.6:10)
>
> Command them to do good, to be rich in good deeds, and to be generous and willing to share. (1 Tim.6:18)
>
> And do not forget to do good and to share with others, for with such sacrifices God is pleased. (Heb.13:16)

5. The rich person is to lay up wealth for the world to come. How does a rich person lay up wealth for the world to come?

⇒ By distributing and giving generously and sacrificially (v.18).

⇒ "By giving it away" (A.T. Robertson. *Word Pictures in the New Testament*, Vol.4, p.596).

⇒ By using "their wealth to do good [and being]...ready to share...[remembering] that a Christian is essentially a man who is a member of a fellowship" (William Barclay. *The Letters to the Philippians, Colossians, and Thessalonians*, p.159).

⇒ "By work of charity" (Matthew Henry. *Matthew Henry's Commentary*, Vol.5, p.83).

> But store up for yourselves treasures in heaven, where moth and rust do not de-

stroy, and where thieves do not break in and steal. (Mt.6:20)

Jesus answered, "If you want to be perfect, go, sell your possessions and give to the poor, and you will have treasure in heaven. Then come, follow me." (Mt.19:21)

Sell your possessions and give to the poor. Provide purses for yourselves that will not wear out, a treasure in heaven that will not be exhausted, where no thief comes near and no moth destroys. (Lk.12:33)

What is more, I consider everything a loss compared to the surpassing greatness of knowing Christ Jesus my Lord, for whose sake I have lost all things. I consider them rubbish, that I may gain Christ (Ph.3:8)

Again, think of all the desperate needs of the world and of our own communities and cities. Any example of any need could be taken, but consider a person who is starving to death. If a rich person does not reach out and save the starving person and give life to him, how can the rich person expect God to give life to him in the next world? The only way we—any of us who are rich—can lay hold of eternal life is to give life to those who are dying in the sins and deprivations of their world.

The charge is militarily strong: charge them that are rich in this world, that they lay up treasure for themselves as a firm foundation against the time to come.

2 (6:20-21) **Minister**: the final charge to the minister. The charge is twofold.

1. Guard what has been entrusted to your care. What is it that has been entrusted to the minister? What is the trust committed to him?

> *"It is the deposit of truth delivered to him....It is the teaching which Paul imparted to Timothy, 'the sound words' [of the truth]"* (Kenneth Wuest. The Pastoral Epistles, Vol.2, p.102f).
>
> *"The truths of God, the ordinances of God, keep these"* (Matthew Henry. Matthew Henry's Commentary, Vol.5, p.831).
>
> *"Let nothing cause you to deviate from the Gospel message of the grace of God"* (Oliver Greene. The Epistles of Paul the Apostle to Timothy and Titus, p.241).

The great trust committed to the minister of God is...
- the faith.
- the glorious truth of God which God has revealed to men in His Word and in the Lord Jesus Christ.
- the wonderful gospel of God—the gospel that is revealed in the sending of God's Son to earth in order to save men.

The picture here is that of a *deposit*, of a faithful and diligent banker who looks after the money *deposited* into his care. The minister of God is to guard and keep, look after and care for the faith and truth of God, the faith and truth of His Son and of His Word, of His Revelation and of His gospel. The minister must never forget that God has deposited—actually laid—the truth of God into his hands. The minister has been entrusted with the gospel of God, the glorious message of His Son, the Lord Jesus Christ.

The Pulpit Commentary has an excellent comment on this fact:

> *"Timothy here is to keep diligent and watchful guard over the faith committed to his trust; to preserve it unaltered and uncorrupt, so as to hand it down to his successors exactly the same as he had received it. Oh that the successors of the apostles had always kept this precept"* (A.C. Hervey. *First Timothy*. "The Pulpit Commentary, Vol.21, ed. by HDM Spence and Joseph S. Exell. Grand Rapids, MI: Eerdmans, 1950, p.124).

William Barclay's comments are also worthy of quote:

> *"If in our day the Christian faith were to be twisted and distorted, it would not only be we who were the losers; those of generations still to come would be robbed of something infinitely precious. We are not only the possessors, we are also the trustees of the faith. That which we have received, we must also hand on"* (The Letters to Timothy, Titus, and Philemon, p.161).

If I preach voluntarily, I have a reward; if not voluntarily, I am simply discharging the trust committed to me. (1 Cor.9:17)

I have become its servant by the commission God gave me to present to you the word of God in its fullness-- (Col.1:25)

On the contrary, we speak as men approved by God to be entrusted with the gospel. We are not trying to please men but God, who tests our hearts. You know we never used flattery, nor did we put on a mask to cover up greed--God is our witness. (1 Th.2:4-5)

And we also thank God continually because, when you received the word of God, which you heard from us, you accepted it not as the word of men, but as it actually is, the word of God, which is at work in you who believe. (1 Th.2:13)

That conforms to the glorious gospel of the blessed God, which he entrusted to me. I thank Christ Jesus our Lord, who has given me strength, that he considered me faithful, appointing me to his service. (1 Tim.1:11-12)

And at his appointed season he brought his word to light through the preaching entrusted to me by the command of God our Savior. (Tit.1:3)

2. The minister is to turn away from false teaching. The description of false teaching is graphic.
   a. False teaching is described as godless chatter.
      ⇒ The word "godless" (bebelos) means common, irreverent, and irreligious talk.
      ⇒ The word "chatter" means empty and meaningless.

Therefore, the charge is to take all *empty talk* and turn away from it. Have absolutely nothing to do with common, irreverent, godless, and *empty*

voices—no matter who is sounding forth the words. This would, of course, include:
⇒ false claims to truth
⇒ worldly philosophy
⇒ suggestive talk
⇒ all forms of false teaching
⇒ novel ideas of religion
⇒ off-colored jokes
⇒ cursing
⇒ criticism
⇒ gossip

b. False teaching is described as *opposing ideas* and *false knowledge*.
⇒ The phrase "opposing ideas" (antitheseis) means antithesis, that is, to stand against some thesis, truth, or fact. What is being condemned is the false knowledge of men, the things that men teach that are contrary to God's glorious revelation in Christ and in the Word of God. The minister of God—in fact, any person—is a fool to stand against truth and fact, whether of God or of true knowledge.

The charge is strong, very strong: turn away from men and their teachings when they stand against Christ and the teachings of God's Word. Have nothing to do with the false knowledge of men. The men and their false teachings may concern philosophy, psychology, education, sociology, religion—any area of knowledge—but turn away from them if they are false. How do you tell if it is false? By the Word of God, the revelation and record of Christ and of the truth of God. If knowledge stands in opposition to the Word of God, turn away from it.

Note that some professing church members had turned to false teaching. The seriousness of the situation is seen in that these are the last words of this letter. The very last thing that Paul says to Timothy is to turn away from false teaching. What a warning to us!

Because of the increase of wickedness, the love of most will grow cold. (Mt.24:12)

Those on the rock are the ones who receive the word with joy when they hear it, but they have no root. They believe for a while, but in the time of testing they fall away. (Lk.8:13)

Jesus replied, "No one who puts his hand to the plow and looks back is fit for service in the kingdom of God." (Lk.9:62)

"When an evil spirit comes out of a man, it goes through arid places seeking rest and does not find it. Then it says, 'I will return to the house I left.' When it arrives, it finds the house swept clean and put in order. Then it goes and takes seven other spirits more wicked than itself, and they go in and live there. And the final condition of that man is worse than the first." (Lk.11:24-26)

But now that you know God--or rather are known by God--how is it that you are turning back to those weak and miserable principles? Do you wish to be enslaved by them all over again? (Gal.4:9)

But my righteous one will live by faith. And if he shrinks back, I will not be pleased with him." (Heb.10:38)

Yet I hold this against you: You have forsaken your first love. (Rev.2:4)

THE
OUTLINE & SUBJECT INDEX

REMEMBER: When you look up a subject and turn to the Scripture reference, you have not only the Scripture, you have *an outline and a discussion* (commentary) of the Scripture and subject.

This is one of the *GREAT VALUES* of **The Preacher's Outline & Sermon Bible**®. Once you have all the volumes, you will have not only what all other Bible indexes give you, that is, a list of all the subjects and their Scripture references, *BUT* you will also have...

- An outline of *every* Scripture and subject in the Bible.
- A discussion (commentary) on every Scripture and subject.
- Every subject supported by other Scriptures or cross references.

DISCOVER THE GREAT VALUE for yourself. Quickly glance below to the very first subject of the Index of First Timothy. It is:

ACCEPTANCE - ACCEPTABLE
Who - what is **a**.
Children caring for parents. 5:4-8; 5:16

Turn to the reference. Glance at the Scripture and outline of the Scripture, then read the commentary. You will immediately see the GREAT VALUE of the INDEX of **The Preacher's Outline & Sermon Bible**®.

OUTLINE AND SUBJECT INDEX

ABOVE REPROACH
Meaning. 3:2-3

ACCEPTANCE - ACCEPTABLE
Who - what is **a**.
Children caring for parents. 5:4-8; 5:16
Prayer. 2:1-8

ADAM
And Eve. Function of each in God's creation. 2:12-14
Fact.
Bore greater sin than Eve. 2:14
Sinned willfully. Was not deceived. 2:14
Illustrates orderly function in the family. 2:13
Meaning. 2:9-10
Sinned willfully. 2:14

ADORN
Meaning. 2:9-10

ALCOHOL (See **DRUNKENNESS**)

ALEXANDER
Discussed. A believer with shipwrecked faith. 1:19-20

AMBITION - AMBITIOUS
Evil **a**. causes. Pride. 3:6

ANGELS
Nature. Elect. 5:21
Purpose. To minister to Christ. 3:16

APOSTASY
Discussed. 4:1-5
Marks of - Characteristics of.
Asceticism. 4:3-5
Seared consciences. 4:1-2
Source of.
Doctrines of devils. 4:1-2
False prophets & teachers. 4:1-2
Seducing spirits. 4:1-2

APOSTLE
Meaning. 1:1; 2:3-7

ARGUE - ARGUMENTS
Discussed. 4:7; 6:20-21

BACKSLIDING - BACKSLIDERS
Described as. Shipwrecked faith. 1:19
Results. Can **b**. so far that one is turned over to Satan. 1:20

BEHAVE (See **CONDUCT**)

BEHAVIOR, GOOD
Meaning. 3:2-3

BELIEVER
Duty. To be a man of God. Marks of. 6:11-16

BISHOP (See **OVERSEER**)

BLAMELESS (See **ABOVE REPROACH**)

BODY
Duty.
To exercise. 4:8
To take care of **b**. 3:2-3

BRAWLER (See **QUARELSOME**)

BROTHER - BROTHERHOOD
Among various ages. 5:1-2

CALL - CALLED (See **MINISTER**)
Purpose of. To lay hold of eternal life. 6:12

CHARGE (See **COMMAND**)

CHILDBEARING
Promise to women in **c**. 2:15

CHURCH
Described.
Church of the living God. 3:14-15
Family of God. 3:14-15
Pillar & ground of the truth. 3:14-15
Discussed. 3:14-16
Behavior & relationships in the **c**. 3:14-6:21
Duties, order, & organization of the **c**. 2:1-3:13
Spirit & discipline of relationships. 5:1-2
Women of the **c**. 2:9-15
Duty.
First **d**. To pray. 2:1-8
Ministries of.
To various age groups. 5:1-2
To widows. 5:3-16
Names - Titles.
C. of the living God. 3:15
House of God. 3:15
Three pictures. 3:15
Nature.
Described. 3:14-16
Symbolized in the family. 3:4
Officers of. Bishop. Discussed. 3:1-7
Organization.
Deacons. 3:8-13
Elders or officials. 4:14
Government, policy of. 3:1-7; 3:8-13
Ministers - Overseers - Bishops. 3:1-7
Presbytery. 4:14
Who the **c** is. 3:14-15
Worship. An early **w**. service. 4:13

CHURCH DISCIPLINE
How to *rebuke*. 5:1
Of a minister. 5:19-20

CITIZENSHIP
Duty.
To leave judgment up to God. 5:24-25
To pray for authorities. 2:2

INDEX

CIVIL AUTHORITIES
    Duty toward. To pray for all in authority. 2:2

CLOTHING (See **DRESS**)
    Meaning. 6:17-19

COMMAND
    Meaning. 6:17-19

CONDUCT
    Meaning. 3:14-15

CONSCIENCE
    Discussed. 1:19
    Function - Purpose - Work. To approve behavior. 1:5; 1:19
    How not to offend.
        By holding a pure, good **c**. 1:5; 1:19
        By not shipwrecking. 1:19
    Kinds of.
        Good - clear. 1:5; 1:19
        Pure. 1:5
        Seared. 4:2
    Reaction to. Hardening, searing. 4:2
    Warning. Can be put away, neglected. 1:19-20

CONTENTMENT
    Discussed. Secret to **c**. 6:6-10
    Meaning. 6:6-8
    Source of. Godliness, not wealth. 6:6-10

CONVERSION
    Illustration. Paul's **c**. to show God's mercy for great sinners. 1:15-16

COVETOUS - COVETOUSNESS
    Described as. Root of all evil. 6:10
    Meaning. 3:2-3
        Love of money. 6:10
        Willing to be rich. 6:9
    Results.
        Acute mental anguish. 6:10
        Disqualification of pastoral call. 3:3
        Enslavement. 6:9
        Many hurtful lusts. 6:9
        Many temptations. 6:9
        One to fall. 6:9
        Wandering. 6:9

DEACONS
    Discussed. 3:8-13
    Qualifications. 3:8-13
    Wife of. Discussed. 3:11-12

DISCIPLESHIP
    Duty. To make disciples. 1:1-2

DISCIPLINE, CHURCH
    Described. Delivered to Satan. 1:19-20

DOUBLETONGUED
    Meaning. 3:8

DRESS
    Duty.
        Not to dress to attract attention. 2:9-10
        To be modest. 2:9-10
    Can cause problems.
        Attracting & being subjected to someone other than own spouse. 2:9-10
        Immodesty & insensitivity. 2:9-10
        Rebellion (unfaithfulness). 2:9-15
    Discussed. 2:9-15
    Proper **d**.
        Must be based upon faith & love. 2:15
        To be modest & sensitive. 2:9-10
        To **d**. as a godly person. 2:9-10
        To watch one's adorning - demeanor. 2:9-10
    Results of proper dress.
        Discussed. 2:9-15
        Saves one in childbearing. 2:15
    Warning against. Being overly dressed - living extravagantly. 2:9

DRUNKENNESS
    Duty. To abstain. 3:2-3

ELDER
    Discussed. 3:1-7; 5:17-20
    Qualifications. 3:1-7

ELDERLY
    Ministry to. Discussed. 5:1-2

EMPLOYEE
    Discussed. 6:1-2
    Duty. Toward a Christian. Supervisor. 6:1-2

EVANGELISM
    Duty. To reach the world for Christ. 3:16

EVE
    And Adam. Function of both in creation. 2:12-14
    Fact. Was deceived, but not Adam. 2:14
    Was deceived; Adam was not. 2:14

EVIL SPIRITS
    Work of. To seduce into false teaching. 4:1-2

EXHORT - EXHORTATION
    Meaning. 2:1

FABLES (See **MYTHS**)

FAITH
    Meaning. 6:11
    Warning. Can be shipwrecked. 1:19-20

FAITHFUL - FAITHFULNESS
    Duty. To be **f**. in all things. 3:11-12
    Meaning. 6:11

FALSE TEACHERS (See **TEACHERS, FALSE**)

FAMILY
    Duties. Function of husband & wife. 2:12-14
    Leaders must rule **f**. well. 3:4-5; 3:11-12
    Nature.
        Miniature of the church. 3:4-5, cp. Eph.5:22-33
        Woman more easily deceived. 2:14
        Orderly arrangement necessary. 2:12-14
    Parents. Aged **p**. to be cared for. 5:2-8

FAVORITISM
    Duty. Of minister. Not to show **f**. 5:21

FILTHY LUCRE
    Meaning. 3:2-3

GENEALOGIES
    Error. Discussed. 1:4

GENTLE
    Meaning. 3:2-3

GENTLENESS
    Meaning. 6:11

GIFTS, SPIRITUAL
    Purpose. To predict & encourage Timothy in his call to the ministry. 1:18

GNOSTICISM
    Discussed. 4:3

GOD
    Deity. One God. 2:3-7
    Names - Titles. God our Savior. 1:1; 2:3
    Nature.
        One God. 2:3-7
        Is perfect—no imperfection whatsoever. 2:3-7

GOD'S HOUSEHOLD
    Described.
        House of God. 3:14-15

GODLINESS
    Meaning. 6:11
    Mystery of. 3:16
    Results. Contentment. 6:6-8

GOVERNMENT (See **CIVIL AUTHORITIES**)
    To be prayed for. 2:1-3

GRAVE (See **RESPECT**)

HOPE
    Comes through Christ. 1:1

HOSPITALITY
    Meaning. 3:2-3

HUMANISM
    Fact. Preached by some ministers. 6:5

HYMENAEUS
    Discussed. 1:19-20

IMMORTALITY
    Source. Jesus Christ. 6:14-16

IMPERFECTION
    Discussed. Man is imperfect, therefore unacceptable to a perfect God. 2:3-7

INCARNATION
    Discussed. Six facts. 3:16

INTERCESSION
    Meaning. 2:1

JESUS CHRIST
    Ascension. To be crowned with glory. 3:16
    Death.
        To give Himself a ransom. 2:3-7
        To save man. 2:3-7
    Deity.
        Did the works of God. 3:16
        God incarnated in human flesh. 3:16
        Incarnation. 3:16
        Lived a sinless & perfect life. 3:16
        Proven by the resurrection. 3:16
        Proven by three things. 3:16
    Exalted. To rule & reign. 3:16

INDEX

Humanity. Begotten as man - sent by God. 2:5
Life. Ministered to by angels. 3:16
Mediator. Discussed. 2:3-7
Mission. To save man. 1:15-16
Names - Titles.
   Christ Jesus our hope. 1:1
   The one mediator. 2:5
Nature - Origin.
   Immortal, King of kings & Lord of lords. 6:13-16
   Sinless, perfect. The Ideal Man. 2:3-7
Work of - Mission of.
   Redemption. (See **REDEEM - REDEMPTION**) 2:5-7
   To save man to the uttermost. 1:15

JUDGMENT
Duty. To leave j. up to God. 5:24-25

LABOR - LABORERS
Duty. Toward employers. 6:1-2

LAW
Purpose. Discussed. 1:8-11

LEADERS - LEADERSHIP (See **DEACONS; MINISTERS**; and Related Subjects)
Of the church.
   Deacons. 3:8-13
   Ministers - Overseers. Bishops. 3:1-7

LUCRE, FILTHY
Meaning. 3:2-3

MAN
Depravity.
   Hunger for material things. 6:9-10
   Imperfect; therefore, unacceptable to God. 2:3-7
Errors. Hunger for material things. 6:9-10
Nature.
   Craves God & His Word. 6:4
   Imperfect; therefore, unacceptable to God. 2:3-7

MATERIALISM
Discussed. 6:6-10
The passion for wealth. 6:6-10
The rich man. 6:17-19
What m. does. Causes many harmful desires. 6:9-10

MEEK – MEEKNESS (See **GENTLENESS**)

MEN, ELDERLY
How to treat in the church. 5:1

MERCY
Meaning. 1:2
Purpose. To show God's great m. for sinners. 1:15-17

MINISTER
Call.
   Credentials. 1:1
   Enabled & counted worthy. 1:12-17
   Entrusted with the gospel. 1:11
Call.
   Must be c. by God, not just choosing a profession. 1:18
   Ordination by God. 2:7
   To guard ordination. 5:22
Commission - Mission. Enabled & counted worthy. 1:12-17
Described as.
   Good. 4:6-16
   Man of God. 6:11
   True. 1:12-17
Discipline of. Discussed. 5:19-20
Discussed. 3:1-7
   A good m. Twelve qualities. 4:6-16
   Four charges. 5:21-25
   Restoring a fallen m. 5:22
   Testimony of a true m. 1:12-17
   Charge to the young m. To be a warrior. 1:18-20
Duty.
   Discussed. 6:11-16
   Fourfold. 6:11-16
   Must not fear the face of man. 5:21
   Not to neglect the gift that is in him. 4:14
   Not to ordain others too quickly. 5:22
   Primary duty. to devote himself to public worship. 4:13
   To be a good m. 6:6-16
   To be an example to believers. In six areas. 4:13
   To be a man of reason & purpose. 4:11
   To be a trusted son. 6:20-21
   To be a warrior. 1:18-20
   To be honored. 5:17-18
   To be impartial. 5:21-25
   To exercise physically & spiritually. 4:7-8
   To fight & lay hold of eternal life. 6:12
   To guard himself & his teaching. 4:16
   To guard ordination. 5:22
   To instruct believers about false teachers. 4:6
   To keep the commandments of God. 6:13-16
   To labor strenuously. 4:10
   To leave judging others up to God. 5:23
   To meditate & to wholly give himself to the Scriptures. 4:15
   To nourish himself in the faith. 4:6
   To reject false teaching, that is, profane & old wives fables. 4:7
   To take care of his body. 5:23
   To various ages. 5:1-2
   Toward m. 5:19-20
   To widows. 5:3-16
   Twelve duties. 4:6-16
   Twofold duty. 6:20-21
False m. (See **TEACHERS, FALSE**)
Financial support. To be paid double. 5:17-20
Names - Titles. Elders. 5:17
Qualifications. 3:1-7

MINISTER, FALSE (See **TEACHERS, FALSE**)

MONEY
Discussed. Love of. Causes four things. 6:9-10
Duty. Must not be a lover of. 3:2-3

MYSTERY
Of the faith. Discussed. 3:9-10
Of godliness.
   Discussed. 3:16
   Six facts. 3:16

MYTHS
Meaning. 1:4

NOVICE (See **RECENT CONVERT**)

ORDINATION
Duty.
   Not to o. a fallen minister too quickly. 5:22
   Not to o. too quickly. 5:22
Source. God is the One who ordains. 2:7
To be guarded. 5:22

OVERSEER
Discussed. 3:1-7
Qualifications. 3:1-7

PARTIALITY
Duty. Of minister. Not to show p. 5:21

PASTORAL EPISTLES
Purpose for writing. 3:14-15

PATIENT (See **GENTLE**)

PAUL
Conversion & call of. 1:12-17
   To be a pattern of God's mercy & longsuffering. 1:15-16
Former life of. Discussed. 1:13-14

PEACE
Meaning. 1:2

PERSECUTION - PERSECUTORS (See **PAUL**, Sufferings & Trials)

PRAY - PRAYER - PRAYING
Different kinds of p. 2:1
Discussed. 2:1-8
Duty.
   First duty of the church: to pray. 2:1-8
   To pray for all men to be saved. 2:3-7
   To pray for all rulers. 2:2
How to pray. Three essentials. 2:8
Who is to p. The church: its first duty. 2:1-8

PREACHER
Meaning. 2:3-7

PREJUDICE
Duty. Of minister. Not to show p. 5:21

PRIDE
Caused by. Being "lifted up" - given responsibility too soon. 3:6
Of the false minister. What he takes p. in. 6:4
Results. To be condemned with the devil. 3:6

PROPHECY, GIFT OF
Work—exercise of. Predicted Timothy's call to the ministry. 1:18

QUARRELSOME
Meaning. 3:2-3

RANSOM - REDEEM - REDEMPTION
Discussed. 2:3-7
Purpose. To redeem men. 2:3-7
Source. Christ. 2:3-7

REBUKE
Meaning. 5:1

INDEX

RECENT CONVERT
Meaning. 3:6

RELATIONSHIPS
Discussed. Spirit & discipline of r. 5:1-2

REPENTANCE
Of a fallen minister. Discussed. 5:22

RESPECT
Meaning. 3:8

RESTORATION, SPIRITUAL
Of a fallen minister. Discussed. 5:22

REAVEST
Meaning. 2:1

RICHES (See **MONEY**)
Dangers of. Three dangers. 6:17-19
Discussed.
    Charges to the rich man. 6:17-19
    Secret to contentment. 6:9-10
Duty. Discussed. 6:17-19
Results. Four significant r. 6:9-10

RIGHTEOUSNESS
Meaning. 6:11

RULERS
Duty toward. To pray for all r. 2:2

SALVATION - SAVED
Duty. To pray for s. of all men. 2:1-8
Source - How one is s.
    By Christ. 1:15-16
    By Christ the Mediator. 2:3-7
    By God our Savior. 1:1; 2:3-7

SATAN
Fell by pride. 3:6
Work - strategy of. Seduces men - through evil spirits. 4:1-2

SELF-CONTROLLED
Meaning. 3:2-3

SIN
List of. 1:9-10
Results - Penalty. Imperfection. Makes man unacceptable to God. 2:3-7

SLANDER - SLANDERER
Meaning. 3:11-12

SLAVES
Discussed. 6:1-2
Duty. Toward a Christian supervisor. 6:1-2

SOBER (See **SELF-CONTROLLED**)

SPECULATIONS (See **TEACHERS, FALSE**)
Discussed. 4:7; 6:20-21

SPIRIT, MAN'S
More important than physical. 4:8

SPIRITUAL STRUGGLE & WARFARE
Discussed. To be a warrior. 1:18-20
Duty. To fight a good warfare. 1:18
Weapons. Faith & a good conscience. 1:18

SPORTS
Exhortations to. Exercise for godliness. 4:8

STEWARDSHIP
Duty. To support minister. Double honor. 5:17-20

STRIKER (See **VIOLENT**)

SUPPLICATION (See **REAVEST**)

TEACH
Duty. Must be appointed, qualified to t. 2:3-7

TEACHER
Meaning. 2:3-7

TEACHERS, FALSE (See **APOSTASY; DECEIVE - DECEPTION; JUDAIZERS; LEGALISM; RELIGIONISTS**
Characteristics - Marks.
    Five c. 6:3-5
    Does not preach the words of the Lord Jesus Christ. 6:3
    Pride. What he takes p. in. 6:7
Description of false t. & their apostasy. 4:1-5; 6:20-21
Discussed. 4:1-5; 6:3-5; 6:20-21
    Danger of. 1:3-11
Errors of.
    Are seduced by evil spirit. 4:1-2
    Consciences are seared. 4:1-2
    Deception & seduction. 4:1-2
Protection against.
    Knowing their danger. 1:3-11
    Turning away from. 6:20-21
Teachings of.
    Are profane & old wives tales. 4:7
    Discussed. 1:3-11; 4:3-5
    Vs. true teaching. 1:3-20; 6:3-5
What he teaches. Self-help; self-esteem; humanism. 6:5
Where are false teachers. Within the church. 1:3-20

TEACHING, FALSE
Teachings of.
    Are falsely called & knowledge. 6:20-21
    Are profane & godly chatter. 6:20-21

TEMPERATE
Meaning. 3:2-3

THANKSGIVING
Meaning. 2:1

TIMOTHY
Call of. To ministry. 1:18
Discussed. 1:2

TRUST
Meaning. 6:20

VIGILANT (See **TEMPERATE**)

VIOLENT
Meaning. 3:2-3

WEALTH (See **MONEY**)
Danger - problem of.
    Passion for. 6:6-10
    The root of all evil. 6:10

WIDOWS
Discussed. Treatment of. 5:3-16
Duty. To be cared for by children. 5:3-8; 5:16
Traits. Gossipers, idle, busybodies. 5:13

WINE
Duty. To abstain. 3:2-3

WITNESS - WITNESSING
Duty. To proclaim Christ. 3:16

WORD OF GOD
Fact. Man's heart craves God & His Word. 6:4

WORKMEN (See **EMPLOYEE**)

WORLD
Reached by earlier church. 3:16

WOMEN
Duties of w.
    In childbearing. 2:15
    In dress & clothing. 2:9-10
    In the church. 2:11; 2:12-14
Duties of w.
    Not to teach or take authority over a man. 2:11; 2:12-14
    To be submissive before men in church leadership. 2:11; 2:12-14
Elderly. How to treat within the church. 5:2
In the church. Discussed. 2:9-15
Leadership of.
    Example after example. 2:12-14
    Place in the church. 2:12-14

WORSHIP
Of early church. Services. Described. 4:13

YOKE
Meaning. 6:1

YOUTH
Men. How to treat within the church. 5:1
Women. How to treat within the church. 5:2

SECOND

TIMOTHY

2 TIMOTHY

INTRODUCTION

AUTHOR: Paul, the Apostle.

DATE: Uncertain. Probably A.D. 65-68.

A reconstruction of what happened determines the date of *Second Timothy* (see *Date—Introduction—1 Timothy*). The reconstruction is based upon Paul's original plans and the few facts given by him. When he was released from prison (A.D. 63), the way was opened for him to again visit the churches in Asia.

The exact order in which his visits took place is not known. After so long a period in prison, his heart would naturally turn toward Ephesus. There he left Timothy behind (1 Tim.1:3). At some point he went to Troas where he visited Carpus. There he left some books, parchments, and a cloak with him (2 Tim.4:13). He traveled to Miletum where Trophimus was left sick; to Crete where Titus was pastor (Tit.1:5); and to Corinth (2 Tim.4:20). Then he journeyed to Nicopolis in Macedonia (Tit.3:12). Some place along the route two significant events took place: first, Paul wrote the epistles to Timothy and to Titus; and second, Paul returned to Rome where he was imprisoned for the second and final time. It should be mentioned that several of the early church fathers say that Paul carried the gospel to Spain as he had originally planned (Ro.15:24, 28). If Paul were able to carry out this mission, he must have visited Spain right after being released from his first imprisonment. The time necessary for the events mentioned above to happen and the closing years of Nero's reign would necessitate this. (See Introduction, Date—First Timothy for more discussion.)

TO WHOM WRITTEN: "To Timothy, my dear son" (1:2). (See *Introduction—1 Timothy*.)

PURPOSE: Paul was in prison in Rome when he wrote Second Timothy. He had already appeared for his preliminary hearing before the Supreme Court of Rome, before Nero himself. During his trial, no man stood with him. He had to face the charges all alone (2 Tim.4:16-17). Some were forsaking the faith (2 Tim.2:17; 4:10), and others were publicly opposing Paul (2 Tim.4:14-15). He was about to be sentenced to death—and he knew it (2 Tim.4:6-8). He would never be able to write again. This was to be his last will and testament—the last words he would ever pen. Several things were weighing heavily upon his heart.

1. Paul's heart ached for Timothy's companionship. He needed Timothy. He wanted "his dear son" by his side in his final hour.

2. Paul wished to share some final matters with his son and successor—just in case Timothy did not arrive in time.

3. Paul wanted his son, Timothy, to equip himself as well as possible for his great call—to fulfill the tremendous task begun by Paul: "Guard the good deposit that was entrusted to you—guard it with the help of the Holy Spirit who lives in us" (2 Tim.1:14).

4. Paul felt the need to fortify the courage of his dear son. Timothy was trustworthy, but he was sometimes weak in courage (2 Tim.1:6-7) and physical strength (1 Tim. 5:23). He needed to take care of himself physically and spiritually in order to more adequately minister.

5. Paul wanted to prepare his *son* for the perilous times coming upon the earth in the last days (2 Tim.3:1f).

SPECIAL FEATURES:

1. *Second Timothy* is "A Pastoral Epistle." There are two other Pastoral Epistles: *First Timothy* and *Titus*. They are called Pastoral Epistles because they deal primarily with the pastoral care, oversight, and organization of the church. They tell believers how they ought to behave in the house of God (2 Tim.3:15). Interestingly, the term *pastoral* has a long history. It was first used by Thomas Aquinas in A.D. 1274. He called First Timothy "an epistle of pastoral rule" and Second Timothy "an epistle of pastoral care." The term "Pastoral Epistles," however, began to be widely used only after D.N. Berdot (A.D. 1703) and Paul Anton (A.D. 1726) so described them (Donald Guthrie. *The Pastoral Epistles*. "Tyndale New Testament Commentaries," p.11).

2. *Second Timothy* is "A Personal Epistle." It was written to a young disciple who was loved as a son. The epistle is filled with warm and affectionate feelings and filled with instructions that were to govern Timothy's personal behavior.

3. *Second Timothy* is "An Ecclesiastical Epistle." It was written to answer questions about church organization, doctrinal purity, and personal behavior. Two things were happening. First, the number and sizes of churches were growing rapidly, and second, the apostles were aging. In both cases the apostles were just unable to personally reach and instruct all the churches; therefore, they had to write if the churches were to be rooted and grounded in the Lord.

4. *Second Timothy* is "An Apologetic Epistle." It is a defense of the faith. The first rumblings and early development of false teaching had just begun to appear (Gnosticism. See Colossians, Introductory Notes, Purpose.) Therefore, Paul warns the believers and defends the truth against heretical and false teaching.

OUTLINE OF 2 TIMOTHY

THE PREACHER'S OUTLINE & SERMON BIBLE® is *unique*. It differs from all other Study Bibles & Sermon Resource Materials in that every Passage and Subject is outlined right beside the Scripture. When you choose any *Subject* below and turn to the reference, you have not only the Scripture, but you discover the Scripture and Subject *already outlined for you—verse by verse*.

For a quick example, choose one of the subjects below and turn over to the Scripture, and you will find this marvelous help for faster, easier, and more accurate use.

In addition, every point of the Scripture and Subject is *fully developed in a Commentary with supporting Scripture* at the bottom of the page. Again, this arrangement makes sermon preparation much easier and faster.

Note something else: The Subjects of Second Timothy have titles that are both Biblical and *practical*. The practical titles sometimes have more appeal to people. This *benefit* is clearly seen for use on billboards, bulletins, church newsletters, etc.

A suggestion: For the quickest overview of Second Timothy, first read *all the major titles* (I, II, III, etc.), then come back and read the subtitles.

OUTLINE OF 2 TIMOTHY

GREETING: PAUL'S GREAT GLORY, 1:1-5

I. **THE STRONG CHARGES TO TIMOTHY, 1:6-2:26**

   A. Charge One: Endure Abuse for the Gospel, 1:6-12
   B. Charge Two: Hold Fast to the Lord Jesus Christ, 1:13-18
   C. Charge Three: Be Strong in the Lord Jesus Christ, 2:1-7
   D. Charge Four: Remember Jesus Christ is the Resurrected Lord, 2:8-13
   E. Charge Five: Remind the Church About the Danger of Words and The Foundation of God, 2:14-21
   F. Charge Six: Flee Youthful Lusts and Follow After the Lord, 2:22-26

II. **THE PREDICTIONS OF THE LAST DAYS, 3:1-17**

   A. The Godless Marks of the Last Days, 3:1-9
   B. The Contrasting Marks of Godly Believers, 3:10-13
   C. The Godly Mark of Living in the Scripture, 3:14-17

III. **THE TRIUMPH OF PREACHING, 4:1-8**

   A. The Awesome Charge to Preach and to Minister, 4:1-5
   B. The Triumphant Testimony of Paul, 4:6-8

IV. **THE FINAL FAREWELL OF PAUL TO THE WORLD, 4:9-22**

2 TIMOTHY

CHAPTER 1

GREETING: PAUL'S GREAT GLORY, 1:1-5

1 His great call
2 His son in the faith
3 His clear conscience

Paul, an apostle of Christ Jesus by the will of God, according to the promise of life that is in Christ Jesus,
2 To Timothy, my dear son: Grace, mercy and peace from God the Father and Christ Jesus our Lord.
3 I thank God, whom I serve, as my forefathers did, with a clear conscience, as night and day I constantly remember you in my prayers.
4 Recalling your tears, I long to see you, so that I may be filled with joy.
5 I have been reminded of your sincere faith, which first lived in your grandmother Lois and in your mother Eunice and, I am persuaded, now lives in you also.

4 His privilege of praying for a disciple
5 His remembrance of Timothy's tears
6 His memory of Timothy's family—their genuine faith

GREETING: PAUL'S GREAT GLORY, 1:1-5

(1:1-5) **Introduction**: a believer is highly privileged by God. Paul knew this and he gloried in those privileges. But note: he does not glory in the things of this earth; he glories in the things that relate to God.
1. His great call (v.1).
2. His son in the faith (v.2).
3. His clear conscience (v.3).
4. His privilege of praying for a disciple (v.3).
5. His remembrance of Timothy's tears (v.4).
6. His remembrance of Timothy's family—their genuine faith (v.5).

1 (1:1) **Call—Paul—Minister**: the first glory of Paul was his great call, the call God had given him. Paul did not glory in the things of this earth; he gloried in the things of God. God had called him out of sin and institutional religion to be a messenger of His. Paul uses the word *apostle*. He says that he was an "apostle [apostolos] of Christ Jesus by the will of God." The word apostle means one called and sent forth on a very special mission (see DEEPER STUDY # 5, *Apostle*—Mt.10:2 for more discussion). The mission given to Paul was that of a messenger. It was God's will that Paul proclaim "the promise of life that is in Christ Jesus." The promise of life—real life, true life, the only true life there is—is in Christ Jesus. There is no life apart from Christ. There is existence, mere survival, but no real life. Therefore, Paul was a messenger, an apostle, a man who was sent by God to proclaim the promise of God, the promise that God makes to man: He will give life to any person who trusts His Son, the Lord Jesus Christ.

Just imagine being called by God Himself. What a privilege! No matter what the call is, it is a privilege just to be called by God. But imagine being called to proclaim the glorious promise of God's very own Son, the promise of life that is in Him. That call is the greatest of privileges. That was the call of Paul. That was the glory of Paul: the great call that God had given him.

> **Thought 1.** What a glorious privilege the messenger of God has: to proclaim the promise of life. Every servant of God should bow in humble adoration and submission—to proclaim the promise of life as never before.

> You did not choose me, but I chose you and appointed you to go and bear fruit—fruit that will last. Then the Father will give you whatever you ask in my name. (John 15:16)

> 'Now get up and stand on your feet. I have appeared to you to appoint you as a servant and as a witness of what you have seen of me and what I will show you. (Acts 26:16)

> All this is from God, who reconciled us to himself through Christ and gave us the ministry of reconciliation: that God was reconciling the world to himself in Christ, not counting men's sins against them. And he has committed to us the message of reconciliation. We are therefore Christ's ambassadors, as though God were making his appeal through us. We implore you on Christ's behalf: Be reconciled to God. God made him who had no sin to be sin for us, so that in him we might become the righteousness of God. (2 Cor 5:18-21)

> I thank Christ Jesus our Lord, who has given me strength, that he considered me faithful, appointing me to his service. (1 Tim 1:12)

> In him was life, and that life was the light of men. (John 1:4)

> The thief comes only to steal and kill and destroy; I have come that they may have life, and have it to the full. (John 10:10)

> Jesus said to her, "I am the resurrection and the life. He who believes in me will live, even though he dies; (John 11:25)

> Jesus answered, "I am the way and the truth and the life. No one comes to the Father except through me. (John 14:6)

> Who has saved us and called us to a holy life—not because of anything we have done but because of his own purpose and grace. This grace was given us in Christ Jesus before the beginning of time, but it has now been revealed through the appearing of our Savior, Christ Jesus, who has destroyed death and has brought life and immortality to light through the gospel. (2 Tim 1:9-10)

> He who has the Son has life; he who does not have the Son of God does not have life. (1 John 5:12)

2 TIMOTHY 1:1-5

2 (1:2) **Paul—Timothy**: the second glory of Paul was Timothy, his son in the faith (see note, *Discipleship—*1 Tim.1:2 for discussion).

3 (1:3) **Conscience—Paul**: the third glory of Paul was his clear conscience. This is a phenomenal statement: Paul says that he served God with a *clear conscience*. God had called Paul to serve His Son, the Lord Jesus Christ, and Paul was faithful and diligent in his service and ministry. In serving Christ, Paul...
- did not slumber and sleep late.
- did not waste and abuse time.
- did not prepare half-heartedly at the last minute.
- did not neglect the ministry and the needs of people.
- did not question or deny the Word of God and its gospel.
- did not deviate from the truth of the Lord Jesus Christ, the very Son of God Himself.
- did not fail to proclaim the whole gospel and the whole counsel of God.

Paul did not have a conscience that caused him to question his actions and life—its purpose and meaning and significance. Paul did not have a conscience that questioned, bothered, nagged, and pricked him. Paul was faithful to Christ and His ministry; therefore, he could forcefully declare: "I serve...with a clear conscience." This was the boast of Paul: a clear conscience.

Thought 1. Every minister of God should ask: "Do I serve God with a clear conscience? If not, why?" We must correct every failure and every shortcoming. We must serve Christ faithfully and diligently. A clear conscience must be the glory of the minister.

> **So I strive always to keep my conscience clear before God and man. (Acts 24:16)**
> **Now this is our boast: Our conscience testifies that we have conducted ourselves in the world, and especially in our relations with you, in the holiness and sincerity that are from God. We have done so not according to worldly wisdom but according to God's grace. (2 Cor 1:12)**
> **The goal of this command is love, which comes from a pure heart and a good conscience and a sincere faith. (1 Tim 1:5)**
> **Holding on to faith and a good conscience. Some have rejected these and so have shipwrecked their faith. (1 Tim 1:19)**
> **Keeping a clear conscience, so that those who speak maliciously against your good behavior in Christ may be ashamed of their slander. (1 Pet 3:16)**

4 (1:3) **Prayer—Paul**: the fourth glory of Paul was his privilege of praying for a disciple. Of course, prayer itself was a privilege for Paul, as prayer is for every believer. But the very thought of taking prayer and zeroing in on a *young disciple* is a special privilege. Why? Because we can concentrate on the young disciple's life, and the hand of God can be seen moving upon his life. Genuine believers know that one of the greatest privileges and comforts of life is being able to carry the needs of a loved person before the Lord and...
- experience the Lord removing the burden from our hearts.
- experience the Lord answering our prayer and meeting the need of our loved one.
- experience the growth and ministry of our loved one for Christ.

The glorious privilege of praying for a young disciple is a privilege indeed, a privilege that needs to be laid hold of more and more. Prayer for young disciples was one of the great glories of Paul. It should be for us as well.

> **If you believe, you will receive whatever you ask for in prayer." (Mat 21:22)**
> **And pray in the Spirit on all occasions with all kinds of prayers and requests. With this in mind, be alert and always keep on praying for all the saints. (Eph 6:18)**
> **Night and day we pray most earnestly that we may see you again and supply what is lacking in your faith. (1 Th 3:10)**

5 (1:4) **Tears—Paul**: the fifth glory of Paul was his remembrance of Timothy's tears. This is a warm and touching statement: Paul yearned and longed to see Timothy. Why? Because of Timothy's tears. Timothy was apparently a man with a strong and tender heart, a heart that was soft and warm and that felt deeply and was easily touched and moved to compassion and tears. There is no question about his strength and courage, for he was chosen by Paul to be Paul's successor. Paul would have never chosen a weakling, someone who was not the strongest among the strong. But something else would appeal to Paul as well: a man with a tender and compassionate heart, a man who was not afraid to show the warmth and softness of tears as he ministered and struggled in prayer before God.

What a man to covet! What a companion in ministry Timothy must have been! No wonder Paul coveted his presence, longing and yearning to join him in ministry.

> **I thank my God every time I remember you. because of your partnership in the gospel from the first day until now, (Phil 1:3, 5)**
> **But if we walk in the light, as he is in the light, we have fellowship with one another, and the blood of Jesus, his Son, purifies us from all sin. (1 John 1:7)**
> **I am a friend to all who fear you, to all who follow your precepts. (Psa 119:63)**
> **A friend loves at all times, and a brother is born for adversity. (Prov 17:17)**
> **Two are better than one, because they have a good return for their work: If one falls down, his friend can help him up. But pity the man who falls and has no one to help him up! (Eccl 4:9-10)**

6 (1:5) **Family—Parents—Lois—Eunice**: the sixth glory of Paul was his memory of Timothy's family—their genuine faith. Timothy had one of the greatest privileges that a child can have: strong Christian parents. His mother and grandmother were staunch believers who were faithful to God's Word every day of their lives. This was and still is the key in any family: faithfulness to God's Word every day. Timothy's mother and grandmother had taught Timothy the Scriptures from earliest childhood.

And how from infancy you have known the holy Scriptures, which are able to make you wise for salvation through faith in Christ Jesus. (2 Tim 3:15)

The point is this: Timothy's faith in Christ was genuine and sincere; it was real and true. He honestly trusted Christ as his Savior and Lord, and he lived for Christ day by day. One of the major reasons for his strength in the Lord was the strong faith of his mother, Eunice, and his grandmother, Lois. They had rooted and grounded him in the faith. Note: their faith had been strong; Paul mentions this as the very reason he could trust the faith of Timothy so much.

Thought 1. What a glorious testimony, yet an awesome responsibility. Parents must be godly, possessing the strongest of faiths—a faith that is genuine and true, real and sincere. Parents must trust the Lord Jesus Christ and rear their children to trust Christ. They must root their children in the Scripture so that they will know how to walk in Christ day by day.

Fathers, do not exasperate your children; instead, bring them up in the training and instruction of the Lord. (Eph 6:4)
I thank God, whom I serve, as my forefathers did, with a clear conscience, as night and day I constantly remember you in my prayers. (2 Tim 1:3)
And how from infancy you have known the holy Scriptures, which are able to make you wise for salvation through faith in Christ Jesus. (2 Tim 3:15)
Impress them on your children. Talk about them when you sit at home and when you walk along the road, when you lie down and when you get up. (Deu 6:7)
Train a child in the way he should go, and when he is old he will not turn from it. (Prov 22:6)

2 TIMOTHY 1:6-12

	I. THE STRONG CHARGES TO TIMOTHY, 1:6-2:26	called us to a holy life—not because of anything we have done but because of his own purpose and grace. This grace was given us in Christ Jesus before the beginning of time, 10 But it has now been revealed through the appearing of our Savior, Christ Jesus, who has destroyed death and has brought life and immortality to light through the gospel.	called us 1) Not by works 2) By His purpose b. Because God's purpose for salvation is eternal c. Because God has now revealed His purpose 1) By Christ's appearance 2) By destroying death 3) By revealing life
	A. Charge One: Endure Abuse for the Gospel, 1:6-12		
1 Stir up the gift of God: Fan into flame the gift of God	6 For this reason I remind you to fan into flame the gift of God, which is in you through the laying on of my hands.		
2 Do not fear—God has not given us the spirit of timidity	7 For God did not give us a spirit of timidity, but a spirit of power, of love and of self-discipline.	11 And of this gospel I was appointed a herald and an apostle and a teacher. 12 That is why I am suffering as I am. Yet I am not ashamed, because I know whom I have believed, and am convinced that he is able to guard what I have entrusted to him for that day.	5 Look at Paul's example a. He was appointed & called to serve the gospel b. He was not ashamed to suffer for the gospel 1) He knew that his faith was sure 2) He was persuaded of God's keeping power c. He was sure that judgment was coming
3 Do not be ashamed of the gospel nor of strong believers	8 So do not be ashamed to testify about our Lord, or ashamed of me his prisoner. But join with me in suffering for the gospel, by the power of God,		
4 Share in the sufferings of the gospel			
a. Because God has saved &	9 Who has saved us and		

DIVISION I

THE STRONG CHARGES TO TIMOTHY, 1:6-2:26

A. Charge One: Endure Abuse for the Gospel, 1:6-12

(1:6-12) **Introduction**: this passage begins a series of strong charges—charges directed to Timothy but applicable to us all. Charge one is an eye-opener; it strikes fear in some believers. Nevertheless, it is a charge that must be heeded by everyone of us: *endure abuse for the gospel*.

1. Stir up the gift of God: fan into flame the gift of God. (v.6).
2. Do not fear—God has not given us the spirit of timidity (v.7).
3. Do not be ashamed of the gospel (v.8).
4. Share in the sufferings of the gospel (v.8-10).
5. Look at Paul's example (v.11-12).

1 (1:6) **Believer—Minister—Gifts, Spiritual**: first, stir up the gift of God, fan into flame the gift of God. What is the "gift of God?" This probably refers to spiritual gifts, the gifts which the Holy Spirit gives to every believer—the spiritual gifts which equip the believer to minister. The word "stir up" or "fan into flame" (anazopureo) can mean to keep blazing and to keep the flame of the fire burning. But it can also mean to rekindle and to restir the flame, indicating that the flame was about to go out. Which is meant here? No doubt Timothy faced what we sometimes face: times when he needed to be restirred and rekindled. But there is no indication that Timothy's flame was about to go out.

Keep this is mind: Paul was facing death; he was about to be executed. He clearly states this fact (2 Tim.4:6-8). Therefore, Paul sensed the need to give Timothy charge after charge. One of the very first things Timothy needed to do was to keep his spiritual gifts blazing and burning to the hottest point possible. The idea is present tense, which means it is progressive and continuous action. The believer is to *keep on* stirring up his gift, never letting its flame lose any of its intensity. He is to use his gift to minister and minister, never slacking up nor losing his zeal. God has gifted the believer to minister, gifted him in a very, very special way; therefore, he must minister. He must do exactly what God has gifted him to do.

> **Thought 1.** Note: the problem with most believers is that they do not even know what their spiritual gifts are. There is a great need within the church to study the gifts and the great price God has paid to secure the gifts for His people. (See outline and notes—Ro.12:3-8; 1 Cor.12:4-11; Eph.4:7-16 for more discussion.)

> The man who had received the five talents brought the other five. 'Master,' he said, 'you entrusted me with five talents. See, I have gained five more.' (Mat 25:20)

> Do not neglect your gift, which was given you through a prophetic message when the body of elders laid their hands on you. (1 Tim 4:14)

> For this reason I remind you to fan into flame the gift of God, which is in you through the laying on of my hands. (2 Tim 1:6)

> We have different gifts, according to the grace given us. If a man's gift is prophesying, let him use it in proportion to his faith. If it is serving, let him serve; if it is teaching, let him teach; if it is encouraging, let him encourage; if it is contributing to the needs of others, let him give generously; if it is leadership, let him govern diligently; if it is showing mercy, let him do it cheerfully. (Rom 12:6-8)

> But eagerly desire the greater gifts. And now I will show you the most excellent way. (1 Cor 12:31)

2 TIMOTHY 1:6-12

Follow the way of love and eagerly desire spiritual gifts, especially the gift of prophecy. (1 Cor 14:1)

2 (1:7) **Fear—Power—Love**: second, do not fear. God has not given us the spirit of timidity. Too often believers—laymen and ministers alike—fear using their gifts. They fear speaking up for Christ and the gospel—they fear...

- ridicule
- criticism
- embarrassment
- opposition
- mockery
- abuse

Being very honest, we have all experienced these fears at one time or another. We failed to witness—to use our gift in speaking up for Christ and in proclaiming the gospel lest we suffer persecution. But note the charge; it is clear and forceful: we are not to fear.

⇒ We are not to fear the face of man.
⇒ We are not to fear the trials that may come our way because we are living for Christ.
⇒ We are not to fear the ridicule and persecution that may be launched against us because we are witnessing and ministering for Christ.

Is it possible to keep from fearing if we live for Christ in this world, a world that is so evil and abusive? How can we keep from being apprehensive if we witness for Christ day by day? How can we keep from being cowardly when the world thinks that religion is to be kept in the church and not out in the world? How can we stand up for Christ when people mock and poke fun at anyone who lives for Christ?

This verse tells us how: we let God equip us. God's equipment does not include fear. The fact is clearly stated: God does not give us the spirit of timidity; God gives us the spirit of love and power, and of self discipline. The word *spirit* means the believer's spirit: the Holy Spirit of God actually injects power, love, and self discipline into the spirit of the believer.

1. The Holy Spirit actually infuses power into the believer's spirit. But note: we do not receive power until we begin to minister. Power is not needed if we just sit around and remain silent about Christ. The Holy Spirit gives us power only when we begin to minister and actually need it. It is when we begin to live for Christ—to use our gifts to bear witness for Him—that the Spirit of God injects power into our spirit. When we begin to live and proclaim Christ, the Holy Spirit endows us with power, enormous power...

- power to face the strain of difficulties and trials.
- power to stand tall in living and witnessing for Christ.
- power to take on the job and to do it well—to the very best of our ability.

But you will receive power when the Holy Spirit comes on you; and you will be my witnesses in Jerusalem, and in all Judea and Samaria, and to the ends of the earth." (Acts 1:8)

With great power the apostles continued to testify to the resurrection of the Lord Jesus, and much grace was upon them all. (Acts 4:33)

I pray also that the eyes of your heart may be enlightened in order that you may know the hope to which he has called you, the riches of his glorious inheritance in the saints, and his incomparably great power for us who believe. That power is like the working of his mighty strength, (Eph 1:18-19)

I pray that out of his glorious riches he may strengthen you with power through his Spirit in your inner being, (Eph 3:16)

Now to him who is able to do immeasurably more than all we ask or imagine, according to his power that is at work within us, (Eph 3:20)

Being strengthened with all power according to his glorious might so that you may have great endurance and patience, and joyfully (Col 1:11)

For God did not give us a spirit of timidity, but a spirit of power, of love and of self-discipline. (2 Tim 1:7)

But as for me, I am filled with power, with the Spirit of the LORD, and with justice and might, to declare to Jacob his transgression, to Israel his sin. (Micah 3:8)

2. The Holy Spirit infuses love into the believer's spirit. This is *agape* love, the kind of love that loves people even if they are sinners and enemies. It is a love that arises within the mind and will, not in the emotions. It is the kind of love that says, "I will love this person no matter what he does to me. I will care for, nourish, and nurture him. I will share Christ with him. I will treat him just as I would want him to treat me if he knew Christ. I will love him and be responsible to him, no matter how he treats me."

Note: this kind of love—the kind of love that can love sinners and enemies—is a gift of God's Spirit. No man can stir or work up *agape* love. *Agape* love is God's love. God alone possesses it; therefore, God alone can give it to men. He gives it to all who live for His Son, the Lord Jesus Christ, and who proclaim Him (cp. v.8-10).

"A new command I give you: Love one another. As I have loved you, so you must love one another. By this all men will know that you are my disciples, if you love one another." (John 13:34-35)

But the fruit of the Spirit is love, joy, peace, patience, kindness, goodness, faithfulness, gentleness and self-control. Against such things there is no law. (Gal 5:22-23)

And live a life of love, just as Christ loved us and gave himself up for us as a fragrant offering and sacrifice to God. (Eph 5:2)

And over all these virtues put on love, which binds them all together in perfect unity. (Col 3:14)

And so we know and rely on the love God has for us. God is love. Whoever lives in love lives in God, and God in him. (1 John 4:16)

3. The Holy Spirit infuses self-discipline into the believer's spirit. "Self-discipline" (sophronismou) means self-control; the ability to control one's emotions, feelings, and thoughts in the midst of trials and circumstances, no matter how severe and stressful. It is just as it says, self-discipline—the mastery over one's mind, over one's heart and life despite the trial or opposition. When the believer

begins to live and bear testimony for Christ, the Holy Spirit gives him self-discipline—a most glorious gift.

Thought 1. Think for a moment. Picture a genuine believer...
- who is living for Christ: walking in Christ and sharing Christ all day every day.
- who honestly loves people and treats people just like he should—no matter how they treat him.
- who is controlled—who controls his passions, feelings, behavior, and thoughts.

Picture such a person: Could God let that person live in timidity? Could God fail to keep from giving that person strength, that is, spiritual power and love and self-discipline? The answer is obvious. The person who truly lives for Christ and bears testimony for Christ is delivered from timidity:
⇒ he is given power, enormous power.
⇒ he is given love, great love for people, no matter who they are.
⇒ he is given self-discipline, peace, stability, and security in a dying and insecure world.

> Those who live according to the sinful nature have their minds set on what that nature desires; but those who live in accordance with the Spirit have their minds set on what the Spirit desires. The mind of sinful man is death, but the mind controlled by the Spirit is life and peace; the sinful mind is hostile to God. It does not submit to God's law, nor can it do so. (Rom 8:5-7)

> So then, let us not be like others, who are asleep, but let us be alert and self-controlled. For those who sleep, sleep at night, and those who get drunk, get drunk at night. (1 Th 5:6-7)

> For God did not give us a spirit of timidity, but a spirit of power, of love and of self-discipline. (2 Tim 1:7)

> Similarly, encourage the young men to be self-controlled. (Titus 2:6)

> Therefore, prepare your minds for action; be self-controlled; set your hope fully on the grace to be given you when Jesus Christ is revealed. (1 Pet 1:13)

> The end of all things is near. Therefore be clear minded and self-controlled so that you can pray. (1 Pet 4:7)

3 (1:8) **Gospel—Witnessing**: third, do not be ashamed of the gospel nor of strong believers who are living and witnessing for Christ. The point and verse are clear enough. No believer is to shrink...
- from identifying with the gospel and the Lord of the gospel.
- from identifying with strong believers who are living for and sharing Christ.

We are to share the gospel—share by living for Christ and by speaking up for Him, bearing testimony of His saving grace. We are to stand up for those who share Christ when they are being ridiculed and persecuted. In fact, note the verse: we are to share in the sufferings of the gospel. Any of us who truly live for the gospel will be opposed and misunderstood by the world. Why? Because we do not live like the world; we do not live sensual, immoral, ungodly, and worldly lives. We do not follow after the things of the world. Therefore, our righteous and godly lives convict the world of its ungodly deeds. Hence, the world ridicules and persecutes us. But we are not to let this stop us: we are not to shrink from living for and sharing the gospel. We are to jump right in with the strong believer and share the gospel with a starving and lost world that reels under the weight of evil, corruption, and death.

> Remember the words I spoke to you: 'No servant is greater than his master.' If they persecuted me, they will persecute you also. If they obeyed my teaching, they will obey yours also. (John 15:20)

> "All this I have told you so that you will not go astray. They will put you out of the synagogue; in fact, a time is coming when anyone who kills you will think he is offering a service to God. They will do such things because they have not known the Father or me. I have told you this, so that when the time comes you will remember that I warned you. I did not tell you this at first because I was with you. (John 16:1-4)

> For it has been granted to you on behalf of Christ not only to believe on him, but also to suffer for him, (Phil 1:29)

> So that no one would be unsettled by these trials. You know quite well that we were destined for them. (1 Th 3:3)

> In fact, everyone who wants to live a godly life in Christ Jesus will be persecuted, (2 Tim 3:12)

> Do not be surprised, my brothers, if the world hates you. (1 John 3:13)

> Dear friends, do not be surprised at the painful trial you are suffering, as though something strange were happening to you. But rejoice that you participate in the sufferings of Christ, so that you may be overjoyed when his glory is revealed. (1 Pet 4:12-13)

4 (1:8-10) **Gospel**: fourth, share in the sufferings of the gospel. As stated above, this is the duty of believers. If we live for Christ—live for the gospel, live godly lives—the ungodly of the world will persecute us. There is no escape from it. But we are not to shrink from our duty. We are not to fear, nor are we to be ashamed of the gospel. We are to live for the gospel and proclaim the gospel. Scripture gives three strong encouragements, three strong reasons why we should stand up for Christ and the gospel.

1. We are to stand up for the gospel because God has saved us and called us with a holy calling. And note: God saved us by grace, that is, freely. We did not have to work one iota for salvation. We did not have to pay a cent nor do a single thing for salvation. God Himself saved us...
- He has delivered us from sin and the bondages of the flesh (sinful nature).
- He has delivered us from death. Think about it: we shall never die. When our time comes—at the last moment, in an instant of time, in a split second—God will transfer us from this world into His presence. We are saved from ever having to taste death.
- He has saved us from judgment and condemnation, from the punishment of hell.

2 TIMOTHY 1:6-12

God has done all this for us, and He has done it by grace—freely—simply because He loves us and wills to save us. How, then, can we deny Him? How can we dare be ashamed of Him and fear living for Him? How can we be ashamed of telling the world about His glorious salvation?

> **Therefore no one will be declared righteous in his sight by observing the law; rather, through the law we become conscious of sin. (Rom 3:20)**
>
> **For it is by grace you have been saved, through faith—and this not from yourselves, it is the gift of God—not by works, so that no one can boast. (Eph 2:8-9)**
>
> **But when the kindness and love of God our Savior appeared, he saved us, not because of righteous things we had done, but because of his mercy. He saved us through the washing of rebirth and renewal by the Holy Spirit, (Titus 3:4-5)**

2. We are to stand up for the gospel because God's purpose for salvation is eternal. Salvation was planned by God before the world was ever created. The gospel of salvation was given to us *in Christ* before the world was ever created. The point is this: the gospel of salvation—wrought through His Son, the Lord Jesus Christ—is God's eternal plan. It is the only plan God has whereby people may be saved. If a person misses this plan, he will miss salvation; he will never be acceptable to God. Therefore, we—all believers—must not be ashamed nor fear proclaiming Christ. Salvation through Christ and the gospel of Christ is the only way any person can ever be saved. We must proclaim the gospel even if men oppose it, for they shall forever be lost if we fail to lead them to Christ.

> **I told you that you would die in your sins; if you do not believe that I am the one I claim to be, you will indeed die in your sins." (John 8:24)**
>
> **Jesus answered, "I am the way and the truth and the life. No one comes to the Father except through me. (John 14:6)**
>
> **Salvation is found in no one else, for there is no other name under heaven given to men by which we must be saved." (Acts 4:12)**
>
> **For there is one God and one mediator between God and men, the man Christ Jesus, who gave himself as a ransom for all men—the testimony given in its proper time. (1 Tim 2:5-6)**

3. We are to stand up for the gospel because God has *now revealed* His purpose of salvation to the world. Note how God did this: "through the appearing of our Savior Christ Jesus." What did Jesus Christ do to reveal God's purpose?

a. Jesus Christ destroyed death. How? How *in this world* can anyone ever destroy death? Very simply, Jesus Christ died *for man*. All that is within man—all that causes man to die—Jesus Christ took upon Himself. Jesus Christ took all the evil, sin, and corruption that causes death—took it all upon Himself and died for man. Now think for a moment: since He has died for man, man does not have to die. Death is destroyed for man: man is freed from death; death no longer has a hold on man. (See note, *Jesus Christ, Mediator*—1 Tim. 2:3-7 for more discussion.)

b. Jesus Christ has brought life and immortality to light through the gospel. Man can now live forever and receive immortality. How? Through the gospel of life and immortality provided by Jesus Christ. When a person believes in Jesus Christ— truly believes by committing his life to Christ— God takes that person's belief and counts it as the life of Christ. God actually counts the person as being *in* Christ. Christ is eternal and immortal; therefore, if a person is *in Christ*, he becomes eternal and immortal. He is immortal because he is *in Christ*. How can such a thing be? Because God *counts* it so. God takes our faith in Christ and counts it as immortality. God loves His Son, the Lord Jesus Christ, so much that He will honor any person who honors His Son. God will honor that person who truly honors His Son by believing in Him—honor the person by doing exactly what the person believes about Christ. Christ proclaimed that any person who believed in Him would never die, but have eternal life. Therefore, if a person believes in Christ, believes the gospel of Christ, God gives that person life and immortality. (See note, *Justification*—Ro.5:1 for more discussion.)

This is the *light of the gospel*—the glorious revelation of the gospel. Jesus Christ has destroyed death and brought life and immortality to man.

> **"For God so loved the world that he gave his one and only Son, that whoever believes in him shall not perish but have eternal life. For God did not send his Son into the world to condemn the world, but to save the world through him. Whoever believes in him is not condemned, but whoever does not believe stands condemned already because he has not believed in the name of God's one and only Son. (John 3:16-18)**
>
> **"I tell you the truth, whoever hears my word and believes him who sent me has eternal life and will not be condemned; he has crossed over from death to life. (John 5:24)**
>
> **I tell you the truth, if anyone keeps my word, he will never see death." (John 8:51)**
>
> **And whoever lives and believes in me will never die. Do you believe this?" (John 11:26)**
>
> **Therefore, there is now no condemnation for those who are in Christ Jesus, (Rom 8:1)**
>
> **Since the children have flesh and blood, he too shared in their humanity so that by his death he might destroy him who holds the power of death—that is, the devil—and free those who all their lives were held in slavery by their fear of death. (Heb 2:14-15)**

5 (1:11-12) **Testimony—Paul, Example**: fifth, look at Paul's example. Paul endured abuse for the gospel. Paul says two significant things about himself.

2 TIMOTHY 1:6-12

1. Paul had been appointed and called to serve the gospel of the Lord Jesus Christ. Three appointments are mentioned.
    a. Paul was appointed to be a preacher of the gospel. The preacher is a herald, a person who is appointed by a king to go forth and proclaim the message of the king. The minister is a preacher who is sent forth by God to preach the truth about Jesus Christ…
        • that He has destroyed death.
        • that He has brought life and immortality to light.
    b. Paul had been appointed an apostle of the Lord Jesus Christ. The apostle is a person who has been sent as a very special witness and on a very special mission. The minister is sent forth on the special mission to bear witness that Jesus Christ is the Mediator between God and men. Jesus Christ has paid the ransom price for man.
    c. Paul had been appointed as a teacher of the Lord Jesus Christ. The teacher is a person who instructs people in the faith and truth of God's Word. It is the gift to root and ground people in doctrine, reproof, correction, and righteousness. God had called him to proclaim and teach the salvation that is in Christ Jesus.
2. Paul was not ashamed to suffer for the gospel.
    a. He knew that his faith was sure; he knew Christ. The point is this: Paul knew Christ on a personal and intimate basis. He walked with Christ day by day—was in fellowship and communion with Him. He had a personal relationship with Christ; therefore, he knew that his belief in Christ was true. This was the reason he was willing to suffer for the gospel: the gospel was true. A person could actually be saved from death and receive life and immortality; a person could actually live face to face with God forever and ever. Paul knew this—knew it beyond a shadow of a doubt. How? Because he knew Christ personally and intimately.

> **The Spirit himself testifies with our spirit that we are God's children. Now if we are children, then we are heirs—heirs of God and co-heirs with Christ, if indeed we share in his sufferings in order that we may also share in his glory. (Rom 8:16-17)**
>
> **And you also were included in Christ when you heard the word of truth, the gospel of your salvation. Having believed, you were marked in him with a seal, the promised Holy Spirit, who is a deposit guaranteeing our inheritance until the redemption of those who are God's possession—to the praise of his glory. (Eph 1:13-14)**
>
> **Because our gospel came to you not simply with words, but also with power, with the Holy Spirit and with deep conviction. You know how we lived among you for your sake. (1 Th 1:5)**
>
> **That is why I am suffering as I am. Yet I am not ashamed, because I know whom I have believed, and am convinced that he is able to guard what I have entrusted to him for that day. (2 Tim 1:12)**
>
> **We proclaim to you what we have seen and heard, so that you also may have fellowship with us. And our fellowship is with the Father and with his Son, Jesus Christ. (1 John 1:3)**
>
> **We know that we have come to know him if we obey his commands. The man who says, "I know him," but does not do what he commands is a liar, and the truth is not in him. But if anyone obeys his word, God's love is truly made complete in him. This is how we know we are in him: (1 John 2:3-5)**
>
> **We know that we live in him and he in us, because he has given us of his Spirit. (1 John 4:13)**
>
> **Anyone who believes in the Son of God has this testimony in his heart. Anyone who does not believe God has made him out to be a liar, because he has not believed the testimony God has given about his Son. (1 John 5:10)**

   b. Paul was persuaded of God's keeping power. Paul had entrusted both his life and work to Christ—all that Paul was as a person and all that Paul did upon earth was entrusted to Christ. The word "entrusted" (paratheke) means to deposit. A.T. Robertson says that Paul means, " 'My deposit' as in a bank, the bank of heaven which no burglar can break (Mt.6:19f)" (*Word Pictures in the New Testament*, Vol.4, p.614). Paul had deposited, turned everything he was and had over to Christ. Why? Because he knew that Christ could keep it and take care of it forever and ever. What exactly did Paul turn over to Christ? His life and work. Imagine!
   ⇒ Paul deposited his life into the hands of Christ; therefore, Christ *increased* his life, guided his life to bear the richest interest and the greatest return. Paul's *deposit of life was increased* to eternal life.
   ⇒ Paul deposited his work into the hands of Christ; therefore, Christ increased his work to bear the richest interest and the greatest return. Paul's *deposit of work was increased* to eternal responsibility and management for God. (See note, *Rewards*—Lk.16:10-12 for more discussion.)

> **Such people we command and urge in the Lord Jesus Christ to settle down and earn the bread they eat. (2 Th 3:12)**
>
> **Who through faith are shielded by God's power until the coming of the salvation that is ready to be revealed in the last time. (1 Pet 1:5)**
>
> **To him who is able to keep you from falling and to present you before his glorious presence without fault and with great joy— (Jude 1:24)**

3. Paul was sure that judgment was coming. Therefore, he committed his life and work to Christ in order to receive the reward of God and not the judgment of God. Paul knew that he had to stand before Christ some day and give an account for his life and work. This is the reason Paul did exactly what Christ said: he trusted Christ, and gave Christ his life—totally. He deposited his life and work with Christ; staked everything he was and had upon Christ. Why? Because he knew that Christ would keep him and

present him faultless in that day. Christ would present him to God as a follower of His, and God would accept Paul because Paul had followed God's one and only Son. Paul knew beyond question who it was that he was following: he was following the Lord Jesus Christ, the very Son of God Himself.

> For the Son of Man is going to come in his Father's glory with his angels, and then he will reward each person according to what he has done. (Mat 16:27)
> For we must all appear before the judgment seat of Christ, that each one may receive what is due him for the things done while in the body, whether good or bad. (2 Cor 5:10)
> Since you call on a Father who judges each man's work impartially, live your lives as strangers here in reverent fear. (1 Pet 1:17)
> "I the LORD search the heart and examine the mind, to reward a man according to his conduct, according to what his deeds deserve." (Jer 17:10)

2 TIMOTHY 1:13-18

	B. Charge Two: Hold Fast to the Lord Jesus Christ, 1:13-18	deserted me, including Phygelus and Hermogenes.	

1 Hold fast to sound teaching
  a. By faith—in Christ alone
  b. By love—in Christ alone
2 Hold fast one's trust—by the power of the Holy Spirit
 	
3 Hold fast without deserting, for many have deserted
	13 What you heard from me, keep as the pattern of sound teaching, with faith and love in Christ Jesus.
	14 Guard the good deposit that was entrusted to you—guard it with the help of the Holy Spirit who lives in us.
	15 You know that everyone in the province of Asia has
		16 May the Lord show mercy to the household of Onesiphorus, because he often refreshed me and was not ashamed of my chains.
		17 On the contrary, when he was in Rome, he searched hard for me until he found me.
		18 May the Lord grant that he will find mercy from the Lord on that day! You know very well in how many ways he helped me in Ephesus.
			4 Hold fast following the example of those who have proven faithful: Onesiphorus
			
			  a. He had searched hard for Paul until he found Paul
			
			  b. He was assured of mercy in the great day of judgment

DIVISION I

THE STRONG CHARGES TO TIMOTHY, 1:6-2:26

B. Charge Two: Hold On to the Lord Jesus Christ, 1:13-18

(1:13-18) **Introduction**: this is the second charge given to believers, both ministers and laymen alike. Note that the charge is strong, of a critical nature: *hold fast*. In a world that is filled with wickedness and false teaching, believers must hold fast to the Lord Jesus Christ.

1. Hold fast to sound teaching (v.13).
2. Hold fast one's trust—by the power of the Holy Spirit (v.14).
3. Hold fast without deserting, for many have deserted (v.15).
4. Hold fast following the example of those who have proven faithful: Onesiphorus (v.16-18).

1 (1:13) **Scripture—Gospel—Doctrine—Teaching—Minister**: first, hold fast to sound teaching. The word "sound" (hugiainonton) is interesting. It means healthful, health giving. Believers must hold fast to sound, health giving teaching, that is, to teaching that will make them sound and healthy. What *teaching* will make a person sound and healthy? The teaching just covered by the Scripture:

⇒ the teaching of the gospel (v.8).
⇒ the teaching of salvation (v.9).
⇒ the teaching about Jesus Christ, the glorious message that He has abolished death and brought life and immortality to man (v.9-10).
⇒ the teaching that Paul himself taught, the words that he taught to Timothy and to the believers of the early church (v.13).

Simply stated, believers are to hold fast to the Holy Scriptures, to the very Teachings of God Himself, for the Word of God alone can bring health and life to the human soul.

1. We must hold fast to sound teaching in *faith*. That is, we must believe in Christ, surrender our hearts and lives to Him, and we must be loyal to Christ. If we do not believe the words and message about Christ—if we do not have faith in Christ—then we are not holding fast to sound teaching. The very first sign of sound teaching is faith in Christ; the very first sign that a person is clinging to sound teaching is his *faith in Christ*. If a person does not believe in Christ, he is not holding fast to sound teaching. He is believing a false doctrine, a false philosophy of life and will thereby perish. The only words that can bring health and soundness to a person are the words of Christ—the life-giving words of His salvation. A person must hold fast to sound teachings by believing in Christ Jesus, the only Savior who has brought the life-giving words of God to earth.

2. We must hold fast to sound teaching *in love*. It is not enough to believe in the sound teachings about Christ; we must also love everyone in Christ and love the world through Christ. A person who truly believes the gospel believes in Christ, and he loves both Christ and the words of the gospel.

The point is this: it is impossible to truly believe Christ and His gospel without loving Christ and His Word. A person who truly loves Christ sees the people of the world through the eyes of Christ: he loves everyone even as Christ loves everyone. He holds fast to sound teachings in love: he seeks to share the teachings of health and soundness with all men. He wants all men to know the sound teachings of salvation that bring health and soundness to the human soul.

> **"I tell you the truth, whoever hears my word and believes him who sent me has eternal life and will not be condemned; he has crossed over from death to life. (John 5:24)**
>
> **But these are written that you may believe that Jesus is the Christ, the Son of God, and that by believing you may have life in his name. (John 20:31)**
>
> **Consequently, faith comes from hearing the message, and the message is heard through the word of Christ. (Rom 10:17)**
>
> **What you heard from me, keep as the pattern of sound teaching, with faith and love in Christ Jesus. (2 Tim 1:13)**
>
> **All Scripture is God-breathed and is useful for teaching, rebuking, correcting and training in righteousness, (2 Tim 3:16)**
>
> **In everything set them an example by doing what is good. In your teaching show integrity, seriousness and soundness of speech that cannot be condemned, so that those who oppose you may be ashamed because they have nothing bad to say about us. (Titus 2:7-8)**

2 TIMOTHY 1:13-18

2 (1:14) **Minister—Believer, Duty**: second, hold fast the trust God has placed into your hands—hold fast your trust—guard it by the power of the Holy Spirit. William Barclay has an excellent comment on this point:

> "Not only do we put our trust in God: God also puts His trust in us. The idea of God's dependence on men is never far from New Testament thought. When God wants something done, He has to find a man to do it. If God wants a child taught, a message brought, a sermon preached, a wanderer found, a sorrowing one comforted, a sick one healed, he has to find some agent and some instrument to do His work" (*The Letters to Timothy, Titus, and Philemon*, p.176).

Matthew Henry says:

> "The Christian doctrine is a trust committed to us....It is committed to us to be preserved pure and entire, and to be transmitted to those who shall come after us, and we must keep it, and not contribute any thing to the corrupting of its purity, the weakening of its power, or the diminishing of its perfection" (*Matthew Henry's Commentary*, Vol.5, p.836).

Note that the believer can guard his trust and do the work of God only by the power of the Holy Spirit. It is the Spirit of God who gifts the believer and calls him to work for the Lord. Every genuine believer is given specific work to do for the Lord, but the believer cannot do the work in his own strength. No man can penetrate the heart of another person; only the Holy Spirit of God can do that. Therefore, the believer must stay close to the Spirit of God and depend upon Him for the power to do good and effective work. The Holy Spirit alone has the power to change a man's heart; therefore, the believer must depend upon the Holy Spirit to help him in his work. (See note—1 Tim.6:20-21 for more discussion.)

> "Again, it will be like a man going on a journey, who called his servants and entrusted his property to them. To one he gave five talents of money, to another two talents, and to another one talent, each according to his ability. Then he went on his journey. (Mat 25:14-15)
>
> So he called ten of his servants and gave them ten minas. 'Put this money to work,' he said, 'until I come back.' (Luke 19:13)
>
> Now it is required that those who have been given a trust must prove faithful. (1 Cor 4:2)
>
> You were bought at a price. Therefore honor God with your body. (1 Cor 6:20)
>
> Timothy, guard what has been entrusted to your care. Turn away from godless chatter and the opposing ideas of what is falsely called knowledge, (1 Tim 6:20)
>
> Each one should use whatever gift he has received to serve others, faithfully administering God's grace in its various forms. (1 Pet 4:10)

3 (1:15) **Backsliding—Desertion—Ministering**: third, hold fast without deserting, for many have deserted. Paul was facing the crisis of his life: he was standing trial on a capital charge, that of being an insurrectionist, a disturber of the peace against the Roman empire. It was dangerous to be associated with Paul; there was the chance that a person would be identified as an associate of Paul. Because of this, most of the believers throughout Asia deserted Paul. They actually turned away from the minister who had done so much for them.

The leaders of the desertion were Phygellus and Hermogenes. This is the only time these two men are mentioned in Scripture; therefore, the only thing we know about them is what is shared here. Apparently, there was a time when they followed the Lord and supported Paul; but now, when the chips were down and the minister of God really needed them, they deserted him and began to oppose him and to lead others to desert him. Paul was deeply hurt; those whom he had loved and done so much for were now turning their backs upon him.

Thought 1. Oliver Greene paints a descriptive application of this event:

> "This reminds us of our Lord. As He broke the loaves and fishes, He had thousands at His feet; but when He fell beneath the weight of His cross, not one person volunteered to carry it for Him—and the Scripture tells us that Simon the Cyrenian was compelled to bear His cross (Mark 15:21). Many pastors know better than I that when a person needs a friend and stands condemned by those in authority, he will always learn who his real friends are. Many times a dear pastor believes that the majority of his church members stand with him—but when the enemies of the Gospel are ready to vote him out, he discovers that his friends are few and that the visible church embraces many spineless Christians. Paul had many converts and professing friends in Asia; but when the testing time came, like the disciples of Jesus they turned back and walked with him no more" (*The Epistles of Paul the Apostle to Timothy and Titus*, p.287).

> But this has all taken place that the writings of the prophets might be fulfilled." Then all the disciples deserted him and fled. (Mat 26:56)
>
> "But a time is coming, and has come, when you will be scattered, each to his own home. You will leave me all alone. Yet I am not alone, for my Father is with me. (John 16:32)
>
> For Demas, because he loved this world, has deserted me and has gone to Thessalonica. Crescens has gone to Galatia, and Titus to Dalmatia. (2 Tim 4:10)
>
> My intercessor is my friend as my eyes pour out tears to God; (Job 16:20)
>
> All my intimate friends detest me; those I love have turned against me. (Job 19:19)

4 (1:16-18) **Onesiphorus—Believers, Faithful**: hold fast, following the example of those who have proven faithful. Note the resounding tenderness heaped upon one man and his household, the man Onesiphorus. Onesiphorus is a dynamic example of a courageous man, a man who was committed to helping people even if it did endanger his life. This passage gives every indication that he dearly loved Paul. When Onesiphorus heard that Paul had been arrested and imprisoned in Rome, he apparently struck out for Rome to see what he could do to help. Note the word "searched" (v.17). This indicates that he had some difficulty finding the prison where Paul was chained. It is true that for two years Paul had been allowed to live in a rented house and to use it as his living quarters despite the fact that he was a prisoner. But apparently at some point he was put behind bars in one of the security prisons where the most notorious criminals were imprisoned. Whatever the case, Onesiphorus did not give up his search. He "searched hard for me [Paul]." The idea is that he searched and searched against great difficulty until he found Paul. Note his ministry to Paul:

⇒ He refreshed Paul, refreshed him *often*. This would certainly include visits and the encouragement and comfort of sharing Scripture and prayer. And, if allowed, it would include food and clothing and the provision of any medical or financial needs Paul might have had.

⇒ He was not ashamed of Paul's imprisonment—not ashamed to be identified with Paul as a friend and fellow believer in the Lord Jesus Christ. He stood by the side of Paul as a follower of the gospel of the Lord Jesus Christ.

Note one other point: Paul's deep appreciation and love for Onesiphorus. He prays that God will have mercy upon this dear saint in the day of judgment—that God will reward Onesiphorus for the many things he did for him when he was a prisoner.

Thought 1. "*The majority of friends (so-called) will forsake us in the darkest hour of need; but the friend who is to be treasured as a jewel is the man who stands with us when we need encouragement, when all others are against us, and seemingly we have lost the battle. No words could ever express the worth of such a friend!*" (Oliver Greene, *The Epistles of Paul the Apostle to Timothy and Titus*, p.228f).

Just as the Son of Man did not come to be served, but to serve, and to give his life as a ransom for many." (Mat 20:28)

In everything I did, I showed you that by this kind of hard work we must help the weak, remembering the words the Lord Jesus himself said: 'It is more blessed to give than to receive.'" (Acts 20:35)

We who are strong ought to bear with the failings of the weak and not to please ourselves. (Rom 15:1)

Carry each other's burdens, and in this way you will fulfill the law of Christ. (Gal 6:2)

Remember those in prison as if you were their fellow prisoners, and those who are mistreated as if you yourselves were suffering. (Heb 13:3)

Religion that God our Father accepts as pure and faultless is this: to look after orphans and widows in their distress and to keep oneself from being polluted by the world. (James 1:27)

2 TIMOTHY 2:1-7

	CHAPTER 2	Jesus.	a. Must endure hardness
		4 No one serving as a soldier gets involved in civilian affairs—he wants to please his commanding officer.	b. Must not become entangled with the affairs of every day life
	C. Charge Three: Be Strong in the Lord Jesus Christ, 2:1-7		c. Must please or obey his commander
1 The source of strength—the Lord's grace	You then, my son, be strong in the grace that is in Christ Jesus.	5 Similarly, if anyone competes as an athlete, he does not receive the victor's crown unless he competes according to the rules.	4 Picture 3: A strong athlete a. Must be disciplined b. Must follow the rules
2 Picture 1: A strong teacher a. Must receive the truth b. Must train others to carry on the truth	2 And the things you have heard me say in the presence of many witnesses entrust to reliable men who will also be qualified to teach others.	6 The hardworking farmer should be the first to receive a share of the crops.	5 Picture 4: A hard working farmer
3 Picture 2: A strong soldier of Jesus Christ	3 Endure hardship with us like a good soldier of Christ	7 Reflect on what I am saying, for the Lord will give you insight into all this.	6 Conclusion: Think over these things

DIVISION I

THE STRONG CHARGES TO TIMOTHY, 1:6-2:26

C. Charge Three: Be Strong in the Lord Jesus Christ, 2:1-7

(2:1-7) **Introduction**: believers must be strong in the Lord. This passage gives an excellent picture of what being *strong in the Lord* means.
1. The source of strength—the Lord's grace (v.1).
2. Picture 1: a strong teacher (v.2).
3. Picture 2: a strong soldier of Jesus Christ (v.3-4).
4. Picture 3: a strong athlete (v.5).
5. Picture 4: a hard working farmer (v.6).
6. Conclusion: think over these things (v.7).

1 (2:1) **Grace**: the source of strength is found in the Lord Jesus Christ. In particular it is found "in the *grace* that is in Christ Jesus." Remember that Paul was facing death; he was to be executed by the Romans on the false charge that he was a revolutionary against the state. Timothy was to be Paul's successor; he would soon have to take over the main responsibility for the churches scattered all over the world. The responsibility for spreading the gospel across the earth would soon be his. Could he stand up under the pressure? Could he handle all the problems and circumstances that would arise? Would he work enough, study enough, learn enough, pray enough, witness enough, preach enough, teach enough, endure enough, strive enough, and war enough in the spirit? There was only one hope for Timothy, just as there is only one hope for any of us. Timothy needed an *unlimited strength*, a strength that could drive him to conquer any circumstance and to work at any task until it was accomplished. That strength could come from only one source, and Paul knew the fact.

⇒ That strength is the strength of God.

The strength of men is no stronger than man, and man ends up in the dust of the ground. His strength ceases to be. And not only this, but all along the path of life, man comes short and fails time after time—no matter who the man is. The weakness of his strength is constantly showing itself.

However, the strength of God is entirely different. God's strength is all sufficient and all powerful. It can and does conquer all, including death itself. Therefore, if a man can tap into God's strength, he can conquer all the circumstances of life, including death; and he can achieve his task upon earth, the very task that God wants him to fulfill while he is on earth. This is what Paul knew. But Paul knew something else: the strength of God can be tapped only through "the *grace that is in Christ Jesus*."

Grace means the *undeserved* favor and blessings of God. Man does not deserve the favor and blessings of God, but God loves man. Therefore, God has provided the way for man to receive His favor and blessings—the greatest way possible—through His Son, the Lord Jesus Christ. Man can receive the blessings of God through the very Son of God Himself. And this includes the strength of God, the strength to conquer and overcome all trials and to fulfill his task upon earth, no matter how much work it involved or how difficult the task may be.

The point is this: we must do just what Paul told Timothy to do. We must be strong—not strong in our own strength, but strong in the grace (favor) of Christ. We must look up to Christ, not to ourselves nor to other people. We must trust the sufficiency of Christ, not our own strength.

Note: Paul paints four pictures to illustrate what he means by being strong in Christ Jesus. These pictures are covered in the next four notes.

> **But by the grace of God I am what I am, and his grace to me was not without effect. No, I worked harder than all of them—yet not I, but the grace of God that was with me. (1 Cor 15:10)**
>
> **Finally, be strong in the Lord and in his mighty power. (Eph 6:10)**
>
> **I can do everything through him who gives me strength. (Phil 4:13)**

2 (2:2) **Teacher—Discipleship**: picture one is that of a strong teacher. A strong teacher has two very basic duties.

1. A strong teacher receives the truth. Timothy had heard Paul preach and teach the truth. How did Timothy know that the preaching and teaching of Paul were true? By the many witnesses who bore testimony to the same thing. Many proclaimed that the promises of Christ were true. When they trusted Jesus Christ as their Savior and Lord, something happened to them.

⇒ They received a changed life, a transformation of life so dramatic that they became as *new persons* and *new creations*.
⇒ They received a deep sense of God's presence.
⇒ They received the absolute assurance of salvation from sin, death, and judgment to come.
⇒ They received the indwelling presence of God's Holy Spirit.
⇒ They received the assurance of living forever.

Simply stated, many witnesses confirmed just what Paul taught; therefore, Timothy could trust what Paul taught. And when he did, Timothy himself was converted. He experienced the truth of Christ and of salvation.

Thought 1. The truth of God and of salvation are established forever. Christ Jesus, the very Son of God Himself, came to earth to reveal God and the way of salvation. Witness after witness down through the centuries confirm the truth. It is up to men to hear and receive it. A *strong teacher* will hear, receive, and transmit the truth to others. He transmits the truth to others so that they in turn may teach others and pass the truth on down to future generations.

2. A strong teacher trains others to transmit the truth. William Barclay gives an excellent description of this point:

> "Every Christian must look on himself as a link between two generations. Not only has he received the faith; he must also pass it on. E.K. Simpson writes on this passage: 'The torch of heavenly light must be transmitted unquenched from one generation to another, and Timothy must count himself an intermediary between apostolic and later ages....The teacher is a link in the living chain which stretches unbroken from this present moment back to Jesus Christ. The glory of teaching is that it links the present with the earthly life of Jesus Christ' " (*The Letters to Timothy, Titus, and Philemon*, p.181f).

Note that the truth is to be committed to *faithful* or "reliable" believers. By reliable (pistos) is meant a person...
• who *believes* in Christ and in the Word of God.
• who is loyal, reliable, dependable, and trustworthy.

Naturally, a person who does not believe in God or in God's Word cannot be said to be faithful to God. He is unfaithful and disloyal. God cannot trust or rely on him.

The point is this: a strong teacher will not commit the truth to an unfaithful or unreliable person. The strong teacher will look for faithful people and commit the truth to them. As Matthew Henry says:

> "Faithful men [are those] who will sincerely aim at the glory of God, the honour of Christ, the welfare of souls, and the advancement of the kingdom of the Redeemer among men" (*Matthew Henry's Commentary*, Vol.5, p.837).

> **Therefore go and make disciples of all nations, baptizing them in the name of the Father and of the Son and of the Holy Spirit, and teaching them to obey everything I have commanded you. And surely I am with you always, to the very end of the age." (Mat 28:19-20)**

> **The third time he said to him, "Simon son of John, do you love me?" Peter was hurt because Jesus asked him the third time, "Do you love me?" He said, "Lord, you know all things; you know that I love you." Jesus said, "Feed my sheep. (John 21:17)**

> **Keep watch over yourselves and all the flock of which the Holy Spirit has made you overseers. Be shepherds of the church of God, which he bought with his own blood. (Acts 20:28)**

> **Be shepherds of God's flock that is under your care, serving as overseers—not because you must, but because you are willing, as God wants you to be; not greedy for money, but eager to serve; (1 Pet 5:2)**

3 (2:3-4) **Soldier—Believer**: picture two is that of a strong soldier. The Christian believer is to be a strong soldier for Jesus Christ.

1. A strong soldier endures, suffers, and shares hardship with all other soldiers. He does not..
• lay behind
• shirk his duty
• seek to escape the battle
• refuse to carry his load
• give in to the enemy
• deny the cause
• reject the commander
• hide from the toil

A strong soldier stands with the other soldiers and suffers the hardships of the struggle with them. He sacrifices all that he is and has for Christ and His cause.
⇒ He gives all of his mind, body, and soul to Christ and His cause of salvation.
⇒ He gives all of his time and energy to Christ and His promise of eternal life.
⇒ He gives all of his money and possessions to Christ and His mission of world evangelism.

The strong soldier of Jesus Christ suffers hardship—no matter what the hardship is. He suffers hardship so that men and women, boys and girls may be saved from sin and starvation, evil and disease, corruption and emptiness, wrong and loneliness, death and judgment.

> **All men will hate you because of me, but he who stands firm to the end will be saved. (Mat 10:22)**

> **Therefore, my dear brothers, stand firm. Let nothing move you. Always give yourselves fully to the work of the Lord, because you know that your labor in the Lord is not in vain. (1 Cor 15:58)**

> **Whatever happens, conduct yourselves in a manner worthy of the gospel of Christ. Then, whether I come and see you or only hear about you in my absence, I will know that you stand firm in one spirit, contending as one man for the faith of the gospel (Phil 1:27)**

> **Timothy, my son, I give you this instruction in keeping with the prophecies once made about you, so that by following**

them you may fight the good fight, (1 Tim 1:18)

Fight the good fight of the faith. Take hold of the eternal life to which you were called when you made your good confession in the presence of many witnesses. (1 Tim 6:12)

By faith Moses, when he had grown up, refused to be known as the son of Pharaoh's daughter. He chose to be mistreated along with the people of God rather than to enjoy the pleasures of sin for a short time. (Heb 11:24-25)

Blessed is the man who perseveres under trial, because when he has stood the test, he will receive the crown of life that God has promised to those who love him. (James 1:12)

Resist him, standing firm in the faith, because you know that your brothers throughout the world are undergoing the same kind of sufferings. (1 Pet 5:9)

2. A strong soldier does not become entangled with the affairs of day to day living. He stays focused upon the cause of Christ—that of reaching a dying world with the message of life. People can have life now—a life that is abundant and overflowing. And they can live eternally—knowing beyond any question that they are going to live forever, never tasting death. But note: they have to hear about the commander-in-chief who can give them this life. This is the task of the Christian soldier; this is the great cause of the Christian soldier. And the strong soldier never diverts from this cause. He does not become entangled with the affairs of this world. His purpose is not...

- to make money
- to party
- to seek possessions
- to focus upon this life
- to covet position
- to indulge the flesh (sinful nature)
- to live in pleasure

His purpose is to focus upon the campaign of Christ, of carrying forth the message of the King of kings, the message of the Lord Jesus Christ Himself. What is that message? The message of eternal salvation. Man can live both now and forever. There is no greater purpose on earth than fighting to carry that message forth. The strong soldier focuses upon his cause and not upon the world. He does not become entangled with the world and its day to day affairs.

Do not conform any longer to the pattern of this world, but be transformed by the renewing of your mind. Then you will be able to test and approve what God's will is—his good, pleasing and perfect will. (Rom 12:2)

Those who use the things of the world, as if not engrossed in them. For this world in its present form is passing away. (1 Cor 7:31)

"Therefore come out from them and be separate, says the Lord. Touch no unclean thing, and I will receive you." "I will be a Father to you, and you will be my sons and daughters, says the Lord Almighty." (2 Cor 6:17-18)

Be imitators of God, therefore, as dearly loved children (Eph 5:1)

In the name of the Lord Jesus Christ, we command you, brothers, to keep away from every brother who is idle and does not live according to the teaching you received from us. (2 Th 3:6)

Endure hardship with us like a good soldier of Christ Jesus. No one serving as a soldier gets involved in civilian affairs—he wants to please his commanding officer. (2 Tim 2:3-4)

Therefore, dear friends, since you already know this, be on your guard so that you may not be carried away by the error of lawless men and fall from your secure position. (2 Pet 3:17)

Do not love the world or anything in the world. If anyone loves the world, the love of the Father is not in him. For everything in the world—the cravings of sinful man, the lust of his eyes and the boasting of what he has and does—comes not from the Father but from the world. (1 John 2:15-16)

3. A strong soldier pleases or obeys his commander-in-chief. He seeks to please the king who has chosen him to be a soldier. A strong soldier focuses upon his commander and his words. He does not look to anyone else...

- not to another commander. Another commander is a false commander.
- not to himself, seeking to satisfy the lusts of his own desires.
- not to loved ones who would have his time and waste his energies.
- not to those in the world who seek his energies and pleasures.

A strong soldier is loyal and committed to his commander-in-chief. He obeys his commander and focuses upon pleasing him and him alone.

"Not everyone who says to me, 'Lord, Lord,' will enter the kingdom of heaven, but only he who does the will of my Father who is in heaven. (Mat 7:21)

On the contrary, we speak as men approved by God to be entrusted with the gospel. We are not trying to please men but God, who tests our hearts. (1 Th 2:4)

Finally, brothers, we instructed you how to live in order to please God, as in fact you are living. Now we ask you and urge you in the Lord Jesus to do this more and more. (1 Th 4:1)

And we urge you, brothers, warn those who are idle, encourage the timid, help the weak, be patient with everyone. (1 Th 5:14)

By faith Enoch was taken from this life, so that he did not experience death; he could not be found, because God had taken him away. For before he was taken, he was commended as one who pleased God. (Heb 11:5)

And do not forget to do good and to share with others, for with such sacrifices God is pleased. (Heb 13:16)

"Blessed are those who wash their robes, that they may have the right to the tree of life and may go through the gates into the city. (Rev 22:14)

Do not let this Book of the Law depart from your mouth; meditate on it day and night, so that you may be careful to do everything written in it. Then you will be prosperous and successful. (Josh 1:8)

4 (2:5) **Athlete—Believers**: picture three is that of a strong athlete. The Christian believer is to be like a strong athlete in the cause of Christ.

1. The athlete is strong in discipline and self-denial. Note the phrase "competes as an athlete." The picture is that of a professional athlete, a person who has dedicated his life—all that he is and has—to the contest. The Christian is not to be an amateur in life; he is to be a professional. The struggle is not a part-time thing; it requires all the dedication, energy, and effort that the Christian athlete has, and then some. The Christian must go until he can go no more; then he must go on and on. How? The same way a professional athlete does: through discipline and self-control. There must be no such thing as...
- an undisciplined believer.
- an uncontrolled believer.
- a flabby believer.
- an indulgent, overeating believer.
- a lustful, immoral believer.
- a licentious believer.
- a part-time believer.
- a lethargic believer.
- a half-hearted, complacent believer.

The believer must be totally committed to live for Christ—every moment of every day. He must be disciplined and controlled in mind, body, and soul.
⇒ His body may ache from tiredness, but he must push on and on even beyond his limit.
⇒ He may wish to indulge, but he must reject the temptation.
⇒ He may desire to look, touch, taste, and have, but he must refuse and focus his thoughts and energies upon the race for Christ.

The Christian believer must seek Christ, to become more and more like Him; and he must seek to make Christ known to every man, woman, and child. No matter how he feels, the Christian believer must be disciplined and controlled every day of his life—disciplined and controlled...
- in the worship of God through Bible study and prayer.
- in bearing testimony to the glorious news of Christ Jesus our Lord—the glorious news of life eternal.

2. The athlete competes according to the rules or else he is disqualified from the contest. This is critical to know; it is the very point at which so many people fail. It is not enough to declare that one is entering the contest, nor is it enough to begin running the race. A person has to compete according to the rules. Kenneth Wuest says:

"The Greek athlete was required to spend ten months in preparatory training before the contest. During this time he had to engage in the prescribed exercises and live a strictly separated life in regard to the ordinary and lawful pursuits of life, and he was placed on a rigid diet. Should he break training rules, he would...be a castaway (1 Cor.9:27), adokimos, 'disqualified,' barred from engaging in the athletic contest" (*The Pastoral Epistles*, Vol.2, p.129f).

Any person who wishes to enter the Christian contest has to obey the rules laid down by the official of the contest. That official is the Lord Jesus Christ, the very Son of God Himself. What are the rules? Very simply stated...
- a person must believe in Christ.
- a person must follow Christ, that is, obey the Word of God.

"For God so loved the world that he gave his one and only Son, that whoever believes in him shall not perish but have eternal life. (John 3:16)

"I tell you the truth, whoever hears my word and believes him who sent me has eternal life and will not be condemned; he has crossed over from death to life. (John 5:24)

So then, just as you received Christ Jesus as Lord, continue to live in him, (Col 2:6)

Whoever claims to live in him must walk as Jesus did. (1 John 2:6)

Thought 1. How many people declare that they are entering the Christian race, but they do not run by the rules? The terrible tragedy is this: they are disqualified.

Do you not know that in a race all the runners run, but only one gets the prize? Run in such a way as to get the prize. Everyone who competes in the games goes into strict training. They do it to get a crown that will not last; but we do it to get a crown that will last forever. Therefore I do not run like a man running aimlessly; I do not fight like a man beating the air. No, I beat my body and make it my slave so that after I have preached to others, I myself will not be disqualified for the prize. (1 Cor 9:24-27)

You were running a good race. Who cut in on you and kept you from obeying the truth? (Gal 5:7)

I press on toward the goal to win the prize for which God has called me heavenward in Christ Jesus. (Phil 3:14)

Therefore, since we are surrounded by such a great cloud of witnesses, let us throw off everything that hinders and the sin that so easily entangles, and let us run with perseverance the race marked out for us. (Heb 12:1)

I have fought the good fight, I have finished the race, I have kept the faith. Now there is in store for me the crown of righteousness, which the Lord, the righteous Judge, will award to me on that day—and not only to me, but also to all who have longed for his appearing. (2 Tim 4:7-8)

5 (2:6) **Farmer—Believer**: picture four is that of a farmer, a farmer who really works. The word "hardworking" (kopiao) means work that is diligent, laborious, exhausting. It is the picture of a farmer who toils to the point of becoming weary, so tired that he cannot put one foot in front of the other.

Note a most significant point: it is the diligent farmer who arduously works—who works to the point of exhaustion—that shall be the *first* to partake of the fruit. The slothful farmer...
- is the last to receive the reward of his harvest and fruit.
- never bears a full harvest and never receives the reward of a full harvest.

The reason is because the slothful farmer either plants less seed or plants later than he should. And he never weeds or harvests the fields like he should. Note the point: it is the diligent farmer who shall be the first to be rewarded. He shall be the first to partake of the fruit of the harvest.

The point is true of the Christian believer as well. The diligent believer shall be rewarded first by God; that is, he shall be given a greater reward by God. Oliver Greene says:

> "Many Christians think that all will share alike in the rewards on that day when the righteous Judge will reward His faithful servants; but these dear people have a tremendous surprise in store for them! Each believer will be rewarded according to his faithful stewardship....I am sure there will be many in heaven without a reward" (*The Epistles of Paul the Apostle to Timothy and Titus*, p.298).

> **For we must all appear before the judgment seat of Christ, that each one may receive what is due him for the things done while in the body, whether good or bad. (2 Cor 5:10)**

> **For no one can lay any foundation other than the one already laid, which is Jesus Christ. If any man builds on this foundation using gold, silver, costly stones, wood, hay or straw, his work will be shown for what it is, because the Day will bring it to light. It will be revealed with fire, and the fire will test the quality of each man's work. If what he has built survives, he will receive his reward. If it is burned up, he will suffer loss; he himself will be saved, but only as one escaping through the flames. (1 Cor 3:11-15)**

Matthew Henry says:

> "If we would be partakers of the fruits, we must labour; if we would gain the prize, we must run the race. And, further, we must first labour as the husbandman does, with diligence and patience, before we are partakers of the fruit; we must do the will of God, before we receive the promises" (*Matthew Henry's Commentary*, Vol.5, p.838).

> **Therefore, my dear brothers, stand firm. Let nothing move you. Always give yourselves fully to the work of the Lord, because you know that your labor in the Lord is not in vain. (1 Cor 15:58)**

> **You need to persevere so that when you have done the will of God, you will receive what he has promised. (Heb 10:36)**

> **Be patient, then, brothers, until the Lord's coming. See how the farmer waits for the land to yield its valuable crop and how patient he is for the autumn and spring rains. You too, be patient and stand firm, because the Lord's coming is near. (James 5:7-8)**

6 (2:7) **Conclusion**: the believer needs to think over these things, and he needs the Lord in order to understand them.

> **"Have you understood all these things?" Jesus asked. "Yes," they replied. (Mat 13:51)**

> **He who has ears, let him hear. (Mat 11:15; 13:9, 43 etc.)**

> **To the Jews who had believed him, Jesus said, "If you hold to my teaching, you are really my disciples. (John 8:31)**

2 TIMOTHY 2:8-13

	D. Charge Four: Remember Jesus Christ is the Resurrected Lord, 2:8-13	thing for the sake of the elect, that they too may obtain the salvation that is in Christ Jesus, with eternal glory.	3 The gospel stirs endurance
1 The gospel proclaims the humanity & deity of Jesus Christ a. The descendant of David: Man b. The risen Lord: God, v.8 2 The gospel carries one thru suffering & assures the victory of one's purpose: The spread of God's Word	8 Remember Jesus Christ, raised from the dead, descended from David. This is my gospel, 9 For which I am suffering even to the point of being chained like a criminal. But God's word is not chained. 10 Therefore I endure every	11 Here is a trustworthy saying: If we died with him, we will also live with him; 12 If we endure, we will also reign with him. If we disown him, he will also disown us; 13 If we are faithless, he will remain faithful, for he cannot disown himself.	4 The gospel assures eternal glory & eternal judgment a. The glory b. The judgment c. The surety of God's Word

DIVISION I

THE STRONG CHARGES TO TIMOTHY, 1:6-2:26

D. Charge Four: Remember Jesus Christ is the Resurrected Lord, 2:8-13

(2:8-13) **Introduction**: this is one of the most important charges ever given to believers—remember the gospel, that Jesus Christ is the resurrected Lord. Jesus Christ was raised from the dead.
1. Remember—the gospel proclaims the humanity and deity of Jesus Christ (v.8).
2. Remember—the gospel carries one through suffering and assures the victory of one's purpose: the spread of God's Word (v.9).
3. Remember—the gospel stirs endurance (v.10).
4. Remember—the gospel assures eternal glory and eternal judgment (v.11-13).

1 (2:8) **Jesus Christ, Humanity; Deity—Gospel**: remember—the gospel proclaims the humanity and deity of Jesus Christ.

1. Jesus the Messiah was man. He was born a descendant David; He was a man just like David, born of the roots of David. God sent His Son into the world in human flesh. The Son of God became a man—flesh and blood—just like all other men. He had a human nature, and because He had a human nature, He knows...
- the sufferings of life.
- the trials of life.
- the temptations of life.
- the problems and difficulties of life.
- the sorrows and griefs of life.
- the struggles and pains of life.

The point is this: Jesus Christ knows exactly what we face in life. Therefore, He is able to help us through all the trials of life. No matter what the sufferings are, Jesus Christ can deliver us through the sufferings and cause us to triumph over them.

> The Word became flesh and made his dwelling among us. We have seen his glory, the glory of the One and Only, who came from the Father, full of grace and truth. (John 1:14)
>
> Since the children have flesh and blood, he too shared in their humanity so that by his death he might destroy him who holds the power of death—that is, the devil—and free those who all their lives were held in slavery by their fear of death. For surely it is not angels he helps, but Abraham's descendants. (Heb 2:14-16)
>
> For this reason he had to be made like his brothers in every way, in order that he might become a merciful and faithful high priest in service to God, and that he might make atonement for the sins of the people. Because he himself suffered when he was tempted, he is able to help those who are being tempted. (Heb 2:17-18)
>
> For we do not have a high priest who is unable to sympathize with our weaknesses, but we have one who has been tempted in every way, just as we are—yet was without sin. Let us then approach the throne of grace with confidence, so that we may receive mercy and find grace to help us in our time of need. (Heb 4:15-16)

2. Jesus the Messiah was divine; He was of the very nature of God Himself. How do we know this? Because He was raised from the dead. The resurrection from the dead declares that Jesus is the Son of God. All other men are dead and gone. The proof is demonstrated by one simple question: "Where are they? Where are our mothers, our fathers, our sisters, and ancestors?" Once they have left this world, they are gone. But not Christ. He died, but He arose and lives forever in the presence of God. Death could not hold Him because He was the Son of God and possessed the perfect spirit of holiness. (See DEEPER STUDY # 4, *Jesus Christ, Resurrection*—Acts 2:24 for more discussion.)

William Barclay has an excellent comment on this point:

> "The tense of the Greek verb which Paul uses does not imply one definite act in time, but a continued state which lasts for ever. Paul is not so much saying to Timothy: 'Remember the actual resurrection of Jesus', rather he is saying: 'Remember Jesus for ever risen and for ever present; remember your risen and your ever-present Lord.' Here is the great Christian inspiration. We do not depend on the inspiration of a memory, however great. We enjoy the power of a presence. When a Christian is summoned to a great task, a task that he cannot but feel is beyond

him, he must go to it in the certainty that he does not go to it alone, but that there is with him for ever and for ever the presence and the power of his risen Lord. When fears threaten, when doubts assail, when inadequacy depresses, remember the presence of the risen Lord" (The Letters to Timothy, Titus, and Philemon, p.189).*

But God raised him from the dead, freeing him from the agony of death, because it was impossible for death to keep its hold on him. (Acts 2:24)

"Therefore let all Israel be assured of this: God has made this Jesus, whom you crucified, both Lord and Christ." (Acts 2:36)

The God of our fathers raised Jesus from the dead—whom you had killed by hanging him on a tree. God exalted him to his own right hand as Prince and Savior that he might give repentance and forgiveness of sins to Israel. (Acts 5:30-31)

And who through the Spirit of holiness was declared with power to be the Son of God by his resurrection from the dead: Jesus Christ our Lord. (Rom 1:4)

For this very reason, Christ died and returned to life so that he might be the Lord of both the dead and the living. (Rom 14:9)

[God's power] Which he exerted in Christ when he raised him from the dead and seated him at his right hand in the heavenly realms, (Eph 1:20)

And being found in appearance as a man, he humbled himself and became obedient to death— even death on a cross! Therefore God exalted him to the highest place and gave him the name that is above every name, (Phil 2:8-9)

2 (2:9) **Suffering—Gospel**: remember—the gospel carries one through suffering and assures the victory of one's purpose—the spread of God's Word. Paul was in prison because he preached the Word of God. At this particular time, Christians were hated with a fierce passion by many throughout the Roman empire. Many reacted against the message of morality and purity, righteousness and justice for all. In addition, one of the worst disasters ever suffered by a city, the burning of Rome, was blamed upon the Christian believers in Rome. Nero, in one of his moments of insanity, was guilty of ordering the fire so that he would be known as the great emperor who rebuilt the city. But the senate could never blame Nero. Therefore they sought a scapegoat, and the scapegoat chosen was the new religious sect, the Christians. As a result, a great persecution of Christian believers began. Paul, of course, was one of the major leaders of the Christians.

"But all human efforts, all the lavish gifts of the emperor, and the propitiations of the gods did not banish the sinister belief that the conflagration was the result of an order. Consequently, to get rid of the report, Nero fastened the guilt and inflicted the most exquisite tortures on a class hated for their abominations, called Christians by the populace" (Tacitus, Annals, 15:44 as quoted by William Barclay. *The Letters to Timothy, Titus, and Philemon*, p.192).

As stated, Paul was in prison for having preached the gospel. He was true to his call, the very purpose for which God had put him on earth: to proclaim the gospel of the Lord Jesus Christ. But note a glorious fact: the Word of God could never be bound. Paul himself could be stopped by men, but the purpose of Paul could never be stopped. The Word of God cannot be stopped. Its message will continue on and on down through history. The message of God's great love for the world—the message of the cross, of the death of God's Son for the world—that message will never be stopped until the world ends. There will always be some believers who will be proclaiming the Word of God—that God will save any person who comes to Him through the Lord Jesus Christ.

I am not ashamed of the gospel, because it is the power of God for the salvation of everyone who believes: first for the Jew, then for the Gentile. (Rom 1:16)

For the word of God is living and active. Sharper than any double-edged sword, it penetrates even to dividing soul and spirit, joints and marrow; it judges the thoughts and attitudes of the heart. (Heb 4:12)

So is my word that goes out from my mouth: It will not return to me empty, but will accomplish what I desire and achieve the purpose for which I sent it. (Isa 55:11)

Therefore this is what the LORD God Almighty says: "Because the people have spoken these words, I will make my words in your mouth a fire and these people the wood it consumes. (Jer 5:14)

"Is not my word like fire," declares the LORD, "and like a hammer that breaks a rock in pieces? (Jer 23:29)

3 (2:10) **Endurance—Gospel**: the gospel stirs one to endure all things. How? By results. God has promised to save people by the gospel. When we preach and teach salvation in Christ Jesus—salvation with eternal glory—God saves people. This is the only hope for people, and no greater hope could exist. Just imagine living forever in eternal glory! Such a life is beyond our imagination, yet it is exactly what the gospel is all about. Therefore, no matter what it costs—no matter how much suffering we have to bear—we must endure it all for the salvation of people. This is the point of Paul: the gospel—the glorious truth that people could actually be saved and receive eternal glory—stirred Paul to suffer all things. Paul longed for people to hear the gospel so that they could be saved. This, too, must be our purpose and objective in life. We, too, must proclaim the gospel—no matter the suffering and sacrifice. We must pay any price to see that people hear the gospel, for the gospel is the only way people can be saved and receive eternal glory.

For whoever wants to save his life will lose it, but whoever loses his life for me will find it. (Mat 16:25)

Peter said to him, "We have left everything to follow you!" (Mark 10:28)

In the same way, any of you who does not give up everything he has cannot be my disciple. (Luke 14:33)

Now I want you to know, brothers, that what has happened to me has really served to advance the gospel. As a result, it has become clear throughout the whole palace guard and to everyone else that I am in chains for Christ. Because of my chains, most of the brothers in the Lord have been encouraged to speak the word of God more courageously and fearlessly. (Phil 1:12-14)

What is more, I consider everything a loss compared to the surpassing greatness of knowing Christ Jesus my Lord, for whose sake I have lost all things. I consider them rubbish, that I may gain Christ (Phil 3:8)

4 (2:11-13) **Confession—Denial—Judgment**: the gospel assures eternal glory and eternal judgment. Most commentators say these three verses were one of the first hymns of the early church.

1. Note the glorious promise: if we die with Christ, we shall also live with Him. How can a person die with Christ? (See notes, pt.3—2 Tim.1:8-10; pt.4—1 Tim.2:3-7. See Deeper Study #1, *Believer, Position in Christ*—Ro.8:1 for detailed discussion.)

When the believer suffers and endures for Christ, he is assured of reigning forever with Christ.

> **But he who stands firm to the end will be saved. (Mat 24:13)**

2. Note the tragic result of denying Christ. "If we disown Him, He also will disown us."

"Whoever acknowledges me before men, I will also acknowledge him before my Father in heaven. But whoever disowns me before men, I will disown him before my Father in heaven. (Mat 10:32-33)

If anyone is ashamed of me and my words in this adulterous and sinful generation, the Son of Man will be ashamed of him when he comes in his Father's glory with the holy angels." (Mark 8:38)

They claim to know God, but by their actions they deny him. They are detestable, disobedient and unfit for doing anything good. (Titus 1:16)

But there were also false prophets among the people, just as there will be false teachers among you. They will secretly introduce destructive heresies, even denying the sovereign Lord who bought them—bringing swift destruction on themselves. (2 Pet 2:1)

Who is the liar? It is the man who denies that Jesus is the Christ. Such a man is the antichrist—he denies the Father and the Son. (1 John 2:22)

3. Note that God means what He says: He will keep His Word. His promise of glory and His pronouncement of judgment are sure. Some people will be saved and glorified, and others will be disowned and condemned.

> "*If we believe not, yet he abideth faithful; he cannot deny himself. He is faithful to his threatenings, faithful to his promises; neither one nor the other shall fall to the ground, no, not the least jot or tittle of them. If we be faithful to Christ, he will certainly be faithful to us. If we be false to him, he will be faithful to his threatenings: he cannot deny himself, cannot recede from any word that he hath spoken, for he is yea, and amen, the faithful witness....If we deny him, out of fear, or shame, or for the sake of some temporal advantage, he will deny and disown us, and will not deny himself, but will continue faithful to his word when he threatens as well as when he promises*" (Matthew Henry. *Matthew Henry's Commentary*, p.839).

Whoever believes in the Son has eternal life, but whoever rejects the Son will not see life, for God's wrath remains on him." (John 3:36)

I told you that you would die in your sins; if you do not believe that I am the one I claim to be, you will indeed die in your sins." (John 8:24)

See to it, brothers, that none of you has a sinful, unbelieving heart that turns away from the living God. (Heb 3:12)

Let us, therefore, make every effort to enter that rest, so that no one will fall by following their example of disobedience. (Heb 4:11)

2 TIMOTHY 2:14-21

		E. Charge Five: Remind the Church About the Danger of Words & About the Foundation of God, 2:14-21	18 Who have wandered away from the truth. They say that the resurrection has already taken place, and they destroy the faith of some.	1) They spiritualize the resurrection 2) They undermine the faith of some
1	Reminder 1: Do not argue over words that do not profit the hearers—speculations, theories, & petty matters	14 Keep reminding them of these things. Warn them before God against quarreling about words; it is of no value, and only ruins those who listen.	19 Nevertheless, God's solid foundation stands firm, sealed with this inscription: "The Lord knows those who are his," and, "Everyone who confesses the name of the Lord must turn away from wickedness."	4 Reminder 4: The foundation of God's house is firm a. God's great house has two inscriptions
2	Reminder 2: Study—seek to be a true teacher of God's Word a. To be approved of God b. To be unashamed c. To correctly teach the Word	15 Do your best to present yourself to God as one approved, a workman who does not need to be ashamed and who correctly handles the word of truth.	20 In a large house there are articles not only of gold and silver, but also of wood and clay; some are for noble purposes and some for ignoble.	b. God's earthly house (church) has a variety of articles 1) There are both noble & base articles
3	Reminder 3: Shun godless chatter and discussions a. It leads to ungodliness b. It eats away as a cancer c. Two examples	16 Avoid godless chatter, because those who indulge in it will become more and more ungodly. 17 Their teaching will spread like gangrene. Among them are Hymenaeus and Philetus,	21 If a man cleanses himself from the latter, he will be an instrument for noble purposes, made holy, useful to the Master and prepared to do any good work.	2) There has to be a cleansing in order to become a useful instrument

DIVISION I

THE STRONG CHARGES TO TIMOTHY, 1:6-2:26

E. Charge Five: Remind the Church About the Danger of Words and the Foundation of God, 2:14-21

(2:14-21) **Introduction**: more trouble is stirred and brewed by words than by any other act. This fact alone stresses the importance of this passage: remember the danger of words and the foundation of God.
1. Reminder 1: do not argue and strive over words that do not profit the hearers—speculations, theories, and petty matters (v.14).
2. Reminder 2: study—seek to be a true teacher of God's Word (v.15).
3. Reminder 3: shun godless chatter and discussions (v.16-18).
4. Reminder 4: the foundation of God's house is firm (v.19-21).

1 (2:14) **Words—Talk—Speculation**: reminder one—do not argue over words that do not profit the hearers. That is, do not argue and quarrel about petty matters nor over religious theories, speculations, and ideas. Time is short, and we are not able to fellowship nor to be together that much. Therefore, when we are together, we must be communicating and sharing words that profit us all. However, this is often not the case. Too often, our words are useless and unprofitable, and sometimes they are even upsetting and destructive. Picture both the unprofitable and the upsetting words that go on in the church and among believers, the arguments and quarrels that have no value to those who listen. There are…
- the words over petty matters. (Just think of some of the petty matters that go on in the church.)
- the words over buildings, traditions, and rituals.
- the words about people, the rumors, gossip, and criticism.
- the words about trivial day-to-day matters.
- the words that waste and pass the time.
- the words that focus on debating theological positions, speculation, and ideas.
- the words over pet ideas and theories.

There are essentially three kinds of unprofitable talk that go on among believers.
⇒ First, there is the trivial talk that passes the time away, talk that fails to build up the believer.
⇒ Second, there is the talk that engages in criticism and gossip, talk that tears a person down.
⇒ Third, there is the talk that enjoys discussing the theories and speculations of theology. William Barclay has such an excellent discussion of this fact that it merits being read by every believer, especially by the students and teachers of the gospel:

> "Discussion can be stimulating and invigorating for those whose approach to the Christian faith is intellectual, for those who have a background of knowledge and of culture, for those who are characteristically students, for those who have a real knowledge of, or interest in, theology. But it sometimes happens that a simple-minded person finds himself in a group which is tossing heresies about, and propounding unanswerable questions, and it may well be that the faith of that simple person, so far from being helped, is upset….And it may well happen that clever, subtle, speculative, destructive, intellectually reckless discussion may have the effect of demolishing, and not building up, the faith of some simple person who happens to become involved in it. As in all things, there is a time

to discuss, and a time to be silent" (*The Letters to Timothy, Titus, and Philemon*, p.197).

> **Nor to devote themselves to myths and endless genealogies. These promote controversies rather than God's work—which is by faith. (1 Tim 1:4)**
>
> **He is conceited and understands nothing. He has an unhealthy interest in controversies and quarrels about words that result in envy, strife, malicious talk, evil suspicions (1 Tim 6:4)**
>
> **Don't have anything to do with foolish and stupid arguments, because you know they produce quarrels. (2 Tim 2:23)**
>
> **But avoid foolish controversies and genealogies and arguments and quarrels about the law, because these are unprofitable and useless. (Titus 3:9)**

The point is this: the preacher and teacher must remind believers—do not argue and quarrel: "it is of no value, and only ruins those who listen." Do not upset or tear down people with your words.

2 (2:15) **Word of God—Study**: reminder two—study to be a true teacher of God's Word. Note the words "do your best" to set your heart upon—be diligent, hurry, rush, and seek the approval of God. Note that it is the approval of God that is to be the believer's concern. A believer is a fool if he does not seek the *approval of God*. To be disapproved is to be displeasing and unacceptable to God. How then can we secure the approval of God?

⇒ By being a workman—the idea is a diligent worker who toils and labors to the point of exhaustion.

But note: our work is pinpointed and identified. We are to study the Word of God and rightly divide it. The words "correctly handles" (orthotomounta) mean to cut straight. Believers are to cut straight to the truth; they are not to take crooked paths and side tracks to the truth. We are to study the truth and correctly handles it. Once we have studied and learned the Word of God, we are to *accurately teach* the Word of God. We are not to teach...

- our own ideas
- the theories of other people
- what we think
- what other men think

We are not to mishandle the Word of God: twist it to fit what we think or want it to say; over-emphasize or under-emphasize its teachings; add to or take away from it. Any person who mishandles God's Word is not approved of God. This is the point of this verse: if we want God's approval—if we want to be acceptable to God—we must study, rush and seek to be a true teacher of God's Word. We must be *workmen* who study God's Word, workmen who study diligently: *who correctly analyze and accurately divide—rightly handle and skillfully teach—the Word of Truth* (Amplified New Testament). This is the believer who will not be ashamed when he faces the Lord Jesus Christ in the great day of judgment.

> **Now the Bereans were of more noble character than the Thessalonians, for they received the message with great eagerness and examined the Scriptures every day to see if what Paul said was true. (Acts 17:11)**
>
> **Keep watch over yourselves and all the flock of which the Holy Spirit has made you overseers. Be shepherds of the church of God, which he bought with his own blood. (Acts 20:28)**
>
> **"Now I commit you to God and to the word of his grace, which can build you up and give you an inheritance among all those who are sanctified. (Acts 20:32)**
>
> **All Scripture is God-breathed and is useful for teaching, rebuking, correcting and training in righteousness, (2 Tim 3:16)**
>
> **Like newborn babies, crave pure spiritual milk, so that by it you may grow up in your salvation, now that you have tasted that the Lord is good. (1 Pet 2:2-3)**
>
> **Be shepherds of God's flock that is under your care, serving as overseers—not because you must, but because you are willing, as God wants you to be; not greedy for money, but eager to serve; (1 Pet 5:2)**
>
> **He humbled you, causing you to hunger and then feeding you with manna, which neither you nor your fathers had known, to teach you that man does not live on bread alone but on every word that comes from the mouth of the LORD. (Deu 8:3)**
>
> **I have not departed from the commands of his lips; I have treasured the words of his mouth more than my daily bread. (Job 23:12)**
>
> **How sweet are your words to my taste, sweeter than honey to my mouth! (Psa 119:103)**
>
> **Then I will give you shepherds after my own heart, who will lead you with knowledge and understanding. (Jer 3:15)**
>
> **When your words came, I ate them; they were my joy and my heart's delight, for I bear your name, O LORD God Almighty. (Jer 15:16)**

3 (2:16-18) **Talk—Speech—Rationalization—Teaching, False**: reminder three—shun, avoid, keep away from godless chatter and discussion. This is descriptive language picturing so much talk that goes on among people.

⇒ So much talk is "godless" (bebelos): common, irreverent, and foul.

⇒ So much talk is chatter: empty and meaningless. It is nothing more than empty voices chattering away in empty and godless discussions.

The charge is direct and forceful: avoid, shun, keep away from godless and empty talk. What are some examples of talk that is godless and empty? There is such talk as...

- false teaching
- cursing
- immoral suggestions
- criticism
- gossip
- worldly philosophy
- theological theories
- off-colored conversations
- indecent insinuations
- suggestive enticements

Note that such talk is not only ungodly and empty, it leads to more and more ungodliness. Such talk actually increases ungodliness in the heart and life of a person. In fact, the picture could be no more descriptive: ungodly talk eats away at a person just like gangrene or a cancerous growth.

This is often ignored and neglected by most people, for most people want to go about doing their own thing. And if we took this charge seriously, just think how it would affect the control of...

- television
- films
- music
- discussions
- opinions
- differences
- positions (theological, social, political)
- decisions
- arguments

This charge affects every form of communication and relationship imaginable. Imagine—no communication and no talk is ever to take place that is ungodly and empty. Why? Because ungodly and empty talk eats like a cancer. It leads a person into more and more ungodliness and emptiness.

> *"Here then is the test. If at the end of our talk and discussion, we are closer to one another and closer to God, then all is well. But if at the end of our discussion, we have erected barriers between each other and we have left God more distant and our view of Him befogged, then all is wrong. The aim of all Christian discussion and of all Christian action is to bring a man nearer to God"* (William Barclay. *The Letters to Timothy, Titus, and Philemon*, p.199).

Note that an example of two men who were engaged in godless talk or teaching is given: Hymenaeus and Philetus. Apparently, these two men were church members who spiritualized the coming resurrection of believers. They were probably saying one of three things: that the resurrection was a spiritual experience that took place...

- at conversion when a believer is counted by God to be raised with Christ.
- at baptism when a person is lifted up out of the water.
- at the birth of the believer's children; that is, his life was being resurrected and living on in the lives of his children.

The point is this: all such godless talk, whether false teaching or just meaningless and empty chatter, is to be shunned, avoided, and turned away from. The believer is to do what verse fifteen says: study, rush, and seek the approval of God. He is to live and move and have his being in the Word of God, concentrating and focusing upon God. God and His Word are to be the obsession of the believer—the very life and breath of the believer.

> **Would he argue with useless words, with speeches that have no value? (Job 15:3)**

> **When words are many, sin is not absent, but he who holds his tongue is wise. (Prov 10:19)**

> **Because of the increase of wickedness, the love of most will grow cold, (Mat 24:12)**

> **Those on the rock are the ones who receive the word with joy when they hear it, but they have no root. They believe for a while, but in the time of testing they fall away. (Luke 8:13)**

> **Jesus replied, "No one who puts his hand to the plow and looks back is fit for service in the kingdom of God." (Luke 9:62)**

> **"When an evil spirit comes out of a man, it goes through arid places seeking rest and does not find it. Then it says, 'I will return to the house I left.' When it arrives, it finds the house swept clean and put in order. Then it goes and takes seven other spirits more wicked than itself, and they go in and live there. And the final condition of that man is worse than the first." (Luke 11:24-26)**

> **But now that you know God—or rather are known by God—how is it that you are turning back to those weak and miserable principles? Do you wish to be enslaved by them all over again? (Gal 4:9)**

> **But my righteous one will live by faith. And if he shrinks back, I will not be pleased with him." (Heb 10:38)**

> **Yet I hold this against you: You have forsaken your first love. (Rev 2:4)**

4 (2:19-21) **Foundation, Spiritual**: reminder three—the foundation of God's house is firm. Some may turn away from Christ; the faith of some may be overthrown and undermine godless teaching and talk. "Nevertheless God's solid foundation of God stands firm." What is meant by the foundation of God? It means the household of God or the household of faith. It means the great house of believers that God is building. It is the family and church of God—the *true family and true church of God*. Note two facts about the great house of believers.

1. The great house of God has two inscriptions written upon it that seal and guarantee its security.

    a. The first inscription is this: "The Lord knows those who are his." There are no false professions and no hypocrites in God's household—not in His real household. No one fools God. Within the earthly church, there are both wheat and tares, both believers and unbelievers. But when God looks upon us, He knows those who are truly His. He knows those who have really entered into His household and those who are only saying that they have entered.

    The point is this: if a person is living within the household of God—remaining steadfast and loyal—he is a true believer, a true member of God's household. And he is secure within God's house. But if a person has forsaken the family of God, he is not of God's household. God is not taken by surprise by any of us. *God knows those who are His*, and those who are His will remain faithful and loyal.

> **The watchman opens the gate for him, and the sheep listen to his voice. He calls his own sheep by name and leads them out. (John 10:3)**

> **"I am the good shepherd; I know my sheep and my sheep know me— (John 10:14)**

> **But the man who loves God is known by God. (1 Cor 8:3)**

> **Nevertheless, God's solid foundation stands firm, sealed with this inscription: "The Lord knows those who are his," and, "Everyone who confesses the name of the Lord must turn away from wickedness." (2 Tim 2:19)**

b. The second inscription is this: "Everyone who confesses the name of the Lord must turn away from wickedness." The sign that a person is of the household of God is a pure and righteous life. A person who follows Christ does not live in sin. If a person lives in sin, he is not following Christ. Therefore, if we name the name of Christ, we must depart from iniquity. If we continue in sin, then we are only making a false profession. We are not of God's household—not really. Our sinful behavior proves the fact.

The point is this: the foundation of God is sure; His household is established forever and it is built upon the principle of righteousness:

⇒ Everyone that names the name of Christ repents and turns away from wickedness (unrighteousness).

This is a fact; it is an eternal principle established by God. His household is built upon righteousness. Righteousness is the inscription that is written across the face of His household. Therefore, if a person is a member of His household, they have forsaken and turned away from wickedness. They do not live in sin.

Thought 1. Common sense tells us that if a person has departed from God, he is not living with God. To be apart from God is not to be with God; it is to be separated from God, out of the presence and house of God.

Common sense tells us that if a person has turned away from wickedness and lives in the righteousness of God, then he belongs to the household of God. To be living like God—righteously—is to be with God, in the presence and house of God.

> You were taught, with regard to your former way of life, to put off your old self, which is being corrupted by its deceitful desires; (Eph 4:22)
>
> Therefore, since we are surrounded by such a great cloud of witnesses, let us throw off everything that hinders and the sin that so easily entangles, and let us run with perseverance the race marked out for us. (Heb 12:1)
>
> Dear friends, I urge you, as aliens and strangers in the world, to abstain from sinful desires, which war against your soul. (1 Pet 2:11)
>
> If you put away the sin that is in your hand and allow no evil to dwell in your tent, (Job 11:14)
>
> Let the wicked forsake his way and the evil man his thoughts. Let him turn to the LORD, and he will have mercy on him, and to our God, for he will freely pardon. (Isa 55:7)

2. God's earthly house (the church) has a variety of articles, both noble and base. The church has some articles or people who are like gold and silver; that is, they honor Christ. But the church also has some articles or people who are like wood and clay; that is, they dishonor Christ. The church has a mixture of people...
   - some are good and some are bad.
   - some are true and some are false.
   - some are genuine and some are counterfeit.
   - some are clean and some are dirty.
   - some are pure and some are tarnished.
   - some are clear and some are stained.
   - some illuminate light and some illuminate darkness.

Note what it takes to become a noble instrument: it takes a cleansing. A person has to cleanse himself from...
   - behavior that is dishonorable and unrighteous.
   - words that are corruptible and dirty.
   - talk that is unclean and contaminating.
   - teaching that is false and cancerous.

A person who cleanses himself from these will become an instrument for noble purposes...
   - made holy, that is, set apart unto Christ and His service.
   - useful to the Master; that is, Christ will be able to use him.
   - prepared to do any good work; that is, Christ will be able to use him for any work.

> **Therefore, I urge you, brothers, in view of God's mercy, to offer your bodies as living sacrifices, holy and pleasing to God—this is your spiritual act of worship. Do not conform any longer to the pattern of this world, but be transformed by the renewing of your mind. Then you will be able to test and approve what God's will is—his good, pleasing and perfect will. (Rom 12:1-2)**
>
> **"Therefore come out from them and be separate, says the Lord. Touch no unclean thing, and I will receive you." "I will be a Father to you, and you will be my sons and daughters, says the Lord Almighty." (2 Cor 6:17-18)**
>
> **Have nothing to do with the fruitless deeds of darkness, but rather expose them. (Eph 5:11)**
>
> **In the name of the Lord Jesus Christ, we command you, brothers, to keep away from every brother who is idle and does not live according to the teaching you received from us. (2 Th 3:6)**
>
> **Do not love the world or anything in the world. If anyone loves the world, the love of the Father is not in him. For everything in the world—the cravings of sinful man, the lust of his eyes and the boasting of what he has and does—comes not from the Father but from the world. (1 John 2:15-16)**

		F. Charge Six: Flee Youthful Lusts & Follow After the Lord, 2:22-26	24 And the Lord's servant must not quarrel; instead, he must be kind to everyone, able to teach, not resentful.	4 **Do not argue or fight with others** a. Be kind b. Be prepared to teach
1	**Flee youthful lusts**	22 Flee the evil desires of youth, and pursue righteousness, faith, love and peace, along with those who call on the Lord out of a pure heart.	25 Those who oppose him he must gently instruct, in the hope that God will grant them repentance leading them to a knowledge of the truth,	c. Do not be resentful v.24 d. Correct others in gentleness 1) That the opponents may be led to repentance
2	**Pursue—follow after the Lord**			
3	**Avoid foolish arguments**	23 Don't have anything to do with foolish and stupid arguments, because you know they produce quarrels.	26 And that they will come to their senses and escape from the trap of the devil, who has taken them captive to do his will.	2) That the opponents may escape from the trap of the devil

DIVISION I

THE STRONG CHARGES TO TIMOTHY, 1:6-2:26

F. Charge Six: Flee Youthful Lusts and Follow After the Lord, 2:22-26

(2:22-26) **Introduction**: this is a critical charge to young people. Any young person who fails to heed this charge is doomed to a barren and empty life and to a lost eternity.
1. Flee youthful lusts (v.22).
2. Follow after the Lord (v.22).
3. Avoid foolish arguments (v.23).
4. Do not argue or fight with others (v.24-26).

1 (2:22) **Youth—Lusts**: first, flee youthful lusts. The Greek word "desires" (epithumai) means passionate lusts and cravings. It can mean either good or bad desires, and its meaning is always to be determined by the context (Wuest). The point is this: passionate desire and craving is normal and natural. God made us to desire and crave. It is when we use our passions to hurt and damage that they become evil. What are the *lusts* or *desires* of youth?

⇒ *The desires of the eye*: youth desire to have and possess. To have and possess are normal desires, but the normal desire can lead to the lust for possessions and people.

⇒ *The desires of the flesh* (*sinful nature*): youth desire the companionship of the opposite sex. Attraction is normal and leads to marriage and the carrying on of the human race. However, the normal desire can lead to illicit sex and immorality.

⇒ *The desire for acceptance*: youth want friends. They want to fit in with their peers. They want approval, and they want to be recognized. This is normal, but it can lead to compromise—the compromise of one's values and morality and of the truth. It can also lead to rebellion against authority.

⇒ *The desire to achieve*: youth desire to be successful, to find their place in the world. However, this can lead to seeking authority and power over people and to the manipulation and using of people for one's own ends.

⇒ *The desire for recognition*: youth desire to be the *top gun*, the star, the best looking, the smartest, the most popular. They constantly picture themselves as winning the game in the last second; winning the beauty pageant; winning the contest; being the one most recognized, and a host of other daydreams. This can lead to either pride and arrogance or to a sense of inferiority and low self-image. It can lead either to the hurting of the less gifted or to the downing of oneself.

⇒ *The desire to act and to act now*: youth, bursting with energy and idealism, want to see things done now. This can lead to impatience and to the mistreatment of people: bypassing and disregarding the peace and security of other people.

⇒ *The desire to be original and creative*: youth want to have the new and fresh idea, the better thought, and the better way for doing things. This can lead to a critical and argumentative spirit. It can also lead to cheating in order to be recognized. It can lead to the restating and rewording of things and ideas and claiming that they are creative ideas.

The charge to youth is direct and forceful: flee youthful lusts—flee the evil desires of youth.

> **But among you there must not be even a hint of sexual immorality, or of any kind of impurity, or of greed, because these are improper for God's holy people. For of this you can be sure: No immoral, impure or greedy person—such a man is an idolater—has any inheritance in the kingdom of Christ and of God. (Eph 5:3, 5)**
>
> **For we brought nothing into the world, and we can take nothing out of it. But if we have food and clothing, we will be content with that. People who want to get rich fall into temptation and a trap and into many foolish and harmful desires that plunge men into ruin and destruction. For the love of money is a root of all kinds of evil. Some people, eager for money, have wandered from the faith and pierced themselves with many griefs. (1 Tim 6:7-10)**
>
> **People will be lovers of themselves, lovers of money, boastful, proud, abusive, disobedient to their parents, ungrateful, unholy, (2 Tim 3:2)**
>
> **"You have heard that it was said, 'Do not commit adultery.' But I tell you that anyone who looks at a woman lustfully has already committed adultery with her in his heart. (Mat 5:27-28)**
>
> **Do not love the world or anything in the world. If anyone loves the world, the love of the Father is not in him. For everything in the world—the cravings of sinful**

man, the lust of his eyes and the boasting of what he has and does—comes not from the Father but from the world. (1 John 2:15-16)

It is God's will that you should be sanctified: that you should avoid sexual immorality; that each of you should learn to control his own body in a way that is holy and honorable, not in passionate lust like the heathen, who do not know God; (1 Th 4:3-5)

Flee the evil desires of youth, and pursue righteousness, faith, love and peace, along with those who call on the Lord out of a pure heart. (2 Tim 2:22)

But each one is tempted when, by his own evil desire, he is dragged away and enticed. Then, after desire has conceived, it gives birth to sin; and sin, when it is full-grown, gives birth to death. (James 1:14-15)

Dear friends, I urge you, as aliens and strangers in the world, to abstain from sinful desires, which war against your soul. (1 Pet 2:11)

2 (2:22) **Church—Believers**: second, follow after the Lord. But note a significant point: join with other believers in following after Him. As a youth, you need the companionship and fellowship, the experience and maturity, the direction and guidance of others. Other believers can help you; therefore, join with them and pursue, follow after the Lord. However, make sure they are genuine believers—that they "call on the Lord out of a *pure heart*." Only the pure in heart—only the genuine seeker—is really following after the Lord. It is the genuine believer with whom we are to fellowship and walk through life. Note what a genuine believer follows after: the very things for which men long and crave.

1. Righteousness (see note 2, pt.1—1 Tim.6:11 for discussion).
2. Faith: (see note 2, pt.3—1 Tim.6:11 for discussion).
3. Love: (see note, *Love*—1 Th.3:12 for discussion).
4. Peace: (see note 2, pt.3—1 Tim.1:2 for discussion).

3 (2:23) **Talk—Tongue**: avoid foolish arguments, speculations, and senseless controversy. There are two things that need to be said and heeded about this verse.

1. Far too much time is wasted on foolish arguments, foolish speculations, especially among ministers and teachers and those who are preparing for the ministry. Too many...
   - ignore the Word of God for the speculations of theology.
   - neglect the study of God's Word for a discussion of theory.
   - reject God's Word for the ideas of men.
   - take the easier road of theological discussion over the more difficult road of studying God's Word.

Too many sit around reading and discussing the speculations of theology instead of focusing upon God's Word and the mission of reaching and growing people for Christ. Too many substitute discussion for deeds. Discussion and speculation may be stimulating and invigorating to the mind, but it does not get the job done. Just think of the time we waste in the speculations of the latest religious craze instead of ministering to the lost and needy of the world.

2. Far too much time is wasted on senseless controversy, especially among members of churches. Think of the things that church members sometimes argue and get upset over—things that matter so little. Think about this: controversy and differences in the church are seldom over the great issues and doctrines of God's Word. They are usually over...
   - buildings and facilities
   - position and authority
   - likes and dislikes
   - opinions and preferences
   - personalities and traits
   - abilities and gifts
   - desires and wants
   - recognition and acceptance

The list could go on and on, but the point is well made. Too many within the church are embroiled in senseless controversy and hurt feelings while multitudes within every community are dying from loneliness, emptiness, neglect, abuse, rejection, disease, hunger, and sin.

The charge is direct and forceful: avoid foolish arguments, speculations and senseless controversy.

Do nothing out of selfish ambition or vain conceit, but in humility consider others better than yourselves. (Phil 2:3)

Nor to devote themselves to myths and endless genealogies. These promote controversies rather than God's work—which is by faith. (1 Tim 1:4)

If anyone teaches false doctrines and does not agree to the sound instruction of our Lord Jesus Christ and to godly teaching, he is conceited and understands nothing. He has an unhealthy interest in controversies and quarrels about words that result in envy, strife, malicious talk, evil suspicions and constant friction between men of corrupt mind, who have been robbed of the truth and who think that godliness is a means to financial gain. (1 Tim 6:3-5)

Keep reminding them of these things. Warn them before God against quarreling about words; it is of no value, and only ruins those who listen. (2 Tim 2:14)

Don't have anything to do with foolish and stupid arguments, because you know they produce quarrels. And the Lord's servant must not quarrel; instead, he must be kind to everyone, able to teach, not resentful. (2 Tim 2:23-24)

But avoid foolish controversies and genealogies and arguments and quarrels about the law, because these are unprofitable and useless. Warn a divisive person once, and then warn him a second time. After that, have nothing to do with him. You may be sure that such a man is warped and sinful; he is self-condemned. (Titus 3:9-11)

4 (2:24-26) **Arguing—Quarreling—Strife**: fourth, do not argue or fight with others. This charge is to "the Lord's servant"—the person who really wishes to serve the Lord. We cannot argue and fight and at the same time serve the Lord. A person who argues and fights is not serving the

Lord, no matter what he may claim. The charge is clear: "the Lord's servant must not quarrel."

1. He must be kind (epion): gentle, reasonable, considerate, soft, tender.
    ⇒ When people oppose him, he does not react, he reaches out in gentleness.
    ⇒ When he has to correct people and point out their weaknesses, he is not mean but gentle.

> **Be completely humble and gentle; be patient, bearing with one another in love. (Eph 4:2)**
>
> **Bear with each other and forgive whatever grievances you may have against one another. Forgive as the Lord forgave you. (Col 3:13)**
>
> **But we were gentle among you, like a mother caring for her little children. (1 Th 2:7)**
>
> **And the Lord's servant must not quarrel; instead, he must be kind to everyone, able to teach, not resentful. (2 Tim 2:24)**
>
> **To slander no one, to be peaceable and considerate, and to show true humility toward all men. (Titus 3:2)**
>
> **But the wisdom that comes from heaven is first of all pure; then peace-loving, considerate, submissive, full of mercy and good fruit, impartial and sincere. (James 3:17)**

2. He must be able to teach: prepared and ready, able and capable, skillful and qualified to teach. Remember: he cannot teach the truth unless he knows the truth; he cannot settle disputes and help those who oppose him...
    - unless he knows what God says about handling problems.
    - unless he walks in the Lord day by day.

> **And teaching them to obey everything I have commanded you. And surely I am with you always, to the very end of the age." (Mat 28:20)**
>
> **Now the overseer must be above reproach, the husband of but one wife, temperate, self-controlled, respectable, hospitable, able to teach, (1 Tim 3:2)**
>
> **Command and teach these things. (1 Tim 4:11)**
>
> **Those who oppose him he must gently instruct, in the hope that God will grant them repentance leading them to a knowledge of the truth, (2 Tim 2:25)**

3. He must be patient, not resentful (see note, pt.11—1 Tim.3:2-3 for discussion).

4. He must correct others in a spirit of gentleness. Within the church there are those who often oppose the minister and the ministries and actions of the church. How are opponents to be approached? Not in a spirit of reaction and meanness; not in a spirit that criticizes, reproaches, whips, and berates. We must approach opponents in a spirit of gentleness (see note, pt.6—1 Tim.6:11 for discussion). There are two reasons for this.
    a. A gentle approach is the only approach that can lead a person to repentance. Arguing and fighting with them will only drive them further away from us and the church. In fact, if we argue with them, we are guilty of the same wrong that they have committed, and we give them reason to cry "hypocrite."
    b. A gentle approach is the only approach that can free a person from the trap of the devil. People who are controversial and argumentative, critical and gossiping may not like to think that they are ensnared by the devil, but Scripture clearly says they are. Note the verse—argumentative and quarrelsome persons are said to be caught in the trap of the devil. Such persons are even said to be taken by the devil at the devil's will.

What is the hope for the argumentative and criticizing person? His only hope is for the minister and believers to approach him in a spirit of gentleness—to reach out to him, attempting to lead him to repentance.

> **Brothers, if someone is caught in a sin, you who are spiritual should restore him gently. But watch yourself, or you also may be tempted. Carry each other's burdens, and in this way you will fulfill the law of Christ. (Gal 6:1-2)**
>
> **It was he who gave some to be apostles, some to be prophets, some to be evangelists, and some to be pastors and teachers, to prepare God's people for works of service, so that the body of Christ may be built up until we all reach unity in the faith and in the knowledge of the Son of God and become mature, attaining to the whole measure of the fullness of Christ. (Eph 4:11-13)**
>
> **Do nothing out of selfish ambition or vain conceit, but in humility consider others better than yourselves. I plead with Euodia and I plead with Syntyche to agree with each other in the Lord. Yes, and I ask you, loyal yokefellow, help these women who have contended at my side in the cause of the gospel, along with Clement and the rest of my fellow workers, whose names are in the book of life. (Phil 4:2-3)**
>
> **Keep reminding them of these things. Warn them before God against quarreling about words; it is of no value, and only ruins those who listen. (2 Tim 2:14)**
>
> **I have seen his ways, but I will heal him; I will guide him and restore comfort to him, (Isa 57:18)**
>
> **"Return, faithless people; I will cure you of backsliding." "Yes, we will come to you, for you are the LORD our God. (Jer 3:22)**
>
> **But I will restore you to health and heal your wounds,' declares the LORD, 'because you are called an outcast, Zion for whom no one cares.' (Jer 30:17)**
>
> **"I will heal their waywardness and love them freely, for my anger has turned away from them. (Hosea 14:4)**
>
> **You will again have compassion on us; you will tread our sins underfoot and hurl all our iniquities into the depths of the sea. (Micah 7:19)**

2 TIMOTHY 3:1-9

	CHAPTER 3 **II. THE PREDICTIONS OF THE LAST DAYS, 3:1-17** **A. The Godless Marks of the Last Days, 3:1-9**	5 Having a form of godliness but denying its power. Have nothing to do with them. 6 They are the kind who worm their way into homes and gain control over weak-willed women, who are loaded down with sins and are swayed by all kinds of evil desires,	3 Mark 2: A powerless religion 4 Mark 3: A corrupt ministry a. They lead the gullible astray
1 In the last days terrible times will come 2 Mark 1: A godless world	But mark this: There will be terrible times in the last days. 2 People will be lovers of themselves, lovers of money, boastful, proud, abusive, disobedient to their parents, ungrateful, unholy, 3 Without love, unforgiving, slanderous, without self-control, brutal, not lovers of the good, 4 Treacherous, rash, conceited, lovers of pleasure rather than lovers of God—	7 Always learning but never able to acknowledge the truth. 8 Just as Jannes and Jambres opposed Moses, so also these men oppose the truth—men of depraved minds, who, as far as the faith is concerned, are rejected. 9 But they will not get very far because, as in the case of those men, their folly will be clear to everyone.	b. They oppose the truth c. They & their corrupt religion will be exposed

DIVISION II

THE PREDICTIONS OF THE LAST DAYS, 3:1-17

A. The Godless Marks of the Last Days, 3:1-9

(3:1-9) **Introduction**: this is a picture of future society—a terrible picture of what the last days of human history will be like. But note a shocking fact: it sounds very much like the society of today. We just do not think of our day as being so terrible; we seldom sit down and study the godless marks of society. But this is exactly what this passage does: it discusses the godless marks of the last days, marks that come close to painting a picture of our day and time. This fact points to our day as being part of the last days. It is very possible that the Lord's return is at hand. One thing is sure, we must do just what Christ said: be prepared for His return, for He can return at any moment. (Note: a person may need to split this passage because of its length. Points one and two could be the first study, and points three and four the second study.)

1. In the last days terrible times will come (v.1).
2. Mark 1: a godless world (v.2-4).
3. Mark 2: a powerless religion (v.5).
4. Mark 3: a corrupt ministry (v.6-9).

1 (3:1) **Perilous Times—End Time**: in the last days terrible times will come. *Terrible times* means difficult, troublesome, trying, uneasy, hard, violent, threatening, and dangerous days. The picture is that of people turning to and fro, here and there, not knowing which way to turn. "The last days" is a Biblical term that points to the *end* of the present age, the days right before the return of Christ, and the end of the world. It should be noted, however, that the marks of the end time are somewhat characteristic of all ages, but they are to be intensified in the last days (cp. Mt.24:1-25:46).

2 (3:2-4) **Godless**: the first mark of the last days will be a godless world. Why will the last days be terrible? Because the world will be godless. Note how the terrible marks of the last days sound very much like a picture of today.

1. People will be *lovers of themselves* (philoutos): this does not mean the normal and natural love of life and of oneself that we should all have. It means selfishness and self-centeredness...
   - to focus upon oneself and one's own pleasure and flesh instead of upon God and other people.
   - to put oneself before others: wife, husband, parent, child, friend, neighbor, God.
   - to put one's own will before God's will.
   - to seek one's own desires without considering others.
   - to go after what one wants even if it is unwise and hurts others.
   - to feel that everyone and everything should revolve around oneself.
   - to focus upon one's own pleasure and flesh and ignore the crying needs of the desperate and dying.

Self-love sets one up like a god and feels that nothing matters as much as the pleasure of oneself. In the last days people will love themselves more than they love anyone else. Selfishness will be one of the terrible marks of the last days.

> I was a stranger and you did not invite me in, I needed clothes and you did not clothe me, I was sick and in prison and you did not look after me.' (Mat 25:43)
>
> But mark this: There will be terrible times in the last days. People will be lovers of themselves, lovers of money, boastful, proud, abusive, disobedient to their parents, ungrateful, unholy, (2 Tim 3:1-2)
>
> If anyone has material possessions and sees his brother in need but has no pity on him, how can the love of God be in him? (1 John 3:17)

2 TIMOTHY 3:1-9

2. People will be *lovers of money* (philarguroi): the word means lovers of money and *possessions*. People will want more and more and bigger and bigger and better and better, and they will seldom be satisfied with what they have. In the last days people will focus upon…
- money, banking more and more.
- houses in the best neighborhoods, on the seashore, in the mountains, and by the rivers.
- furnishings and property.
- possessions—such as clothes, jewelry, antiques, art, and vehicles.
- travel, seeing more and more sights.
- property, stocks and bonds—owning more and more.
- power—controlling more and more.

Men will love money, what it buys and allows them to do, and they will covet more and more of it and the things it buys. Their eyes and hearts will be focused upon money instead of God. They will indulge and hoard instead of meeting the desperate needs of the poor and lost of the world.

> **For the love of money is a root of all kinds of evil. Some people, eager for money, have wandered from the faith and pierced themselves with many griefs. (1 Tim 6:10)**
>
> **Your gold and silver are corroded. Their corrosion will testify against you and eat your flesh like fire. You have hoarded wealth in the last days. (James 5:3)**
>
> **Whoever loves money never has money enough; whoever loves wealth is never satisfied with his income. This too is meaningless. (Eccl 5:10)**
>
> **Like a partridge that hatches eggs it did not lay is the man who gains riches by unjust means. When his life is half gone, they will desert him, and in the end he will prove to be a fool. (Jer 17:11)**

3. People will be *boastful* (alazones): braggarts, pretenders, vaunters, swaggerts. It is a person who…
- boasts in what he has.
- pretends to have what he does not have or to do what he has not done.

Bragging may involve a job, a deal, a possession, an achievement—anything that may impress others. It is a person who feels the need to push himself above others even if it involves pretension, deception, make believe, and lies.

The world is full of boasters and braggarts:
⇒ teachers who pretend to be wise.
⇒ politicians who pretend to have the utopian state.
⇒ business people who pretend to have the product that brings health, beauty, and happiness.
⇒ religionists who pretend to have the revelation and gifts and to be more spiritual than others.

> **Now for some time a man named Simon had practiced sorcery in the city and amazed all the people of Samaria. He boasted that he was someone great, (Acts 8:9)**
>
> **Furthermore, since they did not think it worthwhile to retain the knowledge of God, he gave them over to a depraved mind, to do what ought not to be done. They have become filled with every kind of wickedness, evil, greed and depravity. They are full of envy, murder, strife, deceit and malice. They are gossips, slanderers, God-haters, insolent, arrogant and boastful; they invent ways of doing evil; they disobey their parents; (Rom 1:28-29, 30)**
>
> **As it is, you boast and brag. All such boasting is evil. (James 4:16)**
>
> **For they mouth empty, boastful words and, by appealing to the lustful [sensuality] desires of sinful human nature, they entice people who are just escaping from those who live in error. (2 Pet 2:18)**
>
> **He boasts of the cravings of his heart; he blesses the greedy and reviles the LORD. (Psa 10:3)**
>
> **Those who trust in their wealth and boast of their great riches? No man can redeem the life of another or give to God a ransom for him— (Psa 49:6-7)**
>
> **Like clouds and wind without rain is a man who boasts of gifts he does not give. (Prov 25:14)**
>
> **Do not boast about tomorrow, for you do not know what a day may bring forth. (Prov 27:1)**

4. People will be *proud* (huperephanoi): self-exaltation, conceit, arrogance; being haughty; putting oneself above others and looking down upon others; scorn, and contempt. It means to show oneself; to lift one's head above another; to hold contempt for another; to compare oneself with others. Pride can be hidden in the heart as well as openly displayed.

Very simply stated, the proud person feels that he is better than others. Note that this is a feeling within the heart. The proud person may appear quiet and humble, but within his heart he secretly feels better than others. God opposes the proud.

> **For whoever exalts himself will be humbled, and whoever humbles himself will be exalted. (Mat 23:12)**
>
> **Live in harmony with one another. Do not be proud, but be willing to associate with people of low position. Do not be conceited. (Rom 12:16)**
>
> **If anyone thinks he is something when he is nothing, he deceives himself. (Gal 6:3)**
>
> **In his arrogance the wicked man hunts down the weak, who are caught in the schemes he devises. (Psa 10:2)**
>
> **When pride comes, then comes disgrace, but with humility comes wisdom. (Prov 11:2)**
>
> **Pride goes before destruction, a haughty spirit before a fall. (Prov 16:18)**
>
> **Haughty eyes and a proud heart, the lamp of the wicked, are sin! (Prov 21:4)**
>
> **A greedy man stirs up dissension, but he who trusts in the LORD will prosper. (Prov 28:25)**
>
> **You said in your heart, "I will ascend to heaven; I will raise my throne above the stars of God; I will sit enthroned on the**

mount of assembly, on the utmost heights of the sacred mountain. (Isa 14:13)

Though you soar like the eagle and make your nest among the stars, from there I will bring you down," declares the LORD. (Oba 1:4)

5. People will be *abusive* (blasphemoi): the word means to blaspheme, slander, insult, rail, revile, reproach, curse. Verbal abuse, blasphemy is usually thought to be against God, and it is. But it is also a sin against men. People can verbally abuse, blaspheme others. Think of the cursing and insults thrown against God and men today. Practically everyone is cursing and reviling someone: mothers, fathers, children, teachers, professionals, actors, comedians, politicians, even some professing religionists feel the need to occasionally curse in order to be acceptable.

Why is there so much cursing today? Because there is a loss of respect for both self and others, for both position and authority. People rail, revile, insult, reproach, and curse when they are disturbed within—when they sense dissatisfaction, disapproval, unacceptance, bitterness, emptiness, loneliness, and reaction within their heart. A disturbed and dissatisfied heart causes people to verbally abuse or blaspheme God and man, including themselves (blaming and cursing themselves when they fail and come ever so short).

But I tell you, Do not swear at all: either by heaven, for it is God's throne; (Mat 5:34)

"Their mouths [men] are full of cursing and bitterness." (Rom 3:14)

But no man can tame the tongue. It is a restless evil, full of deadly poison. With the tongue we praise our Lord and Father, and with it we curse men, who have been made in God's likeness. (James 3:8-9)

Above all, my brothers, do not swear—not by heaven or by earth or by anything else. Let your "Yes" be yes, and your "No," no, or you will be condemned. (James 5:12)

"You shall not misuse the name of the LORD your God, for the LORD will not hold anyone guiltless who misuses his name. (Exo 20:7)

"'Do not swear falsely by my name and so profane the name of your God. I am the LORD. (Lev 19:12)

His mouth is full of curses and lies and threats; trouble and evil are under his tongue. (Psa 10:7)

For the sins of their mouths, for the words of their lips, let them be caught in their pride. For the curses and lies they utter, (Psa 59:12)

He loved to pronounce a curse— may it come on him; he found no pleasure in blessing— may it be far from him. (Psa 109:17)

For you know in your heart that many times you yourself have cursed others. (Eccl 7:22)

6. People will be *disobedient to parents* (goneusin apeitheis): refusing to do what one's parents say; rebelling against one's parents; showing disrespect to parents; rejecting parental instruction; dishonoring parental example. If a child will not honor and respect his mother and father, who will he respect? If a child will mistreat his parents—those who are the closest to him—who else will he mistreat? If a child will not obey his parents, those who love and care for him most, who then will be obey? Parents are the ones who gave birth, loved and cared for the children of the world. If the children are not loyal to them, then the children will not be loyal to anyone. The home, society, and civilization will crumble.

"Honor your father and your mother, so that you may live long in the land the LORD your God is giving you. (Exo 20:12)

"'Each of you must respect his mother and father, and you must observe my Sabbaths. I am the LORD your God. (Lev 19:3)

"Cursed is the man who dishonors his father or his mother." Then all the people shall say, "Amen!" (Deu 27:16)

Come, my children, listen to me; I will teach you the fear of the LORD. (Psa 34:11)

Listen to your father, who gave you life, and do not despise your mother when she is old. (Prov 23:22)

"The eye that mocks a father, that scorns obedience to a mother, will be pecked out by the ravens of the valley, will be eaten by the vultures. (Prov 30:17)

For God said, 'Honor your father and mother' and 'Anyone who curses his father or mother must be put to death.' (Mat 15:4)

Children, obey your parents in the Lord, for this is right. "Honor your father and mother"—which is the first commandment with a promise—"that it may go well with you and that you may enjoy long life on the earth." (Eph 6:1-3)

But if a widow has children or grandchildren, these should learn first of all to put their religion into practice by caring for their own family and so repaying their parents and grandparents, for this is pleasing to God. (1 Tim 5:4)

7. People will be *ungrateful* (acharistoi): no sense of gratitude or appreciation for what one has and receives; no giving of thanks to God or man. Many persons feel that the world and society or business and government owe them the good things of life. They have little if any sense of debt to others. This is the reason many waste time on the job, do mediocre work, and feel little obligation to the world and society. They fail to see how privileged they are to be alive and to live in such a beautiful world and to have a job and friends and neighbors. They fail to see how good God has been to them, and how caring and responsible some people are. Therefore, they reach out to get more and more without sensing any need to express thanks and appreciation. They take and take and forget all about the thanksgiving—the debt and contribution—they owe to God and men.

For although they knew God, they neither glorified him as God nor gave thanks to him, but their thinking became futile and their foolish hearts were darkened. (Rom 1:21)

Giving thanks to the Father, who has qualified you to share in the inheritance of the saints in the kingdom of light. (Col 1:12)

Give thanks in all circumstances, for this is God's will for you in Christ Jesus. (1 Th 5:18)

When you have eaten and are satisfied, praise the LORD your God for the good land he has given you. (Deu 8:10)

Enter his gates with thanksgiving and his courts with praise; give thanks to him and praise his name. (Psa 100:4)

Let them sacrifice thank offerings and tell of his works with songs of joy. (Psa 107:22)

8. People will be *unholy* (anosioi): profane, indecent, shameless, given over to the most base passions, being blind to modesty, decency, purity, and righteousness. The unholy person...
- is mastered by passion.
- seeks constant gratification of the flesh (sinful nature).
- senses little shame.
- is blind to decency.
- seeks his pleasure in the abnormal. (Just think of the abnormal sex that is flaunted today.)

Thought 1. Oliver Greene has a very practical and straightforward comment on unholiness:

"This is an unholy age. People have lost respect for their bodies. Women (even church members, professing Christians) dress indecently and expose their nakedness. Men do the same. Men and women tear down the temple of the Holy Spirit.

" 'What? know ye not that your body is the temple of the Holy Ghost which is in you, which ye have of God, and ye are not your own? For ye are bought with a price: therefore glorify God in your body, and in your spirit, which are Gods' (1 Cor.6:19-20).

"A person who tears down and destroys his body through drink, tobacco, foods, and habits is unholy in his living.

"This is an age when people have lost respect and reverence for a holy God, the holy Bible, and holy living. If you are 'a good mixer,' if you can play cards, dance, drink, dress indecently, laugh at a filthy joke, you are a wonderful fellow, a number one citizen; and you can teach a Sunday school class, pray in public, sing in the choir, and hold any number of responsible positions in the church. But the church member who refuses to drink cocktails, use tobacco, attend dances and parties, and who believes in old-time Christianity is called a fanatic or a 'religious square'" (The Epistles of Paul the Apostle to Timothy and Titus, p.335).

To rescue us from the hand of our enemies, and to enable us to serve him without fear (Luke 1:74)

Since we have these promises, dear friends, let us purify ourselves from everything that contaminates body and spirit, perfecting holiness out of reverence for God. (2 Cor 7:1)

Make every effort to live in peace with all men and to be holy; without holiness no one will see the Lord. (Heb 12:14)

For it is written: "Be holy, because I am holy." (1 Pet 1:16)

Since everything will be destroyed in this way, what kind of people ought you to be? You ought to live holy and godly lives (2 Pet 3:11)

I am the LORD who brought you up out of Egypt to be your God; therefore be holy, because I am holy. (Lev 11:45)

9. People will be *without love* (astorgoi): abnormal affection and love; heartless, without human emotion or love; a lack of feeling for others; abuse of normal affection and love. Others become little more than pawns for a man's own use and benefit, pleasure and purposes, excitement and stimulation.

Man has been created to be affectionate—to have affection for others. It is normal and natural for a person to have affection for his family, friends, neighbors, co-workers, and to a certain extent for the stranger and fellow-citizens of the world. But in the end time, people will be so set on satisfying their flesh and pleasure that they will forget family, friends, and everything else. They will be so set on doing their own thing and so self-centered that they will have little affection for anyone or anything else.

⇒ There will be little affection for the normal and natural. People will turn to the abnormal and unnatural in relationships and behavior, pleasures and sex.

⇒ There will be little affection for the home. Home will be nothing more than a place to change clothes and sleep.

⇒ There will be little affection between husband and wife. A spouse will be little more than a person to help pay the bills and to keep up a front for social acceptance. Men and women will become unfaithful and perverted.

⇒ There will be little affection for friends, country, and earth. All will be abused and ignored, neglected and polluted. Selfishness will be the law of the last days.

⇒ There will be little affection for God and the church. God and church will be fitted in when they do not interfere with personal desires and pleasures, rest and recreation.

Love the Lord your God with all your heart and with all your soul and with all your mind and with all your strength.' The second is this: 'Love your neighbor as yourself.' There is no commandment greater than these." (Mark 12:30-31)

"A new command I give you: Love one another. As I have loved you, so you must love one another. By this all men will know that you are my disciples, if you love one another." (John 13:34-35)

Love must be sincere. Hate what is evil; cling to what is good. Be devoted to one another in brotherly love. Honor one another above yourselves. (Rom 12:9-10)

Wives, submit to your husbands as to the Lord. (Eph 5:22)

Husbands, love your wives, just as Christ loved the church and gave himself up for her (Eph 5:25)

Children, obey your parents in the Lord, for this is right. "Honor your father and mother"—which is the first commandment with a promise—"that it may go well with you and that you may enjoy long life on the earth." (Eph 6:1-3)

And this is his command: to believe in the name of his Son, Jesus Christ, and to love one another as he commanded us. (1 John 3:23)

10. People will be *unforgiving* or *trucebreakers* (aspondoi): breakers of promises and agreements; untrustworthy, faithless, treacherous, untruthful, and unforgiving. An unforgiving person or a trucebreaker is a person or some organization or body of people who tragically do not keep their word or promise and they are unforgiving. They are simply unforgiving, untrustworthy and undependable. What happens when a person's word can no longer be accepted?

⇒ What happens in a home when the husband or wife breaks the truce of marriage?
⇒ What happens between parent and child when one of them breaks their promise time and again?
⇒ What happens when an employer breaks his promise to his workers?
⇒ What happens when a worker breaks his truce and slacks up in his work?
⇒ What happens when a nation breaks its agreement with another nation?

The last days will see what we are seeing in our society today: a barrage of broken truces, covenants, promises, and an unforgiving spirit.

Therefore each of you must put off falsehood and speak truthfully to his neighbor, for we are all members of one body. (Eph 4:25)

Truthful lips endure forever, but a lying tongue lasts only a moment. (Prov 12:19)

The earth is defiled by its people; they have disobeyed the laws, violated the statutes and broken the everlasting covenant. (Isa 24:5)

These are the things you are to do: Speak the truth to each other, and render true and sound judgment in your courts; (Zec 8:16)

True instruction was in his mouth and nothing false was found on his lips. He walked with me in peace and uprightness, and turned many from sin. (Mal 2:6)

11. People will be *slanderous* (diaboloi): slanderers. Note that the Greek word is *diabolos*, the very word for the devil. William Barclay says:

"The devil is the patron saint of all slanderers, and of all slanderers he is chief. There is a sense in which slander is the most cruel of all sins. If a man's goods are stolen, he can set to and build up his fortunes again; but if a man's good name is taken away, irreparable damage has been done to him. It is one thing to start an evil and untrue report on its malicious way; it is entirely another thing to stop it....Many a man, and many a woman, who would never dream of putting his or her hand in other peoples' pockets and stealing their money or their belongings, thinks nothing—even finds a pleasure—in passing on a story which ruins someone else's good name, without even trying to find out whether or not the story is true. There is slander enough in every village, and not infrequently in many a Church, to make the recording angel weep as he records these cruel words" (The Letters to Timothy, Titus, and Philemon, p.217).

12. People will be *without self-control* (akrateis): undisciplined and uncontrolled; having no self-control or no power to discipline. It is being given over...
• to pleasure and indulgence
• to passion and sexual craving
• to lust and lewdness

It is a person who cannot control his passion for food, sex, pornography, sensuality, drink, drugs, smoking, whatever. It is a passion that grips and enslaves a person until it becomes an unbreakable habit and bondage.

Therefore do not let sin reign in your mortal body so that you obey its evil desires. (Rom 6:12)

"Everything is permissible for me"— but not everything is beneficial. "Everything is permissible for me"—but I will not be mastered by anything. (1 Cor 6:12)

Everyone who competes in the games goes into strict training. They do it to get a crown that will not last; but we do it to get a crown that will last forever. (1 Cor 9:25)

But the fruit of the Spirit is love, joy, peace, patience, kindness, goodness, faithfulness, gentleness and self-control. Against such things there is no law. (Gal 5:22-23)

Better a patient man than a warrior, a man who controls his temper than one who takes a city. (Prov 16:32)

He who loves pleasure will become poor; whoever loves wine and oil will never be rich. (Prov 21:17)

When you sit to dine with a ruler, note well what is before you, and put a knife to your throat if you are given to gluttony. (Prov 23:1-2)

If you find honey, eat just enough— too much of it, and you will vomit. (Prov 25:16)

13. People will be *brutal* (anemeroi): savage and untamed. It is the word that describes the savage beast of the wild that is unrestrained in its fierceness. It is a word that should never be true of people, yet tragically it is. Never in the history of the world have men become as brutal and savage as they are today.

a. People no longer just murder...
• they mutilate

2 TIMOTHY 3:1-9

- they torture
- they kill at random
- they kill by twos and threes and by thousands and millions (for example, Hitler, Stalin)

...and they take pleasure in their torture and savagery.

b. People no longer just correct and rebuke children, spouse, friend, neighbor, employee, or stranger...
- they curse
- they abuse
- they attack
- they damage
- they act violently

The last days will see an increase in brutal and savage behavior.

> **Be kind and compassionate to one another, forgiving each other, just as in Christ God forgave you. (Eph 4:32)**
>
> **Therefore, as God's chosen people, holy and dearly loved, clothe yourselves with compassion, kindness, humility, gentleness and patience. (Col 3:12)**
>
> **Anyone who hates his brother is a murderer, and you know that no murderer has eternal life in him. (1 John 3:15)**
>
> **But the cowardly, the unbelieving, the vile, the murderers, the sexually immoral, those who practice magic arts, the idolaters and all liars—their place will be in the fiery lake of burning sulfur. This is the second death." (Rev 21:8)**

14. People will not be *lovers of* the good (aphilagathoi): this refers to people despising both good people and good things. In the last days people will be embarrassed...
    - to speak up for what is right.
    - to take a stand for what is good.
    - to be known as a good person.
    - to be a friend to good people.

People will want to fulfill their desires and to satisfy their flesh (sinful nature); they will want to party, indulge, look, feel, taste, experience, possess, take, and fit in and be acceptable with the crowd. They will let morality and justice go and reject whatever restraint they feel. They will actually despise righteousness and want nothing to do with anyone who speaks up for what is right.

Think how far a person and a society have fallen when they...
- are embarrassed to say "no" to what they know is wrong and not good for them (cp. drinking, smoking, cursing, immorality).
- are embarrassed to stand up for what is good.
- are embarrassed to speak up for what is right.
- are embarrassed to be a friend to a good person.

> **Take care that what the prophets have said does not happen to you: "'Look, you scoffers, wonder and perish, for I am going to do something in your days that you would never believe, even if someone told you.'" (Acts 13:40-41)**
>
> **Or do you show contempt for the riches of his kindness, tolerance and patience, not realizing that God's kindness leads you toward repentance? (Rom 2:4)**
>
> **How much more severely do you think a man deserves to be punished who has trampled the Son of God under foot, who has treated as an unholy thing the blood of the covenant that sanctified him, and who has insulted the Spirit of grace? (Heb 10:29)**
>
> **This is especially true of those who follow the corrupt desire of the sinful nature and despise authority [discipline]. Bold and arrogant, these men are not afraid to slander celestial beings [leaders]; (2 Pet 2:10)**

15. People will be *treacherous* (prodotai): betraying a trust refers to a person who...
    - betrays his country
    - betrays his team
    - betrays his friends
    - betrays his family

It refers to a person who betrays any trust or any commitment. The most tragic betrayal of all is the person who betrays Christ and the church—who turns his back upon Christ and returns to the world and its crowd. The last days will see an increase in traitors.

> **Going at once to Jesus, Judas said, "Greetings, Rabbi!" and kissed him. (Mat 26:49)**
>
> **"Brother will betray brother to death, and a father his child. Children will rebel against their parents and have them put to death. (Mark 13:12)**
>
> **Anyone, then, who knows the good he ought to do and doesn't do it, sins. (James 4:17)**
>
> **If they have escaped the corruption of the world by knowing our Lord and Savior Jesus Christ and are again entangled in it and overcome, they are worse off at the end than they were at the beginning. (2 Pet 2:20)**
>
> **Therefore, dear friends, since you already know this, be on your guard so that you may not be carried away by the error of lawless men and fall from your secure position. (2 Pet 3:17)**
>
> **They went out from us, but they did not really belong to us. For if they had belonged to us, they would have remained with us; but their going showed that none of them belonged to us. (1 John 2:19)**
>
> **Yet I hold this against you: You have forsaken your first love. Remember the height from which you have fallen! Repent and do the things you did at first. If you do not repent, I will come to you and remove your lampstand from its place. (Rev 2:4-5)**

16. People will be *rash* (propeteis): headstrong and reckless, rash and hasty—all without giving thought to the consequences. Reckless is probably the best description. A rash person is a person who thinks he knows best and can live and act recklessly, without paying any attention to the consequences. The reckless person thinks little about what he is doing; he just enjoys the feeling and pleasure. He

enjoys the stimulation and excitement; the consequences matter little in the midst of the pleasure and excitement.

Think how much hurt and damage is done when a person lives for the pleasure of the moment. Think of the hurt and damage done because of the pleasure of...
- reckless driving and boating
- reckless work and recreation
- reckless passion and lust
- reckless eating and drinking

Being rash—thinking that one knows best and can live and act recklessly without consequence—has led to more hurt, accidents, damaged bodies, and death than could ever be imagined.

> And I'll say to myself, "You have plenty of good things laid up for many years. Take life easy; eat, drink and be merry."' (Luke 12:19)
>
> There is only one Lawgiver and Judge, the one who is able to save and destroy. But you—who are you to judge your neighbor? (James 4:12)
>
> It is not good to have zeal without knowledge, nor to be hasty and miss the way. (Prov 19:2)
>
> The plans of the diligent lead to profit as surely as haste leads to poverty. (Prov 21:5)
>
> Do not boast about tomorrow, for you do not know what a day may bring forth. (Prov 27:1)
>
> Do you see a man who speaks in haste? There is more hope for a fool than for him. (Prov 29:20)
>
> Do not be quick with your mouth, do not be hasty in your heart to utter anything before God. God is in heaven and you are on earth, so let your words be few. (Eccl 5:2)

17. People will be *conceited* (tetuphomenoi): puffed up and high minded; having feelings of self-importance. It is a person who feels so educated, so scientific, so advanced, so high in position and authority, ability, and gifts that he feels completely self-sufficient. He feels no need for God. He is above God and above most people.

> Live in harmony with one another. Do not be proud, but be willing to associate with people of low position. Do not be conceited. (Rom 12:16)
>
> The man who thinks he knows something does not yet know as he ought to know. (1 Cor 8:2)
>
> If anyone thinks he is something when he is nothing, he deceives himself. (Gal 6:3)
>
> Do nothing out of selfish ambition or vain conceit, but in humility consider others better than yourselves. Each of you should look not only to your own interests, but also to the interests of others. (Phil 2:3-4)
>
> "Let us break their chains," they say, "and throw off their fetters." The One enthroned in heaven laughs; the Lord scoffs at them. (Psa 2:3-4)
>
> In his arrogance the wicked man hunts down the weak, who are caught in the schemes he devises. (Psa 10:2)

> Therefore pride is their necklace; they clothe themselves with violence. (Psa 73:6)
>
> Do not be wise in your own eyes; fear the LORD and shun evil. (Prov 3:7)
>
> When pride comes, then comes disgrace, but with humility comes wisdom. (Prov 11:2)
>
> Pride goes before destruction, a haughty spirit before a fall. (Prov 16:18)
>
> Haughty eyes and a proud heart, the lamp of the wicked, are sin! (Prov 21:4)
>
> Do you see a man wise in his own eyes? There is more hope for a fool than for him. (Prov 26:12)
>
> Woe to those who are wise in their own eyes and clever in their own sight. (Isa 5:21)

18. People will be *lovers of pleasure rather than lovers of God*.

> Matthew Henry says, *"When there are more [pleasure seekers] than true Christians, then the times are bad indeed. God is to be loved above all. That is a carnal mind, and is full of enmity against him, which prefers any thing before him, especially such a sordid thing as carnal pleasure"* (*Matthew Henry's Commentary*, Vol.6, p.844).
>
> Oliver Green says, *"The average church member today does not allow the church service to come between him and his pleasure. Prayer meeting, revival or church duties no longer interfere with social activities. Almost any minister in this country would agree with this, for it is the simple truth that the average church member does not let church interfere with his social life nor with anything he or she wants to do in the line of pleasure"* (*The Epistles of Paul the Apostle to Timothy and Titus*, p.339f).

3 (3:5) **Religion—Godliness—Last Days**: the second mark of the last days will be a powerless religion. Note: there will be religion in the last days. It will be just like today, churches and temples and worship centers will be everywhere. People will claim and profess *godliness*, but their worship will be only a form, only an outward profession, only an appearance of godliness. They will not possess God; they will not have God in their hearts and lives. They will...
- profess God and Christ
- be baptized in the Christian faith
- attend worship services
- participate in the rituals and ceremonies
- recite the creeds
- sometimes talk about God

But they will deny the power of God. What is the power of God? It is the power to deliver men from the bondage of sin, death, and hell—all through the Lord Jesus Christ. It is the power of the cross and resurrection of the Lord Jesus Christ—the power to save people from perishing and to give them eternal life. This is exactly what Scripture says.

> Just as Moses lifted up the snake in the desert, so the Son of Man must be lifted up

[upon the cross], that everyone who believes in him may have eternal life. "For God so loved the world that he gave his one and only Son, that whoever believes in him shall not perish but have eternal life. (John 3:14-16)

I am not ashamed of the gospel, because it is the power of God for the salvation of everyone who believes: first for the Jew, then for the Gentile. (Rom 1:16)

But God demonstrates his own love for us in this: While we were still sinners, Christ died for us. Since we have now been justified by his blood, how much more shall we be saved from God's wrath through him! For if, when we were God's enemies, we were reconciled to him through the death of his Son, how much more, having been reconciled, shall we be saved through his life! (Rom 5:8-10)

Now, brothers, I want to remind you of the gospel I preached to you, which you received and on which you have taken your stand. By this gospel you are saved, if you hold firmly to the word I preached to you. Otherwise, you have believed in vain. For what I received I passed on to you as of first importance : that Christ died for our sins according to the Scriptures, that he was buried, that he was raised on the third day according to the Scriptures, (1 Cor 15:1-4)

For Christ did not send me to baptize, but to preach the gospel—not with words of human wisdom, lest the cross of Christ be emptied of its power. For the message of the cross is foolishness to those who are perishing, but to us who are being saved it is the power of God. (1 Cor 1:17-18)

Yet when I preach the gospel, I cannot boast, for I am compelled to preach. Woe to me if I do not preach the gospel! (1 Cor 9:16)

The point is this: in the last days there will be a powerless religion—a religion of form, ritual, and ceremony. The religionists will deny the power of the cross and resurrection of Jesus Christ. They will deny that Jesus Christ can save men from perishing and give them eternal life. In describing the religion of the last days, Donald Guthrie says:

> "Religion is not entirely denied, but it amounts to no more than an empty shell. There is an outward form...but no power....Its adherents [ministers and followers] are denying the power thereof which suggests a positive [deliberate] rejection of its...power. They have no conception of its generating force" (*The Pastoral Epistles*. "Tyndale New Testament Commentary," p.158).

The Pulpit Commentary says:

> "The meaning is that by their life and character and conversation they gave the lie to the Christian profession. Christianity with them was an outward form, not an inward living power of godliness" (*The Pulpit Commentary*, Vol.21, p.41).

Matthew Henry says:

> "They will assume the form of godliness...but they will not submit to the power of it, to take away their sin. Observe here:
> "Men may be very bad and wicked...they may be lovers of themselves...yet have a form of godliness.
> "A form of godliness is a very different thing from the power of it; men may have the one and be wholly destitute of the other....
> "From such good Christians must withdraw themselves" (*Matthew Henry's Commentary*, Vol.5, p.844).

William Barclay says:

> "The final condemnation of these people is that they retain the outward form of religion, but they deny its power. That is to say, they recite the orthodox creeds, they go through the movements of a correct and dignified ritual and liturgy and worship; they maintain all the external forms of religion; but they know nothing of religion as a dynamic power which changes the lives of men" (*The Letters to Timothy, Titus, and Philemon*, p.219).

4 (3:6-9) **Ministers—Last Days**: the third mark of the last days will be a corrupt ministry. Three things are said about corrupt ministers.

1. Corrupt ministers lead gullible followers astray. Note the phrase "weak-willed women" (gunaikaria). The Greek word means *little women*, *little* in the sense of being spiritually dead, weak, immature, and unstable. However, it should always be remembered that men are just as gullible as women, just as spiritually dead, weak, immature, and unstable. The present passage zeros in on women because of the local situation in Ephesus; some of the women in the Ephesian church were following the corrupt ministers. But the warning is applicable to us all: both men and women must guard against corrupt ministers.

Note what the corrupt minister does. He seeks after people...

- who are laden or burdened down with sins and guilt.
- who are easily swayed and led away by all kinds of desires and lusts.
- who are seeking after truth—who are listening and learning all they can from anybody who claims to have the truth.

This is the person the false minister goes after and eventually captivates. When a person begins to seek the truth because he senses a need in his life, senses that he has been living only for his own selfish desires and lusts—that person is wide open for a corrupt minister to step in and lead him astray. Unfortunately, this is exactly what happens ever too often. And note the great tragedy: the person never comes to the knowledge of the truth. Why? Because they never seek the truth in Christ. They only seek a "form of godliness," not true godliness. True godliness is found in Christ alone and nowhere else.

> Beyond all question, the mystery of godliness is great: He appeared in a body, was vindicated by the Spirit, was seen by angels, was preached among the nations, was believed on in the world, was taken up in glory. (1 Tim 3:16)

Note another point that needs to be given close attention: who the corrupt or false minister is. He is "the kind"—one of those who has "a form of godliness, but denying its power." He has the form and appearance of godliness: he...

- is a minister and fills the position of a minister.
- professes God and Christ.
- practices the rituals and ceremonies of religion.
- talks about and uses religious terms, perhaps even the terms of the Bible.

But he denies the power of godliness by his life and preaching. He does not live in nor preach the power of the cross and resurrection of Jesus Christ. If he does not vocally deny the power, he denies it by what he preaches and teaches: a religion of works and self-effort and of new light—a religion for a new age of men, men who are enormously advanced in science and technology and in the understanding of man—a religion that can reach such levels of growth that God will accept him. In the simplest of terms...

- a corrupt minister is a minister who preaches and teaches that man can be good enough and do enough good to make himself acceptable to God; that man can secure the approval of God by doing certain works and keeping certain rules (laws); that man can reach such a level of growth that God will accept him.
- a corrupt minister is a minister who denies the power of godliness, that is, the power of the cross and resurrection of Jesus Christ to save men and to give them eternal life.

Every generation has felt that it was a *new age*—that it saw more light and truth and was more enlightened than the former generation. In the area of science and technology this is true, BUT IT IS NOT TRUE IN HUMAN LIFE AND BEHAVIOR.

How can we say this? Because man has not been changed. Man is still corruptible, aging, deteriorating, dying, and decaying. And he will continue to be a *corruptible creature* until his heart and soul are changed and made anew. This is where God's Son comes in, only Christ can change the human heart and soul; only He can make a person into a new creature.

The truth of human behavior (sin and death) and of its deliverance from evil and death through Christ has been revealed. This truth never changes. Advancements in science and technology, psychology and medicine cannot stop the process of sin and death. Only Christ—the power of His cross and resurrection—can change man and give him eternal life. Any minister who preaches any other message is a corrupt minister. He is a minister who is preaching and teaching a corrupt and false message.

2. Corrupt ministers oppose the truth. Why? Because their *minds are depraved*, that is, their understanding of the gospel is twisted, distorted, and corrupted. They do not follow the glorious news and power of the death and resurrection of the Lord Jesus Christ.

Note the reference to Jannes and Jambres, two religious leaders in Egypt who opposed Moses when he went to Pharaoh to deliver Israel out of slavery. They stood toe to toe with Moses and resisted the truth, but in the end they were destroyed (cp. Ex.7:1; 8:7; 9:11. The two men are not named in the Old Testament, but they are mentioned in other Jewish religious writings. Their names were apparently well known to all Jews.)

Thought 1. William Barclay clearly describes the resistance to the truth of the gospel:

> *"The Christian leader will never lack his opponents. There will always be those who prefer their ideas to God's ideas. There will always be those who wish to exercise power and influence over people and who will stoop to any means to do so. There will always be those who have their own twisted ideas of the Christian faith, and who wish to win others to their mistaken belief. But of one thing Paul was sure—the days of the deceivers were numbered. Their falsity would be demonstrated; and they would receive their own appropriate place and reward"* (The Letters to Timothy, Titus, and Philemon, p.223).

3. Corrupt ministers and their corrupt religion will be exposed. In the end all false teachers and their teaching will be tracked down and exposed. God will catch and expose every corrupt minister. It will happen when the Lord Jesus Christ returns. Corrupt ministers and their corrupt teaching will *not get very far*.

> **And give relief to you who are troubled, and to us as well. This will happen when the Lord Jesus is revealed from heaven in blazing fire with his powerful angels. He will punish those who do not know God and do not obey the gospel of our Lord Jesus. They will be punished with everlasting destruction and shut out from the presence of the Lord and from the majesty of his power on the day he comes to be glorified in his holy people and to be marveled at among all those who have believed. This includes you, because you believed our testimony to you. (2 Th 1:7-10)**

2 TIMOTHY 3:10-13

		B. The Contrasting Marks of Godly Believers, 3:10-13	and Lystra, the persecutions I endured. Yet the Lord rescued me from all of them.		a. Paul suffered severe persecution
1	Mark 1: Following a godly example	10 You, however, know all about my teaching, my way of life, my purpose, faith, patience, love, endurance,	12 In fact, everyone who wants to live a godly life in Christ Jesus will be persecuted,		b. Believers will suffer persecution
2	Mark 2: Enduring persecution	11 Persecutions, sufferings—what kinds of things happened to me in Antioch, Iconium	13 While evil men and impostors will go from bad to worse, deceiving and being deceived.	3	Mark 3: Guarding against evil men & imposters

DIVISION II

THE PREDICTIONS OF THE LAST DAYS, 3:1-17

B. The Contrasting Marks of Godly Believers, 3:10-13

(3:10-13) **Introduction**: this passage is a contrast with the former passage which dealt with the godless marks of the last days. Here we have the contrasting marks of godly believers.
1. Mark 1: following a godly example (v.10).
2. Mark 2: enduring persecution (v.11-12).
3. Mark 3: guarding against evil men (v.13).

1 (3:10) **Testimony—Godliness**: a godly person follows a godly example. This is a sharp contrast from the godless marks of false teachers (v.1-9). Timothy had known (parakoloutheo) and had closely observed and followed the godly example of Paul. Kenneth Wuest points out that the Greek word means to follow a person so closely that one is always by the person's side, conforming his life to the person (*The Pastoral Epistles*, p.148). It means to join oneself to the person, to become his disciple and to follow his example. Paul had lived a godly life, and Timothy had followed in his footsteps. Paul mentions seven things about his life that stand out as a dynamic example, eight things that a person must focus upon and follow if he wishes to live a godly life.

1. There is *teaching*. What was the source of Paul's teaching? What was it that Paul had taught? The Scriptures, the very Word of Christ and of God. Paul declared this time and again.

> Paul, a servant of Christ Jesus, called to be an apostle and set apart for the gospel of God— the gospel he promised beforehand through his prophets in the Holy Scriptures regarding his Son, who as to his human nature was a descendant of David, and who through the Spirit of holiness was declared with power to be the Son of God by his resurrection from the dead: Jesus Christ our Lord. (Ro.1:1-4)
>
> I am not ashamed of the gospel, because it is the power of God for the salvation of everyone who believes: first for the Jew, then for the Gentile. (Ro.1:16)
>
> Now, brothers, I want to remind you of the gospel I preached to you, which you received and on which you have taken your stand. By this gospel you are saved, if you hold firmly to the word I preached to you. Otherwise, you have believed in vain. For what I received I passed on to you as of first importance: that Christ died for our sins according to the Scriptures, that he was buried, that he was raised on the third day according to the Scriptures. (1 Cor.15:1-4)
>
> And we also thank God continually because, when you received the word of God, which you heard from us, you accepted it not as the word of men, but as it actually is, the word of God, which is at work in you who believe. (1 Th.2:13)
>
> All Scripture is God-breathed and is useful for teaching, rebuking, correcting and training in righteousness, (2 Tim.3:16)
>
> He must hold firmly to the trustworthy message as it has been taught, so that he can encourage others by sound doctrine and refute those who oppose it. (Tit.1:9)
>
> You must teach what is in accord with sound doctrine. (Tit.2:1)

The point is this: the godly person must follow the teaching of godly teachers. He must have nothing to do with the teaching of false teachers (v.1-9).
⇒ A person cannot live godly unless he knows godliness.
⇒ A person cannot teach godliness unless he follows after godliness.

A godly person closely observes and follows after those who live godly lives. He is a disciple of godly examples. He follows the godly teaching of godly people.

2. There is *godly behavior* and conduct. Paul practiced what he preached. He lived what he taught. He professed to be a follower of Christ; therefore, he followed Christ.
⇒ He did not live in sin; he lived in righteousness.
⇒ He did not profess one thing and do another.

Timothy was to do the same, and so are all other believers. A godly person is to behave himself—to conduct his life like he should. He is to live what he professes. He is not to pull down what he teaches by what he does. The believer is to teach godliness, *but first* he is to live godly.

> In everything I did, I showed you that by this kind of hard work we must help the weak, remembering the words the Lord Jesus himself said: 'It is more blessed to give than to receive.'" (Acts 20:35)
>
> Therefore I urge you to imitate me. (1 Cor.4:16)
>
> Follow my example, as I follow the example of Christ. (1 Cor.11:1)
>
> Join with others in following my example, brothers, and take note of those who

live according to the pattern we gave you. (Ph.3:17)

Whatever you have learned or received or heard from me, or seen in me—put it into practice. And the God of peace will be with you. (Ph.4:9)

For you yourselves know how you ought to follow our example. We were not idle when we were with you. (2 Th.3:7)

What you heard from me, keep as the pattern of sound teaching, with faith and love in Christ Jesus. (2 Tim.1:13)

3. There is *purpose* or what Donald Guthrie calls a person's "chief aim in life" (*The Pastoral Epistles*. "Tyndale New Testament Commentaries," p.160). The chief aim of believers is to be one thing and one thing only: Christ and His great mission—the mission of saving people from sin, death, and judgment, and of ministering to people. Eternal life—the glorious privilege of never dying and of living forever—is now possible. Christ made it possible. That was His every purpose for coming to earth—to die for man and to set man free from the terrible sufferings and evils of this corruptible world. Just imagine! Every person on the face of the earth can now be delivered from suffering and evil and live forever. But they have to know how. This was the mission of Christ: to tell them how. And it is to be the mission of the believer: to tell people how to conquer evil and to live forever. The believer's very purpose for living—his chief aim in life—is to proclaim the glorious news of salvation: there is deliverance from death and evil; man can now live and live forever.

Thought 1. William Barclay has some very practical questions to ask:

"As individuals, we should sometimes pause and ask ourselves: what is our aim in life? Have we got one at all? As teachers we should sometimes ask ourselves: what am I trying to do with these people whom I teach? Once Agesilaus, the Sparta king, was asked, 'What shall we teach our boys?' His answer was: 'That which will be most useful to them when they are men.' Is it knowledge, or is it life, that we are trying to transmit? As members of the Church, we should sometimes ask ourselves: what are we trying to do in the Church? It is not enough to be satisfied when a Church is humming like a dynamo, and when every night in the week has its own crowded organisation. Sometimes we should be asking: what, if anything, is the unifying purpose which binds all this activity together?" (The Letters to Timothy, Titus, and Philemon, p.225f).

As Christian believers, the unifying purpose of our lives is set: it is Christ and His great mission of life, life now and life eternal (Jn.10:10; Jn.3:16).

"Just as the Son of Man did not come to be served, but to serve, and to give his life as a ransom for many." (Mt.20:28)

Therefore go and make disciples of all nations, baptizing them in the name of the Father and of the Son and of the Holy Spirit, and teaching them to obey everything I have commanded you. And surely I am with you always, to the very end of the age." (Mt.28:19-20)

He said to them, "Go into all the world and preach the good news to all creation. (Mk.16:15)

For the Son of Man came to seek and to save what was lost." (Lk.19:10)

"For God so loved the world that he gave his one and only Son, that whoever believes in him shall not perish but have eternal life." (Jn.3:16)

The thief comes only to steal and kill and destroy; I have come that they may have life, and have it to the full. (Jn.10:10)

Again Jesus said, "Peace be with you! As the Father has sent me, I am sending you." (Jn.20:21)

4. There is *faith* (see note 2, pt.3—1 Tim.6:11 for discussion).

5. There is *patience* or *longsuffering* (makrothumiai), which means bearing and suffering a long time, persevering, being constant, steadfast, and enduring. Patience or longsuffering never gives in; it is never broken no matter what attacks it.

⇒ Pressure and hard work may fall upon us, but the Spirit of God helps us suffer long under it all.
⇒ Disease or accident or old age may afflict us, but the Spirit of God helps us to suffer long under it.
⇒ Discouragement and disappointment may attack us, but the Spirit of God helps us to suffer long under it.
⇒ Men may do us wrong, abuse, slander, and injure us; but the Spirit of God helps us to suffer long under it all.

Two significant things need to be noted about patience or longsuffering. Patience or longsuffering never strikes back. Common sense tells us that a person who is attacked by others could strike back and retaliate. *But* the Christian believer is given the power of patience—the power to suffer the situation or person for a long, long time.

The point is this: a godly person closely observes and follows after those who are patience. A godly person is a disciple; he follows after those who know how to plow through the trials and problems of life. He learns from the longsuffering of others.

6. There is *love* (see DEEPER STUDY # 1, *Love*—1 Th.3:12 for discussion).

7. There is *endurance* (hupomone). Endurance means fortitude, steadfastness, constancy, perseverance. The word is not passive; it is active. It is not the spirit that just sits back and puts up with the trials of life, taking whatever may come. Rather it is the spirit that stands up and faces life's trials, that actively goes about conquering and overcoming them. When trials confront a man who is truly justified, he is stirred to arise and face the trials head on. He immediately sets out to conquer and overcome them. He knows that God is allowing the trials in order to teach him more and more endurance.

The godly person follows the example of those who persevere, who endure by walking through the trials of life, conquering all for Christ.

⇒ He learns to endure with people no matter what they do.
⇒ He learns to endure in trials no matter how severe they are.

By standing firm you will gain life. (Lk.21:19)

Be joyful in hope, patient in affliction, faithful in prayer. (Ro.12:12)

You need to persevere so that when you have done the will of God, you will receive what he has promised. (Heb.10:36)

Consider it pure joy, my brothers, whenever you face trials of many kinds, because you know that the testing of your faith develops perseverance. Perseverance must finish its work so that you may be mature and complete, not lacking anything. (Jas.1:2-4)

Be patient, then, brothers, until the Lord's coming. See how the farmer waits for the land to yield its valuable crop and how patient he is for the autumn and spring rains. (Jas.5:7)

2 (3:11-12) **Persecution**: a godly person endures persecution. Note two points.

1. Paul suffered severe persecution and affliction. He mentions three experiences that Timothy knew about.
   ⇒ In Antioch the civil leaders of the city had risen up against Paul and expelled him from their city (Acts 13:50).
   ⇒ In Iconium a large mob with the city officials set out to arrest and to stone Paul. He had to flee for his life (Acts 14:4-6).
   ⇒ In Lystra a rioting mob stoned Paul and dragged his limp body out of the city thinking that he was dead. Apparently God worked a miracle and raised him up (Acts 14:19-20).

Paul was constantly persecuted, attacked time and again. But the Lord delivered him. Paul never failed to witness for Christ; therefore, Christ never failed to deliver Paul. But note: deliverance does not mean *deliverance from persecution, but deliverance through persecution.* God strengthens and carries the believer through persecution, not out of persecution. This is what Paul is declaring.

2. The believer will suffer persecution; he cannot escape it, not if he is a genuine believer. (See notes—2 Tim.1:8; 1:8-10 for more discussion.) Believers suffer persecution because they are not like the world; they do not live like the world lives. Therefore, the world persecutes them. Scripture gives four specific reasons why believers will suffer persecution.

   a. Believers will suffer persecution because they are not of this world. They are *called out* of the world. They are in the world, but they are not of the world. They are separated from the behavior of the world. Therefore, the world reacts against them by ridicule and mockery, by verbal and physical abuse, and by discrimination.

   If you belonged to the world, it would love you as its own. As it is, you do not belong to the world, but I have chosen you out of the world. That is why the world hates you. (Jn.15:19)

   b. They will suffer persecution because believers strip away the world's excuse for sin. They live and demonstrate a life of righteousness and they do not compromise with the world and its sinful behavior. They live pure and godly lives, having nothing to do with the sinful pleasures of a corruptible world. Such living exposes the sins of people, and this exposure stirs them to react against believers.

   "If the world hates you, keep in mind that it hated me first...If I had not come and spoken to them, they would not be guilty of sin. Now, however, they have no excuse for their sin. (Jn.15:18, 22).

   In fact, everyone who wants to live a godly life in Christ Jesus will be persecuted. (2 Tim.3:12).

   c. They will suffer persecution because the world does not know God nor Christ. The ungodly of the world want no God other than themselves and their own imaginations. They want to do just what they want—to fulfill their own desires, not what God wishes and demands. However, the godly believer dedicates his life to God, to His worship and service. The ungodly wants no part of God; therefore, they oppose those who talk about God and man's duty to honor and worship God.

   They will treat you this way because of my name, for they do not know the One who sent me. (Jn.15:21)

   They will do such things because they have not known the Father or me. (Jn.16:3)

   d. They will suffer persecution because the world is deceived in its concept and belief of God. The world conceives God to be the One who fulfills their earthly desires and lusts (Jn.16:2-3). Man's idea of God is that of a *Supreme Grandfather*. They think that God protects, provides, and gives no matter what a person's behavior is, just so the behavior is not too far out. They think God will accept them and work all things out in the final analysis. However, the true believer teaches against this. God is love, but He is also just and demands righteousness. The world rebels against this concept of God.

   They will put you out of the synagogue; in fact, a time is coming when anyone who kills you will think he is offering a service to God. They will do such things because they have not known the Father or me. (Jn.16:2-3)

   Remember the words I spoke to you: 'No servant is greater than his master.' If they persecuted me, they will persecute you also. If they obeyed my teaching, they will obey yours also. (Jn.15:20)

   "All this I have told you so that you will not go astray. They will put you out of the synagogue; in fact, a time is coming when anyone who kills you will think he is offering a service to God. They will do such things because they have not known the Father or me. I have told you this, so that when the time comes you will remember that I warned you. I did not tell you this at first because I was with you. (Jn.16:1-4)

So that no one would be unsettled by these trials. You know quite well that we were destined for them. (1 Th.3:3)

For it has been granted to you on behalf of Christ not only to believe on him, but also to suffer for him. (Ph.1:29)

In fact, everyone who wants to live a godly life in Christ Jesus will be persecuted. (2 Tim.3:12)

Do not be surprised, my brothers, if the world hates you. (1 Jn.3:13)

Dear friends, do not be surprised at the painful trial you are suffering, as though something strange were happening to you. But rejoice that you participate in the sufferings of Christ, so that you may be overjoyed when his glory is revealed. If you are insulted because of the name of Christ, you are blessed, for the Spirit of glory and of God rests on you. (1 Pt.4:12-14)

3 (3:13) **Unbelievers—Ungodly, The—Deceivers—Hypocrites—Imposters**: a godly person guards against evil men and imposters.

⇒ Evil men refers to those who actively oppose righteousness and morality; those who live immoral and ungodly lives—who curse, lie, steal, cheat, injure, and live in carnal pleasures and immorality.

⇒ Imposters refers to imposters and deceivers; those who live hypocritical lives—who call themselves Christians and join the church for what they can get out of it. They join the church seeking acceptability, a good image, friends, fellowship, popularity, business clientele, self-image, a following, and a host of other benefits.

The point is that both evil men and imposters will grow worse and worse. Men will become *more and more evil*, more and more...

- ungodly
- lawless
- pleasure-minded
- recreational-minded
- immoral
- unclean
- addicted to drugs
- party-minded
- selfish
- foul-minded
- murderous
- violent

Men will also become more and more of an imposter religiously. They will be religious, professing belief in God, but they will deny the power of godliness. (See note—2 Tim.3:5 for more discussion.) Note: they will deceive themselves and deceive others. They will think that they are acceptable to God, and others will even think they are acceptable to God. But both they and their friends are deceived; they are not acceptable to God.

And this is his command: to believe in the name of his Son, Jesus Christ, and to love one another as he commanded us. (1 Jn.3:23)

The only way to be acceptable to God is by believing on the name of the Lord Jesus Christ. Believing means to follow Christ—to live soberly, righteously, and godly in this present world and to love others even as Christ loved them—to love them to such a point that we give all that we are and have to minister to their desperate needs. But note the point: men will become more and more religious, but as imposters—as men who use religion for their own selfish purposes and for a livelihood and profession.

For false Christs and false prophets will appear and perform signs and miracles to deceive the elect—if that were possible. (Mk.13:22)

Even from your own number men will arise and distort the truth in order to draw away disciples after them. (Acts 20:30)

I urge you, brothers, to watch out for those who cause divisions and put obstacles in your way that are contrary to the teaching you have learned. Keep away from them. For such people are not serving our Lord Christ, but their own appetites. By smooth talk and flattery they deceive the minds of naive people. (Ro.16:17-18)

For such men are false apostles, deceitful workmen, masquerading as apostles of Christ. And no wonder, for Satan himself masquerades as an angel of light. It is not surprising, then, if his servants masquerade as servants of righteousness. Their end will be what their actions deserve. (2 Cor.11:13-15)

Then we will no longer be infants, tossed back and forth by the waves, and blown here and there by every wind of teaching and by the cunning and craftiness of men in their deceitful scheming. (Eph.4:14)

The Spirit clearly says that in later times some will abandon the faith and follow deceiving spirits and things taught by demons. (1 Tim.4:1)

While evil men and impostors will go from bad to worse, deceiving and being deceived. (2 Tim.3:13)

I am writing these things to you about those who are trying to lead you astray. (1 Jn.2:26)

Many deceivers, who do not acknowledge Jesus Christ as coming in the flesh, have gone out into the world. Any such person is the deceiver and the antichrist. (2 Jn.7)

2 TIMOTHY 3:14-17

	C. The Godly Mark of Living in the Scripture, 3:14-17	Scriptures, which are able to make you wise for salvation through faith in Christ Jesus.	
1 A believer must live in the Scripture	14 But as for you, continue in what you have learned and have become convinced of, because you know those from whom you learned it,	16 All Scripture is God-breathed and is useful for teaching, rebuking, correcting and training in righteousness,	3 Scripture is God-breathed inspired by God 4 Scripture is profitable to man
2 Scripture makes a person wise for salvation	15 And how from infancy you have known the holy	17 So that the man of God may be thoroughly equipped for every good work.	5 Scripture equips a man for every good work

DIVISION II

THE PREDICTIONS OF THE LAST DAYS, 3:1-17

C. The Godly Mark of Living in the Scripture, 3:14-17

(3:14-17) **Introduction**: Christians have always stressed the importance of the Bible or of the Scripture. Why? What is the importance and value of Scripture? This passage explains, declaring in no uncertain terms: the godly mark of a believer is that he lives in the Scripture.
1. A believer must live in the Scripture (v.14).
2. Scripture makes a person wise for salvation (v.15).
3. Scripture is God-breathed, inspired by God (v.16).
4. Scripture is useful to man (v.16).
5. Scripture equips a man for every good work (v.17).

1 (3:14) **Scripture—Study—Teachers, Godly**: believers are to live in the Scriptures. Timothy had been taught the Scriptures all of his life. When he was only a child, his mother Eunice and his grandmother Lois had rooted him in the Scriptures (2 Tim.1:5; 3:15). They were both strong believers in the Lord. Paul had also grounded Timothy in the Scriptures. But note a most critical point:
⇒ it is not enough to have learned the Scripture.
⇒ it is not enough to be assured that the teachings of Scripture are true.
⇒ it is not enough to know that your teachers teach the truth.

Timothy knew all this. He had learned the Scriptures and he had found the Scriptures to be true. The claims and promises of Scripture had worked in his own life. Timothy also knew his teachers; their lives bore testimony to the truth of Scripture. But this was not enough.

Note the word "continue" (mene). It means to abide, dwell, remain, and stay in the Scripture. Simply stated, Timothy had to *live* in the Scripture—live, move, and have his being in the Scripture. And more, he had to *live out* the Scripture—continue to walk and live in the truths of the Scripture. He had to do what Scripture said.

Thought 1. Note four significant points in this verse.
1) A person is to learn the Scripture.
2) A person is to be assured of the Scriptures, apply them to his life, and experience the truth and assurance of them.
3) A person is to know his teachers—make sure that they teach the truth of the Scripture.
4) A person is to continue in the Scripture: abide and dwell, remain and stay in the Scripture. He is to live and move and have his being in Scripture.

2 (3:15) **Scripture**: Scripture makes a person wise for salvation. If man needs anything, he needs wisdom, wisdom about how to be saved. Death and every other evil imaginable rushes about and floods the world of man. The strongest among men are swept about and drowned by...

- drugs
- disease
- broken homes
- bad habits
- pride
- license
- selfishness
- greed
- envy
- war
- murmuring
- loneliness
- crime
- accident
- loss
- enslavements
- conceit
- power
- extravagance
- gluttony
- jealousy
- death
- grumbling
- purposelessness
- lawlessness
- immorality
- broken health
- lusts
- indulgence
- prejudice
- discrimination
- drunkenness
- murder
- gossip
- emptiness

There is no end to the evil that is drowning man and his world. What man and his world need is wisdom, the wisdom to save himself and his world. Is such a wisdom available? This is the glorious message of this verse, "Yes!" The Holy Scriptures are able to make man wise for salvation. The Holy Scriptures can save man and his world. How? "Through faith in Christ Jesus." It is the Holy Scriptures that tell us about God's great plan of salvation for man, about how God saves man through faith in His Son, the Lord Jesus Christ. It is the Holy Scriptures alone and no other book...

- that tells us that God loves the world—that He loves the world so much that He sent His one and only Son, the Lord Jesus Christ, into the world to reveal and tell us the truth.
- that tells us that Jesus Christ has taken care of the problem of righteousness and perfection—that He lived a perfect life and secured the ideal and perfect righteousness for man—that when a man believes in Jesus Christ, God takes that man's faith and counts it as righteousness.
- that tells us that Jesus Christ has taken care of the problem of sin and death—that He took all the sins of men upon Himself and bore the penalty and punishment of those sins—that He died for man—that when a person believes in Jesus Christ, God takes that person's faith and counts it as the death of Christ—that God counts the person as having died in Christ and thereby he never has to die.

⇒ that tells us that Jesus Christ has taken care of the problem of living forever—that He has been raised from the dead to live eternally in the presence of God the Father—that when a person believes in Jesus Christ, God takes that person's faith and counts it as the resurrection of Jesus Christ—that the person is counted as having been raised in Christ and is thereby given eternal life.

The point is this: the Holy Scripture tells us how we can be saved through God's Son, the Lord Jesus Christ. No other book reveals this to man. The only wisdom that can ever save this world is the wisdom of God Himself, and that wisdom is found in His Holy Scriptures, the Holy Bible.

> **You are already clean because of the word I have spoken to you. (John 15:3)**
>
> **Sanctify them [set them apart to God] by the truth; your word is truth. (John 17:17)**
>
> **But these are written that you may believe that Jesus is the Christ, the Son of God, and that by believing you may have life in his name. (John 20:31)**
>
> **I am not ashamed of the gospel, because it is the power of God for the salvation of everyone who believes: first for the Jew, then for the Gentile. (Rom 1:16)**
>
> **For everything that was written in the past was written to teach us, so that through endurance and the encouragement of the Scriptures we might have hope. (Rom 15:4)**
>
> **These things happened to them as examples and were written down as warnings for us, on whom the fulfillment of the ages has come. (1 Cor 10:11)**
>
> **And we have the word of the prophets made more certain, and you will do well to pay attention to it, as to a light shining in a dark place, until the day dawns and the morning star rises in your hearts. (2 Pet 1:19)**
>
> **I write these things to you who believe in the name of the Son of God so that you may know that you have eternal life. (1 John 5:13)**
>
> **How can a young man keep his way pure? By living according to your word. (Psa 119:9)**
>
> **Your word is a lamp to my feet and a light for my path. (Psa 119:105)**
>
> **The unfolding of your words gives light; it gives understanding to the simple. (Psa 119:130)**

3 (3:16) **Scripture**: Scripture is God-breathed, inspired by God. This is an extremely important verse in understanding the nature of Scripture, that is, in understanding just what the Scripture is, its nature and authority. Note several facts.

1. Paul was, of course, referring to the Old Testament Scriptures; the New Testament Scriptures had not yet been completed. However, this passage is certainly applicable to the New Testament.

William Barclay says: "If what Paul claims for Scripture is true of the Old Testament, how much truer it is of the still more precious words of the New Testament" (*The Letters to Timothy, Titus, and Philemon*, p.229).

A.T. Robertson, the great Greek scholar, says: "There is no doubt that the apostles claimed to speak by the help of the Holy Spirit (1 Th.5:27; Col.4:16) just as the prophets of old did (1 Pt.1:20f.)....Peter thus puts Paul's epistles on the same plane with the O.T." (*Word Pictures in the New Testament*, Vol.6, p.179).

The point is this: all Scripture—both the Old and New Testament—is inspired by God.

2. Scripture is God-breathed, inspired by God; (theopneustos). What does this mean? What does it mean to say that *God-breathed* the Holy Scriptures? No one can say for sure, but this much can be said.

⇒ The idea is that *God breathed out* the Scripture or *God produced* the Scripture somewhat like He did creation.

> **By the word of the LORD were the heavens made, their starry host by the breath of his mouth. (Psa 33:6)**

Note: it is the Scripture that is inspired, not the man. The Bible does not claim to be written by inspired men. It does claim that the writing is supernaturally given or breathed by God. The Scripture is *breathed out by God*, *not breathed into by God*. The meaning is this: the writing is supernaturally given or breathed by God. The Bible claims to be the Word given by the creative breath of God.

The great Greek scholar A.T. Robertson again says: "God-breathed...[this] is in contrast to the commandments of men" (*Word Pictures in the New Testament*, Vol.4, p.179).

The great Bible expositor Matthew Henry says: "It [Scripture] is a divine revelation, which we may depend upon as infallibly true. The same Spirit that breathed reason into us breathes revelation among us: For the prophecy came not in old time by the will of man, but holy men spoke as they were moved or carried forth by the Holy Ghost, 2 Pt.1:21. The prophets and apostles did not speak from themselves, but what they received of the Lord that they delivered unto us" (*Matthew Henry's Commentary*, Vol.5, p.846f).

The excellent preacher Oliver Greene says: "God Almighty is sovereign; and if we are saved through the power of the Gospel; if the Gospel makes us wise unto salvation; if it is not God's will that any man perish but that all come to repentance, we can rest assured that He has preserved and protected His holy Scriptures down through the centuries!...Anything we need to know about our relationship to God and His relationship to us is found in the Bible. We need no added books, and we cannot afford to take any away. If we add to or take from His Word, God will take away our part out of the book of life. All Scripture is given by inspiration of God. 'Given by inspiration of God,' according to the Greek dictionary, is one Greek word, meaning 'God-breathed'" (*The Epistles of Paul the Apostle to Timothy and Titus*, p.355).

3. The accuracy and dependability of Scripture is clearly seen when one studies what Scripture has to say about itself. (See note and DEEPER STUDY # 1—1 Th.2:13; note and DEEPER STUDY # 1,2—2 Pt.1:19-21.)

a. The Holy Spirit is the author of the Scriptures (2 Pt.1:19-21, esp.21). The *word of the prophets* is more accurately translated *prophetic word*. The origin of Scripture is not found in the will of man, that is, in his attempt to find truth and to interpret truth. But it is found in the Word of the Holy

Spirit who reveals truth to man (cp. Jn.16:12-15; 1 Cor.2:9-10).

b. The writers of the Old Testament claim that the Bible is the Word of God (2 Sam.23:1-3; Is.8:1, 11; Jer.1:9; 5:14; 7:27; 13:12; Ezk.3:4-11; Mic.3:8; Jer.23:29; Hab.2:2; Zech.4:8). They refer to Scripture as "the Word," "the Statutes," "the Law," and "the Testimonies" (cp. Ps.19:1f; 119:1f). "This is what the Lord says" or an equivalent phrase is used over two thousand times in the Old Testament alone.

The writers of the New Testament confirm the claims of the Old Testament writers (Heb.1:1; cp.Mt.1:22; 2:15; Acts 1:16; 28:25; Eph.4:8; 1 Tim.1:18-20). They show the high authority of the Scriptures when they use phrases such as, "It is written" and "Scripture says." They expected the readers and hearers to be bound by Scripture.

c. The writers of the New Testament claim that the Bible is the Word of God (Acts 15:28; 1 Cor.2:13; 3:1; 11:23; 14:37; 15:1-4; Gal.1:11-12; 1 Th.2:13; 2 Pt.3:2). Paul affirmed in behalf of all the apostles that their words were divinely taught (1 Cor.2:13, note the word *we*). Peter asserts the same level of authority for the writings of the apostles as for the Old Testament Scriptures (2 Pt.3:2). The view of inspiration was clear in the early church: the first church council stated that the conclusions of the council were given by the Holy Spirit through the leaders (Acts 15:28f).

d. Jesus Christ claims that the Bible is the Word of God. He contrasts the Scriptures and the commandments of God with the traditions and instructions of men (Mk.7:6-13). He equates the word of Moses with Scripture and His own word with the word of Moses and both as the Word of God (Jn.5:38, 45-47). He says, "the Scripture cannot be broken" (Jn.10:35). He validated the most minute portions of Scripture (Mt.5:18; Lk.16:17). He continually argued the validity of Scripture (Mt.4:4, 7, 10; 22:29, 32, 43; Mk.12:24; Lk.4:4, 8). He saw Himself as the focus and fulfillment of Scripture (Lk.24:25-27). He asserted that what was written must be fulfilled (Lk.22:36-37). He predicted and approved the New Testament and assured His apostles that they would be kept from error (Jn.16:13).

f. The Bible is absolutely trustworthy (Mt.24:35). "The Scripture cannot be broken" (Jn.10:34-35).

> **And we also thank God continually because, when you received the word of God, which you heard from us, you accepted it not as the word of men, but as it actually is, the word of God, which is at work in you who believe. (1 Th 2:13)**
>
> **All Scripture is God-breathed and is useful for teaching, rebuking, correcting and training in righteousness, (2 Tim 3:16)**
>
> **For prophecy never had its origin in the will of man, but men spoke from God as they were carried along by the Holy Spirit. (2 Pet 1:21)**

4 (3:16) **Scripture**: Scripture is profitable to man. The word useful (*ophelimos*) means profitable, beneficial, and helpful. Simply stated, the Bible is for man; God gave it to help man. There are four very specific helps found in the Bible.

1. The Bible is useful for teaching. God wants man to know beyond doubt who God is; who man is; and the beginning, meaning, and end of all things. The Scripture reveals the truth—the nature, meaning, and significance of truth. The Bible gives man the principles and rules for life. It gives him the teachings and doctrines for the foundations of life.

> **You diligently study the Scriptures because you think that by them you possess eternal life. These are the Scriptures that testify about me, (John 5:39)**
>
> **Jesus answered, "My teaching is not my own. It comes from him who sent me. If anyone chooses to do God's will, he will find out whether my teaching comes from God or whether I speak on my own. (John 7:16-17)**
>
> **To the Jews who had believed him, Jesus said, "If you hold to my teaching, you are really my disciples. Then you will know the truth, and the truth will set you free." (John 8:31-32)**
>
> **For everything that was written in the past was written to teach us, so that through endurance and the encouragement of the Scriptures we might have hope. (Rom 15:4)**

2. The Bible is useful for rebuking. God wants man to sense conviction and to be rebuked when he is disobedient to God's will. The Scripture reveals God's will and the consequences of disobedience to His will.

> **But I tell you the truth: It is for your good that I am going away. Unless I go away, the Counselor will not come to you; but if I go, I will send him to you. When he comes, he will convict the world of guilt in regard to sin and righteousness and judgment: But when he, the Spirit of truth, comes, he will guide you into all truth. He will not speak on his own; he will speak only what he hears, and he will tell you what is yet to come. (John 16:7-8, 13)**
>
> **For the word of God is living and active. Sharper than any double-edged sword, it penetrates even to dividing soul and spirit, joints and marrow; it judges the thoughts and attitudes of the heart. (Heb 4:12)**
>
> **Therefore this is what the LORD God Almighty says: "Because the people have spoken these words, I will make my words in your mouth a fire and these people the wood it consumes. (Jer 5:14)**
>
> **"Is not my word like fire," declares the LORD, "and like a hammer that breaks a rock in pieces? (Jer 23:29)**

3. It is useful for correcting. God wants man to be set aright when he is wrong. The Bible teaches obedience by teaching a person to discipline himself, even to the point of suffering (Heb.5:8).

> **You are already clean because of the word I have spoken to you. (John 15:3)**

> Sanctify them by the truth; your word is truth. (John 17:17)
>
> To make her holy, cleansing her by the washing with water through the word, (Eph 5:26)
>
> Now that you have purified yourselves by obeying the truth so that you have sincere love for your brothers, love one another deeply, from the heart. (1 Pet 1:22)
>
> How can a young man keep his way pure? By living according to your word. (Psa 119:9)

4. It is useful for training in righteousness. God wants man to know the right things to do, to think and to say. The Bible reveals how to live "self-control, upright and godly lives in this present age, while we wait for the blessed hope—the glorious appearing of our great God and Savior, Jesus Christ" (Tit.2:12-13).

> Keep reminding them of these things. Warn them before God against quarreling about words; it is of no value, and only ruins those who listen. Do your best to present yourself to God as one approved, a workman who does not need to be ashamed and who correctly handles the word of truth. (2 Tim 2:14-15)
>
> Like newborn babies, crave pure spiritual milk, so that by it you may grow up in your salvation, now that you have tasted that the Lord is good. (1 Pet 2:2-3)
>
> And at that time I told you everything you were to do. (Deu 1:18)
>
> I have hidden your word in my heart that I might not sin against you. (Psa 119:11)

5 (3:17) **Scripture**: Scripture equips—thoroughly equips—a man for every good work. By "thoroughly" (artios) is meant complete, matured, filled. No person is complete or mature apart from Scripture. Man was made for God and he is to live by the Word of God. If he tries to live without God and His Word, man fails in life. He lives an incomplete, immature, and misfitted life. This is particularly true of the *man of God*, the person who claims to be a minister or teacher of God's Word.

> **Thought 1.** Scripture alone, the very Word of God itself, can make a person thoroughly complete and equip him for every good work. William Barclay's comments on this point pierce the heart and need to be *heeded* by everyone of us:
>
> *"The study of the Scriptures trains a man in righteousness until he is equipped for every good work. Here is the essential conclusion. The study of the Scriptures must never be selfish; it must never be simply for the good of a man's own soul. Any change, any conversion which makes a man think of nothing but of the fact that he has been saved is no true change and no true conversion. He must study the Scriptures to make himself useful to God and useful to his fellow men. He must study, not simply and solely to save his own soul, but that he may make himself such that God will use him to help to save the souls and comfort the lives of others. No man is saved unless he is on fire to save his fellow men"* (The Letters to Timothy, Titus, and Philemon, p.232).

What a convicting statement: "He must study... that God will use him to help to save the souls and comfort the lives of others. No man is saved unless he is on fire to save his fellow men." What an indictment that every *man of God must* heed. We must study more and more—we must allow the Scripture to stir us more and more so that we will reach out to save souls and to minister more and more.

> Therefore go and make disciples of all nations, baptizing them in the name of the Father and of the Son and of the Holy Spirit, and teaching them to obey everything I have commanded you. And surely I am with you always, to the very end of the age." (Mat 28:19-20)
>
> You diligently study the Scriptures because you think that by them you possess eternal life. These are the Scriptures that testify about me, (John 5:39)
>
> Now the Bereans were of more noble character than the Thessalonians, for they received the message with great eagerness and examined the Scriptures every day to see if what Paul said was true. Many of the Jews believed, as did also a number of prominent Greek women and many Greek men. (Acts 17:11-12)
>
> We who are strong ought to bear with the failings of the weak and not to please ourselves. Each of us should please his neighbor for his good, to build him up. For even Christ did not please himself but, as it is written: "The insults of those who insult you have fallen on me." For everything that was written in the past was written to teach us, so that through endurance and the encouragement of the Scriptures we might have hope. (Rom 15:1-4)
>
> It [God's word] is to be with him, and he is to read it all the days of his life so that he may learn to revere the LORD his God and follow carefully all the words of this law and these decrees (Deu 17:19)

2 TIMOTHY 4:1-5

	CHAPTER 4 III. THE TRIUMPH OF PREACHING, 4:1-8 A. The Awesome Charge to Preach the Word & to Minister, 4:1-5	and encourage—with great patience and careful instruction. 3 For the time will come when men will not put up with sound doctrine. Instead, to suit their own desires, they will gather around them a great number of teachers to say what their itching ears want to hear. 4 They will turn their ears away from the truth and turn aside to myths. 5 But you, keep your head in all situations, endure hardship, do the work of an evangelist, discharge all the duties of your ministry.	

1 Preach the Word—for the eyes of God & Christ watch you
  a. Christ will judge
  b. Christ will appear
  c. Christ will set up His kingdom
2 Preach the Word—the Word of God is to be preached
	In the presence of God and of Christ Jesus, who will judge the living and the dead, and in view of his appearing and his kingdom, I give you this charge:
	2 Preach the Word; be prepared in season and out of season; correct, rebuke
			3 Preach the Word—for the great apostasy is coming
			  a. People will reject
			
			  b. People will turn away
			
			4 Preach the Word—for you must complete & fulfill your ministry
			  a. Watch & endure
			  b. Work & fulfill

DIVISION III

THE TRIUMPH OF PREACHING, 4:1-8

A. The Awesome Charge to Preach the Word and to Minister, 4:1-5

(4:1-5) **Introduction**: the world is bombarded with message after message offering hope after hope. But above all the messages and above all the hopes that bombard the world, there is one that is more needed by man than all the others—one that is so important that it supersedes all the others combined. What is that message? It is the message of the Word of God. The Word of God offers the *only lasting* hope for man. For this reason the Word of God must be preached. The minister of God must commit himself to the awesome charge to preach the Word of God and to minister as never before.

1. Preach the Word—for the eye of God and of Christ watches you (v.1).
2. Preach the Word—the Word of God is to be preached (v.2).
3. Preach the Word—for the great apostasy is coming (v.3-4).
4. Preach the Word—for you must completely fulfill your ministry.

1 (4:1) **Preaching—Judgment—Jesus Christ, Return**: preach the Word—for the eyes of God and of Christ watch you. The thrust of this great passage is the previous verse:

> **All Scripture is God-breathed and is useful for teaching, rebuking, correcting and training in righteousness, (2 Tim 3:16)**

Therefore, "I give you this charge: Preach the word" (v.1-2). You must preach the Word, for God and Christ are watching. Their eyes are upon you. They are watching to see if you preach the Word. Note: the minister is not to be preaching his own ideas nor the ideas of other men. The message of the gospel is not the message of human philosophy, psychology, sociology, or education. It is not the message of self-image and personal development. As helpful as these subjects may be, they are not the gospel; they are not the Word of God.

The Word is the very Word of God, the glorious gospel of our salvation. The Word is the Scripture which we hold in our hands and study and teach to all who give their lives to Christ Jesus our Lord. The Word that we are to preach is...

- the very revelation of God Himself, the record of what God wants us to know, the record that is recorded in the Holy Scriptures, the Holy Bible (See notes—2 Tim.3:16; 3:17).
- the unbelievable love of God that tells us about Jesus Christ, the Son of God, who came to earth to save man from the sin and suffering and death of this world (see outline, note, and DEEPER STUDY #1,2—Jn.3:16; Ro.5:1-5; 5:6-11).
- the great mercy of God that He has poured out upon us through the death of His Son, the Lord Jesus Christ (see note—Eph.2:4-7).
- the coming resurrection and judgment of all men (see notes—Mt.25:31-46; Jn.5:28-30; 1 Cor. 15:1-58).

This is the Word that we are to preach, and we are to proclaim it from the housetops ever so boldly and courageously. No matter the trials or the threats of men, we are to "preach the Word"—the Word of our living God.

There are three strong reasons given to make sure that we preach the Word of God.
1. The Lord Jesus Christ will judge the living and the dead. If we are living when He returns, He is going to judge us. If we die before He returns, He is going to judge us. The idea is twofold.
⇒ First, He is going to judge us as to whether or not we preached. If He calls us to preach and we do not preach, we will be judged and condemned.
⇒ Second, He is going to judge us as to whether or not we preached the Word. If we preach the ideas of men instead of God's Word, we will be judged and condemned. If we preach a mixture of men's ideas and God's Word, we will be judged and condemned.

> *"Some day Timothy's work will be tested, and that test will be carried out by none other than Jesus Christ Himself. A Christian's work must be good enough, not to satisfy men, but to satisfy Jesus. He must do every task in such a way that he can take it and offer it to*

245

2 TIMOTHY 4:1-5

Christ. He is not concerned with either the criticism or the verdict of men. The one thing he covets is the 'Well done!' of Jesus Christ. If we all within the Church and within the world did our work in that spirit, the difference in life would be incalculable.

⇒ *"It would save us from the touchy spirit which is offended by the criticisms of men.*

⇒ *"It would save us from the self-important spirit which is concerned with matters of personal rights and personal prestige.*

⇒ *"It would save us from the self-centered spirit which demands thanks and praise from men for its every act.*

⇒ *"It would even save us from being hurt by the ingratitude of men.*

"The Christian concentration is on Christ" (William Barclay. *The Letters to Timothy, Titus, and Philemon, p.232f.* Note: paragraphs are marked and set off by us for emphasis.)

For the Son of Man is going to come in his Father's glory with his angels, and then he will reward each person according to what he has done. (Mat 16:27)

He commanded us to preach to the people and to testify that he is the one whom God appointed as judge of the living and the dead. (Acts 10:42)

For he has set a day when he will judge the world with justice by the man he has appointed. He has given proof of this to all men by raising him from the dead." (Acts 17:31)

You, then, why do you judge your brother? Or why do you look down on your brother? For we will all stand before God's judgment seat. (Rom 14:10)

For we must all appear before the judgment seat of Christ, that each one may receive what is due him for the things done while in the body, whether good or bad. (2 Cor 5:10)

2. The Lord Jesus Christ will appear in glory as "the returning conqueror" (William Barclay. *The Letters to Timothy, Titus, and Philemon*, p.233). This is seen in the word "appearing" (epiphaneian). It means the glorious and visible appearance of the Lord Jesus (Kenneth Wuest. *The Pastoral Epistles*, Vol.2, p.153). The history of the word is found in the appearance of the great Roman Emperors, especially when they were scheduled to visit a city. Thorough preparations were made: buildings and streets were scrubbed and cleaned; they were worked hard to prepare themselves and their city for their coming king. They were excited about his coming and focused their attention and energy upon his coming. This is exactly what the minister must do: he must preach the Word, keeping his mind upon the return of the Lord Jesus Christ. He must be prepared for His return, and the minister of the Lord prepares by preaching the Word. The conquering Lord is returning; if we fail to preach the Word, we will stand before Him unprepared—embarrassed and ashamed. If we fail to be subjected to Him now—fail to preach His Word—we shall be subjected and judged by Him.

Therefore God exalted him to the highest place and gave him the name that is above every name, that at the name of Jesus every knee should bow, in heaven and on earth and under the earth, and every tongue confess that Jesus Christ is Lord, to the glory of God the Father. (Phil 2:9-11)

So you also must be ready, because the Son of Man will come at an hour when you do not expect him. (Mat 24:44)

So he called ten of his servants and gave them ten minas. 'Put this money to work,' he said, 'until I come back.' (Luke 19:13)

Therefore you do not lack any spiritual gift as you eagerly wait for our Lord Jesus Christ to be revealed. (1 Cor 1:7)

Therefore judge nothing before the appointed time; wait till the Lord comes. He will bring to light what is hidden in darkness and will expose the motives of men's hearts. At that time each will receive his praise from God. (1 Cor 4:5)

While people are saying, "Peace and safety," destruction will come on them suddenly, as labor pains on a pregnant woman, and they will not escape. (1 Th 5:3)

To keep this command without spot or blame until the appearing of our Lord Jesus Christ, (1 Tim 6:14)

It teaches us to say "No" to ungodliness and worldly passions, and to live self-controlled, upright and godly lives in this present age, while we wait for the blessed hope—the glorious appearing of our great God and Savior, Jesus Christ, (Titus 2:12-13)

And now, dear children, continue in him, so that when he appears we may be confident and unashamed before him at his coming. (1 John 2:28)

3. The Lord Jesus Christ will set up His kingdom forever and ever. The true minister of God will be a citizen of the Lord's kingdom. His position and rank (the amount of responsibility) in that kingdom is based upon his faithfulness in this world. Therefore, the minister of God must preach the Word faithfully. He must keep his eye upon the kingdom of Christ even as Christ is keeping His eye upon the minister's faithfulness. "So live and so work that you will rank high in the roll of citizens of the Kingdom when the Kingdom comes" (William Barclay. *The Letters to Timothy, Titus, and Philemon*, p.234). (See note, *Rewards*—Lk.16:10-12 for a complete list of the promised rewards.)

And I confer on you a kingdom, just as my Father conferred one on me, so that you may eat and drink at my table in my kingdom and sit on thrones, judging the twelve tribes of Israel. (Luke 22:29-30)

2 (4:2) **Preaching—Minister, Work of**: preach the Word—for this is the Lord's call to you. Preaching the Word is to be the consuming passion of the minister's life. Note how forcefully this is brought out in this verse:

⇒ "Preach the Word."

⇒ "Be prepared in season and out of season": keep a sense of urgency; grasp the opportunities and make opportunities to preach.

2 TIMOTHY 4:1-5

⇒ "Correct."
⇒ "Rebuke."
⇒ "Encourage—with great patience and careful instruction."

1. First, preach the Word. The whole thrust is obsession—the minister is to be obsessed with preaching. Preaching is to burn within his soul; he is to be consumed with preaching—a burning passion to preach the unsearchable riches of Christ. Why?

⇒ Because preaching is God's chosen method to save men.

> **For the message of the cross is foolishness to those who are perishing, but to us who are being saved it is the power of God. For since in the wisdom of God the world through its wisdom did not know him, God was pleased through the foolishness of what was preached to save those who believe. (1 Cor 1:18, 21)**

⇒ Because the minister is held accountable to preach.

> **Yet when I preach the gospel, I cannot boast, for I am compelled to preach. Woe to me if I do not preach the gospel! (1 Cor 9:16)**

It is impossible to overemphasize preaching. It is even impossible to fully grasp the importance of preaching. This is the whole thrust of this passage. Just think about the solemn charge and warning that has just been covered in verse one:

⇒ God and Christ both have their eyes on the minister—to see if he is preaching the Word.
⇒ The minister will be judged by the Lord Jesus Christ as to whether or not he preached the Word.
⇒ The minister will face Christ when Christ returns in glory as the conquering Lord—face Him and give an account of his preaching.
⇒ The minister's place and position in the Lord's kingdom will be determined by how faithful he was in preaching the Word.

Therefore, the charge is to preach the Word. Note two very significant points.

a. The word "preach" (kerusso) is the picture of the minister standing before people in all the dignity and authority of God Himself. It is the word that was used of the ambassador who was sent forth by the king to proclaim his message in all of the authority and dignity of the king himself.

> *"This should be the pattern for the preacher today. His preaching should be [with dignity]...that dignity which comes from...the fact that he is an official herald of the King of kings. It should be...[with] authority which will command the respect, careful attention, and proper reaction of the listeners"* (Kenneth Wuest. *The Pastoral Epistles*, Vol.2, p.154).

b. The minister is to preach "*the Word.*" What is meant by "*the Word*"?
⇒ "All Scripture"—all Scripture that is God-breathed, inspired by God (2 Tim.3:16).

The Word means the Scripture, the very Word of God itself. It is "the whole body of revealed truth" (Kenneth Wuest. *The Pastoral Epistles*, Vol.2, p.154). It is the whole counsel of God that comprises what men call *The Holy Bible*. The minister is to preach the Word, the Holy Scripture, the very Word of God Himself. He is not to preach…
- his own ideas
- the ideas of other men
- philosophy
- psychology
- self-image
- self-righteousness
- sociology
- science
- educational development
- personal efforts
- ego-boosters
- man-made religion

The great Greek scholar Kenneth Wuest has one of the most challenging descriptions of the word *preach* ever penned by man:

> *"The word [preach is a] command to be obeyed at once. It is a sharp command as in military language….The preacher must present, not book reviews, not politics, not economics, not current topics of the day, not a philosophy of life denying the Bible and based upon unproven theories of science, but the Word. The preacher as a herald cannot choose his message. He is given a message to proclaim by his Sovereign. If he will not proclaim that, let him step down from his exalted position"* (Kenneth Wuest. *The Pastoral Epistles*, Vol.2, p.154).

Matthew Henry uses striking language:

> *"It is not their own notions and fancies that they are to preach, but the pure plain Word of God; and they must not corrupt it"* (*Matthew Henry's Commentary*, Vol.5, p.848).

> **As you go, preach this message: 'The kingdom of heaven is near.' What I tell you in the dark, speak in the daylight; what is whispered in your ear, proclaim from the roofs. (Mat 10:7, 27)**

> **He said to them, "Go into all the world and preach the good news to all creation. (Mark 16:15)**

> **"Go, stand in the temple courts," he said, "and tell the people the full message of this new life." (Acts 5:20)**

> **Preach the Word; be prepared in season and out of season; correct, rebuke and encourage—with great patience and careful instruction. (2 Tim 4:2)**

2. Second, be prepared in season and out of season. There are two things to note in this point.

a. The word "prepared" (epistethi) means to "take a stand, to stand upon it or up to it, to carry on, to stick to it" (A.T. Robertson). As Robertson says, "There are all sorts of seasons…some difficult…some easy" (*Word Pictures in the New*

Testament, Vol.4, p.629). The task of the minister is to stand and stick to preaching no matter the circumstances, easy or difficult.

b. "The preacher is to proclaim the Word when the time is auspicious, favorable, opportune, and also when the circumstances seem unfavorable. So few times are still available for preaching that the preacher must take every chance he has to preach the Word. There is no closed season for preaching" (Kenneth Wuest. *The Pastoral Epistles*, Vol.2, p.155).

Matthew Henry says:

> "Do this work with all fervency of spirit. Call upon those under [your] charge to take heed of sin, to do their duty: call upon them to repent, and believe, and live a holy life and this both in season and out of season....
>
> "We must do it in season, that is, let slip no opportunity; and do it out of season, that is, not shift off the duty, under pretence that it is out of season" (*Matthew Henry's Commentary*, Vol.5, p.848).

William Barclay says:

> "The Christian teacher is to be urgent. The message he brings is literally a matter of life and death. The teacher and the preacher who really get their message across to people are those who have the tone of earnestness in their voice....
>
> "The Christian teacher is to be persistent. He is to urge the *claims of Christ* 'in season and out of season.' As someone has put it: 'Take or make your opportunity.' As Theodore of Mospeustia put it: 'The Christian must count every time an opportunity to speak for Christ.' It was said of George Morrison of Wellington Church in Glasgow that with him wherever the conversation started, it went straight across country to Christ" (*The Letters to Timothy, Titus, and Philemon*, p.234f).

The Amplified New Testament says:

> "Keep your sense of urgency (stand *by*, be at hand and ready, whether the opportunity seems to be favorable or unfavorable, whether it is convenient or inconvenient, whether it be welcome or unwelcome, you as preacher of the Word are to show people in what way their lives are wrong)."

3. Third, correct (elegxon). The word means to stir a person to correct himself; to put a person under conviction; to lead a person to see his sin and to feel guilt over it. It means to put a person under conviction of sin and to lead him to confession and repentance.

> "The preacher is to deal with sin, both in the lives of his unsaved hearers and in those of the saints to whom he ministers, and he is to do it in no uncertain tones. The word 'sin' is not enough in the vocabulary of our preaching today. And as he deals with the sin that confronts him as he preaches, he is to expect results, the salvation of the lost and the sanctification of the saints" (Kenneth Wuest. *The Pastoral Epistles*, Vol.2, p.155).

4. Fourth, rebuke (epitimeson). This is a strong word, very strong. It is a "sharp, severe rebuke with possibly a suggestion in some cases, of impending penalty. Even where the preacher has experienced failure after failure in bringing sinners or saints to forsake their sin" (Kenneth Wuest. *The Pastoral Epistles*, Vol.2, p.155).

> "A word of warning and rebuke would often save a brother from many a sin and many a shipwreck. But, as someone has said, that word must always be spoken as 'brother setting brother right.' It must be spoken with a consciousness of our common guilt. It is not our place to set ourselves up as the moral judge of anyone; nonetheless it is our duty to speak that warning word when it needs to be spoken" (William Barclay. *The Letters to Timothy, Titus, and Philemon*, p.236f).

> "Convince wicked people of the evil and danger of their wicked courses. Endeavour, by dealing plainly with them, to bring them to repentance. Rebuke them with gravity and authority, in Christ's name, that they may take [your] displeasure against them as an indication of God's displeasure" (Matthew Henry. *Matthew Henry's Commentary*, Vol.5, p.848).

Those who sin are to be rebuked publicly, so that the others may take warning. (1 Tim 5:20)

He must hold firmly to the trustworthy message as it has been taught, so that he can encourage others by sound doctrine and refute those who oppose it. (Titus 1:9)

These, then, are the things you should teach. Encourage and rebuke with all authority. Do not let anyone despise you. (Titus 2:15)

5. Fifth, encourage—with great patience and careful instruction. The word "encourage" (parakaleo) has the idea of "please, I beg of you, I urge you" (Kenneth Wuest. *The Pastoral Epistles*, Vol.2, p.155). It means to beseech, encourage, comfort, and help. It is not enough to reprove and rebuke people. The minister must encourage and comfort, help and carry the person to Christ. Note how crucial this point is.

a. The minister must "encourage with great patience" (makrothumia). The idea is that the minister patiently endures in exhorting people—no matter the circumstances. He exhorts and exhorts, encourages and encourages. He suffers a long, long time with people...
- enduring whatever weaknesses and failings they have.
- enduring whatever evil and injury is done.

The minister suffers a long, long time without resentment or anger, and he never gives up, for he knows the power of Christ to change lives.

b. The minister "encourages with careful instruction." He does not teach bits and pieces of God's Word. He does not focus upon subjects...
- that are popular

- that are favorites
- that arouse curiosity
- that he thinks are needed

He focuses upon all the instructions of God—the whole counsel of God. He encourages people in all the doctrine of God.

The third time he said to him, "Simon son of John, do you love me?" Peter was hurt because Jesus asked him the third time, "Do you love me?" He said, "Lord, you know all things; you know that I love you." Jesus said, "Feed my sheep. (John 21:17)

Love is patient, love is kind. It does not envy, it does not boast, it is not proud. (1 Cor 13:4)

But encourage one another daily, as long as it is called Today, so that none of you may be hardened by sin's deceitfulness. (Heb 3:13)

Be shepherds of God's flock that is under your care, serving as overseers—not because you must, but because you are willing, as God wants you to be; not greedy for money, but eager to serve; (1 Pet 5:2)

3 (4:3-4) **Preaching—Ministers**: preach the Word—for the great apostasy is coming. Even as Paul was writing these words some false teaching had already seeped into the church, and the future was not too bright. This is a prediction of Scripture; Paul was prophesying that the false teaching was to spread. The day was coming when apostasy was to sweep throughout the church. The idea is that the apostasy would be great—many would follow after the false teaching and the whole church would be affected.

We know from church history that this is exactly what happened to the churches in Asia. The Asian churches were the very churches who were warned in the Book of Revelation (Rev.1:11-3:22). There were seven churches, and out of the seven only one remained faithful to the preaching of the Word—the Philadelphian church (Rev.3:7-13). The other six became apostate; many of the people turned away from the pure preaching and teaching of God's Word. Why? What caused the apostasy? What caused so many people and churches to turn away from Christ and from the pure Word of God? This present passage gives the answer, and remember: it was a prediction. The apostasy had not yet happened. Two clear reasons are given why people turn away from Christ and why churches turn away from the preaching of the pure Word of God.

1. People will not put up with sound doctrine. By doctrine, of course, is meant the doctrines, teaching, and instructions of God's Word, the Holy Scriptures. The place of Scripture in the lives of believers has just been discussed in the previous passage (cp. 2 Tim.3:14-17). Note the word "sound" (hugiaino). It means wholesome and healthy doctrine and teaching. The only doctrine and teaching that is sound is that of God's Word.

The point is this: people turn away from sound doctrine because they do not want to hear the truth. What truth? In all honesty, the truth that none of us enjoys hearing.

⇒ We do not enjoy hearing that we are sinful and depraved, dirty and unclean, selfish and immoral, unjust and unworthy, ever failing and always coming up short. No person enjoys hearing this, no matter who he is. Yet the message is true, and a person is foolish not to be honest and acknowledge it. Why? Because the sin and depravity of our hearts is the very reason we live in such an evil world and die. And being honest about the fact is the only way the problem of evil and death can ever be solved. Nevertheless, despite all this it is not enjoyable to confess that we are sinners and hopelessly depraved.

⇒ We do not enjoy hearing that we can do nothing whatsoever to become acceptable to God. This idea just does not make sense to most people, for there are some good people in the world. It is just not a pleasing thought to hear that man cannot do enough good to be acceptable to God. Think about it: no matter who the person is—no matter how good and moral he is—no matter how much good he does, he is not acceptable and cannot make himself acceptable to God. As stated, this is not a pleasant thought, not to any person. Therefore, men do not want to hear such doctrine preached.

⇒ Most people do not like hearing that Jesus Christ is the *only Savior*, the *only Mediator*, the *only way* a person can be saved and acceptable to God. They ask about the people who never hear about Him (like the native in the jungle) and about other religions.

The teaching of Scripture could go on and on, but the point is clear. People turn away from sound doctrine for a very simple reason: they do not want to hear the truth. They either do not agree with it, or else they do not want to be reminded or to think about it.

Jesus answered, "My teaching is not my own. It comes from him who sent me. If anyone chooses to do God's will, he will find out whether my teaching comes from God or whether I speak on my own. (John 7:16-17)

Why is my language not clear to you? Because you are unable to hear what I say. You belong to your father, the devil, and you want to carry out your father's desire. He was a murderer from the beginning, not holding to the truth, for there is no truth in him. When he lies, he speaks his native language, for he is a liar and the father of lies. (John 8:43-44)

He who belongs to God hears what God says. The reason you do not hear is that you do not belong to God." (John 8:47)

There is a judge for the one who rejects me and does not accept my words; that very word which I spoke will condemn him at the last day. (John 12:48)

I urge you, brothers, to watch out for those who cause divisions and put obstacles in your way that are contrary to the teaching you have learned. Keep away from them. (Rom 16:17)

Then we will no longer be infants, tossed back and forth by the waves, and blown here and there by every wind of teaching and by the cunning and craftiness of men in their deceitful scheming. (Eph 4:14)

As I urged you when I went into Macedonia, stay there in Ephesus so that you may command certain men not to teach

false doctrines any longer nor to devote themselves to myths and endless genealogies. These promote controversies rather than God's work—which is by faith. (1 Tim 1:3-4)

Anyone who runs ahead and does not continue in the teaching of Christ does not have God; whoever continues in the teaching has both the Father and the Son. (2 John 1:9)

2. People will want teachers who will allow them to live like they desire. The Greek actually says that people will be *dominated* "by their own lusts" (epithumia). They will be living lives of lusts, cravings, and gratifications—lives that seek the gratification of the flesh through...

- sex and immorality
- recognition and honor
- power and authority
- status and position
- money and possessions
- image and approval
- discipline and control
- religion and personal righteousness
- good works and benevolence

Such desires—lusts and cravings—will so dominate people's lives that they will seek ministers and teachers who will tickle their ears with the message of personal development and self-image.

Note this: the messages of personal development and self-image, of philosophy and psychology, of religion and good works are messages that benefit men. But they do not go far enough. They do not solve the problems of evil and selfishness within the human heart nor do they solve the problem of death. Any person who is truly honest and thoughtful knows that no person and no group of persons—not even the whole human race—can keep a single person from dying nor infuse a serum into a person that will make him live forever. Neither can anyone recreate the earth and the heavens into a perfect world. Man is far short of perfection. If there is to be such a thing as salvation—as being delivered from evil and death and given eternal life in a new heavens and earth—it has to come from God Himself. This is the message, the glorious gospel of God's Word: there is salvation through His love—His love that has been demonstrated in His Son, the Lord Jesus Christ.

The point is this: men do not want to be honest. They want the right to live like they want and to do their own thing. They want the right to be comfortable, at ease, recognized, honored, esteemed, and to secure position, authority, wealth, and power. They want pleasure and stimulation—the gratification of their lusts when they want them gratified. Therefore, they want teachers who will tickle their ears and assure them...

- that the building up of their discipline, image, and personal development is good and acceptable just so God is honored and acknowledged.
- that immorality and carnality are forgivable.

As stated, both messages are true, but they are not the whole truth. And the only way a person can be saved, truly saved, is by surrendering his life to the whole truth of God's Word. Note what Scripture says: false teaching is nothing more than fables. The Amplified New Testament says that people "will turn aside from hearing the truth and wander off into myths and man-made fictions."

I am astonished that you are so quickly deserting the one who called you by the grace of Christ and are turning to a different gospel—which is really no gospel at all. Evidently some people are throwing you into confusion and are trying to pervert the gospel of Christ. But even if we or an angel from heaven should preach a gospel other than the one we preached to you, let him be eternally condemned! As we have already said, so now I say again: If anybody is preaching to you a gospel other than what you accepted, let him be eternally condemned! (Gal 1:6-9)

Anyone who breaks one of the least of these commandments and teaches others to do the same will be called least in the kingdom of heaven, but whoever practices and teaches these commands will be called great in the kingdom of heaven. (Mat 5:19)

They worship me in vain; their teachings are but rules taught by men.'" (Mat 15:9)

Unlike so many, we do not peddle the word of God for profit. On the contrary, in Christ we speak before God with sincerity, like men sent from God. (2 Cor 2:17)

Rather, we have renounced secret and shameful ways; we do not use deception, nor do we distort the word of God. On the contrary, by setting forth the truth plainly we commend ourselves to every man's conscience in the sight of God. (2 Cor 4:2)

In which you used to live when you followed the ways of this world and of the ruler of the kingdom of the air, the spirit who is now at work in those who are disobedient. (Eph 2:2)

They want to be teachers of the law, but they do not know what they are talking about or what they so confidently affirm. (1 Tim 1:7)

The Spirit clearly says that in later times some will abandon the faith and follow deceiving spirits and things taught by demons. Such teachings come through hypocritical liars, whose consciences have been seared as with a hot iron. (1 Tim 4:1-2)

If anyone teaches false doctrines and does not agree to the sound instruction of our Lord Jesus Christ and to godly teaching, (1 Tim 6:3)

For the time will come when men will not put up with sound doctrine. Instead, to suit their own desires, they will gather around them a great number of teachers to say what their itching ears want to hear. They will turn their ears away from the truth and turn aside to myths. (2 Tim 4:3-4)

For there are many rebellious people, mere talkers and deceivers, especially those of the circumcision group [legalists]. They must be silenced, because they are ruining whole households by teaching things they ought not to teach—and that for the sake of dishonest gain. (Titus 1:10-11)

But there were also false prophets among the people, just as there will be false

2 TIMOTHY 4:1-5

teachers among you. They will secretly introduce destructive heresies, even denying the sovereign Lord who bought them—bringing swift destruction on themselves. (2 Pet 2:1)

He writes the same way in all his letters, speaking in them of these matters. His letters contain some things that are hard to understand, which ignorant and unstable people distort, as they do the other Scriptures, to their own destruction. (2 Pet 3:16)

Thought 1. Timothy and all true ministers of the gospel must preach the Word, for a great turning away is coming. God's ministers must preach now while there is still time—preach with all the fervency and power of God's indwelling Spirit.

4 (4:5) **Preaching—Ministers**: preach the Word—for you must complete and fulfill your ministry—you must "fill your ministry to the brim" (Charles B. Williams. *The New Testament in the Language of the People.* "The Four Translation New Testament," p.607). Tragically...
- not every minister completes his ministry.
- not every minister fills his ministry to the brim.
- not every minister does everything Christ wants Him to do.
- not every minister undertakes every ministry that God desires for him.
- not every minister fills every ministry he undertakes to the brim.

Some do; we can look around and see some ministers who serve ever so faithfully. Some are not as gifted as others, and they serve in what men call small ministries, but they serve faithfully and well. How can we all become faithful and fulfill our ministries? How can we fill our ministries to the brim? Paul told Timothy that he had to do four things to complete his ministry.

1. The minister must watch and keep his head in all situations. The phrase "watch, keep your head" (nephe) means to be sober, calm, and alert; to keep a cool, calm, and collected mind; to maintain a controlled and disciplined life and spirit. And note: the minister is to be this way in all things: in body, mind, and spirit—in thought, word and behavior. The minister is to always watch and keep his head—always be alert, calm, controlled, and disciplined—no matter the activity or behavior.

"Watch and pray so that you will not fall into temptation. The spirit is willing, but the body is weak." (Mat 26:41)

So be on your guard! Remember that for three years I never stopped warning each of you night and day with tears. (Acts 20:31)

So, if you think you are standing firm, be careful that you don't fall! (1 Cor 10:12)

Be on your guard; stand firm in the faith; be men of courage; be strong. (1 Cor 16:13)

Devote yourselves to prayer, being watchful and thankful. (Col 4:2)

Be self-controlled and alert. Your enemy the devil prowls around like a roaring lion looking for someone to devour. (1 Pet 5:8)

2. The minister is to "endure hardship" (kakopatheo). The word means to suffer hardships, troubles, problems, difficulties, and evils. Kenneth Wuest gives an excellent discussion of this point, a discussion that merits attention by every minister who has any concern for people whatsoever.

"The verb [endure afflictions] is aorist imperative. It is a sharp command given with military snap and curtness. Timothy needed just that. He was not cast in a heroic mold. How we in the ministry of the Word need that injunction today. What 'softies' we sometimes are, afraid to come out clearly in our proclamation of the truth and our stand as to false doctrine, fearing the ostracism of our fellows, the ecclesiastical displeasure of our superiors, or the cutting off of our immediate financial income. I would rather walk a lonely road with Jesus than be without His fellowship in the crowd, wouldn't you? I would rather live in a cottage and eat simple food, and have Him as Head of my house and the Unseen Guest at every meal, than to live in royal style in a mansion without Him" (*The Pastoral Epistles*, Vol.2, p.159).

All men will hate you because of me, but he who stands firm to the end will be saved. (Mat 10:22)

Therefore, my dear brothers, stand firm. Let nothing move you. Always give yourselves fully to the work of the Lord, because you know that your labor in the Lord is not in vain. (1 Cor 15:58)

Indeed he was ill, and almost died. But God had mercy on him, and not on him only but also on me, to spare me sorrow upon sorrow. (Phil 2:27)

For it has been granted to you on behalf of Christ not only to believe on him, but also to suffer for him, (Phil 1:29)

Therefore, since we are surrounded by such a great cloud of witnesses, let us throw off everything that hinders and the sin that so easily entangles, and let us run with perseverance the race marked out for us. (Heb 12:1)

Blessed is the man who perseveres under trial, because when he has stood the test, he will receive the crown of life that God has promised to those who love him. (James 1:12)

Be self-controlled and alert. Your enemy the devil prowls around like a roaring lion looking for someone to devour. Resist him, standing firm in the faith, because you know that your brothers throughout the world are undergoing the same kind of sufferings. (1 Pet 5:8-9)

3. The minister is to do the work of an evangelist. This does not mean that the minister is to become a traveling or professional evangelist. It means that his work is to be evangelistic—he is to seek to win souls in all that he does. He is to share the love and judgment of God in all of his preaching and teaching and in everything else he does. The very thrust of his ministry is to be that of reconciling people to God, that of sharing the glorious news of God's love

and of coming judgment: that God saves and shall judge people through His Son, the Lord Jesus Christ.

> But you will receive power when the Holy Spirit comes on you; and you will be my witnesses in Jerusalem, and in all Judea and Samaria, and to the ends of the earth." (Acts 1:8)
>
> For we cannot help speaking about what we have seen and heard." (Acts 4:20)
>
> It is written: "I believed; therefore I have spoken." With that same spirit of faith we also believe and therefore speak, (2 Cor 4:13)
>
> For this reason I remind you to fan into flame the gift of God, which is in you through the laying on of my hands. For God did not give us a spirit of timidity, but a spirit of power, of love and of self-discipline. So do not be ashamed to testify about our Lord, or ashamed of me his prisoner. But join with me in suffering for the gospel, by the power of God, (2 Tim 1:6-8)
>
> But in your hearts set apart Christ as Lord. Always be prepared to give an answer to everyone who asks you to give the reason for the hope that you have. But do this with gentleness and respect, (1 Pet 3:15)

4. The minister is to discharge his duties, complete and fulfill his ministry, fill it to the brim. He is to carry his ministry out to the end, fully perform all the duties of it. Again, Kenneth Wuest has an excellent comment on this point:

> "'Ministry' is from a Greek word (diakonia) which speaks of Christian work in general, covering every mode of service. One of the chief temptations of the pastorate is laziness and neglect. Paul lives an intense and tremendously active life. The word 'drive' characterizes him perfectly. As the saying goes: 'It is better to wear out for the Lord than to rust out'" (*The Pastoral Epistles*, Vol.2, p.159f).

> "My food," said Jesus, "is to do the will of him who sent me and to finish his work. (John 4:34)
>
> I have brought you glory on earth by completing the work you gave me to do. (John 17:4)
>
> The third time he said to him, "Simon son of John, do you love me?" Peter was hurt because Jesus asked him the third time, "Do you love me?" He said, "Lord, you know all things; you know that I love you." Jesus said, "Feed my sheep. (John 21:17)
>
> However, I consider my life worth nothing to me, if only I may finish the race and complete the task the Lord Jesus has given me—the task of testifying to the gospel of God's grace. (Acts 20:24)
>
> Keep watch over yourselves and all the flock of which the Holy Spirit has made you overseers. Be shepherds of the church of God, which he bought with his own blood. (Acts 20:28)
>
> I thank Christ Jesus our Lord, who has given me strength, that he considered me faithful, appointing me to his service. (1 Tim 1:12)
>
> Now the overseer must be above reproach, the husband of but one wife, temperate, self-controlled, respectable, hospitable, able to teach, (1 Tim 3:2)
>
> For I am already being poured out like a drink offering, and the time has come for my departure. I have fought the good fight, I have finished the race, I have kept the faith. Now there is in store for me the crown of righteousness, which the Lord, the righteous Judge, will award to me on that day—and not only to me, but also to all who have longed for his appearing. (2 Tim 4:6-8)
>
> Be shepherds of God's flock that is under your care, serving as overseers—not because you must, but because you are willing, as God wants you to be; not greedy for money, but eager to serve; (1 Pet 5:2)
>
> I have posted watchmen on your walls, O Jerusalem; they will never be silent day or night. You who call on the LORD, give yourselves no rest, (Isa 62:6)
>
> Then I will give you shepherds after my own heart, who will lead you with knowledge and understanding. (Jer 3:15)
>
> I will place shepherds over them who will tend them, and they will no longer be afraid or terrified, nor will any be missing," declares the LORD. (Jer 23:4)

2 TIMOTHY 4:6-8

	B. The Triumphant Testimony of Paul, 4:6-8

1 His death
  a. An offering
  b. A departure, cp. 18
2 His testimony
  a. A *good* fight
  b. A *finished* race
  c. A *kept* faith
3 His reward: The crown of righteousness
  a. To be given by the Lord, the righteous Judge
  b. To be given to all believers who love and look for the Lord's return
	6 For I am already being poured out like a drink offering, and the time has come for my departure.
	7 I have fought the good fight, I have finished the race, I have kept the faith.
	8 Now there is in store for me the crown of righteousness, which the Lord, the righteous Judge, will award to me on that day—and not only to me, but also to all who have longed for his appearing.

DIVISION III

THE TRIUMPH OF PREACHING, 4:1-8

B. The Triumphant Testimony of Paul, 4:6-8

(4:6-8) **Introduction—Paul—Death**: Paul is sitting in the drab dungeon of a Roman prison. He is facing the capital charge of insurrection against the Roman government. He has had his preliminary hearing before Nero; therefore, he is soon to stand before Nero in his final trial and hear the fateful verdict: "Execution." How soon? We do not know, but these verses indicate very soon. Paul knew that the end of his life upon earth was immediately at hand. This is the reason he had just passed the banner of the gospel over to Timothy—the reason he had just given Timothy the most awesome charge that can be given to a man: the awesome charge to preach the Word of God and to minister to a world that is lost and dying—a world that is reeling under the weight of so many desperate needs. Timothy must go forth and preach the gospel with all the might and commitment of his being. Note how Paul encourages Timothy even in discussing his own coming death. He wants Timothy to look ahead to the end of his own life and to be able to bear the same testimony. What a challenge to us all: Paul's triumphant testimony.

1. His death (v.6).
2. His testimony (v.7).
3. His reward: the crown of righteousness (v.8).

1 (4:6) **Paul—Death**: Paul's confrontation with death.

1. Paul says that his life is being offered and sacrificed to God in one last act—the act of death. What a view of death! Seeing death as an offering and sacrifice being presented to God. The Greek word for offering or sacrifice (spendomai) is striking: it refers to the drink offering that was presented to God. When a person wanted to make a sacrifice to God, he often took a cup of wine or oil and poured it out as an offering and sacrifice to God. The drink offering symbolized the Lord Jesus pouring out His soul—dying—for us.

Paul is saying, "I am pouring out my soul through death for the Lord Jesus Christ. The life and blood of my body is being sacrificed for the preaching of God's Word. I am laying down my life as an offering to Christ Jesus my Lord—laying it down in the supreme act of sacrifice. I am dying for Him."

The great Biblical writer William Barclay describes the scene with words that should challenge us all:

> "Paul did not think of himself as going to be executed; he thought of himself as going to offer his life to God. His life was not being taken from him; he was laying it down. Ever since his conversion Paul had offered to God—his money, his scholarship, his strength, his time, the vigour of his body, the acuteness of his mind, the devotion of his passionate heart. Only life itself was left to offer, and gladly Paul was going to lay life down" (*The Letters to Timothy, Titus, and Philemon*, p.240).

2. Paul says that the time for his departure from this world has come. The word "departure" (analuo) is striking in its meaning. (The following meanings are taken from W.E. Vine. *Expository Dictionary of New Testament Words*.)

   a. To depart is the picture of a ship hoisting the anchor and loosening the mooring ropes and departing one country for another country. Paul had been anchored and tied to this world, but the anchor and ropes of this world were now being loosed, and Paul was about to set sail for the greatest of all ports—heaven itself.

   b. To depart is the picture of "breaking up an encampment" (W.E. Vine). Paul had been camping in this world. If any man has ever known what it is like to be unsettled and moving about from place to place, it was Paul. And unfortunately it was often not by choice. Many times the opposition to the gospel had been so violent, he had been forced to break camp and move on, sometimes fleeing for his life. But now, Paul was to break camp and depart for the last time, and what a departure it was to be. He would never again have to move. He was departing this world for his permanent residence: heaven itself.

   c. To depart is the picture of the unyoking of an animal from the burden of the cart, plough, or millstone which it had been pulling to grind the grain.

2 TIMOTHY 4:6-8

Paul was to be released from the yoke and burden of labor and toil in this life. He was being released and set free to depart for the pastures and still waters and rest of heaven and eternity.

Matthew Henry says:

> "Observe...with what pleasure he [Paul] speaks of dying. He calls it his departure: though it is probable that he foresaw he must die a violent bloody death, yet he calls it his departure, or his release. Death to a good man is his release from the imprisonment of this world and his departure to the enjoyments of another world; he does not cease to be, but is only removed from one world to another" (*Matthew Henry's Commentary*, Vol.5, p.849).

> "For God so loved the world that he gave his one and only Son, that whoever believes in him shall not perish but have eternal life. (John 3:16)
>
> If we live, we live to the Lord; and if we die, we die to the Lord. So, whether we live or die, we belong to the Lord. (Rom 14:8)
>
> For to me, to live is Christ and to die is gain. If I am to go on living in the body, this will mean fruitful labor for me. Yet what shall I choose? I do not know! I am torn between the two: I desire to depart and be with Christ, which is better by far; (Phil 1:21-23)
>
> All these people were still living by faith when they died. They did not receive the things promised; they only saw them and welcomed them from a distance. And they admitted that they were aliens and strangers on earth. (Heb 11:13)
>
> Then I heard a voice from heaven say, "Write: Blessed are the dead who die in the Lord from now on." "Yes," says the Spirit, "they will rest from their labor, for their deeds will follow them." (Rev 14:13)
>
> Even though I walk through the valley of the shadow of death, I will fear no evil, for you are with me; your rod and your staff, they comfort me. (Psa 23:4)
>
> Precious in the sight of the LORD is the death of his saints. (Psa 116:15)
>
> When calamity comes, the wicked are brought down, but even in death the righteous have a refuge. (Prov 14:32)

2 (4:7) **Paul, Life—Death**: Paul's glorious testimony. The way Paul describes his life is also full of meaning. He quickly glances back over his life and uses three pictures to describe it, the pictures of a soldier, an athlete, and a steward or manager.

1. Paul says that he had lived life just like a faithful soldier: "I have fought the good fight." Paul had responded to the call of the Lord Jesus Christ...
- He had volunteered to serve Christ.
- He had separated himself from this world, sacrificing all that he was and had to be a soldier for Christ—a soldier totally committed to the mission of Christ.
- He had suffered through the threats, scrapes, and wars launched by the enemies of Christ.
- He had fought the "good" (kalos) fight: the fight that was worthy, honorable, noble, and commendable.
- He had done his time, stuck to the mission of Christ to the very end.

Therefore, Paul could victoriously declare, "I have fought the good fight." He was being released from his service as a soldier for the King, released to go home to live at peace in the kingdom of his Lord forever and ever.

> For our struggle is not against flesh and blood, but against the rulers, against the authorities, against the powers of this dark world and against the spiritual forces of evil in the heavenly realms. (Eph 6:12)
>
> Timothy, my son, I give you this instruction in keeping with the prophecies once made about you, so that by following them you may fight the good fight, (1 Tim 1:18)
>
> Fight the good fight of the faith. Take hold of the eternal life to which you were called when you made your good confession in the presence of many witnesses. (1 Tim 6:12)
>
> No one serving as a soldier gets involved in civilian affairs—he wants to please his commanding officer. (2 Tim 2:4)
>
> Remember those earlier days after you had received the light, when you stood your ground in a great contest in the face of suffering. (Heb 10:32)

2. Paul says that he had run and finished the race of his life; he had completed the course of life just like the athlete runs and finishes the course of his race. This is powerful, for it means that Paul disciplined and controlled his life to the utmost—just like the Olympian athlete.
⇒ He controlled what he ate and drank and what he did with his body and mind.
⇒ He focused upon the course of life, how he ran it. He could not run the risk of being distracted by the things of the world and of the flesh, (sinful nature) lest he become disqualified from running the race.

> I do all this for the sake of the gospel, that I may share in its blessings. Do you not know that in a race all the runners run, but only one gets the prize? Run in such a way as to get the prize. Everyone who competes in the games goes into strict training. They do it to get a crown that will not last; but we do it to get a crown that will last forever. Therefore I do not run like a man running aimlessly; I do not fight like a man beating the air. No, I beat my body and make it my slave so that after I have preached to others, I myself will not be disqualified for the prize. (1 Cor 9:23-27)
>
> You were running a good race. Who cut in on you and kept you from obeying the truth? (Gal 5:7)

I press on toward the goal to win the prize for which God has called me heavenward in Christ Jesus. (Phil 3:14)

I have fought the good fight, I have finished the race, I have kept the faith. (2 Tim 4:7)

Therefore, since we are surrounded by such a great cloud of witnesses, let us throw off everything that hinders and the sin that so easily entangles, and let us run with perseverance the race marked out for us. (Heb 12:1)

3. Paul says that he had kept the faith. He had looked after the faith just like a good steward looks after the estate of his master. The Lord had *entrusted* the faith to Paul, and he had kept the faith. He had proven faithful; he had faithfully managed the faith for his Master, the Lord Jesus Christ. The idea is that of a trust, of a management contract between Christ and Paul. Paul is saying that he had kept the terms of the contract; he had managed and looked after the trust faithfully and well. Think about this for a moment—all the sufferings that Paul went through—the terrible trials—the times that he could have...

- dumped the trust of the faith or laid it aside and ignored it. But he never did. He had been chosen by the Lord and Master of life to manage the trust of God, even the faith of our Lord Jesus Christ. Therefore, Paul took the trust and managed it through all—both good and bad times. He never forsook the faith. And because he had been faithful, it was time for him to bear the fruit of his labor. He was now to reap the benefits of the faith; he was to be given all the rights and privileges of the Lord's estate—to live and enjoy its pleasures forevermore.

So he called ten of his servants and gave them ten minas. 'Put this money to work,' he said, 'until I come back.' "'Well done, my good servant!' his master replied. 'Because you have been trustworthy in a very small matter, take charge of ten cities.' (Luke 19:13, 17)

Now it is required that those who have been given a trust must prove faithful. (1 Cor 4:2)

Timothy, guard what has been entrusted to your care. Turn away from godless chatter and the opposing ideas of what is falsely called knowledge, (1 Tim 6:20)

Each one should use whatever gift he has received to serve others, faithfully administering God's grace in its various forms. (1 Pet 4:10)

3 (4:8) **Paul—Reward**: Paul's unbelievable reward—The crown of righteousness. Imagine! There is a crown of righteousness—a crown that a person can receive, a crown that will make him acceptable to God. No person can ever be accepted by God unless he is crowned with righteousness—completely covered with righteousness and made perfect. Why? Because God is perfect and only perfection can live in the presence of God. Therefore, the only way a person can ever become acceptable to God is by receiving the crown of righteousness from God. Paul was to receive the crown of righteousness because he had given his life...

- to be a soldier for Christ and His warfare.
- to be an athlete for Christ and His race (life).
- to be a steward or manager for Christ and His faith.

Think about it: Paul was to be given the crown of righteousness that makes a person perfect before God—righteous and perfect so that he can live before God forever and ever. What a contrast with the fading and deteriorating crowns and trophies given by this world. Note two points.

1. The crown of righteousness will be given by the Lord, the righteous Judge. He is the righteous and perfect judge, the only judge who knows the truth about all men. He knows the heart of every man, and He has seen every man every day and hour of his life. In fact, the Lord has seen every act and heard every word every person has ever done or spoken. He knows all. The Lord knew all about Paul...

- that he had been a good soldier for Christ.
- that he had been a good athlete for Christ.
- that he had been a good steward (manager) for Christ.

The Lord is righteous and just; therefore, Paul knew that the Lord would give him the crown of righteousness in that glorious day of redemption.

2. The crown of righteousness will be given to all who love and look for the Lord's appearing. This is a striking truth. Who is it that loves the Lord's *appearing*? The person who loves the Lord Himself. Who is it that loves the Lord? The person who truly believes in the Lord and the glorious salvation He has provided. Who is a true believer? The person who has committed his life...

- to be a soldier for Christ and His mission.
- to be an athlete for Christ and His course (race and life).
- to be a steward or manager for Christ and His faith.

This is the person who loves and looks for the coming of the Lord Jesus Christ, and this is the person who shall receive the crown of righteousness. As the Greek scholar Kenneth Wuest says:

> *"To those who have considered precious His appearing and therefore have loved it, and...are still holding that attitude in their hearts, to these the Lord Jesus will also give the victor's garland [crown] of righteousness"* (The Pastoral Epistles, Vol.2, p.163).

The effective preacher Oliver Greene says:

> *"No man knows the day or the hour when Jesus will come; we do not know the day or the hour when we will be called to meet the Lord in death. If this should be the day of the Lord's return, or if this should be the day death comes for me, could I testify as Paul did in the face of death? Have I really fought a good fight? Have I kept the faith? Have I been a good minister, true to the Word and to those to whom I preached? Will I have a crown to cast at the feet of Jesus when we crown Him Lord of all?"* (The Epistles of Paul the Apostle to Timothy and Titus, p.371f).

Thought 1. What an indictment against false profession. It is not what we profess about Christ; it is what we do for Christ.

> Everyone who competes in the games goes into strict training. They do it to get a crown that will not last; but we do it to get a crown that will last forever. (1 Cor 9:25)
> Now there is in store for me the crown of righteousness, which the Lord, the righteous Judge, will award to me on that day—and not only to me, but also to all who have longed for his appearing. (2 Tim 4:8)
> Blessed is the man who perseveres under trial, because when he has stood the test, he will receive the crown of life that God has promised to those who love him. (James 1:12)
> And when the Chief Shepherd appears, you will receive the crown of glory that will never fade away. (1 Pet 5:4)
> I am coming soon. Hold on to what you have, so that no one will take your crown. (Rev 3:11)
> The twenty-four elders fall down before him who sits on the throne, and worship him who lives for ever and ever. They lay their crowns before the throne and say: (Rev 4:10)
> And if anyone gives even a cup of cold water to one of these little ones because he is my disciple, I tell you the truth, he will certainly not lose his reward." (Mat 10:42)
> "His master replied, 'Well done, good and faithful servant! You have been faithful with a few things; I will put you in charge of many things. Come and share your master's happiness!' (Mat 25:23)
> But glory, honor and peace for everyone who does good: first for the Jew, then for the Gentile. (Rom 2:10)
> Because you know that the Lord will reward everyone for whatever good he does, whether he is slave or free. (Eph 6:8)

2 TIMOTHY 4:9-22

	IV. THE FINAL FAREWELL OF PAUL TO THE WORLD, 4:9-22	16 At my first defense, no one came to my support, but everyone deserted me. May it not be held against them.	7) When deserted by others
1 A personal message—needing help	9 Do your best to come to me quickly,	17 But the Lord stood at my side and gave me strength, so that through me the message might be fully proclaimed and all the Gentiles might hear it. And I was delivered from the lion's mouth.	b. The experience of God helping him
a. There are special times when believers need help	10 For Demas, because he loved this world, has deserted me and has gone to Thessalonica. Crescens has gone to Galatia, and Titus to Dalmatia.		
1) When a loved one has forsaken God			
2) When left alone because loved ones have gone to their own ministry			
3) When help is needed in the ministry	11 Only Luke is with me. Get Mark and bring him with you, because he is helpful to me in my ministry.	18 The Lord will rescue me from every evil attack and will bring me safely to his heavenly kingdom. To him be glory for ever and ever. Amen.	c. The assurance of God's eternal deliverance—of being rescued & transported into God's heavenly kingdom^{DS1}
4) When a fellow laborer has to be sent forth to his own ministry	12 I sent Tychicus to Ephesus.		
5) When personal items are needed & are out of reach	13 When you come, bring the cloak that I left with Carpus at Troas, and my scrolls, especially the parchments.	19 Greet Priscilla and Aquila and the household of Onesiphorus.	2 A personal greeting—showing personal interest
6) When men actively oppose & cause trouble	14 Alexander the metalworker did me a great deal of harm. The Lord will repay him for what he has done.	20 Erastus stayed in Corinth, and I left Trophimus sick in Miletus.	a. He greeted others
			b. He supplied information about others
		21 Do your best to get here before winter. Eubulus greets you, and so do Pudens, Linus, Claudia and all the brothers.	c. He requested help himself
			d. He passed on the greetings of others
	15 You too should be on your guard against him, because he strongly opposed our message.	22 The Lord be with your spirit. Grace be with you.	e. He gave the benediction of Christ & of grace

DIVISION IV

THE FINAL FAREWELL OF PAUL TO THE WORLD, 4:9-22

(4:9-22) **Introduction—Paul, Writings**: since Second Timothy is Paul's last writing (so far as we know), this is his final message to the outside world.

1. A personal message—needing help (v.9-18).
2. A personal greeting—showing personal interest (v.19-22).

1 (4:9-18) **Ministering—Paul**: there are times when every believer needs help. Even the apostle Paul faced such times—times when he desperately needed the help of other believers. His present situation was one of those times. He was in prison waiting to face his final trial on the charges of being an insurrectionist and trouble-maker for Rome. He was to appear before the emperor Nero, and he was expecting to be executed. Whatever weight and pressure hangs over a man's head—whatever needs are created by being imprisoned and facing execution—all this and much more pressed ever so heavily upon Paul. The present passage gives a glimpse into the heart of Paul as he faced such a terrible trial. It shows what kind of help he needed and how his needs were to be met. The lesson for us to note is this: there are times when we all need help. When those times come, we should not hesitate to ask for help, nor should we hesitate to reach out and help a person who cries for our help.

1. There are some special times when believers need help. Note that Paul asks Timothy to do everything he can to come and visit him. Paul needed Timothy's presence and encouragement in his final hours. Of all the people on earth, Timothy was the dearest to Paul's heart. Facing his final days upon earth, Paul needed and wanted the company of his dear friend. However, there were some very specific reasons why Paul needed Timothy. Only one person was still with Paul—that person was Luke. Looking at why everyone had left Paul gives us a picture into what it is that creates some of the needs in our lives as believers.

   a. Help is needed when a loved one has deserted us (v.10). Note the name Demas. Demas had been a faithful believer and a fellow worker to Paul (Phile.24). He had even been in Rome with Paul for some time. Imagine! He had even served with Paul in some of Paul's most trying moments—while Paul was a prisoner in Rome. What happened? He began to *love this world*. What does this mean?
   ⇒ Does it mean that he began to love the life of this world more than the promise of life in heaven? That he began to fear that he might be persecuted because he, too, professed Christ? That he might be arrested and imprisoned because of his association with Paul?
   ⇒ Does it mean that he began to love the pleasures and comfort, possessions and things of this world more than the sacrifice demanded by Christ?

   Herbert Lockyer gives an excellent picture of what could have happened to Demas:

   > "Under the strong influence of Paul's personality, Demas was [converted]... Becoming a disciple, he was carried away by the enthusiasm of sacrifice. He wanted to live with Paul and die with him, and have a throne and a halo among the martyred saints.
   >
   > "But when Demas came up to the great capital of the then known world in company

with the Lord's prisoners, Paul and Epaphras, it was a different story. He was not a prisoner, and gradually the contrast between the cell and the outer world became intolerable to him. He saw the magnificent halls of the Caesars, the gorgeous homes of the rich and the glitter of a world of music, venal loves, jest and wine. Such a gay world cast its glamour over Demas, and he yielded to its charms. The prison where his friends were languishing seemed wretched alongside the music-haunted, scented, dazzling halls of Rome. Thus Paul had to write one of the most heartbreaking lines in his letters:*

"'Demas hath forsaken me, having loved this present world.' This man of wavering impulse who surrendered the passion of sacrifice and sank in the swirling waters of the world, is a true reflection of the thought that where our love is, there we finally are" (*All the Men of the Bible*). Grand Rapids, MI: Zondervan, 1958, p.91f).

The point is this: when Demas forsook Paul, it cut Paul to the core. It left a vacuum in his heart, and that emptiness needed to be filled by someone else. Paul was facing the darkest hour of his life; therefore, some other believer needed to step in and be a companion to Paul. Paul needed Timothy.

b. Help is needed when loved ones have to move on to their own ministries and we are left alone. Note that both Crescens and Titus had been with Paul, but they had to return to their own ministries. Nothing else is known about Crescens. This is the only reference to him in the Bible. However, tradition does say that he was one of the seventy sent forth to minister by Christ and that he became the bishop of Chalcedon (Herbert Lockyer. *All the Men of the Bible*, p.86).

Titus was a constant companion of Paul during the last fifteen years or more of Paul's life. (see Introduction—Titus for more discussion). He had been sent by Paul to Dalmatia or what was once known as Yugoslavia or Serbia.

The absence of these two dear servants left a deep sense of loneliness in Paul. They needed to return to their own ministries, for the churches and God's dear people needed their ministry. But their departure left an emptiness within Paul's heart. He needed companionship, the encouragement of believers as he faced death.

c. Help is needed when we have a ministry to carry on for the Lord. Note that only Luke was left with Paul. And note that Paul tells Timothy to bring Mark with him. Why? Because Paul needs him to help with the ministry which Paul was carrying on in prison. This is significant, for it tells us that Paul ministered wherever he was, even when he was in prison. His faithfulness is a dynamic example to us. We should minister wherever we are, no matter the circumstances.

The point is this: when we faithfully minister, we need help. We cannot do the work of the ministry alone. We must seek and ask for the help of other believers. (See notes, *Luke*—Col.4:14; *Mark*—Col.4:10 for more discussion.)

d. Help is needed when a fellow-laborer has to be sent to his own ministry. Note that Paul was the one who sent Tychicus to minister in Ephesus (see note and DEEPER STUDY # 1—Eph.6:21-22 for more discussion). When he sent him, it meant that only Luke would remain with Paul. What courage! What a focus upon Christ and the ministry! Imagine facing death and being so focused upon the ministry that you begin to send all your companions off to take care of the needs of others. That was the heart and focus of Paul. Yet he himself had need as he faced death—the need for the companionship of believers.

e. Help is needed when personal items are lacking. Paul needed three things. The prison dungeon was no doubt dark and cold and damp, and Paul needed more clothing (cp. v.21). He also needed "my scrolls especially the parchments." William Barclay suggests that the scrolls were the gospels (Biblia), and the parchments either his legal documents, perhaps proving his Roman citizenship, or else the Hebrew Scriptures. He leans toward the parchments being the Hebrew Scriptures because the Hebrews had written their sacred Scriptures on parchment made from animal skins. As he says, "It was the word of Jesus and the word of God that Paul wanted most of all when he lay in prison awaiting death" (*The Letters to Timothy, Titus, and Philemon*, p.252).

Thought 1. The point is this: we all have practical needs, needs that we sometimes cannot provide for ourselves due to illness, poverty, age, lack of access, lack of know-how, or a host of other reasons. As believers, we need to ask for the help of other believers; and as believers, we need to help when others have need.

f. Help is needed when others actively oppose and do evil and cause trouble for us. In looking at Alexander the metalworker, Barclay's comments are suggestive.

"We do not know what Alexander had done; but perhaps we can deduce what harm he did. The word that Paul uses for did me much evil is the Greek verb endeiknumi. That verb literally means to display; and it was in fact often used for the laying of information against a man. Informers were one of the great curses of Rome at this time. They sought to curry favour for themselves and to receive rewards by laying information. And it may well be that Alexander was a renegade Christian, who went to the magistrates with false and slanderous information against Paul. It may be that Alexander turned against Paul and sought to ruin him in the most dishonourable way" (*The Letters to Timothy, Titus, and Philemon*, p.252).

How many believers turn against other believers? Begin to criticize, gossip, murmur, grumble, and oppose others?—all to gain their own way? How many seek the favor of others by tearing someone else down? Paul needed the help of some courageous believer who would stand with him. He needed someone who would stand by his side and stand against the evil and false charges of Alexander.

g. Help is needed when we are forsaken by all others. Remember: Paul was facing a capital charge, the charge of being a trouble-maker or insurrectionist against Rome. He was appearing before Nero, the Emperor himself, which was the *Supreme Court of Rome*. Two trials were necessary: the preliminary trial or examination where the charges were laid out and briefly examined, and then the trial itself where the defendant was either found guilty or not guilty.

Paul had already faced the preliminary trial, and it is this trial to which he refers. Unbelievably and tragically, the very same thing that had happened to Christ happened to Paul. Not a single person—not one believer and not one friend—attended court with Paul. No one stood with Paul.

When a believer faces such a terrible trial, he needs help. He needs courageous believers standing with him. What an indictment! What a challenge for us to be courageous and faithful to each other in the dark hours of trial and need!

2. There is the experience of God helping the believer. Even when others do not help us, God will be with us. No greater declaration could be made: "But the Lord stood at my side." Men may not stand with us, but the Lord will. He will never desert us no matter how grave and threatening the situation may be. He will stand right by our side. But note a critical fact: we must be faithful. Christ will stand with us just as we stand with Him. Paul declares that Christ was with him because he was not ashamed of Christ. He continued to preach Christ and His mission of eternal life for all men, even to the Roman Supreme Court, to Nero himself. The result: Paul "was delivered from the lion's mouth" (Nero and the devil).

3. There is the assurance of God's eternal deliverance—of being rescued from death and transported into the Lord's heavenly kingdom. Humanly, the situation seemed bleak for Paul. He was not guilty, yet he was being condemned to death on false charges because the civil and state religious leaders were set on stamping out Christ and His church. Paul was doomed to death in the eyes of the world. But note the glorious truth: not in the eyes of Paul. In the eyes of Paul, he was going to his *coronation*. The Lord Jesus Christ was going to preserve him and transport him into the kingdom of God, the kingdom that is gloriously perfected and that lasts forever. Paul has only one final statement about the matter: "To him [Christ] be glory forever and ever."

And teaching them to obey everything I have commanded you. And surely I am with you always, to the very end of the age." (Mat 28:20)

No temptation has seized you except what is common to man. And God is faithful; he will not let you be tempted beyond what you can bear. But when you are tempted, he will also provide a way out so that you can stand up under it. (1 Cor 10:13)

He has delivered us from such a deadly peril, and he will deliver us. On him we have set our hope that he will continue to deliver us, (2 Cor 1:10)

Since the children have flesh and blood, he too shared in their humanity so that by his death he might destroy him who holds the power of death—that is, the devil—and free those who all their lives were held in slavery by their fear of death. (Heb 2:14-15)

Keep your lives free from the love of money and be content with what you have, because God has said, "Never will I leave you; never will I forsake you." So we say with confidence, "The Lord is my helper; I will not be afraid. What can man do to me?" (Heb 13:5-6)

If this is so, then the Lord knows how to rescue godly men from trials and to hold the unrighteous for the day of judgment, while continuing their punishment. (2 Pet 2:9)

The LORD replied, "My Presence will go with you, and I will give you rest." (Exo 33:14)

The LORD is my strength and my shield; my heart trusts in him, and I am helped. My heart leaps for joy and I will give thanks to him in song. (Psa 28:7)

Yet I am poor and needy; may the Lord think of me. You are my help and my deliverer; O my God, do not delay. (Psa 40:17)

So do not fear, for I am with you; do not be dismayed, for I am your God. I will strengthen you and help you; I will uphold you with my righteous right hand. (Isa 41:10)

When you pass through the waters, I will be with you; and when you pass through the rivers, they will not sweep over you. When you walk through the fire, you will not be burned; the flames will not set you ablaze. (Isa 43:2)

Even to your old age and gray hairs I am he, I am he who will sustain you. I have made you and I will carry you; I will sustain you and I will rescue you. (Isa 46:4)

Do not be afraid of them, for I am with you and will rescue you," declares the LORD. (Jer 1:8)

DEEPER STUDY # 1

(4:18) **Death, Deliverance From—Preserve—Eternal Life**: the phrase "will bring me safely to his heavenly kingdom" is a picture of God transporting Paul right through this world into the next world. It is the picture of time—of unbroken time. God preserves Paul right through time into eternity. In one moment of time, Paul is living in this world, conscious and aware; but within the same moment—in a split second—he is transported into God's heavenly kingdom. That one moment of time happens quicker than the blinking of an eye (11/100 of a second). Just imagine! There is no loss of consciousness, no experience or awareness of death. One moment Paul is a citizen of this world, and within the same split moment he stands before the Lord as a citizen of His kingdom (2 Cor.5:6-8). It is the beautiful picture of the believer never having to taste death. (See notes—Col.3:1-4; Heb.2:9; see 2 Cor.5:5-8.)

2 (4:19-22) **Paul—Believers, Hall of Fame**: believers need to always show personal interest in each other. This is a lesson that can be learned from the closings of Paul's letters to the churches. He always sent greetings from believers who were with him as well as greeting believers in the churches to which he was writing. Remember these were the very last words that Paul ever wrote.

1. Paul greeted other believers. There was no sense of competitiveness or jealousy whatsoever in him. He loved and cared for all.
   ⇒ Prisca and Aquila (see DEEPER STUDY # 2—Acts 18:2 for discussion).
   ⇒ Onesiphorous (see note—2 Tim.1:16-18 for discussion).

2. Paul supplied information about others. He was concerned for those who longed for information about other ministers. Again, note how he lifts others up, sharing whatever he can about other dear believers.
   ⇒ Erastus (see note—Ro.16:23 for discussion).
   ⇒ Trophimus (see note—Acts 20:4-6 for discussion).

3. Paul requested help for himself. He needed Timothy's presence and encouragement (see note—2 Tim.4:9-18).

4. Paul passed on the greetings of others. Who were these? Paul had just said that Luke alone was with him. They were probably believers who lived in Rome and who occasionally visited Paul, but who did not visit him too often nor really minister to his needs.
   ⇒ Eubulus and Pudens and Claudia: this is the only mention of these in the New Testament. However, they and Timothy must have known each other for them to be sending greetings to Timothy.
   ⇒ Linus: this, too, is the only mention of him in the New Testament. However, early Christian writers say that he was the first bishop of Rome and that he served as bishop for about twelve years (Herbert Lockyer. *All the Men of the Bible*, p.218).

5. Paul gave the benediction of Christ and of grace. These are the last words ever written by God's dear servant, the servant who loved the Lord and people so much, yet who suffered so much at the hands of people. He loved everyone and he loved everyone deeply. All he wanted for men was two simple but glorious things:
   ⇒ that the Lord Jesus Christ, God's own dear Son, might be with their spirit.
   ⇒ that the grace of God—His favor and blessings—be with all.

> No! We believe it is through the grace of our Lord Jesus that we are saved, just as they are." (Acts 15:11)
>
> And are justified freely by his grace through the redemption that came by Christ Jesus. (Rom 3:24)
>
> In him we have redemption through his blood, the forgiveness of sins, in accordance with the riches of God's grace (Eph 1:7)
>
> In order that in the coming ages he might show the incomparable riches of his grace, expressed in his kindness to us in Christ Jesus. For it is by grace you have been saved, through faith—and this not from yourselves, it is the gift of God—not by works, so that no one can boast. (Eph 2:7-9)
>
> And my God will meet all your needs according to his glorious riches in Christ Jesus. (Phil 4:19)
>
> For the grace of God that brings salvation has appeared to all men. It teaches us to say "No" to ungodliness and worldly passions, and to live self-controlled, upright and godly lives in this present age, while we wait for the blessed hope—the glorious appearing of our great God and Savior, Jesus Christ, (Titus 2:11-13)
>
> So that, having been justified by his grace, we might become heirs having the hope of eternal life. (Titus 3:7)

THE

OUTLINE & SUBJECT INDEX

REMEMBER: When you look up a subject and turn to the Scripture reference, you have not only the Scripture, you have *an outline and a discussion* (commentary) of the Scripture and subject.

This is one of the *GREAT VALUES* of **The Preacher's Outline & Sermon Bible®**. Once you have all the volumes, you will have not only what all other Bible indexes give you, that is, a list of all the subjects and their Scripture references, *BUT* you will also have...

- An outline of *every* Scripture and subject in the Bible.
- A discussion (commentary) on every Scripture and subject.
- Every subject supported by other Scriptures or cross references.

DISCOVER THE GREAT VALUE for yourself. Quickly glance below to the very first subject of the Index of Second Timothy. It is:

ABUSIVE
Meaning. 3:2-4

Turn to the reference. Glance at the Scripture and outline of the Scripture, then read the commentary. You will immediately see the GREAT VALUE of the INDEX of **The Preacher's Outline & Sermon Bible®**.

OUTLINE AND SUBJECT INDEX

ABUSIVE
Meaning. 3:2-4

ACCUSERS, FALSE (See **SLANDEROUS**)

AFFECTION, WITHOUT (See **WITHOUT**)

ALEXANDER THE METALWORKER
Discussed. 4:14-15

APOSTASY
Deliverance found in.
  Continuing in the Scriptures. 3:14-17
  Preaching the Word. 4:2
Described as.
  A great **a**. 4:3-4
  A time existing now.
    In the church now. 3:13
    Men creeping into the church. 3:6-9
  A time in the future. The last times. 3:1-9
  Perilous times (that) shall come. 3:1
  Waxing worse and worse. 3:13
Discussed. 3:1-9; 4:3-4
Examples.
  Demas. 4:10
  Hymeneus and Philetus. 2:16-18
  Jannes and Jambres. 3:8-9
Fate - End of. To be exposed. 3:9
Marks of - Characteristics of.
  A corrupt ministry 3:6-9
  Being deceived. 3:1-9
  Having a form of godliness, but denying the power. 3:5
  Loving the world. 4:10
  Religious but powerless. 3:5
  Turning from the truth. 4:3-4
Source of. False prophets and teachers. 4:3-4

APOSTLE
Meaning. 1:11-12

APPOINT - APPOINTED
The believer is **a**. to Death. 4:6-8; cp. Job 14:14

APPROVED - APPROVAL
Secured by. Study & diligent work. 2:15

AQUILA
Paul sent greetings to **A**. when a prisoner. 4:19

ARGUE - ARGUMENTS
Discussed. 2:14; 2:16-18; 2:23; 2:24-26

ASHAMED
Caused by.
  Abuse & persecution. 1:6-12
  Being **a**. of bold believers. 1:8
  Failure to study the Word. 2:15
How not to be **a**.
  Bearing abuse. 1:8
  Confidence in God's keeping power. 1:11-12
  Stirring up the gift of God. 1:6
  Studying the Word. 2:15
Things not to be **a**. of.
  Being abused. 1:6-12
  Bold believers. 1:8
  Studying the Word. 2:15
  The gospel. 1:8
  Witnessing. 1:8

ASSURANCE
Comes by.
  God's faithfulness. 2:19
  Gospel, The. 2:11-13, 19
  Purging one's self. 2:19-21
Fact.
  Believers are preserved eternally. 4:18
  Believers are to be transferred into heaven. 4:18
Needed in.
  Being transported into eternity. 4:18
  Facing evil. 4:16-18
  Salvation. 2:11-13; 2:19
  Standing all alone. 4:16-18

ATHLETE
Traits. Discussed. 2:5

BACKSLIDING
Caused by. Two things. 4:3-4

BELIEVER
Described.
  As a farmer. 2:6
  As a soldier. 2:3-4
  As a teacher. 2:2
  As an athlete. 2:5
Duty - Behavior.
  Threefold. 3:10-13
  To be strong in Christ. 2:1-7
  To endure abuse for the gospel. 1:6-12
  To flee youthful lusts. 2:22-26
  To guard against impostors. 3:13
  To hold fast. 1:13-18
  To remember the resurrected Lord. 2:8-13
Purpose. To be committed to Christ & His mission. 3:10-11

BIBLE (See **SCRIPTURES - WORD OF GOD**)
Discussed. 3:16
Inspired. 3:16
Purpose of. 3:16

BLASPHEMY (See **ABUSIVE**)

BOASTERS - BOASTFUL
Meaning. 3:2-4

BROTHERHOOD
Duty. Not to forsake when persecuted. 1:15-18

BRUTAL
Meaning. 3:2-4

CALL - CALLED
Described as. A holy **c**. 1:8-10

CARPUS
Paul had forgotten & left some personal items at the home of **C**. 4:13

CHILDREN
Duties toward. To be taught the Scriptures. 1:5; 3:10; 3:16-17
Sins of. Disobedience to parents. 3:2-4

INDEX

CHRISTIAN (See **BELIEVER**)

CHURCH
  Local c.
    A great house. 2:19-21
    Foundation of God. 2:19
    God's building. 2:19-21
  Mission. To disciple & teach faithful men. 2:2
  Names - Titles.
    A great house. 2:20
    Foundation of God. 2:19
    God's building. 2:19-21
  Problems. End times - to face a great turning away. 3:1-9; 4:3-4
  Security of.
    Basis of. 2:19-21
    Discussed. 2:19-21
  Universal c.
    A great house. 2:20
    Foundation of God. 2:19
    God's building. 2:19-21
    Vessels. 2:20-21

CHURCH DISCIPLINE
  Of whom. Opposition. 2:24-26

CLAUDIA
  Visited Paul in prison & knew Timothy. 4:21

COMMISSION
  Described. As preaching. 4:1-6
  Given. To preachers. 4:1-6

CONCEIT
  Meaning. 3:2-4

CONCEITED
  Meaning. 3:2-4

CONSCIENCE
  Duty. To have a clear c. 1:3

COURAGE - COURAGEOUS
  Failure in c. In standing with Paul. 4:16-18

COVENANTBREAKERS
  Discussed. 3:2-4

COVETOUS (See **LOVERS OF MONEY**)

CRESCENS
  Sent by Paul to minister. 4:10

CRITICISM - CRITICIZING (See **DIVISION**)
  Described as.
    Showing satanic enslavement. 2:24-26
    The snare of the devil. 2:24-26
  Nature. Is being enslaved by Satan. 2:24-26
  Source of. The devil. 2:24-26

CROWN OF RIGHTEOUSNESS
  Discussed. 4:8

DEATH
  Confronting - Facing. Reviewing one's life. 4:6-8
  Of believer.
    Delivered from d. Quicker than the blink of an eye (11/100 of a second). 4:18
    Never tastes d. 4:18
    Picture of. 4:6

DECEIVERS
  Duty. To guard against d. 3:13

DEMAS
  Discussed. Forsook Christ for the world. 4:9

DEPARTURE
  Meaning. 4:6

DESERTION
  Of Paul. By all believers when Paul was a prisoner. 1:15-18; 4:16

DESPITE - DESPISERS
  Discussed. 3:2-4

DISCIPLESHIP
  Discussed. 2:2

DISCIPLINE
  Duty.
    To d. like an Olympic athlete. 2:5
    To maintain military d. 2:3-4
    To work like a hard working farmer. 2:3-6
  Without d. Meaning. 3:2-4

DISOBEDIENCE
  To parents. Discussed. 3:2-4

DIVISION - DISSENSION (See **CRITICISM; JUDGING; UNITY**)
  Answer to d. Discussed. Four answers. 2:14-26
  Caused by. The devil. 2:24-26

DOCTRINE
  Duty. To preach sound doctrine. 4:2
  Rejected. Last days, people will reject sound d. 4:3-4
  Source. To be the Word of God. 3:14-17

ENCOURAGE
  Meaning. 4:2

END TIME
  Predictions. 3:1-17
  Signs of - Events.
    Eighteen signs. 3:2-4
    Godless vs. godly men. 3:1-17
    Godlessness. 3:2-4
    Perilous times. 3:1
    Powerless religion. Form of godliness, but deny the power. 3:5
    Will not endure sound doctrine. 4:3-4

ERASTUS
  Ministered in Corinth. 4:20

ETERNAL LIFE
  Assurance of. God preserves believer for eternal life. 4:18
  Fact.
    Are preserved eternally. 4:18
    To be transferred into. 4:18

EUBULUS
  Visited Paul in prison & knew Timothy. 4:21

EUNICE
  Grandmother of Timothy. 1:5

EVIL
  God delivers from. 4:16-18

EXHORT – EXHORTATION (See **ENCOURAGE**)

FALSE ACCUSERS (See **SLANDEROUS**)

FAMILY (See **CHILDREN; HUSBAND; MARRIAGE; WIFE**)
  Examples of. Strong faith. 1:5; 3:15
  Parents.
    To instill a strong faith in children. 1:5; 3:15
    To teach the Scriptures. 1:5; 3:15

FARMER
  Traits. Discussed. 2:6

FEAR
  Cause of.
    F. to witness. 1:7-8
    Persecution. 1:6-12
  Causes one to.
    Be ashamed, embarrassed. 1:7-8
    Be silent - failing to witness. 1:7-8
  Discussed. 1:6-12
  Duty. Not to fear. Reasons. 1:7
  Overcome by. God's power, hope, and of self-discipline. 1:7

FIERCE (See **BRUTAL**)

FOOLISH
  Discussed. 3:3

FOUNDATION
  Of God's building or church. Discussed. 2:19-21

GENTLE - GENTLENESS
  Meaning. 2:24-26

GIFTS, SPIRITUAL
  Described as. A trust - to hold on to. 1:14
  Duty.
    To hold on to. 1:14
    To stir up the g. of God. 1:6

GOD
  Faithfulness of. Even if one does not believe. 2:11-13
  Purpose.
    Discussed. 1:8-10
    Is eternal. 1:8-10

GODLESS
  Sign of end time. 3:2-4; 3:5

GODLINESS
  Sign of the end time. But deny the power. 3:5

GOSPEL
  Duty.
    Not to be ashamed of the g. 1:8
    To endure abuse for the g. 1:6-12

GRACE
  Discussed. 2:1

HATE - HATRED
  Discussed. 3:3

HAUGHTY (See **PROUD**)

HEADY (See **Rash**)

INDEX

HEAVEN (See **ETERNAL LIFE; IMMORTALITY; KINGDOM OF HEAVEN; RESURRECTION**)
  Believers.
    Are preserved for. 4:18
    Are to be transported into. 4:18

HEIRS (See **INHERITANCE**)

HERMOGENES
  Forsook Paul. 1:15

HIGHMINDED (See **CONCEITED**)

HOLY SPIRIT
  Work of. Enables the believer to hold fast. 1:13

HYMENAEUS
  Taught that the resurrection of believers had already passed. 2:16-18

INCONTINENT (See **SELF-CONTROL**)

INGRATITUDE (See **UNGRATEFUL**)

INSTANT
  In season, out of season. Meaning. 4:2

INTELLIGENCE
  Weakness of. 3:6-9

JESUS CHRIST
  Death. Purpose. 1:8-10
  Deity. Proven by the resurrection. 2:8
  Humanity. Born as a Man, of the seed of David. 2:8
  Resurrection.
    Duty toward. To be remembered. 2:8-13
    Effects upon believers. 2:8
    Power of. In believers. 2:8
  Return.
    Described. Glory of. 2:12-13
    Duty.
      To look for the blessed hope of Christ's return. 2:12-13
      To preach the Word. 4:2
    Results of. Eight **r**. 2:12-13
    Word "appearing" (epiphaneian). Meaning. 4:1
  Work of.
    Has abolished death. 1:8-10
    To give life and immortality. 1:8-10
    To stand with and strengthen believers. 4:16-18

KILL - KILLING
  Discussed. 3:1-4, esp. 3

KNOWLEDGE
  Weakness of. 3:6-9

LIFE
  Purpose of. To be committed to Christ & His mission. 3:10-11

LINUS
  Discussed. 4:19-22

LOIS
  Mother of Timothy. 1:5

LONGSUFFERING (See **PATIENCE**)

LOVE, SELF
  Discussed. 3:2-4

LOVE, WITHOUT
  Meaning. 3:2-4

LOVERS OF MONEY
  Meaning. 3:2-4

LUKE
  Only believer to stay with Paul in his final days. 4:11

LUSTS
  Duty. To flee youthful **l**. 2:22
  Meaning. 2:22

MAN
  Weakness & powerlessness of. Strength & self-sufficiency ends up in the grave. 2:1

MARK
  Paul asked for Mark to visit him when he was in prison. 4:11

MEDICINE
  Weakness of. 3:6-9

MIND
  Described. Self-discipline. Meaning. 1:7

MINISTERS
  Described as.
    Athlete. 2:5
    Farmer. 2:6
    Soldier. 2:3-4
  Discussed. Corrupt **m**. 3:6-9
  Duty.
    Fivefold duty. 1:6-12
    To avoid petty arguments & speculations. 2:14-21
    To be strong. 2:1-7
    To endure abuse for the gospel. 1:6-12
    To flee lusts & follow after the Lord. 2:22-26
    To fulfill the ministry—fill up to the brim. 4:5
    To have a clear conscience. 1:3
    To hold fast in three areas. 1:13-18
    To hold fast sound words, that is, the Word of God. 1:13
    To pray for disciples. 1:3
    To preach the Word. 4:1-5
    To remember the resurrected Lord. 4:16-18

MINISTERS, FALSE (See **TEACHERS, FALSE**)

MINISTRY - MINISTERING
  Duty. To hold fast one's trust, one's **m**. 1:14
  Example. Onesiphorus. **M**. to Paul while Paul was a prisoner. 1:15-18

MONEY
  Love of. Discussed. 3:2-4

MURDER
  Discussed. 3:2-4

NEEDS - NECESSITIES
  Times when help is needed. 4:9-18

OFFERING
  Meaning. 4:6

PARENTS
  Disobedience to. Discussed. 3:2-4
  Duty. To rear children in the Scriptures. 1:5; 3:15

PATIENCE
  Meaning. 3:10-11; 4:2

PAUL
  Call of.
    To be a preacher, apostle, & teacher. 1:11-12
    To be an apostle. 1:1
  Life.
    Eight traits. 3:10-13
    Senses his coming death. 4:6-8
    Triumphant at end of life. 4:6-8
  Ministry.
    Discipled young men. 1:2
    Final farewell of **P**. to the world. 4:6-8
    Glory of **P**.'s ministry. 1:1-5
    Unashamed of the gospel. 1:6-12
  Sufferings - Traits of.
    Deserted by all when imprisoned. 1:15-18
    Discussed. 3:11-12
  Testimony. Triumphant at end of life. 4:6-8

PERILOUS TIMES (See **TERRIBLE TIMES**)

PERSECUTION
  Duty.
    To endure for the gospel. 1:6-12; 3:11-12

PERSEVERANCE (See **ENDURANCE**
  Discussed. 1:13-18
  Duty. To **p**. for the gospel. 1:6-12
  Why **p**.
    Assures God's presence. 4:16-18
    Discussed. 2:8-13
    God stands by when others forsake. 4:16-18

PHILETUS
  Taught that the resurrection of believers had already taken place. 2:16-18

PHILOSOPHY (See **MIND**)
  Duty. To avoid speculations & petty arguments. 2:14-24; 2:23; 2:24-26

PHYGELLUS
  Forsook Paul. 1:15

PLEASURE
  Discussed. 3:2-4

PREACH - PREACHING
  Discussed. 4:1-5
  Duty - Compulsion. The charge to **p**. 4:1-5
  Meaning. 4:2
  Results. Triumphs. 4:6-8

PREACHER
  Meaning. 1:11-12

PRISCILLA
  Paul sent greetings to **P**. while a prisoner. 4:19

INDEX

PROFANE
Meaning. 3:2-4

PROUD
Meaning. 3:2-4

PSYCHOLOGY
Weakness of. 3:6-9

PUDENS
Visited Paul in prison & knew Timothy. 4:21

PURPOSE
In life. To be committed to Christ & His mission. 3:10-11

RASH
Meaning. 3:2-4

RATIONALISM
To avoid. Discussed. 2:14-21

REBUKE
Meaning. 4:2

RECKLESS (See **RASH**)

RELIGION
Discussed. R. in the last days. To be corrupt. 3:1-9
Problem with. Powerless. Form of godliness, but deny the power. 3:5
Weakness of. 3:6-9

REPROVE
Meaning. 4:2

REWARD
Described.
  Being transported to heaven. 4:18
  Crown of righteousness. 4:8

RIGHTEOUSNESS
Crown of. Discussed. 4:8
Results - Reward. A crown of r. 4:8

SACRIFICE
Meaning. 4:6

SALVATION
Source. Christ. 1:8-10

SATAN
Work - Strategy of. Snares, captures men. 2:26; cp. 22-26

SAVAGE – SAVAGERY (See **BRUTAL**)

SCIENCE
Weakness of. 3:6-9

SCRIPTURES
Discussed. 3:14-17; 3:16
Duty.
  To live & continue in the S. 3:14-17
  To preach. 4:2
  To rear children in S. 1:5
  To study. 2:15; 3:15-17
Effect - Work of. Enables the believer. 3:15-17
Inspiration. Discussed. 3:16
Purpose of. Discussed. 3:16

SECURITY (See **ASSURANCE**)
Source. God's knowledge. 2:19-21

SELF-CONTROL
Without self-control. Meaning. 3:2-4

SELF-CONTROL, WITHOUT
Meaning. 3:2-4, esp. 3

SELF-LOVE
Discussed. 3:2-4

SELFISHNESS
Discussed.
  A sign of a godless society. 3:2-4
  A sign of the end time. 3:2-4

SEPARATED - SEPARATION
Duty. Not to be entangled with the world. 2:3-4

SIN
Deliverance. God delivers believers from evil. 4:18
List of. In last days. Eighteen sins listed. 3:1-9

SLANDEROUS
Meaning. 3:2-4

SLANDERERS (See **ABUSIVE**)

SOLDIER
Traits. Discussed. 2:3-4

SPECULATIONS (See **TEACHERS, FALSE**)
Discussed. 2:14; 2:16-18; 2:23

SPORTS
Exhortations.
  Fight a good fight. 4:7
  Finish the course of life. 4:7
  Reward. Receives a crown. 4:8

STIR UP
Meaning. 1:6

STRENGTH (See **POWER**)
Source. Grace of Christ. 2:1

STRIFE
Discussed. 2:14; 2:16-18; 2:23

TEACH, APPOINTED TO
Meaning. 2:24-26

TEACHER (See **TEACHERS, FALSE; MINISTERS**)
Duty.
  Fivefold duty. 1:6-12
  To avoid petty arguments & speculations. 2:14-21
  To be strong. 2:1-7
  To endure abuse for the gospel. 1:6-12
  To flee lusts & follow after the Lord. 2:22-26
  To fulfill the ministry—fill up to the brim. 4:5
  To have a clear conscience. 1:3
  To hold fast in three areas. 1:13-18
Duty.
  To hold fast sound words, that is, the Word of God. 1:13
  To pray for disciples. 1:3
  To preach the Word. 4:1-5
  To remember the resurrected Lord. 4:16-18

Meaning. 1:11-12
Traits. Discussed. 2:2

TEACHERS, FALSE
Behavior.
  To go from bad to worse. 3:13
  Turn people away from the truth. 3:3-4
Characteristics - Marks. Discussed. 3:1-3; 3:13
Danger of. Disturb & destroy some. 2:14; 2:16-18
Discussed.
  Corrupt. 3:6-9
  Sign of the end time. 3:6-9

TEACHING
Duty. To be ready to teach. 2:24-26
Source. To be the Word of God. 3:10-13

TECHNOLOGY
Weakness of. 3:6-9

TERRIBLE TIMES
Meaning. 3:1

TESTIMONY
Example. Of Paul. Triumphant t. of Paul. 4:6-8
Mark of a godly t. 3:10-13

TITUS
Sent by Paul to minister. 4:10

TONGUE
Duty.
  To avoid petty arguments & speculations. 2:14-21
  To shun useless chatter. 2:16-18

TRAITORS
Discussed. 3:2-4

TROPHIMUS
Became sick & had to be left behind by Paul. 4:20

TRUCEBREAKERS
Meaning. 3:2-4

TYCHICUS
Sent by Paul to minister. 4:12

UNBELIEF
God is still faithful despite unbelief. 2:13

UNBELIEVERS
Discussed. Life without God. Eight traits. 3:3
Names - Titles. Impostors, deceivers. 3:13

UNGRATEFUL
Meaning. 3:2-4

UNHOLY
Meaning. 3:2-4

UNTHANKFUL (See **UNGRATEFUL**)

UNITY (See **BROTHERHOOD; DIVISION**)
Reasons for. Not arguing or striving over words and false doctrine. 2:14-26

INDEX

WITNESS - WITNESSING
  Duty. Not to be ashamed to **w**. 1:8; 1:8-10
  How to go.
    As an evangelist. 4:1-5
    Preaching the Word. 4:1-5
    Unashamed. 1:6-12

WORD OF GOD
  Duty.
    To study & rightly divide. 2:15
    To teach to a child. 1:5; 3:15
  Inspiration & purpose of. 3:16-17
  Nature of.
    Cannot be bound. 2:9
    Inspired. 3:16-17
  Power of. To save. Is not bound. 2:9
  Surety of. Nothing can stop. 2:9

WORDS (See **TONGUE**)
  Danger of. Discussed. 2:14-21
  Duty.
    To hold fast sound & healthy **w**. 1:13
    To preach. 4:1-5
  Rejected. In last days. 4:3-4

WORKS, LEGALISTIC (See **LAW; LIBERTY**)
  Danger. Believing one is saved because of **w**. 1:9
  Vs. salvation. 1:9

WORLD
  Deliverance from. Not to be entangled with. 2:3-4
  Described. As godless in the end time. 3:2-4
  Paul's final farewell to the **w**. 4:6-8; 4:9-22

YOUTH
  Discussed.
    Desires of. Normal & sinful **d**. 2:22
    Lusts of **y**. 2:22
  Duty. To flee youthful lusts & follow after Christ. 2:22-26

TITUS

TITUS

INTRODUCTION

AUTHOR: Paul, the Apostle.

DATE: Uncertain. Probably A.D. 64-66, some time after he wrote First Timothy. The books of *First Timothy* and *Titus* seem to have been written while Paul was traveling and ministering between two Roman imprisonments. The date depends upon the answer to this question: Did Paul suffer one or two Roman imprisonments? The book of Acts mentions only one imprisonment and closes with Paul in prison in Rome. It says nothing about his death. As one discusses this question, one major thing needs to be kept in mind. Paul prayed fervently that God would release him from prison. And he asked others to pray fervently for his release (Ph.1:25-26; Phile.22). Did God answer his prayer as requested? No one knows for sure. However, several factors point rather decisively to his being released and later suffering a second imprisonment.

1. The Life and Movements of Paul. Paul says in Tit.1:5 that he had been to Crete on a mission tour. And in Tit.3:12 he says that he was spending the winter in Nicopolis. These events do not fit in with any of the accounts in *Acts*. The evidence seems to be that God answered his prayer and had him released from prison.

2. The Life and Movements of Paul's Companions. Note the following two examples, and there are others. In 1 Tim.1:3 Paul says that he told Timothy to stay in Ephesus. But there is no record of this event in Scripture. Paul had made only two visits to Ephesus. One was a very short visit with little, if any, ministry. There is no mention whatsoever about Timothy (Acts 18:19-22). The second was his three year ministry in which Timothy had a part. But when it came time for Paul to move on, he sent Timothy and Erastus to Macedonia. He did not ask Timothy to stay in Ephesus. When then did Paul tell Timothy to stay in Ephesus? There just is no record of such a visit in Scripture. Thus all indications point to a third visit by Paul and Timothy—a visit after his first imprisonment and before an unrecorded second imprisonment.

Again, in 2 Tim.4:20 Paul writes, "I left Trophimus sick in Miletus." Paul was in Miletus before his first Roman imprisonment, but he did not leave Trophimus there sick (Acts 20:17). Trophimus went on to Rome with Paul (Acts 21:29). When then was Trophimus left at Miletus sick? The only clear answer seems to be that Paul made another visit to Miletus—after his first imprisonment and right before a second unrecorded imprisonment.

3. The Time Sequence Between the Writing of the Prison Epistles and the Pastoral Epistles. The Prison Epistles (*Ephesians, Philippians, Colossians,* and *Philemon*) were written while Paul was in prison in Rome. He says so in each epistle. Note the following example: Philemon 24 says that Demas is a follower of Christ, but 2 Tim.4:10 says that he had deserted. The letter to Timothy was definitely written after the prison letter to Philemon. When? The evidence points toward a time after his first imprisonment and before a second unrecorded imprisonment. This seems to be the only clear explanation.

As stated above, *1 Timothy* and *Titus* seem to have been written right after Paul had been released from his first imprisonment in Rome and was traveling about ministering. At some point in those few years he was rearrested and imprisoned in Rome for a second time. During this second imprisonment he wrote Second Timothy before he was executed. His execution was probably between A.D. 65-68.

TO WHOM WRITTEN: "To Titus, mine true son in our common faith" (Tit.1:4). These facts are known about Titus.

⇒ He was a Gentile, a Greek (Gal.2:3).
⇒ He was led to Christ by Paul (Tit.1:4).
⇒ His conversion was such a testimony that he was personally used as an example of God's work among the Gentiles before the Jerusalem Council (Gal.2:12f).
⇒ He became a missionary partner to Paul and served with Paul for the last fifteen years of Paul's life (2 Cor.7:6-16; 8:16f; 2 Cor.2:13; 7:6, 13; 8:23; 12:18; 2 Tim.4:10).
⇒ He apparently served with Paul in Ephesus and was sent by Paul to Corinth: sent to deliver the Second Epistle to the Corinthians from Paul and to help the church straighten out the divisions within the church (2 Cor.8:6).
⇒ He was in charge of the churches on the island of Crete (Tit.1:5). Crete was one of the most difficult mission fields in the ancient world. Its people had one of the worst reputations imaginable—so much so that the very name *Cretian* was used as a byword, "to cretize." "To cretize" meant that a person was a cheat and a liar. The Cretians were "famed as a drunken, insolent, untrustworthy, lying, gluttonous people" (William Barclay. *The Letters to Timothy, Titus, and Philemon*, p.277).
⇒ He was with Paul for a while when Paul was in prison in Rome (2 Tim.4:10).
⇒ The last word about *Titus* is that he was sent by Paul to minister in Dalmatia or what was once called Yugoslavia or Serbia (2 Tim.4:17)

PURPOSE: Paul had three purposes for writing *Titus*.

1. To warn against false teachers.
2. To set in order the organization of the churches and the behavior of the believers (Tit.1:5).
3. To encourage Titus to proclaim the message of sound doctrine.

SPECIAL FEATURES:

1. *Titus* is "A Pastoral Epistle." There are two other Pastoral Epistles: First and Second Timothy. They are called Pastoral Epistles because they deal primarily with the pastoral care, oversight, and organization of the church. They tell believers how they ought to behave in the house of God (1 Tim.3:15). Interestingly, the term *pastoral* has a long history. It was first used by Thomas Aquinas in A.D. 1274. He called First Timothy "an epistle of pastoral rule" and 2 Timothy "an epistle of pastoral care." The term "Pastoral Epistles," however, began to be widely used only after D.N. Berdot (A.D. 1703) and Paul Anton (A.D. 1726) so described them (Donald Guthrie. *The Pastoral Epistles*, p.11).

2. *Titus* is "A Personal Epistle." It was written to a young disciple who was loved as a son. The epistle is filled with feelings of warmth and affection and filled with instructions that were to govern Titus' personal behavior.

3. *Titus* is "An Ecclesiastical Epistle." It was written to answer questions about church organization, doctrinal purity, and personal behavior. Two things were happening. First, the number and sizes of churches were growing rapidly, and second, the apostles were aging. In both cases the apostles were just unable to personally reach and instruct all the churches; therefore, they had to write if the churches were to be properly instructed.

4. *Titus* is "An Apologetic Epistle." It is a defense of the faith. The first rumblings and early development of false teaching had just begun to appear (Gnosticism. See Colossians, Introductory Notes, Purpose.) Therefore, Paul warns the believers and defends the truth against heretical and false teaching.

OUTLINE OF TITUS

THE PREACHER'S OUTLINE & SERMON BIBLE® is *unique*. It differs from all other Study Bibles & Sermon Resource Materials in that every Passage and Subject is outlined right beside the Scripture. When you choose any *Subject* below and turn to the reference, you have not only the Scripture, but you discover the Scripture and Subject *already outlined for you—verse by verse*.

For a quick example, choose one of the subjects below and turn over to the Scripture, and you will find this marvelous help for faster, easier, and more accurate use.

In addition, every point of the Scripture and Subject is *fully developed in a Commentary with supporting Scripture* at the bottom of the page. Again, this arrangement makes sermon preparation much easier and faster.

Note something else: The Subjects of Titus have titles that are both Biblical and *practical*. The practical titles sometimes have more appeal to people. This *benefit* is clearly seen for use on billboards, bulletins, church newsletters, etc.

A suggestion: For the quickest overview of *Titus*, first read *all the major titles* (I, II, III, etc.), then come back and read the subtitles.

OUTLINE OF TITUS

GREETING: THE MINISTRY OF GOD'S SERVANT, 1:1-4

I. **THE TRUE AND FALSE CHURCH OFFICIALS, 1:5-16**

   A. The True Elders or Ministers, 1:5-9
   B. The Contrasting False Teachers, 1:10-16

II. **THE MESSAGE OF SOUND DOCTRINE, 2:1-3:11**

   A. Message 1: The Behavior of Believers, 2:1-10
   B. Message 2: The Grace of God, 2:11-15
   C. Message 3: The Civic Duties of Believers, 3:1-2
   D. Message 4: Life Without God, 3:3
   E. Message 5: Life With God—Salvation, 3:4-7
   F. Message 6: The Warning to Believers, 3:8-11

III. **THE CONCLUDING REMARKS: SOME COMMITTED CHRISTIAN BELIEVERS, 3:12-15**

TITUS

CHAPTER 1

GREETING: THE MINISTRY OF GOD'S SERVANT, 1:1-4

1. His great call
2. His purpose: To stir believers
   a. In their faith
   b. In the knowledge of the truth
3. His message: The hope of eternal life
   a. Promised by God
   b. Revealed in God's Word through preaching
   c. Entrusted into the hands of Paul & other believers.
   d. Promised by God our Savior
4. His reward: Bearing sons in the faith

Paul, a servant of God and an apostle of Jesus Christ for the faith of God's elect and the knowledge of the truth that leads to godliness—
2 A faith and knowledge resting on the hope of eternal life, which God, who does not lie, promised before the beginning of time,
3 And at his appointed season he brought his word to light through the preaching entrusted to me by the command of God our Savior,
4 To Titus, my true son in our common faith: Grace and peace from God the Father and Christ Jesus our Savior.

GREETING: THE MINISTRY OF GOD'S SERVANT, 1:1-4

(1:1-4) **Introduction**: Paul always declared his relationship to God and the Lord Jesus Christ when writing a letter. He wanted no question about who he was nor about what his purpose was. He was focused upon Christ and His glorious gospel that offered eternal life to men. From the first to the last, Paul was the servant of God and the messenger of the Lord Jesus Christ. This is the purpose of these introductory words to Titus: to declare that he is God's servant. This is an excellent passage on the ministry of God's servant.

1. His great call (v.1).
2. His purpose: to stir believers (v.1).
3. His message: the hope of eternal life (v.2-3).
4. His reward: bearing sons in the faith (v.4).

1 (1:1) **Slave—Apostle—Paul**: God's servant receives the greatest of calls. God's true servant is called to be a slave of God and an apostle or messenger of Jesus Christ. Note two striking points.

1. Paul says that he was *a slave of God*. This is striking, for the last thing that a person wants to be is a slave to anybody. Yet this is exactly what Paul claimed. In fact, he proudly declared that he was the slave of God. What did Paul mean?

   a. He meant that he was totally possessed by God. God had looked upon Paul and seen his degraded and needful condition; God had seen Paul in the slave-market of the world, held in bondage by sin and death, the trouble and trials of life. And God was moved with compassion toward Paul; therefore, God *bought and purchased* Paul. Paul was now the slave of God—totally possessed by God.

   b. He meant that his will belonged totally to God. He was completely subservient to God and owed total allegiance to the will of God. As Kenneth Wuest says, "His will was swallowed up in the sweet will of God" (*The Pastoral Epistles*, Vol.2, p.181).

   c. He meant that he had the highest and most honored and kingly profession in all the world. Men of God, the greatest men of history, have always been called "the servants of God." It was the highest title of honor. The believer's slavery to God is no cringing, cowardly, or shameful subjection. It is the position of honor—the honor that bestows upon a man the privileges and responsibilities of serving the King of kings and Lord of lords.

   ⇒ Moses was the slave of God (Dt.34:5; Ps.105:26; Mal.4:4).
   ⇒ Joshua was the slave of God (Josh.5:14).
   ⇒ David was the slave of God (2 Sam.3:18; Ps.78:70).
   ⇒ Paul was the slave of God (Ro.1:1; Ph.1:1; Tit.1:1).
   ⇒ James was the slave of God (Jas.1:1).
   ⇒ Jude was the slave of God (Jude 1).
   ⇒ The prophets were the slaves of God (Amos 3:7; Jer.7:25).
   ⇒ Christian believers are said to be the slaves of Jesus Christ (Acts 2:18; 1 Cor.7:22; Eph.6:6; Col.4:12; 2 Tim.2:24).

Thought 1. The great need today is for men and women to become *slaves* of the Lord Jesus Christ. We must become His slaves and do what He says. Then and only then will the world be reached with the glorious news of eternal life. Then and only then will the desperate needs of the world be met.

> Whoever serves me must follow me; and where I am, my servant also will be. My Father will honor the one who serves me. (John 12:26; cp. Ro.12:1; 1 Cor.15:58)
>
> Obey them not only to win their favor when their eye is on you, but like slaves of Christ, doing the will of God from your heart. Serve [laboring] wholeheartedly, as if you were serving the Lord, not men, (Eph 6:6-7)
>
> Whatever you do, work at it with all your heart, as working for the Lord, not for men, since you know that you will receive an inheritance from the Lord as a reward. It is the Lord Christ you are serving. (Col 3:23-24)
>
> Therefore, since we are receiving a kingdom that cannot be shaken, let us be thankful, and so worship God acceptably with reverence and awe, (Heb 12:28)
>
> Worship the LORD your God, (Exo 23:25)
>
> And now, O Israel, what does the LORD your God ask of you but to fear the LORD your God, to walk in all his ways, to love him, to serve the LORD your God with all your heart and with all your soul, (Deu 10:12)

TITUS 1:1-4

> Serve the LORD with fear and rejoice with trembling. (Psa 2:11)
> Worship the LORD with gladness; come before him with joyful songs. (Psa 100:2)

2. Paul says that he was an apostle of Jesus Christ. The word "apostle" means a person who is sent out or sent forth. An apostle is a representative, an ambassador, an envoy, a person who is sent out into one country to represent another country. Three things are true of the apostle:

⇒ he belongs to the king or country who sends him out.
⇒ he is commissioned to be sent out.
⇒ he possesses all the authority and power of the person who sends him out.

Thought 1. The very same things are true of any minister or teacher of Christ: the minister or teacher is the representative, ambassador, envoy, and messenger of Jesus Christ and only of Jesus Christ. As William Barclay says:

> "The man who preaches the gospel of Christ or teaches the truth of Christ, if he is a truly dedicated soul, does not talk about his own opinions, or offer his own conclusions; he comes with the message of Christ and with the word of God. The true envoy of Christ has reached past the stage of perhapses and maybes and possiblys, and speaks with the accent of the certainty and the authority of one who knows" (*The Letters to Timothy, Titus, and Philemon*, p.260).

> You did not choose me, but I chose you and appointed you to go and bear fruit—fruit that will last. Then the Father will give you whatever you ask in my name. (John 15:16)
> We are therefore Christ's ambassadors, as though God were making his appeal through us. We implore you on Christ's behalf: Be reconciled to God. (2 Cor 5:20)
> Paul, an apostle—sent not from men nor by man, but by Jesus Christ and God the Father, who raised him from the dead— (Gal 1:1)
> I want you to know, brothers, that the gospel I preached is not something that man made up. I did not receive it from any man, nor was I taught it; rather, I received it by revelation from Jesus Christ. (Gal 1:11-12)
> I desire to do your will, O my God; your law is within my heart." (Psa 40:8)
> Then I heard the voice of the Lord saying, "Whom shall I send? And who will go for us?" And I said, "Here am I. Send me!" (Isa 6:8)

2 (1:1) **Minister, Purpose—Faith—Truth**: the purpose of God's servant is to stir believers. Note that believers are called "God's elect." They are the persons whom God has chosen to be His "holy and beloved" people.

⇒ Believers have been elected to be *holy*. The word "holy" (hagios) means separated or set apart. God called believers out of the world and away from the old life it offered, the old life of sin and death. He called believers to be separated and set apart unto Himself and the new life He offers, the new life of righteous-ness and eternity.

⇒ Believers have been elected to be the *beloved* of God. God has called believers to turn away from the old life that showed hatred toward God, the old life that rejected, rebelled, ignored, denied, and was constantly cursing in the face of God. God has called believers to be the beloved of God, the persons who receive His love in Christ Jesus and who allow Him to shower His love upon them.

Very simply stated, the elect of God, the holy and beloved of God, are those who have really believed and trusted Jesus Christ as their Savior. It is these persons, the believers, who really have faith in God and acknowledge the truth which leads to godliness.

The point is this: the servant of God builds upon the faith of believers. He and they both believe in God and have committed their lives to the Lord Jesus Christ. Therefore, his whole purpose for existing is twofold.

1. The servant of God stirs believers to have more and more faith in God. He stirs them to build their faith—to increase it—to grow more and more in their trust of God and of Christ. He labors day and night to turn men to Christ and to stir them to trust Him. He knows that their only hope to overcome the sin and death of this world is to trust Christ; therefore, He does all he can—laboring day and night—to teach them to trust His death and resurrection to deliver them.

> Then they asked him, "What must we do to do the works God requires?" Jesus answered, "The work of God is this: to believe in the one he has sent." (John 6:28-29)
> In addition to all this, take up the shield of faith, with which you can extinguish all the flaming arrows of the evil one. (Eph 6:16)
> And without faith it is impossible to please God, because anyone who comes to him must believe that he exists and that he rewards those who earnestly seek him. (Heb 11:6)
> And this is his command: to believe in the name of his Son, Jesus Christ, and to love one another as he commanded us. (1 John 3:23)
> For everyone born of God overcomes the world. This is the victory that has overcome the world, even our faith. Who is it that overcomes the world? Only he who believes that Jesus is the Son of God. (1 John 5:4-5)
> Early in the morning they left for the Desert of Tekoa. As they set out, Jehoshaphat stood and said, "Listen to me, Judah and people of Jerusalem! Have faith in the LORD your God and you will be upheld; have faith in his prophets and you will be successful." (2 Chr 20:20)

TITUS 1:1-4

2. The servant of God stirs believers to acknowledge the truth; that is, he stirs them to grow in the knowledge of the truth: to study the truth; to learn it, and to practice it. Note why. Because of godliness. Godliness is to be the end, the very reason why we are to learn the truth. We are to live godly lives. God wants His people to be godly, that is, to be like Him; to live like He lives. We shall be with Him eternally—living face to face with Him—conformed to His godly nature. Therefore, He wants us to live like Him now—to live godly, holy, and righteous lives. He wants us to show the world that He is real—show them by letting His godliness live itself out in our lives.

> **Since we have these promises, dear friends, let us purify ourselves from everything that contaminates body and spirit, perfecting holiness out of reverence for God. (2 Cor 7:1)**
>
> Have nothing to do with godless myths and old wives' tales; rather, train yourself to be godly. (1 Tim 4:7)
>
> But you, man of God, flee from all this, and pursue righteousness, godliness, faith, love, endurance and gentleness. (1 Tim 6:11)
>
> It teaches us to say "No" to ungodliness and worldly passions, and to live self-controlled, upright and godly lives in this present age while we wait for the blessed hope—the glorious appearing of our great God and Savior, Jesus Christ, (Titus 2:12-13)
>
> Make every effort to live in peace with all men and to be holy; without holiness no one will see the Lord. (Heb 12:14)
>
> For it is written: "Be holy, because I am holy." (1 Pet 1:16)
>
> Since everything will be destroyed in this way, what kind of people ought you to be? You ought to live holy and godly lives (2 Pet 3:11)

3 (1:2-3) **Ministers, Motivation—Eternal life—Word of God**: the message of God's servant is the hope of eternal life. Unbelievable! Too good to be true! Yet it is true. There is eternal life. The glorious message of God's servant is nothing less than the message of deliverance from death—of living forever and ever. Note four points.

1. First, the hope of eternal life has been promised by God Himself. There are two reasons.
   a. God cannot lie. God cannot lie because of His perfect nature. Think about these facts for a moment.
      ⇒ God's nature is perfect love and love does not lie. God loves perfectly; therefore, He always tells the truth. He has promised us eternal life because He loves us, because He is the God of love and truth; therefore, we shall receive eternal life. We shall live with Him forever and ever.
      ⇒ God's nature is perfect morality and righteousness. Morality and righteousness do not lie. A moral and righteous person tells the truth. And just think: God is perfect; therefore, He is always moral and righteous. He can never be immoral by deceiving nor be unrighteous by lying. Therefore, we shall receive eternal life—live forever just as He has promised.
      ⇒ God's nature is perfect truth. Once He speaks He has spoken, and it shall be so. His Word can never be anything but what has been spoken. Therefore, when God promised eternal life to those who believe, then all who believe shall live forever.
   b. God gave the promise of eternal life before the world began. Eternal life was His very purpose for creating man. Therefore when He created man, He purposed that every person who believed in Him—who truly believed in Him—would live with Him eternally. God cannot lie; therefore, what He promised before the world began WILL BE. If we truly believe in God's Son, the Lord Jesus Christ, we shall live forever and ever.

> He is the Rock, his works are perfect, and all his ways are just. A faithful God who does no wrong, upright and just is he. (Deu 32:4)
>
> O Sovereign LORD, you are God! Your words are trustworthy, and you have promised these good things to your servant. (2 Sam 7:28)
>
> For the word of the LORD is right and true; he is faithful in all he does. (Psa 33:4)
>
> The Maker of heaven and earth, the sea, and everything in them— the LORD, who remains faithful forever. (Psa 146:6)
>
> Not at all! Let God be true, and every man a liar. As it is written: "So that you may be proved right when you speak and prevail when you judge." (Rom 3:4)
>
> God did this so that, by two unchangeable things in which it is impossible for God to lie, we who have fled to take hold of the hope offered to us may be greatly encouraged. (Heb 6:18)

2. Second, the hope of eternal life was revealed in God's Word—revealed through preaching. God has given man a record of His promise—a record of eternal life. Where? Where can man find this record? In God's Word and in the preaching of God's Word. God has recorded forever the glorious message of eternal life in His Word and in the preaching of His Word. As long as the earth stands His Word will stand, and some believers will be preaching the glorious message of eternal life. Therefore, if a person wants to find the record of eternal life, he must not go to the records of men, but to the Word of God and to the preaching of that Word.

> **Anyone who believes in the Son of God has this testimony in his heart. Anyone who does not believe God has made him out to be a liar, because he has not believed the testimony God has given about his Son. And this is the testimony: God has given us eternal life, and this life is in his Son. He who has the Son has life; he who does not have the Son of God does not have life. I write these things to you who believe in the name of the Son of God so that you may know that you have eternal life. (1 John 5:10-13)**

> "I tell you the truth, whoever hears my word and believes him who sent me has eternal life and will not be condemned; he has crossed over from death to life. (John 5:24)
>
> You know the message God sent to the people of Israel, telling the good news of peace through Jesus Christ, who is Lord of all. (Acts 10:36)
>
> For we do not preach ourselves, but Jesus Christ as Lord, and ourselves as your servants for Jesus' sake. (2 Cor 4:5)

3. The hope of eternal life has been entrusted into the hands of Paul and to all other believers—to all the servants and ministers of God. Note exactly what this verse says: God's Word and the preaching of God's Word have been entrusted to men by the command of God. God's Word and the preaching of His Word are not an option. God commands that we take care of His Word and that we preach it—all believers—all the servants and ministers of God. The message of eternal life is to be proclaimed.

> Therefore go and make disciples of all nations, baptizing them in the name of the Father and of the Son and of the Holy Spirit, and teaching them to obey everything I have commanded you. And surely I am with you always, to the very end of the age." (Mat 28:19-20)
>
> He said to them, "Go into all the world and preach the good news to all creation. (Mark 16:15)
>
> Again Jesus said, "Peace be with you! As the Father has sent me, I am sending you." (John 20:21)
>
> I have become its servant by the commission God gave me to present to you the word of God in its fullness— (Col 1:25)
>
> On the contrary, we speak as men approved by God to be entrusted with the gospel. We are not trying to please men but God, who tests our hearts. You know we never used flattery, nor did we put on a mask to cover up greed—God is our witness. (1 Th 2:4-5)
>
> That conforms to the glorious gospel of the blessed God, which he entrusted to me. I thank Christ Jesus our Lord, who has given me strength, that he considered me faithful, appointing me to his service. (1 Tim 1:11-12)
>
> And at his appointed season he brought his word to light through the preaching entrusted to me by the command of God our Savior, (Titus 1:3)

4. The hope of eternal life has been promised by God our Savior. It is God the Father, as well as Christ, who loves and saves us. Therefore, we never have to die. God delivers us from sin, death, and judgment to come. The point to see is that God is not like He is sometimes pictured.

⇒ God is not way off in space someplace, unconcerned and disinterested in the world and trials of men. Neither is God stern and severe, always looking over the shoulders of men just waiting to punish them when they go astray and do something wrong. God is not a hovering Judge, filled with anger and madness at men. God is love; God is our Savior and He longs to save us—to give us eternal life.

> And my spirit rejoices in God my Savior, (Luke 1:47)
>
> This is good, and pleases God our Savior, who wants all men to be saved and to come to a knowledge of the truth. For there is one God and one mediator between God and men, the man Christ Jesus, who gave himself as a ransom for all men—the testimony given in its proper time. (1 Tim 2:3-6)
>
> (And for this we labor and strive), that we have put our hope in the living God, who is the Savior of all men, and especially of those who believe. (1 Tim 4:10)
>
> A faith and knowledge resting on the hope of eternal life, which God, who does not lie, promised before the beginning of time, and at his appointed season he brought his word to light through the preaching entrusted to me by the command of God our Savior, (Titus 1:2-3)
>
> But when the kindness and love of God our Savior appeared, he saved us, not because of righteous things we had done, but because of his mercy. He saved us through the washing of rebirth and renewal by the Holy Spirit, whom he poured out on us generously through Jesus Christ our Savior, so that, having been justified by his grace, we might become heirs having the hope of eternal life. (Titus 3:4-7)
>
> To the only God our Savior be glory, majesty, power and authority, through Jesus Christ our Lord, before all ages, now and forevermore! Amen. (Jude 1:25)
>
> Surely God is my salvation; I will trust and not be afraid. The LORD, the LORD, is my strength and my song; he has become my salvation." (Isa 12:2)
>
> In that day they will say, "Surely this is our God; we trusted in him, and he saved us. This is the LORD, we trusted in him; let us rejoice and be glad in his salvation." (Isa 25:9)

4 (1:4) **Minister**: the reward of God's servant is that of fruit, of bearing others in the faith. Titus was a spiritual son of Paul; that is, Paul had apparently led Titus to the Lord. (See Introduction, *Author*—for discussion on Titus.) Note the phrase "common faith." Titus believed in the Lord Jesus Christ just as Paul did. His faith was common to Paul's; it was placed in the same Person—in the Lord Jesus Christ. The point is powerful: *the common faith* in Christ is the faith that brings eternal life to all believers. All persons who believe in Christ have one thing in common: their faith. Therefore, they are the ones who shall live eternally.

The point is this: a true servant of God will bear fruit; he will bear sons and daughters in the faith. This is part of their reward: to see others trust Christ Jesus as their Savior and grow in the grace and peace of God and Christ. Note these terms.

⇒ Grace (see Deeper Study # 1, *Grace*—Tit.2:11-15 for discussion).
⇒ Peace (see note, *Peace*—1 Tim.1:2 for discussion).

While walking upon earth, a servant of God can have no greater reward than to see others receive Christ and grow spiritually.

> Therefore go and make disciples of all nations, baptizing them in the name of the Father and of the Son and of the Holy Spirit, and teaching them to obey everything I have commanded you. And surely I am with you always, to the very end of the age." (Mat 28:19-20)
>
> It was he who gave some to be apostles, some to be prophets, some to be evangelists, and some to be pastors and teachers, to prepare God's people for works of service, so that the body of Christ may be built up (Eph 4:11-12)
>
> And the things you have heard me say in the presence of many witnesses entrust to reliable men who will also be qualified to teach others. (2 Tim 2:2)

TITUS 1:5-9

	I. THE TRUE & FALSE CHURCH OFFICIALS, 1:5-16	disobedient. 7 Since an overseer is entrusted with God's work, he must be blameless—not overbearing, not quick-tempered, not given to drunkenness, not violent, not pursuing dishonest gain. 8 Rather he must be hospitable, one who loves what is good, who is self-controlled, upright, holy and disciplined. 9 He must hold firmly to the trustworthy message as it has been taught, so that he can encourage others by sound doctrine and refute those who oppose it.	**3 His personal qualifications** a. What he is: The overseer or steward of God b. What he is not to be c. What he is to be **4 His preaching qualifications** a. Holding firm to the Word b. Reason: He must encourage & correct
	A. The True Elders or Ministers,^{DS1} **1:5-9**		
1 Two critical needs in the church a. To straighten out things b. To appoint elders **2 His family qualifications**	5 The reason I left you in Crete was that you might straighten out what was left unfinished and appoint elders in every town, as I directed you. 6 An elder must be blameless, the husband of but one wife, a man whose children believe and are not open to the charge of being wild and		

DIVISION I

THE TRUE AND FALSE CHURCH OFFICIALS, 1:5-16

A. The True Elders or Ministers, 1:5-9

(1:5-9) **Introduction**: this passage is a strong picture of the office-holder in the church—just what the office-holder should be and do. It spells out in no uncertain terms the qualifications of the elder (overseer or minister, whatever the title is that he is known by).

1. Two critical needs in the church (v.5).
2. His family qualifications (v.6).
3. His personal qualifications (v.7-8).
4. His preaching qualifications (v.9).

DEEPER STUDY # 1
(1:5-9) **Elder (presbuteros)—Overseer (episkopos)**: note the terms elder and overseer are used interchangeably in this passage (v.5, 7). (See outline and notes—1 Tim.3:1-7 for more discussion.) The elder or overseer was probably the same office as the pastor-teacher or minister of a church. The gift of pastor-teacher refers to only one gift which is given to the same person (Eph.4:11). The focus of the gift is to *pastor, oversee*, and *shepherd* believers in the local church. William Barclay points out that elder was more of a Jewish name and overseer was more of a Greek name, each referring to the same office (*The Letters to Timothy, Titus, and Philemon*, p.80-81). The word *elder* was used to refer to the man, to his standing, to his years of faithfulness and service. The word overseer (episkopas) and the gift *pastor-teacher* were used to refer to the man's duties and his work of overseeing and supervising the church. In comparison, a man today is often called minister, pastor, preacher, or reverend. Usually reverend is used to refer to the man personally and minister, pastor, or preacher is used to refer to the man's functions.

The pastoral gift is the gift that is directly ascribed to the Lord Jesus. He called Himself the Good Shepherd (Jn.10:11, 14). Others called Him the Great Shepherd of the sheep (Heb.13:20), the Shepherd of men's souls (1 Pt.2:25), and the Chief Shepherd (1 Pt.5:4). The pastoral gift is an ordained office; the elder is the basic office of the church.

1. Elders are called and set apart by the Holy Spirit (Acts 20:28; 13:2).
2. Elders are ordained officers (Acts 14:23; Tit.1:5).
3. Elders shepherd and oversee the flock of God (Acts 20:28-29; 1 Pt.5:2-3).
4. Elders are to guard and preach the Word (Tit.1:9).
5. Elders have a healing ministry through prayers and the anointing with oil (Jas.5:14).
6. Elders took a leading part in the decisions of the Jerusalem Council. They are identified along with the apostles as the chief authorities of the church (Acts 15:2; 16:4).
7. Elders are the ones to whom Paul reports when returning from his third missionary journey, and they are the ones who advise him how to combat the Judaizers (Acts 21:18-25).
8. Elders are the ones to whom Paul delivers the offering that had been taken for the Jerusalem Church during the great famine (Acts 11:30).

1 (1:5) **Church, Needs**: two critical needs exist in the church. Note: the church in Crete had these two needs. Crete was an island in the Mediterranean Sea, an island with many cities. William Barclay quotes Homer as calling the island, "Crete of the hundred cities" (*The Letters to Timothy, Titus, and Philemon*, p.268). No doubt, Paul had led people to Christ all over the island in city after city, and had established churches in the cities in which the converts lived. However, he had left to carry on the work of evangelism, but he had left Titus behind to root and ground the church in Christ. Paul spells out two critical needs of the churches, two needs that exist in every church.

1. There was the need to straighten out the things that are *defective and left unfinished*. This refers to all that Paul covers in the letter to Titus:

⇒ How to set up true officials in the church and how to deal with false teachers (Tit.1:5-16).
⇒ How men and women in the church are to live and behave (Tit.2:1-3:11).

Thought 1. No matter the church, there are still some defects and some things to be done. Every church still has a long way to go before it reaches the full stature of what it should be before its Lord. But even more than this, tragically too many churches have two serious defects and flaws: they are not adequately organized for ministry and they have allowed false teaching in their ranks. As a result they are not reaching people for Christ and, in some cases, they are facing terrible division and splits and destruction of their testimony.

The point is this: the very need of a church is to set in order the things that are defective and left undone. A church must be constantly growing in Christ or else it begins to slip back and to lose its message of eternal life for mankind.

2. There was the need to appoint elders in every city. The term *elder* refers to the minister of the church. No church, no matter how small, should remain without a minister for too long. This was the concern of Paul for the churches in Crete, and it should be our concern. One of the two critical needs of a church is for committed ministers who love the Lord with all their heart. (See DEEPER STUDY #1, *Elder*—Tit.1:5-9 for more discussion.)

2 (1:6) **Elder—Minister—Overseer**: the minister or elder of a church must be qualified. He must meet some family qualifications.

1. The minister or elder must be blameless (see note, pt.1—1 Tim.3:2-3 for discussion).

> Everyone has heard about your obedience, so I am full of joy over you; but I want you to be wise about what is good, and innocent about what is evil. (Rom 16:19)
>
> So that you may be able to discern what is best and may be pure and blameless until the day of Christ, (Phil 1:10)
>
> So that you may become blameless and pure, children of God without fault in a crooked and depraved generation, in which you shine like stars in the universe (Phil 2:15)
>
> The Lord will rescue me from every evil attack and will bring me safely to his heavenly kingdom. To him be glory for ever and ever. Amen. (2 Tim 4:18)
>
> Such a high priest meets our need—one who is holy, blameless, pure, set apart from sinners, exalted above the heavens. (Heb 7:26)
>
> To him who is able to keep you from falling and to present you before his glorious presence without fault and with great joy— (Jude 1:24)

2. The minister or elder must be the husband of one wife (see note, pt.2—1 Tim.3:2-3 for discussion).

> "Haven't you read," he replied, "that at the beginning the Creator 'made them male and female,' and said, 'For this reason a man will leave his father and mother and be united to his wife, and the two will become one flesh'? So they are no longer two, but one. Therefore what God has joined together, let man not separate." (Mat 19:4-6)
>
> Now the overseer must be above reproach, the husband of but one wife, temperate, self-controlled, respectable, hospitable, able to teach, (1 Tim 3:2)
>
> An elder must be blameless, the husband of but one wife. (Titus 1:6)
>
> He must not take many wives, or his heart will be led astray. He must not accumulate large amounts of silver and gold. (Deu 17:17)

3. The minister or elder must have children who believe. By this is meant believing in the Lord Jesus Christ and remaining faithful to Him. The minister's children are to be above reproach; they are not to be "loose in morals and conduct or unruly and disorderly" (Amplified New Testament).

William Barclay gives an excellent description of this point:

> *"The family of the elder must not be undisciplined. Nothing can made up for the lack of parental control. The training of children is ultimately in the hands of the parent"* (*The Letters to Timothy, Titus, and Philemon*, p.268f).

Oliver Greene also gives an excellent picture of what Scripture is saying about the minister and his children:

> "What Paul is saying here is that an elder or bishop must have a well-governed family, a family which fully respects him, a family well trained in spiritual matters. If the family of a bishop were insubordinate and opposed to spiritual matters, or if members of the family were unbelievers or scoffers, that man could not be entrusted with the government of the church of the living God.
>
> "It is clearly set forth here that an elder or bishop must be a family man, with a wife and children who respect him to the fullest degree. His family must be spiritually minded; they must love the church and the things of God and cooperate with the head of the family in all things. If a man cannot rule his own house and lead his own family concerning spiritual matters, how could he direct the church? If he were a man who did not have the respect of his family, he could not hope to have the respect of the church" (*The Epistles of Paul the Apostle to Timothy and Titus*, p.415).

> So then, let us not be like others, who are asleep, but let us be alert and self-controlled. For those who sleep, sleep at night, and those who get drunk, get drunk at night. But since we belong to the day, let us be self-controlled, putting on faith and love as a breastplate, and the hope of salvation as a helmet. (1 Th 5:6-8)
>
> Now the overseer must be above reproach, the husband of but one wife, temperate, self-controlled, respectable, hospitable, able to teach, (1 Tim 3:2)
>
> In the same way, their wives are to be women worthy of respect, not malicious talkers but temperate and trustworthy in everything. (1 Tim 3:11)
>
> Rather he [an overseer] must be hospitable, one who loves what is good, who is

self-controlled, upright, holy and disciplined. (Titus 1:8)

Teach the older men to be temperate, worthy of respect, self-controlled, and sound in faith, in love and in endurance. to be self-controlled and pure, to be busy at home, to be kind, and to be subject to their husbands, so that no one will malign the word of God. (Titus 2:2, 5)

For the grace of God that brings salvation has appeared to all men. It teaches us to say "No" to ungodliness and worldly passions, and to live self-controlled, upright and godly lives in this present age, while we wait for the blessed hope—the glorious appearing of our great God and Savior, Jesus Christ, (Titus 2:11-13)

Therefore, prepare your minds for action; be self-controlled; set your hope fully on the grace to be given you when Jesus Christ is revealed. (1 Pet 1:13)

The end of all things is near. Therefore be clear minded and self-controlled so that you can pray. (1 Pet 4:7)

3 (1:7-8) **Elder—Minister**: the minister—elder or an overseer must measure up personally; there are some personal qualifications that he must meet. Note the elder is here called an overseer. The two words are used interchangeably. Note also the critical importance placed upon his being blameless; he must live a blameless life. The reason is clearly stated: he is "entrusted with God's work."

1. An *overseer* or *steward* is the person who is placed in charge of the household and estate of the owner. The overseer or minister is the steward of God's church and God's people. He does not own the church, nor does he possess the people of the church. But he is in charge of their provision and education, of their nourishment and growth, of their behavior and duties. He must see that the household of God is cared for and looked after and that their energies and lives are directed to the will of the Master. Above all else, the steward must do the will of the Master, carry out His Word without any deviation whatsoever. This is what is meant by being "blameless." The steward exists solely for the Master—solely to see that the Word of God is done. He must be blameless when it comes to the will of God. (See note, *Ministers*—1 Cor.4:1-2 for more discussion.)

2. Note: there are some things—very important things—that the minister or overseer of God *must not do*.

   a. He must not be overbearing (authade): self-pleasing, arrogant, haughty, and self-centered. It is a person who thinks too highly of himself, who looks at his own things and ignores or neglects the things of others. It is a person who is harsh to others; who criticizes, grumbles, and condemns others; who downs others and elevates himself in his own mind.

Therefore, whoever humbles himself like this child is the greatest in the kingdom of heaven. (Mat 18:4)

But you are not to be like that. Instead, the greatest among you should be like the youngest, and the one who rules like the one who serves. (Luke 22:26)

Do not offer the parts of your body to sin, as instruments of wickedness, but rather offer yourselves to God, as those who have been brought from death to life; and offer the parts of your body to him as instruments of righteousness. (Rom 6:13)

For by the grace given me I say to every one of you: Do not think of yourself more highly than you ought, but rather think of yourself with sober judgment, in accordance with the measure of faith God has given you. (Rom 12:3)

Do nothing out of selfish ambition or vain conceit, but in humility consider others better than yourselves. Each of you should look not only to your own interests, but also to the interests of others. (Phil 2:3-4)

Submit yourselves, then, to God. Resist the devil, and he will flee from you. (James 4:7)

Young men, in the same way be submissive to those who are older. All of you, clothe yourselves with humility toward one another, because, "God opposes the proud but gives grace to the humble." Humble yourselves, therefore, under God's mighty hand, that he may lift you up in due time. (1 Pet 5:5-6)

b. He must not be quick-tempered (orge): a long-lasting anger; an anger that is deeply rooted and has been held for a long time; an anger against someone that a person just refuses to let go; the person refuses to forgive the other person. The minister must not be quick tempered or hot-headed, nor given over to long-lasting anger.

But I tell you that anyone who is angry with his brother will be subject to judgment. Again, anyone who says to his brother, 'Raca, ' is answerable to the Sanhedrin. But anyone who says, 'You fool!' will be in danger of the fire of hell. (Mat 5:22)

"In your anger do not sin" : Do not let the sun go down while you are still angry, (Eph 4:26)

But now you must rid yourselves of all such things as these: anger, rage, malice, slander, and filthy language from your lips. (Col 3:8)

Since an overseer is entrusted with God's work, he must be blameless—not overbearing, not quick-tempered, not given to drunkenness, not violent, not pursuing dishonest gain. (Titus 1:7)

My dear brothers, take note of this: Everyone should be quick to listen, slow to speak and slow to become angry, (James 1:19)

Refrain from anger and turn from wrath; do not fret—it leads only to evil. (Psa 37:8)

A man's wisdom gives him patience; it is to his glory to overlook an offense. (Prov 19:11)

Do not be quickly provoked in your spirit, for anger resides in the lap of fools. (Eccl 7:9)

TITUS 1:5-9

c. He must not be given to drunkenness (see note, pt.8—1 Tim.3:2-3 for discussion).

> For he [John the Baptist] will be great in the sight of the Lord. He is never to take wine or other fermented drink, and he will be filled with the Holy Spirit even from birth. (Luke 1:15)
> It is better not to eat meat or drink wine or to do anything else that will cause your brother to fall. (Rom 14:21)
> "You and your sons are not to drink wine or other fermented drink whenever you go into the Tent of Meeting, or you will die. This is a lasting ordinance for the generations to come. (Lev 10:9)
> He [the Nazarite] must abstain from wine and other fermented drink and must not drink vinegar made from wine or from other fermented drink. He must not drink grape juice or eat grapes or raisins. (Num 6:3)
> Do not gaze at wine when it is red, when it sparkles in the cup, when it goes down smoothly! (Prov 23:31)
> "It is not for kings, O Lemuel— not for kings to drink wine, not for rulers to crave beer, (Prov 31:4)
> But they replied, "We do not drink wine, because our forefather Jonadab son of Recab gave us this command: 'Neither you nor your descendants must ever drink wine. (Jer 35:6)
> But Daniel resolved not to defile himself with the royal food and wine, and he asked the chief official for permission not to defile himself this way. (Dan 1:8)

d. He must not be violent, a person given over to violence (see note, pt.9—1 Tim.3:2-3 for discussion).

> Do nothing out of selfish ambition or vain conceit, but in humility consider others better than yourselves. Each of you should look not only to your own interests, but also to the interests of others. (Phil 2:3-4)
> Keep reminding them of these things. Warn them before God against quarreling about words; it is of no value, and only ruins those who listen. (2 Tim 2:14)
> And the Lord's servant must not quarrel; instead, he must be kind to everyone, able to teach, not resentful. (2 Tim 2:24)
> Do not accuse a man for no reason— when he has done you no harm. (Prov 3:30)
> Starting a quarrel is like breaching a dam; so drop the matter before a dispute breaks out. (Prov 17:14)
> It is to a man's honor to avoid strife, but every fool is quick to quarrel. (Prov 20:3)

e. He must not pursue dishonest gain (see note, pt.12—1 Tim.3:2-3 for discussion).

> For the love of money is a root of all kinds of evil. Some people, eager for money, have wandered from the faith and pierced themselves with many griefs. (1 Tim 6:10)
> Your gold and silver are corroded. Their corrosion will testify against you and eat your flesh like fire. You have hoarded wealth in the last days. (James 5:3)

3. Note: there are some very important things that the minister or steward of God must be.

a. He must be hospitable (see note, pt.6—1 Tim.3:2-3 for discussion).

> Share with God's people who are in need. Practice hospitality. (Rom 12:13)
> Now the overseer must be above reproach, the husband of but one wife, temperate, self-controlled, respectable, hospitable, able to teach, (1 Tim 3:2)
> And is well known for her good deeds, such as bringing up children, showing hospitality, washing the feet of the saints, helping those in trouble and devoting herself to all kinds of good deeds. (1 Tim 5:10)
> Rather he must be hospitable, one who loves what is good, who is self-controlled, upright, holy and disciplined. (Titus 1:8)
> Do not forget to entertain strangers, for by so doing some people have entertained angels without knowing it. (Heb 13:2)
> Offer hospitality to one another without grumbling. (1 Pet 4:9)

b. He must be one who loves what is good (philagathos): the Greek means a lover of good things as well as of good people. The minister of God loves good no matter where he finds it, in people or things. He loves the poor and the homeless, the weak and the suffering, as well as the wealthy and healthy. And the minister loves to do good things for everyone, no matter who they are—good things such as...
- expressing appreciation
- encouraging
- giving gifts
- helping when help is needed
- ministering and serving
- preaching and teaching the truth of God's Word

Very simply stated, a minister loves good men and good things; therefore, he is always ministering. He is always involved in the lives of good people and always involved in doing good things for everyone he can.

> "A new command I give you: Love one another. As I have loved you, so you must love one another. By this all men will know that you are my disciples, if you love one another." (John 13:34-35)
> Love must be sincere. Hate what is evil; cling to what is good. (Rom 12:9)
> May the Lord make your love increase and overflow for each other and for everyone else, just as ours does for you. (1 Th 3:12)

TITUS 1:5-9

Now that you have purified yourselves by obeying the truth so that you have sincere love for your brothers, love one another deeply, from the heart. (1 Pet 1:22)

c. He must be self-controlled (see note, pt.4—1 Tim.3:2-3 for discussion).

So then, let us not be like others, who are asleep, but let us be alert and self-controlled. For those who sleep, sleep at night, and those who get drunk, get drunk at night. But since we belong to the day, let us be self-controlled, putting on faith and love as a breastplate, and the hope of salvation as a helmet. (1 Th 5:6-8)

Now the overseer must be above reproach, the husband of but one wife, temperate, self-controlled, respectable, hospitable, able to teach, (1 Tim 3:2)

In the same way, their wives are to be women worthy of respect, not malicious talkers but temperate and trustworthy in everything. (1 Tim 3:11)

Rather he must be hospitable, one who loves what is good, who is self-controlled, upright, holy and disciplined. (Titus 1:8)

Teach the older men to be temperate, worthy of respect, self-controlled, and sound in faith, in love and in endurance. to be self-controlled and pure, to be busy at home, to be kind, and to be subject to their husbands, so that no one will malign the word of God. (Titus 2:2, 5)

For the grace of God that brings salvation has appeared to all men. It teaches us to say "No" to ungodliness and worldly passions, and to live self-controlled, upright and godly lives in this present age, while we wait for the blessed hope—the glorious appearing of our great God and Savior, Jesus Christ, (Titus 2:11-13)

Therefore, prepare your minds for action; be self-controlled; set your hope fully on the grace to be given you when Jesus Christ is revealed. (1 Pet 1:13)

The end of all things is near. Therefore be clear minded and self-controlled so that you can pray. (1 Pet 4:7)

d. He must be upright (dikaion): honest, just, fair, above board in his behavior and dealings with both God and man. There is no deception, lying, cheating, stealing, meanness, misbehavior, or irresponsibility whatsoever in the minister's dealings—none with men or with God.

Give everyone what you owe him: If you owe taxes, pay taxes; if revenue, then revenue; if respect, then respect; if honor, then honor. (Rom 13:7)

To do what is right and just is more acceptable to the LORD than sacrifice. (Prov 21:3)

This is what the LORD says: "Maintain justice and do what is right, for my salvation is close at hand and my righteousness will soon be revealed. (Isa 56:1)

Follow justice and justice alone, so that you may live and possess the land the LORD your God is giving you. (Deu 16:20)

e. He must be holy (hosion): pure, clean, moral, unpolluted from the dirt and filth of sin. The minister must be a person who is clean and pure before the eyes of God.

Since we have these promises, dear friends, let us purify ourselves from everything that contaminates body and spirit, perfecting holiness out of reverence for God. (2 Cor 7:1)

Make every effort to live in peace with all men and to be holy; without holiness no one will see the Lord. (Heb 12:14)

Therefore, prepare your minds for action; be self-controlled; set your hope fully on the grace to be given you when Jesus Christ is revealed. As obedient children, do not conform to the evil desires you had when you lived in ignorance. But just as he who called you is holy, so be holy in all you do; for it is written: "Be holy, because I am holy." (1 Pet 1:13-16)

Since everything will be destroyed in this way, what kind of people ought you to be? You ought to live holy and godly lives (2 Pet 3:11)

f. He is disciplined in all things. He must have power over his body, mind, and life. He must be vigilant and watchful, controlling and guarding his behavior both when alone and when with others. He must control his eyes, ears, tongue, flesh, body, appetites, thoughts, hands, and feet—watching where he goes, what he does, says, thinks, eats, hears, looks at, and desires.

"Watch and pray so that you will not fall into temptation. The spirit is willing, but the body is weak." (Mat 26:41)

So be on your guard! Remember that for three years I never stopped warning each of you night and day with tears. (Acts 20:31)

So, if you think you are standing firm, be careful that you don't fall! (1 Cor 10:12)

Be on your guard; stand firm in the faith; be men of courage; be strong. (1 Cor 16:13)

Be self-controlled and alert. Your enemy the devil prowls around like a roaring lion looking for someone to devour. (1 Pet 5:8)

4 (1:9) **Minister—Preaching**: the minister or elder must measure up in his preaching; there is a preaching qualification that he must meet.

1. The elder or minister must hold firmly to the faithful Word. What Word? Note what the verse says: the "trustworthy message," that he must preach, the "trustworthy message," or teaching of God's Word. The minister of God must take the Word of God and cling to it in the face of all temptation and opposition—no matter what men may say or claim. The minister of God is a minister of God; he is not called to be the minister of anyone else. Therefore,

his mission is to cling to the Word of God. He is to hold fast to the pure Word of God; he is to be taught the "sound doctrine" of the Word. He is to be a person who has studied and studied the Word and is deeply rooted and grounded in the Word of God. His measurement is not how good a speaker he is, how charismatic and appealing; it is how well he has taught the Word of God. How much has he rooted his people in the doctrines of God's Word?

> But these are written that you may believe that Jesus is the Christ, the Son of God, and that by believing you may have life in his name. (John 20:31)
>
> Now the Bereans were of more noble character than the Thessalonians, for they received the message with great eagerness and examined the Scriptures every day to see if what Paul said was true. (Acts 17:11)
>
> "Now I commit you to God and to the word of his grace, which can build you up and give you an inheritance among all those who are sanctified. (Acts 20:32)
>
> For everything that was written in the past was written to teach us, so that through endurance and the encouragement of the Scriptures we might have hope. (Rom 15:4)
>
> Do your best to present yourself to God as one approved, a workman who does not need to be ashamed and who correctly handles the word of truth. (2 Tim 2:15)
>
> All Scripture is God-breathed and is useful for teaching, rebuking, correcting and training in righteousness, so that the man of God may be thoroughly equipped for every good work. (2 Tim 3:16-17)
>
> Like newborn babies, crave pure spiritual milk, so that by it you may grow up in your salvation, now that you have tasted that the Lord is good. (1 Pet 2:2-3)
>
> I write these things to you who believe in the name of the Son of God so that you may know that you have eternal life. (1 John 5:13)

2. There is a strong reason why the elder or minister must hold fast to the Word of God: he must be able to encourage and to refute those who oppose God and Christ.

⇒ People need to be exhorted, that is, encouraged to trust Christ and to follow Him.
⇒ People need to be refuted, especially those who stand opposed to God and curse him and refuse to surrender to Him. The word refute (elegchein) means *"to rebuke a man in such a way that he is compelled to see and to admit the error of his ways. Trench says that it means 'to rebuke another, with such an effectual wielding of the victorious arms of the truth, as to bring him, if not always to a confession, yet at least to a conviction of his sin'....Christian rebuke means far more than 'giving a man a row'...means far more than merely speaking to him in such a way that he sees the error of his ways and accepts the truth. The aim of Christian rebuke is not to humiliate a man, but to enable him to see and recognize and admit the duty and the truth to which he has been either blind or disobedient"* (William Barclay. *The Letters to Timothy, Titus, and Philemon*, p.274).

Note how the minister of God is to encourage and refute people: "by sound doctrine." And note the words "so that:" he is to be so grounded in God's Word that he can encourage and refute people *out of God's Word*.

> Those who sin are to be rebuked publicly, so that the others may take warning. (1 Tim 5:20)
>
> He must hold firmly to the trustworthy message as it has been taught, so that he can encourage others by sound doctrine and refute those who oppose it. (Titus 1:9)
>
> These, then, are the things you should teach. Encourage and rebuke with all authority. Do not let anyone despise you. (Titus 2:15)
>
> Those who sin are to be rebuked publicly, so that the others may take warning. (1 Tim 5:20)

TITUS 1:10-16

	B. The Contrasting False Teachers, 1:10-16	Therefore, rebuke them sharply, so that they will be sound in the faith	a. To become sound in the faith

1 They oppose the truth
  a. Are undisciplined
  b. Are talkers & deceivers
  c. Are only religionists
  d. Must be silenced
  e. Upset whole families
  f. Teach error
	10 For there are many rebellious people, mere talkers and deceivers, especially those of the circumcision group.
	11 They must be silenced, because they are ruining whole households by teaching things they ought not to teach—and that for the sake of dishonest gain.
		14 And will pay no attention to Jewish myths or to the commands of those who reject the truth.
		15 To the pure, all things are pure, but to those who are corrupted and do not believe, nothing is pure. In fact, both their minds and consciences are corrupted.
			b. To cease their myths & man-made rules
			
			3 They are impure—totally
			  a. To the pure all is pure
			  b. To the corrupt & unbelieving
			    1) Nothing is pure
			    2) Conscience & minds are corrupted

g. Are gripped by greed
  h. Have a sorry reputation
 	
2 They must be rebuked
	12 Even one of their own prophets has said, "Cretans are always liars, evil brutes, lazy gluttons."
	13 This testimony is true.
		16 They claim to know God, but by their actions they deny him. They are detestable, disobedient and unfit for doing anything good.	**4 They claim to know God, but their works deny God**
			  a. They deny God
			  b. They are detestable & disobedient

DIVISION I

THE TRUE AND FALSE CHURCH OFFICIALS, 1:5-16

B. The Contrasting False Teachers. 1:10-16

(1:10-16) **Introduction**: this is a clear picture of false teachers, a picture that every believer and church should diligently study.
1. They oppose the truth (v.10-12).
2. They must be rebuked (v.13-14).
3. They are impure—totally (v.15).
4. They claim to know God, but their works deny God (v.16).

1 (1:10-12) **False Teachers**: they oppose the truth. There were *many false teachers* throughout the churches of Crete, and there have been many down through the centuries. The church has always had to combat false teaching. Note: the false teachers come from within the churches, not from without. They were of the circumcision, that is…
 • they were religionists (v.10).
 • they claimed to know God (v.16).
 • they were ruining whole households (v.11).
Remember: the churches met in homes; they did not have buildings in which to meet. The point to see is that they opposed the truth.

1. They were *rebellious* (anupotaktoi): undisciplined, unruly, disloyal, insubordinate against God and the truth. They refused to submit to God and to the truth of the gospel and of God's Word.

> "Not everyone who says to me, 'Lord, Lord,' will enter the kingdom of heaven, but only he who does the will of my Father who is in heaven. (Mat 7:21)
> For if the message spoken by angels was binding, and every violation and disobedience received its just punishment, how shall we escape if we ignore such a great salvation? This salvation, which was first announced by the Lord, was confirmed to us by those who heard him. (Heb 2:2-3)
> But there were also false prophets among the people, just as there will be false teachers among you. They will secretly introduce destructive heresies, even denying the sovereign Lord who bought them—bringing swift destruction on themselves. (2 Pet 2:1)

2. They were *mere talkers* (mataiologoi): empty talkers, saying and teaching things that amount to nothing and are worthless. Their teaching helped no one—not permanently and not eternally. Their teaching was not able to overcome sin and death—not able to bring true forgiveness of sin and eternal life to a person.

> Would he argue with useless words, with speeches that have no value? (Job 15:3)
> At the beginning his words are folly; at the end they are wicked madness— (Eccl 10:13)
> What you heard from me, keep as the pattern of sound teaching, with faith and love in Christ Jesus. (2 Tim 1:13)
> And soundness of speech that cannot be condemned, so that those who oppose you may be ashamed because they have nothing bad to say about us. (Titus 2:8)

3. They were *deceivers* (phrenapatai): "mind-deceivers" (A.T. Robertson. *Word Pictures in the New Testament*, Vol.4, p.600), misleaders. They misled themselves and misled others away from the truth. They turned away from the truth and followed error; they followed a false belief.

> For such people are not serving our Lord Christ, but their own appetites. By smooth talk and flattery they deceive the minds of naive people. (Rom 16:18)
> For such men are false apostles, deceitful workmen, masquerading as apostles of Christ. And no wonder, for Satan himself masquerades as an angel of light. It is not surprising, then, if his servants masquerade as servants of righteousness. Their end

will be what their actions deserve. (2 Cor 11:13-15)

While evil men and impostors will go from bad to worse, deceiving and being deceived. (2 Tim 3:13)

Many deceivers, who do not acknowledge Jesus Christ as coming in the flesh, have gone out into the world. Any such person is the deceiver and the antichrist. (2 John 1:7)

4. They were of the circumcision; that is, they were Jewish religionists. (See notes—Gal.2:3-5; DEEPER STUDY # 1—2:4; 5:2-4 for more discussion.) They professed Christ, but they refused to accept the all-sufficiency of Christ and His cross.

⇒ They refused to accept that Christ died for their sins—actually bore the judgment and punishment for their transgressions against God.
⇒ They refused to accept that God accepted them by faith and only by faith—that God took their faith and counted it as righteousness; that God required nothing more and nothing less than a person's total trust, the laying of the person's life into the hands of God, all the person is and has, his total being—and that is all that was needed to be saved.

Very simply, the false teachers—the religionists—taught that man made himself acceptable...
- by doing the best he could.
- by being good and doing good.
- by being as religious as he could.
- by keeping the laws and rules of religion.
- by undergoing the basic ritual of religion (circumcision, baptism, confirmation, church membership, etc.).
- by observing and practicing the ceremonies and rules of religion.
- by being faithful in worship and stewardship.

"Not everyone who says to me, 'Lord, Lord,' will enter the kingdom of heaven, but only he who does the will of my Father who is in heaven. (Mat 7:21)

Since they did not know the righteousness that comes from God and sought to establish their own, they did not submit to God's righteousness. (Rom 10:3)

All who rely on observing the law are under a curse, for it is written: "Cursed is everyone who does not continue to do everything written in the Book of the Law." (Gal 3:10)

Many a man claims to have unfailing love, but a faithful man who can find? (Prov 20:6)

5. They had mouths that needed to be silenced. Their false teaching needed to be stopped, but not by physical force. The word "silenced" (epistomizein) means to muzzle or bridle, but it should be by reason and argument, not by physical force. False teachers must always be silenced. Their teaching is misleading and erroneous; therefore, their teaching must be restrained, stopped dead in its tracks. Their tongues must be silenced. False teachers must not be allowed to sow the seeds of their error.

And soundness of speech that cannot be condemned, so that those who oppose you may be ashamed because they have nothing bad to say about us. (Titus 2:8)

For it is God's will that by doing good you should silence the ignorant talk of foolish men. (1 Pet 2:15)

6. They were ruining, that is, upsetting and disrupting whole households. They were turning some away from the truth and tearing families apart. In other cases they were overthrowing the faith of whole families. Whole families were following the false teaching and leaving the church. This was, of course, the objective of the false teachers: to secure a following for themselves by turning people away from the truth of Christ.

I am astonished that you are so quickly deserting the one who called you by the grace of Christ and are turning to a different gospel— which is really no gospel at all. Evidently some people are throwing you into confusion and are trying to pervert the gospel of Christ. But even if we or an angel from heaven should preach a gospel other than the one we preached to you, let him be eternally condemned! As we have already said, so now I say again: If anybody is preaching to you a gospel other than what you accepted, let him be eternally condemned! (Gal 1:6-9)

Anyone who breaks one of the least of these commandments and teaches others to do the same will be called least in the kingdom of heaven, but whoever practices and teaches these commands will be called great in the kingdom of heaven. (Mat 5:19)

7. They were teaching things that they should not teach (see pt.4 above).

8. They were seeking dishonest gain. They had entered the church and religion and were teaching a false doctrine...
- to gain a livelihood or money.
- to gain recognition.
- to gain a following.
- to gain acceptance.
- to gain the satisfaction of being in a reputable profession.

9. They had a sorry reputation. They were professing religionists, but they were living no better than the rest of society. This is clearly seen by looking at three traits of Cretian society. Note that the traits are taken from a Cretian poet. (Grecian poets were considered prophets in that day, men who were under the inspiration of the gods.) Paul does not give his name, but he was Epimenides who lived somewhere around 600 B.C. and was ranked as one of the seven wisest men of Greece (William Barclay. *The Letters to Timothy, Titus, and Philemon*, p.277).

   a. The false teachers were chronic liars. They were not living for Christ nor following after the truth. They were just like Cretian society, living false lives and following lies. And they were teaching a false, lying doctrine—teaching it right inside the church, leading believers to follow their lies.

b. The false teachers were evil beasts. That is, they were savage and malicious in standing against the truth of Christ and of salvation by grace through faith. Just like wild beasts, they savagely attacked the church and its believers, attempting to consume them in their false teaching and doctrine.

c. The false teachers were idle gluttons. This does not mean that they were inactive and never industrious nor that they were fat and lazy. Some, no doubt, were just as some are in every society—lazy, gluttonous, slothful, and too complacent to study the Word of God and to seek the truth. What it means in this context is that...

- they were idle in dealing with the truth. They had nothing to do with the truth. They had turned away from it. When it came to Christ and the truth, they were idle and inactive.
- they were gluttons, that is, greedy and seeking to fill their lust for whatever they were after: recognition, a following, money, self-image. Honoring Christ and reaching people for Christ and sharing the truth was not the focus of their lives.

> **The Spirit clearly says that in later times some will abandon the faith and follow deceiving spirits and things taught by demons. Such teachings come through hypocritical liars, whose consciences have been seared as with a hot iron. (1 Tim 4:1-2)**
>
> **If anyone teaches false doctrines and does not agree to the sound instruction of our Lord Jesus Christ and to godly teaching, (1 Tim 6:3)**
>
> **For the time will come when men will not put up with sound doctrine. Instead, to suit their own desires, they will gather around them a great number of teachers to say what their itching ears want to hear. They will turn their ears away from the truth and turn aside to myths. (2 Tim 4:3-4)**

2 (1:13-14) **False Teachers:** they must be rebuked. The witness just given against society and false teachers is true. And remember: the false teachers were in the church, professing to be followers of Christ. But they were not following Christ—not fully and wholly. Therefore, they had to be sharply rebuked. The idea is that they had to be corrected with sternness and even in severity. This is understandable, for false teaching is one of the greatest sins and dangers facing believers. False teaching hurts the church and its believers as much as any sin, for it turns men away from God and Christ and destroys the church and its mission. But note a most significant point: there were two reasons why the false teachers and their followers were to be rebuked.

1. False teachers and their followers were to be rebuked so that they would become sound in the faith.

> *"Here precisely is the wonderful thing....Paul does not say to Timothy: 'Leave them alone. They are hopeless and all men know it.' He says: 'They are bad and all men know it. Go and convert them.' There are few passages which so demonstrate the divine optimism of the Christian missionary and evangelist, who refuses to regard any man as hopeless. The greater the evil, the greater the challenge. It is the Christian conviction that there is no sin which is too great for the grace of Jesus Christ to encounter and to conquer"* (William Barclay. *The Letters to Timothy, Titus, and Philemon*, p.278).

The false teachers were not sound in the faith; they were not standing with Christ nor for Christ. They were not following Christ nor teaching the Word of God in its purity and simplicity. They were in danger of being lost, and condemned from the presence of God forever. In addition they were leading others down the same false road. If the false teachers and their followers were not corrected, then more and more lives would be corrupted and destroyed. Therefore, the false teachers had to be dealt with; there was no choice. Confronting them with the truth of Christ and of the Word was their only hope. An attempt to root them in sound doctrine had to be made—both for Christ and their own eternal salvation.

2. False teachers and their followers were to be rebuked so they might cease from their myths and man-made religious rules. Note: what false teachers follow are only fables and myths, imaginations within man's mind, and man-made rules of religion.

> **Have nothing to do with the fruitless deeds of darkness, but rather expose them. (Eph 5:11)**
>
> **And we urge you, brothers, warn those who are idle, encourage the timid, help the weak, be patient with everyone. (1 Th 5:14)**
>
> **Those who sin are to be rebuked publicly, so that the others may take warning. (1 Tim 5:20)**
>
> **Preach the Word; be prepared in season and out of season; correct, rebuke and encourage—with great patience and careful instruction. (2 Tim 4:2)**
>
> **This testimony is true. Therefore, rebuke them sharply, so that they will be sound in the faith (Titus 1:13)**
>
> **These, then, are the things you should teach. Encourage and rebuke with all authority. Do not let anyone despise you. (Titus 2:15)**
>
> **"Shout it aloud, do not hold back. Raise your voice like a trumpet. Declare to my people their rebellion and to the house of Jacob their sins. (Isa 58:1)**
>
> **When I say to a wicked man, 'You will surely die,' and you do not warn him or speak out to dissuade him from his evil ways in order to save his life, that wicked man will die for his sin, and I will hold you accountable for his blood. (Ezek 3:18)**
>
> **But if you do warn the wicked man to turn from his ways and he does not do so, he will die for his sin, but you will have saved yourself. (Ezek 33:9)**

3 (1:15) **False Teachers:** they are impure, totally impure. The basic question of life is this: How does a person become pure and righteous before God? Men try to become acceptable to God by works—by doing the works of religion, by doing good and being good. This is where so many of the laws, rules, rituals, and ceremonies of religion come from. They are merely man's desire to become acceptable to God. Man feels the way to become acceptable is to be religious and keep all the rules of religion. But note a critical fact: no religion and no man-made rule or work can save a man from sin and death. Everything that is made by man dies and decays—ends up just like he does, as nothing more than the dust of the ground. Man cannot do enough good nor do enough works to create a pure mind and conscience within himself, not a mind and conscience that has the absolute assurance of living forever.

But note another fact: there is a way to become pure and righteous before God. How? By Jesus Christ—by believing in Jesus Christ...

- by trusting His purity and righteousness to cover us.
- by trusting His death and resurrection to cover us.

When we believe that Jesus Christ died for us, God accepts the death of Christ *for us*. He forgives our transgressions and never charges them against us. We are free from sin in Christ; through our faith in Christ God counts us pure and righteous.

This is what the verse means. If we are pure in Christ, then all things are pure to us. We do not have to worry about doing things to become pure. We are pure—perfectly righteous and acceptable to God because we are *in Christ*. Our faith is *in Christ* to make us pure, not in religious rules.

Therefore false teachers and their followers—in fact all unbelievers—lack the absolute assurance of forgiveness and of eternal life—of being acceptable to God. Their minds and consciences are corrupted. No matter what their man-made religious rules are—rules governing food, discipline, do's and don'ts, washings, baptisms, ceremonies, rituals—they are all impure. They are only physical and material and man-made substances—all to perish after they are used.

Thought 1. "*'Unto the pure all things are pure'* does not mean that dope and alcoholic beverages which will dull the mind and destroy the body are pure. There is probably a direct teaching here concerning ceremonial meats and drinks among the Jews. (In this connection, study the entire fourteenth chapter of Romans.) Some foods were regarded as clean and could be eaten, while others were considered unclean and were therefore forbidden. What Paul is saying is that those distinctions ceased when Christ died and rose again: 'Christ is the end of the law for righteousness to every one that believeth' (Rom.10:4). In this Christian era, it is not what we eat or drink that saves us or damns us; it is 'What think ye of Christ? Whose Son is He?' 'As many as received Him, to THEM gave He power to become the sons of God, even to them that believe on His name: which were born...born of God' (John 1:12, 13).

"In Paul's day, under the Law of Moses, a Jew dare not eat pork nor drink certain drinks; but in this day, meats and drinks neither save nor damn—although a child of God, led by the Spirit of God, will not eat or drink those things that will destroy the body. God puts His law in our hearts and leads us by His Spirit (Rom.8:14), and if we are led by the Spirit we will not fulfill the lust of the flesh. Truth makes free; and when we know and obey the truth, we eat and drink those things that are wholesome, good, and profitable to body and soul.

"A person who is a true child of God will not use this passage to attempt to prove that all things are right and lawful for the Christian. There are those who say that if you think something is not sin, then to you it is not sin; but such reasoning is not to be found in the Word of God. The Bible clearly teaches that we are to 'have no fellowship with the unfruitful works of darkness, but rather reprove them' (Eph.5:11). 'Love not the world, neither the things that are in the world. If any man love the world, the love of the Father is not in him' (1 John 2:15). 'Abstain from all appearance of evil' (1 Thess.5:22). 'Prove all things; hold fast that which is good' (1 Thess.5:21). 'Whether therefore ye eat, or drink, or whatsoever ye do, do all to the glory of God' (1 Cor.10:31).

"The principle here involved is a pure, truly pious mind; and if we have such a mind we will not eat or drink those things that will destroy our testimony. The believing heart does not major on the distinction of food and drink, festivals, ceremonies, rites, holy days, holidays. These things have nothing to do with purity of heart and spirit, and the conscience of the believer is not to be burdened with nor enslaved by them. The heart of a believer is to be controlled by the Holy Spirit of God and by the laws of God laid down in the New Testament. We are not under the Law of Moses. We live by faith, not by sight. We live as the Holy Spirit leads us into the paths of righteousness" (Oliver Greene, *The Epistles of Paul the Apostle to Timothy and Titus*, p.429f).

Thought 2. "'*But unto them that are defiled and unbelieving is nothing pure.*' This statement is very clear: The unbeliever is lost, totally depraved, without strength, hopeless, helpless, without God and eternally damned unless he embraces Christianity by faith in the finished work of Christ. To the sinner, NOTHING is pure. Proverbs 21:4 tells us, '...The plowing of the wicked is sin.' James 4:17 says, '...To him that knoweth to do good, and doeth it not, to him it is sin!'...

"To the unbeliever, everything is made the means of increasing his depravity, his unrighteousness and his ungodliness. It makes no difference what ordinances of religion unbelievers may observe and practice; it matters not what distinctions they may make concerning meats, drinks, days, ceremonies or religious events; such observances will not change their state of depravity. Making distinctions in food, drinks, and clothing only fosters pride and produces self-righteousness. Those who do these things are attempting to justify themselves through their own goodness and labors, following the commandments of men instead of submitting to the love of God. They push aside the mercies of God and satisfy their own lusts. They are corrupt at heart, and observance of ordinances, ceremonies, abstinence from food and drink makes them no better; it simply leads to deeper depravity and greater damnation" (Oliver Greene, *The Epistles of Paul the Apostle to Timothy and Titus*, p.431f).

Blessed are the pure in heart, for they will see God. (Mat 5:8)

All these evils come from inside and make a man 'unclean.'" (Mark 7:23)

Furthermore, since they did not think it worthwhile to retain the knowledge of God, he gave them over to a depraved mind, to do what ought not to be done. (Rom 1:28)

Since we have these promises, dear friends, let us purify ourselves from everything that contaminates body and spirit, perfecting holiness out of reverence for God. (2 Cor 7:1)

So I tell you this, and insist on it in the Lord, that you must no longer live as the Gentiles do, in the futility of their thinking. (Eph 4:17)

Do not let anyone who delights in false humility and the worship of angels disqualify you for the prize. Such a person goes into great detail about what he has seen, and his unspiritual mind puffs him up with idle notions. (Col 2:18)

The goal of this command is love, which comes from a pure heart and a good conscience and a sincere faith. (1 Tim 1:5)

To the pure, all things are pure, but to those who are corrupted and do not believe, nothing is pure. In fact, both their minds and consciences are corrupted. (Titus 1:15)

Now that you have purified yourselves by obeying the truth so that you have sincere love for your brothers, love one another deeply, from the heart. (1 Pet 1:22)

4 (1:16) **False Teachers**: they make a claim that they know God, but their works deny Him. The false teachers openly professed Christ, claimed to be Christian, and to belong to the church. And note: they were preaching, teaching, and filling the pulpits and seats of instruction in the churches. But their works betrayed them. Their behavior clearly showed that they were hypocrites. They were not teaching the pure Word of God, not teaching the truth about Jesus Christ. Note the final terrible fact: by their works they were denying God and Christ. No matter what they professed and claimed, if they did not teach the pure Word of God and the pure truth about God and His Son, Jesus Christ, then they were denying God.

⇒ They were being detestable: vile and repulsive to both God and true believers. They were corrupting the truth, and corruption always sends up a foul smell.

⇒ They were being *disobedient*: refusing to submit to God and to follow and teach the truth of Christ and of God's Word.

⇒ They were *unfit*: useless and worthless; failing to meet the test of God. In God's eyes they were of no value. They were fit only to be rejected.

"Not everyone who says to me, 'Lord, Lord,' will enter the kingdom of heaven, but only he who does the will of my Father who is in heaven. (Mat 7:21)

He replied, "Isaiah was right when he prophesied about you hypocrites; as it is written: "'These people honor me with their lips, but their hearts are far from me. (Mark 7:6)

They claim to know God, but by their actions they deny him. They are detestable, disobedient and unfit for doing anything good. (Titus 1:16)

They remembered that God was their Rock, that God Most High was their Redeemer. But then they would flatter him with their mouths, lying to him with their tongues; (Psa 78:35-36)

My people come to you, as they usually do, and sit before you to listen to your words, but they do not put them into practice. With their mouths they express devotion, but their hearts are greedy for unjust gain. Indeed, to them you are nothing more than one who sings love songs with a beautiful voice and plays an instrument well, for they hear your words but do not put them into practice. (Ezek 33:31-32)

TITUS 2:1-10

		CHAPTER 2 II. THE MESSAGE OF SOUND DOCTRINE, 2:1-3:11 A. Message 1: The Behavior of Believers, 2:1-10	pure, to be busy at home, to be kind, and to be subject to their husbands, so that no one will malign the word of God. 6 Similarly, encourage the young men to be self-controlled. 7 In everything set them an example by doing what is good. In your teaching show integrity, seriousness 8 And soundness of speech that cannot be condemned, so that those who oppose you may be ashamed because they have nothing bad to say about us. 9 Teach slaves to be subject to their masters in everything, to try to please them, not to talk back to them, 10 And not to steal from them, but to show that they can be fully trusted, so that in every way they will make the teaching about God our Savior attractive.	b. To keep God's message from being slandered
1	Preach & teach sound doctrine	You must teach what is in accord with sound doctrine. 2 Teach the older men to be temperate, worthy of respect, self-controlled, and sound in faith, in love and in endurance. 3 Likewise, teach the older women to be reverent in the way they live, not to be slanderers or addicted to much wine, but to teach what is good. 4 Then they can train the younger women to love their husbands and children, 5 To be self-controlled and		5 The behavior of younger men

2	The behavior of older men
	  a. An example of maturity
	  b. To show a sound faith
				6 The behavior of teachers & young ministers

3	The behavior of older women
	  a. An example in holiness and reverence
	  b. To teach younger women
				7 The behavior of Christian workmen
				  a. An example of obedience
				
				  b. To make God's teaching attractive

4	The behavior of younger women a. An example in purity			

DIVISION II

THE MESSAGE OF SOUND DOCTRINE

A. Message 1: The Behavior of Believers, 2:1-10

(2:1-10) **Introduction**: What is a believer to be like? How is a believer to live in the world? This passage discusses in clear and direct terms just what the behavior of believers is to be. And note: it discusses every age group and the important positions of the teacher and minister and of the Christian workman.

1. Preach and teach sound doctrine (v.1).
2. The behavior of older men (v.2).
3. The behavior of older women (v.3).
4. The behavior of younger women (v.4-5).
5. The behavior of younger men (v.6).
6. The behavior of teachers and young ministers (v.7-8).
7. The behavior of Christian workmen (v.9-10).

1 (2:1) **Minister—Teacher—Doctrine—Word of God**: the minister must preach and teach *sound doctrine*. This is in contrast to the false teachers just covered in the former passage (Tit.1:10-16). The word "sound" means wholesome and healthy. Therefore, *sound doctrine* means the doctrines and teachings of God's Word—the wholesome and healthy teachings of God's Word in contrast to the diseased teachings of false teachers. The teachings of false teachers will only implant a cancerous disease into the human heart and result in death and destruction. Therefore, the exhortation to Titus was urgent, and it is urgent to every minister of God. The health and destiny of God's people and of the church are at stake.

> **Thought 1.** Preach and teach sound doctrine—the teachings of God's Word. Do not preach and teach your own ideas or opinions nor the latest fads of theology. Do not add anything to the Word of God nor take anything away from it. Take the teachings of God's Word in all their soundness and preach and teach them.

> They worship me in vain; their teachings are but rules taught by men.'" (Mat 15:9)

> And we also thank God continually because, when you received the word of God, which you heard from us, you accepted it not as the word of men, but as it actually is, the word of God, which is at work in you who believe. (1 Th 2:13)

> As I urged you when I went into Macedonia, stay there in Ephesus so that you may command certain men not to teach false doctrines any longer nor to devote themselves to myths and endless genealogies. These promote controversies rather than God's work—which is by faith. (1 Tim 1:3-4)

> If you point these things out to the brothers, you will be a good minister of Christ Jesus, brought up in the truths of the faith and of the good teaching that you have followed. (1 Tim 4:6)

> Watch your life and doctrine closely. Persevere in them, because if you do, you will save both yourself and your hearers. (1 Tim 4:16)

2 (2:2) **Men, Older—Church—Age Groups**: the behavior of older men. What are older men to be like in the world? How are they to live? Six traits are given.

1. Older men are to be *temperate* (nephalios): sober and moderate. It is the opposite of over-indulgence in anything such as eating, drinking, recreation, or whatever.

TITUS 2:1-10

So then, let us not be like others, who are asleep, but let us be alert and self-controlled. (1 Th 5:6)

It teaches us to say "No" to ungodliness and worldly passions, and to live self-controlled, upright and godly lives in this present age, while we wait for the blessed hope—the glorious appearing of our great God and Savior, Jesus Christ, (Titus 2:12-13)

Therefore, prepare your minds for action; be self-controlled; set your hope fully on the grace to be given you when Jesus Christ is revealed. (1 Pet 1:13)

The end of all things is near. Therefore be clear minded and self-controlled so that you can pray. (1 Pet 4:7)

2. Older men are to be *worthy of respect* (semnos): serious, honorable, worthy, reverent, noble. It has to do with seriousness of purpose and life. It is the opposite of being flippant and shallow, non-purposeful and uncommitted. Older men are to be men of such strong purpose and behavior that they inspire reverence and awe. Older men are not to enter a *second childhood* and act like children.

"My food," said Jesus, "is to do the will of him who sent me and to finish his work. Do you not say, 'Four months more and then the harvest'? I tell you, open your eyes and look at the fields! They are ripe for harvest. Even now the reaper draws his wages, even now he harvests the crop for eternal life, so that the sower and the reaper may be glad together. (John 4:34-36)

But seek first his kingdom and his righteousness, and all these things will be given to you as well. (Mat 6:33)

Brothers, I do not consider myself yet to have taken hold of it. But one thing I do: Forgetting what is behind and straining toward what is ahead, I press on toward the goal to win the prize for which God has called me heavenward in Christ Jesus. All of us who are mature should take such a view of things. And if on some point you think differently, that too God will make clear to you. Only let us live up to what we have already attained. (Phil 3:13-16)

3. Older men are to be *self-controlled* (sophron): sober-minded, disciplined, able to curb desires and emotions. Older men are to have minds that are sound, sensible, and chaste—minds that have complete control over all sensual desires. Neither age nor retirement gives the elderly a right to live a life of license, neither in drink, eating, sex, recreation, travel, play nor in any other area of life. The elderly who really know the Lord are not to waste time and fritter their life away. Too many people—children, men, women—are destitute, poor, hurting, and dying from hunger, poor housing, loneliness, emptiness, and sin.

As Paul discoursed on righteousness, self-control and the judgment to come, Felix was afraid and said, "That's enough for now! You may leave. When I find it convenient, I will send for you." (Acts 24:25)

Do you not know that in a race all the runners run, but only one gets the prize? Run in such a way as to get the prize. Everyone who competes in the games goes into strict training. They do it to get a crown that will not last; but we do it to get a crown that will last forever. Therefore I do not run like a man running aimlessly; I do not fight like a man beating the air. No, I beat my body and make it my slave so that after I have preached to others, I myself will not be disqualified for the prize. (1 Cor 9:24-27)

But the fruit of the Spirit is love, joy, peace, patience, kindness, goodness, faithfulness, gentleness and self-control. Against such things there is no law. (Gal 5:22-23)

He who loves pleasure will become poor; whoever loves wine and oil will never be rich. (Prov 21:17)

When you sit to dine with a ruler, note well what is before you, (Prov 23:1)

4. Older men must be *sound* (*healthy*) *in the faith*: this means to be strong in the Christian faith—in one's faith in Christ and in the Word of God and its promises. It means the whole body of Christian doctrine—all the teachings of God's Word. Older men are to have a strong faith in Christ and in God's Word. They are to love Him and His Word more and more as the years pass, ever growing in faith.

Then they asked him, "What must we do to do the works God requires?" Jesus answered, "The work of God is this: to believe in the one he has sent." (John 6:28-29)

Consequently, faith comes from hearing the message, and the message is heard through the word of Christ. (Rom 10:17)

And without faith it is impossible to please God, because anyone who comes to him must believe that he exists and that he rewards those who earnestly seek him. (Heb 11:6)

In the same way, faith by itself, if it is not accompanied by action, is dead. (James 2:17)

And this is his command: to believe in the name of his Son, Jesus Christ, and to love one another as he commanded us. (1 John 3:23)

For everyone born of God overcomes the world. This is the victory that has overcome the world, even our faith. Who is it that overcomes the world? Only he who believes that Jesus is the Son of God. (1 John 5:4-5)

5. Older men must be *sound* (*healthy*) *in love* (see notes, *Love*—1 Th.1:3; Deeper Study # 1—3:12; note 5—2 Th.1:3 for discussion).

6. Older men must be *sound in endurance* (hupomeno): (see notes, pt.7—2 Tim.3:10 for discussion).

3 (2:3) **Women, Older—Church**: the behavior of older women. What are older women to be like in the world? How are they to live?

1. Older women are to be *reverent* (hieroprepes): holy, devout, different and set apart in purity of behavior and

thought. They are to live and move about in a spirit of holiness and be focused upon sacred things. Matthew Henry says that elderly women are to keep "a pious [holy] decency and decorum in clothing and gesture, in looks and speech, and in all their deportment [behavior]" (*Matthew Henry's Commentary*, p.862).

> To rescue us from the hand of our enemies, and to enable us to serve him without fear in holiness and righteousness before him all our days. (Luke 1:74-75)
>
> Since we have these promises, dear friends, let us purify ourselves from everything that contaminates body and spirit, perfecting holiness out of reverence for God. (2 Cor 7:1)
>
> And to put on the new self, created to be like God in true righteousness and holiness. (Eph 4:24)
>
> Make every effort to live in peace with all men and to be holy; without holiness no one will see the Lord. (Heb 12:14)
>
> As obedient children, do not conform to the evil desires you had when you lived in ignorance. But just as he who called you is holy, so be holy in all you do; for it is written: "Be holy, because I am holy." (1 Pet 1:14-16)
>
> Since everything will be destroyed in this way, what kind of people ought you to be? You ought to live holy and godly lives (2 Pet 3:11)

2. Older women are not to be *slanderers* (diabolos): talebearers, gossipers, a person who goes about talking about others, stirring up mischief and disturbance. This is so terrible a sin that the devil himself is called *the slanderer* (diabolos). This—slanderer (diabolos)—is one of the very names of the devil.

> Get rid of all bitterness, rage and anger, brawling and slander, along with every form of malice. (Eph 4:31)
>
> We hear that some among you are idle. They are not busy; they are busybodies. (2 Th 3:11)
>
> Besides, they get into the habit of being idle and going about from house to house. And not only do they become idlers, but also gossips and busybodies, saying things they ought not to. (1 Tim 5:13)
>
> If anyone considers himself religious and yet does not keep a tight rein on his tongue, he deceives himself and his religion is worthless. (James 1:26)
>
> The tongue also is a fire, a world of evil among the parts of the body. It corrupts the whole person, sets the whole course of his life on fire, and is itself set on fire by hell. (James 3:6)
>
> Brothers, do not slander one another. Anyone who speaks against his brother or judges him speaks against the law and judges it. When you judge the law, you are not keeping it, but sitting in judgment on it. (James 4:11)

> Therefore, rid yourselves of all malice and all deceit, hypocrisy, envy, and slander of every kind. (1 Pet 2:1)
>
> For, "Whoever would love life and see good days must keep his tongue from evil and his lips from deceitful speech. (1 Pet 3:10)
>
> Whoever slanders his neighbor in secret, him will I put to silence; whoever has haughty eyes and a proud heart, him will I not endure. (Psa 101:5)
>
> With his mouth the godless destroys his neighbor, but through knowledge the righteous escape. (Prov 11:9)
>
> A perverse man stirs up dissension, and a gossip separates close friends. (Prov 16:28)
>
> The words of a gossip are like choice morsels; they go down to a man's inmost parts. (Prov 26:22)

3. Older women are *not to be addicted to much wine* (see note, pt.8—1 Tim.3:2-3 for discussion).

4. Older women are to *teach what is good* (kalodidaskalos): this refers to ministry in the home (Donald Guthrie. *The Pastoral Epistles*. "Tyndale New Testament Commentaries," p.193). Older women are to live such godly lives that they teach by their very example and testimony within the home. Note: they are to teach the younger women how to live for Christ in a sinful and corruptible world.

> When they had finished eating, Jesus said to Simon Peter, "Simon son of John, do you truly love me more than these?" "Yes, Lord," he said, "you know that I love you." Jesus said, "Feed my lambs." (John 21:15)
>
> Then they can train the younger women to love their husbands and children, (Titus 2:4)
>
> Impress them on your children. Talk about them when you sit at home and when you walk along the road, when you lie down and when you get up. (Deu 6:7)
>
> Their children, who do not know this law, must hear it and learn to fear the LORD your God as long as you live in the land you are crossing the Jordan to possess." (Deu 31:13)
>
> Train a child in the way he should go, and when he is old he will not turn from it. (Prov 22:6)

4 (2:4-5) **Younger Women—Church**: the behavior of younger women. What are younger women to be like in the world? How are they to behave as they walk day by day? Seven traits are given.

1. Younger women are to love their husbands. Note: this particular command is to *young women* which means that her marriage is a young marriage. The only way a young married couple can become united and bound together and have the kind of life they desire is by loving each other. Therefore, the young wife must love her husband...

- with a selfless and unselfish love.
- with a giving and sacrificial love.
- with a quiet and peaceable love.

- with a love of the will as well as of the heart.
- with a love of commitment as well as of affection.

The word used here for love (phileo) actually stresses affection, care, tenderness, warmth, and feelings. The young wife is to have *affection* for her husband.

Thought 1. A young wife may live in a mansion and have the finest of furnishings—she may be the most beautiful woman in the world and have the very best wardrobe—she may have a husband who loves her ever so dearly—but if she does not love her husband, they are both unhappy and often miserable. Young women are to love—to learn to love their husbands. Christ can help her and teach her to love him.

> **In this same way, husbands ought to love their wives as their own bodies. He who loves his wife loves himself. (Eph 5:28 Applies to wife as well.)**
>
> **Husbands, love your wives and do not be harsh with them. (Col 3:19)**
>
> **Isaac brought her into the tent of his mother Sarah, and he married Rebekah. So she became his wife, and he loved her; and Isaac was comforted after his mother's death. (Gen 24:67)**
>
> **So Jacob served seven years to get Rachel, but they seemed like only a few days to him because of his love for her. (Gen 29:20)**
>
> **Now the king was attracted to Esther more than to any of the other women, and she won his favor and approval more than any of the other virgins. So he set a royal crown on her head and made her queen instead of Vashti. (Est 2:17)**
>
> **Many waters cannot quench love; rivers cannot wash it away. If one were to give all the wealth of his house for love, it would be utterly scorned. (Song 8:7)**

2. Young women are to love their children. There is no greater call or task on earth than that of being a mother. William Barclay points this out in descriptive language:

> *"It is the simple fact that there is no greater task and responsibility and privilege in this world than to make a home....In the last analysis there can be no greater career than the career of homemaking. How many a man, who has set his mark upon the world, has been enabled to do so simply because there was someone at home who cared for him and loved him and tended him. It is infinitely more important that a mother should be at home to put her children to bed and to hear them say their prayers than that she should attend all the public and Church meetings in the world.*
>
> *"It has been said that consecration is that which makes drudgery divine; and there is no place where consecration can be more necessarily and beautifully shown than within the four walls of the place which we call home. The world can do without its committee meetings; it cannot do without its homes; and a home is not a home when the mistress of the home is absent from it"* (*The Letters to Timothy, Titus, and Philemon*, p. 286f).

Despite the great call and privilege of motherhood, there are two problems about this command that must be covered—the problems of child abuse and of putting profession before children. Oliver Greene states it well:

> *"This verse seems unnecessary—and yet it is very important. Most animals will fight and die to protect their young, but some men and women are so totally depraved that they lose all respect and love for their own flesh and blood—their children [cp. child abuse]. The aged saints are to teach the younger women to love their children. Any precious mother with a baby in the home has a full time job twenty-four hours a day, seven days a week. No other person will ever love your child as you love it if you are a true mother. No other person can train and discipline that child as you will if you are a true mother. No person can take the place of a mother; therefore, mothers should love their children above fame, fortune, beauty, houses, or social prestige. Children should come first in the heart of a mother; and she should forsake all except her husband to give her love, time, and attention to her children. The best friend any child will ever have on the face of this earth is a godly, consecrated mother who loves him"* (*The Epistles of Paul the Apostle to Timothy and Titus*, p 442f).

Matthew Henry says that young mothers are "to love their children, not with a natural affection only, but a spiritual, a love springing from a holy sanctified heart and regulated by the word; not a fond foolish love, indulging them in evil, neglecting due reproof and correction where necessary, but a regular Christian love, showing itself in their pious education, forming their life and manners aright, taking care of their souls as well as of their bodies, of their spiritual welfare as well as of their temporal" (*Matthew Henry's Commentary*, Vol.5, p.863).

> **Who wants all men to be saved and to come to a knowledge of the truth. (1 Tim 2:4)**
>
> **I have been reminded of your sincere faith, which first lived in your grandmother Lois and in your mother Eunice and, I am persuaded, now lives in you also. (2 Tim 1:5)**
>
> **Discipline your son, for in that there is hope; do not be a willing party to his death. (Prov 19:18)**
>
> **Train a child in the way he should go, and when he is old he will not turn from it. (Prov 22:6)**
>
> **Folly is bound up in the heart of a child, but the rod of discipline will drive it far from him. (Prov 22:15)**
>
> **Do not withhold discipline from a child; if you punish him with the rod, he will not die. (Prov 23:13)**

TITUS 2:1-10

3. Younger women are to be self-controlled (sophronos): this is the same Greek word translated self-controlled in verse two. (See note, pt.3—Tit.2:2 for discussion and verses.) Simply stated, young women are not to live a life of license within the home or out in public: partying, drinking, overeating, indulging in any sense of the word. She is to curb her desires and emotions.

4. Younger women are to be pure (agnas): pure morally and sexually; to be pure in thought and act.

> **But I tell you that anyone who looks at a woman lustfully has already committed adultery with her in his heart. (Mat 5:28)**
> **It is God's will that you should be sanctified: that you should avoid sexual immorality; (1 Th 4:3)**
> **To be self-controlled and pure, to be busy at home, to be kind, and to be subject to their husbands, so that no one will malign the word of God. (Titus 2:5)**

5. Younger women are to be busy: homemakers. No better exposition of this command could be given than that written by Oliver Greene:

> *"This does not mean that the wife is never to go out of the home, never to take part in any outside interests; but she is not to neglect the duties of the home in order to participate in things outside the home. In other words, she is not to be better known outside the home than in the home, by her own husband and family. She is to be diligent at home—not lazy or slothful, not unconcerned about the home and the things pertaining thereto—but to give her best to the home, seeing that things are in order and that the home is kept as becomes a Christian. Young wives are not to omit their own duties and become 'busybodies' in others' affairs.... Christianity puts the right kind of pride in the heart—and a woman who is a believer should take pride in her home, which is her castle. She should keep that home clean, neat, and presentable. A young married woman with a baby and a home, if she does her duty, has a full time job.*
> *"Dear ladies should never forget that God made woman to make this world a sweeter, brighter, happier place in which to live. Adam was lonely; his life was empty. He found not a helpmate as he named the animals. Therefore, God removed a rib from Adam's side and made Eve and gave her to Adam to be his helpmate. God did not give Eve to Adam for his slave. Wives are not to be chattels or slaves. They are to love and esteem their husband, their children, love their home and be diligent in that field. A young woman who is not willing to make a home for her husband and her family should stay single.*
> *"Husbands are commanded to love their wives as Christ loved the Church and gave Himself for it; and in like manner, wives are commanded to be in subjection to their own husbands, because the husband is the head of the wife even as Jesus is the head of the Church (Eph.5:25ff). Therefore, Christianity is the patron of domestic virtues....There can never be a great local church without great Christian families; and there will never be a great Christian family without Christian fathers and mothers—not only Christian in word, but in deed and in truth. Great homes make great churches; great homes and great churches make great nations. A Christian home is a place of contentment—a place of peace; and when domestic duties are neglected, the home suffers severely. Regardless of how much a mother may do outside the home, whatever self-denial and zeal she may contribute to outside interests, and regardless of how much good she may accomplish outside the home, if she neglects her home she has brought reproach upon Christianity. The duty of a Christian mother is first to her home, and these other interests must be secondary"* (*The Epistles of Paul the Apostle to Timothy and Titus*, p.444f).

> **But I tell you that anyone who looks at a woman lustfully has already committed adultery with her in his heart. (Mat 5:28)**
> **It is God's will that you should be sanctified: that you should avoid sexual immorality; (1 Th 4:3)**
> **To be self-controlled and pure, to be busy at home, to be kind, and to be subject to their husbands, so that no one will malign the word of God. (Titus 2:5)**

6. Younger women are to be *kind* (agathos): of the highest quality and character; virtuous through and through; kind, good natured and caring. There is no vice, no dirt or pollution in her life; she is pure and clean, of the highest character. And she is good to people, that is, kind and caring. She is not an idle person, going from house to house being a gossiper and busy body. She is purposeful, moving in and among people doing good, showing care and kindness, helping people wherever she can (cp. 1 Tim. 5:13).

> **In the same way, let your light shine before men, that they may see your good deeds and praise your Father in heaven. (Mat 5:16)**
> **In everything set them an example by doing what is good. In your teaching show integrity, seriousness (Titus 2:7)**
> **And let us consider how we may spur one another on toward love and good deeds. (Heb 10:24)**
> **And do not forget to do good and to share with others, for with such sacrifices God is pleased. (Heb 13:16)**

7. Younger women are to be *subject to their husbands*. There is to be a *partnership* and *order* between men and women. Neither is independent of the other. Both are from

the other, and the relationship that exists between them has come from God.

> **In the Lord, however, woman is not independent of man, nor is man independent of woman. For as woman came from man, so also man is born of woman. But everything comes from God. (1 Cor 11:11-12)**

There is neither male nor female in God's eyes. He sees both men and women as one, each as significant as the other.

> **There is neither Jew nor Greek, slave nor free, male nor female, for you are all one in Christ Jesus. (Gal 3:28)**

a. When God talks about man being the head of the woman, He is not talking about ability or worth, competence or value, brilliance or advantage. God is talking about function and order within an organization. Every organization has to have a head for it to be operated in an efficient and orderly manner. There are no greater organizations than God's universe, His church, and His Christian family. Within God's order of things there is a partnership, but every partnership must have a head, and God has ordained that man is the head of the partnership.

b. The great pattern for the wife to follow is Christ and the church. Christ is the head of the church. This simply means that Christ has authority over the church. So long as the church lives by this rule, the church experiences love and joy and peace—orderliness—and it is able to carry out its function and mission on earth to the fullest. So it is with the husband; he is the head of the family, the ultimate authority in the family. The wife is to be submissive to that authority just as the church is to be submissive to Christ. So long as she and the rest of the family live by this rule, the family experiences love, joy, and peace—orderliness—and it fulfills its function and purpose on earth. This, of course, assumes that the husband is fulfilling his part in the family. As in any organization, each member must do his part for the organization to be orderly and accomplish its purpose.

c. The husband is the savior of the body just as Christ is the Savior of the church. Christ is the great Protector and Comforter of the church. So the husband is to be the *protector and comforter* of the wife. By nature, that is, by the constitution and build of the body, the husband is stronger than the wife. Therefore, in God's order of things, he is to be the main *protector* and *comforter* of the wife. These two functions are two of the great benefits which the wife receives from a loving husband who is faithful to the Lord.

> **To the married I give this command (not I, but the Lord): A wife must not separate from her husband. (1 Cor 7:10)**
> **Wives, submit to your husbands, as is fitting in the Lord. (Col 3:18)**
> **A woman should learn in quietness and full submission. I do not permit a woman to teach or to have authority over a man; she must be silent. For Adam was formed first, then Eve. (1 Tim 2:11-13)**
> **In the same way, their wives are to be women worthy of respect, not malicious talkers but temperate and trustworthy in everything. (1 Tim 3:11)**
> **Then they can train the younger women to love their husbands and children, (Titus 2:4)**
> **Wives, in the same way be submissive to your husbands so that, if any of them do not believe the word, they may be won over without words by the behavior of their wives, (1 Pet 3:1)**
> **She watches over the affairs of her household and does not eat the bread of idleness. (Prov 31:27)**
> **To the woman he said, "I will greatly increase your pains in childbearing; with pain you will give birth to children. Your desire will be for your husband, and he will rule over you." (Gen 3:16)**

Note why young women must live and behave as God says: that the Word of God will not be maligned, that is, dishonored, reproached and slandered. The young woman who professes Christ but does not live for Him brings reproach upon God's Word. How? It stirs the world to think within their minds:

> *"There must be no power in the Word of God, no power to change lives—no power to give love, joy, peace, and hope. There must be no advantage to believing Christ and to trusting the promises of God's Word. The promises mean nothing to this hypocritical young woman—not enough to stir her to follow Christ. Therefore, there must be nothing to this thing called Christianity. The promises of the Word of God must be meaningless and powerless. They have made no difference in her life."*

But note: this is not true. The Word of God is alive and powerful; it does change lives (Heb.4:12). The problem is with some wives: they just...

- do not spend time in genuine study of God's Word, learning how they are to live.
- do not spend time in genuine prayer, asking God to help them to live victorious lives over the temptations and trials of this life.
- do not discipline their lives nor control their tongues as the Word of God demands.

The result is, of course, the charge of hypocrisy, and the Word of God is reproached and slandered.

Thought 1. What an indictment against a young lady: being a hypocrite and being the cause for the Word of God being maligned.

> **You who brag about the law, do you dishonor God by breaking the law? As it is written: "God's name is blasphemed among the Gentiles because of you." (Rom 2:23-24)**
> **Many will follow their shameful ways and will bring the way of truth into disrepute. (2 Pet 2:2)**

> But because by doing this you have made the enemies of the LORD show utter contempt, the son born to you will die." (2 Sam 12:14)
>
> So I continued, "What you are doing is not right. Shouldn't you walk in the fear of our God to avoid the reproach of our Gentile enemies? (Neh 5:9)

5 (2:6) **Younger Men—Church**: the behavior of younger men. Note that only one encouragement is specifically directed to young men. This is not because they are more saintly and need fewer instructions (smile, young men), nor because they are less important and merit less attention and space in God's Word. Remember: Timothy was a young man, so what is said to him in the next two verses applies to young men as well. All young men are included in the encouragements to Timothy.

The specific encouragement to young men is to be self-controlled (sophroneo): temperate, controlled, disciplined, restrained; curbing emotions, passions, and desires. It means to have a mind that is sound, sensible, and focused upon pure and clean thoughts and meaningful things. It means to control one's mind and life and to keep them focused upon the purpose, meaning, and significance of life. It means to control everything in life. This is critical for young men. Three reasons tell us why.

1. The bodies of young men are becoming more and more sexually alive as they move on toward middle age. Attraction and passion increases and stirs the young man to pay attention to the opposite sex. This is normal and natural; it is the way God has chosen to cause young men and women to become attracted to each other and to marry and carry on the human race. But always remember this: this is the very reason for this exhortation. Young men must control themselves. They must be men—real men—noble and honorable—disciplined and controlled, keeping themselves pure for the sake of their family and for Christ and His church. Passion can engulf a young man and drown him and his family if he is married.

2. The young men are discovering themselves, searching for and finding their place in society. Three of the biggest decisions ever made have to be made when a man is young:

⇒ the decision of *leaving home*: when to leave home and take on the total responsibility for oneself and perhaps a family.

⇒ the decision regarding *marriage*: who and when to marry and to take on a family.

⇒ the decision regarding *employment or profession*: what work to do in life.

Youth—up until middle age—is usually a seeking and an unsure time for young men, a time when they have to fight to secure their place in the world. This is the reason for the charge: young men must control themselves.

⇒ The urge to attack, run over, bypass, neglect, ignore, and abuse people in order to move ahead must be controlled.

⇒ The urge to back off, fall into line, go along, and compromise must be controlled. Young men are not to lose their vitality and energy, ambition, and dreams. They are to seek to move ahead and to make the greatest contribution they can both for society and Christ. But they are to stay under control and not do it in a rampaging, passionate, and inconsiderate way.

3. Young men are full of vision and dreams and energy, but they lack experience. The result is that they often become reckless and inconsiderate and unfeeling. And they often make mistakes. This is the reason for this charge: young men must be adventuresome and must pursue their dreams with all the energy they have, but they must be sober-minded, self-controlled, and disciplined as they move forward in life.

> So then, let us not be like others, who are asleep, but let us be alert and self-controlled. (1 Th 5:6)
>
> It teaches us to say "No" to ungodliness and worldly passions, and to live self-controlled, upright and godly lives in this present age, while we wait for the blessed hope—the glorious appearing of our great God and Savior, Jesus Christ, (Titus 2:12-13)
>
> Therefore, prepare your minds for action; be self-controlled; set your hope fully on the grace to be given you when Jesus Christ is revealed. (1 Pet 1:13)
>
> The end of all things is near. Therefore be clear minded and self-controlled so that you can pray. (1 Pet 4:7)

6 (2:7-8) **Ministers—Teachers—Young Men—Church**: the behavior of young ministers and teachers. Remember: these two verses can be made a continuation of the charge to young men (v.6). What are young ministers or teachers to be like in the world? How are they to behave? Five traits are given.

1. Young ministers and teachers are to set an example by doing what is good. The word "example" (tupos) literally means to make an impression with a die, to mould or form, to strike an impression. Therefore, it means that the young minister and teacher must be a model example of good works. This can be forcefully stated in several ways:

⇒ He must live what he preaches.
⇒ His behavior must match his teaching.
⇒ His life must not tear down what his words build up.
⇒ His deeds must show the light which he proclaims
⇒ His example must be his first concern; his instruction must be his second concern.

Teaching others is a necessity, but being an example to others is an *absolute* essential. Words mean nothing without the behavior to back up the words. When people see a life that is strong and full of love, joy, peace, and righteousness, they are far more likely to receive Christ and to live righteous lives themselves.

Thought 1. People have a right to expect the minister and teacher to live what they preach and teach. The great tragedy is that too few live what they profess. Too few pray—really pray—and too few really study the Scriptures devotionally, and even fewer consistently witness and share Christ with the lost. The great cry of God is for ministers and teachers who will live like they should and who will be a pattern, a *dynamic example of good works*. This is the only way laymen will ever become the witnesses for Christ that they should.

> "You are the salt of the earth. But if the salt loses its saltiness, how can it be made salty again? It is no longer good for

anything, except to be thrown out and trampled by men. (Mat 5:13)

In the same way, let your light shine before men, that they may see your good deeds and praise your Father in heaven. (Mat 5:16)

Don't let anyone look down on you because you are young, but set an example for the believers in speech, in life, in love, in faith and in purity. (1 Tim 4:12)

In everything set them an example by doing what is good. In your teaching show integrity, seriousness (Titus 2:7)

Brothers, as an example of patience in the face of suffering, take the prophets who spoke in the name of the Lord. (James 5:10)

And let us consider how we may spur one another on toward love and good deeds. (Heb 10:24)

Live such good lives among the pagans that, though they accuse you of doing wrong, they may see your good deeds and glorify God on the day he visits us. (1 Pet 2:12)

2. Young ministers and teachers are to set an example in doctrine and teaching. As stated above, living for Christ and being a dynamic pattern of good works is always to precede preaching and teaching, but preaching and teaching are important as well. In fact, if a person is truly living for Christ, he will preach and teach; he will share Christ. There is no way to live for Christ and not share the glorious message of salvation in Him. Living for Christ and preaching and teaching Christ go hand in hand. But note this: how a person preaches and teaches is critical. There is a right way and a wrong way to preach and teach.

    a. Young ministers and teachers are to have integrity; that is, they are to have pure motives and preach a pure doctrine. The young minister or teacher faces enormous temptations in his preaching and teaching, especially the temptation to impress people and win their approval and favor. How does this happen? By thinking about preaching and teaching in order to show one's…
- preaching ability
- charisma
- education
- authority
- intelligence
- insight
- mastery of the language
- knowledge

There is one other temptation that professional ministers and teachers in particular face, a temptation that must be guarded against at all times. That is the temptation to use the ministry as a means of livelihood. There is the temptation to *hold back on the message of God*, on what should be done, lest the people disapprove and one's livelihood be affected.

The ministers and teachers of God must have integrity; they must have pure motives every time they walk into the pulpit and classroom. They must preach and teach only for the purpose of reaching and ministering to people. They must not deviate from preaching the pure doctrine of God's Word; they must be true to the Holy Scripture (cp. 2 Tim.3:16).

    b. Young ministers and teachers are to preach and teach with seriousness, that is, with dignity and sincerity. They must approach the ministry and the function of preaching and teaching with *seriousness*. This does not mean that a preacher or teacher…
- is above others.
- is more important than others.
- is more highly privileged than others.
- is to be elevated in the minds of others.
- is to hold position over others.

Dignity does not mean a sense of privilege, but a sense of responsibility. The minister and teacher of God must be aware that he is duty-bound to proclaim the message of God to a lost and dying world. To preach and teach with gravity, dignity and seriousness means…
- to esteem the message of God's Word with the highest regard.
- to have the strictest regard for the truth of God's Word.
- to be honest and above reproach in proclaiming God's Word.

Note that the focus is not the preacher or teacher. It is the doctrine and message of God's Word. The preacher and teacher *proclaims it with integrity and seriousness*.

    c. Young ministers and teachers are to preach and teach with "soundness of speech." The word *soundness* means healthy and whole. The message must be true to God's Word, for only God's Word can make people sound, healthy, and whole.

Note the two results of living for Christ and of preaching and teaching for Christ.

⇒ The preacher and teacher cannot be condemned. Others may accuse him, but the accusation will be false and God will know the truth.

⇒ Opponents to the preacher or teacher will be put to shame by their gossip and accusations. If the preacher or teacher suffers, he will suffer because of the evil doing of others, not because he has done evil. Oliver Greene has an excellent conclusion to these verses:

"He was to preach a Gospel that is the power of God unto salvation—not weak or anemic, not unsound; but pure in every detail—a Gospel with which no one could find fault. He was to speak pure words, serious words….The enemy will be ashamed that he opposed such a message, because the Word of God will not return void; it will accomplish that whereunto it is sent. Any minister who defends the faith and preaches the pure Gospel of the marvelous grace of God will never be forced to apologize for the message he has delivered, because it will always bring forth fruit. Paul wanted Titus to be a fruitful minister; he wanted those to whom Titus preached to be healthy, strong believers" (The Epistles of Paul the Apostle to Timothy and Titus, p.451f).

We had previously suffered and been insulted in Philippi, as you know, but with

the help of our God we dared to tell you his gospel in spite of strong opposition. For the appeal we make does not spring from error or impure motives, nor are we trying to trick you. On the contrary, we speak as men approved by God to be entrusted with the gospel. We are not trying to please men but God, who tests our hearts. You know we never used flattery, nor did we put on a mask to cover up greed—God is our witness. We were not looking for praise from men, not from you or anyone else. As apostles of Christ we could have been a burden to you, (1 Th 2:2-6)

If you point these things out to the brothers, you will be a good minister of Christ Jesus, brought up in the truths of the faith and of the good teaching that you have followed. (1 Tim 4:6)

He must hold firmly to the trustworthy message as it has been taught, so that he can encourage others by sound doctrine and refute those who oppose it. (Titus 1:9)

You must teach what is in accord with sound doctrine. (Titus 2:1)

7 (2:9-10) **Slaves—Employees**: the behavior of Christian slaves or workmen. (See outlines and notes—1 Tim.6:1-2; Eph.6:5-9; Col.3:22-4:1 for more discussion.) There were millions and millions of slaves in the Roman Empire during the days of Paul. One source says that there were over sixty million (William Barclay. *The Letters to the Galatians and Ephesians*, p.212). The gospel was bound to reach many of these, and the churches all over the Empire were bound to be filled with slaves. For this reason the New Testament has much to say to slaves (1 Cor.7:21-22; Col.3:22; 4:1; 1 Tim.6:1-2; Tit.2:9-10; 1 Pt.2:18-25 and the whole book of Philemon are written either to or about a slave). However, slavery is never directly attacked by the New Testament. If it had been, there would have probably been so much bloodshed the scene would have been unimaginable! The slave owners and government would have...

- attacked the church, its preachers and believers, seeking to destroy such a doctrine.
- imprisoned and executed any who refused to be silent about such a doctrine.
- reacted and killed all of the slaves who professed Christ.

The Expositors Greek Testament (Vol.4, p.377f) has an excellent statement on how Christianity went about destroying slavery:

"Here, as elsewhere in the NT, slavery is accepted as an existing institution, which is neither formally condemned nor formally approved. There is nothing to prompt revolutionary action, or to encourage repudiation of the position...the institution is left to be undermined and removed by the gradual operation of the great Christian principles of...

- the equality of men in the sight of God
- a common Christian brotherhood
- the spiritual freedom of the Christian man
- the Lordship of Christ to which every other lordship is subordinate."

The instructions to slaves and masters in the New Testament are applicable to every generation of workman. As Francis Foulkes says, "...the principles of the whole section apply to employees and employers in every age, whether in the home, in business, or in the state" (*The Epistle of Paul to the Ephesians*. "Tyndale New Testament Commentaries," p.167).

Note five instructions governing the behavior of Christian workmen.

1. The Christian workman is to be obedient. He is to follow the instruction of the person over him. Note: he is to obey "in everything." In the workplace there is to be no instruction that is not to be obeyed. This, of course, does not mean he is to obey orders that are contrary to the teaching of the Lord and damaging to His people and creation. However, it does mean that the Christian workman is to do what he is told to do when he has been given the privilege of a job, the privilege...

- to earn a livelihood and provide for himself and his family.
- to serve humanity through providing some needed product or service.
- to earn enough to help meet the desperate needs of the world and to carry the gospel to the world.

The attitude of the Christian workman is that the energy and effort he puts into his job is important to the Lord.

2. The Christian workman is to go beyond the call of duty: he is to actually please his master in all things. This includes such things as...

- *attitude*: he has an attitude of appreciation for the job and for the livelihood it provides him.
- *spirit*: he shows commitment and loyalty, eagerness and diligence in his work.
- *thoughts*: he thinks about his work, how to improve it and to be more efficient.
- *talk and words*: he builds up the company and the work it does.
- *relationships*: he seeks to build good relations with all fellow employees and management.
- *work and labor*: he is on time and gives a full day of labor *plus* some. He actually seeks to increase his own productivity and that of the whole workplace. He helps the company when extra effort or hours are needed and goes well beyond what is required.

3. The Christian workman does not answer back, talk back, or contradict his manager (master). He recognizes the need for orderliness and for levels of supervision in order to get the job done. Therefore, he follows the instructions of those above him in order to get the job done.

4. The Christian workman does not steal. The Greek word actually stresses the stealing of small, petty items. How many have stooped to stealing, to doing what so many in the world do. How many feel that they are not getting what is due them, therefore, they are justified in taking a little here and a little there. The Christian workman is not to steal—*not ever*.

5. The Christian workman is to show that they can be fully trusted, that is, trustworthiness, loyalty, and faithfulness. He is to be...

- totally trustworthy
- completely loyal
- utterly faithful

The manager (master) is to know that he can depend upon the Christian workman in all that he does.

6. The Christian workman is to make the teaching about God our Savior attractive. What a beautiful, descriptive way to state this truth! The Christian workman is to take the teaching of God our Savior and make the teaching so attractive that no matter where he walks or moves, the teaching of God our Savior is noticed, given attention. The Christian workman lives and moves and has his being in the teachings of God. Therefore, everyone in the workplace who looks at him is attracted to the teachings of God.

Thought 1. William Barclay makes a point that every Christian workman needs to note:

> *"It may well be that the man who takes his Christianity to his work with him will run into trouble; but, if he sticks to it, he will end by winning the respect of all men.*
>
> *"E.F. Brown tells of a thing which happened in India. 'A Christian servant in India was once sent by his master with a verbal message which he knew to be untrue. He refused to deliver it. Though his master was very angry at the time, he respected the servant all the more afterwards and knew that he could always trust him in his own matters.'*
>
> *"The truth is that in the end the world comes to see that the Christian workman is the only workman worth having. In one sense, it is hard to be a Christian at our work; in another sense, if we would try it, it is much easier than we think, for there is not a master under the sun who is not desperately looking for workmen on whose loyalty and efficiency he can rely"* (*The Letters to Timothy, Titus, and Philemon*, p.292f).

Slaves, obey your earthly masters with respect and fear, and with sincerity of heart, just as you would obey Christ. Obey them not only to win their favor when their eye is on you, but like slaves of Christ, doing the will of God from your heart. Serve wholeheartedly, as if you were serving the Lord, not men, because you know that the Lord will reward everyone for whatever good he does, whether he is slave or free. (Eph 6:5-8)

Slaves, obey your earthly masters in everything; and do it, not only when their eye is on you and to win their favor, but with sincerity of heart and reverence for the Lord. Whatever you do, work at it with all your heart, as working for the Lord, not for men, since you know that you will receive an inheritance from the Lord as a reward. It is the Lord Christ you are serving. Anyone who does wrong will be repaid for his wrong, and there is no favoritism. (Col 3:22-25)

All who are under the yoke of slavery should consider their masters worthy of full respect, so that God's name and our teaching may not be slandered. Those who have believing masters are not to show less respect for them because they are brothers. Instead, they are to serve them even better, because those who benefit from their service are believers, and dear to them. These are the things you are to teach and urge on them. (1 Tim 6:1-2)

Teach slaves to be subject to their masters in everything, to try to please them, not to talk back to them, (Titus 2:9)

Slaves, submit yourselves to your masters with all respect, not only to those who are good and considerate, but also to those who are harsh. (1 Pet 2:18)

The LORD God took the man and put him in the Garden of Eden to work it and take care of it. (Gen 2:15)

By the sweat of your brow you will eat your food until you return to the ground, since from it you were taken; for dust you are and to dust you will return." (Gen 3:19)

Whatever your hand finds to do, do it with all your might, for in the grave, where you are going, there is neither working nor planning nor knowledge nor wisdom. (Eccl 9:10)

He who has been stealing must steal no longer, but must work, doing something useful with his own hands, that he may have something to share with those in need. (Eph 4:28)

TITUS 2:11-15

	B. Message 2: The Grace of God,DS1 2:11-15		
1 The grace of God brings salvation	11 For the grace of God that brings salvation has appeared to all men.	appearing of our great God and Savior, Jesus Christ,	of our great God and Savior, Jesus Christ
2 The grace of God teaches us how to live	12 It teaches us to say "No" to ungodliness and worldly passions, and to live self-controlled, upright and godly lives in this present age,	14 Who gave himself for us to redeem us from all wickedness and to purify for himself a people that are his very own, eager to do what is good.	4 The grace of God is demonstrated in the death of Christ a. To redeem us b. To set us apart as a special people c. To inspire good works
a. Teaches us to deny some things			
b. Teaches us things to be		15 These, then, are the things you should teach. Encourage and rebuke with all authority. Do not let anyone despise you.	5 The grace of God is a message to be proclaimed through preaching, encouraging, & rebuking
3 The grace of God teaches us to look for the return	13 While we wait for the blessed hope—the glorious		

DIVISION II

THE MESSAGE OF SOUND DOCTRINE

B. Message 2: The Grace of God, 2:11-15

(2:11-15) **Introduction**: The great message of the grace of God involves five significant points.
1. The grace of God brings salvation (v.11).
2. The grace of God teaches us how to live (v.12).
3. The grace of God teaches us to look for the return of our great God and Savior, Jesus Christ (v.13).
4. The grace of God is demonstrated in the death of Christ (v.14).
5. The grace of God is a message to be proclaimed through preaching, encouraging and rebuking (v.15).

DEEPER STUDY # 1
(2:11-15) **Grace**: (charis): probably the most meaningful word in the language of men. The Bible means something far more than men mean by grace. To men the word "grace" means three things.
1. Grace is that something, that quality within a thing that is beautiful or joyful. It may be the fragrance of a flower, the rich green of the grass, the beauty of a lovely person.
2. Grace is anything that has loveliness. It may be a thought, an act, a word, a person.
3. Grace is a gift, a favor that someone might extend to a friend. The favor is always freely done, expecting nothing in return, and the favor is always done for a friend.

However, when the early Christians looked at what God had done for men, they had to add a deeper and much richer meaning to the word *grace*. For God had saved sinners, those who had acted against Him. Therefore, grace became the favor of God showered upon men—men who did not deserve His favor. Grace became the kindness and love that God freely gives to His *enemies*—men who are...

- "powerless" (Ro.5:6).
- "ungodly" (Ro.5:6).
- "sinners" (Ro.5:8).
- "enemies" (Ro.5:10).

No other word so expresses the depth and richness of the heart and mind of God. This is the distinctive difference between God's grace and man's grace. Whereas man sometimes does favors for his friends and thereby can be said to be gracious, God has done a thing unheard of among men: He has given His very own Son to die for His enemies (Ro.5:8-10). (See notes—Jn.21:15-17; Eph.2:8-10.)

a. God's grace is not earned. It is something completely undeserved and unmerited.

> For it is by grace you have been saved, through faith—and this not from yourselves, it is the gift of God—not by works, so that no one can boast. (Eph 2:8-9)
> But when the kindness and love of God our Savior appeared, he saved us, not because of righteous things we had done, but because of his mercy. He saved us through the washing of rebirth and renewal by the Holy Spirit, (Titus 3:4-5)

b. God's grace is the free gift of God. God extends His grace toward man.

> And are justified freely by his grace through the redemption that came by Christ Jesus. (Rom 3:24)
> But because of his great love for us, God, who is rich in mercy, made us alive with Christ even when we were dead in transgressions—it is by grace you have been saved. (Eph 2:4-5)
> For the grace of God that brings salvation has appeared to all men. It teaches us to say "No" to ungodliness and worldly passions, and to live self-controlled, upright and godly lives in this present age, while we wait for the blessed hope—the glorious appearing of our great God and Savior, Jesus Christ, who gave himself for us to redeem us from all wickedness and to purify for himself a people that are his very own, eager to do what is good. (Titus 2:11-14)

c. God's grace is the only way man can be saved.

> But the gift is not like the trespass. For if the many died by the trespass of the one man, how much more did God's grace and the gift that came by the grace of the one man, Jesus Christ, overflow to the many! (Rom 5:15)
> I always thank God for you because of his grace given you in Christ Jesus. (1 Cor 1:4)
> For you know the grace of our Lord Jesus Christ, that though he was rich, yet for your sakes he became poor, so that you through his poverty might become rich. (2 Cor 8:9)

> [Salvation] whom he poured out on us generously through Jesus Christ our Savior, so that, having been justified by his grace, we might become heirs having the hope of eternal life. (Titus 3:6-7)

4. Grace means all the favors and gifts of God. It means all the good and perfect gifts of God, all the good and beneficial things He gives us and does for us, whether physical, material, or spiritual (Jas.1:17).

> In him we have redemption through his blood, the forgiveness of sins, in accordance with the riches of God's grace (Eph 1:7)
>
> In order that in the coming ages he might show the incomparable riches of his grace, expressed in his kindness to us in Christ Jesus. (Eph 2:7)
>
> And my God will meet all your needs according to his glorious riches in Christ Jesus. (Phil 4:19)
>
> The grace of our Lord was poured out on me abundantly, along with the faith and love that are in Christ Jesus. (1 Tim 1:14)

1 (2:11) **Grace—Salvation**: the grace of God brings salvation. What does the grace of God mean? Among men grace means the favor and blessing that one person bestows upon another person. But God's grace means something far more. God's grace is the grace that brings salvation to man. God's grace is Jesus Christ, the gift of the Savior to the world. God's grace, the Lord Jesus Christ, saves the person...

- who is in rebellion against God.
- who curses God.
- who stands against God.
- who opposes God.
- who sins against God.
- who lives contrary to God.
- who lives an ungodly life.
- who is lonely.
- who is empty.
- who is powerless.
- who has any lack or need.
- who is without purpose and meaning.

God's grace, the Lord Jesus Christ, reaches down to those who have rejected God: who are doing their own thing and living like they want; it reaches down to those who ignore and neglect God and pay little attention to what God says.

The point is this: God's grace, the gift of His Son to the world, is not deserved. God's grace is not merited. No person deserves the favor of salvation that is in Christ. There are three reasons why we do not deserve God's grace.

1. We come short of God's glory in that we sin. God does not sin or go contrary to His law, but we do. We sin and transgress God's law. God never acts against His glory and nature, but we do. We do all kinds of things against the glory of God's nature; we often shame and curse, neglect and ignore, abuse and reject Him. God dwells in the glory of His perfection; we live in the shame of corruption. Stated as simply as possible: we come short, ever so short of God's glory.

> **For all have sinned and fall short of the glory of God, (Rom 3:23)**
>
> We all, [just] like sheep, have gone astray, each of us has turned to his own way; and the LORD has laid on him the iniquity of us all. (Isa 53:6)
>
> All of us have become like one who is unclean, and all our righteous acts are like filthy rags; we all shrivel up like a leaf, and like the wind our sins sweep us away. (Isa 64:6)
>
> As it is written: "There is no one righteous, not even one; there is no one who understands, no one who seeks God. All have turned away, they have together become worthless; there is no one who does good, not even one." "Their throats are open graves; their tongues practice deceit." "The poison of vipers is on their lips." "Their mouths are full of cursing and bitterness." "Their feet are swift to shed blood; ruin and misery mark their ways, and the way of peace they do not know." "There is no fear of God before their eyes." (Rom 3:10-18)

2. We come short of God's glory in that we die. God does not die, but we do. The glory of God's nature is that He lives forever, but not us. The shame of our nature is that we die; we do not live forever. We have to go through the terrible and agonizing and painful experience of death. We come ever so short of God's eternal glory.

> Therefore, just as sin entered the world through one man, and death through sin, and in this way death came to all men, because all sinned— (Rom 5:12)
>
> For the wages of sin is death, (Rom 6:23)
>
> Just as man is destined to die once, (Heb 9:27)
>
> For, "All men are like grass, and all their glory is like the flowers of the field; the grass withers and the flowers fall, (1 Pet 1:24)
>
> Like water spilled on the ground, which cannot be recovered, so we must die. But God does not take away life; instead, he devises ways so that a banished person may not remain estranged from him. (2 Sam 14:14)
>
> For all can see that wise men die; the foolish and the senseless alike perish and leave their wealth to others. (Psa 49:10)
>
> What man can live and not see death, or save himself from the power of the grave? Selah (Psa 89:48)
>
> You sweep men away in the sleep of death; they are like the new grass of the morning—though in the morning it springs up new, by evening it is dry and withered. (Psa 90:5-6)
>
> As for man, his days are like grass, he flourishes like a flower of the field; the wind blows over it and it is gone, and its place remembers it no more. (Psa 103:15-16)
>
> All go to the same place; all come from dust, and to dust all return. (Eccl 3:20)
>
> No man has power over the wind to contain it ; so no one has power over the

day of his death. As no one is discharged in time of war, so wickedness will not release those who practice it. (Eccl 8:8)

A voice says, "Cry out." And I said, "What shall I cry?" "All men are like grass, and all their glory is like the flowers of the field. The grass withers and the flowers fall, because the breath of the LORD blows on them. Surely the people are grass. (Isa 40:6-7)

3. We come short of God's glory in that we have violated the laws of heaven and are doomed to the prison and judgment of hell. When we die, we do not cease to exist. We exist forever. The very fact that we come short of God's glory makes us *short of heaven*. We are not perfect; therefore, we are not fit to live in a perfect place, that is, in heaven. We are doomed and judged to live outside heaven, away from God's presence in a place called hell. And we must always remember why: if we choose to live without God in this present world, then we condemn ourselves to live without God in the next world. If we reject the privilege of living with God in this world, then we reject the right to live with God in heaven.

Do not be afraid of those who kill the body but cannot kill the soul. Rather, be afraid of the One who can destroy both soul and body in hell. (Mat 10:28)

"Then he will say to those on his left, 'Depart from me, you who are cursed, into the eternal fire prepared for the devil and his angels. (Mat 25:41)

And give relief to you who are troubled, and to us as well. This will happen when the Lord Jesus is revealed from heaven in blazing fire with his powerful angels. He will punish those who do not know God and do not obey the gospel of our Lord Jesus. (2 Th 1:7-8)

Just as man is destined to die once, and after that to face judgment, (Heb 9:27)

If this is so, then the Lord knows how to rescue godly men from trials and to hold the unrighteous for the day of judgment, while continuing their punishment. (2 Pet 2:9)

By the same word the present heavens and earth are reserved for fire, being kept for the day of judgment and destruction of ungodly men. (2 Pet 3:7)

Enoch, the seventh from Adam, prophesied about these men: "See, the Lord is coming with thousands upon thousands of his holy ones to judge everyone, and to convict all the ungodly of all the ungodly acts they have done in the ungodly way, and of all the harsh words ungodly sinners have spoken against him." (Jude 1:14-15)

But this is the glorious news. God's grace, the Lord Jesus Christ, has brought salvation to us. God's grace, the gift of His own dear Son, saves us from sin, death, and hell. We do not deserve it, but God loves us beyond imagination. He has given His very own Son for us—to save us. He did it because He is gracious. His very nature is the embodiment of grace, of favoring and blessing those who do not deserve it. And note: His salvation is for all men—no matter who they are nor what they have done. The person may be a murderer such as Paul or an adulterer such as David, but God's grace is sufficient to cover any and all sins. God will save any person. His grace, the Lord Jesus Christ who brings salvation, is now available to all men. All men can now be saved—saved from sin, death, and hell—no matter who they are.

And all mankind will see God's salvation.'" (Luke 3:6)

And everyone who calls on the name of the Lord will be saved.' (Acts 2:21)

Then Peter began to speak: "I now realize how true it is that God does not show favoritism but accepts men from every nation who fear him and do what is right. (Acts 10:34-35)

No! We believe it is through the grace of our Lord Jesus that we are saved, just as they are." (Acts 15:11)

For there is no difference between Jew and Gentile—the same Lord is Lord of all and richly blesses all who call on him, for, "Everyone who calls on the name of the Lord will be saved." (Rom 10:12-13)

[God] who wants all men to be saved and to come to a knowledge of the truth. (1 Tim 2:4)

For the grace of God that brings salvation has appeared to all men. (Titus 2:11)

The Lord is not slow in keeping his promise, as some understand slowness. He is patient with you, not wanting anyone to perish, but everyone to come to repentance. (2 Pet 3:9)

We also know that law is made not for the righteous but for lawbreakers and rebels, the ungodly and sinful, the unholy and irreligious; for those who kill their fathers or mothers, for murderers, for adulterers and perverts, for slave traders and liars and perjurers—and for whatever else is contrary to the sound doctrine (1 Tim 1:9-10)

In his pride the wicked does not seek him; in all his thoughts there is no room for God. (Psa 10:4)

2 (2:12-13) **Grace—Salvation**: the grace of God teaches us how to live. It teaches us to do two things.

1. God's grace, the Lord Jesus Christ, teaches us to deny ungodliness and worldly lusts or passions, that is, to reject, renounce, give up, and have nothing to do with ungodliness and worldly lusts or passions. God's grace, the Lord Jesus Christ, teaches us "to say 'no' to ungodliness and worldly lusts [passions]" (Beck, *The New Testament in the Language of Today*).

   a. *Ungodliness* (asebeia): anything that is not like God, not holy, righteous or pure; anything that does not honor God by word or deed, that does not show reverence and worship toward God; anything that does not obey God, that violates God's commandments and goes against His will. The grace of God, the Lord Jesus Christ, teaches us to deny ungodliness, to give up and to turn away from everything that is ungodly and does not honor and praise Him.

> What good will it be for a man if he gains the whole world, yet forfeits his soul? Or what can a man give in exchange for his soul? (Mat 16:26)
> "Be careful, or your hearts will be weighed down with dissipation, drunkenness and the anxieties of life, and that day will close on you unexpectedly like a trap. (Luke 21:34)
> Children, obey your parents in everything, for this pleases the Lord. (Col 3:20)
> You adulterous people, don't you know that friendship with the world is hatred toward God? Anyone who chooses to be a friend of the world becomes an enemy of God. (James 4:4)

b. *Worldly lusts or passions* (kosmikai epithumiai): all the desires of this world that are not fit for heaven and could not be presented to God; all the desires that push us away from God; all the desires and lusts of the world that stir us...
- to look when we should not look.
- to do when we should not do.
- to get more when we should give more.
- to be selfish and vicious when we should be sacrificial and kind.
- to be sensual and immoral when we should be disciplined and pure.
- to seek the recognition of men when we should seek the recognition of God.

c. *Worldly lusts* or *passions* are those desires that crave the possessions of this world, that attach us to this world, and that will remain in this world when we leave it. We will go away and move on, but they will be left behind.

d. *Worldly lusts* or *passions* are the desires that crave the sensual and selfish pleasures of this world, the very things that we would never want God to see.

The grace of God, the Lord Jesus Christ, teaches us to deny worldly lusts and to give up and turn away from everything that we cannot take with us and present to God when we meet Him face to face.

> What good will it be for a man if he gains the whole world, yet forfeits his soul? Or what can a man give in exchange for his soul? (Mat 16:26)
> "Be careful, or your hearts will be weighed down with dissipation, drunkenness and the anxieties of life, and that day will close on you unexpectedly like a trap. (Luke 21:34)
> Children, obey your parents in everything, for this pleases the Lord. (Col 3:20)
> You adulterous people, don't you know that friendship with the world is hatred toward God? Anyone who chooses to be a friend of the world becomes an enemy of God. (James 4:4)

2. God's grace, the Lord Jesus Christ, teaches us to live self-controlled, upright, and godly lives in this present age.

a. Self-controlled (sophronos): temperate and disciplined. It is restraining desires, lusts, and appetites. It is never giving in to excess—to the lust for more and more. It is controlling everything and using it for its proper purpose:
⇒ It is controlling the desire for sex and using it for marriage.
⇒ It is controlling the desire for food and using it for health.
⇒ It is controlling the desire for material things and using it to meet both the needs of one's own family and the desperate needs of the world.

> As Paul discoursed on righteousness, self-control and the judgment to come, Felix was afraid and said, "That's enough for now! You may leave. When I find it convenient, I will send for you." (Acts 24:25)
> Do you not know that in a race all the runners run, but only one gets the prize? Run in such a way as to get the prize. Everyone who competes in the games goes into strict training. They do it to get a crown that will not last; but we do it to get a crown that will last forever. Therefore I do not run like a man running aimlessly; I do not fight like a man beating the air. No, I beat my body and make it my slave so that after I have preached to others, I myself will not be disqualified for the prize. (1 Cor 9:24-27)
> But the fruit of the Spirit is love, joy, peace, patience, kindness, goodness, faithfulness, gentleness and self-control. Against such things there is no law. (Gal 5:22-23)
> He who loves pleasure will become poor; whoever loves wine and oil will never be rich. (Prov 21:17)
> When you sit to dine with a ruler, note well what is before you, (Prov 23:1)

b. Upright (dikaios): doing right, treating others like we should, doing good to them, giving them their due share. What an indictment! How selfish we are in our hoarding and banking while a world dies from starvation, disease, war, evil, and sin. Every person is due his share. We are to live righteously, giving and seeing to it that every man is treated right, that every man receives his due share. If they are well-off physically and materially, we are to treat them righteously, just like we would want to be treated. If they are needy, poor, destitute, hungry, diseased, lonely, bed-ridden, and sinful, we are to do right toward them and meet their needs. They are to receive their due share of this earth just as we are.

> Come back to your senses as you ought, and stop sinning; for there are some who are ignorant of God—I say this to your shame. (1 Cor 15:34)

> Filled with the fruit of righteousness that comes through Jesus Christ—to the glory and praise of God. (Phil 1:11)
>
> Command those who are rich in this present world not to be arrogant nor to put their hope in wealth, which is so uncertain, but to put their hope in God, who richly provides us with everything for our enjoyment. Command them to do good, to be rich in good deeds, and to be generous and willing to share. In this way they will lay up treasure for themselves as a firm foundation for the coming age, so that they may take hold of the life that is truly life. (1 Tim 6:17-19)
>
> And do not forget to do good and to share with others, for with such sacrifices God is pleased. (Heb 13:16)
>
> Anyone, then, who knows the good he ought to do and doesn't do it, sins. (James 4:17)

c. *Godly* (eusebos): to be like God; to live as God would live on this earth; to live in the consciousness that God lives within the very body of the believer—that the believer's body is the very temple of God. It is living and moving and having one's being in God. It is living just like God says to live, obeying Him in all things.

> Have nothing to do with godless myths and old wives' tales; rather, train yourself to be godly. (1 Tim 4:7)
>
> But you, man of God, flee from all this, and pursue righteousness, godliness, faith, love, endurance and gentleness. (1 Tim 6:11)
>
> It teaches us to say "No" to ungodliness and worldly passions, and to live self-controlled, upright and godly lives in this present age, (Titus 2:12)
>
> Since everything will be destroyed in this way, what kind of people ought you to be? You ought to live holy and godly lives (2 Pet 3:11)

3 (2:13) **Jesus Christ, Return—Grace:** God's grace, the Lord Jesus Christ, teaches us to look for the return of the Lord. This is a great verse on the coming again of the Lord Jesus Christ, and the Greek points out its greatness even more:

> *"Looking for the blessed hope, even the appearing of the glory of our great God and Savior Jesus Christ"* (Kenneth S. Wuest. *Word Studies in the Greek New Testament*).

The blessed hope and appearing of our Lord Jesus Christ are not two different things; the blessed hope *is* the appearing of our Lord Jesus Christ. He will appear in all the glory and majesty of His Being. What will be so blessed about His return? The word "blessed" (makarios) means to be filled with happiness, prosperity, richness, benefits, the highest good—all the great and glorious benefits imaginable. Therefore, the blessed hope of the Lord's return is to be filled with all that you can imagine and more...

- all the *happiness* imaginable and more.
- all the *prosperity* imaginable and more.
- all the *richness* imaginable and more.
- all the *benefits* imaginable and more.

If you can imagine the highest good and all the richness of life possible, the appearing of the glory of the Lord Jesus Christ will be that and more—much more.

1. The return of Jesus Christ will mean a *glorious union*: we will see Christ for the first time and be united with Him forever (Jn.14:3).

> "Father, I want those you have given me to be with me where I am, and to see my glory, the glory you have given me because you loved me before the creation of the world. (John 17:24)
>
> After that, we who are still alive and are left will be caught up together with them in the clouds to meet the Lord in the air. And so we will be with the Lord forever. (1 Th 4:17)

2. The return of Jesus Christ will mean a *glorious reunion*: the dead in Christ will arise and we who live will be reunited with our loved ones and friends forever.

> The Spirit himself testifies with our spirit that we are God's children. Now if we are children, then we are heirs—heirs of God and co-heirs with Christ, if indeed we share in his sufferings in order that we may also share in his glory. (Rom 8:16-17)
>
> After that, we who are still alive and are left will be caught up together with them in the clouds to meet the Lord in the air. And so we will be with the Lord forever. Therefore encourage each other with these words. (1 Th 4:17-18)

3. The return of Jesus Christ will mean a *glorious transformation of body*: we will receive our new incorruptible and eternal bodies.

> So will it be with the resurrection of the dead. The body that is sown is perishable, it is raised imperishable; it is sown in dishonor, it is raised in glory; it is sown in weakness, it is raised in power; it is sown a natural body, it is raised a spiritual body. If there is a natural body, there is also a spiritual body. (1 Cor 15:42-44)
>
> For the perishable must clothe itself with the imperishable, and the mortal with immortality. (1 Cor 15:53)
>
> But our citizenship is in heaven. And we eagerly await a Savior from there, the Lord Jesus Christ, who, by the power that enables him to bring everything under his control, will transform our lowly bodies so that they will be like his glorious body. (Phil 3:20-21)

4. The return of Jesus Christ will mean a *glorious life of happiness*: we will receive perfect joy and freedom from trials, pain, suffering, evil, and death.

> Then the righteous will shine like the sun in the kingdom of their Father. He who has ears, let him hear. (Mat 13:43)

> When Christ, who is your life, appears, then you also will appear with him in glory. (Col 3:4)
>
> He who was seated on the throne said, "I am making everything new!" Then he said, "Write this down, for these words are trustworthy and true." (Rev 21:5)

5. The return of Jesus Christ will mean a *glorious remaking of the heavens and earth*: we will receive a perfect world of love, joy and peace.

> That the creation itself will be liberated from its bondage to decay and brought into the glorious freedom of the children of God. (Rom 8:21)
>
> But the day of the Lord will come like a thief. The heavens will disappear with a roar; the elements will be destroyed by fire, and the earth and everything in it will be laid bare. Since everything will be destroyed in this way, what kind of people ought you to be? You ought to live holy and godly lives as you look forward to the day of God and speed its coming. That day will bring about the destruction of the heavens by fire, and the elements will melt in the heat. But in keeping with his promise we are looking forward to a new heaven and a new earth, the home of righteousness. (2 Pet 3:10-13)
>
> Then I saw a new heaven and a new earth, for the first heaven and the first earth had passed away, and there was no longer any sea. (Rev 21:1)

6. The return of Jesus Christ will mean a *glorious reward*.

> Now there is in store for me the crown of righteousness, which the Lord, the righteous Judge, will award to me on that day—and not only to me, but also to all who have longed for his appearing. (2 Tim 4:8)
>
> Blessed is the man who perseveres under trial, because when he has stood the test, he will receive the crown of life that God has promised to those who love him. (James 1:12)
>
> Praise be to the God and Father of our Lord Jesus Christ! In his great mercy he has given us new birth into a living hope through the resurrection of Jesus Christ from the dead, and into an inheritance that can never perish, spoil or fade—kept in heaven for you, (1 Pet 1:3-4)
>
> And when the Chief Shepherd appears, you will receive the crown of glory that will never fade away. (1 Pet 5:4)

7. The return of Jesus Christ will mean an *eternity of ruling and reigning*: we will receive the position and responsibility of serving Christ through all eternity.

> Jesus replied, "The one who has dipped his hand into the bowl with me will betray me. (Mat 26:23)
>
> There will be no more night. They will not need the light of a lamp or the light of the sun, for the Lord God will give them light. And they will reign for ever and ever. (Rev 22:5)
>
> "Behold, I am coming soon! My reward is with me, and I will give to everyone according to what he has done. (Rev 22:12)

8. The return of Jesus Christ will mean a *glorious dwelling place and mansions* (*many rooms*).

> In my Father's house are many rooms; if it were not so, I would have told you. I am going there to prepare a place for you. And if I go and prepare a place for you, I will come back and take you to be with me that you also may be where I am. (John 14:2-3)

4 (2:14) **Jesus Christ, Death—Grace**: the grace of God is revealed in the death of Christ. Jesus Christ "gave Himself for us." What does this mean? It means that Jesus Christ died for us. The word "for" (huper) means that He died in our behalf, for our sake, in our place, as our substitute. It means that Jesus Christ took our sins upon Himself, and paid the penalty for them. He bore...

⇒ the verdict of sin, the pronouncement of *guilty* for us.
⇒ the condemnation of our sins for us.
⇒ the punishment of our sins for us.

What was the verdict, the condemnation, and the punishment which He bore for us? The guilt of our sins which is death. Jesus Christ died for us. He died as our substitute; He died for us, and because He died for us we never have to die. This is what Scripture means when it says that Jesus Christ gave Himself for us. This is how God demonstrated His grace to the world: He gave His Son to die for the sins of men.

> But God demonstrates his own love for us in this: While we were still sinners, Christ died for us. (Rom 5:8)

But note a most critical point: why Jesus Christ died for us. He died for us for three critical reasons.

1. Christ died to redeem us from all wickedness. We are guilty of wickedness, that is, of what has just been covered—of ungodliness and worldly passions, of lawlessness, of disobeying and transgressing the law of God. We are sinners—short of God's glory—and we cannot keep from sinning and being short of God's glory. We have been kidnapped, captured, and captivated by lawlessness and imperfection. Therefore, we need to be redeemed (lutroo), that is, set free and delivered. The ransom needs to be paid so that we can be delivered and set free. This is why Jesus Christ gave Himself for us: to redeem us. The death of Jesus Christ was our ransom. His death sets us free from sin. How? God accepts His death for our death. When we believe that Christ died for us—really believe—God accepts our belief as the death of Jesus Christ. God takes our belief and counts it as the death of Jesus Christ. This means that we have already died, that we actually died with Christ when He died. God identifies us with Christ, with His death. Therefore, we are set free from sin and its penalty. We are delivered from the penalty of sin which is death. By faith in Jesus Christ we are redeemed,

that is, set free from sin and death. (See note, *Redemption*—Eph.1:7 for more discussion.)

> And are justified freely by his grace through the redemption that came by Christ Jesus. (Rom 3:24)
>
> Christ redeemed us from the curse of the law by becoming a curse for us, for it is written: "Cursed is everyone who is hung on a tree." (Gal 3:13)
>
> In whom we have redemption, the forgiveness of sins. (Col 1:14)
>
> [Christ] who gave himself for us to redeem us from all wickedness and to purify for himself a people that are his very own, eager to do what is good. (Titus 2:14)
>
> He did not enter by means of the blood of goats and calves; but he entered the Most Holy Place once for all by his own blood, having obtained eternal redemption. (Heb 9:12)
>
> For you know that it was not with perishable things such as silver or gold that you were redeemed from the empty way of life handed down to you from your forefathers, (1 Pet 1:18)
>
> And they sang a new song: "You are worthy to take the scroll and to open its seals, because you were slain, and with your blood you purchased men for God from every tribe and language and people and nation. (Rev 5:9)

2. Christ died so that He might have a people that are His very own, a very special people as His own possession. This is seen in the word "own" (periouson). The word means set apart, possessed over and above, especially selected and reserved for. When a person really grasps what Jesus Christ has done for him, that person can only surrender all he is and has to Christ. The person wants to follow and serve Christ, to do all that Christ says. The person separates himself from the world, sets his life apart to follow Christ, and Christ takes the person and by the power of the Holy Spirit sets the person apart to be His own very special possession. Through the death of Jesus Christ, the believer becomes the very special possession of the Lord Jesus Christ.

> But you are a chosen people, a royal priesthood, a holy nation, a people belonging to God, that you may declare the praises of him who called you out of darkness into his wonderful light. (1 Pet 2:9)
>
> Now if you obey me fully and keep my covenant, then out of all nations you will be my treasured possession. Although the whole earth is mine, (Exo 19:5)
>
> For you are a people holy to the LORD your God. Out of all the peoples on the face of the earth, the LORD has chosen you to be his treasured possession. (Deu 14:2)
>
> And the LORD has declared this day that you are his people, his treasured possession as he promised, and that you are to keep all his commands. He has declared that he will set you in praise, fame and honor high above all the nations he has made and that you will be a people holy to the LORD your God, as he promised. (Deu 26:18-19)
>
> For the sake of his great name the LORD will not reject his people, because the LORD was pleased to make you his own. (1 Sam 12:22)

3. Christ died to stir good works. Again, when a person really grasps what Jesus Christ has done for him, the person is stirred to give his life to Christ—to do all he can to serve Christ and to tell everyone in the world that the Savior has come to save men. The believer works and works, doing all the good he can in order to reach everyone he can with the glorious message of redemption.

> In the same way, let your light shine before men, that they may see your good deeds and praise your Father in heaven. (Mat 5:16)
>
> Command them to do good, to be rich in good deeds, and to be generous and willing to share. (1 Tim 6:18)
>
> In everything set them an example by doing what is good. In your teaching show integrity, seriousness (Titus 2:7)
>
> And let us consider how we may spur one another on toward love and good deeds. (Heb 10:24)
>
> Live such good lives among the pagans that, though they accuse you of doing wrong, they may see your good deeds and glorify God on the day he visits us. (1 Pet 2:12)

5 (2:15) **Preaching—Grace**: the grace of God is to be proclaimed. It is to be proclaimed in three ways.

1. We are to teach about the grace of God: preach, teach, and bear witness to it. There is no argument about the grace of God, about the Lord Jesus Christ; God does love the world. He has sent His Son into the world. Therefore, we are to teach the message of His grace—of the Lord Jesus Christ—utilizing every method of speech there is, and we are to do it day by day.

> "Go, stand in the temple courts," he said, "and tell the people the full message of this new life." (Acts 5:20)
>
> These, then, are the things you should teach. Encourage and rebuke with all authority. Do not let anyone despise you. (Titus 2:15)
>
> But the LORD said to me, "Do not say, 'I am only a child.' You must go to everyone I send you to and say whatever I command you. (Jer 1:7)
>
> "Get yourself ready! Stand up and say to them whatever I command you. Do not be terrified by them, or I will terrify you before them. (Jer 1:17)
>
> You must speak my words to them, whether they listen or fail to listen, for they are rebellious. (Ezek 2:7)
>
> As they moved, they would go in any one of the four directions the creatures faced; the wheels did not turn about as the

creatures went. Their rims were high and awesome, and all four rims were full of eyes all around. When the living creatures moved, the wheels beside them moved; and when the living creatures rose from the ground, the wheels also rose. (Ezek 1:17-19)

2. We are to encourage people in the grace of God. People are lonely, empty, without purpose, discouraged, distressed, and without hope. They need to hear the glorious message of God's grace, of the Lord Jesus Christ, and they need to hear about the wonderful life God gives us now and eternally—all through the Lord Jesus Christ.

> Until I come, devote yourself to the public reading of Scripture, to preaching and to teaching. (1 Tim 4:13)
>
> Preach the Word; be prepared in season and out of season; correct, rebuke and encourage—with great patience and careful instruction. (2 Tim 4:2)
>
> He must hold firmly to the trustworthy message as it has been taught, so that he can encourage others by sound doctrine and refute those who oppose it. (Titus 1:9)
>
> These, then, are the things you should teach. Encourage and rebuke with all authority. Do not let anyone despise you. (Titus 2:15)
>
> But encourage one another daily, as long as it is called Today, so that none of you may be hardened by sin's deceitfulness. (Heb 3:13)
>
> Let us not give up meeting together, as some are in the habit of doing, but let us encourage one another—and all the more as you see the Day approaching. (Heb 10:25)

3. We are to rebuke people in the grace of God. There is no excuse for men rejecting the grace of God in their sin. God has done too much for us in Christ Jesus His Son. A man is a fool to reject eternal life, the glorious redemption and hope which Christ gives. Men need to be told the truth, rebuked and put under conviction by our rebuking them in the grace of God.

> So watch yourselves. "If your brother sins, rebuke him, and if he repents, forgive him. (Luke 17:3)
>
> Have nothing to do with the fruitless deeds of darkness, but rather expose them. (Eph 5:11)
>
> Those who sin are to be rebuked publicly, so that the others may take warning. (1 Tim 5:20)
>
> Preach the Word; be prepared in season and out of season; correct, rebuke and encourage—with great patience and careful instruction. (2 Tim 4:2)
>
> To be self-controlled and pure, to be busy at home, to be kind, and to be subject to their husbands, so that no one will malign the word of God. (Titus 2:5)

TITUS 3:1-2

CHAPTER 3

C. Message 3: The Civic Duties of a Believer, 3:1-2

1 He is to obey the laws
2 He is to do good works
3 He is not to speak evil
4 He is to be peaceable
5 He is to be gentle
6 He is to show humility

Remind the people to be subject to rulers and authorities, to be obedient, to be ready to do whatever is good,
2 To slander no one, to be peaceable and considerate, and to show true humility toward all men.

DIVISION II

THE MESSAGE OF SOUND DOCTRINE

C. Message 3: The Civic Duties of a Believer, 3:1-2

(3:1-2) **Introduction**: the thrust of this passage is not the rulers of government and their behavior; the thrust is the believer and his duty to the state. Usually the believer can do little about how the authorities in government conduct their affairs, but the believer can do a great deal about his behavior as a citizen within the state. And God is very, very clear about the believer's behavior. Keep in mind that such terrible leaders as Nero were ruling when God led Paul to give these instructions to Titus and the believers on the island of Crete. Six duties of the Christian citizen are clearly spelled out.

1. He is to obey the laws (v.1).
2. He is to do good works (v.1).
3. He is not to speak evil (v.2).
4. He is to be peaceable (v.2).
5. He is to be gentle (v.2).
6. He is to show humility (v.2).

1 (3:1) **Citizenship—Law, Civil**: the Christian citizen is to *obey the laws of a nation, both the rulers and their authority*. Note the double command: "to be subject" and "to be obedient." This is strong; God expects believers to keep the command. All civil authority is to be obeyed, even the laws of one's own local community as well as the laws of one's state and nation. Why is this so important? The reason is self-evident; it is perfectly clear: without law and the keeping of the law society would be in utter chaos.

⇒ Lawlessness would run wild.
⇒ No one would be safe to walk the streets.
⇒ People would have to live behind closed doors.
⇒ Abuse, attacks, murder, and war would be a constant threat.
⇒ No property would be safe.
⇒ There would be no public roads, transportation, water, sewage, or electrical systems, for there would be no law to collect taxes. And even if there was, no one would honor it.
⇒ There would be no military police or fire protection for the same reason.

Without law and the keeping of the law there can be no society and no community, no life together, no bond to tie people together. Law, rulers and their authority, are an utter necessity to keep people from becoming wild beasts in a jungle of unrestrained selfishness and lawlessness.

Chaos is not God's will for the world; law and order are God's will. God wills men to live in a world of love, joy, and peace—a world of perfect law and order. Therefore, the believer is to set the example: he is to obey the rulers and the laws of his community and nation. He is to show how *loving and joyful, peaceful and wonderful* life can be if people will obey God and obey the civil authorities of this world. (See notes—Ro.12:18; 13:1; 1 Pt.2:13-17 for the believer's duty when rulers and laws oppose God.)

"Do not blaspheme God or curse the ruler of your people. (Exo 22:28)

Do not revile the king even in your thoughts, or curse the rich in your bedroom, because a bird of the air may carry your words, and a bird on the wing may report what you say. (Eccl 10:20)

Paul replied, "Brothers, I did not realize that he was the high priest; for it is written: 'Do not speak evil about the ruler of your people.'" (Acts 23:5)

Everyone must submit himself to the governing authorities, for there is no authority except that which God has established. The authorities that exist have been established by God. (Rom 13:1)

Submit yourselves for the Lord's sake to every authority instituted among men: whether to the king, as the supreme authority, or to governors, who are sent by him to punish those who do wrong and to commend those who do right. (1 Pet 2:13-14)

Show proper respect to everyone: Love the brotherhood of believers, fear God, honor the king. (1 Pet 2:17)

2 (3:1) **Citizenship—Good Works**: the Christian citizen is to be ready to *do whatever is good, every good work;* is to work and serve within his community for the good of all citizens, and he is to work and serve diligently. The word "ready" (hetoimous) means to be willing; to be prepared; to jump and be the first to diligently serve the community. And note: it is "Whatever is good, every good work" that he is to be ready to do. *Whatever is good, good works* does not refer only to church work; it refers to the day by day employment of people and to the volunteer and service needs of a community. Every community is filled with needs, the needs of the lonely, poor, shut in, elderly, orphaned, homeless, sick—an innumerable list of needs that cry out for community attention. It is the duty of Christian citizens to take the lead in reaching out to meet these needs. The Christian citizen is to be ready and diligent, taking the lead in every good work within the community and nation. Keep in mind that a person's employment, his day-to-day job, is a major work that contributes to society. No matter how mundane, routine, and unimportant a person may feel his work is, it is not. It is very significant, for it contributes and helps to meet the needs of his fellow citizens and community.

> And God is able to make all grace abound to you, so that in all things at all times, having all that you need, you will abound in every good work. (2 Cor 9:8)
> And do not forget to do good and to share with others, for with such sacrifices God is pleased. (Heb 13:16)
> Anyone, then, who knows the good he ought to do and doesn't do it, sins. (James 4:17)
> Trust in the LORD and do good; dwell in the land and enjoy safe pasture. (Psa 37:3)

3 (3:2) **Evil Speaking—Citizenship**: the Christian citizen is *to speak evil of no person*. No citizen is to be slandered or verbally abused and torn down. God's ideal for society is this: all citizens working to build up and enrich the lives of each other and their community and nation. If a person, ruler or citizen, is working to build us up, why would we speak evil of him? We know that in day to day practical living, we live in an evil world where some citizens are selfish and greedy, and others commit some terrible and atrocious acts. It is this that causes chaos in society.

But note: the Christian citizen is not to speak evil against any citizen, not even an evil ruler. The answer to reaching evil people is not cursing, reviling, slandering, criticizing, and tearing them down. Verbal abuse only causes more evil—active retaliation. The only answer to reaching an evil citizen is to reach out to him in kindness, trying to lead him to change and live the way he should as a contributing citizen to the community. But note this: reaching out to evil people and not speaking evil against them does not mean that we do not use firm, strong, and warning words. We are never to give license to evil, nor to indulge the selfish and sinful acts of people. We are to speak with authority and strength against evil and untruth. We are to warn, and the community is to back up the warning with *just control*, even if it means imprisonment.

The point is this: there is no place in a just society for citizens speaking evil against each other. Cursing, reviling, slandering, and railing at each other is not the way to help those in rebellion against God, government, and man. The way to help is to reach out with kindness; and then if kindness fails, to reach out with strong, authoritative warnings—and then back up the warning. There is never a place for evil speaking. Christian citizens are to take the lead in speaking kind and strong words, words that warn against selfish and evil behavior.

> **Thought 1.** What an indictment against society! Even more, what a terrible indictment against those who speak evil against others within the church!

> Whoever slanders his neighbor in secret, him will I put to silence; whoever has haughty eyes and a proud heart, him will I not endure. (Psa 101:5)
> He who conceals his hatred has lying lips, and whoever spreads slander is a fool. (Prov 10:18)
> With his mouth the godless destroys his neighbor, but through knowledge the righteous escape. (Prov 11:9)
> "Beware of your friends; do not trust your brothers. For every brother is a deceiver, and every friend a slanderer. (Jer 9:4)

4 (3:2) **Brawling—Fighting—Contention**: the Christian citizen is to be peaceable, not a brawler (amachos). The Christian is not to be...
- a fighting, contentious person
- a person who is walking around looking for an argument or fight
- a person who walks around with a chip on his shoulder looking for controversy or argument
- a person who is so opinionated and stubborn, thinking everyone else is always wrong
- a person who is always criticizing or talking about others, stirring up trouble and disturbing feelings, causing division.

The Christian citizen is to be the very opposite: he is to be meek and peaceful. This, of course, does not mean that the Christian citizen does not speak up for what is right; he does. And he is strong in his stand, refusing to give in to the license and indulgence of evil. But he seeks peace where it is possible, and he seeks to lead others to be peaceable.

> I am a man of peace; but when I speak, they are for war. (Psa 120:7)
> Who devise evil plans in their hearts and stir up war every day. (Psa 140:2)
> Do not accuse a man for no reason— when he has done you no harm. (Prov 3:30)
> A hot-tempered man stirs up dissension, but a patient man calms a quarrel. (Prov 15:18)
> Starting a quarrel is like breaching a dam; so drop the matter before a dispute breaks out. (Prov 17:14)
> He who loves a quarrel loves sin; he who builds a high gate invites destruction. (Prov 17:19)
> A fool's lips bring him strife, and his mouth invites a beating. (Prov 18:6)
> It is to a man's honor to avoid strife, but every fool is quick to quarrel. (Prov 20:3)
> Do not bring hastily to court, for what will you do in the end if your neighbor puts you to shame? (Prov 25:8)
> Like one who seizes a dog by the ears is a passer-by who meddles in a quarrel not his own. (Prov 26:17)
> As charcoal to embers and as wood to fire, so is a quarrelsome man for kindling strife. (Prov 26:21)
> Do nothing out of selfish ambition or vain conceit, but in humility consider others better than yourselves. (Phil 2:3)
> Keep reminding them of these things. Warn them before God against quarreling about words; it is of no value, and only ruins those who listen. (2 Tim 2:14)

And the Lord's servant must not quarrel; instead, he must be kind to everyone, able to teach, not resentful. (2 Tim 2:24)

5 (3:2) **Gentle—Citizenship**: the Christian citizen must be *considerate, gentle* (epieikeis). The word is difficult to translate into English. It is translated by others as gentleness, forbearance, reasonableness, consideration, agreeableness, courtesy, patience, and softness. There is the tendency to say that either forbearance or gentleness is the better translation. It means that there is *something better than mere justice*—a gracious gentleness. Christian citizens are to be gentle and forbearing in dealing with other citizens.

Thought 1. The point is well-taken: we must be gentle and forbearing in dealing with citizens. The last thing that we must do is to criticize, condemn, censor, neglect, and ignore citizens. We must reach out to the people of the world with the gospel, and we must treat them with a *loving gentleness*. We must be gentle, having absolutely nothing to do with harshness. Too many of us are harsh and critical or neglectful and withdrawn. Too many of us are wrapped in the cloak of religion having nothing to do with reaching out to the lost. The desperate need of the hour is for us to reach out with the gospel in a spirit of *love and consideration, in a spirit of gentleness*.

> Be completely humble and gentle; be patient, bearing with one another in love. (Eph 4:2)
>
> Bear with each other and forgive whatever grievances you may have against one another. Forgive as the Lord forgave you. (Col 3:13)
>
> But we were gentle among you, like a mother caring for her little children. (1 Th 2:7)
>
> And the Lord's servant must not quarrel; instead, he must be kind to everyone, able to teach, not resentful. (2 Tim 2:24)
>
> To slander no one, to be peaceable and considerate, and to show true humility toward all men. (Titus 3:2)
>
> But the wisdom that comes from heaven is first of all pure; then peace-loving, considerate, submissive, full of mercy and good fruit, impartial and sincere. (James 3:17)

6 (3:2) **Humility—Meekness**: the Christian citizen must *show true humility* (prautes) *to all* citizens. The word means to be gentle, tender, humble, mild, considerate, but strongly so. Humility has the strength to control and discipline, and it does so at the right time.

a. Humility has *a humble state of mind*. But this does not mean the person is weak, cowardly, and bowing. The humble person simply loves people and loves peace; therefore, he walks humbly among men regardless of their status and circumstance in life. Associating with the poor and lowly of this earth does not bother the humble person. He desires to be a friend to all and to help all as much as possible.

b. Humility has *a strong state of mind*. It looks at situations and wants justice and right to be done. It is not a weak mind that ignores and neglects evil and wrong-doing, abuse and suffering.

⇒ If someone is suffering, humility steps in and does what it can to help.
⇒ If evil is being done, humility does what it can to stop and correct it.
⇒ If evil is running rampant and indulging itself, humility actually strikes out in anger. However, note a crucial point: the anger is always at the right time and against the right thing.

c. Humility has *strong self-control*. The humble person controls his spirit and mind. He controls the lusts of his flesh (sinful nature). He does not give way to ill-temper, retaliation, passion, indulgence, or license. The humble person dies to himself, to what his flesh would like to do, and he does the right thing—exactly what God wants done.

In summary, the gentle man walks in a humble, tender, but strong state of mind; denies himself, giving utmost consideration to others. He shows a control and righteous anger against injustice and evil. A gentle man forgets self and lives for others because of what Christ has done for him.

⇒ God is gentle.

> But the fruit of the Spirit is love, joy, peace, patience, kindness, goodness, faithfulness, gentleness and self-control. Against such things there is no law. (Gal 5:22-23)

⇒ Jesus Christ was gentle and humble.

> Take my yoke upon you and learn from me, for I am gentle and humble in heart, and you will find rest for your souls. (Mat 11:29)

⇒ Believers are to be gentle.

> Brothers, if someone is caught in a sin, you who are spiritual should restore him gently. But watch yourself, or you also may be tempted. (Gal 6:1)
>
> As a prisoner for the Lord, then, I urge you to live a life worthy of the calling you have received. Be completely humble and gentle; be patient, bearing with one another in love. Make every effort to keep the unity of the Spirit through the bond of peace. (Eph 4:1-3)
>
> Those who oppose him he must gently instruct, in the hope that God will grant them repentance leading them to a knowledge of the truth, (2 Tim 2:25)
>
> To slander no one, to be peaceable and considerate, and to show true humility toward all men. (Titus 3:2)
>
> Therefore, get rid of all moral filth and the evil that is so prevalent and humbly accept the word planted in you, which can save you. (James 1:21)
>
> Who is wise and understanding among you? Let him show it by his good life, by deeds done in the humility that comes from wisdom. (James 3:13)
>
> Instead, it should be that of your inner self, the unfading beauty of a gentle and quiet spirit, which is of great worth in God's sight. (1 Pet 3:4)

TITUS 3:3

	D. Message 4: Life Without God, 3:3
1 Man is foolish,^{DS1} disobedient,^{DS2} & deceived^{DS3} 2 Man is a slave of passions & pleasures 3 Man lives in malice^{DS4} & envy^{DS5} 4 Man is hateful^{DS6} & hated^{DS7}	3 At one time we too were foolish, disobedient, deceived and enslaved by all kinds of passions and pleasures. We lived in malice and envy, being hated and hating one another.

DIVISION II

THE MESSAGE OF SOUND DOCTRINE

D. Message 4: Life Without God, 3:3

(3:3) **Introduction**: this is a terrible picture of what life is like without God. Note that *we who are believers* were living a life just like what is described here before we accepted Christ. This does not necessarily mean that we were actively involved in every sin included in the list, but we are all guilty of at least some of these sins. And being guilty, we stand before God imperfect and short of His glory. Therefore, we need to be saved through the Lord Jesus Christ. Oliver Greene has an excellent introduction to this verse that merits quoting in its entirety:

> "We who are Christians now, once conformed to this picture of wickedness. (The 'we' also includes Paul and Titus.) The verse does not necessarily mean that every believer has been guilty of all the things pointed out here. Some things are mentioned that no doubt Paul was not guilty of before his conversion; but he is simply pointing out to Titus that he should preach to the people in the churches...that they should live holy lives, and especially manifest a spirit of humility, order, peace, kindness, and due subordination to local authorities. Titus should point out to the believers that they were formerly disorderly, wicked, sensual—sinners by nature; but having heard the Gospel, through the power of the Gospel they had been saved from these things by the grace of God, and now they were new creations in Christ Jesus and by their daily practices should prove to unbelievers that they have had a change of heart.
>
> "The minister of the Gospel is never to be proud or arrogant. He is to point unbelievers to Christ—not to his own righteousness or ability to live above the world. The minister is to remember that before his conversion he was in the same condition as the unbeliever to whom he now preaches. The minister is not to forget that he is not superior to others because of HIS ability, but because of the grace of God and the power of God. The minister is to exhort the wicked to repent. Remembering his own life of sin and wickedness will help him to fervently preach the grace of God which worked a miracle in his own heart; and having had a miracle of grace performed in his own heart, he knows what the grace of God can do for all who will receive it" (*The Epistles of Paul the Apostle to Timothy and Titus*, p.472f).

The subject of the verse and of this study is: *life without God*.
1. Man is foolish, disobedient, and deceived (v.3).
2. Man is a slave of passions (lust) and pleasure (v.3).
3. Man lives in malice and envy (v.3).
4. Man is hateful and hated (v.3).

1 (3:3) **Foolish—Disobedient—Deceived—Unwise—Unbelievers—Lost, The**: man is foolish, disobedient, and deceived (v.3) (see DEEPER STUDY # 1, *Foolish*—Tit.3:3; DEEPER STUDY # 3, *Disobedient*—Tit.3:3; DEEPER STUDY # 2, *Deceived*—Tit.3:3).

DEEPER STUDY # 1

(3:3) **Foolish—Unwise—Unbelievers—Lost, The**: a person without God is "foolish" (anoetoi). The word means to be thoughtless, dull, senseless, and without understanding in spiritual matters; to be ignorant of God and unwise in dealing with God.

Note that men sometimes call each other *fools*, using the word as a term of reproach. But believers are forbidden to call other persons fools; God wants no person reproached. But this is not the way the word is being used in the present passage. Scripture is simply saying that a person who denies, ignores, or neglects God is acting foolishly, very unwisely.

⇒ He is thoughtless: not applying his thoughts to God; not thinking through the truth about God.
⇒ He is dull: not being sharp in his thoughts about God. He is being sleepy-minded, slow, and sluggish toward God.
⇒ He is senseless: not using good common sense about God. He is acting contrary to good common sense. He is deficient in his thoughts about God.
⇒ He is without understanding: he does not grasp or comprehend God; he does not have the right ideas or thoughts about God.
⇒ He is ignorant of God: he does not know God. He has not learned God—has not looked at, thought about, studied, nor met, walked and fellowshipped with God.
⇒ He is unwise: he is acting contrary to wisdom; he is acting dangerously and foolishly.

Scripture is as clear as it can be: the person who walks upon earth without God is foolish. And remember: we were one time foolish—all of us—every believer. We walked upon earth most unwisely, thinking little if any about God, ignoring and neglecting Him; and some of us even denied Him.

But thanks be to God our Savior. He has saved us, and He will save any person no matter how foolish and ignorant of God he is. No matter how foolish and far away from God a person is, God will save him if he will just call upon the name of the Lord Jesus Christ.

> **This is the fate of those who trust in themselves, and of their followers, who approve their sayings. Selah (Psa 49:13)**
>
> **The fool says in his heart, "There is no God." They are corrupt, and their ways are vile; there is no one who does good. (Psa 53:1)**
>
> **The wisdom of the prudent is to give thought to their ways, but the folly of fools is deception. Fools mock at making amends for sin, but goodwill is found among the upright. (Prov 14:8-9)**
>
> **He who trusts in himself is a fool, but he who walks in wisdom is kept safe. (Prov 28:26)**
>
> **Like a partridge that hatches eggs it did not lay is the man who gains riches by unjust means. When his life is half gone, they will desert him, and in the end he will prove to be a fool. (Jer 17:11)**
>
> **Then the Lord said to him, "Now then, you Pharisees clean the outside of the cup and dish, but inside you are full of greed and wickedness. You foolish people! Did not the one who made the outside make the inside also? (Luke 11:39-40)**
>
> **"But God said to him, 'You fool! This very night your life will be demanded from you. Then who will get what you have prepared for yourself?' "This is how it will be with anyone who stores up things for himself but is not rich toward God." (Luke 12:20-21)**
>
> **For since the creation of the world God's invisible qualities—his eternal power and divine nature—have been clearly seen, being understood from what has been made, so that men are without excuse. For although they knew God, they neither glorified him as God nor gave thanks to him, but their thinking became futile and their foolish hearts were darkened. Although they claimed to be wise, they became fools (Rom 1:20-22)**
>
> **Be very careful, then, how you live—not as unwise but as wise, (Eph 5:15)**

DEEPER STUDY # 2

(3:3) Disobedient—Unbelievers—Lost, The: a person without God is "disobedient" (apeitheis). The word means to refuse to obey by not doing what one should; to rebel against and to reject instruction; to refuse to be persuaded; to be obstinate against authority. Note a most significant fact: the charge is that man is disobedient in general; that is, he disobeys all authority:

⇒ He disobeys parents, civil authorities, civil laws, and the natural laws of nature—polluting and misusing everything about him.

⇒ He disobeys the laws of personal duty as he walks day by day at home, in the workplace, and throughout his community.

⇒ Most tragic of all, in fact, the cause of all other disobedience, is that he disobeys God and His Word, the very Person who can save him and who has laid down the commandment of life for man.

Man just comes short, disobeying all the laws and duties of life—not all the time, but sometimes. By nature, when a person wants something that is forbidden, he is drawn to go after it despite the fact that it is wrong and disobedient. He is simply drawn to disobey the law of God or the law of the land and the restriction of the parent.

The point is this: all of us—every believer and every unbeliever—have walked in disobedience. We have all disobeyed all authority; we have been lawless and transgressed all authority ranging from parents over to God. We have come short—far short—of what we should have done.

But thanks be to God our Savior, for He has provided the way for us to be forgiven. Our guilt and punishment for having broken the law of God and of man can be completely removed from us. How? Through our Lord Jesus Christ. No matter how disobedient we have been—no matter how lawless we have been—God our Savior will forgive our transgressions. He will forgive them if we genuinely believe that His Son, the Lord Jesus Christ, paid the punishment of our transgression when He died upon the cross.

> **"Therefore everyone who hears these words of mine and puts them into practice is like a wise man who built his house on the rock. The rain came down, the streams rose, and the winds blew and beat against that house; yet it did not fall, because it had its foundation on the rock. But everyone who hears these words of mine and does not put them into practice is like a foolish man who built his house on sand. The rain came down, the streams rose, and the winds blew and beat against that house, and it fell with a great crash." (Mat 7:24-27)**
>
> **Furthermore, since they did not think it worthwhile to retain the knowledge of God, he gave them over to a depraved mind, to do what ought not to be done.... slanderers, God-haters, insolent, arrogant and boastful; they invent ways of doing evil; they disobey their parents; (Rom 1:28, 30)**
>
> **Let no one deceive you with empty words, for because of such things God's wrath comes on those who are disobedient. (Eph 5:6)**
>
> **And give relief to you who are troubled, and to us as well. This will happen when the Lord Jesus is revealed from heaven in blazing fire with his powerful angels. He will punish those who do not know God and do not obey the gospel of our Lord Jesus. (2 Th 1:7-8)**
>
> **We also know that law is made not for the righteous but for lawbreakers and rebels, the ungodly and sinful, the unholy and irreligious; for those who kill their fathers or mothers, for murderers, (1 Tim 1:9)**
>
> **For if the message spoken by angels was binding, and every violation and disobedience received its just punishment, how shall we escape if we ignore such a great**

salvation? This salvation, which was first announced by the Lord, was confirmed to us by those who heard him. (Heb 2:2-3)

The world and its desires pass away, but the man who does the will of God lives forever. (1 John 2:17)

DEEPER STUDY # 3

(3:3) **Deceived—Unbelievers—Lost, The**: a person without God is "deceived" (planomenoi). The word means to be misled and led astray. It means to be seduced away from God and the truth and away from what is right. Man is so easily led astray that Scripture pictures him as a wandering and lost sheep. He is a sheep that must be sought after, found, and saved or else he will be destroyed by the wilderness of the world—destroyed because he was deceived and led away from the eternal pasture of God. Scripture teaches that man is *seduced and led astray* by several things.

⇒ Man is seduced and led astray by immoral and seductive persons.

"Their throats are open graves; their tongues practice deceit." "The poison of vipers is on their lips." (Rom 3:13)

I urge you, brothers, to watch out for those who cause divisions and put obstacles in your way that are contrary to the teaching you have learned. Keep away from them. For such people are not serving our Lord Christ, but their own appetites. By smooth talk and flattery they deceive the minds of naive people. (Rom 16:17-18)

But among you there must not be even a hint of sexual immorality, or of any kind of impurity, or of greed, because these are improper for God's holy people. Nor should there be obscenity, foolish talk or coarse joking, which are out of place, but rather thanksgiving. For of this you can be sure: No immoral, impure or greedy person—such a man is an idolater—has any inheritance in the kingdom of Christ and of God. Let no one deceive you with empty words, for because of such things God's wrath comes on those who are disobedient. (Eph 5:3-6)

While evil men and impostors will go from bad to worse, deceiving and being deceived. (2 Tim 3:13)

Dear children, do not let anyone lead you astray. He who does what is right is righteous, just as he is righteous. (1 John 3:7)

Friend deceives friend, and no one speaks the truth. They have taught their tongues to lie; they weary themselves with sinning. (Jer 9:5)

Her rich men are violent; her people are liars and their tongues speak deceitfully. (Micah 6:12)

⇒ Man is seduced and led astray by false teaching and false systems of religion.

Jesus answered: "Watch out that no one deceives you. For many will come in my name, claiming, 'I am the Christ, ' and will deceive many. (Mat 24:4-5)

For such men are false apostles, deceitful workmen, masquerading as apostles of Christ. And no wonder, for Satan himself masquerades as an angel of light. It is not surprising, then, if his servants masquerade as servants of righteousness. Their end will be what their actions deserve. (2 Cor 11:13-15)

Then we will no longer be infants, tossed back and forth by the waves, and blown here and there by every wind of teaching and by the cunning and craftiness of men in their deceitful scheming. (Eph 4:14)

Don't let anyone deceive you in any way, for that day will not come until the rebellion occurs and the man of lawlessness is revealed, the man doomed to destruction. (2 Th 2:3)

The Spirit clearly says that in later times some will abandon the faith and follow deceiving spirits and things taught by demons. Such teachings come through hypocritical liars, whose consciences have been seared as with a hot iron. (1 Tim 4:1-2)

Avoid godless chatter, because those who indulge in it will become more and more ungodly. Their teaching will spread like gangrene. Among them are Hymenaeus and Philetus, (2 Tim 2:16-17)

Having a form of godliness but denying its power. Have nothing to do with them. They are the kind who worm their way into homes and gain control over weak-willed women, who are loaded down with sins and are swayed by all kinds of evil desires, always learning but never able to acknowledge the truth. (2 Tim 3:5-7)

For there are many rebellious people, mere talkers and deceivers, especially those of the circumcision group. They must be silenced, because they are ruining whole households by teaching things they ought not to teach—and that for the sake of dishonest gain. (Titus 1:10-11)

Many deceivers, who do not acknowledge Jesus Christ as coming in the flesh, have gone out into the world. Any such person is the deceiver and the antichrist. (2 John 1:7)

⇒ Man is seduced and led astray by self.

Do you not know that the wicked will not inherit the kingdom of God? Do not be deceived: Neither the sexually immoral nor idolaters nor adulterers nor male prostitutes nor homosexual offenders nor thieves nor the greedy nor drunkards nor slanderers nor swindlers will inherit the kingdom of God. (1 Cor 6:9-10)

If anyone thinks he is something when he is nothing, he deceives himself. (Gal 6:3)

Do not be deceived: God cannot be mocked. A man reaps what he sows. The one who sows to please his sinful nature, from that nature will reap destruction; the one who sows to please the Spirit, from the Spirit will reap eternal life. (Gal 6:7-8)

Do not merely listen to the word, and so deceive yourselves. Do what it says. (James 1:22)

If anyone considers himself religious and yet does not keep a tight rein on his tongue, he deceives himself and his religion is worthless. (James 1:26)

If we claim to be without sin, we deceive ourselves and the truth is not in us. (1 John 1:8)

So, because you are lukewarm—neither hot nor cold—I am about to spit you out of my mouth. You say, 'I am rich; I have acquired wealth and do not need a thing.' But you do not realize that you are wretched, pitiful, poor, blind and naked. (Rev 3:16-17)

For in his own eyes he flatters himself too much to detect or hate his sin. (Psa 36:2)

The heart is deceitful above all things and beyond cure. Who can understand it? (Jer 17:9)

⇒ Man is seduced and led astray by Satan.

You belong to your father, the devil, and you want to carry out your father's desire. He was a murderer from the beginning, not holding to the truth, for there is no truth in him. When he lies, he speaks his native language, for he is a liar and the father of lies. (John 8:44)

The god of this age has blinded [deceived] the minds of unbelievers, so that they cannot see the light of the gospel of the glory of Christ, who is the image of God. (2 Cor 4:4)

For such men are false apostles, deceitful workmen, masquerading as apostles of Christ. And no wonder, for Satan himself masquerades as an angel of light. (2 Cor 11:13-14)

The coming of the lawless one will be in accordance with the work of Satan displayed in all kinds of counterfeit miracles, signs and wonders, and in every sort of evil that deceives those who are perishing. They perish because they refused to love the truth and so be saved. (2 Th 2:9-10)

And Adam was not the one deceived; it was the woman who was deceived and became a sinner. (1 Tim 2:14)

⇒ Man is seduced and led astray by evil, immoral, and unjust governments and states.

The light of a lamp will never shine in you again. The voice of bridegroom [Christ] and bride [the church] will never be heard in you again [Babylon, the symbol of the godless city or government]. Your merchants were the world's great men. By your magic spell all the nations were led astray. (Rev 18:23)

Woe to the city of blood, full of lies, full of plunder, never without victims! (Nahum 3:1)

⇒ Man is seduced and led astray by sin.

For sin, seizing the opportunity afforded by the commandment, deceived me, and through the commandment put me to death. (Rom 7:11)

You were taught, with regard to your former way of life, to put off your old self, which is being corrupted by its deceitful desires; (Eph 4:22)

But encourage one another daily, as long as it is called Today, so that none of you may be hardened by sin's deceitfulness. (Heb 3:13)

Remember the point of this verse: once we were all deceived. All of us had been led astray from God. But thanks be to God our Savior. He has found us and saved us, and He will find and save any person who will turn toward Him and call out for Him. God our Savior is searching for every person, not willing that any should perish. In fact, God is with the person at all times. All the person has to do is *turn* to God and call upon Him, and God will save him.

2 (3:3) **Lusts—Pleasure—Unbelievers—Lost, The**: a person without God is enslaved by all sorts of *passions and pleasures*.

⇒ The word "passions" (epithumiais) means passionate cravings, desires, urges, and lusts; it means to have a yearning passion for.

⇒ The word "pleasures" (hedonais) can mean either good or bad pleasures. In the present context it means bad pleasures, desiring and indulging in worldly amusements and worldly delights.

Every person knows what it is to have the sinful nature lusting after the pleasures and delights of this world, to have it yearning and yearning to lay hold of the pleasures and delights...

- of having more and more
- of having bigger and better
- of partying
- of lusting
- of intoxicating drugs
- of having power
- of exercising authority
- of indulging in food
- of having recognition
- of having money
- of owning property
- of having possessions
- of getting attention
- of attaining position
- of displaying fashion

Man is enslaved by the things of the world, things that damage his body—that make him greedy and selfish—that destroy his spirit and doom him to destruction.

But thanks be to God our Savior. He has saved us and delivered us from the enslavements of this world, the enslavements of lust and pleasure that destroy our bodies and souls. The wonderful news is that any person can be delivered from the destructive lusts and pleasures of this world. How? Through our Lord Jesus Christ. If a person will turn away from the destructive lusts and pleasures and turn to Christ, God will deliver him. God will give him the power to conquer the passions or lusts and enslavements of this world.

The seed that fell among thorns stands for those who hear, but as they go on their way they are choked by life's worries, riches and pleasures, and they do not mature. (Luke 8:14)

And I'll say to myself, "You have plenty of good things laid up for many years. Take life easy; eat, drink and be merry." ' "But God said to him, 'You fool! This very night your life will be demanded from you. Then who will get what you have prepared for yourself?' (Luke 12:19-20)

But the widow who lives for pleasure is dead even while she lives. (1 Tim 5:6)

But mark this: There will be terrible times in the last days. People will be lovers of themselves, lovers of money, boastful, proud, abusive, disobedient to their parents, ungrateful, unholy....treacherous, rash, conceited, lovers of pleasure rather than lovers of God— (2 Tim 3:1-2, 4)

At one time we too were foolish, disobedient, deceived and enslaved by all kinds of passions and pleasures. We lived in malice and envy, being hated and hating one another. (Titus 3:3)

You have lived on earth in luxury and self-indulgence. You have fattened yourselves in the day of slaughter. (James 5:5)

But I tell you that anyone who looks at a woman lustfully has already committed adultery with her in his heart. (Mat 5:28)

Therefore God gave them over in the sinful desires of their hearts to sexual impurity for the degrading of their bodies with one another. (Rom 1:24)

In the same way the men also abandoned natural relations with women and were inflamed with lust for one another. Men committed indecent acts with other men, and received in themselves the due penalty for their perversion. (Rom 1:27)

For you have spent enough time in the past doing what pagans choose to do—living in debauchery, lust, drunkenness, orgies, carousing and detestable idolatry. (1 Pet 4:3)

The eye of the adulterer watches for dusk; he thinks, 'No eye will see me,' and he keeps his face concealed. In the dark, men break into houses, but by day they shut themselves in; they want nothing to do with the light. (Job 24:15-16)

3 (3:3) **Malice—Envy—Unbelievers—Lost, The**: man lives in malice and envy (v.3) (see Deeper Study # 4, *Malice*—Tit.3:3; Deeper Study # 5, *Envy*—Tit.3:3).

DEEPER STUDY # 4
(3:3) **Malice—Unbelievers—Lost, The**: a person without God lives in malice (kakia). The word means evil disposition or evil in nature. It is a spirit full of evil and malice and injury, a character that is as evil as it can be. It is a person who always looks for the worst in other people and always passes on the worst about them. It is the person who so often ruins other people both in reputation and body and in mind and spirit. It is a person so full of evil that he is always ruining others either by word or violence. There are some people who would not actively strike and harm a person, but everyone has experienced feelings against another person. The feelings arise from some argument or difference within the family, with a neighbor, or at work, school, or play. And the feelings were strong, so strong that one could care less if something bad happened to the person. And most people have even had feelings...

- that wished something bad upon others.
- that downgraded and tore down others.

Tragically, these feelings even occur within families. People hold malice within their hearts; they could care less if something bad happened to others. But thanks be to God our Savior. He has provided forgiveness for this terrible sin—both forgiveness and deliverance. And He will forgive and deliver any person who turns away from his malice and bitterness against others and turns to Him.

Brothers, stop thinking like children. In regard to evil be infants, but in your thinking be adults. (1 Cor 14:20)

Get rid of all bitterness, rage and anger, brawling and slander, along with every form of malice. Be kind and compassionate to one another, forgiving each other, just as in Christ God forgave you. (Eph 4:31-32)

But now you must rid yourselves of all such things as these: anger, rage, malice, slander, and filthy language from your lips. (Col 3:8)

Therefore, rid yourselves of all malice and all deceit, hypocrisy, envy, and slander of every kind. Like newborn babies, crave pure spiritual milk, so that by it you may grow up in your salvation, now that you have tasted that the Lord is good. (1 Pet 2:1-3)

DEEPER STUDY # 5
(3:3) **Envy**: a person without God lives in envy (phthonoi). The word means that a person covets what someone else has, covets it so much that he wants it even if it means that it has to be taken away from the other person. He may even wish that the other person did not have it or had not received it. We may look at people and envy their...

- money
- position
- looks
- possessions
- popularity
- clothes
- social status
- recognition
- authority

The results of envy are terrible; envy takes a terrible toll upon the life and body of a person.

⇒ A person who envies *does not have peace or happiness*. He is dissatisfied with what he is and has, and is always wanting more and more of what others have.

⇒ In addition to this, envy often drives a person into *crime and lawlessness* in order to get what he craves.

⇒ On top of this, envy often leads to *physical problems* such as migraine headaches, high blood pressure, and ulcers.

⇒ Envy also causes *emotional problems* ranging from mild neurosis of depression to psychotic behavior.

But thanks to be to God our Savior. He saves and delivers us from envy. Through Christ He gives us life, real life, and He satisfies our hearts and lives with eternal pleasures (Ps.16:11).

A heart at peace gives life to the body, but envy rots the bones. (Prov 14:30)

Do not let your heart envy sinners, but always be zealous for the fear of the LORD. (Prov 23:17)

Do not envy wicked men, do not desire their company; (Prov 24:1)

Let us behave decently, as in the daytime, not in orgies and drunkenness, not in sexual immorality and debauchery, not in dissension and jealousy. (Rom 13:13)

Love is patient, love is kind. It does not envy, it does not boast, it is not proud. (1 Cor 13:4)

Let us not become conceited, provoking and envying each other. (Gal 5:26)

4 (3:3) **Hate**: man is hateful and hated (v.3) (see Deeper Study #6, *Hate*—Tit.3:3; Deeper Study #7, *Hate*—Tit.3:3).

DEEPER STUDY # 6
(3:3) **Hate**: a person without God is hateful; that is, he is worthy of being hated (stugetoi). This is the only time this terrible word is used in the Bible. It means to be hated—to be worthy of being hated and counted as detestable. This is strong language, to think that we are worthy of being hated. What does this mean?

⇒ It means the selfish, greedy, covetous nature of man is worthy of being hated—the nature that lies, steals, cheats, banks, and hoards while millions of others are dying from hunger, thirst, disease, cold, heat, sin, evil, and from the lack of the gospel which could save the whole world.

⇒ It means the carnal and immoral nature of man is worthy of hatred—the nature that commits fornication and adultery, destroying homes and bodies through broken trusts and disease and emotional and mental traumas—from which many never recover.

The list could go on and on, but the point is clear: the behavior of man is very often worthy of being hated. But thanks be to God, for He has saved and transformed our hateful nature. He has taken our unloving nature and made new men out of us. And He will do it for any person who turns from living a selfish and worldly life and turns to Christ. God will transform any person who trusts and follows His Son, the Lord Jesus Christ.

The Pharisees, who loved money, heard all this and were sneering at Jesus. He said to them, "You are the ones who justify yourselves in the eyes of men, [earthly possessions, things] but God knows your hearts. What is highly valued among men is detestable in God's sight. (Luke 16:14-15)

For the LORD your God detests [extremely hated and disgusting] anyone who does these things, anyone who deals dishonestly. (Deu 25:16)

After the time of mourning was over, David had her brought to his house, and she became his wife and bore him a son. But the thing David had done [adultery] displeased the LORD. (2 Sam 11:27)

You are not a God who takes pleasure in evil; with you the wicked cannot dwell. (Psa 5:4)

The LORD examines the righteous, but the wicked and those who love violence his soul hates. (Psa 11:5)

There are six things the LORD hates, seven that are detestable to him: haughty eyes, a lying tongue, hands that shed innocent blood, a heart that devises wicked schemes, feet that are quick to rush into evil, a false witness who pours out lies and a man who stirs up dissension among brothers. (Prov 6:16-19)

Do not plot evil against your neighbor, and do not love to swear falsely. I hate all this," declares the LORD. (Zec 8:17)

DEEPER STUDY # 7
(3:3) **Hate**: a person without God is the citizen of a world of hate, a world in which people hate one another—a tragic and terrible fact, but a fact nevertheless.

⇒ Race hates race
⇒ Nation hates nation
⇒ Employees hate employers
⇒ Brothers hate brothers
⇒ Wives hate husbands
⇒ Children hate parents

No matter the race, color, creed, class, position, or standing—hate fills the human heart and consumes both man and his world. The result is the worst imaginable world, a world that is ever so beautiful yet is defiled by a human nature and behavior that defies all human explanation—a human nature that chooses to live in a world of...

- war
- murder
- abuse
- fighting
- division
- divorce
- rape
- theft
- argument
- lying
- deception
- slavery

But thanks be to God our Savior. He has saved us and provided an escape for us through His Son, the Lord Jesus Christ. We can be delivered from the hatred of the world and receive a life of love, joy, and peace—a life that will go on and on forever.

"For God so loved the world that he gave his one and only Son, that whoever believes in him shall not perish but have eternal life. (John 3:16)

"I tell you the truth, whoever hears my word and believes him who sent me has eternal life and will not be condemned; he has crossed over from death to life. (John 5:24)

Anyone who claims to be in the light but hates his brother is still in the darkness. (1 John 2:9)

Anyone who hates his brother is a murderer, and you know that no murderer has eternal life in him. (1 John 3:15)

"'Do not hate your brother in your heart. Rebuke your neighbor frankly so you will not share in his guilt. (Lev 19:17)

Hatred stirs up dissension, but love covers over all wrongs. (Prov 10:12)

Better a meal of vegetables where there is love than a fattened calf with hatred. (Prov 15:17)

TITUS 3:4-7

1 Salvation comes from God a. From God's kindness b. From God's love c. Not by good works, the righteous things we do d. By God's mercy	E. Message 5: Life With God—Salvation, 3:4-7 4 But when the kindness and love of God our Savior appeared, 5 He saved us, not because of righteous things we had done, but because of his mercy. He	saved us through the washing of rebirth and renewal by the Holy Spirit, 6 Whom he poured out on us generously through Jesus Christ our Savior, 7 So that, having been justified by his grace, we might become heirs having the hope of eternal life.	**2 Salvation is a rebirth & renewal by God's Spirit**[DS1] **3 Salvation comes through Jesus Christ our Savior** a. He gives the Spirit b. He justifies by His grace c. He makes us heirs of eternal life

DIVISION II

THE MESSAGE OF SOUND DOCTRINE

E. Message 5: Life With God—Salvation, 3:4-7

(3:4-7) **Introduction**: this is one of the greatest summaries on salvation in all Scripture. It is a message that must be preached if people are going to be reached for Christ and if believers are going to be grounded in sound doctrine.

1. Salvation comes from God (v.4-5).
2. Salvation is a rebirth and a renewal by God's Spirit (v.5).
3. Salvation comes through Jesus Christ our Savior (v.6-7).

1 (3:4-5) **Salvation—Kindness—Love**: salvation comes from God. God is the Author of salvation. God is not as most people imagine Him.

⇒ Some people imagine God to be far off in outer space someplace with little if any concern and interest in the affairs and lives of men. They feel God is almost untouchable, and they see little evidence to contradict this. They and others sometimes worship and pray and nothing seems to happen. Their prayers are just not answered. They still suffer and the affairs of the world just keep on as they always have. There is little if any indication that God is really active in their lives and in the world, so if He exists, He must be far off and not too interested in the world. This is the view of many people about God.

⇒ Others imagine God to be some Supreme Being who hovers over people watching their every move. They see God as the Supreme Judge who is always on the lookout for those who do wrong and who is ready to jump on them and condemn them unless they keep the laws and rules of God.

⇒ Some people imagine God to be somewhat like a loving and indulgent grandfather type of being. They see God as the Supreme Being of the universe whose basic nature is love. In fact, they feel He is so loving that He understands a little sin here and there. Therefore, He will indulge and forgive a life of worldliness and some indiscretion here and there and accept all. He will accept a person who does some good. (Note: few people—very, very few—ever think that God will reject them, not in the final analysis.)

Note what this verse says. God is not far off in outer space, disinterested in man; He is not the loving, indulgent grandfather of the human race; He is not some Supreme Judge hovering over men to punish them when they do wrong. God is our Savior. He is vitally concerned with us, so concerned that His very name is *God our Savior*. He has saved us from the sin and evil and the suffering and death of this world and from the condemnation of the next world. Imagine! We are saved from sin and evil, suffering and death, and from ever having to face condemnation. God our Savior has saved us and given us life eternal; we shall live forever and ever, never dying and never being separated from God—not at all—not even for one minute. Note two significant points.

1. Salvation comes from God's "kindness" (chrestotes). This word is often translated *goodness*. It means good, gracious, and kind. But it is a goodness and kindness that is so deep that it always gives whatever is necessary to meet the needs of a person (Barclay). *Kindness* is so deep within God that it is of His very nature. God is so good and kind that He could do nothing else but save us. He had to meet our need; He had to save us from sin, death, and condemnation. Why? Because He is kind; He had to extend His kindness out toward man by saving him.

> Or do you show contempt for the riches of his kindness, tolerance and patience, not realizing that God's kindness leads you toward repentance? (Rom 2:4)
>
> The LORD appeared to us in the past, saying: "I have loved you with an everlasting love; I have drawn you with lovingkindness. (Jer 31:3)
>
> I will betroth you to me forever; I will betroth you in righteousness and justice, in love and compassion. (Hosea 2:19)

2. Salvation comes from God's "love" (philanthropia). This means that God's love reached out toward man; that God has a deep-seated affection for man and that He has showered His affection upon man by saving him. The word has the idea of compassion in it. God loves man so much that His affection and compassion are stirred to save men. God loves us so much that He must act to handle the sin and death problems for man and provide an escape from condemnation.

> "For God so loved the world that he gave his one and only Son, that whoever believes in him shall not perish but have eternal life. (John 3:16)
> "I tell you the truth, whoever hears my word and believes him who sent me has eternal life and will not be condemned; he has crossed over from death to life. (John 5:24)

> But God demonstrates his own love for us in this: While we were still sinners, Christ died for us. (Rom 5:8)
>
> But because of his great love for us, God, who is rich in mercy, made us alive with Christ even when we were dead in transgressions—it is by grace you have been saved. (Eph 2:4-5)
>
> How great is the love the Father has lavished on us, that we should be called children of God! And that is what we are! The reason the world does not know us is that it did not know him. (1 John 3:1)
>
> This is how God showed his love among us: He sent his one and only Son into the world that we might live through him. (1 John 4:9)
>
> And so we know and rely on the love God has for us. God is love. Whoever lives in love lives in God, and God in him. (1 John 4:16)

3. Salvation does not come by good works, not because of righteous things a person does. Men cannot earn righteousness by good works. No person can be good enough or do enough good to make God accept him. This is the great fallacy of most people and most religions. They think that they can secure God's approval by being good and doing good. But this is the great fallacy:
⇒ Man cannot do enough good to make himself perfect.
⇒ Man is already imperfect, so he can never be perfect. Imperfection can never become perfection.

What man fails to see is that God is perfect, and as perfect, He cannot accept anything imperfect. Therefore, no matter how many works of righteousness man does—no matter how much good he does—man is not saved by his own efforts. He cannot earn, win, or merit salvation, not by any self-righteousness or personal goodness which he might attain.

> **Thought 1.** Common sense tells us this, for everything about man passes away and dies. No matter what it is, everything man knows and possesses—even himself—ages, decays, and passes away. Therefore, righteousness or goodness based within man dies and passes away with him. If man is to be saved, then Someone outside of himself and of his world—Someone with the power to penetrate and save this world—has to come to earth and snatch man out of its corruption and save him. The point is this: if man is to ever be saved, he will not be saved by *self*-righteousness nor by anything else that concerns *self*. *Self* and all that concerns *self* only die. Man can only be saved by some *Force* much greater than himself, some Force that is living and personal and kind and loving enough to save him. That Force, of course, is God Himself.
>
> > Many will say to me on that day, 'Lord, Lord, did we not prophesy in your name, and in your name drive out demons and perform many miracles?' Then I will tell them plainly, 'I never knew you. Away from me, you evildoers!' (Mat 7:22-23)
> >
> > Therefore no one will be declared righteous in his sight by observing the law; rather, through the law we become conscious of sin. (Rom 3:20)
> >
> > Know that a man is not justified by observing the law, but by faith in Jesus Christ. So we, too, have put our faith in Christ Jesus that we may be justified by faith in Christ and not by observing the law, because by observing the law no one will be justified. (Gal 2:16)
> >
> > For it is by grace you have been saved, through faith—and this not from yourselves, it is the gift of God—not by works, so that no one can boast. (Eph 2:8-9)
> >
> > But when the kindness and love of God our Savior appeared, he saved us, not because of righteous things we had done, but because of his mercy. He saved us through the washing of rebirth and renewal by the Holy Spirit, (Titus 3:4-5)

4. Salvation comes from God's "mercy" (eleon). The word means feelings of pity, compassion, and kindness. It is a desire to succor, to tenderly draw unto oneself and to care for. Two things are essential in order to have mercy: seeing a need and being able to meet that need. God sees our need for salvation; He sees that we need to be saved from sin, death, and condemnation. Therefore, God acts; He has mercy upon us and provides the way for us to be saved.

> His mercy extends to those who fear him, from generation to generation. (Luke 1:50)
>
> But because of his great love for us, God, who is rich in mercy, made us alive with Christ even when we were dead in transgressions—it is by grace you have been saved. (Eph 2:4-5)
>
> He saved us, not because of righteous things we had done, but because of his mercy. He saved us through the washing of rebirth and renewal by the Holy Spirit, (Titus 3:5)
>
> Because of the Lord's great love we are not consumed, for his compassions never fail. (Lam 3:22)
>
> Who is a God like you, who pardons sin and forgives the transgression of the remnant of his inheritance? You do not stay angry forever but delight to show mercy. (Micah 7:18)

2 (3:5) **Regeneration—Renewal—New Birth—New Man—Salvation—Holy Spirit**: salvation is a rebirth and a daily renewing of life by God's Holy Spirit.

1. The word "rebirth" (palingenesias) means to be regenerated or given new life; to be given a new birth; to be renewed or revived; to be spiritually reborn or converted. Salvation is a spiritual rebirth; it is a person being *born again* by the Spirit of God.

Note that the new birth is so radical a change in a person's life that it is described as a "washing" (loutrou) which means a bath, a complete immersion. Salvation is so dramatic it is just like the washing away of the old life and the receiving of a new life. All that concerns a person's old life is washed away, all the...
- sin and evil
- corruption and injustice
- selfishness and greed

TITUS 3:4-7

- guilt and doubt
- dirt and immorality
- pollution and worldliness
- failure and shortcoming

The Spirit of God cleanses a person—immerses the person in the cleansing blood of Jesus Christ.

> In him we have redemption through his blood, the forgiveness of sins, in accordance with the riches of God's grace (Eph 1:7)
>
> In whom we have redemption, the forgiveness of sins. (Col 1:14)
>
> But if we walk in the light, as he is in the light, we have fellowship with one another, and the blood of Jesus, his Son, purifies us from all sin. (1 John 1:7)
>
> And from Jesus Christ, who is the faithful witness, the firstborn from the dead, and the ruler of the kings of the earth. To him who loves us and has freed us from our sins by his blood, (Rev 1:5)
>
> I answered, "Sir, you know." And he said, "These are they who have come out of the great tribulation; they have washed their robes and made them white in the blood of the Lamb. (Rev 7:14)

The Spirit of God through the blood of Christ washes away the old life and gives the believer a new life. The Spirit of God regenerates a person, saves him from his old life and gives him a new life—a rebirth—spiritually creating him into a new person.

> Yet to all who received him, to those who believed in his name, he gave the right to become children of God—children born not of natural descent, nor of human decision or a husband's will, but born of God. (John 1:12-13)
>
> In reply Jesus declared, "I tell you the truth, no one can see the kingdom of God unless he is born again." Jesus answered, "I tell you the truth, no one can enter the kingdom of God unless he is born of water and the Spirit. (John 3:3, 5)
>
> And that is what some of you were. But you were washed, you were sanctified, you were justified in the name of the Lord Jesus Christ and by the Spirit of our God. (1 Cor 6:11)
>
> Therefore, if anyone is in Christ, he is a new creation; the old has gone, the new has come! (2 Cor 5:17)
>
> He saved us, not because of righteous things we had done, but because of his mercy. He saved us through the washing of rebirth and renewal by the Holy Spirit, (Titus 3:5)
>
> For you have been born again, not of perishable seed, but of imperishable, through the living and enduring word of God. (1 Pet 1:23)
>
> Everyone who believes that Jesus is the Christ is born of God, and everyone who loves the father loves his child as well. (1 John 5:1)

2. The word "renewal" (anakainosis) means to make new again; to renew again; to revive again; to make new spiritually; to begin all over again; to adjust again. Salvation is the Holy Spirit adjusting a person and renewing him all over again. It is the Spirit of God taking a person, readjusting his life and reviving him spiritually. Note that the renewing is done by the Spirit of God just as regeneration is. W.E. Vine says that the stress is "the continual operation of the indwelling Spirit of God." Kenneth Wuest says, "This is the work of the Holy Spirit in sanctification."

The point is a most wonderful truth. The Holy Spirit not only renews a person and gives him a new birth and a new life, but He does much, much more. He renews and revives a person *day by day*. Every day of a person's life is a renewal and a revival—by the Spirit of God. Life—a single day—does not need to be...

- dull
- routine
- drudgery
- without purpose or meaning
- aimless
- complacent

When a person is truly saved, the Holy Spirit renews and revives him day by day. He stirs and energizes the person to follow Jesus more and more closely and to serve Him more and more faithfully.

> Therefore, I urge you, brothers, in view of God's mercy, to offer your bodies as living sacrifices, holy and pleasing to God—this is your spiritual act of worship. Do not conform any longer to the pattern of this world, but be transformed by the renewing of your mind. Then you will be able to test and approve what God's will is—his good, pleasing and perfect will. (Rom 12:1-2)
>
> Therefore we do not lose heart. Though outwardly we are wasting away, yet inwardly we are being renewed day by day. (2 Cor 4:16)
>
> You were taught, with regard to your former way of life, to put off your old self, which is being corrupted by its deceitful desires; to be made new in the attitude of your minds; (Eph 4:22-23)
>
> And have put on the new self, which is being renewed in knowledge in the image of its Creator. (Col 3:10)
>
> He saved us, not because of righteous things we had done, but because of his mercy. He saved us through the washing of rebirth and renewal by the Holy Spirit, (Titus 3:5)

DEEPER STUDY # 1

(3:5) Rebirth—New Birth: the New Testament teaching on the new birth is rich and full.

1. The new birth is a necessity. A person will never see (Jn.3:3) nor ever enter (Jn.3:5) the Kingdom of God unless he is born again (Jn.3:7).

2. The new birth is a spiritual birth, the birth of a new power and spirit in life. It is not reformation of the old

nature (Ro.6:6). It is the actual creation of a new birth within—spiritually (Jn.3:5-6; cp. Jn.1:12-13; 2 Cor.5:17; Eph.2:10; 4:24). (See notes—Eph.1:3; 4:17; Deeper Study #3—4:24.) A person is spiritually born again:

    a. By water, even the Spirit (see Deeper Study # 2—Jn.3:5).
    b. By the will of God (Jas.1:18).
    c. By incorruptible, imperishable, seed through the Word of God (1 Pt.1:23).
    d. By God from above (1 Pt.1:3). The word *again* (ana) in the phrase "born again" also means *above*.
    e. By Christ, who gives both the *power and right* to be born again (Jn.1:12-13).

3. The new birth is a definite experience, a real experience. A person experiences the new birth:
    a. By believing that Jesus is the Christ, the Son of God (1 Jn.5:1; cp. Jn.3:14-15).
    b. By the gospel as it is shared by believers (1 Cor.4:15; Phile.10).
    c. By the Word of God (1 Pt.1:23) or by the Word of Truth (Jas.1:18).

4. The new birth is a changed life, a totally new life. A person proves that he is born again:
    a. By doing righteous acts (1 Jn.2:29; cp. Eph.2:10; 4:24).
    b. By not practicing sin (1 Jn.3:9; 5:18).
    c. By loving other believers (1 Jn.4:7).
    d. By overcoming the world (1 Jn.5:4).
    e. By keeping himself (1 Jn.5:18).
    f. By possessing the divine seed or nature (1 Jn.3:9; 1 Pt.1:23; 2 Pt.1:4; cp. Col.1:27).

3 (3:6-7) **Salvation—Justification—Inheritance**: salvation comes through Jesus Christ our Savior. Jesus Christ has done three wonderful things for us.

1. Jesus Christ is the One who pours out the Holy Spirit so richly upon us. As stated in verse five, it is the Holy Spirit who regenerates us and who revives us day by day. But we would not have the Holy Spirit apart from Jesus Christ. Jesus Christ is the One who gives us the Holy Spirit. Note this:

⇒ It is a man's head that stirs and arouses his spirit to flow through his body and get to the work at hand. So it is with Christ the Head of the church. Christ arouses His Spirit to flow through His body of believers which is His church.

When a person believes in Jesus Christ, Christ puts His Spirit into the new believer. Yea, Christ pours out His Spirit richly and abundantly upon the person. The result is both regeneration or rebirth (a new birth) and a daily renewing or revival (stirred to follow Christ and to serve Him more and more).

Thought 1. The essential power in the life of a believer is the power of the Holy Spirit. It is He and He alone who imparts life to the believer and who arouses the believer to serve Christ day by day (renewal). All the behavior of a believer and all the words of a believer and all the worship of a believer are powerless without the power of the Holy Spirit. It does not matter how high his position, how appealing his profession, how attractive his appearance, how consistent his worship—his life is powerless without the presence and power of the Holy Spirit. He is totally unacceptable to God, both he and his religious work.

The Spirit gives life; the flesh counts for nothing. The words I have spoken to you are spirit and they are life. (John 6:63)

And I will ask the Father, and he will give you another Counselor to be with you forever—the Spirit of truth. The world cannot accept him, because it neither sees him nor knows him. But you know him, for he lives with you and will be in you. I will not leave you as orphans; I will come to you. (John 14:16-18)

You, however, are controlled not by the sinful nature but by the Spirit, if the Spirit of God lives in you. And if anyone does not have the Spirit of Christ, he does not belong to Christ. (Rom 8:9)

And if the Spirit of him who raised Jesus from the dead is living in you, he who raised Christ from the dead will also give life to your mortal bodies through his Spirit, who lives in you. (Rom 8:11)

Don't you know that you yourselves are God's temple and that God's Spirit lives in you? (1 Cor 3:16)

Do you not know that your body is a temple of the Holy Spirit, who is in you, whom you have received from God? You are not your own; (1 Cor 6:19)

But when the time had fully come, God sent his Son, born of a woman, born under law, to redeem those under law, that we might receive the full rights of sons. Because you are sons, God sent the Spirit of his Son into our hearts, the Spirit who calls out, "Abba, Father." (Gal 4:4-6)

As for you, the anointing you received from him remains in you, and you do not need anyone to teach you. But as his anointing teaches you about all things and as that anointing is real, not counterfeit—just as it has taught you, remain in him. (1 John 2:27)

We know that we live in him and he in us, because he has given us of his Spirit. (1 John 4:13)

Thought 2. Barclay makes an excellent point that needs to be heeded by every church and believer:

"All the work of the Church, all the words of the Church, all the sacraments of the Church are powerless and inoperative unless the power of the Holy Spirit is there. However highly a Church be organized, however splendid its ceremonies may be, however beautiful its buildings, and however elaborate its worship, all is ineffective without the power of the Spirit. The more we read the New Testament, the more we come to the conclusion that to the people of the early Church the Spirit and the Risen Christ were one and the same. The lesson is clear. Revival in the Church does not come from increased efficiency in organization; it comes from waiting upon God. It is not that efficiency is not necessary; it is. But no amount of efficiency can breathe life into a body from which the breath of the Spirit has departed" (The Letters to Timothy, Titus, and Philemon, p.301).

2. Jesus Christ is the One who justifies us. In simple terms *justification* means that God takes the believer's faith and counts it as righteousness (Ro.4:3; cp. Gen.15:6; see notes—Ro.4:1-3; Deeper Study # 1—4:1-25; note—5:1. Also see Deeper Study # 4, *Cross*—Jn.12:32 for more discussion.)

When a person *really believes* that Jesus Christ is *his Savior*, God takes that person's faith and counts it for righteousness (Ro.4:3, 5, 9, 11, 22, 24). The person is not righteous; he has no righteousness of his own. He is still imperfect, still sinful, still corruptible, still short of God's glory as a sinful human being. But he does believe that Jesus Christ *is his Savior*. Such belief honors God's Son (whom God loves very much), and because it honors God's Son, God accepts that person's faith for righteousness. God counts that person's faith as righteousness. Therefore, that person becomes acceptable to God. (In a discussion of justification, a person's belief—the right kind of belief—is critical. See Deeper Study # 2—Jn.2:24; note—Ro.10:16-17.)

Note why God justifies a person. God justifies a man because of His Son Jesus Christ. When a man believes in Jesus Christ, God takes that man's faith and counts it as righteousness. The man is not righteous, but God considers and credits the man's faith as righteousness. Why is God willing to do this?

a. God is willing to justify man because He loves man that much. God loves man so much that He sent His Son into the world and sacrificed Him in order to justify man (Jn.3:16; Ro.5:8).
b. God is willing to justify man because of what His Son Jesus Christ has done for man.
⇒ Jesus Christ has secured the *Ideal* righteousness for man. He came to earth to live a sinless and perfect life. As Man He never broke the law of God; He never went contrary to the will of God, not even once. Therefore, He stood before God and before the world as the Ideal Man, the Perfect Man, the Representative Man, the Perfect Righteousness that could stand for the righteousness of every man.
⇒ Jesus Christ came into the world to *die* for man. As the *Ideal Man* He could take all the sins of the world upon Himself and die for every man. His death *could stand* for every man. He exchanged places with man by becoming the sinner (2 Cor.5:19). He bore the wrath of God against sin, bearing the condemnation for every man. Again, He was able to do this because He was the Ideal Man, and as the *Ideal Man* His death could stand for the death of every man.
⇒ Jesus Christ came into the world to *arise from the dead* and thereby to conquer death for man. As the *Ideal Man* His resurrection and exaltation into the presence of God *could stand* for every man's desperate need to conquer death and to be acceptable to God. His resurrected life could stand for the resurrected life of the believer.

Now, as stated above, when a man believes in Jesus Christ—really believes—God takes that man's belief and...

- counts it as the righteousness (perfection) of Christ. The man is counted as *righteous in Christ*.
- counts it as the death of Christ. The man is counted as already having *died in Christ*.
- counts it as the resurrection of Christ. The man is counted as already having been *resurrected in Christ*.

Very simply, God loves His Son Jesus Christ so much that He honors any man who honors His Son by *believing on Him*. He honors the man by taking the man's faith and counting (crediting) it as righteousness and by giving him the glorious privilege of living with Christ forever in the presence of God.

Abram believed the LORD, and he credited it to him as righteousness. (Gen 15:6)

Therefore, since we have been justified through faith, we have peace with God through our Lord Jesus Christ, (Rom 5:1)

Consider Abraham: "He believed God, and it was credited to him as righteousness." (Gal 3:6)

And that is what some of you were. But you were washed, you were sanctified, you were justified in the name of the Lord Jesus Christ and by the Spirit of our God. (1 Cor 6:11)

And be found in him, not having a righteousness of my own that comes from the law, but that which is through faith in Christ—the righteousness that comes from God and is by faith. (Phil 3:9)

3. Jesus Christ makes us heirs of eternal life. Scripture actually says that we are "joint heirs" with Christ. This is an astounding truth and promise. We will inherit all that Christ is and has. We will be given the glorious privilege of sharing in all things with the Son of God Himself.

However note this: to be a joint-heir with Christ does not mean that believers are equal heirs in the sense that they will receive an equal amount of the inheritance with Christ. Rather, it means that believers are fellow-heirs with Christ; that is, believers will share in the inheritance of Christ; they will *share* Christ's inheritance with Him.

Being a fellow-heir with Christ means at least three glorious things: it means that we shall share in the nature, position, and responsibility of Christ. The following chart shows this with a quick glance.

FELLOW HEIRS BY NATURE

Christ is the Son of God, the very being and energy of life and perfection. Therefore, we share in the inheritance of His nature. We receive...

- the adoption as children of God (Gal.4:4-7; 1 Jn.3:1).
- the sinless nature of being blameless (Ph.2:15).
- eternal life (Jn.1:4; 10:10; 17:2-3; Jn.3:16; 1 Tim.6:19).
- lasting possessions (Heb.10:34).
- a glorious body (Ph.3:21; 1 Cor.15:42-44).
- eternal glory and honor and peace (Ro.2:10).
- eternal rest and peace (Heb.4:9; Rev.14:13).
- an eternal body (1 Cor.9:25).
- a righteous being (2 Tim.4:8).

TITUS 3:4-7

FELLOW HEIRS BY POSITION

Christ is the exalted Lord, the Sovereign Majesty of the universe, the Lord of lords and King of kings. Therefore, we share in the inheritance of His position. We receive...

- the position of exalted beings (Rev.7:9-12).
- a citizenship in the Kingdom of God (Jas.2:5; Mt.25:34).
- enormous treasures in heaven (Mt.19:21; Lk.12:33).
- unsearchable riches (Eph.3:8).
- the right to surround the throne of God (Rev.7:9-13; 20:4).
- the position of a king (Rev.1:5; 5:10).
- the position of a priest (Rev.1:5; 5:10; 20:6).
- the position of glory (1 Pt.5:4).

FELLOW HEIRS BY RESPONSIBILITY

Christ is the Sovereign Majesty of the Universe, the One who is ordained to rule and oversee all. Therefore, we share in the inheritance of His responsibility. We receive...

- the rulership over many things (Mt.25:23).
- the right to rule and hold authority (Lk.12:42-44; 22:28-29).
- eternal responsibility and joy (Mt.25:21, 23).
- rule and authority over cities (Lk.19:17, 19).
- thrones and the privilege of reigning forever (Rev.20:4; 22:5).

These passages will give some idea of what Scripture teaches when it speaks of the believer being a *fellow-heir* with Christ. There are an innumerable number of Scriptures that could be added to these. As Paul declares:

However, as it is written: "No eye has seen, no ear has heard, no mind has conceived what God has prepared for those who love him"— (1 Cor 2:9)

Oh, the depth of the riches of the wisdom and knowledge of God! How unsearchable his judgments, and his paths beyond tracing out! "Who has known the mind of the Lord? Or who has been his counselor?" "Who has ever given to God, that God should repay him?" For from him and through him and to him are all things. To him be the glory forever! Amen. (Rom 11:33-36)

TITUS 3:8-11

	F. Message 6: The Warning to Believers, 3:8-11	9 But avoid foolish controversies and genealogies and arguments and quarrels about the law, because these are unprofitable and useless.	2 Warning 2: Turn away from foolish & controversial discussion & from false trusts
1 Warning 1: Do good works & keep on doing them	8 This is a trustworthy saying. And I want you to stress these things, so that those who have trusted in God may be careful to devote themselves to doing what is good. These things are excellent and profitable for everyone.	10 Warn a divisive person once, and then warn him a second time. After that, have nothing to do with him. 11 You may be sure that such a man is warped and sinful; he is self-condemned.	3 Warning 3: Reject a divisive person a. He is to be reached out to and warned b. He is perverted & sinful & self-condemning

DIVISION II

THE MESSAGE OF SOUND DOCTRINE

F. Message 6: The Warning to Believers, 3:8-11

(3:8-11) Introduction: this is a critical message, a message that believers must heed. It gives three warnings to believers.

1. Warning 1: do good works and keep on doing them (v.8).
2. Warning 2: turn away from foolish and controversial discussions and from false trusts (v.9).
3. Warning 3: reject a divisive person (v.10-11).

1 **(3:8) Warnings—Good Works—Believers, Duty**: the first warning—believers must do good works and keep on doing them. The Greek word devote (proistemi) means to set before; to give attention to; to be forward and eager and diligent in doing good works. It means...

- to keep on doing good works.
- to sustain good works.
- to persevere in doing good works.
- to carry on good works.

It even has the idea of sustaining good works against all odds regardless of circumstances and difficulties. It means to persevere in good works even in the midst of opposition or danger. The necessity of doing good works is also brought out by the word "careful." The word means...

- to think upon good works.
- to consider good works.
- to give careful attention to good works.
- to focus upon good works.

The idea is that the very thoughts of a person's mind are to be centered and focused upon doing good works. Good works are to be the very concentration and primary purpose of a person's life. But note: this is not all. The necessity of doing good works is brought out by another factor. The minister is instructed to affirm constantly—to insist that believers persevere in doing good works. The idea is that the minister must...

- earnestly insist
- constantly insist
- steadfastly insist

The minister of God must press believers to maintain good works. Why so much emphasis on good works? Matthew Henry says, "Because a bare, inactive faith will not save a person; only a working active faith will save a person. Saving faith is a faith that bears righteousness and purity; it actively works at being righteous and pure and at leading others to live righteous and pure lives."

Note one other point: good works are good and profitable to men. Good works alone will build the kind of society and world for which the human heart longs: a world of love, joy, and peace. But remember what Scripture says: we are not saved *by our works of righteousness*; we are saved by the mercy and grace of God through faith in Christ Jesus.

> To be self-controlled and pure, to be busy at home, to be kind, and to be subject to their husbands, so that no one will malign the word of God. Similarly, encourage the young men to be self-controlled. (Titus 2:5-6)

However we must never forget this: God saves us *to do good works, to do what is good*. Good works are the purpose for which He saves us.

> For we are God's workmanship, created in Christ Jesus to do good works, which God prepared in advance for us to do. (Eph 2:10)

The whole point of this verse is to stress the absolute necessity for devoting oneself to good works. The very proof that we are saved is that we are maintaining good works. If we are not living righteous and pure lives and encouraging others to trust Christ as their Savior and to live righteously, then Scripture declares that we are *not genuinely saved*. The warning to believers is clear: they must do good works and keep on doing them.

> In the same way, let your light shine before men, that they may see your good deeds and praise your Father in heaven. (Mat 5:16)
> Command them to do good, to be rich in good deeds, and to be generous and willing to share. (1 Tim 6:18)
> In everything set them an example by doing what is good. In your teaching show integrity, seriousness (Titus 2:7)
> And let us consider how we may spur one another on toward love and good deeds. (Heb 10:24)
> In the same way, faith by itself, if it is not accompanied by action, is dead. But someone will say, "You have faith; I have deeds." Show me your faith without deeds,

and I will show you my faith by what I do. (James 2:17-18)

Live such good lives among the pagans that, though they accuse you of doing wrong, they may see your good deeds and glorify God on the day he visits us. (1 Pet 2:12)

And this is his command: to believe in the name of his Son, Jesus Christ, and to love one another as he commanded us. (1 John 3:23)

2 (3:9) **Strife—Time, Wasting—Division—Theological Discussion**: the second warning—believers must turn away from foolish and controversial discussions and from false trusts. Very simply, three things are pictured in this verse.

1. There were some who were spending their time sitting and discussing foolish (moros), useless, and stupid questions—discussions that accomplished nothing for the cause of Christ or for the welfare of humanity. William Barclay has a very descriptive discussion of this point that we all need to heed:

> "It has been said that there is a danger that a man may think himself religious because he discusses religious questions. There is a kind of discussion group which argues simply for the sake of arguing. There is a kind of group which will argue for hours about theological questions. It is much easier to discuss theological questions than it is to be kind and considerate and helpful at home, or efficient and diligent and honest at work. There is no virtue in sitting discussing deep theological questions when the simple tasks of the Christian life are waiting to be done. It is indeed true that such discussion can be nothing other than an evasion of Christian duties.
>
> "Paul was quite certain that the real task of the Christian lay in Christian action. That is by no means to say that there is no place for Christian discussions; but it is to say that the discussion which does not end in action is very largely wasted time" (*The Letters to Timothy, Titus, and Philemon*, p.302).

2. There were some who were wasting time on genealogies, that is, on their roots and heritage. They felt that they were acceptable to God because they had good parents and forefathers. They even felt that the more outstanding they could show their roots to be, the more outstanding they would be in the eyes of society and God.

Thought 1. Note two significant lessons.
1) There are many persons who feel that they are acceptable to God because their parents, wife, husband, children, or family are godly. Others feel that their friendship with some minister or godly friend will rub off on them. They just think that God would never reject them because they are close to a godly person.
2) Many persons, even preachers and teachers, stress the godly heritage of Christianity and the great doctrines of the Christian faith. They think that they are acceptable to God because they profess the doctrines and godly heritage of Christianity and because they are involved in religion and in the worshipping of God. But the great tragedy is this: some are relying upon their profession of Christianity to save them instead of relying upon Christ; some are depending upon their belief in the great heritage and doctrines of Christianity to save them instead of depending upon Christ Himself. They just do not know Christ personally; they have not established a personal relationship with Christ.

3. There were those who were arguing and striving over the law, that is, over the Old Testament Scriptures. The false teachers of Paul's day were just like the false teachers of today and down through the centuries. They professed Christ but Christ was not enough to save them. It took both the law and Christ to save them. To be saved a person had to believe in Christ, yes, but he also had to undergo the basic ritual of the law (circumcision, baptism, church membership, confirmation, etc.) and commit his life to keeping the law of God, including the thousands and thousands of rules surrounding the law.

Paul is saying that believers, including preachers and teachers, should not become embroiled in the controversies of Scripture. They are "unprofitable and useless," useless and empty—of no value whatsoever. Christ is all that is needed. He and His Word are to be proclaimed and controversies turned away from. The proclamation of Christ and His Word is the occupation of the believer, the very purpose for the believer's existence.

Thought 1. Arguing over Christ and the Bible does not reach and build people up; proclaiming Christ and His Word is the only activity that reaches and builds people up.

> Nor to devote themselves to myths and endless genealogies. These promote controversies rather than God's work—which is by faith. (1 Tim 1:4)
>
> He is conceited and understands nothing. He has an unhealthy interest in controversies and quarrels about words that result in envy, strife, malicious talk, evil suspicions (1 Tim 6:4)
>
> Don't have anything to do with foolish and stupid arguments, because you know they produce quarrels. (2 Tim 2:23)
>
> But avoid foolish controversies and genealogies and arguments and quarrels about the law, because these are unprofitable and useless. (Titus 3:9)
>
> Do nothing out of selfish ambition or vain conceit, but in humility consider others better than yourselves. (Phil 2:3)
>
> Keep reminding them of these things. Warn them before God against quarreling about words; it is of no value, and only ruins those who listen. (2 Tim 2:14)
>
> And the Lord's servant must not quarrel; instead, he must be kind to everyone, able to teach, not resentful. (2 Tim 2:24)
>
> Starting a quarrel is like breaching a dam; so drop the matter before a dispute breaks out. (Prov 17:14)

3 (3:10-11) **Heresy—Teaching, False**: the third warning—believers must reject the divisive person, those who forsake the truth of Christ and of God's Word. The Greek word divisive (hairetikos) is interesting. It means to take for oneself; to choose for oneself. Therefore, a divisive person is a person who chooses what he is to believe. He rejects all authority no matter what it is: God, Christ, the Word of God, the church, man. He himself chooses what he is to believe. He and he alone is his authority; he and he alone determines truth—what is and what is not truth.

Note that this divisive person is in the church; he associates with believers. This is the picture of most divisive people. Few reject all the teachings of Christ and of the Bible. Most divisive people remain in the church, holding to some basic teachings but rejecting those doctrines that they do not like. The Scripture is clear: believers are to reach out to the heretic or false teacher. He is not to be lambasted, rejected, and expelled from the church. An attempt is to be made to reach him for Christ. In fact, two strong attempts are to be made to reach him. He is to be shown love and care and admonished to repent and confess the truth of Christ and His Word. But note: there is a limit. On the third try, if he does not repent he is to be rejected, that is, expelled from the church. He is not to be allowed to lead other believers astray. (See outline and notes—Mt.18:15-20 for more detailed discussion on church discipline as taught by Christ.)

The divisive person is "warped" (ektrepo): which means he is twisted or turned out and away from the truth of Christ and His Word. Note that the divisive person sins. The idea is that he sins greatly. Therefore, he condemns himself. He himself has chosen the path of unbelief, and he will be condemned for his unbelief.

Whoever believes in him is not condemned, but whoever does not believe stands condemned already because he has not believed in the name of God's one and only Son. (John 3:18)

Thought 1. The point is clear to the thinking and honest believer, and honesty is as necessary as the willingness to think about the issue. A person who uses the scissors of self-opinion and cuts up Christ and the Word of God, casting away some of the teachings concerning Him and His Word, is considered a divisive person by the Bible. It does not matter who he is—preacher, teacher, or layman—this is the person called divisive by the Bible. If he turns or twists himself out of the truth of Christ and Scripture, he is divisive. Therefore, he is to be approached in love and admonished on two specific occasions. If he rejects the two admonitions, he should be approached a third time, and then rejected if he still refuses to repent. He should be rejected and expelled even if he is a minister and teacher in the church.

A striking and tragic question is this—a question that God will surely answer in that great and terrible day of judgment: How many millions of people have been led astray within our churches by false teachers, those whom the Bible calls divisive—those who have turned away from the truth of Christ and of His Word?

"If your brother sins against you, go and show him his fault, just between the two of you. If he listens to you, you have won your brother over. But if he will not listen, take one or two others along, so that 'every matter may be established by the testimony of two or three witnesses.' If he refuses to listen to them, tell it to the church; and if he refuses to listen even to the church, treat him as you would a pagan or a tax collector. (Mat 18:15-17)

They worship me in vain; their teachings are but rules taught by men.'" (Mat 15:9)

We have heard that some went out from us without our authorization and disturbed you, troubling your minds by what they said. (Acts 15:24)

The Spirit clearly says that in later times some will abandon the faith and follow deceiving spirits and things taught by demons. (1 Tim 4:1)

But there were also false prophets among the people, just as there will be false teachers among you. They will secretly introduce destructive heresies, even denying the sovereign Lord who bought them—bringing swift destruction on themselves. (2 Pet 2:1)

Therefore, dear friends, since you already know this, be on your guard so that you may not be carried away by the error of lawless men and fall from your secure position. (2 Pet 3:17)

TITUS 3:12-15

	III. THE CONCLUDING REMARKS: SOME COMMITTED CHRISTIAN BELIEVERS, 3:12-15	Apollos on their way and see that they have everything they need. 14 Our people must learn to devote themselves to doing what is good, in order that they may provide for daily necessities and not live unproductive lives. 15 Everyone with me sends you greetings. Greet those who love us in the faith. Grace be with you all.	layman 5 Apollos: The evangelist whose witness was needed 6 All believers: A people needing to learn good works
1 Artemas: An unknown but committed minister	12 As soon as I send Artemas or Tychicus to you, do your best to come to me at Nicopolis, because I have decided to winter there. 13 Do everything you can to elp Zenas the lawyer and		
athers are iridescented minister			
3 Titus: A disciple with unusual strength			
4 Zenas: A committed			7 Fellow workers: Servants of God & their support to other believers

DIVISION III

THE CONCLUDING REMARKS: SOME COMMITTED CHRISTIAN BELIEVERS, 3:12-15

(3:12-15) **Introduction**: this is the close of Paul's letter to Titus. As usual Paul closes his letter by sharing his plans and sending greetings to various believers. Hence, the close of Paul's letters always gives us a glimpse of some of the early believers. This present passage mentions several committed believers who stand as dynamic examples of what commitment is all about.

1. Artemas: an unknown but committed minister (v.12).
2. Tychicus: a dedicated minister (v.12).
3. Titus: a disciple with unusual strength (v.12).
4. Zenas: a committed layman (v.13).
5. Apollos: the evangelist whose witness was needed (v.13).
6. Our people or all believers: a people needing to learn good works (v.14).
7. Fellow workers: servants of God and their support to other believers (v.15).

1 (3:12) **Artemas—Commitment**: there was Artemas, an unknown but committed minister. This is the only time Artemas is mentioned in the Bible. Note these facts:

⇒ He was a companion of Paul.
⇒ He was a fellow minister serving *under* Paul, a humble minister willing to serve in second place. His call was to serve Christ, and he served Christ no matter where he was placed—even under other ministers.
⇒ He was a committed minister, a minister who was willing to serve on a foreign field among a very difficult people.
⇒ He was apparently a strong minister, for he was being sent to serve in Crete, a most difficult place whose citizens had one of the worst reputations in the ancient world—a reputation so bad that their very name, *Cretian* became a byword for evil. They were famed as a "drunken, insolent, untrustworthy, lying, gluttonous people" (Barclay). Imagine being sent to serve among a people like that! Artemas had to be ever so strong in the Lord.

Then he said to them all: "If anyone would come after me, he must deny himself and take up his cross daily and follow me. For whoever wants to save his life will lose it, but whoever loses his life for me will save it. (Luke 9:23-24)

And anyone who does not carry his cross and follow me cannot be my disciple. (Luke 14:27)

So then, men ought to regard us as servants of Christ and as those entrusted with the secret things of God. (1 Cor 4:1)

Nobody should seek his own good, but the good of others. (1 Cor 10:24)

Therefore, my dear brothers, stand firm. Let nothing move you. Always give yourselves fully to the work of the Lord, because you know that your labor in the Lord is not in vain. (1 Cor 15:58)

Endure hardship with us like a good soldier of Christ Jesus. No one serving as a soldier gets involved in civilian affairs—he wants to please his commanding officer. (2 Tim 2:3-4)

2 (3:12) **Tychicus—Faithful**: there was Tychicus, a most dedicated minister. Note that nothing is said about Tychicus in this passage except the fact that he may be sent to Crete to replace Titus as the minister to the Cretians. However, Tychicus is mentioned throughout Paul's letters. He was one of Paul's most faithful and trusted ministers. (See outline, note, and DEEPER STUDY # 1—Eph.6:21-22 for detailed discussion.)

⇒ He was commissioned by Paul as a messenger to various churches (Eph.6:21f; Col.4:7; 2 Tim.4:12; Tit.3:12).
⇒ He was entrusted to deliver the letters of Paul to the Ephesians, Colossians, and Philemon (Eph.6:21-22; Col.4:7-8).
⇒ He was sent on a special mission to Ephesus (2 Tim.4:12).
⇒ He was to be sent to Crete for the purpose of relieving Titus (Tit.3:12).
⇒ He was called not only Paul's dear brother and faithful minister, but also his fellow servant (Col.4:7).

The point to see in the present passage is the dedication of Tychicus. He was a man with a worldwide vision, and he had sacrificed his life to reach the people of the world with the glorious news that they could now live forever. And note: there was the possibility that he was going to be sent to one of the most difficult places in the ancient world, the island of Crete. But he was a man of commitment—a man who dedicated his life to Christ. Therefore, he was ready and willing to serve anyplace.

> As long as it is day, we must do the work of him who sent me. Night is coming, when no one can work. (John 9:4)
>
> For we cannot help speaking about what we have seen and heard." (Acts 4:20)
>
> Now it is required that those who have been given a trust must prove faithful. (1 Cor 4:2)
>
> You were bought at a price. Therefore honor God with your body. (1 Cor 6:20)
>
> Yet when I preach the gospel, I cannot boast, for I am compelled to preach. Woe to me if I do not preach the gospel! (1 Cor 9:16)
>
> Therefore, my dear brothers, stand firm. Let nothing move you. Always give yourselves fully to the work of the Lord, because you know that your labor in the Lord is not in vain. (1 Cor 15:58)

3 (3:12) **Titus—Minister**: there was Titus, a strong disciple with special strength. Note that Paul wants Titus to join him in Nicopolis. Why? Paul does not say, but Paul needed him for some special ministry, a ministry so special that the other ministers with Paul could not handle it. This fact plus the fact that Titus had been the disciple left behind to set in order the Cretian churches shows that Titus was a strong disciple, a disciple of unusual strength. He was a pioneer for Christ, a disciple so strong in Christ that he could be the first to reach an area for Christ and to set the churches in order for Christ (Tit.1:5).

> Therefore go and make disciples of all nations, baptizing them in the name of the Father and of the Son and of the Holy Spirit, and teaching them to obey everything I have commanded you. And surely I am with you always, to the very end of the age." (Mat 28:19-20)
>
> He said to them, "Go into all the world and preach the good news to all creation. (Mark 16:15)
>
> Again Jesus said, "Peace be with you! As the Father has sent me, I am sending you." (John 20:21)
>
> But you will receive power when the Holy Spirit comes on you; and you will be my witnesses in Jerusalem, and in all Judea and Samaria, and to the ends of the earth." (Acts 1:8)
>
> I can do everything through him who gives me strength. (Phil 4:13)
>
> But as for me, I am filled with power, with the Spirit of the LORD, and with justice and might, to declare to Jacob his transgression, to Israel his sin. (Micah 3:8)

4 (3:13) **Zenas—Laymen, Committed**: there was Zenas, a committed layman. This is the only time Zenas is mentioned in the Bible. Note these facts:
⇒ He was a lawyer.
⇒ He was a Christian believer, a layman who trusted Christ with all his heart.
⇒ He was a committed believer, so committed that he deserved support from the church despite the fact that he was a lawyer and not a full-time pastor.
⇒ He was a believer who was willing to help and serve with other believers. Note that Paul was telling Titus to bring Zenas to him.

The lesson is clear: Christ needs committed laymen who will commit their lives to serve Him and to help other believers. They need to be so committed that they are worthy of support by the church. The church may not be able to support them in addition to the full time staff, but the laymen should be so committed that they are worthy of the support.

> Then Jesus said to his disciples, "If anyone would come after me, he must deny himself and take up his cross and follow me. (Mat 16:24)
>
> In the same way, any of you who does not give up everything he has cannot be my disciple. (Luke 14:33)
>
> Therefore, I urge you, brothers, in view of God's mercy, to offer your bodies as living sacrifices, holy and pleasing to God—this is your spiritual act of worship. Do not conform any longer to the pattern of this world, but be transformed by the renewing of your mind. Then you will be able to test and approve what God's will is— his good, pleasing and perfect will. (Rom 12:1-2)
>
> "Therefore come out from them and be separate, says the Lord. Touch no unclean thing, and I will receive you." "I will be a Father to you, and you will be my sons and daughters, says the Lord Almighty." (2 Cor 6:17-18)
>
> Endure hardship with us like a good soldier of Christ Jesus. No one serving as a soldier gets involved in civilian affairs—he wants to please his commanding officer. (2 Tim 2:3-4)
>
> Do not love the world or anything in the world. If anyone loves the world, the love of the Father is not in him. For everything in the world—the cravings of sinful man, the lust of his eyes and the boasting of what he has and does—comes not from the Father but from the world. The world and its desires pass away, but the man who does the will of God lives forever. (1 John 2:15-17)

5 (3:13) **Apollos—Evangelism**: there was Apollos, an evangelist whose witness was needed. Apollos is mentioned several times in Scripture (see outline and notes—Acts 18:23-28 for full discussion). Apollos was called to preach Christ and to evangelize the lost. As soon as he knew the truth, he was set aflame to share Christ. The fire of evangelism to reach the world for Christ burned in his heart. This was the fire that Paul apparently needed in Nicopolis. Imagine! To have such a burning zeal for souls that others request our witness. What a dynamic example! What a need today! Men and women burning to reach the lost for Christ. Note that Apollos, the evangelist, is not to be left needing anything. The church is to support him and meet his needs.

It was he who gave some to be apostles, some to be prophets, some to be evangelists, and some to be pastors and teachers, to prepare God's people for works of service, so that the body of Christ may be built up until we all reach unity in the faith and in the knowledge of the Son of God and become mature, attaining to the whole measure of the fullness of Christ. (Eph 4:11-13)

Do you not say, 'Four months more and then the harvest'? I tell you, open your eyes and look at the fields! They are ripe for harvest. (John 4:35)

I am obligated both to Greeks and non-Greeks, both to the wise and the foolish. That is why I am so eager to preach the gospel also to you who are at Rome. I am not ashamed of the gospel, because it is the power of God for the salvation of everyone who believes: first for the Jew, then for the Gentile. (Rom 1:14-16)

For I resolved to know nothing while I was with you except Jesus Christ and him crucified. (1 Cor 2:2)

To this end I labor, struggling with all his energy, which so powerfully works in me. (Col 1:29)

6 (3:14) **Believers**: there were the believers, a people needing to learn good works. Note that Paul calls the believers of Crete "our people" (hoi hemeteroi), an endearing term. *The Amplified Bible* says:

> And let our [own people really] learn to apply themselves to good deeds—to honest labor and honorable employment—so that they may be able to meet necessary demands whenever the occasion may require and not be living idle and uncultivated and unfruitful lives.

The point is that believers are to work and labor in order to make money and then they are to do good with their money. They are to help those in need, ministering to help meet the needs of the world. And they are to support men such as Zenas and Apollos, both layman and minister, who have given their lives and time to serve Christ. They are to financially support the spread of the gospel around the world.

I will give you the keys of the kingdom of heaven; whatever you bind on earth will be bound in heaven, and whatever you loose on earth will be loosed in heaven." Then he warned his disciples not to tell anyone that he was the Christ. For where your treasure is, there your heart will be also. (Mat 6:19-21)

He who has been stealing must steal no longer, but must work, doing something useful with his own hands, that he may have something to share with those in need. (Eph 4:28)

Command those who are rich in this present world not to be arrogant nor to put their hope in wealth, which is so uncertain, but to put their hope in God, who richly provides us with everything for our enjoyment. Command them to do good, to be rich in good deeds, and to be generous and willing to share. In this way they will lay up treasure for themselves as a firm foundation for the coming age, so that they may take hold of the life that is truly life. (1 Tim 6:17-19)

7 (3:15) **Believers**: there were fellow workers, servants of God. Paul had several fellow workers with him. Everyone sent their greeting and prayed for God's grace upon the Cretian believers. The idea is that of support and encouragement. And remember: nothing encourages us and stirs us to serve Christ more and more faithfully than the support of other believers. When things are going bad and trial after trial is confronting us, the very thing we need is a word of support from fellow workers. This is the reason we must be constantly supporting others.

Carry each other's burdens, and in this way you will fulfill the law of Christ. (Gal 6:2)

Remember those in prison as if you were their fellow prisoners, and those who are mistreated as if you yourselves were suffering. (Heb 13:3)

Finally, brothers, pray for us that the message of the Lord may spread rapidly and be honored, just as it was with you. (2 Th 3:1)

Pray for us. We are sure that we have a clear conscience and desire to live honorably in every way. (Heb 13:18)

THE
OUTLINE & SUBJECT INDEX

REMEMBER: When you look up a subject and turn to the Scripture reference, you have not only the Scripture, you have *an outline and a discussion* (commentary) of the Scripture and subject.

This is one of the *GREAT VALUES* of **The Preacher's Outline & Sermon Bible®**. Once you have all the volumes, you will have not only what all other Bible indexes give you, that is, a list of all the subjects and their Scripture references, *BUT* you will also have…

- An outline of *every* Scripture and subject in the Bible.
- A discussion (commentary) on every Scripture and subject.
- Every subject supported by other Scriptures or cross references.

DISCOVER THE GREAT VALUE for yourself. Quickly glance below to the very first subject of the Index of Titus. It is:

AGE
    Aged men. Behavior of. 2:2
    Aged women. Behavior of. 2:3
    Different **a**. Discussed. 2:1-8

Turn to the reference. Glance at the Scripture and outline of the Scripture, then read the commentary. You will immediately see the GREAT VALUE of the INDEX of **The Preacher's Outline & Sermon Bible®**.

OUTLINE AND SUBJECT INDEX

ACCUSERS, FALSE (See **SLANDERS**)

AGE
  Aged men. Behavior of. 2:2
  Aged women. Behavior of. 2:3
  Different **a**. Discussed. 2:1-8

APOLLOS
  Discussed. 3:13

APOSTASY
  Discussed. 3:10-11

APOSTLE
  Meaning. 1:1

ARGUMENTS
  Duty. To turn away from. 3:9

ARTEMAS
  Discussed. 3:12

AUTHORITY (See **JESUS CHRIST**, Authority)
  Civil. Discussed. 3:1-2
  Exercised by. The pastor. 2:15

BELIEVERS
  Age groups. Various ages & their behavior. Discussed. 2:1-10
  Duty.
    Of various age groups. 2:1-10
    To be a good citizen. Six duties. 3:1-2
    To shun controversial teachings. 3:9
  Life - Walk.
    Discussed. 2:11-15
    In light of Jesus' return. 2:11-15
    In this present world. 2:11-15
  Names - Titles. Peculiar possession of Christ. 2:14
  Some early **b**. 3:12-15

BISHOPS (See **OVERSEERS**)

BRAWLER
  Discussed. 3:2

CHURCH
  Age groups. Discussed. 2:1-8
  Organization. Elders & bishops. 1:5-9

CHURCH DISCIPLINE
  Reasons for. False teaching. 1:10-16

CITIZENSHIP
  Duties. Sixfold. 3:1-2

CONTENTION
  Discussed. 3:2
  Duty. To turn away from. 3:9

CONTROVERSY
  Duty. To turn away from. 3:9

CRITICISM - CRITICIZING (See **DIVISION**)
  Instructions governing. 3:2

DECEPTION
  Discussed. 3:3

DECEIVERS
  Meaning. 1:10

DETEST - DETESTABLE
  Discussed. 3:3

DISCREET
  Meaning. 2:4-5

DISOBEDIENCE
  Discussed. 3:3

DIVISION - DISSENSION (See **CRITICISM; JUDGING; UNITY**)
  Discussed. 3:2; 3:9; 3:10-11

DOCTRINE
  The message sound **d**. 2:1-3:11
  Theological basis of. Grace of God. 2:11-15

ELDERS
  Discussed. 1:5-9

END TIME
  Christ's return & the world's end. How to behave while waiting for the Lord's return. 2:11-15

ENVY
  Discussed. 3:3

EPIMENIDES
  Greek poet quoted by Paul. 1:12

ETERNAL LIFE
  Duty. To preach. 1:2-3

EXAMPLE
  Meaning. 2:7-8

GENTLE - GENTLENESS
  Discussed. 3:2

GOD
  Nature.
    Cannot lie. Three reasons. 1:2-3
    Kind & loving. 3:4-5
    Merciful. 3:4-5
    Not far off in outer space, but concerned with men. 3:4-5

GODLY
  Meaning. 2:12-13

GOSPEL
  Message. Discussed. 1:2-3

GOSSIPERS
  Meaning. 2:3

GRACE
  Discussed. 2:11-15
  Meaning. 2:11-15
  Of God. Vs. works. 3:4-7
  Source. Of salvation. 2:11
  Work of.
    To save. 2:11; 3:7
    To teach us how to live. 2:12-13
    To teach us to look for Christ's return. 2:12-13

GRAVE (See **WORTHY OF RESPECT**)

HOLY SPIRIT
  Source of. Jesus Christ. 3:6
  Work of.
    Regeneration. 3:5
    Renewal. Day by day. Tit3:5

HOPE
  Believer's **h**. Eternal life. 1:2-3
  Described as. Blessed. 2:13
  Source - Comes through. God's promises. 1:2-3

INHERITANCE
  Discussed. 3:6
  List of rewards. 3:6

INDEX

JESUS CHRIST
  Death.
    Reason for. 2:11-15
    To redeem man. 2:14
  Work of.
    To give the Holy Spirit. 3:5
    To justify. 3:5
    To make us heirs. 3:5

JUSTIFICATION
  Discussed. 3:5

KINDNESS
  Of God. Discussed. 3:4-5

LABOR - LABORERS
  Duty. Toward employers. 2:9-10

LAW
  Relation to believers. To avoid foolish questions about. 3:9

LAW, CIVIL
  Duties toward. To obey civil laws & rulers. 3:1

LOST, THE
  Discussed. Life of. Eight traits. 3:3

LOVE
  Of God. Discussed. 3:4-5

LUST (See **PASSIONS**)

MALICE
  Discussed. 3:3

MAN
  Depravity.
    Life without God. Eight traits. 3:3
    Worthy of being hated. Reasons. 3:3
  Natural m. Life without God. Eight traits. 3:3
  State - Present. Life without God. 3:3

MARRIAGE
  Duty. To love. 2:4-5

MEEK – MEEKNESS (See **GENTLE – GENTLENESS**)

MEN
  Elderly m. Duties of. 2:2
  Young m. Duties of. 2:6-8

MERCY
  Of God. Discussed. 3:4-5

MINISTER
  Call. To be God's servant & messenger. 1:1-4
  Discussed. Qualifications. 1:5-9
  Duty.
    Discussed. Five points. 1:1-4
    Of young m. 2:7-8
    To look after the Word & preach. 1:2-3
    To preach sound doctrine. 1:9
  False m. (See **TEACHERS, FALSE**)
  Motivation. Discussed. 1:2-3

NEW BIRTH
  Discussed. 3:5

NEW MAN
  Discussed. 3:5

OVERSEERS
  Discussed. 1:5-9

PASSIONS
  Discussed. 3:3

PATTERN (See **EXAMPLE**)

PLEASURE
  Discussed. 3:3

PREACHING
  Duty.
    To preach. 1:2-3; 1:9
    To proclaim the grace of God through every means of speech. 2:15
  How to preach. Discussed. 2:7-8

REBIRTH
  Discussed. 3:5

REBUKE
  Duty. To r. & convict people. 2:15

REDEEM - REDEMPTION
  Discussed. 2:11-15; 2:14
  Purpose.
    To forgive sins. 2:14
    To purify a special people. 2:14

REGENERATION (See **REBIRTH**)

RELIGION - RITUAL
  Described as. Fables & commandments of men. 1:13-14

RENEWAL
  Discussed. 3:5

REVEALED - REVELATION (See **JESUS CHRIST**, Revealed as)
  What is r. God's Word is r. through preaching. 1:3

REWARDS
  List of. 3:6

RIGHTEOUSNESS
  Meaning. 2:12-13

RULERS
  Civic. Duties toward. To obey. 3:1

SALVATION
  Assurance. What it is & does. 3:4-7
  Deliverance - Purpose. What it is & does. 3:4-7
  Discussed. 2:11-15; 3:4-7
  Source.
    God's mercy. 3:4-5
    Grace of God. 2:11; 3:7
    Jesus Christ. 3:7

SELF-CONTROLLED
  Meaning. 2:6; 2:12-13

SERVANT
  Discussed. 1:1

SILENCED
  Meaning. 1:11

SIN - SINS
  Acts - Behavior of. Life before Christ. 3:3

SLANDER
  Meaning. 3:2

SLANDERS
  Meaning. 2:3

SLAVES (See **EMPLOYEES**)
  Duty. Behavior of. 2:9-10

SOBER (See **TEMPERATE**)

SOBER-MINDED (See **SELF-CONTOLLED**)

SOUND
  Meaning. 2:1

SPEAKING EVIL
  Discussed. 3:2

STEWARDSHIP
  Duty. To work in order to have enough to support the gospel. 3:14

STOPPED (See **SILENCED**)

STRIFE
  Duty. To turn away from. 3:9

TALKERS, MERE
  Meaning. 1:10

TALKERS, VAIN & EMPTY (See **TALKERS, MERE**)

TEACHERS (See **TEACHERS, FALSE; MINISTERS**)
  Duty.
    Behavior of. 2:7-8
    Of young t. 2:7-8

TEACHERS, FALSE
  Discussed. 1:10-16

TEACHING
  How to teach. Discussed. 2:7-8

TEACHING, FALSE
  Discussed. How to deal with. 2:10-11
  Duty.
    To reject heretics. 2:10-11
    To turn away from. 2:9

TEMPERATE
  Meaning. 2:2

TESTIMONY
  Examples. Some early believers. 3:12-15

TITUS
  Discussed. 3:12

TONGUE, THE (See **CURSING**)
  Duty.
    Not to be mere talkers & deceivers. 1:10-12; 1:16; 3:9
    Not to speak evil of people. 3:2

TYCHICUS
  Discussed. 3:12

WOMEN
  Aged w. 2:3
  Young w. 2:4-5

WORD OF GOD
  Nature of. The message of preaching. 1:2-3

WORTHY OF RESPECT
  Meaning. 2:2

YOUNG MEN
  Behavior of. 2:4-5

ZENAS
  Discussed. A lawyer called to serve. 3:13

PHILEMON

PHILEMON

INTRODUCTION

AUTHOR: Paul, the Apostle.

DATE: Uncertain. Probably A.D. 60-63 during Paul's first imprisonment in Rome.

TO WHOM WRITTEN: To Philemon, a well-to-do member of the Colossian church.

The letter to Philemon was delivered personally to Philemon by Tychicus, a fellow minister with Paul. He was also delivering Paul's letter to the church at Colosse. Tychicus' traveling companion was Onesimus, Philemon's runaway slave. Onesimus had just recently been converted and was now returning to his master to make restitution and to correct the wrong he had done.

PURPOSE: Paul had a twofold purpose in writing Philemon.
1. To encourage Philemon to personally forgive and receive Onesimus, the runaway slave, as a brother in the Lord.
2. To teach the church the spirit in which masters and slaves are to live and work together (note in v.2, Paul writes to the church at Colosse as well as to Philemon).

Colossians 3:22-4:1 should be studied right along with this letter. It is a straight-forward message to the churches on the subject of masters and slaves and of workers and employers (see also Ephesians 6:5-9).

SPECIAL FEATURES:
1. The Man, Onesimus. Onesimus was a runaway slave from Colosse. For some unknown reason he had stolen some property and had fled from his master, Philemon (cp. v.18-19). Swiftly he made his way to Rome where he could apparently be hidden among the crowded streets. But somehow, someplace, he met Paul. And Paul led him to the Lord. Then, one of three things apparently happened.
   a. Onesimus' conscience began to bother him, and he confessed all to Paul.
   b. Epaphras, a messenger from the Colossian church, visited Paul. He recognized the runaway slave and shared the incident with Paul.
   c. Paul knew Onesimus was a slave. In the discussion of the matter one day, Onesimus confessed his thievery and expressed a desire to correct his wrong.

Whatever the cause, Onesimus wished to return, and return he did. He obediently followed the dictates of his Lord and conscience. Interestingly, the very name Onesimus means "useful." Paul plays upon this. He says formerly, "[Onesimus] was useless to you, but now he has become useful both to you and to me." (v.11).

There is a fact of history that should be noted. If this fact is true, it shows the preciousness and strength of our salvation in Christ. Ignatius was evidently the pastor of the Antioch church about fifty years after Paul wrote the letter to Philemon. He was imprisoned and tried for his faith and condemned to die a martyr. While being escorted from Antioch to Rome, he wrote several letters to the churches of Asia Minor. These letters still survive. One of them is written to the Ephesian church where the very first chapter speaks ever so highly of their bishop. His name? Onesimus. And Ignatius does the same thing Paul did. He refers to the meaning of his name: he is Onesimus, the profitable one to Christ (v.11) (William Barclay. *The Letters to Timothy, Titus, and Philemon*, p.315f).

2. The Man, Philemon. Philemon was the slave owner, an outstanding and wealthy leader in the Colossian church. The church met in his home (v.2). He was a man of great love and faith in the Lord Jesus (v.5), a man who refreshed the hearts of other believers (v.7). And, he is a man who was trusted to make the right decision (vs. 14, 21). Evidently Philemon was led to the Lord by Paul (v.19).

3. The Problem of Slavery. Throughout history, slavery has been callous, savage, brutal, and wretched beyond words. This was never more so than in the days of Philemon and Onesimus. Onesimus above all others knew what he might be returning to: slaves had no rights whatsoever. The master had absolute rights over the lives of his slaves. The slave was not even considered a person. He was just a piece of chattel property. He was deliberately held down. He was a thing, a tool that existed to be used at the whim or wish of the master. Slavery was so much a part of the Roman Empire that it has been estimated that there were over 60,000,000 of them (William Barclay. *The Letters to Timothy, Titus, and Philemon*, p.310). Onesimus was just one among ever so many.

It was into this tragic society that Christianity came with a radical and transforming message—a message of emancipation: of personal emancipation, an emancipation of spirit, of attitude, of conscience, of mind, of relationships, of behavior, of work (see notes—Eph.6:5-9; Col.3:22-4:1; 1 Tim.6:1-2; Phile.9-21).

> "There is neither Jew nor Greek, there is neither bond nor free, there is neither male nor female: for ye are all one in Christ Jesus" (Gal.3:28).
>
> "For by one Spirit are we all baptized into one body, whether we be Jews or Gentiles, whether we be bond or free; and have been all made to drink into one Spirit" (1 Cor.12:13).
>
> "[In Christ] there is neither Greek nor Jew, circumcision nor uncircumcision, Barbarian, Scythian, bond nor free: but Christ is all, and in all" (Col.3:11).

There are no personal differences between men who stand in Christ: no human classes, no social status, no caste systems. Men are brothers—brothers beloved in the Lord (Phile.16; cp. v.10, 12, 15, 17). A whole new structure of human relationships is built. A structure by which men exist *together*, work *together*, and serve *together*.

Now, as Colossians 3:22-4:1 and Ephesians 6:5-9 show, this is not a message of softness. It does not accept laziness, tardiness, slothfulness, idleness, or excuses. It does not allow the abusing of one's rights as a brother or as an equal before the Lord. The new relationship in Christ does not take advantage of one another. Both master and slave have duties to perform. In fact, in the eyes of the Lord, there is no difference between the one called master and the one called slave. The important factor is that each lives responsibly where he is. Each is to perform his duty as to the Lord, and not to men: knowing that whatsoever good thing any man doeth, the same shall be received of the Lord, whether he be bond or free" (Eph.6:7-8).

Simply stated, the thrust of Christ is positive. It is the right of men to share in the labor of one another. All men are to be brothers "in the Lord Jesus Christ." There is absolutely nothing wrong nor immoral in sharing in the fruit of one another. It is the brutal and savage treatment, the abuse of a man's person and self-hood that makes a person lose self-respect. Such abuse and mistreatment causes a man's head to hang low. It bows his shoulders, slumps his back, buckles his knees, and drives him into the ground. He cringes and loses all self-respect. He becomes a beast of burden instead of an active, rational, and creative contributor to society.

For this reason, God insists that the glorious message of Christianity be proclaimed, the glorious message that all men must come to Christ Jesus. It is God's will that all men come to Christ and renew their hearts and receive the power to live as a brother to all other men.

The Old Testament made provision for this kind of spirit. It recognized that a slave might wish to remain in the service of his master because of mutual love and trust. It was a pure and simple matter of a mutual contract of labor and service (cp. Ex.21:5; Dt.15:16).

Slaves are to act like moral, responsible beings: "Slaves, obey you earthly masters in everything (Col. 3:22)."

Masters are to treat their slaves as "dear brothers" (Phile.16). They are to give "right and fair" wages (Col.4:1).

OUTLINE OF PHILEMON

THE PREACHER'S OUTLINE & SERMON BIBLE® is *unique*. It differs from all other Study Bibles & Sermon Resource Materials in that every Passage and Subject is outlined right beside the Scripture. When you choose any *Subject* below and turn to the reference, you have not only the Scripture, but you discover the Scripture and Subject *already outlined for you—verse by verse*.

For a quick example, choose one of the subjects below and turn over to the Scripture, and you will find this marvelous help for faster, easier, and more accurate use.

In addition, every point of the Scripture and Subject is *fully developed in a Commentary with supporting Scripture* at the bottom of the page. Again, this arrangement makes sermon preparation much easier and faster.

Note something else: The Subjects of Philemon have titles that are both Biblical and *practical*. The practical titles sometimes have more appeal to people. This *benefit* is clearly seen for use on billboards, bulletins, church newsletters, etc.

A suggestion: For the quickest overview of Philemon, first read *all the major titles* (I, II, III, etc.), then come back and read the subtitles.

OUTLINE OF PHILEMON

I. A GREAT CHRISTIAN MAN: PHILEMON, v.1-7

II. A MAN GREATLY CHANGED: ONESIMUS, v.8-21

III. A FINAL GREETING: SOME BELIEVERS IN THE EARLY CHURCH, v.22-24

PHILEMON

	I. A GREAT CHRISTIAN MAN: PHILEMON, v.1-7	4 I always thank my God as I remember you in my prayers, 5 Because I hear about your faith in the Lord Jesus and your love for all the saints. 6 I pray that you may be active in sharing your faith, so that you will have a full understanding of every good thing we have in Christ. 7 Your love has given me great joy and encouragement, because you, brother, have refreshed the hearts of the saints.
1 His commitment a. Was counted as a dear friend b. Was a laborer for Christ c. Rooted his family in Christ d. Opened his home to the church **2 His basic need: The grace & peace of God**	Paul, a prisoner of Christ Jesus, and Timothy our brother, To Philemon our dear friend and fellow worker, 2 To Apphia our sister, to Archippus our fellow soldier and to the church that meets in your home: 3 Grace to you and peace from God our Father and the Lord Jesus Christ.	**3 His testimony** a. It elicited prayer b. It was steeped in love c. It was steeped in faith **4 His need for prayer** a. That he might share faith more & more effectively b. Reason: He knows every good thing **5 His love** a. It brings great joy b. It refreshes the saints

I. A GREAT CHRISTIAN MAN: PHILEMON, v.1-7

(v.1-7) **Introduction**: this is the picture of a outstanding Christian man, Philemon. He stands as a great example for all believers.
1. His commitment (v.1-2).
2. His basic need: the grace and peace of God (v.3).
3. His testimony (v.4-5).
4. His need for prayer (v.6).
5. His love (v.7).

1 (v.1-2) **Philemon—Dedication**: the commitment of Philemon. His commitment is seen in four striking facts.

1. Philemon was so committed to Christ that he was counted "beloved" by Paul himself. And even more than this, Paul calls him "our dear friend"—a brother in the Lord who was held ever so close to the heart of Paul. But even this is not all that Paul said. Note the striking title that Paul used for himself: "Paul, a prisoner of Jesus Christ." This is a most unusual opening for Paul's letters. He usually opened his letters by establishing his apostleship, saying that he was "Paul, the apostle of Jesus Christ." Philemon must have been a dear friend of Paul's, a friend who recognized God's call to Paul, a friend who loved and supported Paul so much that Paul did not have to establish his call to the ministry for Philemon. Philemon was a beloved friend and supporter of Paul, one who was so committed to Christ that he was counted as beloved by one of God's choice servants, Paul himself.

> "A new command I give you: Love one another. As I have loved you, so you must love one another. By this all men will know that you are my disciples, if you love one another." (John 13:34-35, cp. Jn.15.12)
> Keep on loving each other as brothers. (Heb 13:1)
> Now that you have purified yourselves by obeying the truth so that you have sincere love for your brothers, love one another deeply, from the heart. (1 Pet 1:22)

2. Philemon was so committed to Christ that he was a laborer for Christ. He served Christ diligently, and note: he labored so diligently that Paul calls him a fellow-laborer. He was working so faithfully for Christ that Paul could acknowledge his labor and count him as a fellow-laborer, as working as diligently as Paul himself in the cause of Christ.

Thought 1. What a dynamic testimony: to be working so hard for Christ that one could be counted as a fellow-laborer with Paul! What a challenge for us! May God grant that we be stirred to serve Christ ever so diligently.

> Therefore, I urge you, brothers, in view of God's mercy, to offer your bodies as living sacrifices, holy and pleasing to God—this is your spiritual act of worship. Do not conform any longer to the pattern of this world, but be transformed by the renewing of your mind. Then you will be able to test and approve what God's will is—his good, pleasing and perfect will. (Rom 12:1-2)
> For we are God's fellow workers; you are God's field, God's building. (1 Cor 3:9; cp. 2 Cor. 6:1)
> Therefore, my dear brothers, stand firm. Let nothing move you. Always give yourselves fully to the work of the Lord, because you know that your labor in the Lord is not in vain. (1 Cor 15:58)
> Therefore, as we have opportunity, let us do good to all people, especially to those who belong to the family of believers. (Gal 6:10)
> But you, keep your head in all situations, endure hardship, do the work of an evangelist, discharge all the duties of your ministry. (2 Tim 4:5)

3. Philemon was so committed to Christ that he rooted his family in Christ. Apphia was apparently the wife of Philemon and Archippus the son of Philemon. Note that Archippus is addressed as a fellowsoldier of Paul. This must mean that at some point in his life he had actually served with Paul on some mission campaign. He was apparently the pastor of the Colossian church (Col.4:17).

The point to see is the dedication of this family to Christ. Philemon, as the husband and father, had rooted his family in Christ and led them to serve Christ. He had even supported his son's call and decision to serve Christ in the ministry. He was so committed to Christ that he took his responsibility to be the spiritual head of the family seriously—very seriously. And from all evidence, his wife supported him in his call to be the spiritual head of the family.

PHILEMON 1-7

Thought 1. What a dynamic example for Christian families: fathers, mothers, and children—each living for Christ and fulfilling his and her function and duty within the family.

4. Philemon was so committed to Christ that he opened his home to the church. Remember that the early church did not have church sanctuaries to meet in; they met in homes of faithful and committed believers. Philemon loved Christ so much that he was willing to open his home night after night and week after week for believers to worship and study God's Word together.

Thought 1. How many today would open their home this much for the church? How many love Christ enough to open their home on a regular basis—enough to forget their tiredness and the housecleaning required? Enough to sacrifice relaxation, rest, and family time together?

2 (v.3). **Grace—Peace**: the basic need of Philemon. Philemon had two basic needs.

1. He needed grace (see Deeper Study # 1, *Grace*—Tit.2:11-15; note and Deeper Study # 1—1 Cor.1:4 for discussion).
2. He needed peace (See notes, *Peace*—1 Th.1:1; Jn.14:27 for discussion).

3 (v.4-5) **Philemon—Love—Faith**: the testimony of Philemon. Note that Paul says, "I always thank my God" for you. Imagine having a testimony so strong in the Lord that Paul would thank God for you! That was Philemon.

1. His testimony was so strong that it stirred Paul to pray for him, not just every now and then, but *always*.
2. His testimony was steeped in love (see note, *Love*—1 Th.1:3; Deeper Study # 1—3:12 for discussion).
3. His testimony was steeped in faith (see note, *Faith*—1 Th.1:3; note 4—2 Th.1:3 for discussion).

4 (v.6) **Witness**: the prayer that Philemon needed. This is actually the prayer that every strong believer needs. The verse is somewhat complex because it has so much packed into one verse. Simply stated, Paul is asking God to help Philemon to *share his faith more actively*. Note that "every good thing" is said to be in Philemon. It is those good things that Paul prays for others to acknowledge and desire in their own lives. What are those good things? They would, no doubt, be the fruit of the Spirit.

⇒ love ⇒ goodness
⇒ joy ⇒ faithfulness
⇒ peace ⇒ gentleness
⇒ patience ⇒ self-control
⇒ kindness

The *good things* would also include life, both abundant and eternal life and the glorious hope of living forever in a new heavens and earth with Christ Jesus our Lord. When unbelievers of the world see the *good things* of life and the great hope of eternal life within us, some are bound to want the same hope we have. Therefore, the great need of every believer is for prayer—prayer that God will help us share the good things and the hope that we have in Christ.

For we cannot help speaking about what we have seen and heard." (Acts 4:20)

And the things you have heard me say in the presence of many witnesses entrust to reliable men who will also be qualified to teach others. (2 Tim 2:2)

We proclaim to you what we have seen and heard, so that you also may have fellowship with us. And our fellowship is with the Father and with his Son, Jesus Christ. (1 John 1:3)

And pray in the Spirit on all occasions with all kinds of prayers and requests. With this in mind, be alert and always keep on praying for all the saints. Pray also for me, that whenever I open my mouth, words may be given me so that I will fearlessly make known the mystery of the gospel, (Eph 6:18-19)

5 (v.7) **Love**: the love of Philemon. He was apparently a man who loved everyone and proved it by helping others. He was a man of compassion and grace who was committed to help those who had need. He refreshed them. Barclay has a striking statement on the point of ministry, a point that should challenge every believer who wants more and more of Christ.

"[This] means that we learn about Christ by giving to others. It means that we receive from Christ by sharing with others. It means that by emptying ourselves we are filled with Christ. It means that the poorer we make ourselves in giving, the richer we are in the gifts of Christ. It means that to be open-handed and generous-hearted is the surest way to learn more and more of the wealth of Christ. The man who knows most of Christ is not the intellectual scholar, not even the saint who shuts himself up and spends his days in prayer, but the man who moves in loving generosity among his fellow-men" (*The Letters to Timothy, Titus, and Philemon*, p.319).

In the same way, let your light shine before men, that they may see your good deeds and praise your Father in heaven. (Mat 5:16)

Do you not say, 'Four months more and then the harvest'? I tell you, open your eyes and look at the fields! They are ripe for harvest. Even now the reaper draws his wages, even now he harvests the crop for eternal life, so that the sower and the reaper may be glad together. (John 4:35-36)

Carry each other's burdens, and in this way you will fulfill the law of Christ. (Gal 6:2)

Therefore, as we have opportunity, let us do good to all people, especially to those who belong to the family of believers. (Gal 6:10)

Command them to do good, to be rich in good deeds, and to be generous and willing to share. (1 Tim 6:18)

And do not forget to do good and to share with others, for with such sacrifices God is pleased. (Heb 13:16)

Anyone, then, who knows the good he ought to do and doesn't do it, sins. (James 4:17)

PHILEMON 8-21

	II. A MAN GREATLY CHANGED: ONESIMUS, v.8-21		
1 Paul wanted to make a special request of Philemon a. Paul's right to demand b. Paul's appeal to love c. Paul's age & imprisonment d. Paul's request: Concerns Onesimus	8 Therefore, although in Christ I could be bold and order you to do what you ought to do, 9 Yet I appeal to you on the basis of love. I then, as Paul—an old man and now also a prisoner of Christ Jesus—	will be spontaneous and not forced. 15 Perhaps the reason he was separated from you for a little while was that you might have him back for good—	**4 Onesimus was a changed man** a. A man changed by the hand & providence of God—changed forever b. A man changed from a slave to a brother—a dear brother
2 Onesimus was a spiritual son of Paul—born again a. Had been useless b. Was now useful	10 I appeal to you for my son Onesimus, who became my son while I was in chains. 11 Formerly he was useless to you, but now he has become useful both to you and to me.	16 No longer as a slave, but better than a slave, as a dear brother. He is very dear to me but even dearer to you, both as a man and as a brother in the Lord. 17 So if you consider me a partner, welcome him as you would welcome me.	**5 Onesimus was to be welcomed & trusted as much as Paul** a. In a spirit of sharing debts b. In a spirit of remembering one's own spiritual debts
3 Onesimus was facing his past—to right his wrong a. He returns b. He ministers—serves others c. He trusts the goodness of other believers	12 I am sending him—who is my very heart—back to you. 13 I would have liked to keep him with me so that he could take your place in helping me while I am in chains for the gospel. 14 But I did not want to do anything without your consent, so that any favor you do	18 If he has done you any wrong or owes you anything, charge it to me. 19 I, Paul, am writing this with my own hand. I will pay it back—not to mention that you owe me your very self. 20 I do wish, brother, that I may have some benefit from you in the Lord; refresh my heart in Christ. 21 Confident of your obedience, I write to you, knowing that you will do even more than I ask.	c. In a spirit of mutual refreshment d. In a spirit of obedience

II. A MAN GREATLY CHANGED, ONESIMUS, V.8-21

(v.8-21) **Introduction**: this is the picture of a man greatly changed—changed by Christ. It shows us the difference that conversion should make in a life and just how we should receive a person who has been converted. And remember: Onesimus was a slave and a thief. Few people would ever want to be seen with a slave much less be known as a brother to him. Yet, this is exactly what we are about to see. No matter how low and base a person is, we are to reach out to him and do all we can to bring that person into the fellowship of Christ and the church. This is a strong picture of a man changed by Christ.
1. Paul wanted to make a special request of Philemon (v.8-9).
2. Onesimus was a son of Paul—born again (v.10-11).
3. Onesimus was facing his past—to right his wrong (v.12-14).
4. Onesimus was a changed man (v.15-16).
5. Onesimus was to be welcomed and trusted as much as Paul (v.17-21).

1 (v.8-9) **Paul**: Paul wanted to make a special request of Philemon. He had the right to demand that Philemon grant the request. Why? How can any believer, even a minister, demand that another believer do anything, especially if the believer differs or does not wish to do what is requested? There are two reasons:
⇒ It is the right thing to do.
⇒ It is a believer's duty to do it.

A believer, no matter who he is, should do the right thing; he should do his duty. Therefore, Paul had the right to make a special request of Philemon. But note: Paul did not demand that Philemon grant the request. Philemon should, but Paul did not demand it. Instead he appealed, urged, and pleaded with Philemon because he loved Philemon. Note that Paul based his plea upon three things that should appeal to the heart of any believer.
⇒ Paul based his appeal upon love: the love of Christ and the love of believers for each other. This should mean that Philemon loved Paul as a brother in Christ, loved him enough to grant the request.
⇒ Paul based his appeal upon his age. He was apparently in his fifties and no doubt his body was somewhat more aged than the average person because of the wear and tear upon his body from the sufferings that had been inflicted upon him through the years.
⇒ Paul based his appeal upon the fact that he was a prisoner for the cause of Christ. He had suffered so much in order to carry the gospel to the lost of the world, to people who were hopeless and lost just as Philemon and his family had been.

Because he was a prisoner for Christ, Philemon should grant his request. Paul was tired and worn, about to close his ministry and life upon earth; therefore, he expected his dear friends to heed his last request.

What was Paul's request? It concerned Onesimus, a former slave of Philemon, a slave who had run away to gain his freedom and had fled to Rome. Imagine Onesimus having just returned to Philemon and having handed this letter to Philemon—and Philemon standing there reading this letter. What were his thoughts? What was the impact upon Philemon, the slave owner who had been converted to Christ? What would he do now? There standing before him was a former slave who had broken the law by running away, broken one of the major laws upon which the Roman empire was built. (Rome kept the peace by enslaving and scattering the people of conquered nations all over the world, breaking their loyalty to their homeland. Death was the punishment for runaway slaves.)

2 (v.10-11) **Onesimus—New Birth**: Onesimus was a changed man, a man who had "become a son to Paul," that is, born again. Paul had led Onesimus to the Lord. Remember that Paul was in prison. How then did Paul come in contact with Onesimus? Was Onesimus recognized as a runaway slave while in Rome and imprisoned himself? No! He could not have been, for he was not in prison. He had returned and was moving about freely and was now standing before his owner, Philemon. When Onesimus reached Rome, he had most likely run across some Christian believers, and they had befriended him and introduced him to Paul. Paul then led him to Christ.

Note that Paul pulled no punches. He readily admitted the wrong that Onesimus had done: he had not been useful. The idea is absolutely of no use, just good for nothing. But now he was useful. He had accepted Christ and he was of the greatest use to Philemon and to Paul for the kingdom of Christ.

> **Thought 1.** Jesus Christ changes lives. He can take a useless, unprofitable, good for nothing person and make the most useful, profitable, and good person imaginable. Jesus Christ can take nothing and make something out of any person—no matter...
> - how low a person is
> - how far a person has sunk
> - how far a person has gone
> - what a person has done
>
> ...Jesus Christ can change a person and make him the most useful person in the world. How? Jesus Christ takes a person and *creates him anew*. Christ gives the person *a new birth*, makes *a new creation, a new person* out of him.
>
> > Yet to all who received him, to those who believed in his name, he gave the right to become children of God—children born not of natural descent, nor of human decision or a husband's will, but born of God. (John 1:12-13)
> >
> > In reply Jesus declared, "I tell you the truth, no one can see the kingdom of God unless he is born again." Jesus answered, "I tell you the truth, no one can enter the kingdom of God unless he is born of water and the Spirit. (John 3:3, 5)
> >
> > Therefore, if anyone is in Christ, he is a new creation; the old has gone, the new has come! (2 Cor 5:17)
> >
> > You were taught, with regard to your former way of life, to put off your old self, which is being corrupted by its deceitful desires; to be made new in the attitude of your minds; and to put on the new self, created to be like God in true righteousness and holiness. (Eph 4:22-24; cp. v. 25-32)
> >
> > But now you must rid yourselves of all such things as these: anger, rage, malice, slander, and filthy language from your lips. Do not lie to each other, since you have taken off your old self with its practices and have put on the new self, which is being renewed in knowledge in the image of its Creator. (Col 3:8-10)
> >
> > But when the kindness and love of God our Savior appeared, he saved us, not because of righteous things we had done, but because of his mercy. He saved us through the washing of rebirth and renewal by the Holy Spirit, whom he poured out on us generously through Jesus Christ our Savior, so that, having been justified by his grace, we might become heirs having the hope of eternal life. (Titus 3:4-7)
> >
> > For you have been born again, not of perishable seed, but of imperishable, through the living and enduring word of God. (1 Pet 1:23)
> >
> > Through these he has given us his very great and precious promises, so that through them you may participate in the divine nature and escape the corruption in the world caused by evil desires. (2 Pet 1:4)

3 (v.12-14) **Onesimus—Restitution**: he faced his past in order to right his wrong. This is clear evidence that the heart of Onesimus had been truly converted to Christ. He wanted to return and right the wrong he had done. Christ always does this to a person when he is truly converted. This is what Christianity is all about: converting and changing the wrong and evil in the world, changing it to a world of love and goodness and justice.

Note how dear this slave was to Paul. Paul says that he was sending a part of his own heart to Philemon. Paul loved this man who had been a law-breaker and thief (cp. v.18-19). This slave had become dear, very dear to Paul's heart. He was so dear that Paul would have preferred to keep Onesimus with him. Paul, who was in prison, desperately needed Onesimus—needed his companionship, encouragement, and assistance. But Paul would not ask him to stay. Why? Because Paul would do nothing without the consent of Philemon. Onesimus owed Philemon and it was up to Philemon where Onesimus should serve: either with Philemon as a slave or to return and serve with Paul as a minister. Note this, for it shows how Paul opened the door for Philemon to face Onesimus to be a servant of the gospel. The strength of Paul's wish is seen in his including Onesimus in the list of some great ministers who had been serving with Paul (Col.4:7-9). Paul elevated Onesimus so highly that he said that Onesimus could share exactly what had been happening to the gospel through Rome (also cp. v.15-16).

> **Thought 1.** A Christian believer is to make restitution, to right whatever wrong he has done—in so far as it is humanly possible. No Christian should ever try to escape from making restitution, from righting whatever wrong he has done. The very cause of Christ upon earth is morality and justice—to make the earth as good a place as possible—to teach and charge as many people as possible to live righteous and godly lives—to sweep the earth with the glorious gospel of love and care and the duty of one another to love and care for each other. If believers shirk their duty to right their own personal wrongs, then of what value is their Christianity? This is the reason Onesimus was returning to Philemon—the reason

Paul was sending him back despite the fact that he himself desperately needed Onesimus.

> I tell you, though he will not get up and give him the bread because he is his friend, yet because of the man's boldness he will get up and give him as much as he needs. "So I say to you: Ask and it will be given to you; seek and you will find; knock and the door will be opened to you. For everyone who asks receives; he who seeks finds; and to him who knocks, the door will be opened. (Luke 11:8-10)
>
> When he thus sins and becomes guilty, he must return what he has stolen or taken by extortion, or what was entrusted to him, or the lost property he found, (Lev 6:4)
>
> Yet if he is caught, he must pay sevenfold, though it costs him all the wealth of his house. (Prov 6:31)
>
> If he gives back what he took in pledge for a loan, returns what he has stolen, follows the decrees that give life, and does no evil, he will surely live; he will not die. (Ezek 33:15)

4 (v.15-16) **Onesimus—Love**: Onesimus was a changed man. And what a change he had experienced.

1. He had been changed by the hand of God, that is, under the providence of God. Paul tells Philemon that Onesimus had left for just a brief time *so that* he could return forever. God was overlooking and overruling the whole event for the sake of Onesimus' salvation. Philemon was now able to be associated with Onesimus forever. The implication is that both shall live forever with Christ, worshipping and serving Christ throughout all eternity.

2. He had been changed from a slave to a brother—a "dear brother." Note what Paul says: Onesimus had left as a slave, but he...
- was now above a slave.
- was now a dear brother.
- was now of great value to Paul.
- was now of much more value to Philemon.

Thought 1. The point is well made: when Christ changes a life, the life is changed eternally. Earthly relationships are changed forever. The changed person becomes a dear *brother*. It does not matter what the relationship has been...
- a master-slave relationship
- a friend-enemy relationship
- a victim-criminal relationship
- a love-hate relationship
- a marriage-divorce relationship
- an abused-hurtful relationship

If the person has been truthfully changed by Christ, then he is to be received as a *dear brother*. Why? Because God has put His hand upon the person and changed him forever.

> 'Love your neighbor as yourself.' (Mat 22:39)
>
> "A new command I give you: Love one another. As I have loved you, so you must love one another. By this all men will know that you are my disciples, if you love one another." (John 13:34-35)
>
> My command is this: Love each other as I have loved you. (John 15:12)
>
> Love must be sincere. Hate what is evil; cling to what is good. (Rom 12:9)
>
> Let no debt remain outstanding, except the continuing debt to love one another, for he who loves his fellowman has fulfilled the law. The commandments, "Do not commit adultery," "Do not murder," "Do not steal," "Do not covet," and whatever other commandment there may be, are summed up in this one rule: "Love your neighbor as yourself." Love does no harm to its neighbor. Therefore love is the fulfillment of the law. (Rom 13:8-10)
>
> You are all sons of God through faith in Christ Jesus, for all of you who were baptized into Christ have clothed yourselves with Christ. There is neither Jew nor Greek, slave nor free, male nor female, for you are all one in Christ Jesus. (Gal 3:26-28)
>
> Consequently, you are no longer foreigners and aliens, but fellow citizens with God's people and members of God's household, (Eph 2:19)
>
> May the Lord make your love increase and overflow for each other and for everyone else, just as ours does for you. (1 Th 3:12)
>
> Both the one who makes men holy and those who are made holy are of the same family. So Jesus is not ashamed to call them brothers. (Heb 2:11)
>
> Now that you have purified yourselves by obeying the truth so that you have sincere love for your brothers, love one another deeply, from the heart. (1 Pet 1:22)

5 (v.17-21) **Onesimus—Brotherhood**: Onesimus was to be received and trusted as much as Paul himself. Paul makes an astounding request. He asked Philemon to receive a slave who was a lawless thief just as he would receive himself. Most people would not even want to be seen with a slave or a lawless thief, much less be to be known as a partner or brother to one. But Paul boldly stepped forward and asked that Onesimus, the slave and thief, be received as a partner and brother. And note how sincere Paul was.

⇒ Paul said that he would personally pay whatever money or goods Onesimus had stolen. Why should Philemon accept this? Because Philemon should always remember the debt he owed for his salvation. Paul had led him to Christ; therefore Philemon owed his very life to Paul (v.19).

⇒ Paul said that he would be filled with joy and refreshed if Philemon would receive Onesimus as a partner and brother in the Lord (v.20).

⇒ Paul said that he had great confidence that Philemon would grant the request and even go beyond and do more (v.21).

Thought 1. The one thing that people need above all else is to be received. No matter how low or base, useless and unprofitable, sinful and derelict, crippled and diseased, ugly and unattractive, unapproachable and distasteful—a person needs to be received and brought into the fellowship of Christ and believers.

For too long, the church and believers have shunned and shut out the lowly. Christ loves and longs for every human being—man, woman and child—to be reached for Him.

We must always remember: we are debtors to Christ and to the world, every man, woman, and child. Christ has saved us and given us the fellowship with Himself and God the Father and with one another. Therefore, we are spiritual debtors to all.

Therefore go and make disciples of all nations, baptizing them in the name of the Father and of the Son and of the Holy Spirit, And teaching them to obey everything I have commanded you. And surely I am with you always, to the very end of the age." (Mat 28:19-20)

He said to them, "Go into all the world and preach the good news to all creation. (Mark 16:15)

But you will receive power when the Holy Spirit comes on you; and you will be my witnesses in Jerusalem, and in all Judea and Samaria, and to the ends of the earth." (Acts 1:8)

I am obligated both to Greeks and non-Greeks, both to the wise and the foolish. That is why I am so eager to preach the gospel also to you who are at Rome. (Rom 1:14-15)

For who makes you different from anyone else? What do you have that you did not receive? And if you did receive it, why do you boast as though you did not? (1 Cor 4:7)

You were bought at a price. Therefore honor God with your body. (1 Cor 6:20)

For you know the grace of our Lord Jesus Christ, that though he was rich, yet for your sakes he became poor, so that you through his poverty might become rich. (2 Cor 8:9)

This is how we know what love is: Jesus Christ laid down his life for us. And we ought to lay down our lives for our brothers. (1 John 3:16)

PHILEMON 22-25

	III. A FINAL GREETING: SOME BELIEVERS IN THE EARLY CHURCH, v.22-25
1 Paul: Eternally optimistic	22 And one thing more: Prepare a guest room for me, because I hope to be restored to you in answer to your prayers.
2 Epaphras: Imprisoned for his faith	23 Epaphras, my fellow prisoner in Christ Jesus, sends you greetings.
3 Mark: Redeemed himself	
4 Aristarchus: Always there	24 And so do Mark, Aristarchus, Demas and Luke, my fellow workers.
5 Demas: Forsook Christ	
6 Luke: Gave all to Christ	
7 The conclusion of a much needed benediction: The grace of Christ	25 The grace of the Lord Jesus Christ be with your spirit.

III. A FINAL GREETING: SOME BELIEVERS IN THE EARLY CHURCH, v.22-25

(v.22-25) **Introduction**: this closes the brief letter of Paul to his dear friend Philemon. As was his usual custom, Paul closed his letter by sending greetings to and from various believers. These closings are always of significant interest as they give us a meaningful glimpse into the lives of some of the believers of the early church—brothers and sisters whom we shall soon meet face to face in heaven and fellowship with. We shall all serve our Lord together for eternity.

1. Paul: was eternally optimistic (v.22).
2. Epaphras: was imprisoned for his faith (v.23).
3. Mark: redeemed himself (v.24).
4. Aristarchus: was always there (v.24).
5. Demas: forsook Christ (v.24).
6. Luke: gave all to Christ (v.25).
7. The Conclusion of a much needed benediction: The grace of Christ

1 (v.22) **Paul—Prayer**: Paul is the first believer seen. The point being stressed is his eternal optimism. He was in prison, yet he believed unreservedly that he could be freed by the prayers of his dear friends. What an impact prayer has. God answers prayer; this is His promise. The problem is that we do not take God at His word: we do not pray. The friends of Paul prayed and Paul was apparently released from prison (see Introduction, *Date*—1 Timothy for discussion).

> **Look to the LORD and his strength; seek his face always. (1 Chr 16:11)**
>
> **"Ask and it will be given to you; seek and you will find; knock and the door will be opened to you. (Mat 7:7)**
>
> **"Watch and pray so that you will not fall into temptation. The spirit is willing, but the body is weak." (Mat 26:41)**
>
> **Then Jesus told his disciples a parable to show them that they should always pray and not give up. (Luke 18:1)**
>
> **If you remain in me and my words remain in you, ask whatever you wish, and it will be given you. (John 15:7)**
>
> **Until now you have not asked for anything in my name. Ask and you will receive, and your joy will be complete. (John 16:24)**

> **And pray in the Spirit on all occasions with all kinds of prayers and requests. With this in mind, be alert and always keep on praying for all the saints. (Eph 6:18)**
>
> **Pray continually; (1 Th 5:17)**
>
> **You do not have, because you do not ask God. (James 4:2)**
>
> **Is any one of you in trouble? He should pray. Is anyone happy? Let him sing songs of praise. (James 5:13)**

2 (v.23) **Epaphras**: he was a servant of the Lord who in the past had been imprisoned with Paul.

⇒ He was the "*minister*" of the Colossian church (Col.1:7).
⇒ He was "*a faithful minister* of Christ" (Col.1:7).
⇒ He was "*a servant of Christ*" (Col.4:12).
⇒ He was a "*fellow servant*" who was ever so dear to Paul's heart (Col.1:7).
⇒ He was so committed and dedicated to Christ that Paul called him "my fellow prisoner in Christ Jesus" (Phile.23).
⇒ He was a believer who fervently labored and toiled in prayer for his dear people in Colosse (Col.4:12). He prayed in particular for one thing: that they might be perfect and complete in all the will of God; that is, that they might *know* the complete will of God and do His will perfectly.

> **And pray in the Spirit on all occasions with all kinds of prayers and requests. With this in mind, be alert and always keep on praying for all the saints. (Eph 6:18)**
>
> **Devote yourselves to prayer, being watchful and thankful. (Col 4:2)**
>
> **Look to the LORD and his strength; seek his face always. (1 Chr 16:11)**

⇒ He was a minister who worked hard for his own church and for all the churches that surrounded him (Col.4:13, Laodicea and Hieropolis). He prayed and prayed much, but he also worked much—so much that his labor was even a testimony to the great minister Paul.

"My food," said Jesus, "is to do the will of him who sent me and to finish his work. Do you not say, 'Four months more and then the harvest'? I tell you, open your eyes and look at the fields! They are ripe for harvest. (John 4:34-35)

As long as it is day, we must do the work of him who sent me. Night is coming, when no one can work. (John 9:4)

Do you not know that in a race all the runners run, but only one gets the prize? Run in such a way as to get the prize. Everyone who competes in the games goes into strict training. They do it to get a crown that will not last; but we do it to get a crown that will last forever. (1 Cor 9:24-25)

To this end I labor, struggling with all his energy, which so powerfully works in me. (Col 1:29)

For this reason I remind you to fan into flame the gift of God, which is in you through the laying on of my hands. (2 Tim 1:6)

3 (v.24) **John Mark**: he was the young man who had redeemed himself. Mark had earlier deserted Paul and the ministry (see DEEPER STUDY # 4, *John Mark*—Acts 12:25; note—13:13 for discussion). But note what Paul says to the Colossian church. He tells the church that they are to receive John Mark if he were able to visit them. Apparently, some earlier instructions had been sent to the churches founded by Paul telling them about Mark's desertion. But now the young man had repented and recommitted his life to Christ. He had redeemed himself; therefore, he was to be welcomed.

Thought 1. When a believer fails and sins, even if it is desertion of Christ, he is to be welcomed back with open arms once he has repented. We must not hold a person's failure and sin against him. Christ has forgiven us for so much—all of us—therefore we must forgive and welcome our brothers and sisters back into our hearts and lives.

Repent of this wickedness and pray to the Lord. Perhaps he will forgive you for having such a thought in your heart. (Acts 8:22)

Offer hospitality to one another without grumbling. (1 Pet 4:9)

Hide your face from my sins and blot out all my iniquity. (Psa 51:9)

"I, even I, am he who blots out your transgressions, for my own sake, and remembers your sins no more. (Isa 43:25)

Let the wicked forsake his way and the evil man his thoughts. Let him turn to the LORD, and he will have mercy on him, and to our God, for he will freely pardon. (Isa 55:7)

4 (v.24) **Aristarchus**: he was the believer who was a faithful companion, one who was always there when needed. He is always seen with Paul and other believers, joining them in their great trials and sufferings.

⇒ He was a member of the Thessalonian church, a citizen of Thessalonica (Acts 19:29; 20:4).
⇒ He was one of the believers attacked by the violent mob in Ephesus. The citizens of Ephesus were rioting against Christianity because so many people were being converted that it was cutting into the sale of idols made to the goddess Diana. The fact that Aristarchus was one of the believers attacked and dragged before the mob shows that he was a leader and spokesman for Christ (Acts 19:29).
⇒ He went with Paul to minister in Asia (Acts 20:4).
⇒ He is seen traveling with Paul to Rome after Paul had been arrested and was being transferred to Rome as a prisoner (Acts 27:2).
⇒ He is seen as a fellow prisoner with Paul in Rome while Paul was awaiting trial on the charge of treason. Apparently he too was being charged with the same crime (Col.4:10; Phile.24).

The point is that he was a *real companion*, a companion who stood by the side of his fellow believers through thick and thin. He would never think of deserting his dear friends or the Lord, no matter how difficult the task or terrible the trial. He would face imprisonment and suffer death before he would be a turncoat. He was a good man to have around when facing trials, for he would stand by the side of his friend even if it meant imprisonment and death.

Carry each other's burdens, and in this way you will fulfill the law of Christ. (Gal 6:2)

Remember those in prison as if you were their fellow prisoners, and those who are mistreated as if you yourselves were suffering. (Heb 13:3)

5 (v.24) **Demas**: he was a man who turned away from Christ back to the world. His life is written in tragedy—a life that serves as a warning to other believers—a life that shows the utter necessity of walking in Christ daily. At first, he is seen as a fellow laborer (Phile.24). Later he is just a name, with no comment at all—perhaps suggesting the detection of some loss of spirit and energy in the work for the Lord (Col.4:14). Finally, he is Demas who "loved this present world" and forsook the Lord's work (2 Tim.4:10).

6 (v.24) **Luke**: he gave all to follow Christ—all that the world had to offer. He was the physician who was beloved by Paul and the church (see Introduction, *Author*—the *Gospel of Luke*; DEEPER STUDY # 2—Acts 16:10 for discussion). Note one other fact in Colossians: Luke is said to be the *"beloved* physician (Col.4:14)"—a physician who was endeared to the hearts of believers. Apparently, his medical treatment of believers was diligent, compassionate, warm, and personal. He had an effective ministry for Christ among the believers.

"A new command I give you: Love one another. As I have loved you, so you must love one another. By this all men will know that you are my disciples, if you love one another." (John 13:34-35)

Love must be sincere. Hate what is evil; cling to what is good. (Rom 12:9)

May the Lord make your love increase and overflow for each other and for everyone else, just as ours does for you. (1 Th 3:12)

Now that you have purified yourselves by obeying the truth so that you have sincere love for your brothers, love one another deeply, from the heart. (1 Pet 1:22)

7 (v.25) **Grace:** The conclusion is a much needed benediction, the grace of our Lord Jesus Christ. Above all else, the one thing needed by every person is the grace of our Lord Jesus Christ (See Deeper Study # 1, *Grace*—Tit 2:11-15 for discussion).

THE
OUTLINE & SUBJECT INDEX

REMEMBER: When you look up a subject and turn to the Scripture reference, you have not only the Scripture, you have *an outline and a discussion* (commentary) of the Scripture and subject.

This is one of the *GREAT VALUES* of **The Preacher's Outline & Sermon Bible®**. Once you have all the volumes, you will have not only what all other Bible indexes give you, that is, a list of all the subjects and their Scripture references, *BUT* you will also have…

- An outline of *every* Scripture and subject in the Bible.
- A discussion (commentary) on every Scripture and subject.
- Every subject supported by other Scriptures or cross references.

DISCOVER THE GREAT VALUE for yourself. Quickly glance below to the very first subject of the Index of Philemon. It is:

APPHIA
Friend of Paul at Colosse. 1:1-2

Turn to the reference. Glance at the Scripture and outline of the Scripture, then read the commentary. You will immediately see the GREAT VALUE of the INDEX of **The Preacher's Outline & Sermon Bible®**.

OUTLINE AND SUBJECT INDEX

APPHIA
Friend of Paul at Colosse. 1:1-2

ARCHIPPUS
A friend of Paul. 1:1-2

ARISTARCHUS
Companion of Paul. 1:24

BELIEVER - BELIEVERS
Example.
A great Christian man. Philemon. 1:1-7
A man greatly changed. Onesimus 1:8-21
Some early **c**. 1:8-21

BORN AGAIN (See **NEW BIRTH; REGENERATION**)
Illust.
A prisoner converted. 1:10-11
Made one useful. 1:10-11

CHURCH
Met in home. Of Philemon. 1:1-2

CONVERSION
Illust. Onesimus' change of life. 1:10-16

DEMAS
Laborer with Paul. 1:24

EPAPHRAS
Imprisoned for his faith. 1:23

FORGIVENESS OF OTHERS
Who is to be **f**. Christian brothers. 1:8-21

HOSPITALITY
How ministers are to be received. 1:22

LOVE (See **BROTHERHOOD**)
Illust. Philemon's reception of his runaway slave. 1:17-21

LUKE
A doctor who left all to be with Paul. 1:24

MARK, JOHN
Greeted by Paul. 1:24

MINISTERS
Examples. Interceding in a dispute. 1:8-21
Financial support. Lodging. 1:22

ONESIMUS
A man greatly changed. 1:8-21

PHILEMON
A great Christian man. 1:1-7

SALVATION
Illust. By Onesimus. 1:10-16

SLAVES (See **EMPLOYEES**)
Treatment of. 1:8-21

STEWARDSHIP
Toward ministers. To care for lodging. 1:22

TESTIMONY
Examples.
A great believer - Philemon. 1:1-7
A man greatly changed. 1:8-21
Some early believers. 1:22-24

Outline Bible Resources

This material, like similar works, has come from imperfect man and is thus susceptible to human error. We are nevertheless grateful to God for both calling us and empowering us through His Holy Spirit to undertake this task. Because of His goodness and grace, *The Preacher's Outline & Sermon Bible*® New Testament is complete and the Old Testament volumes are releasing periodically.

The Minister's Personal Handbook and other helpful **Outline Bible Resources** are available in printed form as well as releasing electronically on WORDsearch software.

God has given the strength and stamina to bring us this far. Our confidence is that as we keep our eyes on Him and grounded in the undeniable truths of the Word, we will continue working through the Old Testament volumes. The future includes other helpful Outline Bible Resources for God's dear servants to use in their Bible Study and discipleship.

We offer this material first to Him in whose Name we labor and serve and for whose glory it has been produced and, second, to everyone everywhere who preaches and teaches the Word.

Our daily prayer is that each volume will lead thousands, millions, yes even billions, into a better understanding of the Holy Scriptures and a fuller knowledge of Jesus Christ the Incarnate Word, of whom the Scriptures so faithfully testify.

You will be pleased to know that Leadership Ministries Worldwide partners with Christian organizations, printers, and mission groups around the world to make Outline Bible Resources available and affordable in many countries and foreign languages. It is our goal that *every* leader around the world, both clergy and lay, will be able to understand God's Holy Word and present God's message with more clarity, authority, and understanding—all beyond his or her own power.

LEADERSHIP MINISTRIES WORLDWIDE
PO Box 21310 • Chattanooga, TN 37424-0310
(423) 855-2181 • FAX (423) 855-8616
info@outlinebible.org
www.outlinebible.org - FREE Download materials

LEADERSHIP MINISTRIES WORLDWIDE

Publishers of Outline Bible Resources

Currently Available Materials, with New Volumes Releasing Regularly

- **THE PREACHER'S OUTLINE & SERMON BIBLE® (POSB)**

NEW TESTAMENT

Matthew I (chapters 1–15)
Matthew II (chapters 16–28)
Mark
Luke
John
Acts
Romans
1 & 2 Corinthians
Galatians, Ephesians, Philippians, Colossians
1 & 2 Thessalonians, 1 & 2 Timothy, Titus, Philemon
Hebrews, James
1 & 2 Peter, 1, 2, & 3 John, Jude
Revelation
Master Outline & Subject Index

OLD TESTAMENT

Genesis I (chapters 1–11)
Genesis II (chapters 12–50)
Exodus I (chapters 1–18)
Exodus II (chapters 19–40)
Leviticus
Numbers
Deuteronomy
Joshua
Judges, Ruth
1 Samuel
2 Samuel
1 Kings
2 Kings
1 Chronicles
2 Chronicles
Ezra, Nehemiah, Esther
Job
Psalms 1 (chapters 1-41)
Psalms 2 (chapters 42-106)
Proverbs
Ecclesiastes, Song of Solomon
Isaiah 1 (chapters 1-35)
Isaiah 2 (chapters 36-66)
Jeremiah 1 (chapters 1-29)
Jeremiah 2 (chapters 30-52), Lamentations
Ezekiel
Daniel, Hosea
Joel, Amos, Obadiah, Jonah, Micah, Nahum
Habakkuk, Zephaniah, Haggai, Zechariah, Malachi

New volumes release periodically

KJV Available in Deluxe 3-Ring Binders or Softbound Edition • NIV Available in Softbound Only

- **The Preacher's Outline & Sermon Bible New Testament** — 3 Vol. Hardcover • KJV – NIV

- *What the Bible Says to the Believer* — **The Believer's Personal Handbook**
  11 Chs. – Over 500 Subjects, 300 Promises, & 400 Verses Expounded - Italian Imitation Leather or Paperback

- *What the Bible Says to the Minister* — **The Minister's Personal Handbook**
  12 Chs. - 127 Subjects - 400 Verses Expounded - Italian Imitation Leather or Paperback

- **Practical Word Studies In the New Testament** — 2 Vol. Hardcover Set

- **The Teacher's Outline & Study Bible™ - Various New Testament Books**
  Complete 30 - 45 minute lessons – with illustrations and discussion questions

- **Practical Illustrations** — **Companion to the POSB**
  Arranged by topic and Scripture reference

- **What the Bible Says Series – Various Subjects**
  Prayer • The Passion • The Ten Commandments • The Tabernacle

- **Software – Various products powered by WORDsearch**
  New Testament • Pentateuch • History • Prophets • Practical Word Studies • Various Poetry/Wisdom

- **Topical Sermons Series – Available online only**
  7 sermons per series • Sermons are from The Preacher's Outline & Sermon Bible

- **Non-English Translations of various books**
  Included languages are: Russian – Spanish – Korean – Hindi – Chinese – Bulgarian – Romanian – Malayalam – Nepali – Italian – Arabic
  - Future: French, Portuguese

— Contact LMW for Specific Language Availability and Prices —

For quantity orders and information, please contact:
LEADERSHIP MINISTRIES WORLDWIDE or Your Local Christian Bookstore
PO Box 21310 • Chattanooga, TN 37424-0310
(423) 855-2181 (9am – 5pm Eastern) • FAX (423) 855-8616
E-mail - info@outlinebible.org Order online at www.outlinebible.org

 LEADERSHIP MINISTRIES WORLDWIDE

PURPOSE STATEMENT

LEADERSHIP MINISTRIES WORLDWIDE exists to equip ministers, teachers, and laymen in their understanding, preaching, and teaching of God's Word by publishing and distributing worldwide *The Preacher's Outline & Sermon Bible*® and related **Outline Bible Resources**; to reach & disciple men, women, boys and girls for Jesus Christ.

MISSION STATEMENT

1. To make the Bible so understandable – its truth so clear and plain – that men and women everywhere, whether teacher or student, preacher or hearer, can grasp its message and receive Jesus Christ as Savior, and...

2. To place the Bible in the hands of all who will preach and teach God's Holy Word, verse by verse, precept by precept, regardless of the individual's ability to purchase it.

The **Outline Bible Resources** have been given to LMW for printing and especially distribution worldwide at/below cost, by those who remain anonymous. One fact, however, is as true today as it was in the time of Christ:

THE GOSPEL IS FREE, BUT THE COST OF TAKING IT IS NOT

LMW depends on the generous gifts of believers with a heart for Him and a love for the lost. They help pay for the printing, translating, and distributing of **Outline Bible Resources** into the hands of God's servants worldwide, who will present the Gospel message with clarity, authority, and understanding beyond their own.

LMW was incorporated in the state of Tennessee in July 1992 and received IRS 501 (c)(3) nonprofit status in March 1994. LMW is an international, nondenominational mission organization. All proceeds from USA sales, along with donations from donor partners, go directly to underwrite our translation and distribution projects of **Outline Bible Resources** to preachers, church and lay leaders, and Bible students around the world.